PHEASANTS, PARTRIDGES AND GROUSE

PHEASANTS, PARTRIDGES AND GROUSE

A GUIDE TO THE PHEASANTS, PARTRIDGES, QUAILS, GROUSE, GUINEAFOWL, BUTTONQUAILS AND SANDGROUSE OF THE WORLD

STEVE MADGE AND PHIL McGOWAN

WITH GUY M. KIRWAN

ILLUSTRATED BY

NORMAN ARLOTT, ROBIN BUDDEN, DANIEL COLE,
JOHN COX, CARL D'SILVA, KIM FRANKLIN AND DAVID MEAD

CHRISTOPHER HELM
LONDON

Published 2002 by Christopher Helm, an imprint of A & C Black (Publishers) Ltd.,
37 Soho Square, London W1D 3QZ

ISBN 0-7136-3966-0

A CIP catalogue record for this book is available from the British Library

Typeset and designed by D & N Publishing, Baydon, Marlborough, Wiltshire, UK
Printed and bound in Spain by Artes Gráficas Toledo S.A.U.
D.L. TO: 1161 - 2001

10 9 8 7 6 5 4 3 2 1

CONTENTS

SYSTEMATIC LIST OF SPECIES

ACKNOWLEDGEMENTS

A work of this nature always relies heavily on those that have gone before, and it is with the greatest respect and admiration that we highlight the marvellous works of Hume and Marshall (1879–81), Ogilvie-Grant (1896–97), Beebe (1918–22), Baker (1930), Delacour (1952), Potapov (1985) and Johnsgard (1983, 1986, 1988 and 1991). These superb monographs demonstrate that the Galliformes have scarcely suffered from neglect over the past 100 years!

Many present-day birders have helped in various ways, reading texts, providing photographs, tape-recordings, answering queries and locating obscure reference materials. They are Sergio Aguilar (Mexico), Mark & Kathleen Van Beirs (Belgium), Geoff Carey (Hong Kong), Phil Carroll, David Christie, Mark Cocker, Darrell Clegg (Plymouth Library Services), Julie & Marc Dando (Fluke Art, Looe), Chris Doughty (who showed SM most of the Australian buttonquails in the field), Tsydyp Dorzhiev (Buryat State University, Ulan Ude), Simon Dowell (World Pheasant Association), Jonathan Eames (Vietnam), Kevin Easley (Costa Rica), Jon Fjeldså (Denmark), Jesper Hornskov (China), Keith Howman (World Pheasant Association), Carol & Tim Inskipp, Sara McMahon (Plymouth University), Pedro Mota (Mexico), Dave Nurney, Alex Randall, Michael Rank, Iain Robertson, Craig Robson, Hadoram Shirihai (Israel), Dave Showler, Hans-Walter Schuster (Germany), Ian Sinclair (South Africa), Y. Robert Tymstra (Canada) and Geoff & Hilary Welch (Djibouti Francolin).

Daniel Cole would like to thank Michel Klat and Steve Bishop of the Old House Bird Gardens, Robert Prys-Jones and Mark Adams at the Natural History Museum, Tring, Professor R. L. Potapov, Eugene Potapov and the 'Scientific Collections of the Zoological Institute', and Pavel Tomkovich of the Zoological Museum of Moscow Lomonosov State University.

Special thanks are due to Guy Kirwan, who not only edited the entire book, but also tackled the sandgrouse, buttonquails and several of the New World quail accounts at the last minute, and with amazing enthusiasm and efficiency. We also express grateful thanks to the staff at the World Pheasant Association at Pangbourne, and especially Keith Howman, for permitting access to the wonderful collection there. Thanks also to the staff of the Natural History Museum (Tring), notably Robert Prys-Jones and Peter Colston (now retired), for overseeing access to the skin collection. At Christopher Helm, thanks must go to those who, over the years, have coped with the trials and tribulations inevitably associated with a project of this type, most notably Robert Kirk (now with Princeton University Press), Jo Hemmings (now at New Holland) who instigated it, and most recently Nigel Redman (who oversaw its completion).

Finally, SM would like to offer his greatest thanks to Penny, Elysia and Bryony for their patience while he was locked in a world of quails and pheasants.

SM and PM

Editor's Acknowledgements

For information, much of it from personal unpublished field observations, help with references, access to sources that were then in press, as well as reviews of several of the sandgrouse, buttonquail and other species accounts, I am indebted to: Desmond Allen, Erick Baur, K. David Bishop, Gary Bletsch, Dan Brooks, Thomas Brooks, David Capper, Peter Castell (who generously supplied Jeffery Coburn's unpublished notes on breeding Lichtenstein's Sandgrouse in Kenya), David Christie, Callan Cohen, Peter Cunningham, Ron Demey, Edward Dickinson, Trevor Ellery, Richard Fairbank, Lincoln Fishpool, Mike Flieg, Anita Gamauf, Martin Goodey, Andrew Hester, Jesper Hornskov, Robert Jones, Peter Lack, Peter Leonard, Phil and Patricia Maher, Rodney Martins, Giuseppe Micali, Jason A. Mobley, Stein Nilsen, Shaun Peters, Otto Pfister, Michael Rank, Nigel Redman, Craig Robson, Danny Rogers (who must be singled out for his particularly invaluable assistance and comments concerning several Australian endemics), Valéry Schollaert, Jevgeni Shergalin (who assisted in accessing a wealth of Russian-language information on Tibetan Sandgrouse), James Smith, Claire Spottiswoode, George and Lindsey Swann, Lisa Thomsen, Joe Tobias, Philip Veerman, Chris Vogel, H. Glyn Young and Ray Ziarno. Many of these correspondents came through postings to the e-mail groups African Birding, MEBirdNet, NEO-ORN (Bulletin board for ornithologists working with Neotropical birds) and Oriental Birding. Thanks are due to the list moderators, Phil Atkinson, Andrew Grieve, Van Remsen and Krys Kazmierczak, for overseeing such valuable means of information exchange.

At BirdLife International (Cambridge), Jeremy Speck and Christine Alder were always more than helpful in keeping me up to date with the periodical literature, and David Wege offered other useful assistance, while at the Natural History Museum (Tring), Effie Warr (though now retired) has always provided outstanding help in tracking down key references. At Muséum National d'Histoire Naturelle, Paris, I am grateful to J. M. Bremond and Eric Pasquet for their invaluable assistance in the library and collection and, similarly, Jorge de Leon at the Peabody Museum of Natural History, Yale University, was helpful in securing access to a couple of last-minute references.

For their good company, in various parts of the world, while supposedly relaxing (though in reality working on texts for this book), I principally thank Arthur Grosset, Alvaro Jaramillo, Arturo Kirkconnell and Rosita Posada, Jeremy Minns and family, Valéria Francisca de Paula, Firdous Raja, and Eduardo Moreira Santos and Ana Lúcia de Almeida Faria. Lastly, I thank my partner, Daylén, for twice bearing with me when Galliformes threatened to become (almost) as important as her.

Guy M. Kirwan

INTRODUCTION

'Gamebirds' and humans have been intimately linked since the start of recorded history and, in many ways, have had a more profound effect on Man than any other group of animals. Not only has the Red Junglefowl given rise to the domesticated chicken and village fowl that provides such an important source of protein throughout the world, but other species also play central roles in local economies, cultures and sport. The Brown Eared-pheasant, for example, has long been a symbol of bravery in China, and feathers of the male were used as battle adornments by many generals between the eras of the Warring States and the Qing Dynasty.

Many species of grouse, partridges and pheasants are shot for 'sport', hence the common generic name for the group, and in several rural economies this provides the economic incentive to maintain the habitat that supports these 'quarry' species. While sustainable use is likely to remain a philosophically controversial area of conservation policy for some time to come, there are clearly some areas where sport-hunting has led to the effectivce protection of habitat suitable for 'gamebirds', and thus for other species that share these places.

Pheasants, especially, have also been sought for the beauty of the male plumages, with several species being introduced to captivity in Europe, particularly during the 18th and 19th centuries. The quest to capture these birds and the efforts of the early hunter-naturalists led to much new information concerning their life histories being obtained and, together with colonial sport-hunting, resulted in a far greater knowledge of the distribution and habits of these species than for many other birds that share their habitats. Nonetheless, they have retained their fascination, no doubt aided by the retiring nature and shyness of many species, and they are now among the most eagerly sought targets of birders. However, despite the wealth of information, there is still much data that can be collected on the Galliformes that may be of great value and practical use in their conservation.

GAPS IN OUR KNOWLEDGE

Contributions waiting to be made are not restricted to determining species distributions and habitat use. Our knowledge of the biology of many species is still very poor and this ignorance ranges from some taxonomic relationships to breeding biology and ecology. For example, species limits within hill-partridge populations are presently largely a matter for conjecture; more data are urgently required in order to make more informed assessments. The breeding requirements of many species are known only from anecdotal information. Even among the relatively well-studied grouse there are significant gaps—though this is perhaps unsurprising in those species largely restricted to high latitudes of Siberia.

All is not bleak, however. This book includes some of the best-studied species in the world: the Red Grouse, Northern Bobwhite and Common Pheasant have been the subject of more research than any other bird species (though in the latter case this only applies to research conducted in those countries where it has been introduced). Consequently, we have learnt many lessons about assessing conservation status and determining what is necessary to ensure the survival of a species. The challenge is to put these into practice and to extend these lessons to the many others about which we know so little.

Even within the past decade significant discoveries have been made, including such staggering finds as a new genus of partridge, *Xenoperdix*, described from Tanzania in 1994, a new species of sage grouse from the USA, formally described only in the year 2000, while mystery still clings to the precise relationships between several taxa of Vietnamese *Lophura* pheasants, and where to draw the line between the various forms of Kalij and Silver Pheasants. On the roof of the world, an undescribed monal was discovered in the Himalayas of Arunachal Pradesh in 1998; its taxonomic status is still being investigated.

These exciting discoveries concerning such large and popular birds indicate the potential for field-workers to contribute to our knowledge of these fascinating species, even in the new millennium.

CONSERVATION

Partly because of the long relationship that these birds have had with Man, they are among the most threatened of all avian groups. A recently completed assessment of the status of the pheasants considered no fewer than 50% to be at risk of extinction, according to the Red List categories used by IUCN—The World Conservation Union. Typically these involve the better studied members of the group: in truth, we really know relatively little of the status of many of the more widespread species usually considered safe from extinction. For example, most francolins have relatively large distributions and are considered habitat generalists, and thus tolerant of moderate changes in their habitat wrought by agricultural changes. However, the increasing intensification of agriculture in many areas suggests that several of these are at greater risk than previously thought. One or two Asian species may be disappearing from some areas as the use of agro-chemicals increases, but measuring the scale of this is very difficult.

While there are almost certainly unknown problems facing many widespread species that occupy managed landscapes (either farmland or areas under forestry in temperate and boreal regions), it is those with restricted distributions and specialised habitat requirements that are at most imminent risk of extinction. Here, new information gained from amateur birding trips can play a really crucial role in helping to safeguard their future. Such instances where the interested birder could play a role include searching for the Himalayan Quail, or locating new populations of the Manipur Bush-quail or Bornean Peacock-pheasant. There are many other examples. Detailed inventories, complete with information concerning galliform habitat use and the extent of available forests, even of existing protected areas are surprisingly few. Some protected areas, of course, are well known, such as Taman Negara in Peninsular Malaysia and the Great Himalayan National Park in India, but many reserves in China and Africa remain comparatively poorly documented.

The World Pheasant Association is dedicated to just this task, and works in partnership with the Species Survival Commission of IUCN and BirdLife International's Specialist Groups for the survival of all species of Galliformes. In addition to the three groups responsible for the species included here (those for grouse, for partridges, quail and francolins, and for pheasants), the Specialist Groups also include bodies responsible for megapodes and cracids. These authoritative networks link those active in the study and conservation of gamebirds and, by providing information and advice on these species, are able to determine current global conservation priorities. Any new information may help considerably and can be sent to the World Pheasant Association, P.O. Box 5, Lower Basildon, Reading RG8 9PF, England.

STYLE AND LAYOUT OF THE BOOK

The book is divided into two major sections; the colour plates, distribution maps and brief caption texts, and the main species accounts presented in systematic order. Both sections employ a species numbering system and are easily cross-referenced.

THE PLATES

The 72 colour plates depict the main plumage stages and extremes of the range of geographical, and age- and sex-related variation observed in each species. As far as possible, sample juvenile stages (very short lived in Galliformes) for each genus have been included, but for many species this stage is unknown, or at least undocumented in the literature. On the facing pages, alongside the distribution maps, short texts highlight useful identification features. Figures on each plate and within each genus are to scale. In-flight depictions have been included for those species primarily observed in flight, i.e. the smaller grouse, quails, buttonquails and sandgrouse.

THE MAPS

All species are mapped. As the majority of species are resident, the predominant colour is green, but where seasonal movements occur these are indicated by the use of yellow (breeding or summer range) and blue (non-breeding or winter range). The maps should be used with some caution, as within a given range, a species may only persist in small pockets of suitable habitat, or be very rare or little known. Furthermore, the maps should be used in conjunction with details presented in the main text, within the Habitat, Distribution and Status paragraphs.

THE SYSTEMATIC SECTION

The species accounts follow a specific format, summarised below.

ENGLISH NAMES These provide a seemingly never-ending problem for those engaged in a work of worldwide coverage, and some compromises have been inevitable as a result. The names employed here largely follow the standard reference for each region concerned, but problems still arise with some widespread species, e.g. Willow Grouse/Willow Ptarmigan. Here, the American 'wood-partridge' has been dropped in favour of the alternative 'tree-quail' to avoid confusion with some Oriental species—this move was also adopted by Carroll (1994). Perhaps the greatest departure from other present-day treatments concerns the hill-partridges, a very distinctive group that has been termed simply as 'partridges' in some recent Oriental field guides. Several hill-partridges have had older, more appropriate names restored to help avoid confusion with other names. Thus, instead of the confusing Chestnut-breasted, Chestnut-bellied and Red-breasted Partridges, we have used Chestnut-breasted, Javan and Bornean Hill-partridges (the two latter names being distinctive and reflective of their restricted distributions). It is hoped that such changes will receive widespread recognition.

ALTERNATIVE NAMES Alternative English names used in other reference books within recent decades are listed.

IDENTIFICATION This section summarises those features of each species that enable a swift identification within that species' range, specifically highlighting the key differences from similar species.

DESCRIPTION A summary description of the main plumages of each species, commencing with the important structural features and bare-part coloration. The particular subspecies being described is stated at the start of the account, unless the species is monotypic. Downy chicks are not described, as they are beyond the scope of this guide. Juvenile plumage is short-lived and is often partially replaced while patches of down remain on the head of young birds. First-year birds of all Galliformes may, apparently, be aged by the retention of the two outermost primaries throughout their first year of life; in contrast to the adult primaries, these juvenile feathers are narrower and soon become faded and worn.

GEOGRAPHICAL VARIATION Many species vary geographically, especially across a broad range. Such variations have often been named as recognisable races or subspecies, and therefore receive a trinomial scientific name. Evolution is an ongoing, gradual process and in many cases the division between what constitutes a separate species, rather than a well-marked subspecies, is a fine one. Some subspecies differ markedly from other populations traditionally deemed to constitute part of the same species, and may be better treated as different species (and have been so considered at times). Red and Willow Grouse offer an extreme example of this problem. Scientific studies of speciation now follow several diverging avenues of thought, with the current trend being to recognise more named forms (or taxa) as species. Here, we are content to summarise all widely acknowledged regional variation, listing those subspecies currently considered valid within this section.

MEASUREMENTS Given that many Galliformes are large, relatively small-billed and have relatively short legs, a comprehensive set of measurements is of limited value for the majority of genera. A few simple measurements are given for comparative reasons. Unless stated otherwise, all measurements are in millimetres and weights in grams.

HABITAT The major vegetation zones and altitudinal ranges occupied by each species are summarised.

VOICE Many species have quite varied vocabularies. It is the advertising call, a form of territorial song, which is the loudest and most significant of these. Transcribing obscure and often varied, garbled sounds is difficult, and is invariably very much a personal interpretation, which should be borne in mind when using this section.

HABITS Foraging, social gatherings, diet and other aspects of behaviour are considered and described within this paragraph. Many genera have complex display postures, and indeed several species possess truly spectacular displays (e.g. peafowl, tragopans, Bulwer's Pheasant, the two argus pheasants and most grouse); these are briefly summarised, but interested readers are recommended to consult the more comprehensive summaries provided by Johnsgard (1983, 1986).

BREEDING This section provides a summary of the breeding habits, including nest construction, clutch size, incubation period and egg-laying seasons.

DISTRIBUTION The geographical range of each species is described in this section.

STATUS Comments on each species' abundance, status and those conservation issues of most importance to its future prospects are considered here. Where appropriate, the section commences with the species' threat category as defined by BirdLife International (2000): Critical, Endangered, Vulnerable, Data Deficient and Near Threatened, in declining order of priority.

REFERENCES The most useful works consulted during the preparation of the species account are listed here. Fuller details, along with a list of all other works consulted, are presented in the Bibliography on p 463.

TOPOGRAPHY

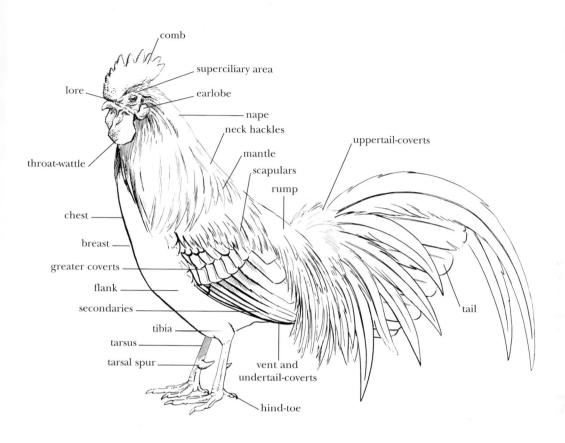

comb
superciliary area
lore
earlobe
nape
neck hackles
throat-wattle
mantle
scapulars
rump
uppertail-coverts
chest
breast
greater coverts
flank
secondaries
tibia
tarsus
tarsal spur
vent and
undertail-coverts
hind-toe
tail

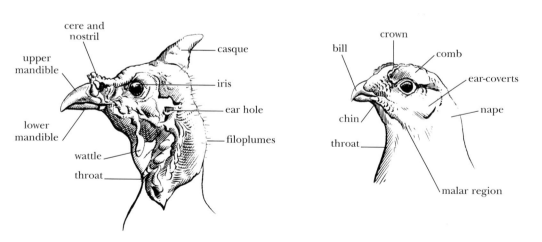

cere and
nostril
casque
upper
mandible
iris
ear hole
lower
mandible
filoplumes
wattle
throat

crown
bill
comb
ear-coverts
nape
chin
throat
malar region

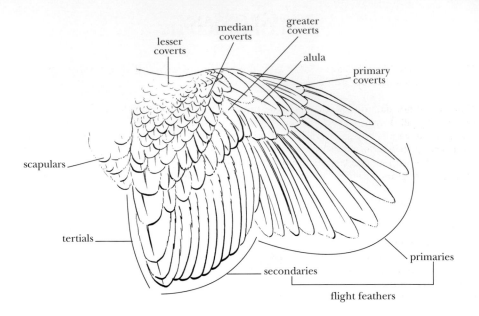

lesser
coverts

median
coverts

greater
coverts

alula

primary
coverts

scapulars

tertials

secondaries

primaries

flight feathers

GLOSSARY

Throughout the book we have tried to keep the number of technical or unfamiliar names to a minimum; nevertheless a few terms require some clarification.

Aberrant Abnormal, usually referring to an unusually plumaged individual.
Advertising call Territorial vocalisation or 'song'.
Afrotropical Faunal region of sub-Saharan Africa, formerly known as the 'Ethiopian' faunal region.
Allopatric Distribution pattern where two or more similar species exist, but geographically replace each other without overlapping. Compare Sympatric.
Altitudinal migrant Montane species which habitually moves to considerably lower elevations in winter.
Arboreal Living in trees.

Clinal variation Where variation between various geographical forms is a gradual, poorly defined intergradation.
Cloud forest Neotropical lush mountain forests, frequently shrouded by clouds.
Comb Fleshy wattle, above eye (e.g. grouse) or along centre of crown (e.g. junglefowl).
Conspecific Of the same species.
Contact notes Calls by which a small, somewhat scattered party of birds frequently utter to keep in contact.
Covey A small flock, usually a family party, of partridges or quails.
Crepuscular Active at twilight of dawn or dusk.
Crop A distensible sac (ingluvies) attached to the gullet (oesophagus) which is well-developed in granivorous birds, used primarily for food storage prior to digestion.
Cryptic Having a pattern or coloration favouring concealment.

Dauria An old name for a region of central Asia between Lake Baikal and north-west China, now referred to as Transbaikalia.
Dimorphic Two colour forms of a species found in the same area, not connected to geographical or racial variation.
Distal At the far end, or towards the tip.
Duetting Male and female calling together, producing a complex cacophony of sound.

Endemic Exclusively confined to a defined area.
'Explode' A sudden 'flushing' of birds at close quarters, usually referring to a covey which scatters in various directions when disturbed, often initially with agitated calling.

Feral Domesticated or introduced species, having become established through deliberate introduction or from escapes.

Gallinaceous Literally 'fowl-like' - a term applied to 'gamebirds'.
Genus (plural Genera) A group of similar species, with shared characters; several genera can be further grouped into a Family.

Hackles Elongated, slender, pointed feathers; usually associated with the neck.
Holarctic Faunal region of the Northern Hemisphere which combines both the Nearctic and Palearctic regions.

Immature A term loosely applied to plumage stages between juvenile and adult; may be applied to juvenile stage also, if precise age not known. Older birds showing strong features of adult plumage may be known as 'subadult'.

Juvenile The first feathered plumage acquired after the downy stage, which is remarkably short-lived in most gallinaceous birds.

Lek A display ground, usually referring to places where several males gather to display.

Monotypic Referring to a classification grouping which is represented by a single form.

Nearctic North American faunal region.
Neotropical Central And South American faunal region.
Nominate race/form The first-named race of a species, indicated by its subspecific name being the same as its specific name

Ocelli 'Eye-spots' as found on the 'trains' of peafowl.
Order A major taxonomic grouping of families with shared features.
Oriental Faunal region of tropical Asia.

Palearctic Faunal region of Europe, North Africa and Asia north of the tropics.
Pectinate Having comb-like 'teeth', as on the toes of grouse.
Polymorphic Having many forms.

Rectrices (singular Rectrix) Tail feathers.
Refulgent Extremely bright and shiny.
Remiges (singular Remex) Flight feathers (primaries and secondaries).

Shaft-streaks A stripe of colour, usually either buff or black along the centre of a feather, typically alongside the feather shaft.
Snood The fleshy projection from the forehead of a male turkey, also known as a 'leader'.
Subadult An imprecise term for a bird of unknown age that is not yet fully adult.
Sympatric Distribution pattern where breeding ranges of two or more similar species overlap. Compare Allopatric.

Taiga Northern, mostly coniferous forests of the Holarctic region.
Taxon (plural Taxa) A named form; it can refer to a subspecies or a species.
Taxonomy The study and classification of named forms.

Wallacea A faunal region comprising the eastern Indonesian regions of Sulawesi, Maluku (the Moluccas) and Nusa Tenggara (Lesser Sundas).
Wattle Naked, fleshy structure on the face or around the eye (see also Comb).

COLOUR PLATES AND MAPS

PLATE 1: SNOW MOUNTAIN QUAIL, SNOW PARTRIDGE AND *AMMOPERDIX* PARTRIDGES

74   Snow Mountain Quail *Anurophasis monorthonyx*   **Text page 246**

Endemic to Snow Mts of Irian Jaya (Indonesian New Guinea), in alpine grasslands above 3000 m. No known overlap with smaller ssp. *lamonti* of Brown Quail of C Highlands of adjacent Papua New Guinea.

74a   Adult male Relatively large barred brown quail with stout yellowish bill and legs.
74b   Adult female Paler, often whitish, and with barring less bold than in male.

1   Snow Partridge *Lerwa lerwa*   **Text page 171**

Dark partridge of Himalayan slopes above tree-line (3000–5500 m). Shares habitat with Tibetan Partridge and Tibetan Snowcock. All plumages similar.

1a   Adult Sexes similar. The intense barring of the head and upperparts is only apparent at close range; in the field it generally appears dark with a red bill. A whitish trailing edge to the secondaries can be striking in flight, especially in fresh plumage.
1b   Juvenile Duller with pale shaft streaks breaking-up plumage barring.

9   See-see Partridge *Ammoperdix griseogularis*   **Text page 180**

Small sandy partridge of desert hills in SW Asia. Very similar to Sand Partridge, with only males safely separable in the field, but ranges do not meet.

9a   Male Shares orange bill, white cheek patches and wavy flank bars with Sand Partridge but note greener legs, black forehead and eye-stripe and whitish chin.
9b   Female Plain greyish-buff, with minute white freckling on head and neck (fine pinkish barring in Sand).
9c   Juvenile Usually has black-and-white head pattern (see text).

10   Sand Partridge *Ammoperdix heyi*   **Text page 182**

Small sandy partridge of desert wadis in E Egypt and Arabian region. Four intergrading races, differing in colour saturation and presence of white on forehead and lores.

10a   Male (nominate; Sinai, Israel, Jordan, Syria and NW Saudi Arabia) Differs from See-see in lacking black on head, but has rufous chin and throat.
10b   Female (nominate) See above for general notes on See-see.
10c   Juvenile Appears to be always plain-headed (see See-see).
10d   Male (*cholmleyi*; SE Egypt, NE Sudan) Distinctly darker than nominate, and lacks white on forehead and lores.

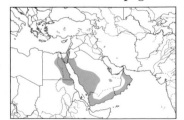

74b

74a

1a

1b

9c

9a

10a

9b

10b

10d

10c

PLATE 2: SNOWCOCKS (WESTERN AND NORTHERN)

Snowcocks are very large, dark greyish partridges of Asiatic mountain ranges, living way above the treeline. Sexes are basically similar in plumage, but females are less well marked, duller and somewhat smaller than the very bulky adult males. Juvenile smaller than adult, even duller than female, with less distinct flank pattern, but become much as adult by first-winter, though not fully adult until second-winter.

4   Caucasian Snowcock *Tetraogallus caucasicus*   Text page 174

Main Caucasus range, separated from Caspian by Kura River Valley, with Caucasian to the north.

4a   **Adult** Darker than Caspian, with breast feathers marked by black chevrons, a rusty nape and ear-coverts patch, and whitish and rufous flank striping.

4b   **Juvenile** Smaller and drabber.

4c   **Adult in flight** White wing-band similar in both Caspian and Caucasian.

5   Caspian Snowcock *Tetraogallus caspius*   Text page 175

Fragmented range over montane E and C Turkey and adjacent regions, including Armenia but not Georgia. Distinctions do not wholly apply to paler races of Caspian (see text). Three races differing principally in colour saturation.

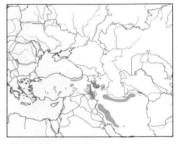

5a   **Adult** (nominate; E Armenia, N Iran) Differs from Caucasian in grey hindneck and cheeks, small black spots on breast, less boldly spotted upperparts, and underparts with finer chestnut streaks. Paler and more buff-toned grey than darkest form *tauricus* (Turkey and W Armenia).

5b   **Juvenile** (nominate) Smaller and drabber than adults.

5c   **Adult** (*semenowtianschanskii*; Zagros Mts of Iran) Paler and overall buffier, with pale grey throat-band interrupted by brown markings.

8   Altai Snowcock *Tetraogallus altaicus*   Text page 179

Altai Mts (chiefly Mongolia), separated from Himalayan by the Zaidam Depression.

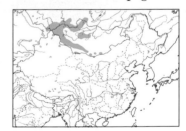

8a   **Adult** Has whitish (not dark grey) flanks, contrasting with blackish vent before white undertail-coverts. In flight, Altai exhibits white chiefly on the primaries, with only a narrow band along the bases of secondaries (latter more extensively white in Himalayan).

8b   **Juvenile** Smaller and drabber than adults.

4a

4b

4c

5a

5b

5c

8a

8b

PLATE 3: SNOWCOCKS (EASTERN) AND MONAL-PARTRIDGES

7   Tibetan Snowcock *Tetraogallus tibetanus*   **Text page 178**

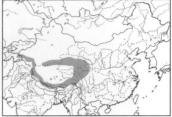

Mountains of C Asia. Range overlaps with Himalayan. Four intergrading races; darker populations in C Tibet, with sandier birds towards both west and east.

7a   Adult (nominate; W Tibet and the Pamirs) A pale sandy-buff form.

7b   Adult (*aquilonifer*; S Tibet, Nepal to Bhutan) Dark grey, with whitest ear-patch. Whitish flanks and mottled undertail-coverts distinctive. In flight has dark wings with white only on tips of secondaries (c.f. Himalayan).

7c   Juvenile (*aquilonifer*) Smaller and drabber than adults.

---

6   Himalayan Snowcock *Tetraogallus himalayensis*   **Text page 177**

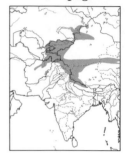

Mountains of C Asia; also introduced Nevada (USA). Range overlaps with Tibetan and almost meets both Altai and Caspian (see text). Six races, differing in colour saturation, which varies according to type of substrate birds inhabit.

6a   Adult (nominate; Afghanistan to Nepal) The darkest form. Dark grey underparts contrast with pale head and breast and white undertail-coverts. In flight has chiefly white primaries and narrow band across base of grey secondaries (c.f. Tibetan).

6b   Juvenile (nominate) Smaller and drabber than adults.

6c   Adult (*grombczewskii*; Kunlun Mts, Tibet) The palest form.

---

2   Verreaux's Monal-partridge *Tetraophasis obscurus*   **Text page 172**

Montane forest from S Gansu to W Sichuan, north of the Yalung River, where inhabits ravines in upper levels of forest.

2   Adult Sexes similar. Both monal-partridges are large brownish partridge-like birds with quite long, broad, white-tipped tails. Best separated by range, but look for rusty throat and whitish belly, and duller grey-brown upperparts of Verreaux's. Juvenile assumed similar to Szechenyi's.

---

3   Szechenyi's Monal-partridge *Tetraophasis szechenyii*   **Text page 173**

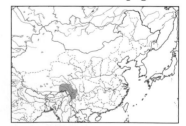

Montane forest of E Tibet and W Sichuan, west of the Yalung River.

3a   Adult Sexes similar. Purer grey rump and uppertail than Verreaux's, buffier belly and yellow-buff (not rusty) throat.

3b   Juvenile Drab, with whitish shaft streaks and dark barring both above and below.

15   Rock Partridge *Alectoris graeca*   Text page 188

SE Europe, Italy and the Alps. Range best distinction from Chukar.
In C Bulgaria and NE Greece virtually overlaps with Chukar; here
(but not elsewhere) Rock is purer grey (less brownish) above and on
breast. Rock has black (not white) lores, with less obvious black spot
at gape, smaller rufous patch behind eye (not boldly interrupting
black band), more rounded (less V-shaped) point to whiter lower
throat (but see text). In Rock, the flank bars are more numerous,
narrower and neater; Chukar has fewer, broader spaced flank bars,
the rear bars often seemingly 'broken'. Three races, two shown.
Sexes similar.

- **15a**   **Adult** (*saxatilis*; Alps) Browner than nominate, latter being purer grey above.
- **15b**   **Juvenile** Typical of genus; this individual has adult flank feathers appearing.
- **15c**   **Adult** (*whitakeri*; Sicily) Has more uniform grey-brown upperparts, and narrower and more pointed border to lower throat, thus approaching Chukar.

14   Chukar *Alectoris chukar*   Text page 186

Most widespread of all partridges (also
introduced N America and elsewhere, see
text). See similar Rock and Przevalski's
(and Red-legged) Partridges for discussion.
Some 16 intergrading races over wide
range, varying in colour saturation and
brown tones to plumage, complicated by
effects of wear and bleaching. Sexes similar.

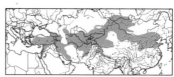

- **14a**   **Adult** (nominate; Himalayas) The darkest form.
- **14b**   **Adult** (*werae*; E Iraq, W Iran) A pale grey and sandy race.
- **14c**   **Adult** (*cypriotes*; Cyprus, Crete, S Turkey, etc.) Strongly toned vinaceous-brown on upperparts.

16   Przevalski's Partridge *Alectoris magna*   Text page 190

Endemic to N China (Qinghai and Gansu) where range virtually
meets Chukar on some mountains, but appears not to directly overlap
(see text).

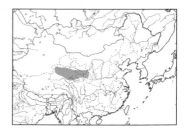

- **16**   **Adult** Sexes similar. Larger than Chukar, with rusty gorget
(narrowly edged black on inner side). Its closely barred flanks
and black lores are suggestive of Rock. Has paler irides than
either.

15a

15c

15b

14b

14a

14c

16

13 Philby's Partridge *Alectoris philbyi*

Text page 185

W Arabia. Local above 2300 m (but occurs to 1400 m). Rocky plateaux and bare mountain slopes. Overlaps with larger Arabian Partridge, but favours more barren biotope at higher elevations.

13a **Adult** Sexes similar. Black face and throat renders it unique in genus.
13b **Juvenile** Attaining adult features.

12 Barbary Partridge *Alectoris barbara*

Text page 184

N Africa, Gibraltar and Sardinia. The only partridge in most of its range. Habitats vary from rocky slopes to open woodlands. Four races (two shown)

12a **Adult** (nominate; N Morocco, N Algeria, Sardinia) Sexes similar. Lacks black border to pale throat, has dark brown crown contrasting with pale supercilium and pale grey face and throat, and chestnut necklace.
12b **Juvenile** Attaining adult features.
12c **Adult** (*barbata*; NE Libya, formerly also NW Egypt) Most distinct race, with reddish-toned upperparts, bluish-grey throat and face, and cinnamon crown and neck patch.

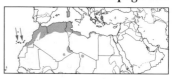

11 Arabian Partridge *Alectoris melanocephala*

Text page 183

W and S Arabia. Favours more bushy slopes at lower elevations than Philby's, but locally occurs to 2800 m.

11a **Adult** Sexes similar. Black crown and grey tail unique in genus. Overlaps with smaller and black-throated Philby's, but unlikely to be confused.
11b **Juvenile** Attaining adult features.

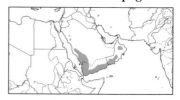

17 Red-legged Partridge *Alectoris rufa*

Text page 191

W Europe, especially Iberia, France and England (where introduced). Favours open country, marginally overlapping with Rock in Alps and widely with Grey elsewhere. Habitats vary, but chiefly open farmland. Sexes similar. Three similar races.

17a **Adult** (nominate) Note band of streaking across upper breast and neck-sides, overall brownish appearance, prominent supercilium and deep rufous belly.
17b **Juvenile** Attaining adult features.

PLATE 6: AFRICAN PARTRIDGES AND ASIAN FRANCOLINS I

105 Stone Partridge *Ptilopachus petrosus*

Text page 273

Dark bantam-like partridge of rocky country in C Africa, also in bushy lowlands in west of range. All plumages similar; despite considerable local variation in tones, only two races generally recognised (see text).

105a **Adult** (nominate; most of range) Rather featureless apart from frequently cocked tail and paler patch in centre of lower breast.

105b **Adult** (*major*, Eritrea) Larger and paler, with broader chestnut flank streaking.

80 Udzungwa Partridge *Xenoperdix udzungwensis*

Text page 252

Endemic to forest undergrowth in the Udzungwa Mts of S Tanzania. Little known and very rare.

80 Small size, barred upperparts, rusty face and blotched underparts together with red bill render it unique. All plumages similar (as far as is known).

21 Grey Francolin *Francolinus pondicerianus*

Text page 196

Indian subcontinent, S Iran and Persian Gulf states (see text for introductions). Painted widely overlaps, but is spotted, not barred, on dark background. All plumages similar. Three races, two extremes shown.

21a **Adult** (nominate; S India, Sri Lanka) Barred plumage with dull orange or whitish throat (varies with race) distinctive, but barring not evident given brief or distant views. Female Black strongly marked by dark barring and scalloping, whereas Grey has pale barring. In flight, note rufous tail (black in Black and Painted). The darkest race, with strong barring and orange throat.

21b **Adult** (*mecranensis*; Pakistan, Iran) The palest race, throat almost whitish.

22 Swamp Francolin *Francolinus gularis*

Text page 197

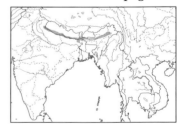

N India and Nepal (and Bangladesh?). Very localised in damp, *terai* grassland. Where habitat meets adjoining dry cultivation Grey also occurs in same areas.

22 All plumages similar. Large francolin with striped underparts and rufous throat. If flushed shows rufous tail like Grey, unlike Black, which has blackish tail.

105a

105b

21b

21a

80

22

Norman Arlott

18 Black Francolin *Francolinus francolinus*

Text page 193

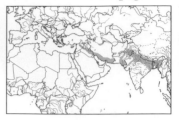

S Asia from Turkey east to Assam (see text for introductions). Sexes differ.

18a **Adult male** (nominate; Turkey, Israel and most of Iran) Black with white ear-patch, intense body spotting and broad chestnut collar. In flight note blackish tail (like Painted and Chinese); flushed birds differ from female Red Junglefowl in having shorter tail and more patterned upperparts.

18b **Adult female** (nominate) Brown, with dark eye-stripe, dark barring and scalloping, and rusty nape (Grey has pale barring).

18c **Adult female** (*arabistanicus*; S Iraq, W Iran) The palest race.

19 Painted Francolin *Francolinus pictus*

Text page 195

India and Sri Lanka. Some overlap with Black in NC India. Three similar races, southern forms darkest.

19a **Adult male** (nominate; S India) Rusty face prevents confusion with male Black, but both sexes resemble female Black; however, Painted has plainer face pattern, lacks rusty nape and has more spotted (less streaked) body. Nominate is intermediate in colour saturation.

19b **Adult female** (nominate) Face pattern often very pale.

20 Chinese Francolin *Francolinus pintadeanus*

Text page 195

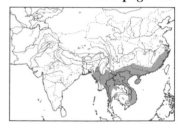

SE Asia (introduced Luzon and Mauritius). Except for tiny overlap with Black in Manipur, this is only francolin in its range. Two similar races.

20a **Adult male** (nominate; China) Striking head pattern, with rusty supercilium and white throat and cheeks separated by black moustachial diagnostic.

20b **Adult female** (nominate) Less strikingly marked but head pattern similar.

18a

18b

18c

19a

19b

20b

20a

Norman Arlott

PLATE 8: AFRICAN FRANCOLINS I

28   Ring-necked Francolin *Francolinus streptophorus*   **Text page 203**

Very local, chiefly N Uganda but isolated population in Cameroon.
Grassy hillsides with rocks.

28a   **Adult male** Suggests Crested, but has yellow (not red) legs,
barred (not spot–streaked) breast and has unmarked area of
chestnut on head and neck. Crested in area of overlap lacks
dark flank stripes of Ring-necked and often carries tail cocked.

28b   **Adult female** Upperparts more barred and streaked than
male.

27   Crested Francolin *Francolinus sephaena*   **Text page 202**

E and SE Africa. At least five similar races, forming two groups (see text).

27a   **Adult male** (nominate; S Africa) Dark crown, whitish supercilium, streaked
neck and breast, plain (but finely streaked in 'Kirk's') lower underparts,
red legs and cocked 'bantam' tail diagnostic.

27b   **Adult female** (nominate) Upperparts more barred than male.

27c   **Adult male** (*rovuma*; coastal Kenya etc) This and similar *spilogaster* (Somalia
etc) are finely streaked on flanks and belly, and are sometimes known as
'Kirk's Francolin'.

26   Latham's Francolin *Francolinus lathami*   **Text page 201**

Equatorial Africa. Forests. Two races, both shown.

26a   **Adult male** (nominate; C Africa east to C Zaïre) Dusky
plumage with pale head-sides unique over most of its range,
but in NE Zaïre overlaps with Nahan's. Yellow legs, and lacks
bare red skin around eye.

26b   **Adult female** (nominate) Drabber and browner than male.

26c   **Adult male** (*schubotzi*; E Zaïre, Uganda) Whiter head-sides and
has darker chestnut markings on upperparts than nominate.

26d   **Adult female** (*schubotzi*) Buffish below, with reddish-brown
breast and rusty face.

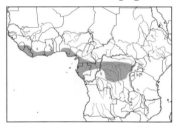

35   Nahan's Francolin *Francolinus nahani*   **Text page 209**

Equatorial Africa. Forests.

35   Blackish francolin, with reddish legs and bare skin around
eye; also note whitish throat. All plumages similar. Lacks
whitish head-sides of Latham's; eastern race *schubotzi* of
Latham's (which overlaps with Nahan's) shows strong sexual
differences, whereas in Nahan's all plumages are similar.

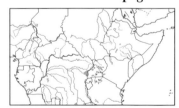

27c

28b

28a

27a

27b

26d

26c

26b

26a

35

Norman Arlott

23 Coqui Francolin *Francolinus coqui*

Text page 198

Africa's most widespread francolin. Bushy grasslands. Habitually walks slowly, with body held low and head up, even when crossing open tracks. Marked variation in underparts barring; a large number of races have been described, but only four generally warranted (two shown).

23a   **Adult male** (nominate; Uganda south to South Africa) Small, with yellow legs, orange-buff head and variably barred underparts. Typical of a darker population (heavily barred Ugandan-type bird shown).

23b   **Adult female** (nominate) Narrow black stripe above eye and border to white throat. A rather dark individual.

23c   **Juvenile** (nominate) More mottled above and below than female.

23d   **Adult male** (*hubbardi*; SW Kenya, NW Tanzania) Unbarred belly typical of western forms.

24 White-throated Francolin *Francolinus albogularis*

Text page 199

WC Africa (with relict populations in Zaïre and Angola). Savanna woodlands. Marked racial variation, with three forms recognised.

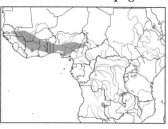

24a   **Adult male** (nominate; Senegal) Small buff-and-rufous francolin, lacking prominent markings. Recalls female Coqui but lacks black stripe above eye and border to throat, has extensive rufous in wings and weak or little barring on underparts.

24b   **Adult female** (nominate) Fine barring on underparts.

24c   **Adult male** (*dewittei*; Zaïre, Angola) Richer, reddish-buff underparts becoming dark chestnut on breast.

24d   **Adult female** (*dewittei*) Lower underparts entirely barred.

24e   **Adult male** (*buckleyi*; Côte d'Ivoire to Cameroon) Rich buff, not whitish supercilium and face; female has barring extending onto belly.

25 Schlegel's Francolin *Francolinus schlegelii*

Text page 200

C Africa. Grassy woodlands.

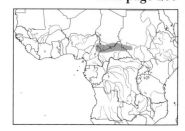

25a   **Adult male** Rich rufous upperparts are an easy distinction from male Coqui, which it resembles (ranges do not overlap). Female White-throated of race *buckleyi* similarly barred, but warmer buff below and rufous normally confined to wings (see text). If flushed, duller brown primaries contrast with rufous rest of wing, primaries rufous in White-throated.

25b   **Adult female** Drabber than male, with diffuse markings on underparts.

23b

23c

23a

23d

24d

24e

24b

24a

24c

25b

25a

Norman Arlott.

PLATE 10: RED-WINGED FRANCOLINS I

A confusing group of African species, the relationships of some forms being open to debate. Sexes are generally similar and all have extensive rufous on upperwing in flight.

32   Moorland Francolin *Francolinus psilolaemus*   Text page 206

Montane grasslands (above 3000 m). Two races. Compare Redwing, Orange River and Shelley's.

32a   **Adult** (nominate; Ethiopia) Dark buffish or rufous, high-elevation francolin, with mottled and freckled plumage. Nominate is rather featureless, except freckling on throat.

32b   **Adult** (*elgonensis*; W Kenya, including Uganda side of Mt Elgon) Extreme rufous bird from Mt Elgon shown, other Kenyan populations are less bright and contrasting.

33   Shelley's Francolin *Francolinus shelleyi*   Text page 207

Savanna and open woodland, with rocky ridges and gorges. At least two subspecies. Compare also Redwing, Orange River and Greywing.

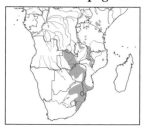

33a   **Adult** (nominate; most of species' range) Has clear white throat, two dark neck-bands (like Orange River), chestnut-striped breast and flanks, and black-and-white patterned belly. Note short white mark behind eye.

33b   **Juvenile** (nominate) Drabber and more weakly patterned than adult.

33c   **Adult** (*whytei*; SE Zaire, N Zambia and N Malawi) Throat buffier, underparts weakly marked and has narrower mottling at lower border to throat patch.

34   Orange River Francolin *Francolinus levaillantoides*   Text page 208

Grasslands, including grassy montane slopes (but in drier regions than Shelley's and ranges probably do not directly overlap). Two disjunct populations, in NE and S Africa, involving at least four subspecies. Compare also Redwing and Greywing.

34a   **Adult** (nominate; most of southern range) Has clear white throat, two dark neck-bands (like Shelley's), but unmarked central underparts. Note longer white line behind eye than Shelley's. Very variable in overall coloration, depending on soils, a dark bird typical of Transvaal is shown.

34b   **Adult** ('*kalaharica*') A pale population of the nominate race from Namibia.

34c   **Adult** (*lorti*; N Uganda, S Sudan, S Ethiopia and Somalia) Very pale, almost creamy-white below, with scaled upper breast; greyish above.

34d   **Adult** (*gutturalis*; Eritrea and N Ethiopia) Pale buff tone to underparts, with neck-bands and breast collar obscure.

34e   **Adult** (*jugularis*; Angola and N Namibia) Pale, but has scaled upper breast.

32a

32b

33c

33b

33a

34b

34e

34c

34a

34d

Norman Arlott.

PLATE 11: RED-WINGED (II) AND HARTLAUB'S FRANCOLINS

In the first three species on this plate, sexes are generally similar and show extensive rufous on upperwing in flight.

29   Finsch's Francolin *Francolinus finschi*   Text page 203

Restricted range. Wooded grassland in hills.

29   Relatively unmarked buff-and-brown francolin, with whitish throat contrasting with dull rufous face and neck, and greyish breast. Overlaps with Redwing in Angola, but latter has more strongly patterned underparts and black-and-white scaled chest and necklace.

31   Redwing Francolin *Francolinus levaillantii*   Text page 205

Grassy habitats and rank vegetation in hills and valleys. Compare Greywing, Finsch's and Moorland. Two subspecies.

31a   **Adult** (nominate; S Africa, N Malawi and NE Zambia) Differs from other similar francolins in having mottled black-and-white chest-band and nape, one (not two) mottled bands on sides of rufous neck and rufous inner throat patch.
31b   **Adult** (*kikuyuensis*; Angola, W Zambia, Zaïre and E Africa) Chest-band narrower, breast striped darker chestnut, lower underparts marked blackish.

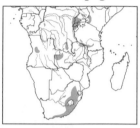

30   Greywing Francolin *Francolinus africanus*   Text page 204

South Africa only but some authorities include Moorland of NE Africa (Plate 10) within this species. Upland grassland and fynbos (coastal heath).

30   **Adult** Relatively featureless francolin, differing from Redwing in being overall greyer (but rufous on head- and neck-sides), has wholly blackish (not yellow-based) bill, distinctively freckled whitish throat and finely barred lower underparts. In flight rufous confined to primaries, not extending across most of secondaries as in Redwing.

36   Hartlaub's Francolin *Francolinus hartlaubi*   Text page 210

Namibia and Angola. A small francolin of rocky hills (kopjes). Overlaps with Red-billed and Orange River Francolins.

36a   **Adult male** Striking sexual dimorphism. Whitish, streaked underparts of male diagnostic within range.
36b   **Adult female** Rufous underparts of female also diagnostic within range.

29

31b

30

31a

36a

36b

Norman Arlott '97.

PLATE 12: AFRICAN FOREST FRANCOLINS

The first three species on this plate are closely related, rather featureless forest francolins, with reddish bill and legs, and are similar in all plumages. Mount Cameroon shows marginally stronger sexual differences and is less closely related to the others.

45 Ahanta Francolin *Francolinus ahantensis*

Text page 216

Replaces Scaly in W Africa (not known east of SW Nigeria). Forest edge and clearings.

45a **Adult** (typical) Almost featureless drab brown francolin with orange bill and legs, and somewhat isolated ear-covert patch, emphasised by dull whitish supercilium and throat, and whitish streaking on underparts (given good views).

45b **Adult** (western birds '*hopkinsoni*') Tend to have clearer whitish streaking below and rufous tone to brown wings.

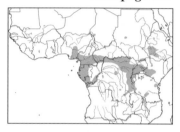

46 Scaly Francolin *Francolinus squamatus*

Text page 217

Equatorial forests. Replaces Ahanta east of River Niger. Compare larger and more chestnut Jackson's (Plate 15) in Kenya. See also Mount Cameroon and Nahan's (Plate 8).

46a **Adult** Reddish-orange bill and legs, and drab dark brownish plumage, with no obvious markings or bare skin around eye. Eastern birds tend to be darker and greyer. Has dull whitish throat, and paler feather edges below (given good views).

46b **Adult** Western birds tend to be paler below and more rufous-toned above.

46c **Juvenile** Duller, and even more weakly patterned than adult.

47 Grey-striped Francolin *Francolinus griseostriatus*

Text page 218

Restricted range. Forest edge and clearings.

47 **Adult** Orange bill and legs and chestnut-streaked buff-and-grey plumage distinctive within limited range.

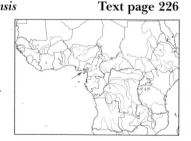

57 Mount Cameroon Francolin *Francolinus camerunensis*

Text page 226

Endemic to forests on Mt Cameroon. Scaly also occurs on the mountain, but Mount Cameroon has bare red skin around eye and shows sexual differences if seen reasonably well.

57a **Adult male** Black streaks on grey underparts and unmarked brown above.

57b **Adult female** Scaled underparts and closely barred upperparts.

45b   45a

46b

46a

46c

47

57b   57a

Norman Arlott

41 Red-billed Francolin *Francolinus adspersus*   Text page 213

Dry savannas of S Africa.

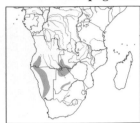

41a   **Adult** Distinctive, finely barred dark grey francolin, with striking
yellow eye-ring and red bill and legs.

41b   **Juvenile** Less distinctive (suggests Natal Francolin), but usually
accompanied by adults at this stage.

42 Cape Francolin *Francolinus capensis*   Text page 214

Endemic to SW Cape, where even forages on roadside verges. Large stocky
dark grey francolin of riverside scrub, fynbos and cultivation.

42   **Adult** Intricately vermiculated when seen close, but large size and
apparent uniformity of very dark plumage prevent confusion. Range
does not overlap with Natal Francolin. All plumages similar.

43 Hildebrandt's Francolin *Francolinus hildebrandti*   Text page 215

Upland shrubby grassland with rocky hillsides. Northern counterpart of
Natal, with ranges almost meeting in C Zambia. Strong sexual dimorphism
a useful feature (Natal has both sexes similar). Compare also smaller
Hartlaub's of Namibia and Angola (Plate 11).

43a   **Adult male** Red bill base and legs and spot-streaked underparts distinctive.

43b   **Adult female** Distinctively rufous below, some populations streaked
on neck and breast but others virtually unmarked (significance of
variation unclear, perhaps merely clinal, no races currently recognised).

44 Natal Francolin *Francolinus natalensis*   Text page 215

Grassy bush with rock outcrops. See also Hildebrandt's.

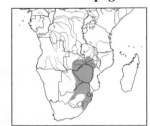

44   **Adult** Appears drab greyish, but plumage intricately scaled and
barred when close, with whitish lower underparts. Reddish legs and
yellowish base to dull red bill help separate from young Red-billed
and Swainson's (Plate 17), which overlap. Occasionally hybridises
with Swainson's in W Zimbabwe; hybrids resemble Natal but have
blackish upper mandible and some bare red skin on throat. All
plumages similar.

41b

41a

43b

42

43a

Norman Arlott

44

These four species geographically replace each other over most of N sub-Saharan Africa. The sexes are similar in all of them.

37   Double-spurred Francolin *Francolinus bicalcaratus*   Text page 211

Bushy grassland. Most widespread francolin in W Africa. Range almost meets Heuglin's in east and Clapperton's in northeast.

37a   **Adult** (nominate; main range) Combination of dull greenish legs and bill, bold supercilium and striped underparts distinctive. More localised Ahanta (Plate 12) has reddish-orange legs and is only weakly patterned on face and underparts. Varies somewhat, with darker birds in higher rainfall areas.

37b   **Adult** (*ayesha*; Morocco, where rare) Larger, darker and more rufous.

39   Heuglin's Francolin *Francolinus icterorhynchus*   Text page 212

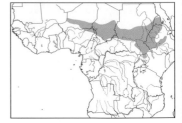

Grassy bush. Replaces Clapperton's over lusher parts of C Africa, but with some overlap in SW Sudan.

39   **Adult** Differs from similar Clapperton's in having orange-yellow legs, bill and bare skin around eye.

38   Clapperton's Francolin *Francolinus clappertoni*   Text page 212

Dry and semi-arid savanna. Marginally overlaps with similar Heuglin's in SW Sudan. In E Uganda compare Hildebrandt's (Plate 13). Variation is clinal, no races recognised.

38a   **Adult** Combination of red bill, legs and bare skin around eye, and spotted underparts distinctive. Western birds, such as this, tend to have whiter underparts.

38b   **Adult** Eastern birds are more heavily marked below.

40   Harwood's Francolin *Francolinus harwoodi*   Text page 213

C Ethiopia (Jemma Valley). Streamside cover in bottom of gorges; visits adjoining cultivation. Compare Erckel's (Plate 16), which occurs in vicinity of Harwood's.

40   **Adult male** Much darker than Clapperton's, lacking latter's whitish throat and supercilium, is scaled rather than blotched below and has buff rear underparts.

37a

37b

38a

39

38b

40

PLATE 15: MONTANE FRANCOLINS I

These are large francolins with red bills and legs. They inhabit montane forests, extending above the tree-line into the alpine heath zone. Sexes are similar.

55   Handsome Francolin *Francolinus nobilis*   **Text page 225**

Mountains bordering E Zaïre.

55   Adult Distinctive large, dark rufous francolin with greyer head and rump; overlaps with smaller, browner Scaly (Plate 12), which lacks red bare skin around eye.

54   Chestnut-naped Francolin *Francolinus castaneicollis*   **Text page 224**

Ethiopia and NW Somalia. Palest suggest Erckel's (Plate 16), but latter has black bill and yellowish legs.

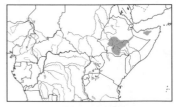

54a   Adult ('*gofanus*' nominate; SW Ethiopia) Red bill and legs, blackish face and rufous head, neck and underparts markings. Nominate shows clinal variation with palest birds ('*ogoennsis*') in Somalia.

54b   Adult ('*kaffanus*' nominate; W Ethiopia) Darkest and most chestnut of nominate populations.

54c   Adult (*atrifrons*; Sidamo, Ethiopia) Lacks rufous, underparts almost unmarked, but blackish face and red bill and legs suggest the species.

56   Jackson's Francolin *Francolinus jacksoni*   **Text page 225**

Montane Kenya. Distinctive within range. Smaller Scaly (Plate 12) is browner, almost unmarked below and occurs at lower altitudes. No races recognised.

56a   Adult ('nominate'; Aberdares) Large reddish francolin.
56b   Adult ('*pollenorum*'; Mt Kenya) Rather darker.
56c   Juvenile Extensively close-barred, typical of the group.

54c

55

54b

54a

56c

56a

56b

Norman Arlott

52   Erckel's Francolin *Francolinus erckelii*   **Text page 222**

Bushy mountain plateaux and hillsides; over most of range it is the
only highland francolin. Introduced Hawaii.

52a   Adult (nominate; Ethiopia and Eritrea) Sexes similar. Large
francolin with black bill, yellowish legs, chestnut crown and
whitish throat.

52b   Adult (*pentoni*; Sudan) Paler and greyer.

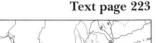

53   Djibouti Francolin *Francolinus ochropectus*   **Text page 223**

Endemic to woodland in Djibouti (where no similar species occur).

53   Adult Darker and smaller than Erckel's, with grey crown centre
and more prominent white spot behind eye; underparts
marked with buff-and-black spotting, rather than rufous and
black.

58   Swierstra's Francolin *Francolinus swierstrai*   **Text page 227**

Endemic to highland forest of W Angola (current status unknown).

58a   Adult male Distinctive whitish face and underparts contrast
with blackish breast and cap; only Red-necked (Plate 17)
overlaps and that occurs at lower altitudes.

58b   Adult female Warmer brown above, finely mottled and
streaked buff.

58c   Juvenile Buff wash to face and throat, flanks scaled.

52a

52b

53

58a

58b

58c

Norman Arlott

PLATE 17: BARE-THROATED FRANCOLINS OR AFRICAN SPURFOWL

50 Red-necked Francolin *Francolinus afer*

Text page 220

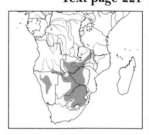

Forest edge and lusher bush than others in group. A large number of local variations occur. Seven subspecies now recognised (see text), falling into two groups:

Black-and-white group (five races, E Africa and W Angola) including:

50a **Adult** (nominate; W Angola) A variable dark, and often white-streaked, francolin with diagnostic red legs, as well as facial and throat skin, and bill.

50b **Adult** ('*cunensis*'; N Namibia) The southernmost and palest end of the cline now included in the nominate race.

50c **Adult** (*swynnertoni*; E Zimbabwe and S Mozambique). Sides of head white. Centre of belly black.

Vermiculated or rufous-striped group (two races, central and north of range):

50d **Adult** (*cranchii*; Lake Victoria to E Angola and SW Tanzania). A finely vermiculated grey race.

---

51 Swainson's Francolin *Francolinus swainsonii*

Text page 221

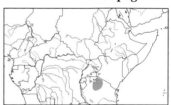

Wooded bush. In Zimbabwe rarely hybridises with Natal (lacks bare skin on face and has partially feathered throat) and *swynnertoni* Red-necked (like Red-necked but has blackish bill and intermediate underparts and head patterns).

51a **Adult** (nominate; most of range, except S Mozambique and W Zimbabwe) Distinctive combination of red facial and throat skin, with blackish upper mandible and legs.

51b **Juvenile** Soon begins to lose throat feathering.

---

49 Grey-breasted Francolin *Francolinus rufopictus*

Text page 219

Bushy plains NW Tanzania. Hybrids with Yellow-necked reported from SE Serengeti.

49 **Adult** Differs from Yellow-necked in having orange bill, orange or pink throat skin, is overall greyer and paler with finer, less obvious, streaking. Red-necked has red legs and lacks chestnut and white markings (ssp. *cranchii*) in area of potential overlap.

---

48 Yellow-necked Francolin *Francolinus leucoscepus*

Text page 219

Dry savannas. Meets Grey-breasted in SE Serengeti National Park, where some hybridisation occurs.

48 **Adult** Dark legs, bare yellow throat and heavily pale-streaked body distinctive. In flight has buff patch over bases of primaries.

50d

50a

50b

50c

51b

49

51a

48

Norman Arlott

PLATE 18: *PERDIX* PARTRIDGES

Medium-sized unspurred Palearctic partridges of open country. They are streaked and barred above, have dark belly patches, rufous tails and flank bars. Sexes are similar.

59 Grey Partridge *Perdix perdix*

Text page 228

Europe and W Siberia; introduced North America. Seven races varying in overall colour saturation; eastern race *robusta* is paler grey, with weaker markings on upperparts.

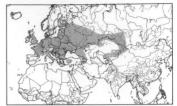

59a **Adult male** (nominate) Dull partridge of open farmland, with finely barred and buff-streaked upperparts, orange face and weak flank barring. Closer views reveal a chestnut belly patch and grey breast. See Daurian for distinctions. Juvenile dull brownish overall, with pale shaft streaks both above and below.

59b **Adult female** Duller orange on face and smaller or no belly patch; scapulars and wing-coverts lack chestnut marks, being more coarsely barred black and buff.

59c **Adult** (rare chestnut mutation '*montana*').

60 Daurian Partridge *Perdix dauurica*

Text page 229

Eastern counterpart of Grey. In overlap zone replaces Grey in bushy foothills, but moves into plains in winter. At least two races, nominate shown.

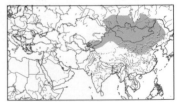

60a **Adult male** Has buffier underparts, especially chest, blackish belly patch and a seasonal 'beard'. An individual with typical extent of buff at breast centre. Where ranges meet, Daurian is darker than *robusta* Grey, with extensive chestnut markings above and bold streaks on scapulars (like nominate Grey).

60b **Adult male** An individual with extensive buff on breast.

60c **Adult female** Duller than male, with smaller belly-patch.

61 Tibetan Partridge *Perdix hodgsoniae*

Text page 230

Tibetan plateau, on rocky slopes. Compare also Chukar (Plate 4) and Snow Partridge (Plate 1). Three races.

61a **Adult** (nominate) Variegated facial pattern contrasting with rufous nape is distinctive, yet the upperparts resemble those of the other two *Perdix*.

61b **Juvenile** (nominate) Featureless buffy-brown, with pale streaks, typical of the genus.

59a

59b

59c

60a

60c

60b

61a

61b

PLATE 19: ABERRANT PARTRIDGES

62   Long-billed Partridge *Rhizothera longirostris*   Text page 232

Dry forest with bamboo. Compare Ferruginous Partridge. Two races; *dulitensis* of Sarawak Mts has greyer and paler underparts.

62a   **Adult male** (nominate) Relatively large partridge with rufous face and underparts and yellowish legs. Easily identified even when rather long, deep-based bill not apparent. Flushes only with great reluctance but when does so shows contrast between pale buffy wings and rump, and dark mantle and back.

62b   **Adult female** (nominate) Lacks grey breast of male.

63   Madagascar Partridge *Margaroperdix madagarensis*   Text page 233

Madagascar. Bushy and grassy habitats.

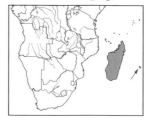

63a   **Adult male** Dark reddish-brown partridge, with striking facial and underparts patterns.

63b   **Adult female** Lacks any strong plumage features, other than being entirely narrowly barred and freckled. Confusion unlikely on Madagascar but on Mauritius and Réunion compare with larger Grey Francolin.

64   Black Wood-partridge *Melanoperdix nigra*   Text page 234

Lowland rainforest. In gloom of forest, other species (i.e. Crimson-headed or even Ferruginous, Plate 29) can look equally as dark or rusty-brown. Juvenile recalls female but has white spots on flanks.

64a   **Adult male** Small all-black partridge with a very stout bill; striking sexual dimorphism a useful clue if pairs seen.

64b   **Adult female** Entirely rusty-brown.

62a

62b

63a

63b

64a

64b

DAVID MEAD

70 Harlequin Quail *Coturnix delegorguei*

Text page 241

African grasslands; influxes often occur following rains. Compare Blue Quail. Two or three races, nominate shown.

70a **Adult male** Rich chestnut and black underparts, contrasting with striking black-and-white facial pattern.

70b **Adult female** Darker than Common, buffier below and has heavier spotting at breast-sides; outer primaries plain brown (barred in Common).

72 Blue Quail *Coturnix adansonii*

Text page 244

African grasslands. Compare larger Harlequin.

72a **Adult male** Differs from King Quail (of Asia) in having blue breast, belly and vent, with chestnut on flanks and forewing (obvious in flight).

72b **Adult female** Similar to King, but has clear barring on wing-coverts (King has plain coverts) and lacks narrow dark cheek bar.

72c **Adult male** In flight. Note chestnut forewing.

73 King Quail *Coturnix chinensis*

Text page 245

Tiny quail of grasslands in Asia and Australia. Compare Blue of Africa. Ten races.

73a **Adult male** (*lineata*; Philippines, Borneo, Sulawesi, Lesser Sundas, Australia) Blue with white throat patches and rufous belly. If flushed tiny size and uniformly brownish forewing diagnostic (only some buttonquails are as small, but have pale panel that contrasts with darker flight feathers).

73b **Adult female** (*lineata*) Barred underparts, plain forewing, yellowish legs and a narrow dark bar below eye.

73c **Adult male** (*lineata*) In flight. Note brown forewing.

71 Brown Quail *Coturnix ypsilophora*

Text page 242

Finely barred dull buffish, greyish or reddish-brown (even blackish in race *dogwa*) Australasian quail. Outside Australia main confusion possibilities are with buttonquails. At least ten races. Nominate Tasmanian race sometimes separated as Swamp Quail (see text).

71a **Adult male** (nominate; Swamp Quail: Tasmania) Note yellow irides.

71b **Adult female** (nominate) More blotched above than male.

71c **Adult male** (*australis*; Brown Quail: Australian mainland) Easily distinguished from Stubble (Plate 20) by stouter bill and dusky ear-smudge within otherwise plain face. Unstreaked underparts marked with fine wavy barring.

71d **Adult male** (*pallidior*; Lesser Sundas on Sumba and Sawu) Has blackish crown, bold pale shaft streaks above, and is quite grey below.

71e **Adult male** (*raaltenii*; rest of Lesser Sundas) Bright rufous underparts, with only weak shaft streaks.

71f **Adult male** (*dogwa*; S New Guinea) An almost slaty-black form.

70a
70b
72c
72a
72b
73c
73a
73b
71a
71b
71c
71d
71e
71f
C.D'S

PLATE 22: BUSH-QUAILS

All members of this genus are confined to grassy habitats in the Indian subcontinent. Marked sexual dimorphism and acquisition of adult male plumage complicates separation of Jungle and Rock.

75 Jungle Bush-quail *Perdicula asiatica*

Text page 247

Dry grassland, often with scattered rocks, amidst tracts of scrub-jungle. Five races (four shown).

75a **Adult male** (nominate; C India) Barred underparts, and masked and capped appearance created by long whitish supercilium and parallel whitish band, separating brownish 'mask' from rufous throat; note also rufous vent. Compare with Rock.

75b **Adult female** (nominate) Grey-brown crown, ear-coverts and upperparts, with variable buff streaking and black markings on scapulars, long whitish supercilium and rich rufous throat.

75c **Adult male** (*vidali*; W India) Darker, with rufous tones above and bolder barring below.

75d **Adult male** (*ceylonensis*; Sri Lanka) Darkest and most coloured form.

75e **Adult male** (*punjaubi*; N India) Paler, sandier than nominate, with finer barring below, and bolder barring on rump.

75f **Immature male** Birds showing mixed sex features are young males (*contra* Rock).

75g **Juvenile** Both sexes female-like, but with whitish streaking on throat and breast.

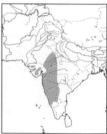

76 Rock Bush-quail *Perdicula argoondah*

Text page 248

Semi-arid or dry stony country, with sparse scrubby cover. Three races (two extremes shown).

76a **Adult male** (*meinertzhageni*; palest race from north of range) Lacks masked and capped effect of Jungle, has upperparts more distinctly barred, rusty ear-coverts and throat merge, and vent buffy-white (but see race *salimalii*).

76b **Adult male** (*salimalii*; red laterite hills of S India) Washed brick-red overall, including ventral region.

76c **Adult female** (*meinertzhageni*) Almost overall unmarked rufous, pale chin and less conspicuous supercilium.

76d **Juvenile** Both sexes barred below (i.e. male-like), older 'intermediate' stages are young females (*contra* Jungle).

77 Painted Bush-quail *Perdicula erythrorhyncha*

Text page 249

Grassy hillsides in lusher habitats than Rock or Jungle. Two races (one shown).

77a **Adult male** (nominate; W India) Bright white throat and supercilium and red bill and legs diagnostic.

77b **Adult female** Recalls darker populations of female Jungle but more richly coloured, with clearer white streaks on upperparts, bold black markings on flanks and red bill and legs.

77c **Juvenile** Both sexes like dull female, with paler legs and bill.

PLATE 23: HIMALAYAN QUAILS AND BAMBOO-PARTRIDGES

78   Manipur Bush-quail *Perdicula manipurensis*   Text page 250

Lowland grassland, NE India. Rare, few recent reports. Two races (nominate shown), northern form *inglisi* (north of Brahmaputra) less boldly marked with black.

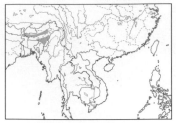

78a   Adult male (nominate; south of Brahmaputra) Dark olive-grey plumage relieved by buffish rear underparts, rufous throat and quite bold black markings. Uniform dark grey upperparts distinctive even when flushed.

78b   Adult female Lacks rufous on face and throat.

79   Himalayan Quail *Ophrysia superciliosa*   Text page 251

Mid-Himalayan steep grassy slopes with scrubby hollows. Probably now extinct, last definite report 1890 but rumours persist. Unlikely to survive in former haunts in NW India but could possibly do so in under-worked northeast. Both sexes relatively full tailed and quite unmistakable. No map.

79a   Adult male Dark brownish-slate, contrasting with whitish forehead, supercilium and face marks; red bill and legs.

79b   Adult female Uniform cinnamon brown, mottled black; red bill and legs.

106   Mountain Bamboo-partridge *Bambusicola fytchii*   Text page 274

Hill-forest edges, scrubby slopes and foothill grasslands of SE Asia. Range does not overlap with Chinese Bamboo-partridge. Two races (both shown).

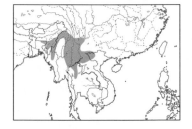

106a   Adult (nominate; NE India and N Myanmar) Sexes similar. Rather large, long-tailed partridge. Whitish supercilium contrasts with blackish or rufous eye-stripe and has rusty-streaked breast and bold black flank spots. In flight rufous primaries and sides to rather long tail distinctive of genus.

106b   Adult (*hopkinsoni*; SW China, N Indochina) Somewhat buffier below and greyer above than nominate.

107   Chinese Bamboo-partridge *Bambusicola thoracica*   Text page 275

Scrubby slopes and foothill grasslands. Sexes similar in both populations.

107a   Adult (nominate; China, introduced Japan) Large grey-breasted and grey-necked partridge with boldly spotted flanks. Has rufous face, throat and neck-sides, bordered by grey supercilium and breast-band; underparts very pale buff marked with black scaly spots.

107b   Juvenile (nominate) Dull brownish, with fine buff shaft streaks. Typical of genus.

107c   Adult (*sonorivox*, Taiwan) Darker, with chestnut, not blackish spots on richer buff flanks and extensively grey head and neck (with rufous restricted to throat centre).

78b

78a

79b

79a

106a

106b

107a

107c

107b

81 Necklaced Hill-partridge *Arborophila torqueola*

Text page 253

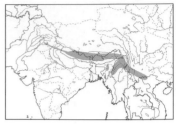

A dark-legged hill-partridge of Himalayan forests, chiefly at 1500–4000 m. Four races (three shown). See text.

81a   **Adult male** (nominate; Garwhal to Arunachal Pradesh) Chestnut crown and ear-coverts and blackish throat, contrasting with white chest patch.

81b   **Adult female** (nominate) Rusty throat, differing from Rufous-throated by barred (not plain or spotted) upperparts, streaked (not spotted) throat, grey (not reddish) legs and browner (not pure grey) breast.

81c   **Juvenile male** (nominate) Young birds are dull, without rufous flank marks, and have whitish breast spotting; sexual differences are apparent from an early age.

81d   **Adult male** (*batemani*; NE India to SW China) Darker, more chestnut below.

81e   **Adult male** (*griseata*; W Tonkin) Greyer above, with slaty breast and more rufous crown and nape.

87 Taiwan Hill-partridge *Arborophila crudigularis*

Text page 258

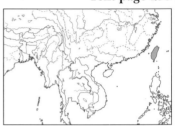

Broad-leaved hill forests on Taiwan, where it is the only hill-partridge.

87a   **Adult male** Superficially similar to White-cheeked but has white (not black) throat and grey (not brown or rusty) mantle in both sexes; the two are also widely separated by range.

87b   **Adult female** Less extensive streaking on neck than male.

86 White-cheeked Hill-partridge *Arborophila atrogularis*

Text page 257

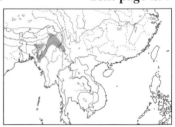

Secondary forest of E Himalayan foothills, chiefly below 1000 m.

86   **Adult** Bold black-and-white head pattern is distinctive in range, comprising white cheeks and whitish supercilium, which contrast with black throat and 'bandit-mask'. Sexes similar.

88 Hainan Hill-partridge *Arborophila ardens*

Text page 259

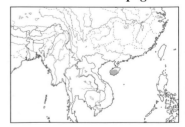

Broad-leaved hill forests on Hainan, where it is the only hill-partridge. Now confined to a few small relict forest patches.

88   **Adult** Combination of blackish head, with gleaming white ear-patch, orange or red breast, and grey underparts is distinctive. Sexes similar.

81b

81c

81a

81e

81d

87a

87b

86

88

C.D'S

90 Orange-necked Hill-partridge *Arborophila davidi*

Text page 261

Low hill forest of NE Cochinchina, Vietnam. Rare.

90 **Adult** Orange-rufous throat and neck-sides broken by bold black collar encircling throat distinctive. Otherwise resembles Brown-breasted of race *albigula* (Plate 26), which occurs as close as S Annam but does not actually overlap. Sexes similar.

92 Cambodian Hill-partridge *Arborophila cambodiana*

Text page 262

Low forested hills of S Cambodia. Little known.

92 **Adult** Bright chestnut face and breast and contrasting bold chequerboard flank pattern are distinctive features; though recalls Bornean, Cambodian has heavily barred upperparts. Sexes similar. Compare Siamese.

91 Siamese Hill-partridge *Arborophila diversa*

Text page 261

Forests of Khao Sabap Mts of SE Thailand.

91 **Adult** Buffy-brown supercilium and face, dusky foreneck, rusty breast and black-and-white spotted underparts distinctive. The boldly patterned flanks are shared by Brown-breasted (Plate 26), which in Thailand is confined to hill regions of the north and west, but Siamese lacks extensive blackish on the neck-sides and has chestnut, not olive-brown breast. Sexes similar. Compare Cambodian.

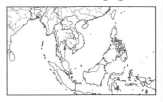

98 Red-billed Hill-partridge *Arborophila rubrirostris*

Text page 267

Montane forests of Sumatra, where overlaps with Sumatran (Plate 26), but latter has black bill and grey head and underparts, bolder black-and-white flank-bands and small white ear-patch.

98a **Adult** Typical black-faced bird. Bright red bill and legs, blackish head (with or without white on face), reddish-brown breast and very narrow white flank bars distinctive. Sexes similar.
98b **Adult** White-throated variant.

97 Bornean Hill-partridge *Arborophila hyperythra*

Text page 266

Thickets in hill and montane forests, chiefly above 1200 m on Borneo. Sexes similar. Two races (both shown).

97a **Adult** (nominate; N Borneo to W Sabah) Very distinctive, being overall dull reddish-brown, with boldly spotted black-and-white flanks. Compare Ferruginous Partridge (Plate 29). Varying amounts of grey on head.
97b **Adult** (*erythrophrys*; Mt Kinabalu, Sabah) Lacks grey on head of nominate.

90

92

91

98b

98a

97b

97a

C.D'S

89   Brown-breasted Hill-partridge *Arborophila brunneopectus*   **Text page 260**

Broad-leaved forests to 1850 m. SE Asia. Three races (all shown).

89a   Adult (nominate; E Myanmar and Thailand east to Yunnan and N Laos) Brownish underparts, barred upperparts and black-and-white flank markings distinctive within range. In Thailand Brown-breasted tends to replace Rufous-throated (Plate 27) below 1200 m. Sexes similar.

89b   Adult (*henrici*; N and C Indochina) Buffier white on face and throat, less blackish on collar and warmer brown above and on breast. Reduced black on flank feathers.

89c   Adult (*albigula*; S Annam) More extensive and whiter pale areas on face, throat, forehead and supercilium than other races.

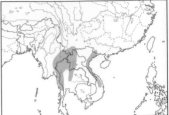

95   Grey-breasted Hill-partridge *Arborophila orientalis*   **Text page 264**

Montane forests of E Java.

95   Adult Basically grey with an almost all-white head. No other hill-partridges overlap, but Javan, which has chestnut belly, grey breast and rufous rather than white face, inhabits montane forest in W and C Java. Sexes similar.

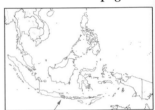

94   Sumatran Hill-partridge *Arborophila sumatrana*   **Text page 264**

Montane forest undergrowth to 2000 m on Sumatra. Sexes similar. Two races, both shown (differences require investigation).

94a   Adult (nominate; C Sumatra) A grey-breasted hill-partridge with black-and-white flank bars and white ear-patch. Overlaps with Red-billed (Plate 25). Similar to Malayan and Grey-breasted (with which formerly considered conspecific), but flank pattern differs.

94b   Adult (*rolli*; N Sumatra) Has blacker throat than nominate, and usually has white loral spot as well as cheek patch; breast more buffy-grey than nominate.

93   Malaysian Hill-partridge *Arborophila campbelli*   **Text page 263**

Hill forest undergrowth, above 1100 m in Peninsular Malaysia where it is the only hill-partridge.

93   Adult Grey with weak black-and-rufous flank bars and white cheek patch and loral spot. Sexes similar.

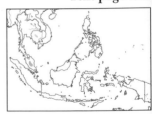

96   Javan Hill-partridge *Arborophila javanica*   **Text page 265**

Hill forest, W and C Java. Three races, two shown (*lawuana* of Mt Lawu has more black on neck than *bartelsi*).

96a   Adult (nominate; W Java) Chestnut flanks and belly contrast with grey breast and rufous, rather than white face distinguishes it from Grey-breasted, which replaces Javan at east end of island. Sexes similar.

96b   Adult (*bartelsi*; WC Java) Less black than other races, with throat and chest almost unmarked rufous.

89a

89b

89c

95

94b

94a

93

96a

96b

C.D'S

83 Rufous-throated Hill-partridge *Arborophila rufogularis*

Text page 255

Montane forests, primarily at 1500–1800 m, of Himalayas and SE Asia. Mid-elevation species, replaced by Necklaced in higher forest. Sexes similar. Seven races, four shown.

83a **Adult male** (nominate; Himalayas east to Mishmi Hills) Lacks intervening collar or belt of colour between rufous throat and grey breast, but note blackish throat in *intermedia* and may be boldly spotted in others (see below). Most likely confusion is with female Necklaced, but Rufous-throated has plain or spotted (not barred) upperparts, spotted or blackish (not streaked) throat, reddish (not grey) legs and grey (rather than brownish) breast. Compare also Chestnut-breasted.

83b **Adult female** (nominate) Similar to male but less spotted on chin and throat and has scattered whitish spots on breast.

83c **Adult** (*intermedia*; Assam, N Myanmar to Yunnan) Upper throat blackish.

83d **Adult** (*annamensis*; S Annam) Throat very pale, almost whitish, and boldly spotted.

83e **Adult** (*guttata*; C Annam) Throat clear rufous, spotted only at sides.

84 Chestnut-breasted Hill-partridge *Arborophila mandellii*

Text page 256

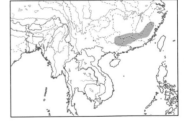

Oak–rhododendron forest of E Himalayas, chiefly at 900–1800 m. Apparently prefers more humid forests than Rufous-throated. Little known.

84 **Adult** Separated from Rufous-throated by chestnut, not grey crown, nape and breast and black and bright white gorget (merely a black line in Rufous-throated). Sexes similar.

85 Collared Hill-partridge *Arborophila gingica*

Text page 257

Moist hill forest in SE China, chiefly at 700–900 m. Overlaps with no other hill-partridge.

85 **Adult** Prominent white forehead, chiefly grey underparts (chestnut flank edging may not be obvious) and chocolate, white and chestnut breast-bands are most important features. Sexes similar.

82 Sichuan Hill-partridge *Arborophila rufipectus*

Text page 254

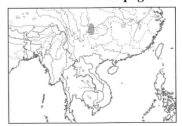

Oak forests in SE Sichuan, chiefly at 1400–1800 m. No other hill-partridge occurs in range.

82a **Adult male** Distinctive, has whitish throat, supercilium and underparts contrasting with broad chestnut breast-band.

82b **Adult female** Greyish-brown breast-band and yellow wash to white throat.

83b

83a

83c

83d

83e

84

85

82a

82b

C.D'S

Members of this group differ from other hill-partridges in being primarily lowland birds, with overall scaly or mottled plumages, lacking any strong patterning, and have yellowish or greenish legs. Their relationships are extremely confused, with some authorities considering them as a single, or two species (see text). Some further taxonomic revision may be desirable, i.e. *tonkinensis*, which has been treated as a form of Scaly-breasted, may deserve specific status.

99 Chestnut-necklaced Hill-partridge *Arborophila charltonii*   Text page 267

Four well-separated subspecies in Malay Peninsula, N Sumatra, NE Borneo and N Vietnam.

99a Adult (nominate; S Thailand and Malay Peninsula) Unmarked chestnut breast-band bordered above by a blackish collar (except *tonkinensis*), a rusty ear-coverts patch (obscured in *tonkinensis*), red orbital skin and yellowish legs (but see Scaly-breasted and Annam for discussion). Race *atjenensis* of N Sumatra very similar but a little brighter.

99b Adult (*graydoni*; NE Borneo) Duller than nominate, with browner ear-patch and greenish-yellow legs.

99c Adult (*tonkinensis*; Tonkin, Vietnam) Duller, with greenish-yellow legs, speckled ear-patch, chestnut of breast only at centre, more spotting on lower breast and lacks dark collar and eye-stripe. This form could be given specific status, conversely it has been treated as a form of Scaly-breasted.

101 Scaly-breasted Hill-partridge *Arborophila chloropus*   Text page 269

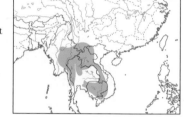

Lowland forests of SE Asia. Four races, two shown.

101a Adult (nominate; Myanmar to Yunnan and N Thailand) Separated from other members of this complex by green (not yellowish) legs and weak scaling on flanks. The otherwise speckled and finely barred plumage, lacking bold patterns distinguishes it from other forest partridges. Sexes similar. Race *peninsularis* (SW Thailand) is similar but has duller buff underparts like *cognacqi*; race *olivacea* (Cambodia to W Tonkin) also similar.

101b Adult (*cognacqi*; Cochinchina, Vietnam) Duller and colder basic plumage tone, with whiter foreneck and drabber buff underparts.

100 Annam Hill-partridge *Arborophila merlini*   Text page 268

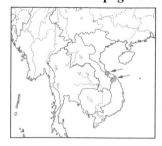

Lowland forests of C Annam. Very restricted (see text). Two races described, both shown, but perhaps best treated as monotypic (see text).

100a Adult (nominate; northern population) Replaced further north by *tonkinensis* form of Chestnut-necklaced, which principally differs in having unmarked chestnut breast-band. To the south and west, it is well isolated from subspecies *cognacqi* and *olivacea* of Scaly-breasted, from which Annam differs in having yellowish legs (not green) and bold dark scaling and spotting on lower breast and flanks. Sexes similar.

100b Adult (*vivida*; Bach Ma National Park) Averages brighter.

99a   99b   99c

101a   101b

100a   100b

C.D'S

102 Ferruginous Partridge *Caloperdix oculea*

Text page 270

Lowland and foothill evergreen forest, of Malaysia, Sumatra and Borneo. Three races, two shown.

102a **Adult** (nominate; Thai-Malay Peninsula) Sexes similar. Rusty forest partridge, with distinctive round black spots on pale brown wings. Blackish upperparts and flanks are clearly scaled rufous, white or buff.

102b **Adult** (*ocellata*; Sumatra) Pale fringes to blackish feathers of mantle and flanks mostly buff, rather than white, but variable. Ssp. *borneensis* of Borneo has more extensive black spotting on rear flanks than other two, with both buff and white fringes to black feathers of flanks and mantle.

102c **Juvenile** Duller than adult, with buffish feather edges, irregular blackish barring and spotting almost forming chest-band, and has blackish scaling on nape.

103 Crimson-headed Partridge *Haematortyx sanguiniceps*

Text page 271

Highland forests, 1000–1500 m. Borneo.

103a **Adult male** Unmistakable black partridge with crimson head and breast. Coloration only approached by male (especially patchy immature male) of rarer Black Wood-partridge (Plate 19), which has much deeper based black bill.

103b **Adult female** Duller than male, with duskier bill.

103c **Juvenile** Dull blackish with brownish-orange head, mottled black on crown; breast blackish-brown, with rusty markings on many feathers. Wing-coverts tipped with small red spots.

104 Crested Partridge *Rollulus rouloul*

Text page 272

Lowland and foothill evergreen forest, of Malaysia, Sumatra and Borneo. Unlikely to be confused.

104a **Adult male** Unmistakable small partridge, shining metallic blue-green, with remarkable red 'shaving-brush' crest and surprisingly obvious white spot on forecrown.

104b **Adult female** May appear equally dark but lacks obvious crest, and is distinctively pea-green, with rufous wings and slate-grey head.

104c **Juvenile male** Crest becomes obvious from an early age.

104d **Juvenile female** Duller than adult, with buff spots on wing feathers.

102b　102a　102c

103c　103a　103b

104a　104b

104c

DAVID MEAD

104d

108 Red Spurfowl *Galloperdix spadicea*

Text page 276

Wooded hills, scrubby thickets. Peninsular India. Sexes differ. Three races, two extremes shown.

108a **Adult male** (*stewarti*; Kerala) Rather long-bodied rufous fowl with relatively long dark tail and red bill, legs and facial skin. Darkest and most richly coloured race. Nominate of C India is rufous with distinctly pale, greyer head and female quite well barred.

108b **Adult female** (*stewarti*) Overall duller, narrowly barred with blackish.

108c **Adult male** (*caurina*; W Rajasthan and Gujarat) Palest race; female almost unmarked.

109 Painted Spurfowl *Galloperdix lunulata*

Text page 277

Dry wooded hills of peninsular India.

109a **Adult male** Much darker than Red, looks blackish in field in usual brief view, the spotting and colour being only apparent with more prolonged views. Has dusky bill and legs and feathered face. Kerala race of Red may appear as dark as Painted, but has red bill, legs and facial skin, and lacks white spotting and metallic blackish of male Painted.

109b **Adult female** Virtually unmarked (many female Red are barred), with buff-ish throat and rear underparts, and bill and legs are blackish, not red.

109c **Immature male** Should be larger than shown, resembles female but male features develop in first year.

109d **Juvenile** Weak barring on upperparts and buff freckling below apparent at close range.

110 Sri Lanka Spurfowl *Galloperdix bicalcarata*

Text page 278

Dense forest in Sri Lanka, where the only spurfowl. Very shy.

110a **Adult male** Chestnut rear body and wings and boldly white-spotted foreparts of male render it unmistakable; better views reveal red legs and facial skin.

110b **Adult female** Overall ruddy-brown, but offers some contrast with whitish throat.

108a

108c

108b

109a

109b

109c

109d

110b

110a

KHEF

PLATE 31: BLOOD PHEASANT AND EASTERN TRAGOPANS

111 Blood Pheasant *Ithaginis cruentus*

Text page 279

High forest, bamboo and alpine scrub (2500–4500 m). Himalayan and Chinese mountains. At least 11 subspecies, falling into two groups (representatives shown here).

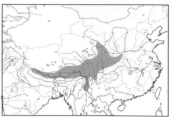

111a **Adult male** (nominate; Nepal and Sikkim) Peculiar short-tailed rotund pheasant, with mop-crest and relatively short tail. Male varies in presence or absence of red on head and breast; some races can appear dull greyish in field, unless seen well. Nominate is typical of green-winged races.

111b **Adult female** (nominate) Crested appearance and relatively unmarked brown plumage distinctive.

111c **Adult male** (*marionae*; W Yunnan) Very crimson race of green-winged group.

111d **Adult male** (*clarkei*; NW Yunnan) Very drab form of green-winged group.

111e **Adult male** (*sinensis*; Shaanxi) Drab grey race of red-winged group.

114 Temminck's Tragopan *Tragopan temminckii*

Text page 283

Mixed forests with bamboo (2500–3600 m). SE Asia.

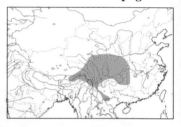

114a **Adult male** Most like Satyr (Plate 32), but has white-spotted red, not brown upperparts, flaming orange collar and pale grey streak–spots (not black-rimmed white eye-spots) from breast down.

114b **Adult female** Bluish orbital skin (like Satyr), but usually overall dull brown lacking rufous tones to tail, and has clearer white spotting on underparts than other tragopans.

116 Cabot's Tragopan *Tragopan caboti*

Text page 285

Evergreen and mixed forests (to 1400 m). SE China. Two similar races, one shown, the other *guangxiensis* of NE Guangxi Zizhiqui is darker, with more extensive maroon-red on back and rump and has yellowish-white rather than buff spotting.

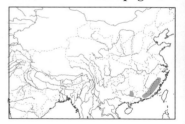

116a **Adult male** (nominate; Zhejiang east to Guangdong) Distinctive, having yellow-orange facial and throat skin and plain buff underparts; upperparts also heavily marked with buff or yellowish-white spotting.

116b **Adult female** (nominate) Quite dark but has much larger pale spotting on underparts than other tragopans and an orange orbital ring.

111a

111b

111e

111c

111d

114a

114b

116b

116a

DAVID MEAD

112 Western Tragopan *Tragopan melanocephalus*

Text page 281

Himalayan forests (2000–3500 m). N Pakistan to NW India. Darkest tragopan.

112a **Adult male** Blackish under- and upperparts contrasting with scarlet nape and orange breast, and red facial and blue gular skin.

112b **Adult female** Duller, more grey-brown than female Satyr, with reddish or orange (not bluish) orbital skin, whiter spotting and streaking, and contrast between darker breast and paler rear underparts.

113 Satyr Tragopan *Tragopan satyra*

Text page 282

Mixed and broad-leaved forests (2500–4000 m). C and E Himalayas.

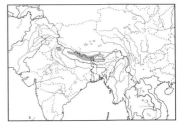

113a **Adult male** Recalls Temminck's (Plate 31), but has brown upperparts, not red, and lacks extensive orange collar of Temminck's; underparts covered by black-rimmed white spots (Temminck's has pearl-grey streak–spots).

113b **Adult female** Bluish orbital skin (like Temminck's), but is usually overall more rufous-brown, and has duller whitish spotting on underparts. Some can be quite dull grey-brown, but even these typically show warm brown tail.

114 Blyth's Tragopan *Tragopan blythii*

Text page 283

Moist forest (2000–3000 m). E Himalayas. Two races.

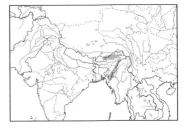

114a **Adult male** (nominate; NE India) Distinctive yellow facial and throat skin, and plain grey underparts from breast down. Bhutan and N Arunachal Pradesh form *molesworthi* darker, but grey of underparts paler and extending higher on breast.

114b **Adult female** (nominate) Yellow orbital skin (blue in Temminck's and Satyr), but is greyer brown than most Satyr and has contrast between distinctly paler belly and darker breast and flanks. Female of Bhutan race darker than nominate Blyth's; both races differ from female Temminck's in lacking bold white spotting on underparts.

112b

112a

113b

113a

114b

114a

DAVID MEAD

PLATE 33: MONALS

Large, heavily built pheasants with broad, flat tails of high-altitude forests in Himalayan region and W China. Blackish males show highly iridescent colours in good light, especially coppery nape. Juvenile resembles female, first-year male patchily plumaged.

118 Himalayan Monal *Lophophorus impejanus*   Text page 288

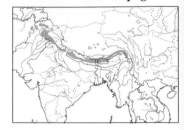

Himalayas. Overlaps with Sclater's in east of range. Monotypic but some individual variation (see text).

118a Adult male A typical individual with 'peacock-crest', white back, black breast and all-rufous tail.
118b Adult male Uncommon green-breasted dark-backed variant.
118c Adult female Separated from other monals by having rump and uppertail-coverts barred brown, concolorous with wings, pale streaks on underparts, as well as upperparts, dark tail bars broader than brown ones, and clean white throat.
118d Adult male In flight.
118e Adult male Green-breasted dark-backed variant. In flight.

119 Sclater's Monal *Lophophorus sclateri*   Text page 290

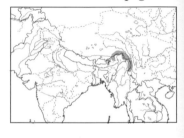

E Himalayas, narrowly meeting Himalayan. Two, perhaps three races.

119a Adult male (nominate; SE Tibet, NE India) Virtually uncrested, with diagnostic white rump and uppertail-coverts and white tail with chestnut band. This individual has an extensive chestnut tail-band (even within range of nominate many have much narrower chestnut band); ssp. *orientalis* (NE Myanmar, NW Yunnan) has narrower tail-band, while newly discovered 'white-tailed monal' (not shown) of W Arunachal Pradesh (marked ? on map) is most likely a form of Sclater's with an all-white tail.
119b Adult female Tail rather shorter than other monals, with conspicuous white tip; underparts close barred (appear uniform brown unless very near) and unstreaked, but upperparts boldly streaked. Pale rump and uppertail-coverts provide strong contrast with dark wings and mantle when flushed.

120 Chinese Monal *Lophophorus lhuysii*   Text page 291

C China. Approaches Sclater's but no known overlap. The largest monal, with the longest tail. Monotypic.

120a Adult male Droopy crest and blue-black tail distinctive; extensive white rump typically concealed when at rest but obvious in flight.
120b Adult female Larger and relatively longer tailed than other monals, with evenly barred tail. Both upper- and underparts clearly pale streaked (recalling Himalayan), but rump and uppertail-coverts pale (like Sclater's).

118e

118d

118b

118a

118c

119a

119b

120a

120b

KHEF

PLATE 34: JUNGLEFOWL

121 Red Junglefowl *Gallus gallus*

Text page 292

Lowland forest undergrowth and second growth (to 2000 m). SE Asia (also widely introduced, especially Pacific islands). Five races, two extremes shown. Compare Grey and Green Junglefowls, which marginally overlap.

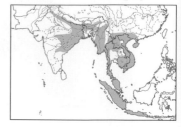

121a Adult male (breeding *murghi*; India, Nepal and Bangladesh) Unmistakable, recalling domestic bantam cock, with fiery golden neck and back hackles (which are shed during eclipse plumage following breeding). Adult plumage assumed in first-year. This race has dark shaft streaks in golden neck hackles and small white 'ear-lobes'.

121b Adult female (*murghi*) Greyish legs, only weakly streaked underparts (*contra* Grey and Sri Lanka Junglefowls) and has noticeable golden fringes to neck feathers forming shawl.

121c Adult male (*jabouillei*; Vietnam, Yunnan and Hainan) Darker and redder than nominate, with all hackles shorter and blunter. Facial wattles small and all red.

122 Grey Junglefowl *Gallus sonneratii*

Text page 294

Forests and second growth (to 1700 m). Peninsular India.

122a Adult male Distinctive with blunt, spangled neck hackles and grey body. Neck hackles and elongated 'tail' feathers 'lost' after breeding and full-male plumage not assumed until second-year.

122b Adult female Easily distinguished from female Red by boldly spotted breast and underparts, and redder legs. Some marginal overlap of the two species in C India.

123 Sri Lanka Junglefowl *Gallus lafayettii*

Text page 295

Forests and second growth, favouring dry forest; at all elevations. Sri Lanka, where the only junglefowl (but beware domestic poultry).

123a Adult male Resembles Red, but entire body plumage chestnut-red, contrasting with glossy black wings; also has yellow centre to comb and red legs. Has only marginally subdued 'eclipse' plumage after breeding. Full-male plumage not assumed until second-year.

123b Adult female Browner breast than female Grey, spotted belly, barred (not plain) wings, reddish legs and rufous 'shawl'.

124 Green Junglefowl *Gallus varius*

Text page 296

Forests and second growth (to 2400 m). Lesser Sundas (Indonesia), overlapping with Red on Java.

124a Adult male Distinctive in its highly glossed dark green plumage, with straight-edged purplish comb and red legs. Lacks 'eclipse' plumage stage; male plumage assumed in first-year.

124b Adult female Barred wings and tail, reddish legs (like female Sri Lanka), and only very indistinctly streaked and scaled on body.

121a

121c

121b

122a

122b

123b

123a

124a

124b

The three Vietnamese forms are very rare, little known and of uncertain taxonomic status.

127 Imperial Pheasant *Lophura imperialis*

Text page 302

Lowland forest. N and C Annam (Vietnam). Very rare.

127a Adult male Wholly dark purplish-blue (including crest), with red legs and facial skin. Larger, with rather more downcurved, longer tail than Edwards's, with less highly glossed plumage (notably less green in wings) and without white crest.

127b Adult female Overall brown, with chestnut fringes to feathers of upperparts and slightly paler underparts; tail darker blackish-brown. Larger than Edwards's, with more distinct crest; paler underparts than Edwards's, chestnut feather edges giving more mottled appearance to body plumage. Tail darker than *annamensis* race of Silver Pheasant (Plate 36).

128A Edwards's Pheasant *Lophura* (*edwardsi*) *edwardsi*

Text page 303

Lowland forest. C Annam (Vietnam). Very rare.

128Aa Adult male Glossy purplish-blue, with striking white crest, red legs and facial skin. Smaller and blunter tailed than Imperial, with more obvious green gloss on wings.

128Ab Adult female Overall uniform dull grey-brown, with chestnut fringes to scapulars and wing-coverts and almost blackish tail (with central feathers more rufous). Compare Imperial and Vietnamese Pheasants (see text).

128B Vietnamese Pheasant *Lophura* (*edwardsi*) *hatinhensis*

Text page 304

Lowland forest. N and C Annam (Vietnam). Very rare.

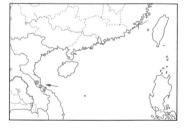

128Ba Adult male Like Edwards's, glossy purplish-blue with striking white (but slightly longer) crest and rather more downcurved white central tail feathers, which are seemingly only attained as second-year.

128Bb First-year female Very much like female Edwards's but perhaps duller, less rufous in tone, and has white or whitish feather either side of tail (but not in centre) when fully adult (i.e. second-year). See text. Older females have white feather either side of tail.

129 Swinhoe's Pheasant *Lophura swinhoii*

Text page 305

Wet lowland forest (to 2800 m) on Taiwan.

129a Adult male Unmistakable glossy blue-black, with white crest, mantle and central tail feathers.

129b Adult female Distinguished from other Taiwan pheasants by blunt tail, spotted upperparts and reddish legs. Compare female Mikado (Plate 41) and Common Pheasants (Plate 42), which also occur on Taiwan.

127b

128Ab

127a

128Aa

128Bb

129b

128Ba

129a

Daniel Cole

PLATE 36: KALIJ AND SILVER PHEASANTS

Between them, these two (perhaps more) polymorphic species inhabit vast stretches of hill and montane forests from Kashmir to Vietnam and E China. In the E Himalayas many are difficult to allocate with confidence to either species, but taking the review by McGowan and Panchen (1994) into consideration, there are 16 subspecies of Silver and 8 of Kalij, with the division between the two basically being the Irrawaddy River in N Myanmar and NW Yunnan (see text).

125 Kalij Pheasant *Lophura leucomelanos*   Text page 298

Mixed forests and secondary scrub. Himalayas east to W Yunnan. The most numerous and widespread Himalayan pheasant, both sexes variable in plumage pattern and coloration.

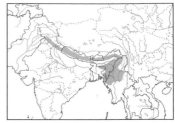

125a **Adult male** (*hamiltoni*; NW India) Blackish tail and upperparts, dusky legs, and relatively shorter tail and slimmer crest than Silver. Pale-chested form, and the only one with a white crest.
125b **Adult male** (*melanota*; E Nepal to W Bhutan) Black-rumped form, but with a pale breast.
125c **Adult male** (*lathami*; E Bhutan to Myanmar) Almost all black, except for whitish barring on the rump (which may be concealed by folded wings); hybridises with Silver in E Myanmar.
125d **Adult female** (*hamiltoni*) Lacks black-and-white markings on underparts shown by most races of Silver. A pale brown subspecies.
125e **Adult female** (*melanota*) A dark brown form with clear whitish scaling.

126 Silver Pheasant *Lophura nycthemera*   Text page 300

Montane forests of China and SE Asia. Very variable. Northern forms distinctive, but separating southern forms from Kalij is open to question. Females very variable, some having boldly spotted or streaked underparts, whereas others are plain brown. Basically, male Silver has denser, more mop-like crest, longer tail (with central feathers whitish), red legs and a finely chevroned pattern on upperparts.

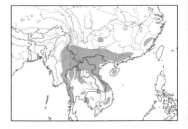

126a **Adult male** (*crawfurdi*; SE Myanmar and SW Thailand) Often treated within Kalij but several features, notably leg colour and close pattern of fine chevrons on upperparts, suggest a closer affinity with Silver.
126b **Adult male** (nominate; SE China and E Tonkin) The largest and whitest race.
126c **Adult male** (*annamensis*; S Vietnam) A small dark race with a relatively long crest, broad white stripes at breast-sides and a relatively short tail.
126d **Adult male** (*engelbachi*; S Laos) Very fine and intense vermiculations make males appear grey above in field, contrasting with clear white band on neck-sides.
126e **Adult female** (nominate) Typical of plain-breasted forms.
126f **Adult female** (*whiteheadi*; Hainan) Very boldly marked below.

125a

125b

125d

125e

125c

126a

126b

126e

126f

126d

126c

130B Hoogerwerf's Pheasant *Lophura (inornata) hoogerwerfi*

Text page 307

Montane forests of N Sumatra (Indonesia); apparently replaces Salvadori's in north of island. Virtually unknown.

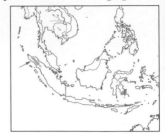

130B Female Only female specimens described; field observations suggest that male is all black like Salvadori's. Perhaps best treated as subspecies of Salvadori's. Female uniformly darker and duller, less chestnut-brown than female Salvadori's, lacking buffish mottling. Legs dark blue-grey.

130A Salvadori's Pheasant *Lophura (inornata) inornata*

Text page 306

Montane forests of S Sumatra (Indonesia). Little known.

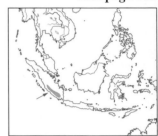

130Aa Adult male All black, with bluish reflections; crestless; has scarlet facial skin and pale grey eye-ring.
130Ab Adult female Overall chestnut-brown with contrasting dusky tail, each body and wing-covert feather with a prominent buff shaft streak, giving mottled appearance; also has extensive red facial skin. Legs pale grey.

131 Crestless Fireback *Lophura erythropthalma*

Text page 308

Lowland and foothill forests (to 1000 m). Sumatra, Malay Peninsula and Borneo. Two races.

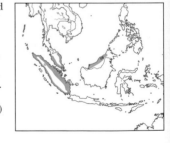

131a Adult male (nominate; Sumatra and Peninsular Malaysia) Dark grey or blue-black (depending on race) with striking cinnamon central tail; distinguished from cinnamon-tailed Bornean race of Crested by red (not blue) facial skin, lack of crest and smaller size. Male of Bornean race *pyronota* has whitish streaking on underparts.
131b Adult female (nominate) Almost wholly blue-black with bare red facial skin, recalls male Salvadori's and Hoogerwerf's (of Sumatra) but is bulkier, lacks metallic blue reflections on wings, has whitish chin and dusky-brownish head, and blackish (not whitish) bill.

132 Crested Fireback *Lophura ignita*

Text page 309

Lowland and foothill forests (to 1000 m). Sumatra, Malay Peninsula and Borneo. Four races.

132a Adult male (nominate; Borneo, except north) Blue-black with prominent crest, coppery-red rump and blue facial skin; colour of legs, underparts and central tail varies according to race. Nominate has flesh or whitish legs and coppery underparts; central tail cinnamon. Other races are *nobilis* of N Borneo, which is like nominate but larger, and variable *macartneyi* of SE Sumatra (possibly not a valid form), which shows a mixture of features linking the two forms depicted.
132b Adult female (nominate) Also crested; has blue facial skin, spotted black-and-white underparts and plain brown upperparts. Note whitish-flesh legs and blackish tail.
132c Adult male (*rufa*; Sumatra, except southeast, and Peninsular Malaysia) Scarlet legs, blue-black underparts (with some white streaks on flanks) and white central tail.
132d Adult female (*rufa*) Note red legs and chestnut tail.

130B

130Aa

130Ab

131b

131a

132d

132c

132a

132b

144 Reeves's Pheasant *Syrmaticus reevesii*

Text page 321

Mixed and deciduous forest in hills, especially in steep-sided valleys (300–1800 m). C and E China (also introduced in parts of Europe and Hawaii).

144a **Adult male** Unmistakable with black-and-white patterned head, scaly golden body and extremely long barred tail.

144b **Adult female** Less obvious, though dusky crown and ear-coverts contrasting with otherwise unmarked whitish or pale buff head and throat distinctive.

133 Siamese Fireback *Lophura diardi*

Text page 310

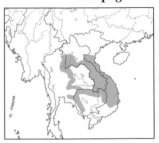

Lowland and foothill forests (to 1000m). SE Asia.

133a **Adult male** Rather slender grey pheasant, with long blackish tail, long red legs and very extensive red facial skin topped by a prominent coronal tuft.

133b **Adult female** Lacks crest, but has striking broadly banded wings and tail, contrasting with rather plain rufous-brown foreparts; also has red legs and facial skin.

134 Bulwer's Pheasant *Lophura bulweri*

Text page 311

Hill and montane forests (300–1500 m) of Borneo.

134a **Adult male** Unmistakable, an incredible blackish pheasant with a stunning white tail and blue facial wattles; legs red.

134b **Adult male** Display posture.

134c **Adult female** Remarkably plain brown, lacking both crest and mottled underparts of Crested Fireback but sharing latter's blue facial skin.

PLATE 39: EARED-PHEASANTS

The sexes are similar in this distinctive genus of montane Chinese species.

136 Tibetan Eared-pheasant *Crossoptilon harmani*

Text page 313

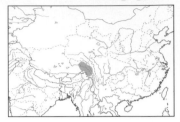

Subalpine meadows and alpine scrub (2400–5000 m). SE Tibet (also just entering NE India). Range meets *drouynii* subspecies of White in Salween Valley, where some interbreeding occurs. The two are perhaps conspecific.

136 **Adult** Dark grey plumage only shared by Blue Eared-pheasant but ranges do not overlap; Tibetan is smaller, lacks white bases to tail feathers and has whitish chin and belly centre, paler grey rump and shorter 'ears'.

135 White Eared-pheasant *Crossoptilon crossoptilon*

Text page 312

Subalpine meadows and alpine scrub (3000–4000 m). SW China. Three or four races, two shown. Meets Tibetan in region of Salween River in SE Tibet with some interbreeding. See text.

135a **Adult** (nominate; SE Tibet, W Sichuan) White plumage distinctive, but some are washed grey on upperparts and ssp. *dolani* (not shown) of S Qinghai has pale grey neck, breast and upperparts. The whitest form, but with grey wings. Those from NW Yunnan have paler grey wings and have been named '*lichiangense*' but this perhaps not a valid race.

135b **Adult** (*drouynii*; E Tibet) Wings almost all white; many show grey wash on mantle.

135c **Juvenile** Eight weeks old, attaining adult features.

138 Blue Eared-pheasant *Crossoptilon auritum*

Text page 315

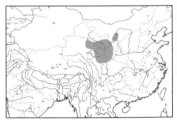

Alpine forests and scrub (2000–4000 m). C China.

138a **Adult** Dark blue-grey plumage, including rump and 'plumes', contrasting with long white 'ears' distinctive. Range disjunct from that of Tibetan, which has paler rump, white central belly and lacks obvious 'ears'.

138b **Juvenile** At about six weeks of age.

137 Brown Eared-pheasant *Crossoptilon mantchuricum*

Text page 314

Alpine forests (1300–2500 m). NE China; very rare (now confined to a handful of fragmented sites).

137a **Adult** Sooty-brown plumage, contrasting with white rump, tail base and long white 'ears' distinctive. Range almost meets Blue Eared-pheasant, which is similarly 'long eared'.

137b **Juvenile** At about six weeks of age.

135b

136

135c

135a

138a

138b

137a

137b

DAVID MEAD

117 Koklass Pheasant *Pucrasia macrolopha*

Text page 287

Montane forests (2000–4000 m). W Himalayas and W and C China. Nine races recognised, falling into three groups (examples of all three shown).

117a Adult male (*nipalensis*; W Nepal) Moderately long tail and crest, a long quill-like tuft on rear of head and a striking white patch on neck-side. Male varies from dark mahogany in N Pakistan to silver-grey in E China (see text). This race typical of dark Himalayan birds, which are darkest in the west (c.f. *castanea* of E Afghanistan and N Pakistan).

117b Adult female (*nipalensis*) Smaller, but longer tailed, than female monals, lacking pale eye surround but with pale supercilium, rusty undertail-coverts and more pointed tail.

117c Adult male (*xanthospila*; N China) Typical of birds from W and N China, which have a golden collar, while feathers of upperparts, breast and flanks are patterned with two black side streaks surrounding a grey shaft streak.

117d Adult female (*xanthospila*) Less richly coloured than Himalayan forms.

117e Adult male (*darwini*; E China) Those from southeast parts of range lack golden collar shown by other Chinese forms, but plumage is otherwise quite variable (see text).

139 Cheer Pheasant *Catreus wallichii*

Text page 315

Scrubby slopes, with crags and secondary tree cover (1200–3000 m). W Himalayas. Rare.

139a Adult male Large pheasant with very long strongly barred tail; latter diagnostic within limited range. Both sexes rather nondescript in plumage, enlivened only by red facial skin and pronounced crest.

139b Adult female Smaller than male, with narrower pale tail-bands (see text).

141 Mrs Hume's Pheasant *Syrmaticus humiae*

Text page 318

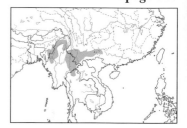

Montane forests (1200–2400 m). E Himalayas. Rare. Two races.

141a Adult male (nominate; NE India and W Myanmar) Long banded tail of both sexes a useful clue in native range, particularly in pale-tailed race *burmanicus*. Chestnut body and metallic blue neck are set-off by white scapular and wing-bars, as well as scaled whitish rump. Race *burmanicus*, of E Myanmar, SW China and N Thailand, similar but male has purplish-blue neck, whiter rump and paler tail.

141b Adult female Nondescript, differs from female Elliot's (Plate 41) in whitish throat and buffier belly and overall warmer plumage tones.

117b

117a

117d

117c

117e

139b

139a

141a

141b

C.D'S

PLATE 41: *SYRMATICUS* PHEASANTS

140 Elliot's Pheasant *Syrmaticus ellioti*

Text page 317

Wooded hills (to 1500 m). SE China.

140a Adult male Chestnut breast and upperparts contrast with white belly and wing-bars, as well as pale nape, black throat and long chestnut-and-white barred tail.

140b Adult female Nondescript, differs from female Mrs Hume's (Plate 40) in having blackish throat and whiter belly.

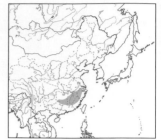

142 Mikado Pheasant *Syrmaticus mikado*

Text page 319

Montane forests (1800–3000 m). Taiwan.

142a Adult male Unmistakable, all blackish (scaled purplish-blue) with very long tail, crossed by narrow white bars.

142b Adult female Darker than congeners, with pronounced whitish mottling on upperparts.

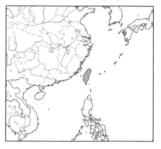

143 Copper Pheasant *Syrmaticus soemmerringii*

Text page 320

Coniferous and mixed forests. Japan. Overlaps with Green Pheasant (Plate 42) but favours denser forests. Five races but because of intergradation and individual variation perhaps only 2–3 valid (see text).

143a Adult male (*scintillans*; N and C Honshu) Rich chestnut pheasant with a very long barred tail. This is the palest and most northerly form, becoming darker towards the south of Honshu.

143b Adult female (*scintillans*) Somewhat between female Elliot's and Mrs Hume's; darker than female Green Pheasant, especially wings in flight, with unbarred shorter, more rufous tail.

143c Adult male (*ijimae*; SE Kyushu) The darkest and most southerly form, similar to nominate of C and S Kyushu, but rump almost entirely white.

140a 140b

142b 142a

143b 143a

143c

C.D'S

145 Common Pheasant *Phasianus colchicus*　　　　　　　　Text page 322

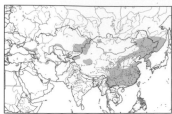

introduced range

The most widespread pheasant, its native range extending over most of temperate Asia and perhaps west to extreme SE Europe. Widely introduced worldwide, including Chile, New Zealand, Tasmania, North America, Japan and Europe (see text). Habitats vary from lowland meadows to farmland and hill forest.

145a　Adult male (nominate; Caucasus region) Plumage variable, with some 30 races recognised. Two main male types shown here (see text).

145b　Adult female (nominate) Females also vary, but scale-spotted underparts and partial tail bars help distinguish from other female pheasants of similar size.

145c　Adult male (*torquatus*; 'Ring-necked Pheasant' of E China).

146 Green Pheasant *Phasianus versicolor*　　　　　　　　Text page 325

Farmland, woodland and riverine grassland. Japan, introduced Hawaii.

146a　Adult male (nominate; SW Honshu and Kyushu) Striking dark green plumage, though beware domesticated melanistic variants of Common Pheasant in areas where latter introduced. Nominate is largest and darkest form. Race *robustipes* (most of Honshu) has paler, greyer crown and rump than nominate and *tanensis* (humid parts of CS Honshu and islands off Kyushu) is somewhat intermediate.

146b　Adult female (nominate) Darker and more intensely marked than Common Pheasant (except melanistic variants) particularly on mantle, which even has green tinge.

147 Golden Pheasant *Chrysolophus pictus*　　　　　　　　Text page 327

Hill forest (chiefly 800–1600 m, but lowlands in Britain). C China; introduced Britain. Small, slender forest pheasant.

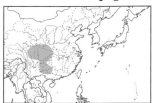

147a　Adult male Unmistakable.

147b　Adult female Very similar to Lady Amherst's but has plainer head and lacks contrasting white throat and belly of latter; bill and legs yellowish. Small size and closely barred, unspotted body plumage and longer, more boldly barred tail are useful distinctions from Common Pheasant.

148 Lady Amherst's Pheasant *Chrysolophus amherstiae*　　　　Text page 328

Hill forest (chiefly 1800–4600 m, but lowlands in Britain). NE Myanmar and SW China; introduced Britain.

148a　Adult male Unmistakable.

148b　Adult female Similar to Golden but slightly larger, warmer brown, more strongly barred, with darker rufous crown contrasting with pale throat, paler belly and has paler but more boldly barred, blunter tipped tail; bill and legs blue-grey.

145a

145b

145c

146b

146a

147b

147a

148b

148a

C.D'S

149 Sumatran Peacock-pheasant *Polyplectron chalcurum*

Text page 329

Hill and mountain forests (800–1700 m) of Sumatra (Indonesia). Two races, *scutulatum* of N Sumatra is more strongly barred.

149a Adult male (nominate; S Sumatra) Elegant dark rusty-brown pheasant, uncrested and lacking ocelli but with long, graduated barred tail. Tail has metallic violet-blue panels on outermost feathers.

149b Adult female (nominate) Shorter tailed, with violet-blue panels on outermost feathers much reduced.

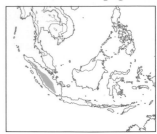

150 Mountain Peacock-pheasant *Polyplectron inopinatum*

Text page 330

Montane forests (900–2000 m) of C Malay Peninsula. Replaced in lowland forests by Malayan (Plate 44).

150a Adult male Long-bodied pheasant, almost blackish on head, neck and underparts, with rusty-brown upperparts marked by small blue ocelli. Uncrested and has long, graduated, vermiculated dark grey tail, sporting large green ocelli.

150b Adult female Smaller with shorter browner tail and upperparts spotted with black ocelli.

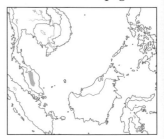

155 Bornean Peacock-pheasant *Polyplectron schleiermacheri*

Text page 335

Lowland forests (to 1100 m) of Borneo. Little known.

155a Adult male Differs from other broad-tailed peacock-pheasants (Plate 44) in being slightly shorter tailed, with blackish underparts, becoming iridescent blue-green at breast-sides, with white throat and stripe on breast centre.

155b Adult female Very similar to female Malayan but smaller, shorter tailed, more rufous-brown and with smaller ocelli.

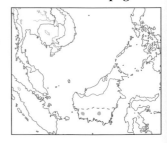

156 Palawan Peacock-pheasant *Polyplectron emphanum*

Text page 336

Lowland and hill forests (to 600 m) of Palawan (Philippines).

156a Adult male Blackish wings and underparts, coupled with upright crest and white cheeks makes identification straightforward.

156b Adult female Almost uniform dark brown with buffy-white cheeks and eyebrow, and shorter, tufted crest, which are equally distinctive.

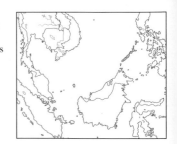

149a

149b

150b

150a

155b

155a

156b

156a

KHEF

PLATE 44: PEACOCK-PHEASANTS II

153 Hainan Peacock-pheasant *Polyplectron katsumatae*

Text page 333

Hill forest on Hainan (China). Now very scarce.

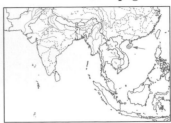

153 Male Smaller, darker and browner than Grey, with shorter crest and larger ocelli on upperparts, the latter shining blue as well as green and have bolder white surround. See text for female.

152 Grey Peacock-pheasant *Polyplectron bicalcaratum*

Text page 332

Lowland and hill forest (to 1800 m). SE Asia, west to Sikkim. Four races.

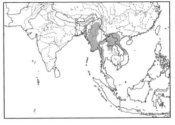

152a Adult male (nominate; E Myanmar through SW China to NW Vietnam) Large peacock-pheasant with a forward-pointing bushy crest and vermiculated grey-brown plumage. Extensive ocelli on upperparts, each spot green with buffish or whitish surround. Upper throat whitish; bare facial skin pinkish or yellowish. Race *bakeri* of NE India (Sikkim to Manipur) is very grey, with buff rings surrounding ocelli; race *bailyi* (possibly from Arunachal Pradesh) is even greyer and darker than *bakeri*, with white spots and streaks. Eastern race *ghigii* of N and C Vietnam and C Laos is browner.

152b Adult female (nominate) Darker, especially head, with ocelli less obvious and virtually absent from tail.

151 Germain's Peacock-pheasant *Polyplectron germaini*

Text page 331

Lowland and hill forest (to 1400 m) of S Vietnam.

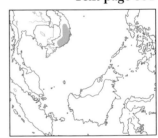

151a Adult male Smaller and darker than Grey (ranges do not overlap), lacks prominent crest, has red facial skin and purplish-blue rather than green ocelli. See text.

151b Adult female Darker than Grey, lacks crest and has reddish skin about the eye.

154 Malayan Peacock-pheasant *Polyplectron malacense*

Text page 334

Lowland forests. Uncommon in Peninsular Malaya and extreme S Tenasserim (perhaps extinct S Thailand). Replaced in C Malayan highland forests by Mountain (Plate 43).

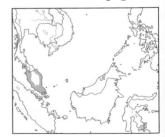

154a Adult male Browner above than Grey (no overlap), with darker ear-coverts, elongated dark crest and brighter pink facial skin. See text.

154b Adult female. Dark like female Germain's but has short crest.

153

152a

152b

151a

151b

154b

154a

KHEF

157 Crested Argus *Rheinardia ocellata*   Text page 337

Dense forest (to 1900 m). C Laos and Annam (Vietnam); also C
Peninsular Malaysia.

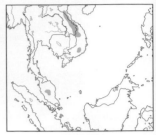

157a Adult male (nominate; Laos and Annam) Both sexes unmistakable,
but especially male with full tail. Prominent droopy black-and-white
crest, whitish surround to dark cheek and dull brown legs identify
the species.
157b Adult female (nominate) Whitish crest and barred wings and tail
distinctive.
157c Adult male (*nigrescens*; Malaysia) Longer, whiter crest and blacker
ground colour to body plumage than nominate.

158 Great Argus *Argusianus argus*   Text page 339

Dense forest (to 950 m). S Thailand, Tenasserim, Malay Peninsula,
Sumatra and Borneo.

158a Adult male (nominate; Malay Peninsula and Sumatra) Both sexes
unmistakable, but especially male with full tail. Prominent bare
blue skin of head, stubbly black crest and redder legs provide
superficial distinctions from Crested Argus.
158b Adult female (nominate) Note bare bluish face and reddish legs.
158c Adult male (*grayi*; Borneo) Averages smaller and greyer than
nominate, with notably brighter rufous underparts.

157b

157c

157a

158c

158b

158a

KHEF

160 Indian Peafowl *Pavo cristatus*

Text page 341

Scrub-jungle, cultivation, villages, ruins, forest edges; to 2000 m. Indian subcontinent; semi-feral populations established many parts of world. Widespread and well known.

160a Adult male Quite unmistakable, with shining blue neck and breast. Immature and non-breeding males have shorter, or may lack 'train'. See also Green Peafowl, especially race *spicifer*, which is probably extinct.

160b Adult female White underparts diagnostic.

161 Green Peafowl *Pavo muticus*

Text page 342

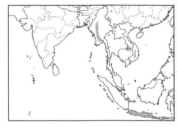

Open woodland, riverine forest and montane grassland; to 3000 m. SE Asia and Java. Rare. Three races.

161a Adult male (*imperator*; Myanmar to S China, Vietnam and Thailand) Easily distinguished from Indian by green neck, breast and flanks and narrow coronal tuft (a bare-shafted fan in Indian). Nominate, now confined to Java, is brighter, more golden-green and has less bluish on upperparts. Race *spicifer* of NE India and NW Myanmar may be extinct, but was duller, with greyish edges to neck and breast feathers and had dark blue foreneck; shape of coronal tuft and dark (not barred) scapulars indicative of this species. See text.

161b Adult female (*imperator*) Dark underparts (white in Indian).

162 Congo Peacock *Afropavo congensis*

Text page 344

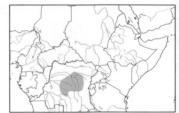

Lowland rainforest. Congo basin. Rare and little known. Unmistakable but rarely encountered. Both sexes iridescent green above.

162a Adult male Remarkable white tuft on crown and bare red skin on neck, black breast and underparts, with violet-blue fringes to feathers.

162b Adult female Russet underparts and wings.

160b

160a

161b

161a

162b

162a

173 Blue Grouse *Dendragapus obscurus*

Text page 359

Coniferous forests. W North America. Larger, slimmer necked and longer tailed than spruce grouses. Eight races form two groups (see text), examples of each group shown. Compare also Ruffed Grouse (Plate 51).

173a **Adult male** (nominate; Wyoming south to N Arizona and New Mexico). Quite uniform bluish-grey to blackish-grey (darkest in Pacific forests) with orange-yellow comb (becoming red during display) and yellowish to purplish (varying with race) cervical sacs. Lacks clear black-and-white patterning of throat and breast, or whitish spotting on uppertail and has greyish (or no) terminal tail-band (not rufous or white of American Spruce).

173b **Adult male** (nominate) Display posture.

173c **Adult male** (*fuliginosus*; Sooty Grouse of W Canada to N California) Display posture.

173d **Adult female** (nominate) Plainer and greyer than female American Spruce, with sparse (not intense) white markings on underparts.

172 American Spruce Grouse *Falcipennis canadensis*

Text page 357

Coniferous forests. N North America. Smaller and shorter tailed than Blue Grouse, with which it overlaps in west of range. Six races, of which *franklinii* most distinct. Compare also Ruffed Grouse (Plate 51).

172a **Adult male** (nominate; Taiga Grouse of most of Canada) Bold black-and-white pattern on throat and underparts. Over most of range tail has rufous or whitish tip, with uppertail-coverts closely barred black. Display posture.

172b **Adult male** (*franklinii*; Franklin's Grouse of NW USA, W Canada) Tail all dark (or narrowly tipped white) and unbarred dark uppertail-coverts with bold white tips.

172c **Adult female** (nominate) Females of all races have two colour phases (grey and rufous); all have boldly barred and spotted underparts (unlike Blue Grouse).

172d **Adult female** (*franklinii*) In flight.

171 Siberian Spruce Grouse *Falcipennis falcipennis*

Text page 356

Coniferous forests. E Siberia. Overlaps with similar Hazel Grouse (Plate 51).

171a **Adult male** Differs from American Spruce in having broad white tip to tail, intensely white-barred central underparts and bold white diamond-shaped spots on flanks (which are weakly streaked and belly more sparsely spotted white in American).

171b **Adult female** Resembles rufous phase of American but has underparts much more boldly spotted white.

171c **Adult female** In flight.

173d

173c

173b

173a

172a

172d

172b

172c

171a

171b

171c

C.D'S

174A and B Willow and Red Grouse *Lagopus lagopus* Text pages 361 & 363

Moorland, tundra and birch/willow scrub. North America and Eurasia. Larger and stouter billed than other *Lagopus*. 19 races have been described.

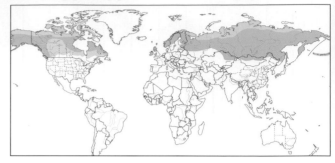

174Ba Adult male (spring *scoticus*; **Red Grouse** of British Isles) British and Irish populations do not acquire white winter garb and have dark wings. They were formerly separated as *L. scoticus* (Red Grouse).

174Bb Adult female (spring *scoticus*). In flight. Less richly coloured than male

174Aa Adult male (spring nominate; **Willow Grouse** of Scandinavia and W Siberia) Other plumages can be confused with ptarmigans, but male Willow is much more chestnut and differs in habitat preference and vocally (see text). Plumage varies with seasonal moults and geographically (see text).

174Ab Adult male (winter nominate) Lacks black eyestripe of male Rock Ptarmigan.

174Ac Adult female (summer nominate). More buffy-yellowish than male with coarser markings.

174Ad Adult male (summer nominate) In flight: wings all white (juvenile Willow has mottled brownish upperwing and tail until first-autumn).

174Ae Adult female (winter nominate) In flight: very like Rock Ptarmigan.

---

175 Rock Ptarmigan *Lagopus mutus* Text page 364

Tundra and alpine zone of mountains. North America and Eurasia. Slightly smaller than Willow Grouse, prefers rocky places. Plumage varies with seasonal moults and geographically (some races become almost blackish on body when worn, see text). 30 races have been described. Black tail an easy distinction from White-tailed but often not obvious until flushed. Juvenile has brownish upperwing and tail until first-autumn.

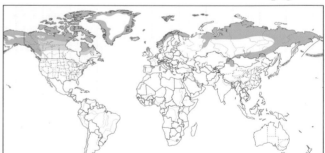

175a/e Adult male (breeding *millaisi*; Scotland). Much greyer than Willow and utters dry rattling belch when flushed.

175b Adult female (autumn *millaisi*). More coarsely barred than male.

175c Adult male (winter *millaisi*) All white, with black eyestripe (absent in female and other *Lagopus*).

175d Adult female (winter *millaisi*) In flight: pattern similar to winter Willow.

175f Adult male (summer *evermanni*; N Canada). One of the darker races.

---

176 White-tailed Ptarmigan *Lagopus leucurus* Text page 366

Tundra and alpine zone of mountains. W North America; the only ptarmigan in USA south of Canadian border. Voice differs from congeners (see text). Juvenile has marbled brownish upperwing and tail until first-autumn.

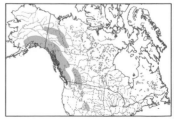

176a/e Adult male (summer nominate; British Columbia and SW Alberta) Slightly smaller than Rock, with white tail diagnostic at all times but often not obvious until flushed.

176b Adult female (summer nominate) Plumage varies with seasonal moults and slightly between five races (see text).

176c Adult male (winter nominate) Both sexes become wholly white at this season, lacking black eyestripe of Rock.

176d Adult female (winter nominate) In flight: wholly white.

174Ba

174Bb

174Aa

174Ae

174Ab

174Ac

174Ad

175a

175d

175f

175c

175b

175e

176c

176b

176d

176a

176e

Norman Arlott.

PLATE 49: BLACK AND SAGE GROUSE

177 Black Grouse *Lyrurus tetrix*

Text page 368

Heathland and mixed forests of N Eurasia. Seven similar races.

177a **Adult male** (nominate) Unmistakable with white vent and wing-bar (latter obvious in flight) contrasting with otherwise black plumage and lyre-shaped tail.

177b **Adult male** (nominate) In display; best seen in communal leks in spring.

177c **Adult female** (nominate) Brown with vermiculations and barring over whole plumage, but in flight look for distinctly notched tail and narrow pale wing-bars.

177d **Adult female** (nominate) In flight.

178 Caucasian Grouse *Lyrurus mlokosiewiczi*

Text page 370

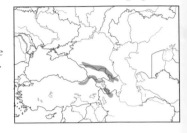

Subalpine and alpine meadows (1700–3300 m) of Caucasus region.

178a **Adult male** Almost all-black male distinctive in range. Differs from Black in lacking white wing-bar and vent and in having longer, slenderer tail. In flight white underwing-coverts can be striking, and often show as a white 'shoulder' spot on ground.

178b **Adult male** In display; best seen in communal leks in spring.

178c **Adult female** Lacks wing-bar of Black, has slightly longer and more square-ended tail and underparts more finely vermiculated.

184 Greater Sage Grouse *Centrocercus urophasianus*

Text page 379

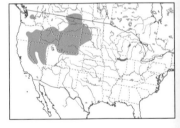

Sagebrush plains. W USA. Large grouse with relatively long tail, which often feeds in open grasslands. See comment under recently separated Gunnison Sage Grouse.

184a **Adult male** Much larger male has distinctive inflatable white ruff on breast, separating black lower underparts from black throat and foreneck.

184b **Adult male** In display; best seen in communal leks in spring.

184c **Adult female** Overall shape not unlike female Common Pheasant, but black central underparts provide easy distinction.

185 Gunnison Sage Grouse *Centrocercus minimus*

Text page 381

Very recently separated from almost identical Greater Sage Grouse, with surviving populations in SW Colorado and SE Utah (where Greater absent).

185a **Adult male** Averages smaller and has broader pale tail bars than Greater; also differs in display posture, voice and genetically. Female very similar to female Greater, apart from smaller size.

185b **Adult male** In display; note impression of having a 'pony-tail'.

177d

177b

177a

177c

178c

178b

178a

185a

184b

185b

184a

184c

C.D'S

179 Western Capercaillie *Tetrao urogallus*

Text page 371

Coniferous and mixed forests. N Eurasia. Shy and elusive forest bird, most easily found in early spring when males lekking. Some 8 races but situation complex (see text).

179a **Adult male** (nominate) Unmistakable dark turkey-like bird with broad tail, shaggy throat and ivory bill; male in S Siberia almost white on underparts below breast (race *taczanowskii*).

179b **Adult male** (nominate) Display posture.

179c **Adult female** (nominate) Mottled and barred brown female is one-third smaller than male and recalls large female Black Grouse, but has more clearly marked, paler underparts, rufous breast and longer, blunt-ended tail.

179d **Adult female** (nominate) In flight.

180 Black-billed Capercaillie *Tetrao parvirostris*

Text page 373

Mixed forests. E Eurasia. Replaces Western in E Siberia but there is considerable overlap in EC Siberia. Three races, of which easternmost *kamschaticus* of Kamchatka has boldest white markings on wings.

180a **Adult male** (nominate) Easily distinguished from Western in being darker (particularly in south of overlap zone where Western has whitish underparts), with smaller black bill and in having bold white spots to tips of uppertail-coverts and on wings.

180b **Adult male** (nominate) Display posture.

180c **Adult female** (nominate) Close to female Western but lacks rusty breast patch, is more barred on breast and has bolder white spots on wings.

179b

179a

179d

179c

180b

180a

180c

PLATE 51: HAZEL AND RUFFED GROUSE

183 Ruffed Grouse *Bonasa umbellus*

Text page 377

Deciduous and mixed forests. North America. Rufous and grey colour types occur which complicates racial determination, currently 14 races accepted.

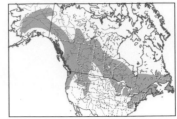

183a **Adult male** (rufous form, *affinis*; NW USA) Shy forest and forest-edge grouse, typically first seen in flight when barred tail with prominent black subterminal band provides easy distinction from American Spruce (Plate 47) and Sharp-tailed (Plate 52) with which it widely overlaps. Bold flank barring, black neck patches, ruff and lack of black on throat make it quite unlike congeners.

183b **Adult male** (grey form, *umbelloides*; most of Canada) Display posture. Most easily found in early spring when males are displaying.

183c **Adult female** (grey form) Sexes similar but female less clearly marked, especially above; has very weak 'combs' and short ruff.

183d **Adult female** (rufous form) In flight.

181 Hazel Grouse *Tetrastes bonasia*

Text page 375

Dense forest of all types. Eurasia. Shy and elusive but high-pitched calls a clue to presence. Compare Siberian Spruce Grouse (Plate 47). Basic colour varies from grey-brown to rufous-brown over wide range, with 12 races recognised (two extremes shown).

181a **Adult female** (nominate; N Europe) Duller than male, without black throat.

181b **Adult female** (nominate) In flight.

181c **Adult male** (*rupestris*; C Europe) Display posture.

181d **Adult male** (*sibiricus*; most of Siberia except far east) If flushed small size, weakly barred tail with prominent black subterminal band and whitish or grey tail tip distinctive within range.

182 Severtzov's Grouse *Tetrastes sewerzowi*

Text page 376

Montane forests (above 1000 m). C China. Two poorly differentiated races (see text).

182a **Adult male** Resembles rufous populations of Hazel Grouse but feathers of underparts have much broader black-and-chestnut centres, giving more narrowly pale-barred appearance. Tail pattern quite different, outer feathers having broad dark bands, with narrow pale intervening bars (Hazel has grey or rufous-brown outertail, almost unmarked except dark subterminal band).

182b **Adult female** Duller than male, with black of throat obscured.

182c **Adult female** In flight.

183b

183d

183a

183c

181b

181c

181d

181a

182a

182b

182c

C.D'S

PLATE 52: PRAIRIE-CHICKENS

187 Greater Prairie-chicken *Tympanuchus cupido*   Text page 383

Shrubby grasslands; localised. North America. Two surviving races
(both shown), nominate now extinct. See also very similar Lesser
Prairie-chicken.

187a Adult male (*pinnatus*; most of range) Display posture. Most
easily found in early spring when males gather for 'booming'
lek and inflate yellow-orange neck sacs. Elongated feathers
form 'shawl' of black and pale buff markings on neck-sides in
both sexes; these are most developed in males and erect into
'rabbit-ears' during display.

187b Adult male (*pinnatus*) Brown and narrowly whitish-barred
grouse, basically similar in all plumages (though male has tail all dark, but mostly concealed by
barred uppertail-coverts).

187c Adult female (*pinnatus*) Tail is barred, rather than all dark, and neck 'shawl' is less well developed.

187d Adult female (*pinnatus*) In flight.

187e Adult male (*attwateri*; coastal Texas) Smaller and darker brown than *pinnatus*.

188 Lesser Prairie-chicken *Tympanuchus pallidicinctus*   Text page 384

Dry shrubby grasslands. C USA. Very similar to Greater Prairie-chicken
but ranges do not overlap.

188a Adult male Display posture. Differences from Greater difficult
to interpret in field; however, lekking males inflate diagnostic
reddish-purple neck sacs.

188b Adult male Slightly smaller than *pinnatus* (but larger than
many *attwateri*) and overall more closely barred, with narrower
black barring on upperparts (merely black edging to brown
bars), but has almost unmarked central belly.

188c Adult female Smaller than male, with barred tail.

188d Adult female In flight.

186 Sharp-tailed Grouse *Tympanuchus phasianellus*   Text page 381

Wooded and bushy grasslands. North America. Six similar races.
Compare also Ruffed Grouse (Plate 51).

186a Adult male (*jamesi*; Alberta S to Wyoming) Display posture.
Sexes similar, but male inflates purplish neck sacs in display.

186b Adult male (*jamesi*) Superficially similar to both prairie-
chickens, but on ground exhibits almost unmarked or, at
most, spotted rather than barred appearance, especially on
underparts.

186c Adult female (*jamesi*) Smaller than male, with weaker facial
pattern and more barred tail centre; sexing of some may be
difficult.

186d Adult female (*jamesi*) In flight. Elongated barred central tail feathers and striking white tail-sides
easily identify flushed birds (prairie-chickens have short, rounded, dark tails).

187b

187d

187a

187c

187e

188d

188b

188a

188c

186b

186d

186a

186c

C.D.S

169 Wild Turkey *Meleagris gallopavo*   Text page 353

Forests and shrubby grasslands. North America and N Mexico. Six races.

169a **Adult male** (*silvestris*; E North America) Sleeker and more agile than its overweight domestic cousin, Wild Turkeys are large dark bronzy brown forest birds with relatively long bodies and long pinkish legs, their bare bluish-grey and rose-pink wrinkled heads and necks are relatively small compared to their overall bulk. Large, broad tails tipped rufous (eastern races) or whitish (southern and western races).

169b **Adult male** (*merriami*; WC USA) Full size may take several years to achieve; southern and western forms have whitish tips to tail-feathers.

169c **Adult female** (*silvestris*) Smaller than male and far less imposing; eastern populations with rufous tail-tip.

170 Ocellated Turkey *Meleagris ocellata*   Text page 354

Forests. Yucatán peninsula (C America) where Wild Turkey absent but beware wandering domestic 'wild turkeys'.

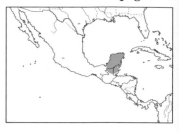

170a **Adult male** Brighter than Wild Turkey, chiefly glossed green and copper, with shining copper and whitish wing panels. Bright blue head has a series of orange 'warts' and lacks reddish dewlap and black 'chest beard' of Wild Turkey. Blue ocelli form bands of blue eye-spots when bird fans its tail in display.

170b **Adult female** Smaller and duller than male, lacking 'snood' and 'horn'.

169a

169c

170b

169b

170a

DAVID MEAD

164 Black Guineafowl *Agelastes niger*   Text page 346

Rainforests of W Equatorial Africa.

164 **Adult male** A full-tailed guineafowl of C African forests, easily
identified by blackish body contrasting with bare pink head
(adult) or white belly (juvenile). Female lacks spurs. Though
it shares forest haunts with larger Plumed Guineafowl and
Congo Peacock, confusion is unlikely if seen well.

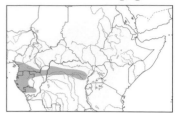

163 White-breasted Guineafowl *Agelastes meleagrides*   Text page 345

Rainforests of W Africa.

163a **Adult male** Easily identified by combination of very restricted
range, white fore body (breast and collar) contrasting with
blackish body and naked red head. Female lacks spurs. Shares
forest with larger Crested Guineafowl (Plate 55) but confusion is unlikely.

163b **Juvenile** Sooty with white belly.

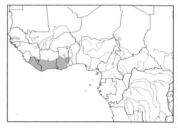

165 Helmeted Guineafowl *Numida meleagris*   Text page 347

Savannas and forest edges, bushy cultivation. Most of Africa. The most familiar
open-country guineafowl. Regional variation complex, with at least nine races
currently recognised, of over 30 described (see text).

165a **Adult male** (nominate; Ethiopia to N Kenya) Combination of lump or
blade-like horny casque on crown (often with some red, depending on race
involved), rather than tuft of feathers, small tail as well as open-country
habitat prevents confusion with others.

165b **Juvenile** Larely brownish with undeveloped head adornment.

165c **Adult male** (*galeata*; W Africa) Short casque and blunt red wattles.

165d **Adult male** (*reichenowi*; Kenya and Tanzania) Tall casque and red wattles.

165e **Adult male** (*mitrata*; Zimbabwe to E African coast) Medium casque and pointed blue wattles tipped
with red.

164

163a

163b

165c

165d

165a

165b

165e

C.D'S

166 Plumed Guineafowl *Guttera plumifera*   Text page 349

Rainforests of Equatorial Africa. Both races shown.

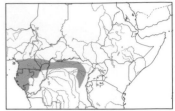

166a Adult (nominate; Cameroon to W Congo) Longer and stiffer topknot than Crested, with much more prominent gape wattles, pure white (not bluish-white) body spotting, boldly spotted (not plain black) collar and lacks red on bare skin of head and neck

166b Adult (*schubotzi*; E Congo) Patches of orange-yellow bare skin on head and neck.

167B Crested Guineafowl *Guttera (pucherani) edouardi*   Text page 350

Lowland forest of Equatorial Africa to Natal. Four well-defined races recognised, but at least 12 have been described; differing in coloration of bare skin of head and purity of white spotting (see text). Compare also Kenya Crested, which is usually treated as conspecific.

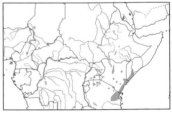

167Ba Adult (nominate; S Africa) Mop of curly black feathers and unspotted black breast and collar provide easy distinctions from Plumed, with which it overlaps in parts of Congo basin (though Crested fonder of forest edge or second growth). See Plumed for further distinctions.

167Bb Adult (*sclateri*; NW Cameroon) Crest straighter, and distinctly shorter on forecrown than at rear.

167Bc Juvenile Drab brownish-grey, with short crest; head downy at first.

167A Kenya Crested Guineafowl *Guttera (pucherani) pucherani*   Text page 350

Thickets and forest edge of E Africa. The only forest guineafowl over most of Kenya east of Rift Valley, marginally overlapping with *verreauxi* race of Crested in north and *barbata* Crested to south (see text). Usually considered conspecific with Crested.

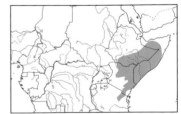

167A Adult Spotted almost to start of bare neck, whereas neck and upper breast of Crested is plain blackish. Kenya Crested has extensive red skin on face as well as throat and brighter blue skin on neck (red only on throat and foreneck, and dingier blue face and neck in Crested). Additional features of Kenya Crested include red eyes (brown in *verreauxi*) and whiter body spotting.

168 Vulturine Guineafowl *Acryllium vulturinum*   Text page 352

Semi-arid savannas. NE Africa.

168a Adult An elegant guineafowl with a slender neck projecting from a cape of metallic blue-and-white striped elongated hackles, this and the relatively long legs and long drooping point of a tail emphasise its elegance and uniqueness, rendering it quite unmistakable.

168b Juvenile Barred rufous body plumage distinctive; head and neck clothed in striped downy feathers at first.

166a

166b

167Ba

167A

167Bb

167Bc

168a

168b

C.D'S

PLATE 56: TREE-QUAILS (AMERICAN WOOD-PARTRIDGES)

189 Bearded Tree-quail *Dendrortyx barbatus*

Text page 385

Humid montane forests (1000–1500 m). NE Mexico. Far more heard than seen (see text).

189a **Adult** Dull brown, rather featureless quail, with relatively long tail (longer in male), grey face and rufous breast. Look for rufous in primaries and tail when flushed, an easy distinction from greyer winged, bar-tailed Long-tailed. Long-tailed overlaps in C Veracruz, but favours higher elevations. Despite name shows no 'beard'.

189b **Juvenile** Duller and less rufous.

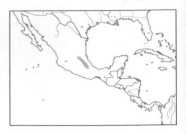

190 Long-tailed Tree-quail *Dendrortyx macroura*

Text page 386

Cloud forests (1200–3300 m). C Mexico. Far more heard than seen (see text). Six races vary in extent of rufous streaking and clarity of head pattern.

190a **Adult** (*oaxacae*, W Oaxaca) Peculiar greyish quail with long barred tail (held cocked when running) and black-and-white head pattern. Unmistakable if seen well but range overlaps with both other tree-quails. Sexes similar but male has longer tail.

190b **Adult** (*striatus*; WC Mexico) Has bolder white facial striping.

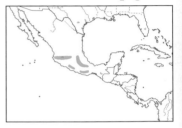

191 Buffy-crowned Tree-quail *Dendrortyx leucophrys*

Text page 387

Humid forests (600–3000 m). C America. Two races. Far more often heard than seen (see text).

191a **Adult** (*hypospodius*; Costa Rica) Rather darker and greyer below than nominate.

191b **Adult** (nominate; S Mexico to Nicaragua) Dull grey-brown, long-tailed quail with black bill (reddish in other tree-quails) and variable rufous streaking on greyish body. Easily distinguished from Long-tailed by reddish-brown (rather than grey) wings and tail, and whitish-buff throat and forehead. Sexes similar though female rather shorter tailed.

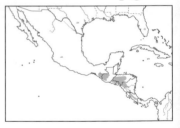

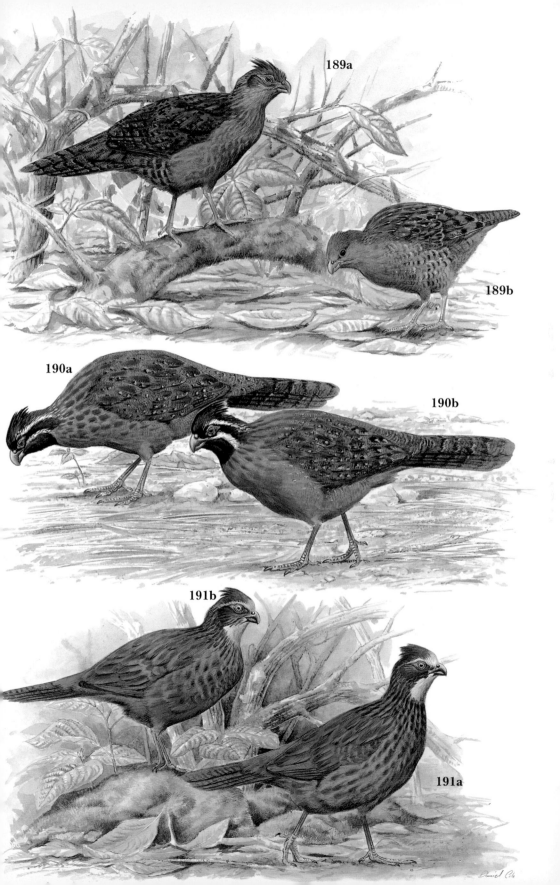

189a

189b

190a

190b

191b

191a

197 Banded Quail *Philortyx fasciatus*

Text page 394

Dry scrubby grasslands. WC Mexico. Has distinctive immature plumage, finally becoming adult at 16–20 weeks.

197a **Adult** Drab brownish and rather long-tailed quail with distinctively barred black-and-white rear underparts and pronounced dark crest. Adults (sexes similar) have dark crest with whitish throat.

197b **Juvenile** At first has whitish shaft streaks and whitish throat, moulting into immature plumage at 8–12 weeks, which is closer to adult but has blackish face and throat.

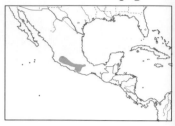

192 Mountain Quail *Oreortyx pictus*

Text page 388

Brushlands and forest edges. W North America. Six similar races recognised differing in degree of colour saturation and extent of brown in body plumage.

192a **Adult** (nominate; SW USA) Typical of browner populations.

192b **Adult** (*eremophila*; W Oregon to C California) Rather large and short-tailed plump quail, with both sexes similarly plumaged. Bold vertical white flank barring diagnostic as is remarkably long, straight crest plume (of two feathers). This race typical of greyer populations.

192c **Juvenile** Drabber than adult, with short plumes.

193 Scaled Quail *Callipepla squamata*

Text page 390

Dry scrubby grasslands. Mexico and S USA. All plumages similar. Four races differing in degree of colour saturation.

193a **Adult** (*pallida*; S USA and NW Mexico) Plump, rather short-tailed quail of semi-arid country. Sandy bluish-grey in overall plumage with short prominent whitish crest. Clearly scaled when close but rather plain looking when further away.

193b **Adult** (*castanogastris*; S Texas and NE Mexico) Darker and browner than other forms with dark chestnut belly centre.

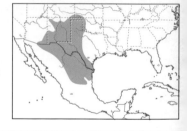

197b

197a

192c

192a

192b

193a

193b

PLATE 58: AMERICAN QUAILS II

194 Elegant Quail *Callipepla douglasii*

Text page 391

Arid scrub and dry secondary woodland. NW Mexico. Range does not overlap with smaller Banded Quail (Plate 57). Five races differing in colour tones and slightly in size.

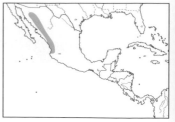

194a **Adult male** (nominate; W Mexico) Plump, greyish quail with bold white spotting on underparts, forward-pointing tawny crest, chestnut on wings and flanks, plus streaking on head and neck.

194b **Adult female** Has dusky crest.

195 California Quail *Callipepla californica*

Text page 392

Bushy grassland and woodland edge. W North America. Eight similar races, differing in colour saturation and degree of brown or grey in plumage, differences being most evident between females.

195a **Adult male** (nominate; W USA) California and Gambel's both have striking black-and-white bridled head pattern and almost ridiculous forward-pointing, drooping crest. Both sexes of California have diagnostic pale or golden scaled belly and central lower underparts (usually becoming chestnut at centre) and strongly speckled nape.

195b **Adult female** (nominate). Short crest and plain head makes sexing easy; female Gambel's lacks scaling on belly.

195c **Juvenile** Duller than female, with buff shaft streaks and spots.

195d **Adult male** (*brunnescens*; N California coast) A brownish form.

196 Gambel's Quail *Callipepla gambelii*

Text page 393

Bushy grassland and woodland edge. W North America. Seven similar races differing in colour saturation and plumage tones.

196a **Adult male** (nominate; W USA) Similar to California Quail, but slightly larger and markedly greyer. Both sexes have plain yellowish-buff belly and central rear underparts, lacking scaly pattern of California. Male also has black (not pale) forehead, brighter chestnut crown and flanks and distinctive blackish belly patch.

196b **Adult male** (*fulvipectus*; N Mexico).

195 × 196 California × Gambel's Quail

Hybrids occur where ranges of these two closely related quails come into contact. Hybrids between Gambel's and Scaled (Plate 57) Quails also occur rarely.

195 × 196 Adult male Such birds show mixed features, such as a combination of black belly patch and scaled underparts.

194b

194a

195a

195d

195c

196a

195b

196b

195 × 196

198 Northern Bobwhite *Colinus virginianus*

Text page 395

North America.

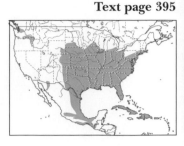

198a **Adult male** (nominate; E USA) Males very variable with some 22 races falling into four groups (examples of each group shown). The nominate is typical of the northern races, which have white or buffish-white throats and supercilia and mottled rufous-brown body plumage quite unlike other North American quails (but compare Montezuma and Ocellated, Plate 64).

198b **Adult female** (nominate) Buff supercilium and throat similar in all forms.

198c **Juvenile** (nominate) Drabber than female, with less distinct head pattern. Typical of the genus.

198d **Adult male** (*ridgwayi*; 'Masked Bobwhite' of C Sonora and SE Arizona) Blackish face contrasts with rufous body.

198e **Adult male** (*pectoralis*; 'Rufous-bellied Bobwhite' of C Veracruz) Southern races are rufous below with variable head patterns, some with all-blackish face and throat.

198f **Adult male** (*coyolcos*; 'Black-headed Bobwhite' of S Mexico) Blackish head and breast typical of males.

199 Yucatan Bobwhite *Colinus nigrogularis*

Text page 397

Yucatán region (where other bobwhites absent). Four races recognised, differing slightly in size and width of black feather fringing on underparts of males.

199a **Adult male** (nominate; Belize) Black throat and eye-band contrasting with bold white supercilium and malar stripe; black-and-rufous underparts heavily spotted white. Adjacent races of Northern Bobwhite are almost unmarked rufous below and have blackish heads.

199b **Adult female** (nominate) Similar to Northern Bobwhite, but has more boldly patterned underparts.

200 Spot-bellied Bobwhite *Colinus leucopogon*

Text page 398

C America. Six races.

200a **Adult male** (nominate; 'White-faced Bobwhite' of SE El Salvador to W Honduras) White supercilium, spotted lower underparts and short crest but vary from having white throat and central underparts to black throat, white malar stripe and spotted underparts.

200b **Adult female** (nominate) Very similar to Crested Bobwhite, but supercilium and throat whiter in Spot-bellied.

200c **Adult male** (*dickeyi*; 'Dickey's Bobwhite' of Costa Rica) Almost meets Crested in Costa Rica (see text), but there Spot-bellied has shorter crest, whitish, not rufous supercilium, mottled throat, and brown, rather than rufous ground colour to underparts.

200d **Adult male** (*hypoleucos*; 'White-breasted Bobwhite' of W El Salvador).

201 Crested Bobwhite *Colinus cristatus*

Text page 399

The only bobwhite in South America. Some 14 races, all with prominent spiky crest but plumage varies over wide range (see text). Could conceivably meet Spot-bellied in the future in Costa Rica, where Crested is spreading from Panama (see text).

201a **Adult male** (nominate; NE Colombia/NW Venezuela) A chestnut throated form.

201b **Adult male** (*panamensis*; Pacific Panama) Whitish cheeks and upper throat, spotted breast.

201c **Adult female** (*panamensis*) Shorter and browner crest than male.

201d **Adult male** (*leucotis*; C Colombia) Whitish cheeks, throat and chest; spotted breast.

201e **Adult male** (*sonnini*; Venezuela to Brazil) Chestnut throat; almost unmarked breast.

198b

198c

198f

198a

198d

198e

199b

200a

200b

199a

201c

200c

200d

201b

201a

201e

201d

202 Marbled Wood-quail *Odontophorus gujanensis*
Text page 400

Lowland rain forest. South America. Eight races varying in basic colour tones.

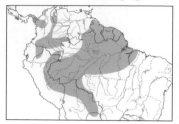

202a Adult (nominate; SE Venezuela to N Paraguay) In C America and W South America the drab brownish plumage and reddish-orange facial skin, lacking any white on head and throat, separates it from most other wood-quails except Starred, which has white spotting on breast, unbarred underparts and relatively plain, pale grey head and throat topped by rufous crown tuft. Sexes similar.

202b Adult (*castigatus*; Costa Rica and W Panama) A brown-bodied race.

203 Spot-winged Wood-quail *Odontophorus capueira*
Text page 402

Lowland forest. E South America. The only quail in its range. Two races, the other, *plumbeicollis* of NE Brazil, is slightly paler below and has less distinct white markings above.

203a Adult: (nominate; over most of range) A dark slate-grey wood-quail with bare red skin around eye and cinnamon supercilium. Differs from Marbled of N Brazil in being plain dark grey below and having clear white spotting above, and ranges do not overlap.

203b Juvenile Has pale shaft-streaks on upperparts, redder bill and mixture of grey and rufous below.

215 Starred Wood-quail *Odontophorus stellatus*
Text page 411

Lowland forest. Upper Amazon basin. The only wood-quail in most of its range, marginally overlapping with Marbled (which see) and possibly Rufous-breasted (Plate 61) in E Ecuador and probably in Peru. Latter at higher elevations and is darker, with blackish face and throat and short crest.

215a Adult male Rufous-and-grey wood-quail with a prominent rufous crest and inconspicuously spotted breast.

215b Adult female Has blackish rather than rufous crown.

216 Spotted Wood-quail *Odontophorus guttatus*
Text page 411

Tropical forests, chiefly in hills. C America. Occurs in both brown and rufous colour phases. Altitudinally overlaps widely only with Black-eared (Plate 61), which lacks spotting, and marginally with darker Black-breasted (Plate 62), which usually has whiter throat; both have an inconspicuous crest. Compare also Singing Quail (Plate 64).

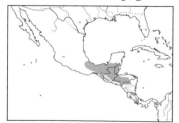

216a Adult male Rufous phase. Rufous-brown wood-quail with orange-rufous crest and heavily white-spotted underparts.

216b Adult female Brown phase. Has blackish rather than rufous crown.

216c Juvenile With smaller, buffer spots below, rufous crown and reddish bill.

202a

202b

203b

203a

215b

215a

216b

216a

216c

DAVID MEAD

205 Rufous-fronted Wood-quail *Odontophorus erythrops*

Text page 403

Lowland forest. Pacific coast of N South America.

205a **Adult** (nominate; SW Ecuador) Throat pattern varies between races, nominate Ecuadorian race is darker and lacks bold white chest-band of Colombian race, and is thus very similar to Black-eared of C America, but latter has black, not chestnut cheeks and rufous or brownish (not blackish) crown. See also text.

205b **Adult male** (*parambae*, most of range) Striking white band across black throat contrasts with otherwise almost unmarked chestnut underparts and dull brown upperparts; note purplish bare orbital skin.

205c **Adult female** (*parambae*) Orbital skin is blackish.

205d **Juvenile** Upperparts with buff shaft streaks, underparts with dark barring and spotting, bill reddish.

204 Black-eared Wood-quail *Odontophorus melanotis*

Text page 402

Lowland tropical forest (450–1600 m). C America. Two races.

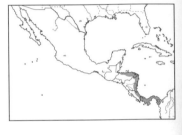

204a **Adult male** Rufous-chestnut crown and underparts, contrast with blackish throat and head-sides, and purplish orbital skin (blackish in female). Range overlaps with Marbled, which has dull underparts, lacking blackish face and throat, and reddish (not purplish or dusky) orbital skin. Also overlaps with Spotted, which has brighter, more orange crest and white-spotted underparts. Suspected to meet *parambae* Rufous-fronted in extreme NW Colombia, which differs in having bold white throat crescent, dusky crown and less extensive black on head-sides. Sexes similar.

204b **Juvenile** Upperparts with buff shaft streaks, underparts with dark barring and spotting, bill reddish.

207 Chestnut Wood-quail *Odontophorus hyperythrus*

Text page 405

Montane tropical forests (1600–2700 m). N Colombia.

207a **Adult male** Unmarked bright rufous-chestnut face and underparts contrast only with whitish spectacles and stripe running back from eye. Female Rufous-fronted has throat pattern dull or lacking and suggests Chestnut, but has blackish bare skin around eye (lacking whitish spectacles). Chestnut also has large black spots on scapulars, which are much more finely marked in Rufous-fronted. See also text.

207b **Adult female** Grey underparts from breast.

209 Rufous-breasted Wood-quail *Odontophorus speciosus*

Text page 407

Lowland tropical forest (to 1700 m). Ecuador and Peru.

209a **Adult male** (nominate; C Peru) Combination of blackish face and throat, whitish eye-stripe and rufous underparts distinctive within range.

209b **Adult female** (nominate) Rufous on underparts confined to breast.

209c **Adult female** (*soederstroemii*; E Ecuador) Female of Ecuadorian race resembles female Chestnut, but latter has rufous head-sides and is only known from Colombia.

209d **Juvenile** (nominate) Confusing, lacking blackish on face and throat but unlikely to be encountered away from company of adults.

205a

205b

205c

205d

204a

204b

207b

207a

209c

209b

209a

209d

DAVID MEAD

PLATE 62: WOOD-QUAILS III

206 Black-fronted Wood-quail *Odontophorus atrifrons*

Text page 404

Montane tropical forest (1200–3100 m). NE Colombia/NW Venezuela.

206a Adult (nominate) Very dark wood-quail with some contrast to even blacker face and throat in good light. Range possibly overlaps only with Marbled (Plate 60), which favours lower altitudes, but latter lacks blackish face and throat and has reddish orbital skin. Other wood-quails in NE Colombia not known to meet its range. Sexes similar.

206b Juvenile Black of face and throat obscured by brownish mottles, bill reddish-brown.

213 Black-breasted Wood-quail *Odontophorus leucolaemus*

Text page 409

Tropical forest (800–1850 m). Costa Rica and W Panama. Range does not meet similar Tacarcuna Wood-quail of E Panama.

213a Adult Blackish forest quail, a typical bird with white throat.

213b Adult ('*smithianus*' variant) has white throat often small, diffuse or even absent.

213c Juvenile Breast more chestnut, less blackish, throat mottled.

210 Tacarcuna Wood-quail *Odontophorus dialeucos*

Text page 407

Subtropical forest (1050–1450 m). E Panama/NW Colombia.

210a Adult Dark brownish wood-quail with striking white supercilium, throat and chest patches; the only wood-quail known from Darién highlands. Unlikely to be confused if seen well, range coming into possible contact only with Rufous-fronted (Plate 61) and Marbled (Plate 60), both of which lack white on head and throat. Similar Black-breasted has white only on throat and only occurs in W Panama.

210b Juvenile Less extensive white on throat, with chin blackish.

212 Venezuelan Wood-quail *Odontophorus columbianus*

Text page 409

Subtropical cloud forest (1100–2400 m). NC Venezuela.

212a Adult male Rufous-brown wood-quail with striking whitish throat and heavy black-edged white spotting on reddish-brown underparts; range does not overlap with two other Venezuelan species of wood-quail. Black-fronted, which is only known from further north (Zulia province), has blackish face and throat, and Marbled (Plate 60) of lower altitudes has unspotted underparts, lacks white throat and has reddish orbital skin.

212b Adult female Reduced white spotting.

212c Juvenile Underparts only weakly spotted, bill reddish.

206a

206b

213b

213a

213c

210a

210b

212c

212a

212b

DAVID MEAD

208 Dark-backed Wood-quail *Odontophorus melanonotus*

Text page 406

Subtropical forests (1200–1500 m). NW Ecuador/SW Colombia.

208a Adult Very restricted range: only overlaps with Rufous-fronted (Plate 61), which Dark-backed appears to replace at higher altitudes. Overall blackish-brown, finely vermiculated rufous, contrasting with clear rufous throat and breast. Entire underparts rufous in Rufous-fronted, which also has black-and-white throat.

208b Juvenile Dull brown with reddish bill.

211 Gorgeted Wood-quail *Odontophorus strophium*

Text page 408

Montane forests (1500–2050 m). C Colombia. Very rare in very restricted range.

211a Adult male Easily distinguished from Rufous-fronted (Plate 61) and Black-fronted (Plate 62) by black-and-white variegated head pattern and white chest-band; Rufous-fronted also has white collar but occurs at lower altitudes, has chestnut head-sides and lacks white breast spotting of male Gorgeted. Closely related Tacarcuna (Plate 62) only occurs near Panama border.

211b Adult female Grey underparts and reduced white spots on breast.

211c Juvenile Duller than female, with fewer, buffer spots below.

214 Stripe-faced Wood-quail *Odontophorus balliviani*

Text page 410

Montane forests (2000–3000 m). N Bolivia and SE Peru.

214 Adult male Only wood-quail in its restricted range. Relatively dark chestnut with prominently white-spotted underparts. Replaced by Starred (Plate 60) much further north in Peru, which lacks extensive white spotting below and has much more conspicuous crest. Sexes similar.

220 Tawny-faced Quail *Rhynchortyx cinctus*

Text page 416

Lowland forest (to 1400 m). C and NW South America. Three similar races, vary only in colour saturation. Compare Singing Quail (Plate 64) in Honduras.

220a Adult male (nominate; Costa Rica and Panama) Very small, short-tailed quail of forest floor. Male has distinctive rufous head-sides, grey breast and buff belly.

220b Adult female (nominate) Brown head and breast, white throat, streak behind eye and belly, with dark scaling on flanks.

208a

208b

211b

211c

211a

214

220b

220a

DAVID MEAD

218 Montezuma Quail *Cyrtonyx montezumae* Text page 414

Bushy grasslands and open woodland (1060–3000 m). Mexico and S USA. Five races (two extremes shown). Compare Ocellated Quail.

218a **Adult male** (nominate; E Mexico) Plump, large-headed quail with ruffle on nape. Male has stunning black-and-white head pattern ('clown-like') and blackish-and-chestnut underparts, the latter profusely spotted white.

218b **Adult female** (nominate) Differs from female bobwhites in head shape, including very stout bill, and by having 'ghost' of male's head pattern.

218c **Adult male** (*sallei*; S Mexico) Approaches Ocellated Quail in underparts coloration.

218b **Juvenile male** Duller than female, with young males soon acquiring underpart spotting.

219 Ocellated Quail *Cyrtonyx ocellatus* Text page 415

Pine–oak woodland and bushy country (750–3050 m). S Mexico to Honduras.

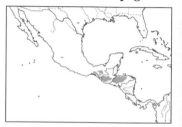

219a **Adult male** Very similar to Montezuma Quail, which it replaces to south (but ranges do not meet). Male differs in having extensive rufous-buff underparts, almost completely obscuring blackish or dark grey, and forming rufous barring on flanks.

219b **Adult female** Probably not safely separable from all populations of Montezuma Quail (see text).

217 Singing Quail *Dactylortyx thoracicus* Text page 412

Hill and montane forests (1000–3000 m). C America. Despite limited range, no fewer than 17 subspecies are recognised, varying in colour saturation and size. Compare Tawny-faced Quail (Plate 63) in Honduras.

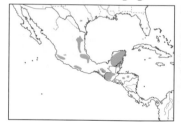

217a **Adult male** (nominate; C Mexico) Very small, short-tailed quail of forest floor. Both sexes overall brownish, marked with fine buff streaks and dark spotting above. Male has buffy-orange head-sides and throat, and greyish underparts, marked by whitish shaft streaks.

217b **Adult female** (nominate). Pale greyish head-sides, becoming whitish on throat, with rest of underparts warm buff.

217c **Adult male** (*sharpei*; SE Mexico and N Guatemala) A richly coloured form.

217d **Juvenile male** (nominate) Duller than female, with blackish spotting on underparts; soon acquires adult features.

PLATE 65: QUAIL-PLOVER AND AFRICAN BUTTONQUAILS

236 Quail-plover *Ortyxelos meiffrenii*

Text page 438

Dry grasslands and open bush. C Africa.

236a **Adult male** Peculiar tiny, rather long-legged quail-like bird, apparently nocturnal by nature. Readily identified when flushed by uniquely patterned rounded wings (like a *Mirafra* lark in shape), which are banded black and white. Flies with erratic lark-like beats, not rapid whirr of quails.

236b **Adult female** Rather larger and brighter than male, with rufous breast.

236c **Adult female** In flight.

221 Small Buttonquail *Turnix sylvatica*

Text page 417

Grasslands and cultivation. SW Europe (very rare), Africa, S Asia, to Java and Philippines. In Africa compare Black-rumped. Nine races differ in colour saturation and strength of upperparts markings, darkest in Philippines. See also Red-backed (Plate 67).

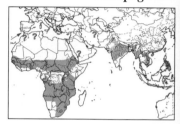

221a **Adult male** (nominate; W Mediterranean) The smallest of three buttonquails of mainland Asia, sharing rufous breast and spotted sides with Yellow-legged (Plate 66), but has grey (not yellow) bill and legs, pale stripes at sides of back, and chestnut feather centres to buffy-edged wing-coverts; latter gives less contrast in flight (but still much stronger contrast than *Coturnix* quails).

221b **Adult female** (nominate) Larger and brighter than male.

221c **Adult female** (nominate) In flight.

227 Madagascar Buttonquail *Turnix nigricollis*

Text page 428

Dry woodland edges and bushy cultivation. Madagascar (introduced Mauritius, Réunion and Glorieuses Is).

227a **Adult male** Barred breast distinctive, especially within range, where it is the only *Turnix*. However, rather larger Harlequin Quail (Plate 21), also present on Madagascar, is typically uniform on upperwing if flushed.

227b **Adult female** Larger and brighter than male, with black throat.

227c **Adult female** In flight.

223 Black-rumped Buttonquail *Turnix hottentotta*

Text page 422

Grasslands and cultivation. C and E Africa. Two well-marked forms, which have occasionally been regarded as separate species.

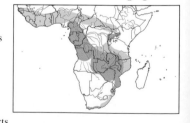

223a **Adult male** (*nana*; most of range) Larger than Small and lacks pale central crown-stripe. Though quite similar in basic coloration, has relatively smaller, scaly (rather than round or heart-shaped) spots at body-sides (more extensive in nominate) and orange-rufous (only on breast in Small) extends over head-sides of head (in female). Irides brown (pale in Small and restricted-range nominate *hottentotta*). In flight has black rump (paler in *hottentotta*) and uppertail-coverts (grey-brown in Small) and some contrast between rusty-buff wing-coverts and dark flight feathers (but less contrast than in Small)

223b **Adult female** (*nana*) Larger and brighter than male.

223c **Adult female** (*nana*) In flight.

223d **Adult male** (nominate; Cape coastal belt of S Africa) For distinguishing features from *nana* see above.

223e **Adult female** (nominate) Larger and brighter than male.

236b

236c

236a

221c

221a

221b

227a

227c

227b

223c

223a

223b

223d

223e

KHEF

PLATE 66: ASIAN BUTTONQUAILS

224 Yellow-legged Buttonquail *Turnix tanki*

Text page 423

Grasslands and cultivation. S and E Asia.

224a **Adult male** (nominate; Indian region) Larger and greyer above than Small (Plate 65), often without pale central crown-stripe and with yellow bill and legs (grey in both Small and Barred). Rufous-orange extends to throat and forms nuchal collar, with bold black spotting at body-sides of body and on pale wing-coverts. Non-breeding female and male usually lack rufous nape.

224b **Adult female** (nominate) Larger and brighter than male, with more obvious nuchal collar.

224c **Adult female** (nominate) In flight has bolder contrast between wing-coverts and flight feathers than Small.

226 Barred Buttonquail *Turnix suscitator*

Text page 426

Grasslands and cultivation. S Asia to Philippines and Sulawesi.

226a **Adult male** (nominate; Sumatra to Bali) Larger and greyer than Small (Plate 65), with distinctive bold barring and scaling on head, breast and fore flanks, contrasting with rufous lower belly and undertail-coverts (in most races). Bill and legs bluish-grey, but more yellowish in some populations.

226b **Adult female** (nominate) Larger and brighter than male. Females of most forms have blackish centre to throat and breast.

226c **Adult female** (*powelli*; Lesser Sundas) Darker grey than mainland forms.

226d **Adult female** (*rufilata*; Sulawesi) Strongly barred flanks; throat white.

226e **Adult female** (nominate) In flight has marked contrast between wing-coverts and flight feathers.

225 Spotted Buttonquail *Turnix ocellata*

Text page 425

Grasslands. Philippines. Two races.

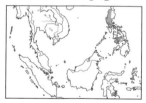

225a **Adult male** (nominate; Luzon) Distinctive large buttonquail with almost unmarked chestnut breast and greenish-yellow bill and legs. Large black spots on wing-coverts and mottled head-sides distinctive.

225b **Adult female** (nominate) Larger and brighter than male, with chestnut nuchal collar and extensive blackish head-sides.

225c **Adult female** (nominate) In flight.

232 Worcester's Buttonquail *Turnix worcesteri*

Text page 434

Highland (only?) grasslands. Endemic to Luzon (Philippines). Little known, confused with Small (Plate 65) which also occurs on Luzon.

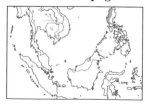

232a **Adult male** Differs from Luzon race, *whiteheadi*, of Small in having much stouter bill, paler upperparts (*whiteheadi* has very slim bill and is darker above), has rufous extending onto throat-sides and malar region, and scaling (not spotting) at breast-sides.

232b **Adult female** Sexes similar, though female averages larger.

232c **Adult female** In flight.

233 Sumba Buttonquail *Turnix everetti*

Text page 435

Grasslands. Endemic to Sumba (Lesser Sundas) but little known.

233a **Adult male** Occurs alongside Sumba race *sumbana* of Red-backed (Plate 67), which also lacks reddish collar. Sumba differs in having stouter bluish bill (slimmer and yellow in *sumbana*), flesh-pink (not yellow) legs and rather plain lightly scaled wing-coverts (boldly black spotted in *sumbana*). Sumba also has a somewhat diffuse dark eye-stripe and upper border to ear-coverts.

233b **Adult female** Slightly brighter and larger than male.

224a

224b

224c

226a

226b

226c

226d

226e

225c

225b

225a

233a

233b

232a

232b

232c

KHEF

222 Red-backed Buttonquail *Turnix maculosa*

Text page 420

Grasslands, forest edges, swampy cover and cultivation. N and E Australia and E Indies. Fourteen races vary in colour saturation and extent of rusty back.

222a Adult male (*melanota*; Lesser Sundas) One of the smallest Australian *Turnix*, pale eyed, yellow legged and with slimmest bill. Duller than female, bill greyer. Dull yellow-buff on face and underparts, with drab grey-brown upperparts. Both sexes have bold black spotting at body-sides and across pale wing-coverts.

222b Adult female (nominate) Yellow bill. Rusty-orange on head-sides and underparts, becoming paler rufous-buff below breast; rich rusty-orange collar encircles mantle (absent in Sumba race).

222c Adult female (*sumbana*; Sumba) Lacks rusty mantle.

222d Adult female (*beccarii*; Sulawesi) Has a narrower rusty collar.

222e Adult female (nominate) In flight.

229 Chestnut-backed Buttonquail *Turnix castanota*

Text page 430

Dry grassy and bushy escarpments and woodland. N Australia.

229a Adult male Large, yellow-eyed, yellow-legged buttonquail with stout greyish-white bill. Rather featureless cinnamon-rufous above and olive-grey below. Marked with indistinct whitish spots and streaks above and below, and weakly scaled black above apart from unmarked rufous rump and uppertail-coverts. Distinctive within range but compare Buff-breasted.

229b Adult female Larger and slightly brighter than male.

229c Adult female In flight.

230 Buff-breasted Buttonquail *Turnix olivei*

Text page 431

Open stony, lightly vegetated country. N Queensland (Australia).

230a Adult male Rather larger and heavier billed even than similar Chestnut-backed, differing in having distinctly buff (not olive-grey) breast, even fewer dark markings on sandy-cinnamon (less rufous) upperparts, and range. Overlaps with Painted.

230b Adult female Larger and slightly brighter than male.

230c Adult female In flight.

231 Painted Buttonquail *Turnix varia*

Text page 432

Scrubland and open woodland. Australia and New Caledonia. Three races; very rare (perhaps extinct) New Caledonia race *novaecaledoniae* small, almost blackish above, with buff fringes to grey breast feathers could have represented a distinct species.

231a Adult male (nominate; Australia) Large, red-eyed, yellow-legged buttonquail with prominent greyish bill. Greyish head and underparts (spotted white) contrast with rusty-brown, well-marked upperparts. In flight has contrast between greyish rump and rusty back (useful on flushed birds within range of Buff-breasted).

231b Adult female Larger and slightly brighter than male.

231c Adult female In flight.

222a

222b

222c

222d

222e

229c

229a

229b

230a

230b

230c

231a

231b

231c

KHEF

PLATE 68: AUSTRALIAN BUTTONQUAILS (II) AND PLAINS-WANDERER

228 Black-breasted Buttonquail *Turnix melanogaster*

Text page 429

Rainforest edges and thickets, especially *Lantana* scrub. E Australia (declining).

228a Adult male Large, distinctive buttonquail, yellow eyed and yellow legged, with white-spotted blackish underparts. Male lacks solid black being heavily mottled or grizzled white (may even appear whitish headed) on blackish background.

228b Adult female Head and breast blackish.

228c Adult female In flight.

234 Red-chested Buttonquail *Turnix pyrrhothorax*

Text page 436

Lush grasslands, forest edges and cultivation. Australia.

234a Adult male Small buttonquail, pale eyed, flesh-coloured legs and has chunky greyish bill. Male much paler below with whitish throat, has marked scaling at breast-sides. Wing-coverts not spotted black (compare Red-backed on Plate 67).

234b Adult female Rusty-orange on throat and breast, not extending onto sides of peppered head.

234c Adult female In flight.

235 Little Buttonquail *Turnix velox*

Text page 437

Grasslands, forest edges and cultivation. Australia.

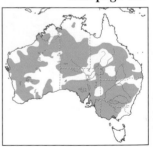

235a Adult male Small buttonquail, pale eyed and flesh-coloured legs with chunky greyish bill. Both sexes pinkish-cinnamon, with contrasting white belly, but male duller with marked scaling at breast-sides. Generally rather featureless.

235b Adult female Rather brighter (see above)

235c Adult female In flight unmarked cinnamon mid-wing panel conspicuous.

237 Plains-wanderer *Pedionomus torquatus*

Text page 440

Grassy plains and fields in treeless country. E Australia. Nocturnal.

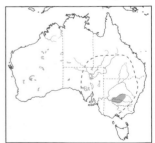

237a Adult male A slim-necked rather long-legged quail-like bird, now considered to be a primitive shorebird. Vermiculated brown plumage relieved by whitish wing panels in flight (recalling miniature thick-knee).

237b Adult female Distinctive black-and-white necklace above chestnut collar.

237c Adult female In flight.

228b

228c

228a

234c

234a

234b

235c

235a

237c

237b

235b

237a

KHEF

Emphasis is placed on features most easily appreciated in flight as most species are typically encountered on the wing. Flight calls are also distinctive (see text).

---

238 Tibetan Sandgrouse *Syrrhaptes tibetanus*

Text page 442

Arid stony plateaux. Tibetan plateau.

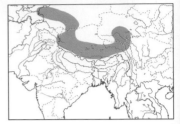

238a Adult male The only northern sandgrouse with a blackish underwing, easily identified by range, though it overlaps with Pallas's (and marginally with Black-bellied, Plate 72) but white belly and dark underwing makes identification straightforward. **238b** In flight, above. **238c** In flight, below.

238d Adult female Barred upperparts, shorter tail than male. **238e** In flight, below.

---

239 Pallas's Sandgrouse *Syrrhaptes paradoxus*

Text page 444

Semi-desert, dry steppe and barren cultivation. C Asia.

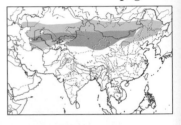

239a Adult male The only northern sandgrouse with almost all-white underwing and underparts, apart from conspicuous (but relatively small) black belly patch. Easily identified by range, though overlaps with Tibetan and Black-bellied (Plate 72); latter has black flight feathers and large black belly patch. **239b** In flight, above. **239c** In flight, below.

239d Adult female Lacks scaled breast-band of male, has black border to yellower throat and has spotting at sides of breast. **239e** In flight, below.

239f Juvenile Duller than female, with scaled foreparts and shorter tail.

---

240 Pin-tailed Sandgrouse *Pterocles alchata*

Text page 445

Dry cultivation, semi-desert and stony plains. SW Europe, N Africa and Middle East. Often in very large flocks. Two races.

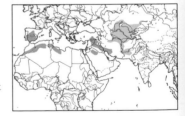

240a Adult male (nominate; Spain and S France) Combination of white belly and underwing contrasting sharply with darker breast quite distinctive in range. Overlaps with Spotted and Crowned (Plate 70), Black-bellied (Plate 72), and Pallas's, all of which have white or very pale underwing-coverts but do not otherwise present identification problems. **240b** In flight, above. **240c** In flight, below.

240d Adult female (nominate) In flight. Shorter tail than male.

240e Adult male (*caudacutus*; most of range) Longer-winged and paler than nominate.

240f Adult female (*caudacutus*) Whitish chin, scaled crown and shorter tail than male.

238e

238c

238b

238a

238d

239b

239e

239c

239f

239d

239a

240d

240c

240a

240b

240f

240e

John Cox

242 Chestnut-bellied Sandgrouse *Pterocles exustus*   **Text page 448**

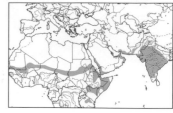

Dry cultivation and semi-desert. C and E Africa and India. Six races, differing in colour tones.

242a **Adult male** (*erlangeri*; Arabia) Combination of all-dark underwing contiguous with dark underparts and pointed tail distinctive throughout range. Flights to drink in mornings. Overlaps with only three others, which have (or appear to have) both dark underwing and bellies, and are short-tailed species: smaller, stumpy reared, dusk-drinking Four-banded and Painted (both Plate 72) and marginally with larger, darker backed Yellow-throated (Plate 71). This race paler than other forms.

242b **Adult male** (*olivascens*; E Africa) Darker than other races. **242c** In flight, above. **242d** In flight, below.

242e **Adult female** (*olivascens*) Barred and spotted underparts and breast, and shorter tail than male. **242f** In flight, below.

243 Spotted Sandgrouse *Pterocles senegallus*   **Text page 450**

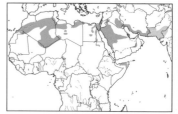

Dry cultivation and semi-desert. N Africa to NW India.

243a **Adult male** Appears sandy with dark flight feathers, a pattern shared by Crowned (with which it often mixes). Crowned has all-dark primaries whereas primaries are pale with darker trailing edge in Spotted (differences difficult to interpret on rapidly beating wings). If overhead look for narrow black belly-stripe and 'pin-tail' of Spotted. Fortunately calls are quite different, Spotted having a liquid, whistled *wittoo, wittoo.* **243b** In flight, above. **243c** In flight, below.

243d **Adult female** Spotted underparts and breast and shorter tail than male. **243e** In flight, below.

246 Crowned Sandgrouse *Pterocles coronatus*   **Text page 454**

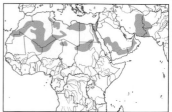

Semi-desert and desert. N Africa to Pakistan. On ground most readily identified by vertical black facial patch in front of eye in male. Five races, differ in colour tones and saturation.

246a **Adult male** (nominate; N Africa) Generally appears pale sandy-buff with blackish primaries and secondaries in flight. At distance very similar to Spotted, but Crowned has more extensive black on primaries and utters a guttural, chattering *chag-chaggara.* **246b** In flight, above. **246c** In flight, below.

246d **Adult female** (nominate) Barred and spotted underparts and breast and lacks face pattern of male. **246e** In flight, below.

246f **Adult male** (*saturatus*; Oman) A richly coloured form.

241 Namaqua Sandgrouse *Pterocles namaqua*   **Text page 447**

Semi-desert and desert. S Africa.

241a **Adult male** The only S African sandgrouse with dark underwing and 'pin tail'. On ground recalls Double-banded (Plate 72), but has plain head, lacking black-and-white patches of male. Female has yellower ground colour to head and neck, and more pointed tail than Double-banded. Drinks mostly in mornings, rarely late in day (Double-banded drinks at night). **241b** In flight, above. **241c** In flight, below.

241d **Adult female** Finely barred and spotted, with a pointed tail. **241e** In flight, below.

242d

242f

242b

242c

242a

242e

243e

243c

243b

243d

243a

246e

246f

246c

246a

246b

246d

241c

241a

241e

241d

241b

John Cox

PLATE 71: AFRICAN SANDGROUSE II

247 Madagascar Sandgrouse *Pterocles personatus*

Text page 455

Dry grasslands, stony lakeshores etc. Madagascar.

247a **Adult male** Identification straightforward as is only sandgrouse on Madagascar. Short-tailed, chunky sandgrouse with distinctive all-blackish underwing in both sexes. On ground male has vertical blackish face patch before eye. **247b** In flight, below. **247c** In flight, above.

247d **Adult female** Lacks black face of male. **247e** In flight, below.

248 Black-faced Sandgrouse *Pterocles decoratus*

Text page 456

Dry savanna and scrubby semi-desert. E Africa. Compare similar sandgrouse on Plate 72: these have black-and-white patches on head (not a complete vertical face-band), while females of these species lack broad whitish breast-band of Black-faced. Drinks at dusk and dawn. Three similar races.

248a **Adult male** (nominate; E Kenya and E Tanzania) Short tailed, blackish rear underparts contrasting with whitish breast-band in both sexes. Underwing coverts buffy-white merging to dusky on axillaries. On ground male has vertical blackish face patch in front of eye (diagnostic in range). **248b** In flight, above. **248c** In flight, below.

248d **Adult female** (nominate) Lacks black face of male. **248e** In flight, below.

248f **Adult male** (*loveridgei*; W Kenya and W Tanzania): a paler, sandier form.

244 Yellow-throated Sandgrouse *Pterocles gutturalis*

Text page 451

Open grasslands. E and S Africa. Two similar races (nominate shown).

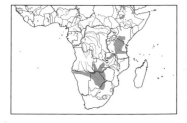

244a **Adult male** (nominate; S Africa) Very large sandgrouse, with all-dark underwing and rear underparts (latter actually dark ruddy-brown) in both sexes. Male very grey above, with cinnamon-rufous wing-coverts and buffy-yellow throat, bordered by black collar. **244b** In flight, above. **244c** In flight, below.

244d **Adult female** (nominate) Lacks collar and is closely speckled above. **244e** In flight, below.

253 Burchell's Sandgrouse *Pterocles burchelli*

Text page 461

Semi-arid savanna. S Africa.

253a **Adult male** Distinctive small sandgrouse, both sexes overall ruddy-cinnamon, including underwing-coverts, which contrast with blackish primaries and secondaries. Closer views reveal profuse whitish spotting in both sexes, though spotting cleaner in male. **253b** In flight, above. **253c** In flight, below.

253d **Adult female** Plumage spotting duller. **253e** In flight, below.

247b

247e

247c

247d

247a

248b

248c

248f

248e

248a

248d

244c

244b

244a

244e

244d

253e

253c

253d

253a

253b

John Cox

PLATE 72: 'BANDED' AND BLACK-BELLIED SANDGROUSE

The first four species are crepuscular or nocturnal in drinking habits. Males of all four have black-and-white crown patches, chest-bands, yellow skin around eye and pink bills. Females are closely barred and are extremely similar. In all species the greyish underwing and barred rear underparts appear dark in flight.

249 Double-banded Sandgrouse *Pterocles bicinctus*

Text page 457

Wooded savanna. S Africa. Three similar races, differ in size and tones.

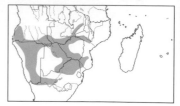

249a Adult male (nominate; Namibia) Unbarred face, neck and upper breast, separated from barred belly by narrow black-and-white bands. The only 'banded' sandgrouse with white spotting on upperparts. Compare Namaqua Sandgrouse (Plate 70). **249b** In flight, above. **249c** In flight, below.

249d Adult female Differs from female Namaqua in having barred (not streaked) breast and blunt tail. **249e** In flight, below.

250 Four-banded Sandgrouse *Pterocles quadricinctus*

Text page 458

Savanna and dry cultivation. C Africa.

250a Adult male Like Double-banded, but has narrow black and broad white chest-bands and lacks white spotting on upperparts. Lichtenstein's differs in having barred face, foreneck and forewing (both sexes) and broad (in male) orange-buff (not white) breast-band. Compare Black-faced (Plate 71). **250b** In flight, above. **250c** In flight, below.

250d Adult female. Lacks face pattern and breast-banding of male. **250e** In flight, below.

251 Painted Sandgrouse *Pterocles indicus*

Text page 459

Semi-arid fields and hills. Pakistan and N India.

251a Adult male Like Double-banded but has broad black-and-buff and narrow chestnut chest-bands. Upperparts broadly barred black, buff and white. Lichtenstein's (no known overlap) prefers more arid rocky country, and differs in barred foreneck and upperparts (both sexes) and (in male) in narrow black (not chestnut) breast-band. **251b** In flight, above. **251c** In flight, below.

251d Adult female Plain face with finely barred body. **251e** In flight, below.

252 Lichtenstein's Sandgrouse *Pterocles lichtensteinii*

Text page 460

Barren rocky hills and wadis with *Acacia*. N Africa to SW Pakistan. Five races differ in colour tones and strength of barring.

252a Adult male (*sukensis*; N Kenya and S Ethiopia) Differs from rest of group in freckled face and barred neck and forewing; broad orange-buff breast-band with narrow black median band and broader one below. Compare Four-banded and Painted. **252b** In flight, above. **252c** In flight, below.

252d Adult female (*sukensis*) Finely barred all over, even face and throat. **252e** In flight, below.

252f Adult male (*ingramsi*; S Yemen) Palest race, with weakest barring.

245 Black-bellied Sandgrouse *Pterocles orientalis*

Text page 452

Dry steppe grasslands. N Africa, SW Europe to C Asia. Two similar races.

245a Adult male (nominate; NW Africa and Spain) Large sandgrouse easily identified by combination of black belly patch and white vent and underwing. Compare Pallas's (Plate 69). **245b** In flight, above. **245c** In flight, below.

245d Adult female Buffy head and underparts, spotted and barred with black, readily separates sexes. **245e** In flight, below.

249e
249c
249d
249a
249b

250d
250e
250c
250a
250b

251e
251b
251c
251a
252e
252c
252b
251d
252d
252a
252f
245b
245e
245c
245a
245d

John Cox

FAMILY PHASIANIDAE
Partridges, Quails and Pheasants
SUBFAMILY PERDICINAE
Partridges, Old World Quails and Spurfowl

A varied assemblage of short-tailed gamebirds, comprising 110 species in 22 genera. *Francolinus* (41 species) and *Arborophila* (21) account for over half of these, whereas no fewer than 11 genera are monotypic.

Genus *LERWA*: Snow Partridge

A monotypic genus containing a heavily-barred Himalayan partridge. Its rather broad wings are strangely pointed for a partridge, and the exceptionally long tertials conceal the wing-tip. The tarsus is short and feathered to halfway at the front. The downy chick is remarkably similar to that of the unrelated Blood Pheasant.

1 SNOW PARTRIDGE
Lerwa lerwa (Hodgson, 1833)   Plate 1

This distinctive close-barred, rear-attenuated partridge of the high Himalayas is unique. Its whistling calls and eggs suggest a distant relationship to snowcocks, but these attributes are perhaps merely indicative of a similar lifestyle. It is even possible that the species is an aberrant francolin.

IDENTIFICATION A dark partridge of the high Himalayas. The intense barring of the head and upperparts is only apparent at close range; in the field it generally appears dark with a red bill, relieved by a whitish frontal collar and white flank striping. If flushed, the whitish trailing edge to the secondaries can be striking, especially in fresh plumage. Confusion with other species unlikely, but shares habitat with Tibetan Partridge, the much larger snowcocks and, at lower elevations, marginally overlaps with Chukar.

DESCRIPTION Bill coral-red (male), pinkish or greyish-pink (female). Irides red or reddish-brown. Legs red or orange-red, relatively short and feathered to midway on tarsus. Wings very broad, sharply pointed at tip. Rear body and tail relatively long. Sexes similar, but female slightly smaller, with bill paler pink than male. Male has a strong, blunt spur, sometimes with a smaller second; female unspurred. **Adult (both sexes)**: Face and throat almost blackish, head and entire upperparts closely-barred black and white, finest on head and neck. Tail barred. Wing-coverts and secondaries similar, the latter broadly tipped white; primaries unbarred blackish with narrow white tips; some scapulars have largely white outer webs; mantle and upper scapulars washed greyish-brown, becoming rusty on tertials, but less evident with wear. White bars on outer part of each feather abrade to produce blacker overall appearance. Breast and underparts rich dark chestnut, becoming whitish on upper chest and vent; flanks boldly striped white. **Juvenile**: Duller, paler buffy-brown below, with pale shaft streaks on both upper- and underparts, breaking the barred pattern above.

GEOGRAPHICAL VARIATION Chinese birds usually larger (male wing 193–213), less rufous-toned

above and slightly paler below. They have been considered as separate subspecies, *major* (Sichuan) and *callipygia* (Gansu), but differences either inconsistent or perhaps clinal, and their validity is doubtful, although Cheng *et al.* (1978) admitted both.

MEASUREMENTS Length 38–40 cm. Male slightly larger than female. Data from India and Nepal. Males: wing 183–204 (mean 194), tarsus 38–40. Females: wing 180–186, tarsus (n=1) 33. Weight (both sexes) 454–709.

HABITAT Open mountainsides above tree-line, favouring steep grassy slopes with scattered shrubs and ferns, interspersed with scree and snow patches. Often just below snow-line or at edges of glaciers. Generally at 3000–5500 m, rarely as low as 2400 m during severe weather. In China, however, it remains above 3800 m in winter.

VOICE Advertising call: the male utters a repeated, loud and clear whistled *jijiu, jijiu, jijiu* gradually quickening and rising in pitch (Li & Lu 1992). It is difficult to equate this with the analogy of Osmaston, who likened this call to the musical clattering made by Grey Francolin (Ali & Ripley 1969). Less often heard female call is shorter (2 seconds), softer and falls in pitch. When flushed, rises noisily, uttering a repeated *huei, huei*.

HABITS Most active in morning and late afternoon. Usually encountered in pairs or small coveys on steep open slopes; larger groups of 20–30 occur in non-breeding season in favoured areas, particularly at roosts. Established breeding territories in China occupied 5 ha. Feeds on various seeds, lichens, mosses and shoots, chiefly from grasses and shrubs; some invertebrates also taken. Generally relatively approachable, exhibiting little fear of humans with which it has little contact in its harsh environment. Indeed, it is often quite inquisitive, standing boldly on an exposed rock or ridge to watch admiring birdwatchers! Flushes noisily, rising with whirring and clapping wings, before flying rapidly downhill, the covey members scattering in various directions. Coveys gather noisily to form communal roosts in rock crevices, caves, under projecting rocks or beneath shrubby cover.

BREEDING Apparently monogamous, with male assisting in chick care. The nest scrape, with or without a lining of moss and leaves, is located on a very steep rocky slope, or near a ridge crest, and well concealed by a rock, grass tuft or low shrub. Clutch 2–5 (mean 3), but sightings of family parties suggest that it can be up to 7; eggs resemble those of snowcocks but smaller; pale buff finely speckled reddish. Breeds in May–July, but season protracted and may vary according to local weather conditions. Incubation solely by female, but no further information.

DISTRIBUTION Almost throughout the higher Himalayas, from extreme N Pakistan east through Kashmir, S Tibet, N India, Nepal and Bhutan to Arunachal Pradesh. In the east, its range extends north into SC China, in E Xizang, W and N Sichuan, north to extreme S Gansu and southeast to the Lijiang Mts in extreme N Yunnan. Some authors (e.g. del Hoyo *et al.* 1994) extend the western limit to Afghanistan, but this lacks foundation and appears to have been perpetuated in error.

STATUS Widespread and locally common. A study area in China held 56 birds per km². Hunting pressure and nest-site disturbance by medicinal herb collectors were adversely affecting this population.

REFERENCES Ali & Ripley (1969), Cheng *et al.* (1978), Fleming *et al.* (1976), del Hoyo *et al.* (1994), Li & Lu (1992).

Genus *TETRAOPHASIS*: monal-partridges

Large partridges with relatively long, broad, wedge-shaped tails of 18 feathers (14 in most other partridge genera). The two species are superficially similar and, as their ranges almost meet in C China, they are usually considered conspecific by Chinese authorities (e.g. Cheng 1987). The genus forms a link between the partridges and the pheasants, and in some respects can be regarded as closer to the latter.

2   VERREAUX'S MONAL-PARTRIDGE
Tetraophasis obscurus (Verreaux, 1870)   Plate 3

Alternative names: Verreaux's Pheasant-partridge or Pheasant-grouse, Chestnut-throated Partridge.

Verreaux's is the more northerly distributed of the two monal-partridges, whose ranges appear to be separated by only 150 km in S Qinghai and W Sichuan.

IDENTIFICATION Distribution is generally the key to specific recognition, although the two species are easily distinguished by throat colour, chestnut in Verreaux's and buff in Szechenyi's. Given exceptionally good views when flushed, Verreaux's should show less contrast between the brownish-grey rump and uppertail and the darker brown mantle than Szechenyi's. Both are large greyish partridge-like birds with rather long, broad, white-tipped tails. The latter feature is unique to the genus, and should be especially obvious when flushed. Comparisons have been made with Koklass Pheasant in basic size and flushing behaviour by observers who know both in life.

DESCRIPTION Bill dusky-brown or blackish. Irides chestnut-brown. Bare skin around eye red. Legs reddish-brown. Sexes generally similar, male has one spur, absent in females. Relatively long, broad, rather graduated tail consists of 18 feathers (14 in other partridges). Elongated axillaries. **Adult (both sexes):** Head, sides and rear of neck, mantle, wings and upperparts medium ashy-grey, tinged brown, darkest on head and mantle. Wing-coverts, scapulars and tertials tipped buffy-white, forming bands of spots on folded wing. Chin and throat rusty-chestnut, narrowly bordered with whitish. Breast slate-grey, spotted with black. Flanks grey with whitish inner webs giving lightly streaked effect, becoming whitish on belly. Undertail-coverts chestnut with white tips giving scaled appearance. Outertail feathers blackish, broadly tipped white; central tail feathers greyish-brown with narrow white tips. **Juvenile:** Apparently undescribed, but presumably much as in Szechenyi's.

GEOGRAPHICAL VARIATION Monotypic.

MEASUREMENTS Length 48 cm. Female smaller than male. Males: wing 214–227 (mean 218), tail 153–175, tarsus c.50, weight (n=1) 938. Females: wing 197–200, tail 150–160, weight (n=2) 720 and 840.

HABITAT Alpine zone of mountain slopes, from borders of tree-line upwards (3000–4100 m). One radio-tagged female moved from 2850 m, in spring, to 3000–3350 m in summer. Occurs on open rocky slopes and among rhododendron and juniper scrub with clearings, meadows and deep ravines.

VOICE Recordings indicate a loud mixture of raucous, guttural, bubbling and grating notes that are apparently similar to those of Szechenyi's. Reported to utter a 'loud cry' when flushed.

HABITS Apparently unstudied. Generally occurs singly or in pairs, feeding in open areas at upper limit of forest. When disturbed, walks away cocking and flirting tail in manner of a snowcock. Behaviour presumed similar to that of slightly better-known Szechenyi's.

BREEDING No information available.

DISTRIBUTION Mountains of C China. From its northern limits in C Gansu, it extends south to Kimar and the Rangta Gol Gorge in the Nan Shan, northeast of Qinghai Hu (Koko Nor) in E Qinghai, and southeast

172

in N (to Songpan) and W Sichuan (to Mupin [Baoxing]). Further west, in this region, it is apparently replaced by Szechenyi's, which occurs as near as the mountains west of the Yalung River.

STATUS Near-Threatened. Apparently not uncommon over much of its range, but its distribution is rather fragmented and perhaps isolated by habitat destruction. Legally protected in China, where it is known from at least 13 localities. No overall population estimates available, but a density of 3.5–4.0 birds per ha reported at Baoxing in W Sichuan. Unknown in captivity. Research into the ecology and status of this poorly-known species is urgently required.

REFERENCES Carey, G. J. (tape recordings), Cheng (1987), Cheng *et al.* (1978), Collar *et al.* (1994), Zhao Zhengjie (1995).

---

3 SZECHENYI'S MONAL-PARTRIDGE
Tetraophasis szechenyii (Madaràsz, 1885)   Plate 3

Alternative names: Szechenyi's Pheasant-partridge or Pheasant-grouse, Buff-throated Partridge.

The more southerly distributed of the two monal-partridges, it being widespread in SE Tibet.

IDENTIFICATION Mountains of E Tibet and W Sichuan, replacing Verreaux's west of the Yalung River. Although distribution is the key to specific identification, given exceptionally good views the two are easily distinguished by throat colour, buff in Szechenyi's and chestnut in Verreaux's. If flushed, Szechenyi's should show a purer grey rump and uppertail, contrasting more with the brownish mantle than in more uniformly brown Verreaux's. Both are large greyish partridge-like birds with comparatively long, broad, white-tipped tails. The latter characteristic is unique to the genus, and should be especially obvious when flushed.

DESCRIPTION Bill dusky-brown or blackish. Irides chestnut-brown. Bare skin around eye red. Legs reddish-brown. Sexes largely similar, male has one spur, absent in females. Relatively long, broad, rather graduated tail consists of 18 feathers (14 in other partridges). Axillaries elongated. **Adult (both sexes):** Head, sides and rear of neck, mantle, wings and upperparts brownish-grey, darkest on head and mantle. Rump and uppertail-coverts purer grey. Wing-coverts, scapulars and tertials have whitish or buff tips, forming bands of spots on folded wing. Chin and throat ochre-buff. Breast grey, spotted with black. Flanks grey with rusty inner webs to feathers giving slightly spotted or streaked pattern. Belly mottled grey, whitish and rufous. Undertail-coverts chestnut with white tips giving scaled appearance. Outertail feathers blackish, broadly tipped with white; central tail feathers greyish-brown with narrow white tips. **Juvenile:** Similar to adult but body feathers with whitish shaft steaks, most prominent on underparts. Upperparts also closely barred black and brown, broken by whitish tips and shaft streaks.

GEOGRAPHICAL VARIATION Monotypic.

MEASUREMENTS Length 50 cm. Female smaller than male. Males: wing 216–236 (mean 226), tail (n=2) 142 and 151, tarsus (n=1) 51, weight (n=2) 1020 and 1500. Females: wing 203–224 (mean 215), tail (n=3) 129–133, weight (n=1) 880.

HABITAT Upper forest and alpine zone of mountain slopes. In mixed coniferous, rhododendron and oak forest at 3200–3700 m, coniferous forest at 3300–3900 m and above the tree-line on grassy, scrubby and rocky slopes to 4878 m.

VOICE Recordings reveal a loud repeated 2–3 note cackling, interspersed with occasional monosyllabic grating notes.

HABITS Little studied. Generally in family parties of 4–12 in non-breeding season. Exceptionally, larger congregations occur, as at Ningguo monastery where a flock of 80 is fed by the monks, and these are so confiding that they even enter the temple in search of food. Elsewhere the species is far less easy to observe. Generally 'freezes' when surprised in the open, or flushes on whirring wings, flying rapidly downhill into forest cover with the speed of a Koklass Pheasant. Often sits quietly in tree until danger has passed, where very difficult to relocate. Also roosts in trees. Feeds on small roots, bulbs, mosses, small fruits and green leaves.

BREEDING Little information. Presumed to be monogamous. Nest and eggs undescribed. Chicks reported in Tibet in late May–August, later broods perhaps being replacements for failed first clutches.

DISTRIBUTION Mountains of SE Tibet north to S Qinghai and W Sichuan south and east to Kulu and the Yalung River, the Lijiang Mts in NW Yunnan, and extreme NE India, in the Upper Subansiri and Siyom drainages of Arunachal Pradesh.

STATUS Near-Threatened. Locally not uncommon and known from 15–20 localities. E Tibet population estimated at 25,000–40,000 birds in 300,000 km². Surveys at three sites in Tibet produced densities between one per 0.23 ha and one per 9 ha. Highest densities were on scrubby or bushy slopes, and it was least numerous in dense forest. Protected both by law and religious taboos in Tibet. Currently unknown in captivity. There is an urgent need for research into the ecology and status of this poorly-known species. Its status in India is unknown, its occurrence there being very marginal and in a politically highly sensitive border region.

REFERENCES Ali & Ripley (1969), Carey, G. J. (tape recordings), Cheng (1987), Cheng *et al.* (1978), Collar *et al.* (1994), Liu Shaochu & Ciren (1993), Ludlow & Kinnear (1944), Rank (1997), Schäfer (1934), Yin Binggao & Liu Wulin (1993), Zhao Zhengjie (1995).

Genus *TETRAOGALLUS*: snowcocks

The five snowcocks are very large grouse-like partridges of high C and S Asian mountains. All are large, relatively long-necked and long-bodied, dark greyish partridges with often striking white undertail-coverts. In general, the sexes are basically similar, but females are less well marked, duller and smaller than the very bulky adult males. When aware of being observed they usually walk away, females tending to depress their tails, whereas males hold the tail more horizontal or even slightly lifted. Territorial males exhibit their undertail-coverts like a white 'powder-puff' when walking with their tails cocked high. Young snowcocks do not attain full size until their second year; first-year males are also often closer to females in plumage coloration.

Their plumage is dense and thick, each feather with a well-developed downy base (as in grouse), this coupled with their large size enables them to survive severe winter temperatures (that fall to –40°C). The body bulk and wing structure of snowcocks is incompatible with flapping flight. Being unable to take-off from a flat surface, they run on their powerful legs to a high point, jump off and glide rapidly across open airspace with necks fully extended, gradually losing altitude (Potapov 1992).

The five species comprise two groups:

WHITE-BELLIED	DARK-BELLIED
Altai Snowcock	Caucasian Snowcock
Tibetan Snowcock	Caspian Snowcock
	Himalayan Snowcock

In view of their basic similarity it is useful to realise that only two species (Himalayan and Tibetan) overlap in range.

LOCATING SNOWCOCKS
Snowcocks usually indicate their presence by their far-carrying curlew-like whistles, which have a ventriloquial quality in the clear mountain air; pinpointing the source is rarely easy. Scanning likely slopes, preferably with a telescope, may be rewarding. Pay particular attention to rock outcrops as calling birds often stand atop such vantage points, or look for slow-moving feeding birds on grassy slopes at the foot of sheer rock walls or crags. They may take to the air after calling, gliding rapidly downwards with hardly a beat, showing extensive white in their wings.

4 CAUCASIAN SNOWCOCK
Tetraogallus caucasicus (Pallas, 1811)   Plate 2

Found only in the main Caucasus range, this species is marginally the smallest and has the most restricted distribution of all snowcocks.

IDENTIFICATION Endemic to the Caucasus. A huge dark grey partridge, twice the size of a Chukar, with long rear body, whitish face and forecrown, and white undertail-coverts. In flight, dark grey forewing contrasts with mostly white primaries and band along length of secondaries. Range separated from similar Caspian Snowcock by Kür River valley, with Caucasian to the north, Caspian to the south. Distinctions from Caspian only visible given optimum views and most marked in adult males, therefore range very important in identification. Caucasian has a dark rusty-brown band running back from eye to merge with dull chestnut hindneck (pure grey in Caspian), pale buffy-grey cheeks (white or grey in Caspian), dark chestnut-brown band at sides of foreneck below ear-coverts (dark grey and extending almost to bill base in Caspian), fine scaly black chevrons on breast (small black spots in Caspian) and more distinct chestnut and whitish flank stripes (narrower reddish stripes, without whitish edges, in Caspian). The grey ground colour is darker in Caucasian, lacking the pale-breasted appearance of Caspian (less evident in darker Turkish birds), but enhancing the pale spotting of the upperparts, especially on the scapulars; spots are larger and whiter in females than males. Rufous and chestnut tones of head and neck can be very indistinct in females, being most obvious in adult males. It also widely overlaps with Chukar.

DESCRIPTION Bill brownish-horn, darker and greyer on upper mandible. Nostril cap and bare skin around eye yellow. Irides brown. Legs orange-yellow. Sexes generally differ but individual variation complicates differences, especially with first-year males. Male has short spur, absent in all but oldest females. **Adult male:** Crown buffy-grey, slightly whiter at sides of forecrown, hindneck and nape dull chestnut, becoming paler rufous on lower nape. Dark reddish-brown band extends from eye down neck-sides, becoming diffuse on hindneck. Ear-coverts pale greyish-buff, neck-sides below ear-coverts white. Chin, throat and foreneck white, separated from white neck-sides by vertical dark chestnut-brown band of irregular shape, broadening lower down, often joining below white forecrown; this band narrows below ear-coverts and has diffuse lower border. Body plumage dark grey, faintly vermiculated; breast and mantle closely scaled with black and warm buff markings; sides of lower breast and flanks have longish stripes of chestnut, interspersed with narrower lines of pale buff and black; undertail-coverts bright white. Tail blackish with chestnut terminal band. Primaries white narrowly tipped dark grey. Secondaries dark grey with white bases. Wing-coverts, scapulars and mantle have conspicuous rufous-buff spots (wearing whiter, especially on scapulars). **First-year male:** Often as dull as female, but ear-coverts buffier and usually showing extensive chestnut in neck-band, which does not yet join on foreneck. **Adult female:** Duller than male, with narrower flank streaks, larger and paler spots on upperparts, mottled grey and dull rufous hindneck and band on neck-sides, the latter not meeting on foreneck. **Juvenile:** Smaller than adult, duller than female, with indistinct flank pattern; much as adult by first winter but not fully mature until second winter.

GEOGRAPHICAL VARIATION Monotypic, but some local variation has been noted; those from more humid west of range (Mt Elbrus) appear slightly darker than populations in the drier east (Dagestan). However, these minor variations have not been recognised subspecifically.

MEASUREMENTS Length 52–56 cm. Marginally the smallest snowcock. Female smaller than male. Males: wing 273–285 (mean 281), tarsus 59–64 (mean 61), mean weight 1932. Females: wing 245–265 (mean 254), tarsus 55–62 (mean 58), mean weight 1734.

HABITAT Montane slopes above both tree- and scrublines, favouring grassy slopes with snow patches and rocky outcrops, interspersed with ravines and cliffs. Most numerous in snow-free zones, generally at 1800–4000 m but will descend lower during or following severe winter snowfall, rarely even into foothills at edge of steppe in Dagestan.

VOICE Advertising call: a clear, far-carrying series of plaintive, ringing whistles not dissimilar to call of Eurasian Curlew *Numenius arquata* but more mellow *cooole-cooole-oouwee-ouweee-weeee*, given by males with neck upstretched and head vertical. Wary birds give periodic single, more rising and piercing *coo-oo-lee*, often prior to flying or soon after take-off. When alarmed utters an emphatic *cok-cok-cok*, which is also given by flushed females, apparently in warning to young. Feeding birds retain contact with a softer clucking.

HABITS Usually in pairs or small parties, chiefly of 3–9; post-breeding males may join non-breeding groups, leaving females once incubation is well advanced. Typically seen perched on rocky outcrop or feeding on grassy slopes below crags, males often walk sedately with tail raised and striking white undertail-coverts fluffed-out. When feeding moves slowly, gradually working uphill. Feeds entirely on plant materials, bulbs, seeds, leaves, especially grass seeds and legumes; latter an important protein-rich component of chicks' diet (which, unlike other gamebird chicks, do not feed on insects). Shy and wary, at sight of predator or human intruder walks or runs uphill to ridge top, flying noisily and rapidly downhill, or across gully, with bursts of wingbeats and prolonged glides. Walks uphill in late afternoon to roost among crags and high rock scree, emerging at dawn to call, before flying downslope to feeding areas. Also rests among rocks in feeding areas during midday period.

BREEDING Monogamous, with sex ratio of 1:1 (see Caspian). Nest a sparsely-lined depression, made by the female, often in open but sometimes partially sheltered by nearby rock. Clutch 5–8, mean 6; nests containing up to 15 are probably the result of two females laying in the same nest; eggs pale greenish-grey or pale blue, with some brown spotting, chiefly at the narrow end. Incubation occupies 28 days, by female only. Probably only female tends young, some broods occasionally merge. Eggs laid April–May, varying according to local conditions, those at highest altitudes laying up to 6 weeks later than those at lowest.

DISTRIBUTION Endemic to the Greater Caucasus, from N Georgia, adjacent regions of Russia flanking northern slopes of Caucasus (Ossetia, Chechnya and Dagestan) and N Azerbaijan. Absent from Armenia, making its reputed occurrence in NE Turkey (Serez 1992, repeated in del Hoyo *et al.* 1994) unlikely and requiring substantiation (Kirwan *et al.* 1999).

STATUS Locally numerous. An overall estimate of 410,000 was made in 1980, when numbers were considered stable. In 1993, 1000 (300–400 pairs) were estimated in Azerbaijan. Despite hunting, the species' remote habitat has meant that only localised pressures have been placed on the overall population.

REFERENCES Baziev (1978), Cramp & Simmons (1980), Dement'ev & Gladkov (1967), del Hoyo *et al.* (1994), Kirwan *et al.* (1999), Serez (1992).

---

5   CASPIAN SNOWCOCK
Tetraogallus caspius (Gmelin, 1784)   Plate 2

The most southerly distributed *Tetraogallus*, it being a western cousin of the Himalayan Snowcock. Its apparently fragmented range encompasses mountains within sight of the Mediterranean, Black and Caspian Seas, and the Persian Gulf.

IDENTIFICATION Mountains of Asia Minor and Iran. Range almost meets, but does not overlap with, similar Caucasian Snowcock. In areas that approach range of

Caucasian (Armenia, Azerbaijan) the two are separated by the Kūr River, with only Caspian to the south. Good views are required to appreciate distinctions from Caucasian. Caspian has slate-grey (not dark chestnut) neck stripe, the crown and hindneck are purer grey, with the lower nape much paler grey (not rufous) forming a pale 'shawl', the cheeks are grey and white (not as buff), and the breast has small black spots (not scaling, although descending to 2500 m in April to breed. Breeds as low as 900 m in extreme north of range (Dzungarian Alatau and Borochoro range), but in Indian subcontinent rarely as low as 2400 m even in severe winters, with one record at 2100 m in Pakistan.

VOICE Very much as Caucasian and Caspian Snowcocks. Advertising call a far-carrying series of 4–7 whistled notes given with head thrown well back, each note slightly rising in pitch and the fourth and subsequent notes about an octave higher than the first few. Pairs can be sexed on call, male has rising call, while that of female is descending. Flushed birds utter far-carrying Eurasian Curlew *Numenius arquata*-like bubbling trills, given repeatedly during their descent flight. Contact calls include a shorter rising *ooeee* and, when agitated, a repeated *kuk, kuk, kuk...* accelerating during delivery with rhythm of a bouncing ping-pong ball (has been likened to the mobbing calls of an agitated Blackbird *Turdus merula*).

HABITS As other snowcocks. Sociable unless breeding, with local populations gathering into winter coveys of 30–40 where density permits. Descends to lower elevations in April to feed on fresh shoots revealed by melting snow. Here, the winter flock becomes fragmented as adult males establish breeding territories and display to attract females. Each pair occupies a territory of c.1 km², which includes a significant proportion of grassy slopes with herb-rich vegetation. Males call from a prominent outcrop on fine mornings between 06:00 and 06:30 hrs, but are generally silent in wet weather. Meanwhile the non-breeding nucleus of the flock moves higher, following the retreating snow-line. During the heat of high summer, in July–August, the new families also move to higher elevations, joining the non-breeders. Feeding groups disperse to traditional resting sites among rocks during midday period, but reassemble to feed in late afternoon. Gait slow while feeding, but when suspicious of danger walks quickly uphill toward rocky outcrop or ridge, ready to take flight if necessary. Feeds on berries, seeds, shoots, roots and small insects.

BREEDING Monogamous. Nest a depression scratched out by the female, sparsely lined with grass, wool and downy feathers, and situated near a ridge top or steep slope, protected by a boulder or projecting cliff face. Clutch 8–10; eggs pale clay to greenish, with scattered reddish or dark brown blotches and speckles. Female alone incubates, for c.30 days. Probably only female tends young but male is in close attendance. Eggs laid late April into May/June. In captivity, females capable of producing 120–150 eggs per annum.

DISTRIBUTION C Asia and western fringes of Tibetan massif, from C and N Afghanistan (south to Safed Koh) and east through N Pakistan, NW India and C Nepal. Also throughout the Tien Shan of Tajikistan, S Uzbekistan, Kyrgyzstan and SE Kazakhstan (north to the Tarbagatay range, Zaysan) and east through adjacent China, in W and S Xinjiang, east to the Nan Shan in NE Qinghai. An introduced population is well established in montane NE Nevada (USA).

STATUS Total population estimated at c.200,000. Although locally common over most of wide range, some decreases have been reported. In area of W China studied by Ma (1992) winter flock sizes decreased from 40 to 20–30 in ten years; this was chiefly attributed to habitat degradation through overgrazing. Another worrying factor is the increased demand for snowcock remains in Chinese medicines as a cure for various ailments including rheumatism. The introduced population in Nevada (USA) is estimated at 250–500.

REFERENCES Ali & Ripley (1970), Bates & Lowther (1952), Dement'ev & Gladkov (1967), Ma (1992), Paludan (1959), Stepanyan (1990).

---

7   TIBETAN SNOWCOCK
Tetraogallus tibetanus (Gould, 1854)   Plate 3

Widespread in the Tibetan massif, widely overlapping with larger Himalayan Snowcock. However, Tibetan forms a species-pair with the more northerly-distributed Altai Snowcock. Both have whitish underparts and reduced white in the wings compared to the other snowcocks.

IDENTIFICATION Mountains of C Asia. Range overlaps with Himalayan Snowcock along northern and southwestern fringes of Tibetan plateau, but their separation is easy. Tibetan has whitish flanks and mottled undertail-coverts, and in flight has dark wings with white only on the tips of the secondaries. Himalayan has dark underparts, contrasting with the pale head and breast and white undertail-coverts, and in flight has largely white primaries and band across base of grey secondaries. Tibetan is, however, similar to Altai Snowcock but their ranges do not overlap (see latter for discussion).

DESCRIPTION *T. t. tibetanus*. Bill, nostril cap and bare skin around eye rose-red. Irides brown. Legs rose-red. Sexes generally similar, individual variation complicating subtle differences, especially in first-year males. Male has short spur, absent in females. **Adult male:** Crown and neck grey, contrasting with pale brownish ear-coverts and whitish centre to throat, lores indistinctly whitish. Upper breast has narrow grey band dividing whitish throat from white of rest of underparts. Flanks and lower underparts white with long undulating black stripes, most striking on flanks; undertail-coverts blackish, heavily spotted and streaked with white. Tail blackish-brown, tipped rufous; central feathers wholly rufous. Upperparts sandy grey, marked with ochre-buff streaks, most noticeable on wing-coverts and scapulars, no streaks on rump and uppertail-coverts, which are greyish-rufous and finely vermiculated. Primaries and secondaries grey-brown, with secondaries broadly tipped white (forming a trailing edge). **First-year male:** As female, but spotting on breast and neck coarser, and with whitish loral area appearing as a weak supercilium. **Adult female:** Duller than male, with head pattern and breast-band more diffuse, invaded by dusky and pale spotting. **Juvenile:** Resembles small dull female. Upperparts have buffish shaft streaks (rather than sides of feathers of adult) and underparts virtually unmarked. Adulthood acquired in second winter.

GEOGRAPHICAL VARIATION Four intergrading races; variation is largely clinal, with darker populations in C Tibet, becoming paler and more sandy toward both the west and east.

T. t. tibetanus Gould, 1854 (includes *tschimenensis* of S Xinjiang) occurs in W Tibet, NW India (Ladakh, N Kashmir) north to the E Pamirs (Tajikistan and S Xinjiang); a rather pale form, strongly toned with sandy-buff.

T. t. aquilonifer R. & A. Meinertzhagen, 1926 occurs in S Tibet, Nepal, Sikkim and Bhutan; darker and greyer than nominate, with whiter ear-coverts.

T. t. henrici Oustalet, 1891 occurs in Xinjiang; darker grey than *aquilonifer*, with greyer tail.

T. t. przewalskii Bianchi, 1907 (includes *centralis* of E Qinghai) occurs in Qinghai and SW Gansu; intergrades with *henrici* in NW Sichuan. Rather pale and sandy, but less so than nominate.

MEASUREMENTS Length 50–56 cm. Female smaller. *T. t. tibetanus*. Males: wing 262–290, tarsus 62–65, weight 1500–1750. Females: wing 251–270, tarsus 62–65, weight 1170–1600.

HABITAT Resident on both high alpine pastures and rather bare or grassy mountain slopes and plateaux up to snow-line; usually well above 3500 m, chiefly 5000–6000 m but in winter sometimes as low as 2450 m. However, avoids forest edge even in the bleakest of weather conditions. Where overlaps with Himalayan Snowcock, Tibetan replaces it at higher elevations.

VOICE Very much as other snowcocks. Advertising call a far-carrying series of 4–5 prolonged, penetrating whistled notes, rather Eurasian Curlew *Numenius arquata*-like in quality. Also a chuckling *chuck-aa-chuck-aa-chuck-chuck-chee-da-da-da*. Flushed birds utter abrupt whistled calls (more subdued than those of

Himalayan Snowcock), which develop into a continuous cackling as they glide downhill.

HABITS As far as is known, social behaviour very similar to other snowcocks, particularly Altai Snowcock. Sociable unless breeding, with local populations gathering into winter coveys of up to 50. Some older references report occasionally massive congregations in autumn, prior to descending to lower elevations, some reputedly involving several thousand. Breeding pairs usually separate from winter gatherings by April. Males call from a prominent outcrop on fine mornings, but are generally silent during wet weather. When suspicious of danger, runs quickly uphill toward rocky outcrop or ridge, ready to take flight if necessary. Feeds on berries, seeds, shoots, roots and small insects.

BREEDING Probably monogamous. Nest a depression sparsely-lined with grass and dead leaves often concealed by a boulder or low shrub. Clutch 4–7; eggs pale clay to reddish-buff, sparsely spotted reddish-brown (often quite heavily marked at smaller end). Laid late May. No information on incubation period or chick care.

DISTRIBUTION Tibetan massif of W China: across most of Tibet (Xizang), extreme S Xinjiang (north to the Kunlun and Astin Tagh ranges), east through Qinghai to S Gansu (the Nan Shan and Min Shan) and adjacent NW Sichuan (Tebbuland). In the south, it reaches SE Tibet and extreme N Assam (Mishmi and Abor Hills), west across the high Himalayas of N Bhutan, Sikkim and N Nepal, to the E Pamirs in Ladakh and N Kashmir, just entering adjacent extreme E Tajikistan.

STATUS Wide range suggests a population of several hundred thousand birds, but no estimates are available. Certainly relatively common at high elevations in Nepal and is presumed to be so over most of range. No specific threats known. Surprisingly little studied compared to other snowcock.

REFERENCES Ali (1962), Ali & Ripley (1970), Baker (1930), Dement'ev & Gladkov (1967).

---

8   ALTAI SNOWCOCK
Tetraogallus altaicus (Gebler, 1836)   Plate 3

The most northerly distributed of the snowcocks, forming a species-pair with the other white-bellied species, Tibetan Snowcock.

IDENTIFICATION Mountains of northern C Asia, centred on the Mongolian Altai, where it is the only snowcock. In extreme E Kazakhstan the northernmost Himalayan Snowcocks are narrowly separated from the westernmost Altai Snowcocks by the Zaysan depression. The two are easily separated by Altai's whitish (not dark grey) flanks that contrast with an extensive blackish area forward of the white undertail-coverts. In flight Altai has white chiefly on the primaries, with only a narrow band on the bases of the secondaries (the secondaries are more extensively white in Himalayan). Altai and Tibetan are separated by the Takla Makan and Gobi

deserts, but the two could be easily distinguished because Altai lacks Tibetan's black flank stripes and, in flight, by Tibetan's lack of white on the primaries, having obvious white only on the trailing edge of the secondaries (white chiefly on primaries in Altai).

DESCRIPTION Bill brownish-horn, darker and browner on upper mandible. Nostril cap and bare skin around eye yellowish-orange. Irides brown. Legs fleshy or orange-red. Sexes generally similar, individual variation complicating subtle differences. Male has short spur, absent in all but oldest females. **Adult (both sexes):** Crown, sides and rear of neck, breast and mantle buffy-grey, faintly freckled with paler buff. Ear-coverts paler. Short supercilium and throat centre whitish, the latter slightly highlighted by a weakly

10   SAND PARTRIDGE
Ammoperdix heyi (Temminck, 1825)

Plate 1

Alternative name: Desert Partridge.

Southern replacement of the See-see, inhabiting desert hills in the Near East, Egypt and Arabia.

IDENTIFICATION Small sandy partridge of Near East and Egypt. Range overlaps with three *Alectoris* partridges, but not with similar See-see (although in Syria, See-see has been recorded from the north and Sand in the south). Males are pinkish-sandy partridges with prominent undulating flank stripes and greyer head, the latter with a striking white patch behind eye; slightly plumper than See-see, without black forehead and with purer yellow (less greenish-yellow) legs. Female probably inseparable from female See-see in field except by range. Birds in Basalt Desert of NE Jordan (and perhaps S Syria) have very dark 'face and cheeks' (I. Andrews pers. comm.).

DESCRIPTION *A. h. heyi*. Bill orange (male) or dull yellowish (female), rather short. Irides reddish-brown or pale brown. Legs yellow, both sexes unspurred. Sexes differ. **Adult male:** Head, neck and entire body and wings pinkish sandy-buff, washed bluish-rose (especially in fresh plumage), paler on vent. Head darker bluish with white patch behind eye on upper ear-coverts and smaller white spot on lores; forehead narrowly whitish; pale rufous chin. Tail rufous. Flank feathers boldly patterned rufous and white, with fine black 'highlights' forming long undulating stripes. **Adult female:** Very plain, lacking bold head and flank pattern of male. Sandy-buff overall, with indistinct grey vermiculations and speckling; indistinct pink barring (rather than white mottling) on rear neck is most reliable plumage difference from female See-see. **Juvenile:** Resembles female, apparently without male plumage features (compare summary of juvenile See-see).

GEOGRAPHICAL VARIATION Chiefly in colour saturation and presence of white on lores and forehead of males. Four races recognised, all of which intergrade with adjacent taxa.

  A. h. heyi (Temminck, 1825) occurs in Jordan, Israel, Sinai (Egypt) and N and C Saudi Arabia; described above.
  A. h. intermedia Hartert, 1917 occurs in W Saudi Arabia, Yemen and Oman; markedly darker, reddish-brown, less sandy, than nominate.
  A. h. nicolli Hartert, 1919 occurs in NE Egypt; lacks white on forehead and lores, much paler than *intermedia*.
  A. h. cholmleyi Ogilvie-Grant, 1897 occurs in SE Egypt and NE Sudan. Lacks white forehead and loral spot like *nicolli*, but much darker overall.

MEASUREMENTS Length 24 cm. Male slightly larger. *A. h. heyi*. Males: wing 126–135 (mean 131), tarsus 32–36 (mean 34). Females: wing 125–132 (mean 128), tarsus 31–33 (mean 32). Weight (both sexes) c.180–200.

HABITAT Rocky and stony hillsides and wadi bottoms in sparsely-vegetated or barren desert hills and canyons. Usually near small or seasonal water source, and often at oases or in wadis with scattered large *Acacia* trees. Avoids active cultivation and plains. Generally below 1000 m but reaches 2000 m in Arabia.

VOICE Advertising call a rising, yelping *kew-kew-kew* or *watcha-watcha-watcha*. Typical call a far-carrying repeated loud, fluty *quip* or *qu-ip*. Also an explosive *wuit-wuit-wuit* when flushed or alarmed.

HABITS Usually encountered in coveys of up to ten in wadis and barren stony hillsides, running rapidly away at sight of intruder, with head held high and body low. When approached, initially crouches then runs rather than flying, the covey scattering in various directions. When flushed, rises suddenly with an audible whirr of wings, flies rapidly downhill or flutters up steep initial slope, then disappears over ridge. Several coveys may assemble to drink, totalling up to 70 individuals, usually in mornings. In Israel location of water important, and leaves areas when water source dries up; however, in most arid parts of Arabia appears to survive for years in very barren regions far from water. Coveys break up into pairs in late winter, but pairs continue to congregate at communal drinking and feeding spots. In spring and summer, family parties with chicks or large young often gather to form quite large flocks, which break up into family parties again later in the year. Feeds primarily on plant material, seeds, corms, bulbs and shoots, but insects form an important part of diet of chicks. Roosts in heat of the day in shade of canyons, rock crevices, under bushes or around abandoned buildings.

BREEDING Apparently monogamous. Minimum distance between nests in Israel c.70 m, rarely only 30 m. Nest a sparsely-lined scrape in shade of rock or bush, sometimes in a hollow crevice at foot of cliff. Clutch 6–14 (chiefly 8–12); nests occasionally containing 18–24 eggs result from two females laying in same scrape; eggs unmarked pale creamy-buff. Incubation, by female only, occupies 21–24 days. After hatching, male helps tend brood. Breeds February–August (Israel), with eggs March–April (Israel, Jordan). Considered occasionally double-brooded in Israel, in seasons following heavy winter rains.

DISTRIBUTION Near East and Egypt. Resident from S Syria (few records), south through Jordan and E Israel, montane W and S Arabia, including Yemen and Oman, and patchily across C Saudi Arabia to UAE. Widespread in S Sinai and Egypt east of the Nile south to NE Sudan. Its reputed occurrence in Eritrea is unproven. A record from Bahrain is thought to relate to an escapee. Vagrant to Lebanon (one record).

STATUS Locally common over most of range, but widely hunted. Protected in Israel, where population estimated at 'a few thousand pairs' in the 1980s. In Egypt, appears to be increasing in Sinai, but rather thinly distributed elsewhere. Locally numerous in Arabia, especially in Oman.

REFERENCES Cramp & Simmons (1980), Shirihai (1996).

Genus *ALECTORIS*: rock partridges

Medium-sized gamebirds of the S and C Palearctic that inhabit open country, including mountains. The genus is characterised by red bills and legs, and striking facial and flank patterns contrasting with the otherwise virtually unmarked body plumage. The sexes are similar but males are larger and possess a short tarsal spur (absent in females). Six of the seven species form a superspecies group, whereas Arabian Partridge differs significantly in overall size and shape, particularly its longer tail.

11   ARABIAN PARTRIDGE
Alectoris melanocephala (Rüppell, 1835)   Plate 5

Alternative names: Arabian Red-legged Partridge, Arabian Chukar.

The most widespread of the *Alectoris* partridges in Arabia, this striking bird is both larger and longer-tailed than the others, and is the only member of the genus to have either a grey tail or a black crown.

IDENTIFICATION Escarpments of W and S Arabia. A large grey partridge with a striking pure white supercilium, face and throat (may appear white-headed at a distance), highlighted by a black central crown and collar. Very distinctive within its range, which overlaps in W Arabia with the smaller, black-throated, Philby's (Chukar nearby in N Saudi Arabia and Musandam, Oman). If flushed, looks larger and greyer than Philby's (or Chukar), with a longer, fuller grey (not rufous) tail. Indeed, within its open habitat, distant individuals may appear remarkably large and long-tailed, recalling rarer (in Arabia) Helmeted Guineafowl *Numida meleagris*.

DESCRIPTION Bill bright red, bare skin around eye and legs rose-red. Irides chestnut-brown. Sexes generally similar, male has one blunt spur, absent in females. Tail relatively long. **Adult (both sexes):** Forehead, crown and upper nape black, broad white supercilium, widest above and in front of eye. Thin black line from base of bill through eye, joining extensively blackish rear ear-coverts, which continue down neck-sides to form black bib. Throat and cheeks pure white, the rather long feathers creating white streaks within black ear-coverts and bib. Flanks boldly barred black and white, each feather grey with a white subterminal band, bordered each side by a narrower black bar. Rest of plumage grey, with pinkish-brown overtones, greyest on rump, mantle and breast. Tail pinkish-grey, becoming dark grey over distal portion. Primaries grey with straw-buff outer webs. **Juvenile:** Poorly documented; overall dull grey-brown, lacking facial pattern or flank bars, ginger-rufous on crown and some vermiculations and fine pale spotting on neck, breast and mantle; bill (and perhaps legs) blackish.

GEOGRAPHICAL VARIATION Monotypic. *A. m. quichardi*, described from the Hadramaut (S Yemen), is usually not considered worthy of recognition.

MEASUREMENTS Length 39 cm. Female smaller. Males: wing 177–210, tail 146–149, weight c.724. Females: wing 166–181, tail 140, weight c.522.

HABITAT Generally prefers lower and more vegetated areas than Philby's, favouring western and southern rainshadow of the Tihamah escarpment. Montane slopes, steep-sided wadis, rocky hillsides and both sandy and stony plains with scattered bushes or trees, including cultivated terraced hillsides and relict montane juniper forest. More varied in both altitude and habitats than Philby's, occurring from 100 m (on coast) to at least 2800 m.

VOICE Call starts as a few evenly spaced notes, gradually increasing in tempo and volume, *cuck, cuck, cuck, owk-owk-owk* or *crowk, crowk, crowk*. Also gives a softer, repeated *cook, cook, cookcookcookcook* to retain contact when foraging or if covey scattered by predator. When flushed gives a *kerkow-kerkow-kerkow* in alarm. Various other soft conversational clucks of less significance. Calls are generally louder and deeper pitched than other members of the genus.

HABITS Generally in pairs or coveys of up to 15 feeding among boulders or bushy cover, rarely venturing completely into the open. Loosely scattered coveys forage uphill, picking grass seeds from both the ground and growing stems, and leaves from bushes. Observed to clamber 1 m from the ground, into a rose bush to feed on hips, and to feed at grain-threshing areas near habitation. Gait slow while feeding but when suspicious of danger walks quickly uphill toward rocky outcrop or ridge, ready to fly if necessary. Most active in early morning and evening, when it walks to drink at local water source.

BREEDING Virtually unstudied. Presumably monogamous. Nest a depression scratched in shade of bush. Eggs white, with very prominent pores. Clutch 5–8, but nests containing at least 11 have been reported. Lays March–May with pair formation in February–March. Former tiny population in Eritrea is reputed to have nested in July–August. Incubation period 25 days (in incubators).

DISTRIBUTION W and S Arabia, from Jeddah, in the Hejaz of Saudi Arabia, south to western highland Yemen, extending east through the coastal hills of S Yemen into montane Dhofar in W Oman. An apparently isolated population exists in Jabal Akhdar in E Oman. Recently reported from near Madinah in N Hejaz (Saudi Arabia), which is a considerable range extension. Formerly reported from the Aseb region of coastal Eritrea, but this population's origins are suspect.

STATUS Not uncommon in much of its range, but distribution rather fragmented, perhaps through extensive hunting, although habitat degradation is currently the greatest threat. Extinct in its very restricted African range (in coastal Eritrea), where unreported since 1890, but this tenuous population perhaps originated from captives.

REFERENCES Castell *et al.* (2001), Gallagher & Woodcock (1980), Jennings (1995), Martins & Kirwan (1996), Meinertzhagen (1954), Porter *et al.* (1996), Rands & Rands (1987).

12 BARBARY PARTRIDGE
Alectoris barbara (Bonnaterre, 1792)

Plate 5

The N African representative of the complex; long isolated from the others, it has developed a unique facial pattern.

IDENTIFICATION The only *Alectoris* partridge in N Africa, with outlying populations on Canary Is, Gibraltar and Sardinia. Barbary lacks a bold black border to the whitish throat, obvious in most others of the genus, but shares the bold flank barring and rusty tail. The grey face and throat and rich chestnut neck patch contrast strongly with the broad pale supercilium and dark chestnut crown (latter cinnamon in reddish race *barbata*). Only similar species in range is very localised Moroccan race of Double-spurred Francolin, but latter possesses indistinct longitudinal flank striping (not vertical bars), streaked (not plain) upperparts and tail uniform with upperparts (not rufous).

DESCRIPTION *A. b. barbara*. Bill bright red, bare skin around eye and legs rose-red. Irides chestnut-brown. Sexes largely similar, male has one blunt spur, absent in females. **Adult (both sexes):** Central forehead, crown and nape dark chestnut, becoming almost blackish on crown-sides. Chin, throat, ear-coverts, lores and supercilium ash-grey, becoming paler on centre of throat. Tuft of rusty-buff feathers obscures narrow chestnut band behind eye; the latter borders rear ear-coverts to join wide neck patch. Broad rich chestnut gorget, speckled white, extends from neck-sides to narrowly join across lower throat. Underparts pinkish-buff, richest on breast and undertail-coverts. Flanks banded black, white and rufous (each feather grey with a broad white subterminal band, bordered each side by a narrower black bar and tipped rufous (black bars narrower than on Red-legged). Rest of upperparts grey, with olive-brown and cinnamon casts; scapulars edged brighter rufous. Tail rufous, with central feathers and bases slate. Primaries straw-buff on outer webs. **Juvenile:** Bill and legs yellowish; very plain overall, lacking head pattern or flank bars but becomes much as adult by autumn; similar to juvenile Red-legged but ear-coverts more rufous, has clearer supercilium and soon begins to attain traces of chestnut neck patch and flank pattern.

GEOGRAPHICAL VARIATION Four races, but variation clinal. Cyrenaican race *barbata* most strongly differentiated.

   A. b. barbara (Bonnaterre, 1792) (includes *theresae*) occurs in NE Morocco, N Algeria, Tunisia, Gibraltar and Sardinia; described above.
   A. b. koenigi (Reichenow, 1899) occurs in Canary Is and NW Morocco; head, neck, chest and upperparts darker and colder grey than nominate.
   A. b. spatzi (Reichenow, 1895) (includes *duprezi*) occurs in S and E Morocco, N Mauritania, S

Algeria, S Tunisia and NW and extreme SW Libya; paler and sandier than nominate, with paler brown crown and gorget, paler grey (almost whitish) throat and supercilium, and less boldly barred flanks; populations intergrade with nominate.
   A. b. barbata (Reichenow, 1896) occurs in NE Libya (Cyrenaica) and (formerly) adjacent NW Egypt; throat and face bluish-grey, heavily black-banded flanks (vestigial rufous tips), paler, almost cinnamon, crown and gorget; the latter with blue-grey (not white) speckles, and reddish upperparts.

MEASUREMENTS Length 34 cm. Female smaller. *A. b. barbara* given. Males: wing 162–171 (mean 166), tail 89–106 (mean 95), weight c.461. Females: wing 149–162 (mean 156), tail 75–91 (mean 84), weight c.376.

HABITAT Almost all bushy cover from sea level to 3300 m (in the High Atlas), from desert wadis and palm groves, through coastal dunes, citrus orchards, olive groves and oak woodland to almost completely denuded stony hillsides and boulder-strewn escarpments. In Morocco, highest densities occur in woodland with clearings and cultivated plots.

VOICE Similar to Chukar and Red-legged Partridge but some (i.e. advertising and alarm) calls differ. Advertising call is a drawn-out, grating *krrraiiik*, rising in tone and often monotonously repeated every 5 seconds in some respects recalling screech of Barn Owl *Tyto alba* but also likened to harsh alarm call of Curlew *Numenius arquata*). Rallying calls similar to others of genus, a repeated guttural, squawking of varying pitches and volumes: *kutchuk kutchuk* or a sharp *kakelik* followed by a slower clucked *chuk-chuk-chuk-chukor-chukor*. When flushed, utters a loud, high-pitched squealed *kree-ah* or loud *chuckachew-chew-chew*, varying in strength.

HABITS Generally in pairs or small coveys of up to ten feeding by dusty tracks or in open areas between bushes. When alarmed, flock scatters, running rapidly in various directions with erect carriage, heading for cover or nearest ridge. Flies reluctantly, but if suddenly flushed may 'explode' with whirring wingbeats, generally flying low for short distance and running off on alighting. In gliding flight wings appear to be held flatter, less bowed than most other partridges. Coveys disband at start of breeding season. Territorial male calls from prominent rock standing erect, almost on 'tiptoe' with neck and legs fully stretched, and chest and flanks puffed out to display patterning. Often aggressive to rivals. Most active early morning and evening, seeking shade in heat of day, when retires to roost among rocks or cliff ledges. Has favoured drinking spots, but can subsist with little water in very dry regions. Indeed, some populations may not drink at

184

all, surviving on moisture obtained from succulent plants (e.g. *Euphorbia* fruits). Feeds primarily on young leaves, shoots and seeds but also small insects, especially ants (latter are important in the diet of chicks). In some areas feeds on spilt grain in stubble fields.

BREEDING Monogamous. Single-brooded. Nest a shallow scrape, either unlined or with scant vegetation, in shade of a bush or boulder, or in long grass. Eggs pale yellow-buff, intensely finely speckled reddish-brown. Clutch 6–20 (chiefly 10–14). Laid January–June depending on location; in NW Morocco commences late February in lowlands but not until late April in mountains; chick reported late January in Egypt; no information from elsewhere. In some locations known not to breed in very dry seasons. Incubation presumed c.24–25 days as in other *Alectoris*.

DISTRIBUTION N Africa. Throughout most of Morocco, south to the Zemmour in N Mauritania, east across N Algeria, Tunisia and N Libya to extreme NW Egypt (no recent records). Outlying populations in Canary Is, Gibraltar and adjacent extreme S Spain, Sardinia, and isolated in the Haggar and Ajjer Mts of SE Algeria and adjacent SW Libya. Also reported from the Tibesti region of N Chad.

STATUS Locally numerous in Morocco, Algeria and Tunisia, but over much of range has declined through hunting pressure and habitat degradation. In S Algeria first reported in the Haggar in 1981, and only recorded in the Tibesti of N Chad in 1936 and 1953. Current status in Libya unknown but is perhaps extinct in Egypt (formerly occurred in Mediterranean coastal desert east to Matruh, where last reported 1964), unless it persists near Salum on the Libyan border. An estimated 600–1000 pairs occur on the Canary Is (Lanzarote, Tenerife and Gomera, where introduced onto Fuerteventura in 1913), but hunting has such a drastic affect on some islands that captive breeding and further introductions are required to 'top-up' the population. Fifty to 75 pairs occur on Gibraltar, with an estimated 50 pairs in adjacent mainland Spain. A larger population (at least 3000 pairs) inhabits Sardinia, where despite regulatory measures, excessive hunting and poaching takes a heavy toll. Other introductions (e.g. in Hawaii and Madeira) have been unsuccessful; occasional specimens taken in S Portugal and England probably result from other such attempts.

REFERENCES Alaoui (1992), Cramp & Simmons (1980), Mocci Demartis (1992), Urban *et al.* (1986).

---

13   PHILBY'S PARTRIDGE
Alectoris philbyi (Lowe, 1934)   Plate 5

Alternative name: Philby's Rock Partridge

Isolated in SW Arabia, this close relative of the Chukar shares its montane range with Arabian Partridge (albeit at different elevations). Its name honours Harry St. John Philby (an English explorer who spent many years in Arabia and crossed the Empty Quarter in 1932).

IDENTIFICATION Endemic to montane SW Arabia. The combination of black face and throat and boldly barred flanks, and its restricted distribution makes identification straightforward. Philby's overlaps only with the larger, longer-tailed and white-throated Arabian Partridge but prefers higher elevations. It is unlikely to be confused given reasonable views. Flushed individuals may be separated by tail colour (rufous as Chukar), unlike the longer, broader, grey tail of Arabian.

DESCRIPTION Bill bright red, bare skin around eye and legs rose-red. Irides chestnut-brown. Sexes similar, male has one blunt spur, absent in females. **Adult (both sexes):** Forehead (apart from narrow black 'nose' band), crown and upper nape grey, washed pale brown. Chin, throat, ear-coverts, lores and narrow band above base of bill black, bordered on lower throat by slightly deeper black 'bib'. Supercilium narrow, whitish and quite contrasting. Flanks boldly banded black, white and rufous (each feather grey with a broad white subterminal band, bordered each side by a narrower black bar and tipped rufous. Rest of plumage grey, with pinkish-brown overtones, greyest on rump and crown. Belly and undertail-coverts rusty-buff. Tail rufous. Primaries have straw-buff outer webs. **Juvenile:** Poorly documented; overall dull brownish, initially lacking blackish face

and throat but soon attaining a dusky 'shadow'; upperparts finely barred; legs pinkish-white.

GEOGRAPHICAL VARIATION Monotypic.

MEASUREMENTS Length 34 cm. Female smaller. Wing (both sexes) 156 (female)–172 (male). Tail (both sexes) 95–114. Weight c.441.

HABITAT Barren rocky slopes and mountain plateaux from 2300 m (locally down to 1400 m) to 3700 m (on Arabia's highest peak). Most abundant in lightly vegetated or (seasonally) denuded slopes of terraced cultivation. Although the two do occur in close proximity, Philby's generally prefers bleaker, more barren slopes at higher elevations than Arabian Partridge.

VOICE Similar to Chukar. A rhythmic repeated *chuk chuk-a-chuk-kar* or *chuk chuk chuk kar*. When alarmed or flushed utters an explosive *chork chork chork*, also a repeated squealing *chuk-a-chuk-a-chuk* and a babbling *chuk-a-chuk-oo*. Contact notes from young include a soft *chuk chuk-a-chuk*. Most vocal in early morning and evening.

HABITS Virtually unstudied. Generally in pairs or small coveys of up to ten feeding on barren terraced slopes.

BREEDING Virtually undocumented. Presumably monogamous. Nests under shade of bush or rock. Eggs white to pale buff spotted or blotched mauve or pale brown. Clutch 5–8 (requires confirmation). Eggs probably laid July–August in N Yemen (6–8 week-old chicks seen 11 October). Late March also reported but requires confirmation. Incubation period 25 days (in incubators).

DISTRIBUTION SW Arabia, from Jeddah, in the Hejaz of Saudi Arabia, south through montane N Yemen, reaching its southern limit around Ta'izz.

STATUS Considered reasonably numerous, although

has doubtless suffered local declines through hunting pressure and habitat degradation.

REFERENCES Castell *et al.* (2001), Hollom *et al.* (1988), Jennings (1995), Martins & Kirwan (1996), Meinertzhagen (1954), Rands (1987).

---

14   CHUKAR
Alectoris chukar (Gray, 1830)   Plate 4

Alternative names: Chukor, Chukar Partridge, Rock Partridge (sic).

The most widespread *Alectoris*, its range extends from the Balkans, across Asia, to E China. Formerly considered a single species with Przevalski's and Rock Partridges within *A. graeca*.

IDENTIFICATION The black gorget encircling the creamy-white chin and throat, banded flanks, and red bill and legs are typical of the genus, of which Chukar is the principal Asian representative. Over much of its wide range there are few identification pitfalls, although in C China (Gansu and Qinghai) it is replaced by the similar Przevalski's Partridge, which has a rusty surround to the narrower black gorget. Przevalski's also has closer and more numerous flank bars, and black lores (features shared by Rock Partridge). In S Bulgaria and NE Greece, Chukar meets its very similar European counterpart, Rock Partridge. Although some hybridisation occurs, Rock tends to replace Chukar at higher elevations. Here, in the Balkans, colour differences between the two are most pronounced, with Rock Partridge being much purer grey above while Chukar has much browner upperparts. These colour tones are not consistent elsewhere. At very close range subtle differences in facial pattern may be visible: Rock has black lores and band from forehead to eye, the black extending narrowly around bill base to gape; Chukar merely has black to forehead with white lores leaving small isolated black spot at gape; behind eye a patch of rufous feathering almost completely interrupts black facial band in Chukar, but this band is scarcely broken in Rock; black gorget forms V on lower throat in Chukar; and lower throat border more rounded in Rock and throat whiter, washed creamy-buff in Chukar (although whiter in some Asian populations). Chukar has fewer flank bars, which are more spaced than in Rock, the rear bars often appearing 'broken'. Voice is also a useful aid; see Rock and Przevalski's Partridges for discussion. Another obstacle to identification is that in many parts of Europe, including Britain, large numbers of hybrid Rock × Red-legged Partridge and Chukar × Red-legged Partridge hybrids have been released for hunting purposes (see Red-legged for discussion).

DESCRIPTION *A. c. kleini*. Bill bright red, bare skin around eye and legs rose-red. Irides chestnut-brown. Sexes similar, male has one blunt spur, absent in female. **Adult (both sexes):** Crown, nape and mantle vinous-brown, becoming blue-grey on neck-sides and breast. Indistinct narrow whitish supercilium. Narrow band on forehead back to eye, widening as a conspicuous black band behind eye, running down neck-sides to

join as a V-shaped collar on chest. Chin, lores, throat and upper chest creamy-white, becoming buff on upper chest where it diffuses slightly into black V. Tiny black spot on upper chin and, more obviously, at gape. Tuft of rusty feathers on upper ear-coverts interrupts black collar line behind eye. Scapulars vinous-brown, with grey centres; wings vinous-brown, darker brown on primaries, which have straw-buff outer webs. Rump and central tail feathers olive-grey. Outertail feathers rufous. Belly warm yellowish-buff, becoming cinnamon-buff on undertail-coverts. Flanks banded black, creamy-buff and rufous (each feather grey at base with a broad creamy-buff subterminal band, bordered each side by a narrower black bar and tipped chestnut). **Juvenile:** Bill and legs pale reddish or brownish-orange; very plain overall, with tiny pale spots on upperparts feather tips and weak bars on underparts. Soon attains traces of black collar and flank pattern and becomes much as adult when c.4 months old; retains two old, abraded outermost primaries for a further year.

GEOGRAPHICAL VARIATION Complex, with marked clinal variation and intergradation. Populations in more humid regions are usually buffier below and more vinous-brown above than paler and greyer birds of more arid habitats. A systematic review is long overdue and would probably invalidate some of the forms listed below (e.g. *koroviakovi*, *shestoperovi*, *subpallida* and *falki*). Plumages of paler and greyer populations are much more subject to bleaching than those of darker and browner populations.

A. c. kleini Hartert, 1925 (includes *caucasica* and *daghestanica*) occurs in SE Bulgaria, NE Greece, N Aegean Is, N Turkey and the Caucasus; described above. Caucasian populations (*caucasica* and *daghestanica*) average a little paler.

A. c. cypriotes Hartert, 1917 (includes *scotti*) occurs in S Turkey, Cyprus and S Aegean Is (e.g. Crete, Rhodes); paler than *kleini*, with crown and upperparts blue-grey, washed buff, rump ashy-grey, belly paler buff. Those in Crete and other S Aegean Is (*scotti*) are smaller and darker.

A. c. sinaica (Bonaparte, 1858) occurs in Syria, Israel, Sinai, Jordan and NW Saudi Arabia; rather larger, especially bill. Very pale grey crown and upperparts, latter washed sandy-buff, bleaching strongly with wear.

A. c. kurdestanica Meinertzhagen, 1923 (includes *armenica*) occurs in E Turkey, Transcaucasia, N Iraq and N and W Iran (including the Elburz); pale with upperparts more vinous-brown than the last and chest purer blue-grey.

A. c. werae (Zarudny & Loudon, 1904) (includes

farsiana) occurs in E Iraq and SW Iran; rather large, like *sinaica*, but crown and upperparts pure pale grey, washed sandy-grey on mantle.

A. c. koroviakovi (Zarudny, 1914) (includes *kirthari*) occurs in E Iran, W and S Afghanistan and W Pakistan; darker and browner than *werae*, more like *kleini* but duller and more olive-grey (less ashy) on rump.

A. c. shestoperovi Sushkin, 1927 (includes *laptevi* and *dementievi*) occurs in Turkmenistan and S Kazakhstan; similar to last, but paler above.

A. c. subpallida (Zarudny, 1914) occurs in Uzbekistan, SE Kazakhstan and SW Tajikistan; slightly paler, more brownish and rufous (less vinaceous) above than *koroviakovi*.

A. c. falki Hartert, 1917 occurs in N Afghanistan, S Uzbekistan, SE Kazakhstan and extreme W China; slightly duller but similar in colour to *koroviakovi* and notably larger (mean male wing 167, 162 in *koroviakovi*).

A. c. dzungarica Sushkin, 1927 (includes *obscurata*) occurs in the Altai Mts of Russia, W Mongolia, NE Kazakhstan and extreme W China; darker and more vinaceous brown on upperparts than *falki*.

A. c. pallescens (Hume, 1873) occurs in NE Afghanistan east through the Karakorums of Pakistan to Ladakh; similar to *werae* in coloration but less greyish above, more tinged with cinnamon.

A. c. pallida (Hume, 1873) (includes *humei*) occurs in W and S Xinjiang Zizhiu; paler and more yellowish-sandy above than *pallescens*, with less greyish, more olivaceous, rump and narrower black flank bars.

A. c. fallax Sushkin, 1927 occurs on the southern slopes of the Tien Shan in Xinjiang Zizhiu; darker than either *pallescens* or *pallida*, but paler than *falki*. More vinaceous on head and nape than *falki*, with greyer rump.

A. c. chukar (Gray, 1830) occurs in E Afghanistan, through Kashmir to W Nepal; the darkest and brownest race.

A. c. pubescens (Swinhoe, 1871) occurs in C and N China; similar to nominate but a little paler (bleaches even paler when worn), with rump and uppertail-coverts tinged olive-grey (rather than brownish-grey).

A. c. potanini Sushkin, 1927 occurs in Mongolia and China, in N Gansu and Nei Mongol Zizhiqu; greyer above than *pubescens*; similar to *falki* but crown more vinaceous and nape browner.

MEASUREMENTS Length 33–36 cm. Female smaller than male. *A. c. kleini*. Males: wing 162–172 (mean 168), tail 76–87 (mean 82), weight 504–595 (mean 536). Females: wing 148–160 (mean 154), tail 74–86 (mean 80), weight 462–545 (mean 501).

HABITAT Favours semi-arid hills and mountain slopes, with sparse grassy cover and scattered bushes. Over extensive range inhabits varied biotopes, from desert plains and sand dunes to scrubby and terraced cultivation, forest clearings, alpine meadows and mountain crags. Reaches 4000 m in W Himalayas (Karakorums and Pamirs) but in many parts of its range it occurs to sea level. Populations inhabiting mountains move to lower elevations in winter to avoid snow cover.

VOICE Similar to Red-legged Partridge. Advertising call a raucous *chuk chuk chuk chuk...chuckARR...chuckARR* with variations. Rallying call similar (as with other *Alectoris*) recalling a clucking chicken, a repeated *chuck... chuck...chuck...chuck* or softer, faster rhythmic *chak chak chak chak chak*. When flushed often utters a repeated *wittoo-wittoo-wittoo*. Various other, short harsh or squealing calls may also be given. Most vocal in morning, particularly when gathering to commence feeding at daybreak.

HABITS Forages in small coveys of 6–10 for much of the year, but post-breeding gatherings of 50–70 or more (chiefly young) form in areas where numerous. During cold winters coveys descend to foothills, valleys and plains and may form large groups; such assemblages have reached 150 in New Zealand (where introduced), 900 in Israel (over 6 km²), 500 in Turkmenistan and 'thousands' by the Vargod River in Tajikistan in adverse weather conditions. Most coveys disband at start of breeding season, although young non-breeders remain in flocks throughout. Diet very similar to Red-legged Partridge, consisting principally of grass seeds and leaves of small plants, plus a proportion of small invertebrates, especially ants and beetles (insects being especially important to the young). In winter scratches and digs for plant bulbs and tubers, e.g. tulips, garlic and berries. Most populations occur near a reliable water source, which is visited early morning after feeding. When alarmed, runs rapidly, wherever possible heading uphill with erect carriage, quickly disappearing over nearest ridge. Loath to fly, but if suddenly flushed 'explodes' with whirr of fast wingbeats, generally flying low downhill following contours of hillside, running off on alighting. Territorial male calls from prominent rock standing erect with the neck upstretched and the chest and flanks puffed out to display patterning. Males generally aggressive to rivals. Indeed, in Afghanistan and Pakistan the practice of trapping them for 'cock-fighting' matches is widespread. Most active dawn to mid-morning and late afternoon to evening, seeking shade in heat of day, when retires to roost among rocks or cliff ledges, or beneath vegetation, often near water.

BREEDING Monogamous; possibly sometimes bigamous. Chiefly single-brooded, but second broods occasionally proven (commenced when first brood seven days old). Nest a shallow scrape lined with scant vegetation, under the shade of a bush or boulder, or in rock crevice. Eggs pale yellow-buff, variably speckled reddish-brown. Clutch 6–24 (chiefly 10–15). Lays late March–June over wide native range, but even as late as August in Israel and Caucasus (replacement broods) and, in Israel, as early as late February, chiefly mid-April to late May in Caucasus and Turkmenistan, May–June in Mongolia, Afghanistan and Kashmir and, in the Southern Hemisphere, chiefly October–November in New Zealand. Incubation 22–25 days, primarily by female but male also incubates occasionally. Chicks tended largely by female, although male may often act as guardian of the covey for at least the first week. At two weeks coveys usually merge to form 'nurseries' tended by 1–2 females. Young become full-sized at c.50 days.

DISTRIBUTION SE Europe, through Asia Minor and C Asia east to the Yellow Sea in E China. A primarily

Asiatic species, it reaches its western extremity in SE Bulgaria (extreme E Stara Planina (Balkan), eastern Rhodope and the Sakar Planina (Brannitza) ranges—chiefly south of the Maritza valley), NE Greece (east of Komotini), European Turkey (Koru and Tekir ranges) and the Aegean Is (including Rhodes and Crete). Range includes Cyprus and extends east across Asiatic Turkey, south through Syria, Lebanon, W Jordan, Palestine and Israel to N Saudi Arabia and Sinai (Egypt). From E Turkey it occurs throughout the Caucasus (including Armenia, Georgia and Azerbaijan) and the Crimea (where introduced). In Iraq it is confined to the foothills of the Zagros Mts in the northeast (but could occur in the extreme west). Widespread in Iran, being absent only from the southern and central deserts and the lush Caspian lowlands. An isolated population exists on the south side of the Strait of Hormuz, in Musandam (Oman), which may have been long introduced. Several other introductions have permitted small numbers to become locally established in coastal UAE, on Bahrain and in Qatar. From Kopet Dagh in NE Iran, it is widespread in C and N Afghanistan and Turkmenistan (north to the Mangyshlak Peninsula in SW Kazakhstan), northeast through S Uzbekistan, Tajikistan, and Kyrgyzstan, to the foothills of the Tien Shan in E Kazakhstan, north to the W Russian Altai (Tuva) and W and S Mongolia (east to the Gobian Altai and north to the Khangai Mts). It is widespread over N China, from N and W Xizang (Tibet) and Xinjiang through SE Gansu, Ningxia, Shaanxi, Shanxi, S Inner Mongolia (Nei Mongol Zizhiqu) and Hebei to S Liaoning and N Shandong. It is largely absent from the Tibetan massif but other populations extend from Afghanistan south into W Pakistan, and east across N Pakistan, through Kashmir, Ladakh and the Indian Himalayas to C Nepal. Long popular as a sporting bird it has been widely introduced, but most attempts have failed (e.g. W Europe, Mexico, Australia) with notable exceptions in W USA (where widespread), Canada (common in British Columbia), Hawaii (all main islands), New Zealand (marginally established at 1–2 sites on North I., quite common on parts of South I.) and on Robben I., South Africa.

STATUS Despite its massive range (one of the most widespread of all partridges), the species appears distinctly uncommon throughout most of it. This is doubtless due to human persecution, as in less accessible montane regions it remains relatively numerous. Persecution clearly determines abundance; it is relatively common in Israel (where well protected), but it has become scarce or very local in adjacent Jordan, Lebanon and Syria. The few population estimates that have been made include, at least 100,000 in Azerbaijan in 1993 (a decrease from 800,000 in 1955), 50,000–200,000 pairs in Turkey, 1000–5000 pairs in Greece, 1000–10,000 pairs in Bulgaria and 100,000–200,000 pairs in Cyprus. Numbers are subject to considerable annual fluctuations, with population crashes evident after prolonged severe winter weather. Habitat degradation, associated with agricultural intensification and a decline in stock grazing on high montane pastures, has been cited as an important factor in areas where known to have declined. The introduced N American population is huge, in 1973 an estimated 500,000 were hunted annually. In contrast the South African population (confined to Robben I.) barely sustains itself without further introductions (there were c.300 in 1983).

REFERENCES Cramp & Simmons (1980), Dement'ev & Gladkov (1967), Dolgushin *et al.* (1962), Johnsgard (1988), Marchant & Higgins (1993), Shirihai (1996), Siegfried (1971), Stokes (1961), Vaurie (1965), Watson (1962a, 1962b).

15   ROCK PARTRIDGE
Alectoris graeca (Meisner, 1804)   Plate 4

Endemic to montane S Europe. It shares a surprising number of plumage features with Przevalski's Partridge of C China.

IDENTIFICATION European counterpart of Chukar, which it marginally meets in SE Bulgaria and NE Greece. Apart from range, the two are most easily separated vocally (see Voice) as plumage differences are small and difficult to interpret under normal field conditions. In SE Europe (where their ranges come close or even overlap), Chukar has a broader whitish but diffuse supercilium, and is browner above and on upper breast than Rock, which is purer grey and has a neat narrow pale line bordering the black facial band. These characters do not generally apply to other races of either species. Other differences are subtler and require careful interpretation. At very close range, facial patterns differ: Rock has the lores and band from forehead to eye black, the black turning down before eye to extend narrowly around bill base to gape (Chukar has the black band turn up onto forehead in front of eye, leaving the lores white apart from an isolated black spot at the gape). The black collar of Rock is neater, cleaner (with only a few greyish feathers hardly breaking into the band behind eye) and becomes U-shaped on the chest (whereas in Chukar a patch of rufous feathering almost completely interrupts the black band behind eye and the gorget forms a V on the chest). The throat is whiter in Rock (creamy-buff in Chukar, although whiter in some Asian populations) and Chukar has a diffuse inner edge to black on lower throat within the V (cleaner in U of Rock). Rock has a block of close, neat flank bars that are equally dark and pale (Chukar has fewer flank bars, which are wider spaced than in Rock, the rear bars seemingly broken). Range also marginally overlaps with Red-legged Partridge as well as with Chukar, and occasional hybrids occur with both. Indeed, the Sicilian race *whitakeri* approaches Chukar in some respects, perhaps suggesting that Sicilian Rocks may have hybridised with Chukar in the distant past (perhaps from long-forgotten Chukar introductions). See also Red-legged Partridge for comment on hybrids and Przevalski's Partridge for comment on plumage similarity.

DESCRIPTION *A. g. graeca*. Bill bright red, bare skin around eye and legs rose-red. Irides chestnut-brown.

Sexes generally similar, male has one blunt spur, absent in female. **Adult (both sexes):** Crown, nape, back and scapulars grey, only slightly washed olive-brown; mantle and chest dark vinous (greyer in worn plumage). Indistinct narrow whitish supercilium. Narrow band on forehead connects with black lores and extends through eye, constricting slightly on upper ear-coverts through intrusion of some grey feathering, but soon widens on neck-sides and joins as a U-shaped collar on chest. Chin, throat and upper chest white, or white with weak grey wash. Wings grey, with slight olive-brown wash when fresh, darker brown on primaries, which have straw-buff outer webs. Rump grey. Tail rufous. Belly warm cinnamon-yellow becoming paler cinnamon on undertail-coverts. Flanks banded black, creamy-buff and, very narrowly, chestnut (each feather grey at base with broad creamy band bordered fore, and less obviously aft, by a black bar and narrowly tipped chestnut). **Juvenile:** Bill and legs pale reddish; overall very plain, much as juvenile Chukar but differs slightly in having whiter throat and darker brown (rather than rufous) ear-coverts. Soon attains traces of black collar and flank pattern, and becomes much as adult when c.4 months of age; retains two old, abraded outermost primaries for a further year.

GEOGRAPHICAL VARIATION Despite similarity to Chukar, with which it was formerly considered conspecific, in the overlap zone in the Balkans the two species differ in basic upperparts colour tones (purer grey in *A. g. graeca*, browner in *A. chukar kleini*). There is a narrow (5–10 km) band of hybridisation in NE Greece, extending 80 km into Bulgaria, but the two largely behave as species, differing vocally as well as in habitat preference. In SE France there is a population of natural hybrids with Red-legged Partridge. Three races are included within *A. graeca*, two of which intergrade in SE Europe.

A. g. saxatilis (Bechstein, 1805) occurs in the Alps, Italy and former Yugoslavia, intergrading with the nominate in W Bulgaria and Macedonia; similar to nominate but crown, back and rump washed olive-brown, less pure grey, chest pinker and less dark vinous. However, intensity of colour tones varies with wear and bleaching (Vaurie 1959, restricted *saxatilis* to the Alps and included other Italian and Yugoslavian populations within the nominate).

A. g. graeca (Meisner, 1804) occurs in Greece, the Ionian Is, S Bulgaria and perhaps Albania; described above.

A. g. whitakeri Schiebel, 1934 occurs in Sicily; upperparts uniform dark grey-brown, central tail feathers mottled dusky, apex of collar narrow, almost broken, less boldly U-shaped than in other forms (thus approaching Chukar in some respects).

MEASUREMENTS: Length 32–35 cm. Female smaller. *A. g. saxatilis.* Males: wing 167–174 (mean 171), tail 82–95 (mean 89), weight 650–850. Females: wing 157–167 (mean 162), tail 76–90 (mean 81), weight 500–720.

HABITAT Rocky and grassy hillsides and mountains, preferring the dry subalpine zone between the tree-line and snow-line. Steep sunny south-facing slopes, including boulder scree, with scattered bushes and stunted trees are especially favoured. Ascends to higher ground post-breeding, but may be forced to lower elevations, including the environs of human settlements, by heavy snow as winter progresses. In Sicily and parts of SE Europe locally occurs to sea level.

VOICE Advertising and rally calls have individual notes more clipped, and far less guttural than either Red-legged Partridge or Chukar, most dominant phrase is a rapidly repeated 3–4-syllable grating *chi-TiTiTi-CHIK*, squeakier, higher pitched and quicker than calls of sibling species. A number of other harsh or squealing calls (18 have been distinguished), several of which are shared with other *Alectoris*. When flushed utters a distinctive shrill whistled *peeyou* followed by a more Chukar-like repeated *wittoo-wittoo-wittoo*. Most vocal in morning, particularly when gathering to commence feeding at daybreak.

HABITS Similar to Chukar and Red-legged Partridge. Pairing begins in February as coveys disband, but unpaired birds form small sexually- and age-segregated flocks for most of the year, that rarely exceed 15 individuals. Formerly (when more numerous), post-breeding gatherings of 50–100 occasionally reported during very severe winter weather. In cold winters coveys descend to valleys and will forage around farmsteads and other habitation. Diet consists principally of seeds and leaves of mountain plants, showing far less dependence on arable weeds than Red-legged Partridge (except, perhaps, in winter); a high proportion of small invertebrates are taken in the breeding season, especially grasshoppers and beetles (insects being important to the young). Territorial male calls from prominent rock standing erect with upstretched neck, and chest and flanks puffed out to display patterning. Most active dawn to mid-morning and late afternoon to evening, when retires to roost site on ground, or more rarely in low trees, often near water.

BREEDING Principally monogamous, with some at least forming long-term pair bonds; occasionally bigamous. Chiefly single-brooded, but infrequent second broods commenced a few days after the first and may be incubated by the male. Nest a shallow scrape lined with scant vegetation by female, in shelter of vegetation or boulder. Eggs creamy-yellow to pale yellow-buff, variably speckled reddish-brown. Clutch 6–21 (chiefly 8–14). Lays mid-May to June in Alps, late April–June further south (Greece). Incubation 24–26 days, primarily by female but male may also incubate if a second clutch is initiated. Chicks tended by both sexes, although male's role is more as a guard rather than a direct helper. Young adult-sized at 50–60 days.

DISTRIBUTION The Alps, Italy and SE Europe. From SE France, through Swiss Alps to Bavarian Alps of S Germany, W Austria (chiefly W Carinthia) and N Italy. Also the Apennines of C and S Italy, and Sicily. From Slovenia, south through Croatia, Bosnia, Yugoslavia (Serbia), Albania, Macedonia and Greece (including the Ionian Is) east to extreme SW Romania and SW and C Bulgaria. Probably widely released around world, but much confusion with Chukar. Failed introduction to Hawaii attempted in 1959. It has recently been released in small numbers in Lebanon where competition with Chukar is inevitable should it become established. Reputed occurrence in Turkey is erroneous and also based on confusion with Chukar.

189

STATUS Local resident, quite numerous in some areas but over most of range has declined by as much as 80% since 1970. Survives most readily in rather inaccessible habitats; hunting pressures and the increasing development and spread into formerly more remote regions of both winter and summer tourism have had an adverse effect in other areas. Populations fluctuate markedly, suffering high mortality rates during wet summers (poor breeding success) and starvation during heavy snowfalls in late winter. An overall decrease in traditional farming methods in montane regions has probably aggravated winter survival rates. The overall total population was estimated at 34,000–64,000 pairs in 1994, with 10,000–20,000 in Italy, 10,000–15,000 in Croatia, 2000–3000 in France, 3000 in Switzerland and 2000–5000 in Greece.

REFERENCES Bernard-Laurent (1984), Bocca (1990), Botev (1980), Cramp and Simmons (1980), Gossow et al. (1992), Lups (1981), Menzdorf (1982), Sara (1988), Schifferli et al. (1980), Tucker & Heath (1994), Vaurie (1964), Watson (1962a, 1962b).

---

16 PRZEVALSKI'S PARTRIDGE
Alectoris magna (Przevalski, 1876) Plate 4

Alternative names: Przevalski's Rock Partridge, Rusty-necklaced Partridge.

Endemic to the C Chinese mountains, it occurs in close proximity to adjacent populations of Chukar and has independently evolved some of the same plumage differences from that species exhibited by Rock Partridge (with which it was formerly considered conspecific).

IDENTIFICATION Przevalski's Partridge replaces Chukar in some arid mountains of C China (primarily in Gansu and Qinghai). Their ranges do not overlap but replace each other geographically. Differences in vocalisations and display postures appear to be the main reproductively isolating factors, rather than habitat differences. Przevalski's differs from all forms of Chukar and Rock Partridge in having a relatively wide rusty surround to an increasingly narrow black inner 'collar' and has pale (not brown eyes). Przevalski's has the lores and band from forehead to eye black, the black turning down before eye to extend narrowly around bill base to gape (in Chukar the black band turns onto the forehead in front of eye, leaving the lores white, apart from an isolated black spot at the gape); this feature is remarkably similar to that of Rock and, like that species, Przevalski's has closer and more numerous flank bars than Chukar. However, unlike Rock, the upperparts coloration of Przevalski's differs little from those of adjacent Chukar populations.

DESCRIPTION Bill bright red, bare skin around eye and legs rose-red. Irides pale yellowish-grey. Sexes similar, male has one blunt spur, absent in female. Adult (both sexes): Crown, nape, back and scapulars sandy-grey, slightly washed brown. Indistinct narrow whitish supercilium. Narrow band on forehead connects with black of lores and extends back to eye. Behind eye, a band of rusty feathering extends down neck-sides and joins at centre of upper breast, inside this rusty gorget is a narrow blackish border to the white throat. This black inner ring narrows and diffuses at the breast centre. Chin, throat and upper chest white or creamy-white. Wings sandy-grey, with slight brown wash when fresh, darker brown on primaries, which have straw-buff outer webs. Rump sandy-grey. Tail rufous. Belly cinnamon-yellow becoming paler cinnamon on undertail-coverts. Flanks banded black, creamy-buff and, very narrowly, chestnut (each feather grey at base

with a broad creamy band, bordered by a black bar and narrowly tipped chestnut). Juvenile: Rather plain, like others in genus, but richly speckled with white. Adult-like plumage (actually a slightly duller first-winter plumage) is attained after c.2 months.

GEOGRAPHICAL VARIATION Monotypic.

MEASUREMENTS Length 36–38 cm. Female only slightly smaller. Males: wing 169–180, tail 105–122, weight 445–710. Females: wing 160–172, tail 90–120, weight 442–615.

HABITAT Barren rugged plateaux and rocky mountain slopes at 1300–4000 m, favouring steep, sparsely vegetated ravines and canyons. Montane populations descend to lower elevations in winter, when often around farmsteads and villages.

VOICE Vocalisations described by Liu (1984, 1992), who emphasised their whistling nature and their closer similarity to Rock Partridge, rather than Chukar. Advertising call of male, a continuously repeated *gala, gala, gala*. Morning call (rallying call) a repeated *ga, ga, ga, gela gela gela*, given at sunrise prior to foraging. Flushed birds utter an excited *fei-ji, fei-ji, fei-ji* or *ja, ja, ja* audible over considerable distances in flight. Alarm call of male given whilst guarding nest, a whistled *dirdir, dirdir, dirdir* likened to the call of Oriental Greenfinch *Carduelis sinica* (Liu 1992).

HABITS In coveys of up to 30 during non-breeding season, which disband from late March to mid-April as pairing takes place. Small coveys of unmated males persist through the summer, until joined by mixed-sex broods in autumn. In cold winter weather coveys descend from higher elevations to valleys and will forage around farmsteads and other habitation, picking fallen grain from animal pens or droppings of domestic animals. Diet consists principally of seeds, bulbs, rhizomes, leaves, seedlings and shoots, with a small proportion of invertebrates, chiefly spiders, grasshoppers and beetles (insects being important to the young). Territorial male calls from prominent rock standing erect, holding head high and drawn back, displaying facial, necklace and flank patterns like others of genus. Most active dawn to mid-morning and late afternoon to evening, when retires to roost site on ground in hollows or crevices, often near water.

BREEDING Monogamous. Single-brooded. Nest a shallow scrape lined with scant vegetation and feathers constructed by both sexes, sheltered by vegetation or boulder. Eggs pale yellow-buff, speckled reddish-brown. Clutch 7–20 (chiefly 12). Lays first half of May until July. Incubation by female alone, occupies 22–24 days (in incubator or under domestic hen). Both sexes tend young, remaining together throughout the autumn and winter, when coveys amalgamate.

DISTRIBUTION NC China through most of N Qinghai (west to W Qaidam basin and south to Zhaling and Eling lakes at the headwaters of the Huang Ho) and east across S Gansu to the Quwu Mts of extreme S Ningxia Huizu Autonomous Region.

STATUS Near-Threatened. Locally numerous but heavily hunted in several areas, resulting in local extinctions. Habitat degradation and extensive use of pesticides are also cited as local threats. Population estimated at c.100,000. Numbers subject to marked fluctuations according to annual rainfall, surviving well in wet years and badly in years of drought, or in more arid parts of range.

REFERENCES Collar *et al.* (1994), Liu (1984, 1992), Liu & Yang (1982), Watson (1962a, 1962b).

17 RED-LEGGED PARTRIDGE
Alectoris rufa (Linnaeus, 1758)   Plate 5

Widely introduced to many parts of the world, its native range makes it one of the few W European endemic bird species (it is often referred to as 'French Partridge').

IDENTIFICATION W European counterpart of Chukar and Rock Partridge, differing from both in having a well-developed necklace of streaks and spots across chest and neck-sides below the black gorget (most evident when viewed head-on) and more earthybrown upperparts (note some races of Chukar are almost as brown). Overlaps widely with slightly smaller Grey Partridge but black border to creamy throat, unmarked upperparts, whitish supercilium and bold flank barring are easy distinctions. Even in flight, the unmarked upperparts are evident and rising birds may permit a glimpse of the patterned head or unmarked belly if it banks. Many of those released for sport in the past have been hybrids with similar Chukar (often termed 'Ogridge'). These are greyer overall and have much less extensive streaking below the black gorget. In the Alpes-Maritimes of S France, populations of natural hybrids with Rock Partridge occur, with similarly intermediate plumages and vocalisations.

DESCRIPTION *A. r. rufa.* Bill bright red, bare skin around eye and legs rose-red. Irides brown. Sexes similar, male has one blunt spur, absent in females. Adult (both sexes): Crown, nape and mantle vinous-brown, becoming blue-grey on forehead and crown sides above diffuse whitish supercilium. Nape, neck-sides and breast rufous-cinnamon, becoming greyer when worn. Very narrow band on forehead back to eye, widens as conspicuous black band behind eye, runs down neck-sides to form collar on chest. Chin, throat and upper chest creamy-white. Tiny black spots on upper chin and gape. Tuft of buff feathers on upper ear-coverts interrupts black collar line behind eye. Extensive necklace of black streaks and spots radiates from lower border of collar across breast and neck-sides, often coalescing to form extensive blackish area on central chest. Rump, wings, uppertail-coverts and central tail dark olive-grey, becoming greyer on rump, especially with wear. Darker brown primaries have straw-buff outer webs. Breast blue-grey; belly and undertail-coverts warm orange-buff. Outertail feathers rufous-chestnut. Flanks banded black, creamy and rufous (each feather grey at base with a whitish or creamy-buff subterminal band, followed by a black bar and tipped chestnut). Juvenile: Bill and legs pale reddish or horn-brown, soon becoming dull reddish. Crown and nape dark olive-brown. Upperparts, including wing-coverts, breast-sides and flanks grey-brown, each feather with a tiny white tip and some a weak sepia subterminal bar. Flanks similar with whitish subterminal bars and central feather streaks. Breast blue-grey, tipped sepia. Whitish throat and chest, bordered by indistinct dusky mottling give suggestion of adult pattern. Central underparts below breast yellowish-buff. Soon attains traces of black collar and flank pattern, and becomes much as adult at c.4 months; retains two old, abraded outermost primaries for a further year.

GEOGRAPHICAL VARIATION Slight and clinal, varying chiefly in colour saturation and slightly in size. Three races recognised.

A. r. rufa (Linnaeus, 1758) (includes *corsa* and *laubmanni*) occurs in France, Corsica, NW Italy, and British Is (introduced); described above.

A. r. hispanica (Seoane, 1894) (includes *maderensis*) occurs in Portugal and adjacent N and W Spain, and introduced Madeira and perhaps Azores; darker, brighter and more richly coloured than nominate, with stouter bill.

A. r. intercedens (Brehm, 1858) (includes *australis*) occurs in E and S Spain, including the Balearic Is, intergrading with *hispanica* in C Spain, and introduced Gran Canaria and Azores; much paler above than *hispanica*, markedly greyer on rump, but brighter below and heavier billed than nominate.

MEASUREMENTS Length 35–38 cm. Female smaller. *A. r. rufa.* Males: wing 161–169 (mean 165), tail 87–97 (mean 93), weight 500–547 (mean 516). Females: wing 152–161 (mean 157), tail 77–92 (mean 84), weight (n=1) 540.

HABITAT Open dry country, locally (in mountains of south of range) to 2000 m. From cultivation, low downs, sandy tracts and maquis to foothills; favours low-intensity cultivation with a mix of fallow and uncultivated areas. Generally in drier habitats than Grey Partridge but the two overlap widely in range.

VOICE Similar to Chukar. Rallying call a rhythmic repeated chicken-like clucking, which develops into a harsh, grating *chuk-chuk-chukAR-CHUKAR*. Advertising call of male recalls rhythmic chuffing of a steam engine in delivery, a repeated *go-CHAK-CHAK, go-CHAK-CHAK, go-CHAK-CHAK*. When alarmed or flushed utters an explosive squealed squeaky *cheeragh, cheeragh, cheeragh*. Contact notes include a soft *chik chik chik chik*. Various other short harsh or squealing calls also given. Most vocal in morning, particularly when gathering to feed at daybreak.

HABITS Generally in small coveys of 6–10, but postbreeding gatherings of up to 70 not infrequent in areas where numerous. Exceptionally large gatherings of 200–300 have been recorded in cold weather. Montane populations tend to descend to lower elevations during winter. Single-sex coveys of 20–40 males recorded in late winter in USA, but most flocks disband at start of breeding season as pairing begins in February–March. Non-breeders flock throughout the breeding season. Diet very similar to Chukar and Grey Partridge, but capable of taking larger food items than latter, chiefly roots (including beet), seeds, beechmast and leaves of small plants, plus a proportion of small invertebrates, especially ants and beetles (insects are especially important to the young). Coveys visit favoured drinking site at or even just before dawn, before feeding. When alarmed, runs rapidly with erect carriage, quickly disappearing over nearest ridge. Often crouches at onset of danger, suddenly 'exploding' in whirr of fast wingbeats, generally flying low and running off on alighting. Territorial male calls from prominent position standing erect with neck stretched, and chest and flanks puffed out to display patterning. Most active dawn to mid-morning and late afternoon to evening, seeking shade during heat of day, when retires to roost among ploughed furrows, stubble, waterside cover or low trees.

BREEDING Monogamous with some at least forming long-term pair bonds; occasionally bigamous. Chiefly single-brooded, but rare second broods commenced simultaneously, with male incubating. Nest a shallow scrape sparsely lined with vegetation, in shade of bush, grass tuft or boulder (several scrapes created by male, while female selects favourite). Eggs pale yellow-buff, variably speckled reddish-brown and grey. Clutch 10–15 (chiefly 11–12). Lays late April–May in England and Portugal, May to mid-June in France. Incubation occupies 23–24 days, primarily by female but male may share these duties and frequently incubates and rears any additional brood. Family coveys stay together throughout first autumn and winter. Youngsters become adult-sized at c.50–60 days.

DISTRIBUTION SW Europe. Native range encompasses most of Portugal, Spain and S and C France (including Corsica, north to E Brittany and S Normandy and east to the Jura), extending into NW Italy (Piedmont, Liguria, Elba, and N Apennines). Its presence on the Balearics, Azores, Madeira and Gran Canaria is considered to be the result of long-established introductions. It is also an established exotic in England and, more locally, in Wales and S Scotland. Marginally established in parts of North and South Is of New Zealand, but frequent and widespread introduction attempts in N America have failed. Native range formerly extended into N Brittany, W and S Switzerland and Germany's Rhineland, but long since extirpated from these regions.

STATUS Considered reasonably numerous, but has suffered marked overall decline since the 1970s, which accelerated in the 1980s. Changes in agricultural practices and consequent habitat loss are the major factors involved, but excessive hunting and the release of large numbers of artificially reared birds (many of which are hybrids with Chukar or Rock Partridge) also threaten the purity of local populations. The French population was estimated at 550,000 pairs in 1980, while in the UK it was considered to be over 90,000 pairs, with c.2 million in Spain, at least 50,000 in Portugal and 1000 in Italy.

REFERENCES Bump (1958), Cramp & Simmons (1980), Goodwin (1953, 1954, 1958), Potts (1988), Vaurie (1965).

Genus *FRANCOLINUS*: francolins

Forty-one francolin species are currently recognised, 36 in Africa and 5 in Asia. Such remarkable diversity is the product of long geographical isolation of many African francolins from their congeners, and many species thus form closely related groups.

Francolin systematics were reviewed by Hall (1963) and Crowe & Crowe (1985). The latter revision has since been thoroughly overhauled, with the added component of DNA analysis of a selection of species (Crowe *et al.* 1992). The new results restrict *Francolinus sensu stricto* to the five Asian francolins and ascribed the 36 African forms to three separate genera: *Peliperdix, Scleroptila* and *Pternistis*. However, this work does not appear to have gained universal acceptance and we have decided to regard these as subgenera of *Francolinus* within the present work.

Subspeciation has been considered to be high within the African taxa, but Urban *et al.* (1986) recognise relatively few forms, considering the majority of subspecies to be described from inadequate material, or that the degree of local and individual variation and general clines in coloration dictate a less expansive approach. As this has become the standard reference on Afrotropical birds, their recommendations have been followed here.

CHARACTERISTICS

These partridge-like birds are basically cryptically coloured, and both sexes usually similar in plumage (exceptions are remarkably few). Juveniles resemble duller versions of adults or females, shaft streaking of the feathers contributing to this impression, disrupting the form of barring or streaking, which appears neater in adults. In many species, age- and sex-related plumage variation is not often a major problem in francolin identification. Males usually possess 1–2 well-developed tarsal spurs, in most females these are absent or so short as to be invisible in the field. However, there are exceptions, as younger males have shorter spurs than older males and females, and males of some species wholly lack spurs. Many of the most similar-looking species are isolated from each other or overlap only marginally; where similar species' ranges do overlap there are generally differences in both habitat and altitude. Distribution and habitat are extremely important identification clues.

HABITS

Like all gamebirds, francolins are shy and cover loving, and most active in early morning and evening when they may feed or dust-bathe along tracks or roadsides. In the heat of the day, many shelter under bushes or boulders and are largely inactive. Most easily located by their noisy advertising calls, typically uttered by males in early morning or evening from a low prominence, such as a mound or bush. Females of some species often respond to the male call, creating a raucous, ventriloquial duet.

IDENTIFICATION FEATURES

As plumages are intricately patterned, it is important to concentrate on a few key features when observing francolins:

  bill and leg colour
  spotting, streaking or barring on underparts (especially flanks)
  barring or streaking on upperparts
  presence of bare skin on throat or around eye
  head pattern and colour
  whether sexes are alike

Stone Partridge of W and C Africa and the recently described Udzungwa Partridge of S Tanzania, despite their superficial appearance, are not closely related to francolins. The almost uniform dark plumage and habit of carrying the tail cocked are distinctive of Stone Partridge, although Crested Francolin shares the latter habit.

Subgenus *FRANCOLINUS*: Asiatic francolins

Black Francolin *F. francolinus*, Painted Francolin *F. pictus*, Chinese Francolin *F. pintadeanus*, Grey Francolin *F. pondicerianus* and Swamp Francolin *F. gularis*.

Although Africa is rich in francolins, the same cannot be said for Asia, which boasts just five that provide few identification problems, there being very little overlap between similar species. Clearly Black, Painted and Chinese Francolins are related, indeed limited hybridisation has been reported between Black and Painted in areas where the two co-occur. This suggests that, although probably derived from a common ancestor, they have been separate for a very long period, with Black extending its range from the west to meet the other two. In contrast, Grey and Swamp Francolins are isolated species of uncertain affinities.

18   BLACK FRANCOLIN
Francolinus francolinus (Linnaeus, 1766)   Plate 7

Alternative name: Black Partridge (India).

A beautifully marked francolin with an extensive range from Europe to Assam.

IDENTIFICATION Sexes differ. Male black with white ear-coverts patch and intensely white-spotted mantle and body sides; a broad deep chestnut collar separates the black breast and black throat but is relatively inconspicuous owing to the overall plumage darkness. Female brown heavily mottled with black feather centres on both body surfaces and has an inconspicuous chestnut nape patch. Marginally overlaps with Chinese Francolin in Manipur and Painted Francolin in NC India; also wide overlap with Grey and Swamp Francolins (which see for discussion). In flight, female could be confused with female Red Junglefowl but is bulkier, with shorter tail and more mottled upperparts.

DESCRIPTION *F. f. francolinus*. Bill blackish. Irides brown. Legs reddish. Sexes differ: female unspurred, male has one spur. **Adult male:** Crown and nape pale brown, with black streaks; head-sides, chin and throat black enclosing white ear-coverts patch; broad deep chestnut collar encircles lower neck. Breast and underparts black, with white flanks spotting and rusty-whitish vent. Mantle black spotted white; rump and uppertail-coverts blackish with close fine whitish barring; rest of upperparts brown with black and buff mottling and streaking. **Adult female:** Crown and nape brown, with dark streaks; head-sides and neck buff with dark brown ear-coverts and whitish throat; breast and rest of underparts buff with dark barring and scalloping, becoming rufous on vent. Lower nape dull chestnut. Upperparts as male but brown replaces black basal colour to rump and uppertail-coverts. **Juvenile:** Recalls dull version of female but underparts paler, only weakly streaked and barred.

GEOGRAPHICAL VARIATION Six subspecies vary in overall size and darkness of plumage (latter most obvious in female). Clinal variation, from largest in Israel to smallest in NE India, with increasing colour saturation from palest populations in Iran to darkest at western and eastern limits of range.

F. f. francolinus (Linnaeus, 1766) (includes *billypani*) occurs in Turkey, the Middle East and Caspian region; large, with female darker than most other races.

F. f. arabistanicus Zarudny & Härms, 1913 occurs in C and SE Iraq and W Iran; slightly smaller (male wing 166–179), female paler, less strongly patterned above and with narrower barring below.

F. f. bogdanovi Zarudny, 1906 (includes *festivus*) occurs in S Iran and Afghanistan; a small race, with palest females. Male has pale sandy upperparts, with bolder white markings than other forms.

F. f. henrici Bonaparte, 1856 occurs in Pakistan; darker than previous form, close to Iraqi race in colour, but smaller (male wing 148–163).

F. f. asiae Bonaparte, 1856 (includes *parkerae*) occurs in India east to C Nepal and W Bengal; intermediate between *henrici* and the next race.

F. f. melanonotus Hume, 1888 occurs from E Nepal east; the darkest and smallest race (male wing 143–155), males have almost blackish-brown upperparts, females very dark, with heavy barring below.

MEASUREMENTS Length 31–36 cm. Male usually larger. *F. f. francolinus*. Males: wing 174–182 (mean 177), tarsus 54–60 (mean 57), weight 450–500. Females: wing 163–171 (mean 167), tarsus 50–55 (mean 52), weight 400–450.

HABITAT Lowland cultivation with extensive bushy cover, tall grassland with bushes, river deltas and lake edges with scrub and reeds. Locally on cultivated montane slopes, where it occurs to 2500 m in India and Nepal, but only a summer visitor at higher altitudes.

VOICE Advertising call very distinctive and far carrying: a strident, penetrating, grating series of notes preceded by a sharp metallic call, *clip, gek-ge-gek, gek-ge-gek*. Very similar to Painted Francolin. Otherwise relatively silent.

HABITS Shy and wary, rarely in open except 'singing' male or when crossing tracks, often with tail slightly cocked. Usually in pairs or family parties, feeding in cover but readily entering cultivation and especially active early morning and evening. Male utters harsh grating 'song' from ground or low perch, e.g. tree or fence post, with head up, wings drooped and broad tail spread; otherwise entirely a ground dweller. Flushes reluctantly, with rapid heavy wing action, interspersed with glides in manner that recalls true pheasants rather than partridges, soon dropping back to cover.

BREEDING Monogamous. Nest a scrape lined with grass, usually hidden in tussock. Mean clutch 6–9 (India), 4 (Pakistan) or 8–12 (Azerbaijan). Eggs yellowish-olive to brown. Breeding chronology varies over wide range but late April–June in Caspian lowlands and in various months in Indian subcontinent.

DISTRIBUTION S Asia and formerly S Europe. Present, fragmented range extends from Cyprus, S Turkey, Israel, Palestine, extreme NW Jordan and Syria through Azerbaijan (and a tiny adjacent area of Armenia) to NW and NE Iran and adjacent SW Turkmenistan. From Iraq, through SW and S Iran east through extreme S Afghanistan, Pakistan, across N India (south to Gwalior and Orissa) and Nepal to Bangladesh, Bhutan (one recent record), Assam and Manipur. Introductions established in USA (S Florida and Louisiana), Hawaii and Guam. Recently reintroduced into Italy (Tuscany) and Portugal (the Algarve).

STATUS Locally common in Indian subcontinent, but considerable decline caused by hunting further west, including Pakistan, and no recent records from Bangladesh. In Azerbaijan massive losses due to hunting: population of 663,000 in 1956 was only 23,300 by 1990. Hunted in Turkey, although theoretically protected: in 1988 just 300–450 calling males in three relict areas of southeast, but additional populations have been subsequently discovered. Locally common where protected, with c.2000 pairs in Israel and Palestine in 1996. Range formerly extended into Europe, but long since extirpated from Spain, Greece and Italy, although recent reintroduction into latter appears successful and reportedly now established in one area of NE Algarve in Portugal.

REFERENCES Ali & Ripley (1969), van den Berk (1988), Cramp & Simmons (1980).

19 PAINTED FRANCOLIN
Francolinus pictus (Jardine & Selby, 1828)   Plate 7

Alternative name: Painted Partridge (India).

Southern counterpart of Black Francolin, favouring drier habitats and occasionally hybridising with latter in limited overlap zone.

IDENTIFICATION A blackish francolin profusely mottled with white from neck downwards, contrasting with tawny-rufous head. Upperparts recall Black Francolin, with which it overlaps in a narrow band across NC India. Head pattern prevents confusion with male Black, but both sexes could be confused with female Black, although latter has rufous nape, dark eyeline, more streaked (less spotted) under- and upperparts (if seen well), and different underparts coloration. Grey Francolin has entire plumage prominently barred, not spotted, narrow black border to pale throat and rufous, not black, tail.

DESCRIPTION *F. p. pictus.* Bill blackish. Irides brown. Legs reddish. Sexes similar, both unspurred. **Adult male:** Crown and nape pale brown with black streaks; head-sides, chin and throat unmarked tawny-rufous. Breast and underparts black with intense white spotting obscuring black ground colour and becoming rusty-whitish on vent. Mantle black, spotted white; rump and uppertail-coverts blackish, finely and closely barred whitish; rest of upperparts brown with black and buff mottling and streaking. Tail black. **Adult female:** Duller, with whiter throat, buffier-toned and slightly barred underparts, and duller bare parts. **Juvenile:** Resembles female but even duller with yellower legs.

GEOGRAPHICAL VARIATION Slight, varying in overall intensity of colour and markings. Three races recognised, but first two clinal.
> **F. p. pictus** (Jardine & Selby, 1828) occurs in S India, south of 20°N; described above.
> **F. p. pallidus** (Gray, 1831) occurs in C India; intergrades with, but paler than, nominate.
> **F. p. watsoni** Legge, 1880 occurs in Uva province of Sri Lanka; very dark with intense blackish underparts markings in both sexes.

MEASUREMENTS Length 31–32 cm. Sexes similar. *F. p. pallidus.* Males: wing 140–149, tarsus 37–45. Females: wing 140–151, tarsus 41–46. Weight (both sexes) 242–340.

HABITAT Intermediate between lusher country favoured by Black and dry scrub of Grey Francolin, preferring dry grassland and scrub–jungle, often in hills, interspersed with streams and water channels. In Sri Lanka restricted to dry, scrub- and grass-covered hills to 1500 m.

VOICE Advertising call very similar to Black Francolin: a strident, high-pitched *click...cheek-cheek-keray.* Usually rather silent and less vocal than Black Francolin.

HABITS Shy and wary, rarely in open except 'singing' male or when crossing tracks, often with tail slightly cocked. Usually in pairs or family parties, feeding within cover but readily entering cultivation and especially active early morning and evening. Male may utter harsh grating 'song' from low perch, including small dead trees or fence posts, with head stretched forward, wings drooped and broad tail spread, but otherwise a ground dweller, although may roost in trees as well as on ground. Flushes reluctantly, with rapid whirring wingbeats.

BREEDING Monogamous. Nest a well-hidden scrape, lined with grass and leaves. Mean clutch 4–6, occasionally 8; eggs olive-brown. Breeding commences at start of rains, March–June in Sri Lanka, April–June in C India, continuing into September further north.

DISTRIBUTION Endemic to Indian subcontinent, from Sri Lanka (Uva) and peninsular India, north to S and E Gujarat, C Rajasthan (e.g. Ranthambore National Park), S Uttar Pradesh and N Madhya Pradesh. Overlaps with Black Francolin in Rajasthan, where hybrids noted.

STATUS Sri Lanka race *watsoni* endangered by hunting and indiscriminate habitat burning within its limited range. Locally common in India although many local decreases have resulted from habitat degradation caused by encroaching cultivation. A mean density of 7.7 birds per km² was recorded in prime habitat in Gujarat.

REFERENCES: Ali & Ripley (1969), Baker (1928), Kaul & Howman (1992).

---

20 CHINESE FRANCOLIN
Francolinus pintadeanus (Scopoli, 1786)   Plate 7

Alternative name: Burmese Francolin (India).

Eastern counterpart of Black Francolin, the two species' ranges meet only in Manipur.

IDENTIFICATION A dark, intensely marked, francolin that recalls Black in its basically blackish plumage profusely mottled with white from neck down; slightly larger and bulkier, especially around head and neck than Black. Male easily distinguished from Black by white throat and head-sides (divided by black malar),

and heavily spotted breast and central underparts (breast and central underparts unmarked black in Black). Female differs from female Black in rufous supercilium (not nape) and paler cheeks. Their ranges only overlap in Manipur (extreme NE India).

DESCRIPTION *F. p. phayrei.* Bill blackish. Irides brown. Legs reddish (breeding male) or yellowish-brown (non-breeding and female). Sexes differ. **Adult male:** Crown and nape dark brown, mottled black, supercilium rufous, ear-coverts, lores, chin and throat white with blackish moustachial and blackish eye-patch. Neck, breast and rest of underparts black, heavily mottled with white spots, these increasing and merging on lower underparts such that white predominates; vent pale rufous. Mantle black, spotted white; rump and uppertail-coverts blackish closely and finely barred whitish; rest of upperparts brown with black and buff mottling and streaking, and quite extensive chestnut on wing-coverts and scapulars. **Adult female:** Crown and nape brown with dark streaks; head-sides and neck buff, with dusky-brownish eye, malar stripes and whitish throat; breast and rest of underparts buff with dense, fine dark barring, becoming broader on lower underparts and rufous on vent. Upperparts as male but brown replaces black basal colour to rump and uppertail-coverts. **Juvenile:** Resembles female but duller, streaked pale above with barred, rather than spotted, hindneck, and lacks, or has ill-defined, eye-stripe and malar.

GEOGRAPHICAL VARIATION Slight. Two races differ in size. An exceptional plumage variant, with black throat and cheeks and blackish vent has been collected once in Tonkin (Vietnam) and was described as a 'new' species '*F. boineti*'.
> **F. p. pintadeanus** (Scopoli, 1786) occurs in SE China; typically larger.
> **F. p. phayrei** (Blyth, 1843) occurs in Manipur (India), Myanmar, Thailand and Indochina; described above.

MEASUREMENTS Length 31–34 cm. Sexes similar. *F. p. phayrei*. Both sexes: wing 132–151, tarsus 42–44, weight 284–397.

HABITAT Favours dry, open forested or scrub-covered hillsides, but local in lowlands. To 1500 m in Thailand.

VOICE Advertising call: 5–6 loud, harsh and metallic resonant notes, the final two more rapidly delivered, *kak-kak-kuich, ka-ka* or *wi-ta-tak-takaa* repeated after prolonged pauses. No other vocalisations have been documented.

HABITS Shy and wary, rarely in open except 'singing' male or when crossing tracks. Usually in pairs or family parties, feeding in cover but readily entering cultivation and especially active early morning and evening. Occasionally perches in trees when flushed, and 'sings' from prominent post or stump in manner of Black Francolin, but otherwise a ground dweller. Flushes reluctantly.

BREEDING Monogamous. Nest a well-hidden scrape, lined with grass and leaves. Mean clutch 4–5, occasionally 7; eggs creamy or olive-cream. Breeding commences at start of rains, March–June in Myanmar but few data from elsewhere.

DISTRIBUTION SE Asia, from SE Manipur (NE India) east across Myanmar and S and SE China (W and S Yunnan, S Guizhou, Guangxi, Hainan, Guangdong, Hong Kong, Fujian and north to Zhejiang). Also south over W and S Thailand (absent from the peninsula) and Indochina, including much of Cambodia, Laos and Vietnam. Introduced populations probably persist on Mauritius but no longer in Luzon (Philippines).

STATUS Locally common and no evidence of substantial decreases. Tolerant of cultivation within its habitat. Continued survival of introduced populations on Mauritius and Luzon (near Manila) requires confirmation.

REFERENCES Ali & Ripley (1969), Baker (1928).

---

21 GREY FRANCOLIN
Francolinus pondicerianus (Gmelin, 1789)   Plate 6

Alternative name: Grey Partridge (India).

One of the most conspicuous Indian gamebirds, its distinctive voice is a characteristic sound in drier parts of the subcontinent.

IDENTIFICATION The overall strongly barred plumage and dull orange or whitish throat (varies with race) with narrow black border prevents confusion with all other gamebirds of the region. However, barring may not be evident in brief or more distant views. Most likely confusion species is Painted Francolin, with which it widely overlaps, but latter is distinctly spotted, not barred, on a darker background colour. Confusion less likely with darker Black Francolin, females of which are strongly mottled with dark barring and scalloping, whereas Grey has entirely pale barred plumage. In flight, the rufous tail easily distinguishes it from both Black and Painted, which have black tails, but not from Swamp with which it marginally overlaps. Swamp has streaked, not barred, flanks, is larger and inhabits damp grassland and reeds. In S Iran and Baluchistan, range overlaps with Chukar, which also has rufous tail,

but latter has strong black flank bars, unmarked sandy-grey upperparts and occurs in rocky habitats (Grey Francolin is a plains species). Compare also overlapping See-see. Voice very distinctive.

DESCRIPTION *F. p. pondicerianus*. Bill dark. Irides brown. Legs orange. Sexes similar, although male larger and has single spur, female unspurred. **Adult (both sexes):** Crown and nape grey-brown to rufous-brown; forehead, head-sides and supercilium rufous-buff; ear-coverts brown; throat whitish or orange-buff with narrow dark border. Rest of underparts pale buff with dark barring, narrowest on neck and breast, broadest on flanks. Rufous or grey-brown above, with whitish shaft streaks on coverts, tertials and scapulars, and whitish and narrow dark barring on entire upperparts; tail rufous with dark subterminal band. **Juvenile:** Resembles adult but duller, lacking dark border to pale throat.

GEOGRAPHICAL VARIATION Three intergrading subspecies.
> **F. p. pondicerianus** (Gmelin, 1789) (includes *ceylonensis*) occurs in S India and Sri Lanka; darkest,

with strong barring and orange throat.

F. p. interpositus Hartert, 1917 (includes *'prepositus'*, *'paganus'* and *'titar'*) occurs in N India and Pakistan; distinctly paler with whitish throat centre.

F. p. mecranensis Zarudny & Härms, 1913 occurs in W Pakistan and S Iran; very pale overall, with throat almost whitish.

MEASUREMENTS Length 30–32 cm. Male slightly larger. *F. p. pondicerianus*. Males: wing 142–161, tarsus 44–46, weight 255–340. Females: wing 142–146, tarsus 41–42, weight 200–312.

HABITAT Favours dry plains and semi-desert, or gently undulating country with dry thorn scrub. Common in scrubby cultivation, often near villages. Local in scrubby slopes and valleys in foothills, but avoids montane regions.

VOICE Advertising call: a loud, metallic, ringing, strident and rapid *kat-ee-la, kat-ee-la, kat-ee-la*, soon repeated and generally preceded by up to four sharp notes that rise in pitch. Female utters a high-pitched, rising *tee-tee-tee* and a weaker version of the male advertising cry, often in a duet with male. When flushed, often gives a sharp, high, agitated *kirr-kirr* in alarm.

HABITS Typically in coveys, feeding on dusty tracks and open patches between scrub. When alarmed flock breaks up, running rapidly in various directions with erect carriage, heading for dense undergrowth. Reluctant to fly, but if suddenly flushed may 'explode' with whirring wingbeats, generally flying low for short distance and running off on alighting. Most active early morning and evening. Coveys split up into pairs at start of breeding season. Uses favoured drinking spots, where available, but able to subsist with little water in very dry country, apparently taking early morning moisture. Occasionally perches in bushes if persistently pursued; roosts in scrubby bushes and on ground. 'Sings' from ground and perch in shrubbery.

BREEDING Monogamous. Nest a well-hidden scrape, lined with grass and leaves, often beneath a bush. Mean clutch 6–9 pale buff eggs. Breeding reported in all seasons, but most usual April–September.

DISTRIBUTION Throughout Indian subcontinent south of the Himalayas to coastal N Sri Lanka and east to Bangladesh. Also west in lowland Pakistan and Baluchistan (one record in SE Afghanistan), through S Iran to Persian Gulf. Isolated populations (perhaps not native) are increasing in UAE, Bahrain, Qatar, E Saudi Arabia and N Oman. Widely introduced, with extant populations on several Indian Ocean islands: Seychelles (now only on Desroches and Coetivy in the Amirantes), Mauritius, Réunion and Rodrigues; but no longer on Diego Garcia I. or Andaman Is. Also introduced onto Hawaii and into parts of SW USA.

STATUS Locally abundant, but decreasing in areas where hunting pressure severe, and in agricultural areas following extensive use of pesticides. Survives well in moderate or broken cultivation, and is increasing in Oman through spread of desert cultivation techniques. First recorded in Bahrain c.1981, Qatar in 1986 (where now common) and extreme E Saudi Arabia in 1991. The increasing UAE population was estimated at 5000–10,000 pairs in 1996.

REFERENCES Ali & Ripley (1969), Aspinall (1996).

---

22   SWAMP FRANCOLIN
Francolinus gularis (Temminck, 1815)   Plate 6

Alternative names: Swamp Partridge, Kyah.

A very local francolin of *terai* grasslands in the NE Indian subcontinent.

IDENTIFICATION Rather large, bulky francolin with closely barred upperparts, streaked underparts and relatively unmarked head and rufous throat. Prominent flank streaking is most striking feature at moderate range, providing an easy distinction from Black or Grey Francolins, with which it overlaps in range. Its preference for damp *terai* grassland excludes Grey Francolin from much of its range, but they occur alongside each other where *terai* meets adjoining dry cultivation. Has rufous tail feathers in flight, like Grey but unlike Black, which has blackish tail. Voice distinctive.

DESCRIPTION Bill black. Irides brown. Legs reddish (dull red or orange-yellow, brightest in breeding male). Sexes similar: male has single short spur, female unspurred. **Adult (both sexes):** Crown and nape brown, finely barred darker; supercilium and band below eye buff; chin, throat, foreneck and head-sides rufous-chestnut. Neck-sides, breast and underparts dark brown with broad creamy feather centres, edged black (most prominently striped on flanks); vent rufous. Upperparts brown with close rufous-buff and narrower dark barring; tail chestnut. **Juvenile:** Resembles adult but duller, with buffier throat and brown, rather than black, edges to underparts streaking.

GEOGRAPHICAL VARIATION None recognised: *ridibundus*, described from extreme west of range, is generally considered unworthy of recognition.

MEASUREMENTS Length 36–38 cm. Sexes similar. Both sexes: wing 162–186, tarsus 60–70, weight (n=1 male) 510.

HABITAT Wet grassland and reedbeds in alluvial lowlands to 250 m, mixed with bushy swamp–jungle vegetation; also mixed grassland, reedbeds and cultivation (e.g. sugar cane fields). Occasionally moves higher, during periods of high floods, exceptionally recorded from Cherrapunji plateau in Assam at 1200 m.

VOICE Advertising call a loud *kaw-care* or *ko-ko-care* that may be accompanied in duet with *kirr-kirr-kirr* from female. Perhaps latter same as that described as a prolonged series of sharp notes, *chuill-chuill-chuillll-chuill...* uttered at rate of ten calls in eight seconds. Also a harsh *chuckeroo-chuckeroo-chuckeroo* preceded by several harsh chuckles and croaks (latter not unlike Grey Francolin, but poorly documented). Flushes late but if pressed rises with chuckles and cackling.

HABITS Shy and difficult to observe, presence indicated by distinctive calls. Most likely to be seen feeding in early morning and evening on tracks or in other open areas, such as edges of cultivation and paddies near damp grassland. Feeds on tubers, bulbs, seeds and flowers of wetland plants, as well as grain and weed seeds in fields. Until they are one month old, chicks feed almost exclusively on insects. Spends most time within tall grassland and reeds by water, even wading in shallows and clambering reed stems while negotiating patches of deeper water. Generally in pairs or family parties. Males indulge in fierce disputes at onset of breeding season. Runs rapidly when disturbed, heading for dense, tall grass. Reluctant to fly, but if flushed rises heavily with whirring wingbeats, generally flying strongly for short distance and dropping into tall dense grass. Roosts in small trees and bushes within grassland or on clumps of broken reeds. During heat of day may also shelter within shade of small plantations. 'Sings' with upstretched neck and body held erect, from ground or small bush.

BREEDING Monogamous. Nest constructed by female, well hidden in dense waterside undergrowth or among flattened reeds close to water's edge; a well-built construction of weeds and grass, with a relatively deep cup. Clutch 4–7, mean six. Eggs pale buff, plain or mottled and blotched reddish, especially at larger end. Breeds February–May, chiefly in March–April before onset of rains. Male helps tend chicks.

DISTRIBUTION N and NE India. Patchily distributed along flood plains of Ganges and Brahmaputra Rivers in N India, west to N Uttar Pradesh and east to W Assam and E Bangladesh, just entering SW and SE Nepal.

STATUS Vulnerable. Its specialised *terai* grassland habitat has been severely exploited since the 1950s, with extensive tracts remaining only in national parks. The species has undergone an associated decline (with perhaps now fewer than 10,000 individuals) and is similarly fragmented (several sites are tiny and highly isolated), but remains locally numerous in natural grassland and nearby swamp–jungle (e.g. in Dudwa and Kaziranga National Parks). Nesting success appears very low, often due to human disturbance. Recently reported from just 24 areas in India (of which 14 are protected) and three in Nepal (all protected); probably persists in Bangladesh but no recent records. Densities appear significantly higher in areas where sparse cultivation and light grazing are interspersed within natural grassland, but grassland burning, to improve habitat for rare mammals especially if conducted in the breeding season may have a serious negative impact.

REFERENCES Ali & Ripley (1969), Baral (1998), BirdLife International (2000, 2001), Grimmett *et al.* (1998), Iqubal *et al.* (1998), Javed (1998, 2001), Javed & Rahmani (1991), Shrestha (1992).

Subgenus *PELIPERDIX*: red-tailed francolins

Coqui Francolin *F. coqui*, White-throated Francolin *F. albogularis* and Schlegel's Francolin *F. schlegelii*.

Two of these three are strongly sexually dimorphic (Schlegel's is the exception). All three have buff-streaked upperparts, buffish head-sides, barred underparts, some rufous in tail (can be visible in flight) and short yellowish legs and black bills. Vocally they have musical trumpeting calls. Two other species are tentatively included here, although they do not appear to sit so easily within this grouping: Latham's *F. lathami* and Crested Francolins *F. sephaena*.

23   COQUI FRANCOLIN
Francolinus coqui (Smith, 1836)   Plate 9

An attractive and very widespread little francolin, most abundant in the southern part of its wide range.

IDENTIFICATION Combination of small size, orange-buff head and barred underparts of male distinctive. Female could be confused with female White-throated, but latter lacks black stripe above eye and border to throat (faint necklace in *buckleyi*), has only weakly barred underparts, paler breast (except more richly coloured *dewittei*) and brighter rufous wings (primaries merely washed rufous in W African Coqui if seen in flight). Coqui Francolin has distinctive habit of walking slowly, with body held low and head up, even when crossing open tracks. Range does not overlap with Schlegel's, but latter has rufous upperparts, and both sexes have buff head-sides without throat pattern of female Coqui. In Ethiopia, compare female with larger Orange River Francolin.

DESCRIPTION *F. c. coqui*. Bill black with yellow base. Irides brown. Legs yellow. Sexes differ in head pattern; male single spurred, female has no, or one very short, spur. **Adult male:** Throat, face and head-sides unmarked ochre-buff, contrasting with whitish underparts and becoming buffier on rear body; underparts from lower neck to flanks closely barred black, most intense on breast, broadest on flanks. Upperparts grey-brown finely streaked buff, tail reddish-brown. **Adult female:** Also barred below, but breast unbarred tawny and head pattern quite different: throat white with black border and has black stripe above eye, bordering crown. **Juvenile:** Resembles female but less streaked above and has narrower, fainter underparts barring on buffier background.

GEOGRAPHICAL VARIATION Marked, especially in degree of barring on lower underparts; a large number of races have been described, but definition obscured by much clinal and local variation. Only four warrant recognition according to Urban *et al.* (1986).

F. c. coqui (Smith, 1836) (includes *ruandae, kasaicus, vernayi, hoeschianus, lynesi, stuhlmanni* and *campbelli*) occurs in S Africa, north to C and NW Tanzania and Uganda; described above but paler and longer tailed in Botswana and Namibia, and more heavily barred populations in Uganda.

F. c. hubbardi Ogilvie-Grant, 1895 occurs in W and S Kenya; has unbarred buff belly and greyish mottling in crown.

F. c. maharao Sclater, 1927 (includes *thikae*) occurs in Ethiopia, Kenya and N Tanzania; small, with unbarred belly and buff wash to entire underparts.

F. c. spinetorum Bates, 1928 (includes *buckleyi* and *angolensis*) occurs in W Africa south to Angola and Zambia; has unbarred buff belly and strong rufous wash to crown and primaries.

MEASUREMENTS Length 21–25 cm. Sexes similar. *F. c. coqui* given. Males: wing 123–147 (mean 134), tarsus 31–45 (mean 38), weight (n=2) 278, 289. Females: wing 118–147 (mean 131), tarsus 31–43 (mean 37), weight 218–259.

HABITAT Dry wooded grasslands to 2200 m. Locally in sand dunes with bushy cover but avoids cultivation, except at edges if unmolested.

VOICE Advertising call (chiefly early morning and evening): 7–10 trumpet-like crowing notes, with second or third note loudest, others diminishing and final notes fading, *kek, KEK, kek, kek, kek, kek, koh, heh, kek*. In some areas (especially W Africa) the call is very rapid (thus recalling Schlegel's). A more frequently uttered call is a high-pitched, squeaky *co-qui, co-qui, co-qui* or *be-quick, be-quick*, which may be repeated 6–8 times. Coveys give a soft *churr-churr* when alarmed. Flushed individuals utter shrill squeaks.

HABITS Usually in pairs or small parties in wooded grassland. Shy and cover loving, very difficult to flush but flies strongly if put-up. Prefers to escape by running, although often crouches and 'freezes' in the open when alarmed. Roosts on ground. Walk has distinctive slow, half-crouching gait with body low and horizontal, and head carried high. Successful in arid grassland and appears to depend little on standing water. Calls from ground; at onset of breeding season males are relatively pugnacious.

BREEDING Monogamous. Nest a scrape, lined with grass and hidden among tufts of grass. Mean clutch 4–5, but 2–8 recorded; eggs pinkish-white to pale brown. Season varies over wide range, chiefly allied to onset of rainy season.

DISTRIBUTION Widespread in suitable habitat in Africa. Patchy and local in W Africa, from S Mauritania to N Nigeria, with an isolated population in S Ethiopia, but more extensive in drier areas south of C Kenya, S Uganda and SE Cameroon, although absent from southwest of continent.

STATUS Locally common in much of its southern range, but distinctly local and uncommon to scarce in W Africa and Ethiopia. Uncommon and local in most of Kenya, where most numerous in Rift Valley. Local decreases attributable to disease (e.g. fowl pox), grass burning and overgrazing to which it appears to be particularly sensitive.

REFERENCES Meyer (1971), Urban *et al.* (1986), Zimmerman *et al.* (1996).

24   WHITE-THROATED FRANCOLIN
Francolinus albogularis Hartlaub, 1854   Plate 9

An uncommon francolin with bright rufous wings, found chiefly in W Africa with relict populations in Zaïre, Angola and Zambia.

IDENTIFICATION Small buffish and rufous francolin lacking prominent markings, although female has fine barring on underparts. Male unlikely to be confused. Female could be mistaken for female Coqui, although latter has black stripe above eye and border to throat (only faint necklace in race *buckleyi* of White-throated), stronger and broader underparts barring, tawny-buff breast (compare richly-coloured race *dewittei* of White-throated) and has rufous wash only to primaries, not entire wing as in White-throated. Range does not overlap with Schlegel's Francolin, although the two almost meet in Cameroon; the latter species has whitish, barred underparts and the entire upperparts, not just wings, rufous.

DESCRIPTION *F. a. albogularis.* Bill black with yellow base. Irides brown. Legs orange-yellow. Sexes differ in underparts markings; male has one spur, female virtually unspurred. **Adult male:** Crown mottled grey and rufous; supercilium and lores whitish; ear-coverts greyish; throat white. Head-sides, neck, breast and underparts buff with sparse rufous streaking on breast and flanks. Upperparts dark greyish-brown with fine buff streaks and faint barring, wing-coverts and flight feathers rufous, the rufous almost concealed when on ground but conspicuous in flight. Limited variation exists as some are distinctly rufous on mantle as well as wings. More richly coloured race *dewittei* has chestnut breast and much warmer buff underparts. **Adult female:** Similar to male, but duller with fine dark and whitish barring on breast and flanks. **Juvenile:** Resembles female but underparts more extensively barred.

GEOGRAPHICAL VARIATION Three races generally recognised.

F. a. albogularis Hartlaub, 1854 occurs in Senegambia; described above.

F. a. buckleyi Ogilvie-Grant, 1892 (includes *gambagae*) occurs in E Côte d'Ivoire to Cameroon; male has buff, not whitish, supercilium; female has underparts barring extending onto belly and forming diffuse border to lower throat.

F. a. dewittei Chapin, 1937 (includes *meinertzhageni*)

199

occurs SE Zaire, E Angola and adjacent NW Zambia; male has much richer, reddish-buff underparts becoming dark chestnut on breast, and female is entirely barred on lower underparts.

MEASUREMENTS Length 23–25 cm. Sexes similar, male usually slightly larger. *F. a. albogularis* given. Males: wing 129–141 (mean 135). Females: wing 122–131 (mean 127), tarsus 37–39 (mean 38). Weight (both sexes) 263–284.

HABITAT Open savanna and rolling, hilly country with sparse scrub cover, favouring recently burnt areas for feeding; also in disused, scrubby fields but avoids active cultivation. Locally in more heavily wooded savanna grassland.

VOICE Advertising call a high-pitched, strident *ter-ink-inkity-ink*, more rapid in delivery than Coqui; another call is a two-syllable *ter-ink, ter-ink* again not unlike *co-qui* of Coqui but faster. Also a distinctive *che-cheer-che, che-cheer-che* and a *kili-kili-kili*. Some references mention a penetrating whistle.

HABITS Usually in pairs or small parties in open grassland. Shy and wary, very difficult to flush but flies strongly on whirring wings, with extended neck, if put-up. Prefers to escape by slinking away through grass. Feeds in open on bare ground, disused cultivation and tracks through grassland. Roosts and calls from ground.

BREEDING Probably monogamous. Nest a scrape in open, lined with grass and leaves. Mean clutch 6, but 4–7 recorded; eggs buff to pale brown with fine speckling. Lays September–October in Senegambia, June in Nigeria and October–December in Zaïre, most usually at end of dry season and start of rains, but breeding reported towards end of rainy season in E Sénégal.

DISTRIBUTION From S Sénégal, E Gambia and Guinea, east through drier parts of W Africa to extreme N Cameroon (Benue Plain). Isolated populations occur much further south in SE Zaïre (Marungu to Upemba National Park), E Angola (E Moxico) and adjacent Zambia (NW Balovale).

STATUS Local and uncommon, most numerous in Tambacounda region of Sénégal and C Nigeria. Very scarce at edges of range (e.g. few recent records from The Gambia) with relict southern populations most at risk and no recent reports from Zambia.

REFERENCES Barlow *et al.* (1997), Urban *et al.* (1986).

---

25   SCHLEGEL'S FRANCOLIN
Francolinus schlegelii Heuglin, 1863   Plate 9

Alternative name: Schlegel's Banded Francolin.

Rare and little-known francolin of wooded savanna in C Africa, which has a close association with the 'Ka' tree. Unlike Coqui and White-throated, the sexes are similar.

IDENTIFICATION Combination of buff head-sides and throat, finely barred pale buffish or whitish underparts and rufous upperparts render this small francolin virtually unmistakable. Most closely resembles male Coqui but ranges do not overlap, and latter has greyish-brown ground colour to upperparts, finer white shaft streaks above and some races have central underparts unbarred whitish. Range almost meets White-throated in Cameroon, female of latter has barred breast and flanks, with a buffier background, a clear white throat and rufous normally confined to wings, occasionally extending onto mantle. If flushed, look for duller brown primaries that should contrast with rufous of rest of wing; in White-throated the primaries are rufous.

DESCRIPTION Bill black with yellow base. Irides brown. Legs yellow. Sexes similar: male has single spur, female almost unspurred. **Adult male:** Crown mottled rufous and grey; lores and ear-coverts grey-brown; supercilium and rest of head and neck ochre-buff. Breast and rest of underparts whitish with close dark barring and rufous blotching on flanks. Upperparts chestnut with buff shaft streaks, scapulars and tertials with black blotches and rump and uppertail-coverts vermiculated with blackish; rufous wing-coverts and secondaries contrast with dull brown primaries. **Adult female:** Similar, but breast and belly barring broken, appearing mottled, and narrower white streaks on browner and more black-blotched upperparts. **Juvenile:** Resembles female, but mantle and scapulars more strongly barred with rufous and black.

GEOGRAPHICAL VARIATION None recognised, but has been treated as a race of Coqui Francolin by some authorities.

MEASUREMENTS Length 22–25 cm. Sexes similar but male usually slightly larger. Males: wing 121–133 (mean 128), tarsus 34–41 (mean 37), weight c.251. Females: wing 118–126 (mean 123), tarsus 31–37 (mean 34), weight c.223.

HABITAT Well-wooded grassland, especially favouring low thick areas of grass within scrubby woodland. Occasionally visits edges of cultivation.

VOICE Advertising call resembles Coqui and White-throated Francolins, but is faster and lower pitched: *ter, ink, terrra*. Other calls undocumented, but reportedly gives a soft *korrr-korrr-korrr*, especially at dusk.

HABITS Probably similar to Coqui, but information sparse. Shy and wary, shunning habitation. Usually in pairs or small parties, but occasionally reported accompanying other francolin species. Closely associated with the 'Ka' tree *Isoberinia doka*, at least in Sudan, feeding on ground on its leaves, but extent of association unstudied. Roosts on ground, beneath trees, huddled together and facing opposite directions.

BREEDING Probably monogamous. Nest a scrape lined with leaves. Clutch 2–5 creamy eggs. Breeds in Sudan in September–November.

DISTRIBUTION C Africa, from NC Cameroon (Adamawa plateau), through S Chad and N Central African Republic to SW Sudan (Bahr el Ghazal).

STATUS Little known. Apparently uncommon or rare

and decidedly local throughout range, but no studies of populations or threats.

REFERENCE Urban *et al.* (1986).

---

26 LATHAM'S FRANCOLIN
Francolinus lathami (Hartlaub, 1854)   Plate 8

Alternative names: Latham's Forest Francolin, Forest Francolin.

A distinctive, but shy and uncommon, species of equatorial forests. Its very dark overall coloration is an anomaly within the *Peliperdix* group but an ideal adaptation to the species' forest environment.

IDENTIFICATION A small dark forest francolin; the combination of blackish or dark brownish plumage and pale head-sides is unique in most of its range, but in NE Zaïre it overlaps with the very localised Nahan's Francolin, which has red (not yellow) legs, lacks pale head-sides or rufous in upperparts, has bare red skin around eye and similarly plumaged sexes (female much browner than male in Latham's).

DESCRIPTION *F. l. lathami.* Bill black. Irides brown. Legs yellow. Sexes differ, but share similar basic pattern; female has no, or short, spur, male single spurred. **Adult male:** Blackish neck and underparts with prominent white spotting, striking whitish or pale greyish-buff head-sides, contrasting with blackish throat and eye-stripe. Upperparts greyish-brown barred and mottled rufous, duller on rump and uppertail-coverts; upper mantle blacker with white spotting. **Adult female:** Blackish parts of male plumage are brown, pale brownish face patch and upperparts mottled black; extensive white spotting on underparts as male. However, females of eastern race are distinctly rufous on head-sides and much less spotted below (see Geographical Variation). **Juvenile:** Resembles female, but has whitish throat and whiter central lower underparts, young females having more extensive white on lower underparts than males and white breast markings form streaks rather than spots.

GEOGRAPHICAL VARIATION Two subspecies.
  F. l. lathami Hartlaub, 1854 occurs in W and C Africa east to C Zaïre; described above.
  F. l. schubotzi Reichenow, 1912 occurs in E Zaïre and adjacent Sudan and Uganda; male whiter on head-sides and has darker chestnut markings on upperparts; female has buffish, rather than white, markings on underparts, almost unmarked rich reddish-brown breast and is distinctly rufous on head-sides.

MEASUREMENTS Length 24–26 cm. Sexes similar. *F. l. lathami* given. Males: wing 128–143 (mean 136), tarsus 37–49 (mean 41), weight (n=1) 254. Females:

wing 127–143 (mean 134), tarsus 37–51 (mean 41), weight (n=1) 284.

HABITAT Lowland primary forest and locally in dense secondary forest; reaches 1400 m in Uganda.

VOICE Advertising call a melodious dove-like *coo*, repeated three times, or a frequently repeated *kwee, coo, coo*. Others refer to a series of prolonged, uniform high-pitched whistles and a flute-like call. A low clucking contact note reported from individuals moving through the forest.

HABITS Very shy and difficult to observe, in pairs or family parties in forest undergrowth, keeping very much within cover. Occasionally feeds on forest tracks, especially after rain. Feeds by scratching in leaf-litter, chiefly on small invertebrates, especially ants and termites. Most active, and certainly most vocal, at night. Runs away through undergrowth if alarmed, or sits 'tight', very difficult to flush, but if surprised underfoot flies fast on whirring wings for only short distance. Probably roosts in trees. Calls from trees and ground.

BREEDING Probably monogamous. Eggs laid on dry leaves between forest tree buttresses, without constructing a true nest. Clutch usually 2, rarely 3, dark buff to rusty-brown eggs. Breeding season varies according to local conditions, probably chiefly in dry season; eggs reported December and February in Cameroon, January–February in Sierra Leone and Ghana, December–April in Zaïre, and August in Uganda.

DISTRIBUTION Lowland SW and C Africa, from Sierra Leone east to extreme W Uganda, south to Cabinda (Angola) at mouth of Congo River. Relict populations are known in S Sudan (Zande district) and SC Uganda (Mabira and Kifu Forests).

STATUS Uncommon, least so in Sierra Leone and Ghana. Shy and retiring habits make it less conspicuous than most francolins. Forest destruction is principal threat, but shooting and trapping are important factors in some areas. Populations in Sudan and Uganda possibly severely threatened as records are few, and their fragmentation suggests a broad decline at eastern edge of range.

REFERENCE Urban *et al.* (1986).

Alternative name: Kirk's Francolin (*rovuma* group).

The precise position of this widespread species has been much debated. Hall (1963) allied it with Ring-necked, but subsequent studies have indicated that the two are only superficially similar and it was placed in *Peliperdix* by Crowe *et al.* (1992).

IDENTIFICATION Striking head pattern, streaked neck and breast, plain or finely-streaked lower under-parts, red legs and cocked tail diagnostic. Most similar to Ring-necked, with which it overlaps in Uganda, but has barred breast, chestnut nape and yellow legs, and occurs in montane terrain.

DESCRIPTION *F. s. sephaena.* Bill black. Irides brown. Legs red. Sexes similar but female smaller and lacks spur (male has one spur). **Adult male:** Crown dark brown, mottled greyish; crown-sides and eye-stripe blackish, rear-crown feathers slightly ruffled (but often sleeked flat); supercilia whitish, almost meeting on nape. Throat whitish, head-sides, neck and upper breast dark rufous, closely spotted and streaked whitish, becoming blacker across breast in some races. Rest of underparts buffish, finely streaked whitish but black on flanks in some races. Upperparts warm rufous-brown with prominent creamy-buff shaft streaks, duller brown, almost unmarked rump and black tail, latter usually conspicuous in flight and when walking, as characteristically held cocked high. **Adult female:** Similar, but has narrower shaft streaks and more vermiculated upperparts. **Juvenile:** Resembles female but paler overall, with broader shaft streaks above.

GEOGRAPHICAL VARIATION Five races recognised, but several others described. Races occupy two groups that were formerly treated as separate species.

Crested Francolins (nominate group): lower underparts finely and usually indistinctly vermiculated.

F. s. *sephaena* (Smith, 1836) (includes *zuluensis*) occurs in S Africa north to S Mozambique, S Zimbabwe and S Botswana; described above.

F. s. *zambesiae* Mackworth-Praed, 1920 (includes *thompsoni, chobiensis* and *mababiensis*) occurs in Mozambique (except coast and south) west to Angola; underparts less strongly marked, back richer reddish-brown, but crown and nape paler.

F. s. *granti* Hartlaub, 1866 (includes *schoanus, ochrogaster, delutescens* and *jubaensis*) occurs in Ethiopia south to C Tanzania (except Horn of Africa and coastal E Africa); smaller, with weaker breast markings.

Kirk's Francolins (*rovuma* group): underparts finely streaked, most strongly in southern races.

F. s. *rovuma* Gray, 1867 occurs in coastal Kenya, south to N Mozambique and S Malawi; underparts strongly streaked.

F. s. *spilogaster* Salvadori, 1888 (includes *somaliensis*) occurs in Somalia, E Ethiopia and NE Kenya; larger than *rovuma*, with finer streaking below.

MEASUREMENTS Length 33–35 cm. Male slightly larger. F. s. *sephaena* given. Males: wing 137–170 (mean 154), tarsus 42–51 (mean 46), weight 320–417 (mean 368). Females: wing 135–166 (mean 145), tarsus 39–52 (mean 43), weight 280–350 (mean 315).

HABITAT Scrubby woodland with grassy areas, riverine thickets, often in relatively dry country but in most arid parts of range dependent on water. In Somalia occurs to 2200 m, but chiefly below 1500 m in most of range.

VOICE Advertising call: a loud, rapidly repeated (5–9 times), high-pitched, two-note cackle, the second note higher pitched, *kerra-kreek* or *kwerri-kwetchi.* Relatively noisy, sometimes even calling in heat of the day, but most vocal at dusk when several may call simultaneously.

HABITS In pairs or small parties of up to seven. Forages near cover, chiefly in early morning and evening, spending heat of day beneath bushes. Walks slowly and deliberately, cocking tail vertically like a bantam; runs rapidly into cover when disturbed, even perching in bushes and trees when pursued by predators. Roosts in trees. Flushes reluctantly, usually flying low only for short distance. Typically wary but if unmolested may become remarkably bold, in Somalia even feeding on outskirts of villages and towns.

BREEDING Monogamous. Nest a shallow depression lined with grasses, well concealed under a bush. Mean clutch 6 but 4–9 recorded. Eggs pinkish-white to cream, speckled pale brown. Season varies over wide range, but chiefly October–March in S Africa, May–July in Kenya and March–May in Ethiopia and Somalia (also August).

DISTRIBUTION E and S Africa, from SE Sudan, C Ethiopia and W Somalia, south through E Africa to the Transvaal. In S Africa extends west through Zimbabwe, S Zambia and E Botswana to NE Namibia; with an isolated population in SE Angola.

STATUS Locally numerous; wide range and local abundance indicates little overall threat to populations, but has decreased in coastal Kenya though habitat destruction.

REFERENCES Clancey (1967), Crowe *et al.* (1992), Hall (1963), Urban *et al.* (1986).

Subgenus *SCLEROPTILA*: red-winged francolins

Ring-necked Francolin *F. streptophorus*, Finsch's Francolin *F. finschi*, Greywing Francolin *F. africanus*, Red-wing Francolin *F. levaillantii*, Moorland Francolin *F. psilolaemus*, Shelley's Francolin *F. shelleyi* and Orange River Francolin *F. levaillantoides*.

Seven species of medium-sized francolins with vermiculated and buff-streaked upperparts, relatively short yellowish legs and blackish bills. The sexes are similarly plumaged in this group. Voices are more musical, less raucous than those of several other francolin groups. Generally they occur in relatively open, often rocky, habitats and where ranges overlap, species are separated by altitude. Relationships within this group are complicated by marked racial variation, certain races having been placed within different species to those given in this work.

28   RING-NECKED FRANCOLIN
Francolinus streptophorus Ogilvie-Grant, 1891   Plate 8

A localised E African species, with an isolated population in Cameroon. Once allied with Crested, recent studies indicate that it is closer to Finsch's and Redwing Francolins, with which it forms a superspecies.

IDENTIFICATION Combination of barred breast and chestnut head and neck-sides distinctive, but white throat and supercilium shared by Crested. Ring-necked, however, has yellow (not red) legs, a barred (not spotted) breast and unmarked area of chestnut on head and neck. Additionally, Crested, in area of overlap lacks dark flank stripes of Ring-necked and often carries its tail cocked.

DESCRIPTION Bill black with yellow base to lower mandible. Irides brown. Legs pale yellow. Sexes similar, both virtually unspurred. **Adult male:** Crown and nape dark grey-brown, supercilium whitish extending towards nape. Head and neck-sides unmarked reddish-chestnut, contrasting with white throat. Upper breast and lower neck white with black barring extending onto mantle and forming a broad collar. Underparts, below breast, buff with dark brown flank striping. Plain greyish-brown upperparts relieved by narrow buff shaft streaks. Tail and flight feathers grey-brown. **Adult female:** Similar but has pale edges to browner crown feathers and upperparts barred rufous-brown with broader pale shaft streaks than male. **Juvenile:** Apparently undocumented.

GEOGRAPHICAL VARIATION Monotypic.

MEASUREMENTS Length 35 cm. Sexes similar. Males: wing 141–167 (mean 150), tarsus 34–46 (mean 41), weight (n=2), 364 and 406. Females: wing 139–160 (mean 152), tarsus 36–50 (mean 42), no weight data.

HABITAT Stony hillsides with sparse grassy and scrub cover, and wooded grasslands at 600–1800 m. In N Uganda favours more vegetated wooded grasslands than Crested. In Cameroon occurs in uninhabited rocky hills covered by thin grass.

VOICE Advertising call distinctive: two soft dove-like *coos*, the second higher pitched, followed by a prolonged piping trill. A noisy flight call also given, but often flushes silently. No other calls described.

HABITS Very shy francolin of stony hillsides, preferring to escape by hard running. Usually in pairs or small (family?) parties. Spends most time within cover and shade of bushes, and is most likely to be seen in early morning by tracks and roadsides. Flushes reluctantly but flight reportedly extremely fast. Feeds at edges of cultivation. Calls usually given from low perch, such as a termite mound, early in morning.

BREEDING Probably monogamous. Nest a scrape, with little or no lining, situated at base of a rock. Clutch 4–5 greyish-buff eggs with finely dark-speckled pores. Reported April in Uganda and December –March in Kenya, apparently in dry season or at start of rains.

DISTRIBUTION E Africa, with an isolated population in W Cameroon (Foumban in highlands). In E Africa, occurs over much of N Uganda (from Kidepo National Park west to the Nile and south to Katonga Valley, also at foot of Mt Moroto), W Kenya (from south slopes of Mt Elgon to Samia Hills and Nyando Valley) and NW Tanzania (Kibondo and Kasulu). Mackworth-Praed & Grant (1957) report occurrence in extreme S Sudan, but this requires confirmation.

STATUS Uncommon and local over most of range, but shy and retiring nature makes it easily overlooked. Locally common in Gulu and Choa districts of Uganda, and fairly common in Tanzania. Rare and little known in Kenya, where scarcity of recent reports suggests that occurrences may only be sporadic.

REFERENCES Mackworth-Praed & Grant (1957), Urban *et al.* (1986), Zimmerman *et al.* (1996).

29   FINSCH'S FRANCOLIN
Francolinus finschi Bocage, 1881   Plate 11

A very local and little-known red-winged francolin of woodland in Zaïre and Angola.

IDENTIFICATION Relatively unmarked buff and brown francolin with whitish throat and rufous flight feathers the most striking features, although latter concealed when at rest. Unlikely to be confused with—

in its limited range, although it overlaps with Redwing Francolin in Angola. Latter, however, has more strongly patterned underparts and necklace of black and white scaling on upper breast.

DESCRIPTION Bill brownish-black, relatively long and stout. Irides brown. Legs yellowish-brown. Sexes similar, with single spur, but female has shorter spur than male. **Adult (both sexes):** Crown and nape greyish-brown; head and neck-sides rufous, contrasting with white throat. Upper breast grey-brown mottled buff; lower breast and belly buff, blotched chestnut; flanks greyer, barred rufous-buff and blotched chestnut. Upperparts dark grey-brown with buff shaft streaks and rufous-buff barring, primaries and outer secondaries rufous-chestnut with grey-brown tips. Tail brownish-grey, barred and vermiculated with buff. **Juvenile:** Undescribed.

GEOGRAPHICAL VARIATION Usually considered monotypic.

MEASUREMENTS Length 34–36 cm. Sexes similar. Males: wing 162–170 (mean 167), tarsus 43–54 (mean 49). Females: wing 158–174 (mean 166), tarsus 40–53 (mean 45). No weight data but estimated c.560.

HABITAT Wooded savanna, *Brachystegia* woodland; in Gungu district of Zaïre in grassland near gallery forest to 600 m, and on bare slopes above tree-line at 2100 m on Mt Moco in Angola.

VOICE Only described vocalisation, presumed to be the advertising call is a loud *wit-u-wit*.

HABITS Unstudied. Reported to be chiefly met with in pairs. Known to eat insects and seeds.

BREEDING Probably monogamous. Nest placed on ground within vegetation. Clutch c.5 pale brown eggs. Reported breeding January, March and July in Zaïre and June–August in Angola.

DISTRIBUTION Three discrete populations: by banks of Congo River on Congo–Zaïre border around Brazzaville and Kinshasa; S Zaïre in Gungu District; and C Angola from Cuanza Norte and S Malanje to N Huíla.

STATUS Near Threatened. No recent information from Angola but considered scarce there. One population was protected within Cagandala National Park but habitat there has probably been decimated during unstable political situation of recent decades. More numerous in Gungu district of S Zaire. No information from Congo.

REFERENCES Jean (2000), Urban *et al.* (1986).

30 GREYWING FRANCOLIN
Francolinus africanus (Stephens, 1819)   Plate 11

Alternative names: Grey-wing, Grey-winged Francolin.

A declining South African Francolin closely related to Redwing and Shelley's, with range overlapping that of former although preferring drier habitats.

IDENTIFICATION A closely vermiculated grey-brown francolin with few field marks, but finely broken-barred underparts and mottled whitish throat are important criteria. Overlaps with much more rufous Redwing Francolin, which has warm buff underparts with more extensive rufous blotching, whiter throat and chestnut primaries (only obvious in flight). Greywing has only faint rufous wash to primaries. Range only just meets that of Shelley's, which has whiter throat with definite mottled border, broader and coarser underparts markings (thus appearing less uniform greyish below) and broader rufous striping on flanks. Northern edge of range also meets Orange River Francolin, which has whiter throat with mottled border, buffish underparts with rufous streaking and rufous-toned upperparts.

DESCRIPTION Bill blackish-brown. Irides brown. Legs brownish-yellow. Sexes similar, although female unspurred (male has single spur). **Adult (both sexes):** Crown and nape dark brown, mottled rufous; supercilium and head- and neck-sides dull rufous; throat dull white, intensely mottled and becoming paler on chin; mottled greyish band down hindneck-sides. Breast tawny-buff, mottled chestnut and forming brighter band of colour contrasting with vermiculated dingy buff-white and dark of rest of underparts, although flanks blotched chestnut. Upperparts grey-brown with buff shaft streaks and dull rufous barring, rump and uppertail-coverts plainer. Wings grey-brown with very weak rufous wash to primaries. Tail

grey-brown, barred buff. **Juvenile:** Similar but duller, with finely barred, rather than mottled, whiter throat, and central underparts spotted (not barred).

GEOGRAPHICAL VARIATION Monotypic following Crowe & Crowe (1985). Former treatments included Moorland and northern races of Orange River Francolin within this species.

MEASUREMENTS Length 31–33 cm. Sexes similar. Males: wing 144–169 (mean 157), tarsus 38–48 (mean 43), weight 411–501. Females: wing 142–163 (mean 153), tarsus 37–47 (mean 42), weight 385–410.

HABITAT Low scrub and open grassy areas on rolling hillsides and hill tops at 1800–2750 m, locally to sea level in SW Cape.

VOICE Distinctive advertising call: a musical, high-pitched whistling *whee-hee-hee, wee-pe-ew* or *squea-kee-oo, squea-kee-oo*, repeated several times with short pauses. Coveys give soft whistling contact note and, when flushed, rise with a series of loud squeals.

HABITS Forages in small coveys of c.8, presumed to be family parties, but larger numbers sometimes congregate at favoured feeding spots. Feeds by digging with bill for bulbs and tubers. Most active in early morning and evening, spending hot part of day within bushy cover. Flushes relatively easily. Calls chiefly in early morning and evening from a low mound or boulder.

BREEDING Monogamous. Nest a scrape lined with grass and feathers placed under a grassy tuft. Mean clutch 5–7, but 3–10 and even 15 recorded, but latter possibly result of two females laying in same nest. Eggs yellowish-brown, sometimes speckled with brown and dark grey. Breeding reported July–

December in Cape and August–March in Natal, with peak in November–December.

DISTRIBUTION South Africa, from SE Transvaal, Swaziland and N Natal, Lesotho and Orange Free State (except north) west over most of Cape Province (except northwest).

STATUS Local and usually uncommon, most numerous in Cape Province and most uncommon in east of range, where it overlaps with Redwing Francolin, suggesting competition between the two species.

REFERENCES Crowe & Crowe (1985), Mentis and Bigalke (1980, 1981), Urban *et al.* (1986).

---

31   REDWING FRANCOLIN
Francolinus levaillantii (Valenciennes, 1825)   Plate 11

Alternative names: Levaillant's Red-winged Francolin, Levaillant's Francolin, Redwing.

A patchily distributed francolin that exhibits remarkably little racial variation despite its disjunct range. Closely related to Greywing, Finsch's and Ring-necked Francolins, with which it marginally overlaps.

IDENTIFICATION Bright rufous neck-sides and rufous-buff underparts contrast with black and white scaled necklace and unmarked rufous-buff and whitish throat (latter lacks border, therefore gives appearance of having only one, not two, mottled bands on neck-sides unlike several other species in this complex). In flight the extensively rufous primaries are conspicuous, but these are more or less hidden at rest. Shelley's has a neat mottled blackish border to white throat, wholly streaked chestnut breast, whiter underparts with coarse black markings and finer buff streaking above. **South Africa:** Greywing has underparts vermiculated grey-brown with less distinct rufous marks on flanks, lacks obvious rufous in primaries, has breast-band of chestnut markings and throat intensely speckled; Orange River has duller rufous neck-sides, dark border to white throat and breast streaked rufous, not scaled black and white. **Kenya:** localised Moorland has chestnut collar and rufous breast with black spotting, lacking scaled upper breast-band and collar of Redwing. **Angola:** Finsch's has similar rufous wings but is much plainer, with almost unmarked greyish-buff underparts, lacking a defined breast-band and collar.

DESCRIPTION *F. l. levaillantii.* Bill blackish-brown with yellower base to lower mandible, stouter and longer than similar francolins. Irides brown. Legs brownish-yellow. Sexes similar but female unspurred (male has single spur). **Adult (both sexes):** Crown and nape dark brown, mottled rufous; head- and neck-sides warm rufous-buff with band of dark mottling extending down centre of neck-sides to join breast-band; throat unmarked rufous-buff becoming whiter in centre, bordered below by band of dark and white scaling on upper breast, the latter encircling base of neck. Underparts below breast warm buff with extensive rufous blotching, most marked on flanks. Upperparts warm dark brown mottled blackish with prominent buff shaft-streaks, primaries and outer secondaries rufous-chestnut with grey-brown tips. Tail dark brownish-grey, finely barred rufous-buff. **Juvenile:** Similar but duller, with less distinct breast-band and collar (buffish and grey-scaled rather than black and white).

GEOGRAPHICAL VARIATION Two races recognised.

F. l. levaillantii (Valenciennes, 1825) (includes *crawshayi*) occurs in South Africa, N Malawi and NE Zambia; described above.
F. l. kikuyuensis Ogilvie-Grant, 1897 (includes *muleme, adolffriederici, benguellensis, clayi* and *momboloensis*) occurs in Angola, W Zambia, Zaïre and E Africa; breast-band narrower, lower breast well streaked with chestnut and central underparts heavily mottled blackish.

MEASUREMENTS Length 34–38 cm. Sexes similar. *F. l. levaillantii.* Male wing 149–171 (mean 162), tarsus 44–53 (mean 48), weight 492–560; female wing 140–168 (mean 158), tarsus 42–49 (mean 46), weight (n=2) 462, 515.

HABITAT Damp montane grassland on steep slope or in sheltered valley with reeds. Also rank grass by streams, scrubby woodland with grassy clearings and locally in grassy cultivation. Below 3000 m, even reaching coastal districts in Cape Province and Natal.

VOICE Advertising call: a series of c.5 musical, high-pitched, piping whistles, followed, after a short pause, by a slurred *heep,* i.e. *whee-hee-hee-hee-whee, heep,* which has also been rendered as *chirrya-cheep, chirrya-cheep, chirrya-cheep* or *pip-pip-peeep-peeep-peeep.* In Kenya rendered as a loud, chanting *ki-al-de-werk.* Female utters a quiet clucking when accompanying chicks. Also gives a *kourrr* in alarm and a loud, shrill squeal if flushed.

HABITS Apparently more confiding than many francolin species. Usually in small parties of up to ten, feeding on tracks and roadsides in early morning and evening. Runs readily if disturbed but flushes only reluctantly, often sitting very 'tight' until almost stepped on. Flight fast and low, generally for considerable distance if flushed. Feeds by digging with strong bill for bulbs and corms. Roosts on ground in small groups. Calls from ground.

BREEDING Monogamous. Nest a scrape lined with roots and grass, under a grassy tuft, often close to surface water. Mean clutch 5, but 3–12 recorded. Eggs olive-brown to yellowish-brown, speckled dark grey or brown, incubated for 22 days (n=1) by female alone. Season variable over wide range but March–July in Cape, December in Transvaal and further north reported to breed principally in rainy season or start of following dry season, e.g. August–March in Mpumalanga Province, South Africa. May nest twice per year.

DISTRIBUTION Local and patchy over S and E Africa, from western highlands of Kenya, S Uganda and adjacent former E Zaïre, Rwanda, Burundi and

NW Tanzania. Also extreme S Tanzania, adjacent N Malawi and NE Zambia with isolated populations in former SE Zaïre, W Zambia and highlands of C Angola. Most widespread in South Africa, from C and S Transvaal, through W Orange Free State and W and N Natal, Lesotho and Swaziland, and coastal mountains of Cape Province.

STATUS Local and uncommon over most of range, but quite common in parts of S Africa. However, even here range has contracted in recent decades due to habitat degradation, chiefly through overgrazing by domestic animals, scrub clearance and burning. Considerable decline in recent decades in Kenya through intensive agricultural development of upland grasslands.

REFERENCES Jansen *et al.* (2001), Urban *et al.* (1986), Zimmerman *et al.* (1996).

---

32   MOORLAND FRANCOLIN
Francolinus psilolaemus Gray, 1867
Plate 10

Alternative names: Montane Red-winged Francolin, Montane Francolin.

A very local francolin of montane heath in Ethiopia, with isolated populations in Kenya and Uganda.

IDENTIFICATION Overall dark buffish-brown high-elevation francolin, with mottled and freckled plumage and bright rufous wings (obvious in flight). Northern populations lack prominent plumage features, although southern populations have a distinct contrast between whitish throat and rufous neck and breast. Restricted range and montane habitat prevents confusion with most other francolins. In Ethiopia overlaps with Orange River, which has unmarked white throat, whiter underparts with fine black barring on lower underparts, and is greyer above. In Kenya overlaps with Redwing Francolin, which has barred black and white (not buff or rufous) nape and lower throat, lacks black breast spotting but has dark spotting on lower underparts. Shelley's also has overlapping range in Kenya but occurs at lower altitudes.

DESCRIPTION *F. p. psilolaemus.* Bill blackish-brown with yellow base to lower mandible. Irides brown. Legs pale yellow. Sexes alike, male with one spur, female unspurred. **Adult (both sexes):** Crown and nape brown, mottled buff, head- and neck-sides buff with profuse black freckling. Breast buff with black spotting, rest of underparts buff with chestnut blotching and fine dark freckling and barring. Upperparts dark brown, with rufous barring and buff shaft streaks, primaries and outer secondaries bright rufous, indistinctly tipped greyish-brown. Tail dark brown, barred warm buff. **Juvenile:** Apparently undescribed.

GEOGRAPHICAL VARIATION Two races recognised. Nominate formerly considered conspecific with Greywing Francolin and *elgonensis* as a race of Shelley's Francolin.

  F. p. psilolaemus Gray, 1867 (includes *ellenbecki*) occurs in Ethiopia; throat freckled, neck and breast dull buff, and smaller (male wing 150–176).

  F. p. elgonensis Ogilvie-Grant, 1896 (includes *theresae*) occurs in Kenya and Uganda; more rufous-buff on head, nape, neck and breast; throat almost unmarked white, and larger than nominate (male wing 168–180).

MEASUREMENTS Length 33–35 cm (*F. p. psilolaemus*), 37–40 cm (*F. p elgonensis*). Sexes similar. *F. p. psilolaemus* given, *elgonensis* larger. Males: wing 150–176 (mean 164), tarsus 38–51 (mean 45), weight (n=2) 510, 530. Females: wing 151–172 (mean 159), tarsus 40–48 (mean 44), weight (n=2) 370, 510.

HABITAT Montane heathland, moorland and grassland, generally at 2400–4000 m, but in Ethiopia locally as low as 1600 m.

VOICE Advertising call: a musical series of four notes, frequently repeated; described as very similar to Shelley's Francolin and, like that species, a calling bird will often trigger responses from others. Most vocal at dusk. When flushed, gives a series of shrill squealing cries as it 'explodes' from almost underfoot.

HABITS Usually in pairs or family parties. Shy and wary, preferring to feed within cover rather than in open. In Ethiopia, feeds in damp grassy areas and sedges by upland pools in open country. If alerted to danger peers above top of low grasses to watch intruder, ducking below cover and moving quietly away upon approach. Flushes reluctantly and only if hard-pressed, flying a considerable distance before dropping back into cover.

BREEDING Monogamous. Nest placed in rough grasses. Clutch 5; egg colour undocumented. Breeding reported most of year, but chiefly in first six months.

DISTRIBUTION Fragmented in E Africa. Mountains of C and SE Ethiopia (Shoa, Arussi, Bale, Sidamo); Mt Elgon on Kenya/Uganda border; and in Kenya also on Mt Kenya, the Aberdares and Mau Narok.

STATUS Generally uncommon and elusive throughout restricted range, apparently most numerous at Mau Narok and Mt Elgon, and not uncommon in parts of Ethiopia.

REFERENCE Urban *et al.* (1986).

33 SHELLEY'S FRANCOLIN
Francolinus shelleyi (Ogilvie-Grant, 1890)   **Plate 10**

Uncommon but widespread in southern half of E Africa, although records from many areas are inexplicably few.

IDENTIFICATION Combination of clear white throat (buffish in *whytei*), broken whitish eye-stripe, extensively chestnut breast, chestnut-striped flanks and barred black and white belly diagnostic (most obvious in nominate). Female Coqui has broader and clearer white eye-stripe running onto neck-sides, lacks chestnut breast and flanks striping and is smaller. Redwing has buff, spotted black, underparts, black and white mottled breast-band and collar, buffish throat and one, not two, mottled bands on neck-sides. **Kenya:** at lower altitudes than Moorland, which is more rufous and buff below, with dark spotting on breast. **South Africa:** marginally overlaps with Orange River, which is paler above and has buff central underparts that lack bold black markings; Greywing has closely barred and vermiculated grey-brown underparts, mottled throat patch and greyish primaries.

DESCRIPTION *F. s. shelleyi*. Bill black with yellow base to lower mandible. Irides brown. Legs dull yellow. Sexes similar, but female duller and virtually unspurred (male has one spur). **Adult (both sexes):** Crown and nape dark grey-brown, mottled greyish-buff; supercilium, head and neck-sides rufous-buff with band of dark mottled feathers down centre of neck-sides; broken whitish patch around eye, running back along head-sides. Throat white (buffish in *whytei*) with border of blackish mottling, widening lower down. Breast and collar chestnut with whitish streaking, and chestnut striping and blotching extending onto flanks. Rest of underparts whitish with blackish blotching and scaling on centre, becoming more finely barred lower down. Upperparts dark greyish-brown with cream shaft streaks, dark mottles and rufous-buff barring; uppertail-coverts plainer greyish-brown with weaker markings; primaries and outer secondaries bright rufous, indistinctly tipped greyish-brown. Tail grey-brown, finely barred buff. **Juvenile:** Similar, but rufous-buff barring on upperparts reduced or absent and black and white markings on underparts more broken.

GEOGRAPHICAL VARIATION Two races currently recognised; up to seven have been described, although most are now included within nominate as clinal or localised variants. Zimmerman *et al.* (1996) recognise *uluensis* and *macarthuri* as valid forms.

F. s. shelleyi Ogilvie-Grant, 1890 (includes *uluensis, macarthuri, canidorsalis, trothae* and *sequestris*) occurs over most of range; described above.

F. s. whytei Neumann, 1908 occurs in SE Zaïre, N Zambia and N Malawi; throat patch buffer, underparts less heavily marked black and white, and narrower mottling at lower border to throat patch.

MEASUREMENTS Length 33–35 cm. Sexes similar. *F. s. shelleyi* given. Males: wing 152–177 (mean 162), tarsus 37–47 (mean 42), weight 420–480. Females: wing 145–172 (mean 157), tarsus 35–47 (mean 40), weight 392–460.

HABITAT Open montane and hilly grasslands, and open woodland, preferring areas with rocky outcrops, including wooded gorges in Kenya. Intolerant of heavy grazing and burning of grassland, but in some areas visits light cultivation. Although southernmost populations occur in coastal hills, is chiefly an upland species, reaching 2200 m in Zimbabwe, and 3000 m in E Africa.

VOICE Advertising call: a musical series of four notes, frequently repeated, with a longer pause between second and third notes, rendered as *I'll-drink-yer-beer* or *klee-klee-kleer* or *ski-UK skiski-eu*. Initial calling bird usually sparks off a response from several others. Only other call reported is a shrill squeal of alarm when flushed.

HABITS Usually in pairs or small parties. Digs for roots and bulbs, creating cone-shaped holes up to 5 cm deep in ground. Runs readily if disturbed but flushes only reluctantly, often sitting very 'tight' until almost stepped on and almost impossible to flush a second time, despite flying only a short distance. Roosts on ground in small groups. Calls from ground.

BREEDING Probably monogamous. Nest a scrape lined with roots and grass, under a grassy tuft or among rocks. Mean clutch 4–5, but up to 7 recorded. Eggs pinkish-white to creamy-buff, sometimes finely spotted. Timing variable over wide range but prefers the dry season.

DISTRIBUTION Relatively patchy. Northernmost population occurs in SC Kenya and N Tanzania; apart from three specimens from S Uganda and a scatter of records from interior Tanzania there appears to be a gap in its range. The central population ranges through Malawi, N Zambia and SE Zaïre. Another occupies C Zambia, extending into S Zaïre and most of Zimbabwe (except extreme south and west). Southern populations occur from S Mozambique to NE Transvaal and most of Natal.

STATUS Relatively uncommon over most of range, but locally common. Range has contracted in many areas through overgrazing and scrub clearance, especially by burning.

REFERENCES Meyer (1971), Urban *et al.* (1986), Zimmerman *et al.* (1996).

34   ORANGE RIVER FRANCOLIN
Francolinus levaillantoides (Smith, 1836)   **Plate 10**

Alternative names: Smith's Francolin (nominate), Archer's Greywing (*lorti* = '*archeri*'), Rüppell's Francolin (*gutturalis*), Acacia Francolin.

This species includes two widely separated populations, in NE and SW Africa. The northern group was formerly treated within Greywing Francolin and the northernmost form, *gutturalis*, may be worthy of species status. This indicates the confusion that exists over the correct allocation of many taxa within the 'red-winged' complex.

IDENTIFICATION Variable over its wide and disjunct range, with useful characters varying according to overlapping species; southern (but not northern) forms have extensive rufous flight feathers, and all are merely finely barred over lower central underparts. **Southern Africa:** range marginally overlaps with Greywing, which has mottled throat, lacking border, vermiculated greyish underparts and is duller grey-brown above, including flight feathers. Redwing has one (not two) mottled bands down brighter rufous neck-sides, with rufous extending onto upper 'shoulder', a buffish throat and scaled black and white breast and nape. Shelley's also marginally overlaps, but is darker above and has bolder black barring and markings on central underparts. **Northern races:** overlaps with Moorland in Ethiopia, which has buff, black-speckled throat, neck and breast, buffier underparts and more rufous flight feathers. Most northerly race, *gutturalis*, overlaps with no similar species.

DESCRIPTION *F. l. levaillantoides* (with references to other southern populations). Bill brownish-black with yellowish base. Irides brown. Legs dull yellow. Sexes similar: male has one spur, much shorter in female. **Adult (both sexes):** Head and neck-sides buff with band of black and white mottles running back from eye down neck-sides; throat white with border of black and white mottling, forming a narrow gorget on upper breast; breast and underparts buff with intense chestnut blotching and streaking across breast, extending onto flanks in most forms. However, races of C and N Botswana and Namibia have pale sandy-buff ground colour to head and underparts, and *jugularis* of N Namibia and Angola has extensive black and white mottled breast-band. All forms have grey-brown upperparts with chestnut blotching (less extensive in pale populations) and buff shaft streaks, primaries and outer secondaries bright rufous, indistinctly tipped greyish-brown. Tail grey-brown, barred and vermiculated with buff. **Juvenile:** Less defined throat border and irregular black barring on underparts.

GEOGRAPHICAL VARIATION Complex, up to 15 races described, but Urban *et al.* (1986) recognise just four. Distinctive Eritrean race *gutturalis* (Rüppell's Francolin) may be a full species. Due to the less extensive rufous in their wings northern races have been treated as races of Greywing Francolin.

Southern races:
    F. l. levaillantoides Smith, 1836 (includes *pallidior*,

ludwigi, *gariepensis*, *watti*, *langi* and *kalaharica*) occurs in S Africa, north to C Namibia; described above. Southern populations are darkest in southeast of range, with palest forms (*pallidior*, *langi* and *kalaharica*) in north and west, *kalaharica* of C Botswana being extremely pale and sandy with much reduced chestnut markings on underparts.
    F. l. jugularis Büttikoffer, 1889 (includes *cunenensis* and *stresemanni*) occurs in N Namibia to Angola; broad breast-band of black and white scaling, whitish underparts and very few chestnut marks on flanks.

Northern races:
Eritrean race *gutturalis* (Rüppell's Francolin) has white throat, lacking border or band of mottling down neck-sides; head and neck-sides rufous; breast greyish-buff with intense chestnut streaking, rest of underparts buff with much black streaking, interspersed by chestnut blotching on flanks. Other northern populations closer to southern forms but with greyer flight feathers, both throat border and band down neck-sides well defined, especially latter; underparts very pale, almost unmarked below chestnut-streaked breast and flanks, except for fine barring or streaking on lower underparts.
    F. l. gutturalis (Rüppell, 1835) (includes *eritreae*) occurs in Eritrea; see above, a very distinct form.
    F. l. lorti Sharpe, 1897 (includes *archeri*, *stantoni* and *friedmanni*) occurs in Sudan, Uganda, S Ethiopia and N Somalia; finer dark markings on lower underparts and greyer flight feathers than southern races.

MEASUREMENTS Length 33–35 cm. Sexes similar. *F. l. levaillantoides* given. Males: wing 142–173 (mean 163), tarsus 39–48 (mean 43), weight 370–538. Females: wing 146–175 (mean 160), tarsus 37–48 (mean 41), weight 379–450.

HABITAT Dry grassland, with or without shrubby cover, dry woodland and grassy, boulder-strewn mountainsides. Reaches c.2500 m in Ethiopia and Uganda.

VOICE Advertising call: similar to Shelley's Francolin, but faster with briefer pauses between notes. A screeching *weecheele-weecheele-weecheele*, *pirrie-perrie* or *ki-be-til-ee*, repeated 5–9 times. Also gives typical 'redwing' squeal of alarm if flushed.

HABITS Shy and elusive. Calls repeatedly toward dawn and dusk; spends little time feeding in open and is therefore far more often heard than seen. Usually in pairs or small parties of up to 12. Flushes very reluctantly, preferring to escape by running away through vegetation and even reported to hide in burrows of ground-dwelling mammals.

BREEDING Monogamous. Nest a scrape under tussock of grass. Clutch 5–8. Eggs pale pink to yellowish-brown, sometimes speckled brown. Timing varies over wide range, e.g. February–May and September–

October in Transvaal, June in Namibia, April, August and December in Angola, February, April and August in Ethiopia, and May–June in Somalia.

DISTRIBUTION Two groups of races, in NE and SW Africa. Southern populations occur from SE Angola, through C Namibia and C Botswana to N South Africa (W and S Transvaal, Orange Free State, Lesotho and N Cape Province). Northern races fragmented: an isolated population in extreme SE Sudan and NE Uganda (Kidepo Valley and Mt Moroto); more extensively from southern highlands of Ethiopia to N Somalia and Djibouti, with an isolated population (*gutturalis*) in Eritrea and Tigre (Ethiopia).

STATUS Reportedly not uncommon in parts of Ethiopia, but no recent records from Djibouti or Sudan. In Somalia known only from the upper Guban and Warsangelle areas where not uncommon. In Uganda more or less confined to Mt Moroto. Southern populations locally not uncommon; stable and perhaps increasing in Namibia and possibly Botswana; distinctly local and uncommon in South Africa with no recent records from Lesotho, upper limit of population in NW Cape estimated at 500,000 but considered to be in decline.

REFERENCES Ash & Miskell (1998), Clancey (1967), Dean (2000), Urban *et al.* (1986).

Subgenus *ACENTRORTYX*: Nahan's Francolin

Despite basic plumage similarity to Latham's Francolin, this species is only distantly related to the latter, and some authorities have even doubted whether Nahan's is a true francolin. Crowe *et al.* (1992) erected its own monotypic subgenus, *Acentrortyx*, within *Pternistis*.

35 NAHAN'S FRANCOLIN
Francolinus nahani Dubois, 1905   Plate 8

Alternative name: Nahan's Forest Francolin.

A rare and little-known dark francolin of C African forests.

IDENTIFICATION Blackish francolin of forest undergrowth in C Africa. Most easily separated from similar Latham's by lack of whitish head-sides (although throat centre whitish), duller less rufous, brown upperparts and by red bare skin around eye and red (not yellow) legs. Perhaps inseparable if poorly seen in forest undergrowth as both are basically blackish below, but another useful clue is that sexes of Latham's differ (especially in eastern race *schubotzi*, which overlaps with Nahan's) whereas sexes are the same in Nahan's.

DESCRIPTION Bill blackish with red base. Irides brown. Extensive area of bare red skin around eye. Legs red. Sexes similar, both unspurred. **Adult (both sexes):** Blackish head, neck and underparts with white mottling, scaling and streaking on throat, foreneck and entire underparts, although blackish-brown coloration predominates and typically appears very blackish overall in forest shade. Back, mantle and scapulars blackish with extensive warm brown barring and vermiculations; rump and uppertail-coverts dull brown with fine black barring; wing-coverts warm brown, each feather with buff central spot; flight feathers dull brown, secondaries extensively barred blackish. **Juvenile:** Similar, but legs duller and greyer, white streaking on neck does not extend to hindneck, and flanks and breast marbled brownish.

GEOGRAPHICAL VARIATION Monotypic.

MEASUREMENTS Length 23–26 cm. Sexes similar. Males: wing 129–141 (mean 135), tarsus 35–41 (mean 37), weight (n=2) 308 and 312. Females: wing 128–142 (mean 135), tarsus 34–41 (mean 37), weight (n=3) 234–260.

HABITAT Dense lowland rainforest, at 1000–1400 m. In Uganda, favours dense vegetation in secondary forest, especially in swampy areas.

VOICE Territorial call a fluid build-up of pairs of notes, gradually rising in frequency and volume, lasting 7–10 seconds, sometimes 16–20 seconds. In Budongo Forest, Uganda, most vocal between 07:30 hrs and 08:30 hrs.

HABITS Poorly known. Very shy and difficult to observe, most observations are of pairs or small groups of up to five, rarely seven. Appears even more retiring than Latham's, keeping to cover of dense undergrowth, apparently loath to venture onto forest tracks. Scratches in leaf-litter and has been noted feeding in association with groups of Crested Guineafowl *Guttera pucherani*.

BREEDING Probably monogamous. Two nests in Uganda were on ground by tree buttresses, partially obscured by vines or epiphytes. The only other nest reported was in tree hollow c.1 m above ground. Clutch 4 (two nests). Eggs pinkish-buff, speckled with pale brown and purple. Individuals in breeding condition taken in April in Uganda and the two nests there had eggs in August and October.

DISTRIBUTION Very local in NE Zaïre (area bounded by Aruwimi, Nepoko and Semliki Rivers) and W and EC Uganda (in Kibale, Bugoma, Budongo and Mabira Forests).

STATUS Endangered. Always rare, its shy nature and limited range make this one of Africa's least known gamebirds. It is less often seen than Latham's, which is highly inconspicuous. Few reports between 1960 and

1990, but since then occurrence reconfirmed in Ituri Forest in Zaïre and, in Uganda, research undertaken in 1996 in Budongo and Mabira Forest Reserves has demonstrated it to be present in reasonably significant numbers (despite continued logging in these forestry managed reserves). Fieldwork in Kibale Forest in February–May 1998 failed to locate the species. Baiting forest trails with grain is evidently successfully employed by hunters to entice them into the open (the species and its eggs are considered to make good eating, and its feathers are used for decorative purposes), but recent work in Uganda used tape playback.

REFERENCES BirdLife International (2000), Collar *et al.* (1994), Crowe *et al.* (1992), Dranzoa *et al.* (1997, 1999), Mackworth-Praed & Grant (1970), Plumptre (1996), Urban *et al.* (1986).

Subgenus *PTERNISTIS* (part): vermiculated francolins

Hartlaub's Francolin *F. hartlaubi*, Double-spurred Francolin *F. bicalcaratus*, Clapperton's Francolin *F. clappertoni*, Heuglin's Francolin *F. icterorhynchus*, Harwood's Francolin *F. harwoodi*, Red-billed Francolin *F. adspersus*, Cape Francolin *F. capensis*, Hildebrandt's Francolin *F. hildebrandti* and Natal Francolin *F. natalensis*.

Members of this large group have dull brownish or greyish-brown upperparts, intensely vermiculated or streaked with buff, lacking strong rufous tones; underparts of many have buff markings. Bills and legs orange or reddish, the latter with two spurs. Apart from Hartlaub's and Hildebrandt's, sexual differences are not striking, although females tend to be smaller than males. Members of this group have raucous, grating calls.

36   HARTLAUB'S FRANCOLIN
Francolinus hartlaubi Bocage, 1869   Plate 11

An uncommon francolin of SW Africa, most easily seen in early morning as it calls from a prominent *kopje*.

IDENTIFICATION Striking sexual dimorphism, small size and close association with rocky outcrops are important identification criteria. Rufous underparts of female and whitish, streaked, underparts of male diagnostic within range. Overlaps with Red-billed and Orange River Francolins.

DESCRIPTION Upper mandible brownish, lower yellowish; bill disproportionately stout and curved. Irides brown. Legs yellow. Sexes strikingly different: male spurs are flattened growths rather than obvious spurs, female has small knobs. **Adult male:** Head, neck and underparts whitish, washed buff and rufous on flanks and undertail-coverts, with extensive dark shaft streaks over entire underparts; ear-coverts rufous, crown and nape dark grey-brown. Upperparts dark grey-brown, streaked, vermiculated and barred rufous-buff. Flight feathers grey-brown vermiculated buff on outer webs. Tail dusky-rufous, paler towards base. **Adult female:** Upperparts similar to male, but head, neck and entire underparts dull rufous, mottled grey across breast, lacking streaking. **Juvenile:** Resembles appropriate sex of adult but young males have narrower and more broken (barred) upperparts streaking and fine buff streaking on underparts; young females have flight feathers more intricately peppered and barred.

GEOGRAPHICAL VARIATION Slight. Races *bradfieldi* and *crypticus* not recognised here. Differences largely clinal but central populations often darker than those from further north or south.

MEASUREMENTS Length 26–28 cm. Male distinctly larger. Males: wing 131–172 (mean 143), tarsus 34–57 (mean 38), weight 245–290. Females: wing 131–148 (mean 135), tarsus 32–40 (mean 35), weight 210–240.

HABITAT Dry grassy hills with granite escarpments, scrub and prominent rock outcrops.

VOICE Advertising call: duet between sexes, combining harsh, grating cackles with high squeaks *kor-rack, keerya, keerya, kew*, the middle two notes repeated several times. Alarm a high, squeaky *kerr-ack* from male, and high *keer* from female. When flushed, male utters a chattering repeated *krak*.

HABITS In small coveys of 3–4 on rocky outcrops (*kopjes*) in bushy country. Close association with rocky outcrops important, usually a pair and previous year's offspring live around their territorial *kopje*. In heat of day, shelters in shadow of ledges and shelves among rocks. Most active early morning and evening when pair duet from highest point of *kopje*. Roosts among rocks. When flushed flies around corner of rocks or runs to far side of outcrop. Digs for bulbs and roots with its large bill. Interesting social relationships: defends territory by duet-calling rather than male undertaking physical disputes with rivals, and both sexes perform courtship behaviour, which is less male dominated than in most gamebirds.

BREEDING Monogamous. Nest a well-hidden hollow on *kopje* ledge, but only one described. Clutch 4–8 creamy eggs. Breeds May–June and November in Namibia.

DISTRIBUTION SW Africa, from Benguela and SW Huíla districts of SW Angola south over northern W Namibia (south to Rehoboth).

STATUS Generally local and uncommon, but few data on numbers.

REFERENCE Komen and Myer (1984).

37 DOUBLE-SPURRED FRANCOLIN
Francolinus bicalcaratus (Linnaeus, 1766)

Plate 14

Widespread in W Africa with a relict population north of the Sahara in Morocco.

IDENTIFICATION The most abundant francolin in W Africa. Distinctive combination of dull greenish legs and bill, white supercilium contrasting with black forehead and crown-sides, and mottled black and rufous underparts with narrow, wavy whitish flanks stripes. Confusion unlikely, if seen reasonably well, but compare more localised Ahanta Francolin, which has red, not dull greenish, legs and less contrasting head pattern. Range almost meets closely related Heuglin's in east and Clapperton's in northeast, but former has yellow legs and facial skin, and latter has bare parts red. In Morocco, only similar species is Barbary Partridge, but latter has vertical flank barring and rufous, not dull brown, tail in flight.

DESCRIPTION *F. b. bicalcaratus*. Bill olive-green with darker upper mandible. Irides brown. Legs olive-green. Sexes similar: male has two spurs absent in female; some females are buffier, less whitish, on face and throat. **Adult (both sexes):** Crown and nape reddish-brown with blackish forehead and crown-sides; supercilium white with black eye-stripe before eye; head-sides and neck whitish with dusky shaft streaks, becoming clearer buffish-white on throat. Neck, breast and entire underparts chestnut with black and white spotting and buffish-white streaks forming undulating narrow, pale stripes on flanks. Upperparts brown finely mottled black, becoming warm brown on hindneck, rump and uppertail; buff shaft streaks to upperparts, except rump and uppertail-coverts. Flight feathers grey-brown, irregularly mottled and streaked buff. Tail grey, barred brown. **Juvenile:** Duller with underparts less clearly marked and flanks more barred.

GEOGRAPHICAL VARIATION Several races described but variation clinal, with darkest birds in wetter biotopes. Urban *et al.* (1986) recognise just two subspecies.

   F. b. bicalcaratus (Linnaeus, 1766) (includes *thornei, adamauae* and *ogilvie-granti*) occurs in most of species' range; described above.
   F. b. ayesha Hartert, 1917 occurs in Morocco; usually larger, darker and more rufous, both above and below, than nominate populations. La Perche (1992) afforded it specific status but as differences are minor this appears unwarranted.

MEASUREMENTS Length 31–34 cm. Male larger. *F. b. bicalcaratus* given. Males: wing 157–185 (mean 170), tarsus 44–65 (mean 56), mean weight 507. Females: wing 142–179 (mean 159), tarsus 43–61 (mean 52), mean weight 381.

HABITAT Various types of bushy and scrubby cover in relatively open country, from scrubby woodland clearings, bushy stream-sides and scrubby cultivation to dry and humid bushy savannas; often near villages and active cultivation.

VOICE Advertising call: rather variable and perhaps geographically significant. In Morocco a far-carrying, deep, grating, repeated *krrrak...krrrak*. In tropical W Africa, variously described as a loud, harsh *kor-ker, kor-ker*, also *kokoye-kokoye* and *bebbrek-ek-kek kek-kek Koak Koak* (final notes loudest and furthest carrying, and possibly same as voice attributed to Moroccan race). Also an irregular *ee-Tek*, the first syllable very quiet, a grating *quare quare* and low croaking when flushed.

HABITS A cover-loving francolin that remains close to dense bush. In Morocco encountered in pairs or small parties of up to 12, but in W Africa may form coveys of up to 40 in areas where numerous. Most readily located by distinctive voice, which is uttered from low perch, such as stunted tree or mound, in early morning and evening. Feeds in open and on tracks in early morning and evening, although active throughout day in rainy season. Otherwise in dense cover and flushes extremely reluctantly, preferring to run away through undergrowth. Roosts in trees after walking to favoured drinking spots in late afternoon.

BREEDING Probably monogamous. Nest a scrape, lined with grass, leaves, twigs and feathers, under bush or tuft of grass. Mean clutch 6 sandy or yellowish-buff eggs, occasionally spotted dark. Mid-February to June (chiefly March–April) in Morocco, January–May and August–December in Senegambia, and in rainy season in drier parts of range.

DISTRIBUTION Tiny relict population in W Morocco. Elsewhere, in bushy country of W sub-Saharan Africa north to N Sénégal, C Mali and SW Niger west to SW Chad and south to N Cameroon.

STATUS Moroccan subspecies endangered by hunting and habitat degradation. Now very local, recently declared extinct in former stronghold of Forest of Marmora and almost gone from Sous, only surviving in reasonable numbers southeast of Rabat where protected. A captive-breeding programme has been initiated. Nominate race, in rest of range, only locally threatened by hunting and overgrazing, being the most numerous francolin over most of W Africa.

REFERENCES Cramp & Simmons (1980), de la Perche (1992), Urban *et al.* (1986).

38   CLAPPERTON'S FRANCOLIN
Francolinus clappertoni Children, 1826   Plate 14

Northern representative of superspecies including Harwood's, Double-spurred and Heuglin's Francolins; red legs and facial skin of Clapperton's prevent confusion with all but the first.

IDENTIFICATION Differs from Double-spurred and Heuglin's in red legs and obvious bare skin around eye; range not known to overlap with Double-spurred but does so with Heuglin's in SW Sudan, where yellow legs and less distinct facial skin of latter are useful distinctions. Range possibly meets very localised Harwood's in C Ethiopia, which see for discussion. In E Uganda almost meets Hildebrandt's, which replaces it in Kenya, but latter lacks red patch around eye and has striking sexual differences. Large size and streaked appearance suggests Yellow-necked Francolin, but confusion unlikely if seen well.

DESCRIPTION Bill black with red base to lower mandible. Irides brown. Bare skin around eye red and quite conspicuous. Legs red. Sexes similar: male has two spurs, one or none in female. **Adult (both sexes):** Crown, nape and ear-coverts reddish-brown; head-sides and neck whitish with fine dark streaks; throat and supercilium unmarked whitish; dark moustachial varies in intensity. Breast and rest of underparts buffish-white, each feather has blackish-brown centre creating heavily spot-streaked appearance. Upperparts greyish-brown with close pale buff scaling formed by pale feather fringes. **Juvenile:** Much as adult but upperparts barring more broken and less clear.

GEOGRAPHICAL VARIATION None recognised, although extreme northeast populations (*sharpii, testis, konnigseggi* and *nigrosquamatus*) lack dark moustachial and eastern birds have underparts more heavily marked than those in west (*cavei, gedgii, heuglini* and nominate).

MEASUREMENTS Length 33–35 cm. Male larger. Males: wing 170–193 (mean 180), tarsus 57–72 (mean 64), mean weight 604. Females: wing 150–178 (mean 166), tarsus 48–63 (mean 56), mean weight 463.

HABITAT Various types of dry savanna and sandy grassland with bushes and small trees, locally in dry cultivation and on rocky hillsides. From sea level to 2300 m.

VOICE Similar to Double-spurred and Heuglin's Francolins. Advertising call: a far-carrying grating *kerak*, repeated up to 6 times, often followed by 4–5 short *kek* notes. A two-note whistle also reported.

HABITS Little studied. Usually in pairs or small family parties. Best located by distinctive call, which is uttered from top of termite mound or low tree; most vocal in early morning and evening. Roosts in tall trees; occasionally flushed from trees in day.

BREEDING Monogamous. Nest a scrape, hidden among grasses. Clutch size unrecorded; eggs dirty white to yellowish-brown. Reported July–September in Mali, Chad and Sudan, February–March in Nigeria and in most months in Ethiopia.

DISTRIBUTION Grasslands of C Africa, from E Mali (Azzawakh) across C and SE Niger, NE Nigeria, S Chad and S Sudan (except southwest), western highlands and Rift Valley of Ethiopia and NE Uganda.

STATUS Locally common but patchily distributed over most of range. Decreasing in some regions (e.g. Ethiopian Rift Valley) through habitat degradation.

REFERENCE Urban *et al.* (1986).

---

39   HEUGLIN'S FRANCOLIN
Francolinus icterorhynchus (Heuglin, 1863)   Plate 14

Alternative name: Yellow-billed Francolin.

Southern counterpart of Clapperton's Francolin, with which it overlaps in SW Sudan.

IDENTIFICATION Differs from Double-spurred and Clapperton's Francolins in yellow legs and bare skin around eye, but latter inconspicuous in field; range not known to overlap with Double-spurred but does so with Clapperton's in SW Sudan, where red legs and facial skin of latter are easily seen field marks.

DESCRIPTION Bill orange-yellow with blackish upper mandible. Irides brown. Bare skin around eye dull yellow and relatively inconspicuous. Legs orange-yellow. Sexes similar: male has two spurs, one or none in female. **Adult (both sexes):** Crown reddish-brown with blacker forehead; head-sides and neck, breast and entire underparts whitish, washed buff on breast and belly, with intense blackish shaft streaks and feath-er centres forming spotting on breast and belly, and scaly barring on flanks; throat unmarked whitish. Upperparts greyish-brown indistinctly vermiculated buff with fine shaft streaks, nape and mantle blackish-brown with buff markings. Flight feathers dark brown, intensely vermiculated buff. **Juvenile:** Duller, with underparts less clearly marked, and flanks and upperparts more barred.

GEOGRAPHICAL VARIATION None recognised, but *ugandensis, emini, grisescens* and *dybowskii* described. Ugandan birds usually darker than more northern populations.

MEASUREMENTS Length 30–32 cm. Male larger. Males: wing 158–181 (mean 169), tarsus 54–65 (mean 57), weight 504–588. Females: wing 145–171 (mean 157), tarsus 44–54 (mean 49), weight 420–462.

HABITAT Various types of open and sparsely-wooded

grassland, from grassy cultivation to wooded savanna, usually at 500–1400 m.

VOICE Advertising call: a far-carrying, hoarse but shrill, slowly repeated *kerak-kerak-kek*. No other calls documented.

HABITS Shy, keeping close to grassy cover but feeding freely at edges of cultivation. Usually in pairs or small family parties of up to five. Best located by distinctive call, given from top of termite mound or low tree; most vocal in early morning and evening. Flushes reluctantly, preferring to run through cover; flight noisy and only over short distance. Roosts in trees.

BREEDING Probably monogamous. Nest a scrape, hidden under a bush. Clutch 6–8 pale greyish-buff eggs. Timing varies in Uganda, but in Zaïre nesting only reported at end of rainy season (September–November).

DISTRIBUTION Grasslands of C Africa, over most of Central African Republic and extreme N Zaïre, to SW Sudan, and Uganda (except extreme south and southeast).

STATUS Locally common over most of range, although easily overlooked unless calling.

REFERENCES Short *et al.* (1990), Urban *et al.* (1986).

---

40 HARWOOD'S FRANCOLIN
Francolinus harwoodi Blundell and Lovat, 1899   Plate 14

A distinctive francolin, known only from a few gorges and valleys in central highlands of Ethiopia.

IDENTIFICATION Range, but not habitat, approached by Clapperton's, which has whitish throat and supercilium, less red on bill, is blotched rather than scaled below and has whiter, less buff, lower underparts. Compare also Erckel's Francolin, which occurs in same region as Harwood's.

DESCRIPTION Bill black with red tip and base to upper mandible and red lower mandible. Irides brown. Bare skin around eye red and quite conspicuous. Legs red. Sexes similar. male has two spurs, one or none in female. **Adult male:** Crown dark brown, forehead and supercilium blackish; ear-coverts grey; throat, head and neck-sides whitish finely streaked dark. Neck and breast buffish-white with intense blackish U-shaped marks, extending onto flanks and sparsely across buff belly. Upperparts grey-brown indistinctly vermiculated and barred buff. Flight feathers grey-brown with intense buffy vermiculations. **Adult female:** Similar but more extensively washed brownish-buff below and belly markings tend to be V-shaped rather than U-shaped. **Juvenile:** Resembles female but upperparts less clearly fine barred; young male has intermediate underparts patterning between sexes.

GEOGRAPHICAL VARIATION Monotypic.

MEASUREMENTS Length 33–35 cm. Male larger. Males: wing 177–187 (mean 181), tarsus 53–58 (mean 56), weight (n=1) 545. Females: (n=2) wing 162 and 165, tarsus 46 and 47, weight (n=1) 446.

HABITAT Favours dense beds of *Typha* with scattered trees along stream sides in bottom of gorges; visits adjoining cultivation. Recent observations demonstrate that thorn scrub is also important and there are recent sight records, of birds considered to be this species away from previously known range, in shrubby cultivation and open woodland within dense grassland in upland areas.

VOICE Advertising call (I. S. Robertson recordings): a very harsh, grating, repeated *kuree*, and possibly a two-note *kureea-kuree* not unlike Clapperton's Francolin. No other vocalisations documented.

HABITS Virtually unstudied. Favours dense streamside vegetation but freely visits adjacent cultivation to feed in early morning. When disturbed, flies back to cover of *Typha*. Best located by distinctive rasping call, given in early morning from low tree. Roosts low in trees, apparently keeping below level of reedmace.

BREEDING Undocumented. From sightings of young, egg-laying probably occurs in December.

DISTRIBUTION Endemic to C Ethiopia south of Lake Tana, where certainly known from only a handful of sites along a 160 km-stretch of the Blue Nile and its tributaries. Recent sight records, apparently of this species, in atypical habitats south and west of previous known range, at Gibe Gorge and near Dembidollo (see Habitat), suggest that it may not be quite so restricted as previously thought.

STATUS Vulnerable. Apparently not uncommon, and discovered at a number of new sites during late 1990s surveys, but its highly restricted range makes it very susceptible to human pressures and it is extensively hunted.

REFERENCES Ash (1978), BirdLife International (2000), Robertson *et al.* (1997), Urban *et al.* (1986).

---

41 RED-BILLED FRANCOLIN
Francolinus adspersus Waterhouse, 1838   Plate 13

A dark francolin of dry thorn savanna, the stunning yellow eye-ring is distinctive and not shared by other genus members.

IDENTIFICATION Unlikely to be confused: a grey, very finely barred francolin with striking yellow eye-ring, red bill and legs. Juvenile has duller eye-ring and bill, but associated adults should assist correct identification. Natal Francolin, which overlaps in W Zimbabwe, has dark-streaked upperparts, is scaled, rather than barred, below, lacks eye-ring and has duller bill. Compare Swainson's and Red-necked Francolins, which have bare red skin on throat; former widely overlaps with Red-billed and also has grey legs. Possibly meets Cape Francolin near Orange River in S Namibia, but latter much larger with dull bill, lacks eye-ring and is scaled and streaked below.

DESCRIPTION Bill red. Irides dark brown. Broad yellow eye-ring. Legs red. Sexes similar but female smaller with shorter or no spur, typically one, but sometimes two in males. **Adult (both sexes):** Head, neck, mantle and entire underparts closely barred blackish-grey and white; forehead and area around eye blackish (enhancing eye-ring), ear-coverts unmarked dark grey. Wings, rump and uppertail-coverts greyish-brown, densely vermiculated with fine buff barring. **Juvenile:** Similar but browner, less grey than adults, with fine buff broken streaking on both upper- and underparts; eye-ring narrow and dull yellow; legs dusky yellow, bill brownish with pale lower mandible.

GEOGRAPHICAL VARIATION None recognised, although eastern populations have been named *kalahari*.

MEASUREMENTS Length 33–38 cm. Male larger. Males: wing 157–194 (mean 177), tarsus 48–60 (mean 54), weight 340–635. Females: wing 150–178 (mean 163), tarsus 44–53 (mean 47), weight 340–549

HABITAT Dry bushy and wooded savanna, flood plains with scattered *Acacia*, especially near water holes and watercourses.

VOICE Advertising call variable: typically a loud low-pitched hoarse crowing, increasing to a frenzied cackling *chak, chak, chak, CHAK, chakitty, chakitty, chakitty-chak, chakittychak,* diminishing in volume at end. Very noisy but other calls not well documented.

HABITS Usually in quite large groups of up to 20, freely mixing with other francolins, notably Swainson's. Coveys disband at onset of breeding season as males select territories. Readily feeds and dust-bathes in open by sandy tracks, running to cover of scrub when alarmed; rarely flies into trees when flushed. Most active at dawn and dusk, calling from termite mound or low tree branch but may call throughout the day if unmated. Spends heat of day in shade of bushes. Roosts in trees.

BREEDING Probably monogamous. Nest a scrape, well concealed under a bush. Clutch 4–10, usually 6–7. Eggs creamy to yellowish-brown; laid chiefly at end of rains or start of dry season, e.g. chiefly April–July in Botswana, January–March and May, July–August in Zimbabwe.

DISTRIBUTION SW Africa, from S Angola (S Huíla), most of Namibia and Botswana east to extreme NW Zimbabwe and SW Zambia. Introduction to Hawaii unsuccessful.

STATUS Locally common in suitable habitat, especially within national parks.

REFERENCES Clancey (1967), Urban *et al.* (1986).

42   CAPE FRANCOLIN
Francolinus capensis (Gmelin, 1789)   Plate 13

A large, dark and noisy francolin of extreme SW Africa that is often remarkably tame around farms.

IDENTIFICATION Restricted range, large size and very dark and almost uniform plumage prevent confusion, the whitish-streaked flanks and darker crown being the most obvious plumage features. Only Grey-wing likely to be confused, but latter smaller and less dark with orange on neck, is buff-streaked above, has some rufous in primaries and brownish, not blackish, tail in flight. Range does not overlap with Natal Francolin.

DESCRIPTION Bill brown with dull to reddish-orange base and lower mandible. Irides brown. Legs dusky-yellow to orange-red. Sexes similar but female smaller with legs and lower mandible duller than those of male; lacks, or has one short, spur, typically two in males. **Adult (both sexes):** Crown, nape and ear-coverts almost unmarked greyish-brown, crown darker. Throat and neck whitish with fine dark streaks, becoming more spotted on neck. Breast and entire underparts dark grey with white shaft streaks and whitish and buff vermiculations on each feather. Upperparts much as underparts but lack white shaft streaks and have buffier vermiculations. **Juvenile:**

Resembles adult but legs duskier and has more clearly defined whitish shaft streaks and vermiculations.

GEOGRAPHICAL VARIATION Monotypic.

MEASUREMENTS Length 40–42 cm. Male larger. Males: wing 203–219 (mean 212), tarsus 62–72 (mean 68), weight 600–915. Females: wing 185–213 (mean 196), tarsus 56–76 (mean 62), weight 435–659.

HABITAT Scrub along stream- and riversides, avoiding dense woodland, also scrubby heathland (*fynbos*) and scrubby rocky outcrops.

VOICE Advertising call: a loud crowing, cackled *kak-keek, kak-keek, kak-keeeeeek,* the notes rising in pitch, before diminishing in volume. Also a 'spluttering' flight call when flushed.

HABITS Usually in pairs or family parties, dust-bathing on tracks. Although favours riverine scrub, feeds on adjacent open ground, including grassy cultivation and, where unmolested, may become remarkably confiding, even feeding with farmyard chickens or visiting suburban lawns. If disturbed, prefers to run rather than fly back to cover. Best located by distinctive cackling call, given at sunrise and sunset, or by waiting near favoured drinking spots, where several coveys may gather to drink in late afternoon. Roosts in trees.

BREEDING Probably monogamous. Nest a grass-lined scrape, well concealed under bush. Clutch usually 6–8 but up to 14 presumably the result of two females laying in same nest. Eggs brownish-cream to pinkish, laid chiefly at end of winter rains or start of dry summer, reported July–February with a peak in September–October.

DISTRIBUTION SW Cape Province of South Africa, from lower Orange River south to Cape Peninsula and east to Uitenhage. Introduced on Robben I. near Cape Town.

STATUS Locally not uncommon and common in some areas where unmolested.

REFERENCES Clancey (1967), Little & Crowe (1997), Urban *et al.* (1986).

---

43 HILDEBRANDT'S FRANCOLIN
Francolinus hildebrandti Cabanis, 1878

Plate 13

Northern counterpart of Natal Francolin, their ranges almost meet in C Zambia.

IDENTIFICATION Combination of red legs, spotted (male) or rufous (female) underparts and lack of pronounced head pattern or bare facial skin prevents confusion with overlapping species. In C Zambia almost meets similar Natal Francolin, which is best distinguished by much finer, smaller underparts markings (therefore less conspicuously spotted), less prominently mottled nape and sexes similar in plumage. At very close range the yellow bill base of Natal should be visible.

DESCRIPTION '*F. h. hildebrandti*'. Bill red with black culmen (appears dull unless close). Irides brown. Legs red. Sexes strikingly different, both usually double spurred. **Adult male:** Throat, neck and underparts whitish, with profuse black spotting created by black centres; spotting most clear on lower breast and flanks; crown, nape and supercilia dark grey-brown, becoming rufous-grey on ear-coverts. Upperparts dark grey-brown, blacker on mantle with rufous and buff vermiculations. Mantle has whitish-buff margins to feathers, giving scaly appearance (not obvious in field). **Adult female:** Head, neck and entire underparts unmarked dull rufous with paler and buffer head-sides and throat; crown, nape and upperparts as male, but mantle less scaled. **Juvenile:** Resembles female but dark underparts spotting on some (presumed young males) and upperparts have more prominent buff and black barring, legs duller, brownish-red.

GEOGRAPHICAL VARIATION Slight. Six forms *altumi, helleri, fischeri, grotei, lindi* and *johnstoni* are unrecognised by Urban *et al.* (1986). Differences chiefly clinal and most marked in females, although precise differences between forms poorly understood and require review. Females of southern populations (*grotei* and *johnstoni*) smallest and lack white streaking on mantle, whereas female *altumi* has chest speckled black (plain rufous-buff in nominate).

MEASUREMENTS Length 34–41 cm. Male usually larger. Males: wing 158–189 (mean 174), tarsus 44–62 (mean 50), weight (n=2) 600, 645. Females: wing 151–179 (mean 162), tarsus 41–56 (mean 46), weight (n=2) 430, 480.

HABITAT Chiefly in montane habitats at 2000–2500 m. Dense bushy thickets and shrubby grassland on rocky hillsides, locally above tree-line in heath zone (Arusha National Park).

VOICE Advertising call: a high-pitched cackling *kek-kekek-kek-kerak*, mostly at dawn and dusk when several may call in unison. Also a single or repeated *kek* and a low grating *chuck-a-chuk* contact call.

HABITS Keeps close to shelter of dense bush. Invariably in pairs or family parties. Shy and wary, its presence is only usually revealed by cackling calls. On steep slopes under cover of trees and bushes. Feeds and dust-bathes close to bushy cover. Roosts in trees. Reluctant flyer, preferring to walk quietly into cover when disturbed.

BREEDING Monogamous. Nest a well-hidden scrape, lined with grass and leaves. Mean clutch 4 but up to 8 recorded, eggs creamy to pale brown. Reported in all months but peaks June–July in Malawi and Zambia.

DISTRIBUTION E Africa, from Marsabit south through W Kenya, most of Tanzania (including introduced population on Bwejuu I. near Mafia) to SE Zaïre (Musosa), C Zambia, and S Malawi (Mt Mulanje).

STATUS Local and uncommon, but shy and retiring habits make it less conspicuous than most other francolins.

REFERENCE Urban *et al.* (1986).

---

44 NATAL FRANCOLIN
Francolinus natalensis Smith, 1834

Plate 13

Southern counterpart of Hildebrandt's Francolin, their ranges almost meet in C Zambia.

IDENTIFICATION Uniform grey-brown plumage, relieved by closely scaled underparts and relatively plain, black-streaked, grey-brown upperparts distinctive over most of range. Overlaps with Red-billed Francolin, which has finely barred plumage, lacks streaking on upperparts, and has redder bill and legs and distinct yellow eye-ring (except young). Confusion with other species less likely, but in C Zambia almost meets Hildebrandt's Francolin, which is very similar but lacks yellow at base of bill, and has larger, clearer, wider-spaced black drop-spotting on underparts, more prominent spotting on nape and exhibits pronounced sexual dimorphism (sexes similar in Natal Francolin). Hybrids with Swainson's Francolin, occasionally found in W Zimbabwe, are closer to Natal but have blackish upper mandible and some bare red skin on throat.

DESCRIPTION Bill orange with yellow base, but not striking unless close. Irides brown. Legs red. Sexes similar. If seen together, female appears slightly smaller than male and often lacks spur (male usually single spurred). **Adult (both sexes):** Head dark grey-brown with paler feather fringes and tips, and blackish patch around eye. Entire underparts whitish with close blackish-scalloped barring, most obvious on flanks and most intense on throat, neck and breast; entire upperparts dull greyish-brown with prominent blackish, well-spaced shaft streaks and indistinct paler vermiculations. **Juvenile:** Duller with buff wash on underparts, dull greenish bill and fleshy legs.

GEOGRAPHICAL VARIATION Slight. Three forms not currently recognised, as differences are clinal and ill defined, with individual variation complicating situation. However, northernmost populations (*naevei*) tend to be paler below, with stronger scaling than nominate and *thamnobium*.

MEASUREMENTS Length 33–38 cm. Male typically larger. Males: wing 150–186 (mean 168), tarsus 42–57 (mean 49), weight 415–650. Females: wing 149–167 (mean 156), tarsus 40–52 (mean 45), weight 370–400.

HABITAT Dense scrubby thickets and wooded hillsides in dry country, although typically close to water. Favours riverine woodland and rocky, scrub-covered slopes but locally at fringes of cultivation. From sea level (Natal) to 1800 m (E Zimbabwe).

VOICE Advertising call: a four-note rasping *ker-kik-kik-kik* with emphasis on three *kik* notes, or a ringing *kwali-kwali-kwali*. Also a rasping *krr-ik-krr*, repeated 4–5 times and a short *kik* in alarm.

HABITS Rarely far from shelter of thickets. Invariably in pairs or small parties of up to 10, often mixing with Red-billed and Swainson's Francolins. On rocky outcrops and steep slopes under cover of trees and bushes. Feeds and dust-bathes close to bushy cover. Roosts in trees. Flight action relatively slow, but only reluctantly takes to wing, preferring to walk sedately into cover when disturbed. Most vocal early morning and late evening.

BREEDING Monogamous. Nest a scrape, lined with grass, under bush. Mean clutch 5, but up to 10 have been found, perhaps the result of two females laying in same nest. Eggs creamy to pale buff. Breeds all months, but chiefly March–May in Zambia and Zimbabwe, and in January–February and April–July in South Africa.

DISTRIBUTION S Africa, from C Zambia, south through Zimbabwe, E Botswana, W Mozambique and E South Africa to coastal Natal and extreme N and E Cape Province.

STATUS Locally numerous but agricultural changes have led to local declines in parts of South Africa.

REFERENCES Clancey (1967), Irwin (1981), Urban *et al.* (1986).

Subgenus *PTERNISTIS* (part): the scaly francolins

Ahanta Francolin *F. ahantensis*, Scaly Francolin *F. squamatus* and Grey-striped Francolin *F. griseostriatus*.

These three species are medium-sized francolins of C and W African forests. Overall, they are relatively uniform dark brownish, lacking prominent markings and their most striking features are whitish throats and reddish or orange-red bills and legs. Sexes similar. Calls are nasal and raucous.

45   AHANTA FRANCOLIN
Francolinus ahantensis Temminck, 1851   Plate 12

Poorly studied W African francolin of forest undergrowth that replaces Scaly Francolin west of the Niger River.

IDENTIFICATION Combination of forest habitat, orange bill and legs and relatively uniform plumage, without striking markings (pale-streaked underparts only obvious when close) distinctive. Range does not overlap with Scaly or Grey-striped Francolins. Double-spurred Francolin has dull greenish legs and more prominent white supercilium. See also Latham's Francolin.

DESCRIPTION Bill orange-red with black base. Irides brown. Inconspicuous pale orange bare patch above ear-coverts. Legs orange. Sexes similar, female unspurred (male has 1–2 spurs). **Adult male:** Head-sides and neck blackish, finely mottled white and buff, contrasting with whitish throat and indistinct pale supercilium; crown, nape and ear-coverts greyish-brown to warm brown. Upperparts greyish-brown finely vermiculated black; warmer brown on wings and rump; mantle and back feathers have buffish-white edges and vermiculations. Underparts greyish-brown, feathers with whitish edges, blackish subterminal line and grey-brown centres, forming relatively prominent streaking at close range. **Adult female:** Smaller than male, with buff spotting on wing-coverts and blacker inner secondaries. **Juvenile:** Distinctly greyer below than adult, with finer, more broken, whitish streaking and broader, more spot-like, black markings on upperparts.

GEOGRAPHICAL VARIATION None recognised, but there is a cline towards paler and more rufous-winged populations (*hopkinsoni*) in west of range.

MEASUREMENTS Length 33–35 cm. Male usually larger. Males: wing 161–181 (mean 172), tarsus 53–59 (mean 56). Females: wing 154–172 (mean 164), tarsus 46–53 (mean 50). Weight, no data.

HABITAT Forest edges and clearings with dense, tangled undergrowth, old plantations and abandoned shrubby cultivation.

VOICE Advertising call: a high-pitched, loud *kee-kee-keree*, also a less raucous *kok-kee-keroo*. Often duets, with presumed female giving *ker-weerk* as male utters squealing advertising call.

HABITS Shy and elusive. Calls repeatedly and noisily

before dawn. Rarely feeds in open. Usually in pairs or family parties, feeding under tangled cover, often near water. Flushes very reluctantly, but sometimes alights in trees when surprised. Roosts in trees well concealed in canopy, occasionally on ground.

BREEDING Probably monogamous. Nest a scrape under thick cover. Clutch 4–6 with up to 12 recorded. Eggs cream to pinkish-buff, reported late December in Ghana and January and September in Senegambia.

DISTRIBUTION W Africa in three disjunct populations. Westernmost is in coastal lowlands of The Gambia, Sénégal and N Guinea-Bissau. Then from S Guinea, Sierra Leone to W Liberia. Easternmost population occurs from NE Côte d'Ivoire and Ghana, through C Togo and Bénin to SW Nigeria.

STATUS Locally quite common in east of range and not uncommon in Sierra Leone and Ghana, but distinctly rare and local in Senegambia, and there are very few records from The Gambia.

REFERENCES Mackworth-Praed & Grant (1970), Urban *et al.* (1986).

46   SCALY FRANCOLIN
Francolinus squamatus (Cassin, 1857)   Plate 12

Numerous in forest undergrowth, being relatively abundant but shy and easily overlooked, although very vocal near dusk.

IDENTIFICATION Combination of forest habitat, reddish-orange bill and legs, and very plain dark brownish plumage without apparent markings or red skin around eye relatively distinctive. Does not overlap with other group members (Ahanta and Grey-striped), but dark plumage and red bill and legs shared by larger and more rufous Jackson's and Handsome Francolins, which have relatively restricted ranges in E Africa, and very range-restricted Mount Cameroon Francolin, which has conspicuous red bare skin around eye. Compare also Nahan's Francolin.

DESCRIPTION Bill dark brown with orange-red lower mandible. Irides brown. Legs orange-red. Sexes similar, female unspurred (male has 1–2 spurs) and smaller. **Adult (both sexes):** Relatively uniform dark buffish-brown or grey-brown, darkest on upperparts, palest on head-sides and central underparts, becoming buffish-white on throat. Upperparts vermiculated and barred black and buff when seen close, but most obvious markings on underparts: dark feather borders give scaled effect at close range. Flight feathers almost uniform grey, although inner secondaries spotted black. Overall plumage tone varies from reddish, through buffish to cold greyish-brown (see Geographical Variation). **Juvenile:** Distinctly warmer, more rufous-brown than adult with broader, more spot-like, black markings on upperparts and fine black and white barring on central underparts.

GEOGRAPHICAL VARIATION No races recognised by Urban *et al.* (1986), in a review that dismissed all

variations as being clinal. The following races have been described: *usambarae*, *doni*, *schuetti*, *uzungwensis*, *tetraoninus*, *zappeyi*, *dowashanus*, *maranensis*, *kapitensis*, *keniensis* and *chyuluensis*. In general, western populations are reddest brown above, with the most intense rufous and buff markings and have the palest central underparts, whereas those in the east are drabbest and darkest; gradual intergradation exists between the two extremes.

MEASUREMENTS Length 30–33 cm. Male typically larger. Males: wing 159–184 (mean 175), tarsus 48–60 (mean 54), weight 432–565. Females: wing 147–182 (mean 163), tarsus 41–59 (mean 49), weight 377–515.

HABITAT Favours evergreen forest edges with dense undergrowth at 800–3000 m, also locally in old abandoned shrubby cultivation, plantations and secondary forest with scrubby undergrowth.

VOICE Advertising call: a high-pitched, nasal *ke-rak* repeated up to 12 times and increasing in volume; also rendered as a rapid guttural, repeated *kwi-kau-ra* and as mixed whistle and grating *hu-hu-hu-hurrrr* (the striking conflict in transcriptions suggests either local variation, or that several call types are involved). Female call more nasal and higher pitched than male. Family parties may produce a guttural *quarek-quarek* and retain contact using a very quiet low clucking. Alarm *karek-kak-kak*.

HABITS Generally shy and elusive but locally confiding. Calls repeatedly towards dawn and dusk; spends little time in open, favouring undergrowth by water but sometimes feeds in forest clearings and on tracks. Usually in pairs or family parties. Flushes very reluctantly, squatting when alarmed, then running through vegetation if closely approached. Well-concealed tree canopy roost. Calls from termite mound or in chorus from tree roost.

BREEDING Probably monogamous. Nest a scrape under tussock of grass, lined with grass and feathers but one found on a termite mound. Clutch 3–8 (mean 6) buffish eggs, often pinkish-buff. Timing varies over wide range, with no defined seasonality but October–March favoured in Cameroon and January–June in Zaïre.

DISTRIBUTION Widely, but patchily, distributed in equatorial Africa, from C Nigeria south through Cameroon to extreme W and N Zaïre, east across northern equatorial forests to Uganda, C Kenya, N, E and W Tanzania (also adjacent Rwanda and Burundi) and N Malawi. Isolated populations in S Zaïre, C Sudan (Jebel Marra) and highlands of S Ethiopia.

STATUS Locally quite common, but forest destruction and hunting have been responsible for dramatic decreases in some areas, contributing to its fragmented distribution.

REFERENCES Mackworth-Praed & Grant (1970), Urban *et al.* (1986).

47 GREY-STRIPED FRANCOLIN
Francolinus griseostriatus (Ogilvie-Grant, 1890)   Plate 12

Endemic to Angola, it is virtually unstudied and presumably severely endangered.

IDENTIFICATION Combination of forest habitat, orange bill and legs and chestnut-streaked plumage render it unmistakable within limited range.

DESCRIPTION Bill orange-red with black distal two-thirds to upper mandible. Irides brown. Legs orange-red. Sexes similar, female unspurred (male has one spur) and smaller. **Adult (both sexes):** Head greyish-brown, paler at sides, becoming more rufous-brown on forehead. Neck-sides, hindneck, mantle, back and scapulars chestnut with grey feather edges, buff streaking and sparse black vermiculations. Rump and upper-tail-coverts grey-brown with fine black barring, much duller than chestnut and grey of scapulars and mantle. Tail chestnut, barred blackish. Wings dull brown, with flight feathers mottled and barred brown and tawny on outer webs. Underparts buff with chestnut shaft streaks, becoming more intensely streaked rufous and grey across breast, contrasting with white chin and throat. **Juvenile:** More uniform rufous-cinnamon above, with dark, not chestnut, feather centres and black spotting on each feather; underparts less strongly streaked chestnut and belly whiter.

GEOGRAPHICAL VARIATION Monotypic. Pinto (1983) regarded those from the more southerly population (in Benguela) as darker than those in the north, but Collar (1998) considered such differences invalid.

MEASUREMENTS Length 29–31 cm. Male typically larger. Males: wing 139–161 (mean 153), tarsus 43–52 (mean 48). Females: wing 144–153 (mean 148), tarsus 40–45 (mean 42). Weight, no data.

HABITAT Dense forest undergrowth, in both secondary and gallery forest at 800–1200 m. May visit adjacent cultivation.

VOICE Advertising call resembles Scaly Francolin (which see).

HABITS Virtually unknown. Feeds within forest undergrowth but reportedly visits adjacent abandoned cotton fields and grassy flats to feed in early morning and evening, flying back to forest if disturbed. Roosts in trees.

BREEDING Undocumented.

DISTRIBUTION Known from two small areas of the W Angolan escarpment: S Cuanza Sul and W Malanje districts north to Bengo and Cuanza Norte, and further south in S Benguela and extreme NE Huíla districts.

STATUS Vulnerable. The political situation in Angola has restricted fieldwork there in recent decades, and this species went unrecorded between 1954 and 1983, when it was reported as still reasonably numerous. A steady reduction in its forest habitat has occurred since then and it is almost certainly extensively hunted. Unknown in captivity and the species' future prospects appear dire; further study and conservation measures are urgently required.

REFERENCES BirdLife International (2000), Collar (1998), Collar *et al.* (1994), Dean (2000), Pinto (1983), Urban *et al.* (1986).

Subgenus *PTERNISTIS* (part): African spurfowl or bare-throated francolins

Yellow-necked Francolin *F. leucoscepus*, Grey-breasted Francolin *F. rufopictus*, Red-necked Francolin *F. afer* and Swainson's Francolin *F. swainsonii*.

Distinctive group of four large francolins with coloured bare throat and foreneck skin and raucous calls. Sexes similar in plumage, although males are larger and have two spurs. Members of this group are also known as 'spurfowl'. To avoid confusion with the Asian spurfowl, they are termed 'francolins' here, following the vernacular names long used in S Africa and adopted by Urban *et al.* (1986).

YELLOW-NECKED FRANCOLIN
Francolinus leucoscepus Gray, 1867   **Plate 17**

Alternative name: Yellow-necked Spurfowl.

Probably the commonest and most conspicuous francolin of arid and semi-cultivated areas in E Africa.

IDENTIFICATION Large and conspicuous francolin of semi-arid bush and cultivation, with dark legs, bare yellow dark-bordered throat patch and heavily streaked plumage; in flight has striking buff patch on primaries. Unlikely to be confused but marginally overlaps with Grey-breasted in SE Serengeti National Park where hybrids known. However, Grey-breasted typically has orange, not black bill, more orange or pink bare throat skin, is greyer and paler overall with narrower and less obvious white streaking on plumage. Confusion with other species very unlikely but compare Red-necked Francolin with which it overlaps in range, but not habitat, in coastal Kenya and parts of Tanzania.

DESCRIPTION Bill black with reddish base. Irides brown. Legs brownish-black. Bare red skin around eye. Bare yellow skin on throat, becoming more orange on chin and has definite dark-feathered border. Sexes similar, female smaller and virtually unspurred (male has two spurs). **Adult (both sexes):** Crown greyish-brown, supercilium whitish, ear-coverts pale grey. Neck, breast, underparts and mantle dark brown with rufous wash on flanks, intensely marked with prominent whitish or pale buff streaks. Rest of upperparts dull olive-brown, with inner webs of primaries pale buff forming prominent patch in flight. **Juvenile:** Duller and overall less clearly marked with greyer and narrowly white-streaked underparts, and more buff-vermiculated upperparts; facial and throat skin paler and duller than adult.

GEOGRAPHICAL VARIATION Slight. A number of races have been described (*tokora, oldowai, infuscatus, kilimensis, keniensis, holtermulleri* and *muhamed-ben-abdullah*) but none were admitted by Urban *et al.* (1986). In general, there appears to be a cline towards those with paler underparts ground colour in the east of range.

MEASUREMENTS Length 33–36 cm. Male larger. Males: wing 184–216 (mean 200), tarsus 61–67 (mean 64), weight 615–896. Females: wing 170–216 (mean 187), tarsus 53–69 (mean 58), weight 400–615.

HABITAT Dry wooded grassland and plains with scattered *Acacia* and bushy cultivation, usually in semi-arid country but locally in relatively lush habitats and forest edges (e.g. lower slopes of Mt Kenya). Where range meets Red-necked and Grey-breasted Francolins, Yellow-necked inhabits drier habitats. Occurs from sea level to 2400 m.

VOICE Advertising call similar to other bare-throated species, although a little lower pitched than Red-necked: a loud, deep, grating *ko-waarrk, ko-warrk, ko-weeark*. Also a more prolonged series, fading in pitch at end: *ko-weerrrk-kweeerrrk-kwerrrk-kwarr-karr-karr*.

HABITS Usually in pairs or small parties, although coveys often congregate into quite large numbers at favoured feeding spots. Prefers cover of bushes, but readily ventures to feed in more open areas, including scrubby cultivation, in early morning and late afternoon; often on dusty tracks, especially in wet weather when it appears to avoid damp vegetation. Often follows large mammals, such as elephants, to feed on undigested seeds in their droppings and may even approach motor vehicles by mistake! Escapes by running through scrubby cover, but flies quite readily if hard-pressed and may resort to trees to escape predators. Roosts in shrubs and low in trees, to where it also retires in heat of day. Most vocal just after dawn, when calls from a termite mound or low tree branch.

BREEDING Monogamous. Nest a scrape virtually unlined but for a few blades of grass and odd feathers. Clutch 3–8 (mean 5) but up to 17 recorded, latter obviously the product of two females laying in same nest. Eggs creamy to pinkish-buff, speckled darker. Breeds January–June over most of range but all months in Tanzania, commencing in latter part of rainy season and early part of following dry season.

DISTRIBUTION E Africa, from Eritrea and Somalia, south through S Ethiopia (except highlands), extreme SE Sudan, NE Uganda, most of Kenya (except more humid extreme west and east) to eastern plateau of NC Tanzania.

STATUS Locally common, and appears to thrive at edges of cultivation in sparsely populated country. However, it is extensively hunted in some areas, e.g. Kenya, where dramatic decreases have been reported from some localities in recent years.

REFERENCE Urban *et al.* (1986).

---

49 GREY-BREASTED FRANCOLIN
Francolinus rufopictus (Reichenow, 1887)   **Plate 17**

Alternative name: Grey-breasted Spurfowl.

Confined to N Tanzanian plains, between the ranges of the other two bare-throated francolins of this region. Despite its intermediate appearance, it is clearly quite distinct and worthy of specific status.

IDENTIFICATION Large, recalling Yellow-necked Francolin, with which it marginally overlaps. Grey-breasted has an orange, not black, bill, more orange or pink bare throat skin, is overall greyer and paler with narrower and less obvious white streaking on body. Hybrids with Yellow-necked Francolin have been reported from SE Serengeti National Park. Red-necked Francolin, in marginal or potential overlap zone, has all-red bill and legs, and is vermiculated grey below. Confusion with other species very unlikely.

DESCRIPTION Bill wholly orange. Irides brown. Legs brownish-black. Bare skin around eye, lores, chin and throat orange-yellow to pink. Sexes similar, female smaller and virtually unspurred (male has two spurs). **Adult (both sexes):** Forehead and crown-sides blackish-brown, becoming paler on crown and nape; head-sides, neck and breast grey with dark shaft streaks and white moustachial. Lower breast and rest of underparts streaked black, chestnut and whitish-buff. Upperparts greyish finely streaked chestnut, buff and black. **Juvenile:** Distinctly more barred underparts than adult and more vermiculated and streaked buff above, lacking chestnut.

GEOGRAPHICAL VARIATION Monotypic.

MEASUREMENTS Length 36–39 cm. Male larger. Males: wing 193–222 (mean 213), tarsus 62–72 (mean 68), weight 779–964. Females: wing 180–199 (mean 190), tarsus 54–63 (mean 58), weight 439–666.

HABITAT Wooded grassland and plains with scattered *Acacia* and bushy cover, in less arid habitats than Yellow-necked and often in streamside thickets.

VOICE Advertising call similar to Yellow-necked

Francolin, a loud grating *ka-waaark, ka-waaark, ka-waaark,* sometimes fading in pitch at end *koarrk-koarrk-karrk-krrk-krrk-krrk-krrr.* Also a high-pitched cackle in alarm if flushed.

HABITS Little studied. Usually in pairs or small parties, although coveys may congregate into quite large numbers at favoured feeding spots. Keeps within cover of bushes and trees but feeds in more open areas in early morning and late afternoon, even at fringes of cultivation. Most vocal near dusk and after dawn, vocalisations intensifying at onset of rainy season. Calls from termite mound or tree stump.

BREEDING Monogamous. Nest a scrape lined with grass and feathers well concealed in long grass. Clutch 4–5 buffish or pale brown eggs. Breeds February–April and in June–July, during rainy season and early part of following dry season.

DISTRIBUTION CN Tanzania, from C Serengeti National Park and Crater Highlands to Wembere steppes, Mwanza and Lake Eyasi.

STATUS Locally common, although local decreases reported as more intensive cultivation encroaches on its grassland environment.

REFERENCE Urban *et al.* (1986).

---

50 RED-NECKED FRANCOLIN
Francolinus afer (Müller, 1776)   Plate 17

Alternative name: Red-necked Spurfowl.

A very variable species that replaces Swainson's and Yellow-necked in wetter, more vegetated habitats, its range separating those two species.

IDENTIFICATION A dark, often white-streaked, francolin, the combination of red facial and throat skin with wholly red bill and legs is diagnostic. Marginally overlaps and co-occurs with Swainson's Francolin, adults of which have black upper mandible and legs, and are largely uniform greyish-brown overall with dark streaking; juveniles are more problematic, but Red-necked is darker than Swainson's; occasional wild hybrids between Swainson's and Red-necked have been reported from Zimbabwe (see Swainson's). No known overlap with Grey-breasted Francolin although almost meet in N Tanzania; latter paler and has black legs and pinkish or orange facial skin. Very marginal overlap with Yellow-necked in Tanzania and coastal Kenya, but here Red-necked inhabits lusher vegetation, and Yellow-necked has black legs, yellow throat skin and rufous in wing. Northern populations overlap with smaller, paler and less streaked Scaly Francolin, which lacks bare facial skin and has black bill.

DESCRIPTION Bill red. Irides brown. Legs red. Bare skin around eye, lores, chin and throat red. Sexes similar, female smaller and virtually unspurred (male has 1–2 spurs). Two marked groups of races that intergrade. **Black-and-white races:** (most of range except north), a very variable complex, see Geographical Variation. **Adult (both sexes):** Forehead and crown-sides blackish

or whitish, head-sides whitish (unmarked or mottled dark). Crown, neck and underparts greyish-black, with white or silvery tips forming streaked and mottled appearance, or whitish with black streaking, in some races central underparts unmarked blackish and contrast with white flank stripes. Upperparts dull brown with blackish streaking. **Vermiculated races:** (northern areas). **Adult (both sexes):** Forehead and supercilium blackish, crown and upperparts dull brown with dark streaking. Head-sides, neck, breast and underparts closely vermiculated grey with dark shaft streaks and rufous or maroon stripes on belly and flanks, latter absent in female. **Juvenile:** Distinctly browner than adult, with bare skin of throat partially covered in pale down and has dark bill and dull yellowish legs.

GEOGRAPHICAL VARIATION Complex, a plethora of races has been described but Urban *et al.* (1986) recognise seven in two groups that freely intergrade within two broad zones (from C Tanzania through C Malawi to E Zambia, and C and N Angola).

Black-and-white group (five races): all are larger than those of vermiculated group.

F. a. **afer** (Müller, 1776) (includes *benguellensis, cunenensis* and *punctulatus*) occurs in W Angola to extreme N Namibia; smallest of group (wing of male 157–181, female 153–175), supercilium and moustachial white, breast brown, lower underparts blackish with broad white streaks or whitish with black streaks (latter, in extreme south of range, formerly recognised as *cunenensis*).

F. a. **castaneiventer** (Gunning & Roberts, 1911)

(includes *krebsi*, *notatus* and *lehmanni*) occurs in coastal Cape Province to Natal; supercilium blackish, head, neck and underparts blackish-grey becoming blacker below, with prominent but narrow whitish streaking.

F. a. swynnertoni (Sclater, 1921) occurs in E Zimbabwe and Mozambique south of Zambezi River; supercilium and head-sides white, neck, breast and underparts greyish-black with fine white streaking, becoming broader on flanks, central underparts unmarked blackish.

F. a. melanogaster (Neumann, 1891) (includes *humboldtii*, *tornowi*, *itigi* and *loangwae*) occurs in Mozambique north of Zambezi, and E Tanzania; resembles last race but lacks white on head.

F. a. leucoparaeus Fischer & Reichenow, 1884 occurs in coastal Kenya; resembles last race but head-sides white with black mottles and supercilium black and white.

Vermiculated or rufous-striped group (two races): smaller than black-and-white group except nominate race.

F. a. cranchii (Leach, 1818) (includes *tertius*, *bohmi*, *intercedens* and *nyanzae*) occurs from W Congo through S Zaïre to S Uganda, in extreme NW Tanzania and W Kenya, south to Angola, C Zambia, N Malawi and S Tanzania; wing of male 157–189, female 149–179, head, neck and underparts vermiculated grey, male has rufous belly stripes.

F. a. harterti (Reichenow, 1909) occurs in W Tanzania, Rwanda and Burundi; similar but smaller (male wing 156–179, female 117–177) with darker, almost maroon, belly stripes.

MEASUREMENTS Length 25–38 cm. Marked size differences between races, with vermiculated group smaller than others except nominate. Data below refers to southernmost race *castaneiventer*; comparative wing lengths for some smaller races are presented under Geographical Variation. Males: wing 171–210 (mean 192), tarsus 56–64 (mean 60). Females: wing 170–188 (mean 182), tarsus 51–64 (mean 56). Weight (both sexes) 444–765.

HABITAT Where range meets Swainson's and Yellow-necked Francolins, generally in moister, more evergreen forests than these dry-country species; however, where no competition with other bare-throated francolins occurs in a much wider range of grassy and scrubby habitats. In parts of S Africa freely mixes with Swainson's, with which it sometimes hybridises. Wooded gorges and evergreen forest edges are favoured in southern range, whereas in Zambia occurs in almost any form of grassy or wooded country. In Tanzania, Uganda and Zaïre in scrubby or wooded grassy plains, and in coastal Kenya in long grass with patches of woodland.

VOICE Advertising call similar to other bare-throated species, but higher pitched: a squealed harsh cackle, *ko-waaark* repeated 4–8 times and fading at end. A loud, raucous *kek-kek-kek* may be given if flushed and a clucking alarm call reported while perched in trees.

HABITS Shy, remaining deeper within thickets or woodland cover than other bare-throated species, but locally feeds in short-cropped grassland and along roadsides in early morning in north of range. In less-populated areas often feeds in cultivation but always keeps close to cover. Usually singly or in small parties but may also associate with other francolins, chiefly Swainson's in S Africa. Most vocal early morning and late afternoon, male calling from ground or termite mound. Roosts in bushes and trees to which it also retires in heat of day for shade. Flushes very reluctantly, preferring to run through cover and usually only flies a short distance before alighting and running on; if chased by mammalian predators may take cover in tree canopy.

BREEDING Monogamous. Nest a scrape lined with grass, leaves and feathers, well concealed in long grass under a bush. Clutch 3–9 pinkish-buff to pale brown eggs. Timing varies over wide range and habitats, but egg-laying usually commences at end of rainy season to take advantage of lush cover at start of following dry season.

DISTRIBUTION SC Africa, from S Uganda, coastal Kenya and east shore of Lake Victoria south over most of Tanzania (except north), Rwanda and Burundi, through E Zaïre, Malawi, Mozambique, E Zimbabwe to SE South Africa in E Cape Province. Absent from arid regions of Namibia (except extreme northwest) and Botswana but widespread in Zambia (except southwest), Angola (except southeast) and across S Zaïre to E Congo. Introduced to Ascension I.

STATUS Locally quite numerous, but cover-loving habit makes it less conspicuous than other bare-throated species. Local decreases reported through hunting (e.g. in Zaïre) or competition with Swainson's Francolin (e.g. in Zimbabwe). Forest destruction may also be a problem locally and it usually disappears from increasingly populated areas.

REFERENCE Urban *et al.* (1986).

---

51 SWAINSON'S FRANCOLIN
Francolinus swainsonii (Smith, 1836)   Plate 17

Southernmost of group, overlapping and occasionally hybridising with Red-necked and Natal Francolins in northeast of range.

IDENTIFICATION Combination of red facial and throat skin with blackish upper mandible and legs diagnostic. Adult Red-necked Francolin in overlap zones has all-red bill and legs and either whitish supercilium and throat-sides and white-striped flanks, or is very grey with rufous-striped underparts; juveniles problematic in areas where mixed flocks occur, but juvenile Swainson's has distinctly paler upperparts than Red-necked. Hybrids with Natal Francolin lack bare skin on face and have partially-feathered throat; those with Red-necked recall latter but have blackish bill and intermediate underparts pattern (see Irwin 1981).

DESCRIPTION *F. s. swainsonii.* Bill blackish with red lower mandible. Irides brown. Legs blackish. Bare skin around eye, lores, chin and throat red. Sexes similar, female darker and smaller, with more heavily marked upperparts and is unspurred (male has 1–2 spurs). **Adult (both sexes):** Overall relatively uniform dark grey-brown, greyest on head and neck, and brownest on underparts and vent. All contour feathers have dark shaft streaks giving sparsely streaked appearance, streaks densest and most speckled on head and neck, and strongest on flanks. **Juvenile:** Warmer and paler brown than adult, with bare skin of throat covered in pale down and has dull yellowish legs.

GEOGRAPHICAL VARIATION Slight. Two sub-species recognised, but those from Botswana and adjacent Namibia and Zimbabwe are intermediate in appearance and have also been accorded various subspecific status.

F. s. swainsonii (Smith, 1836) (includes *damarensis*, *gilli* and *chobiensis*) occurs in most of species range; described above.

F. s. lundazi White, 1947 occurs in S Mozambique and N and W Zimbabwe; slightly smaller, distinctly paler and browner, and with narrower streaking.

MEASUREMENTS Length 34–39 cm. Male larger. *F. s. swainsonii* given. Males: wing 172–208 (mean 191), tarsus 50–68 (mean 60), weight 487–875. Females: wing 158–190 (mean 174), tarsus 47–58 (mean 52), weight 365–650.

HABITAT Dry grassland with varying amounts of bushy cover, from riverine forest edges to dense grassland and cultivation, usually near water but in some areas in very dry habitats.

VOICE Advertising call similar to Red-necked Francolin but lower pitched: a deep, rasping, croaked *kwaaark-kwaaark-kwaaark-kwaark-kwaark-krr-krr-krr* fading at end; occasionally female replies with a high *kwee-ke-ke-kwee.* If flushed may 'explode' giving a *qua-qua-qua-quak* in alarm. Coveys give a conversational clucking while feeding.

HABITS Shy but often feeds in open, including cultivation. Usually alone or in small parties of up to eight, but also freely associates with other francolins, chiefly Red-necked, Red-billed and Natal. Coveys gather at favoured drinking spots in morning and late afternoon. Most vocal early morning and late afternoon, male calling from termite mound or low branch in upright posture, with head up and bare throat inflated. Often sits in bushes and trees in wet weather, and basks in sun on exposed perches to dry-off after rain. Flushes very reluctantly, preferring to run in crouched posture through cover, but capable of strong, surprisingly agile and fast flight, although usually over short distance, running upon alighting. Roosts in bushes and low trees.

BREEDING Monogamous. Nest a scrape lined with grass, leaves and feathers, well concealed under a bush or among grass. Clutch 4–8, but up to 12 recorded (mean 5). Eggs cream to pinkish-buff. Timing varies, perhaps twice a year in some areas, chiefly December–May in South Africa, February–May in Botswana, February–March is peak in Zimbabwe and May–July in Zambia.

DISTRIBUTION S Africa, from NW Malawi, through Luanga Valley over much of S Zambia, Zimbabwe (except extreme east), Botswana (except southwest), extreme SW Angola (Cuando Cubango), N Namibia, SW Mozambique (Tete) and E South Africa, where it extends south and west over E Orange Free State and N Natal.

STATUS Locally common, and increasing in some areas, where it appears to be ousting the closely related Red-necked Francolin.

REFERENCES Irwin (1981), Urban *et al.* (1986).

Subgenus PTERNISTIS (part): montane francolins

Erckel's Francolin *F. erckelii*, Djibouti Francolin *F. ochropectus*, Chestnut-naped Francolin *F. castaneicollis*, Handsome Francolin *F. nobilis*, Jackson's Francolin *F. jacksoni*, Mount Cameroon Francolin *F. camerunensis* and Swierstra's Francolin *F. swierstrai*.

Seven medium to large francolins of montane forest and scrub. Swierstra's and Mount Cameroon are western isolates that form a species-pair. Although superficially different, both are obviously sexually dimorphic medium-sized francolins that appear to have some affinity with the scaly group and may possibly warrant distinct treatment as an intermediate group. The other five have similar plumage patterns, exhibit few differences, other than size, between sexes and live in isolated montane habitats in E Africa.

52   ERCKEL'S FRANCOLIN
Francolinus erckelii (Rüppell, 1835)

Plate 16

A large dark-crowned francolin, the northernmost not only of the montane group but of all E African species, its range extending as far as the Red Sea hills in Sudan.

IDENTIFICATION A large dark francolin with black bill, yellowish legs, chestnut crown and whitish throat; in most of range it is the only highland francolin, but at lower altitudes in the south it possibly meets Clapperton's and Harwood's, although confusion is unlikely with either. Closest to Djibouti Francolin but ranges are mutually exclusive.

DESCRIPTION Bill black. Irides brown. Legs yellowish. Sexes similar but female smaller and virtually unspurred, male has two spurs. **Adult (both sexes):** Forehead, lores and crown-sides blackish; crown and nape chestnut; ear-coverts grey with whitish patch behind eye. Head and neck-sides chestnut with fine white streaks and mottles; throat unstreaked whitish. Breast grey streaked chestnut, flanks and belly whitish with close chestnut and dark streaks. Upperparts dull brown with rufous fringes, becoming richer rufous-chestnut, streaked whitish, on mantle. Flight feathers brownish-grey. Tail dark reddish-brown. **Juvenile:** Similar but duller, with buff streaking and fine barring over most of upperparts.

GEOGRAPHICAL VARIATION Isolated Sudanese population, *pentoni*, distinctly paler and greyer but perhaps unworthy of recognition.

MEASUREMENTS Length 38–43 cm. Male larger. Males: wing 200–227 (mean 216), tarsus 61–75 (mean 66), weight 1050–1590. Females: wing 167–194 (mean 185), tarsus 52–65 (mean 56), weight (n=1) 1136.

HABITAT Scrubby cover on montane plateaux and hillsides, preferring thickets at forest edges, at 2000–3500 m. Sudanese population occurs at much lower altitudes, frequenting wooded cover along stream beds in hills.

VOICE Advertising call: a prolonged series of croaked, cackling notes, the first loud and emphatic, gradually fading in pitch and volume at end *errk-errk-erk-erk-rkkuk-kuk-ku*; also described as a series of low *chuck* notes, accelerating to a climax followed by a winding-down series of clucking notes *chuck-chuck-chuck-chuck-chuck-KRAAAAH-chuckaluck-chuckaluck-chuckaluck*.

HABITS Shy and wary. Generally in dense vegetation, or on cliff slopes, in pairs or small parties. Most active just after dawn, when it may enter edges of cultivation to feed on fallen grain. Difficult to locate except by voice, being most vocal at dawn and dusk, when males call from boulders or cliff tops. If alarmed, runs uphill through dense cover, flushing to fly noisily back downhill. Coveys may converge at favoured drinking spots in late afternoon. Feeds on narrow cliff ledges, flying and walking between ledges even on precipitous, near-vertical faces.

BREEDING Monogamous. Nest a scrape, lined with grass, on ground. Clutch 4–10 whitish to pale brown eggs. Breeds in May and rainy season, September–November, in Ethiopia and April–May (rains) in Sudan.

DISTRIBUTION Highlands of N Ethiopia and Eritrea, north and west of Rift Valley, with an isolated population in Sudan in hills south and west of Port Sudan. Introduced into Hawaii.

STATUS Formerly locally numerous in Ethiopia and Sudan, but has decreased in recent decades through forest destruction. Introduced into Hawaii in 1957, where well established on six largest islands and especially numerous on leeward slope of Mauna Kea on Hawaii and Lanai. Due to wary nature, usually difficult to observe and thus easily overlooked.

REFERENCES Pratt *et al.* (1987), Urban *et al.* (1986).

---

53 DJIBOUTI FRANCOLIN
Francolinus ochropectus Dorst & Jouanin, 1952

Plate 16

Alternative names: Pale-bellied Francolin, Tadjoura Francolin.

Perhaps the most endangered francolin. Endemic to Djibouti, where it occurs in diminishing hill forest in two small areas. Intermediate in overall appearance between Erckel's and *atrifrons* race of Chestnut-naped.

IDENTIFICATION Unlikely to be confused within its restricted range, where it is the only francolin, although Yellow-necked occurs elsewhere in Djibouti. Appears dark in field, and shares yellowish legs, rufous crown and dark face with larger Erckel's, but crown and upperparts markedly darker, and underparts marked with buff spotting, rather than rufous and black. Ranges also differ.

DESCRIPTION Bill dusky with yellowish-horn lower mandible. Irides brown. Legs dull greyish-yellow to yellowish-orange. Sexes similar but female smaller and virtually unspurred, male has two spurs. **Adult (both sexes):** Forehead, crown-sides, lores and head-sides blackish; crown orange-chestnut, central crown and ear-coverts patch grey (darker in autumn); whitish spot behind eye. Lower sides of head rufous mottled pale buff, and very pale buffish or yellowish unstreaked throat. Sides of neck, breast and most of underparts heavily-streaked blackish and buff on whitish background, most intense on breast; central belly and undertail-coverts paler, being more intensely streaked whitish (inconspicuous in field). Upperparts dull grey-brown streaked rufous, contrasting slightly with paler and duller greyish-brown primaries in flight. Tail rufous-brown. **Juvenile:** Similar but duller, with buff barring rather than streaking on upperparts.

GEOGRAPHICAL VARIATION Monotypic.

MEASUREMENTS Length 33–36 cm. Male larger. Males: wing 206–210, tarsus 66–72, mean weight 809. Females: wing 197–205, tarsus 65–70, mean weight 605.

VOICE Advertising call: a loud *Erk* followed by a rapidly repeated and accelerating series of *kak* notes, fading to terminate in a chuckle. Apparently similar to Erckel's Francolin. A low conversational clucking noted from a feeding covey.

HABITAT Dry woodland undergrowth, from market gardens to plateaux with low scrubby trees and bushes; favouring densest undergrowth at 700–1780 m. In Day region principally in juniper forest, but juniper absent from nearby Mabla Mts, which are less vegetated.

HABITS Shy and elusive. Generally in dense vegetation in pairs or small parties but a concentration of c.20 recorded. Most active just after dawn and very difficult to locate except by voice. If alarmed seeks shelter of dense shrubby tree cover from which it is difficult to flush. Presumably roosts in similar cover. Recorded feeding under fig trees and on termites in areas that have been disturbed by warthogs.

BREEDING Probably monogamous. Clutch 7–9 according to local information, but undocumented. Only nest discovered was a shallow depression lined with grasses on a barely accessible mountain ledge (A. Laurent). Probably breeds after winter rains when vegetation most luxuriant, but a small family party was recorded as late as June.

DISTRIBUTION Endemic to Djibouti, where only known from two areas, the Day region of the Goda Mts and in the Mabla Mts 60 km to the east.

STATUS Critical. Most numerous in Day region, with a smaller population in Mabla Mts. Data insufficient to accurately assess population, but considered to have declined to c.500–1000 by 1998. Status of recently located Mabla population unknown but main population in Day region is at risk due to continued habitat degradation through overgrazing by domestic animals and woodcutting, and there is increasing evidence of human persecution. Strict protection of forested areas and an enforced hunting ban is crucial if its survival is to be ensured.

REFERENCES BirdLife International (2000), Blot (1985), Laurent (1990), Welch and Welch (1984, 1985, 1986).

54 CHESTNUT-NAPED FRANCOLIN
Francolinus castaneicollis Salvadori, 1888   Plate 15

Widespread in highlands of S Ethiopia, it also occurs just over the border in adjacent Somalia and has recently been discovered in Kenya.

IDENTIFICATION Unlikely to be confused within its habitat, its red bill and legs and boldly marked plumage are useful distinctions from the more northerly Erckel's, whose range it almost meets in C Ethiopia. Does not overlap with Harwood's, which is smaller, lacks blackish forehead and has red skin around eye. Smaller, drabber, buff-streaked and finely mottled Moorland Francolin occurs in same areas but in higher, more alpine (non-forested) habitats, and also has yellowish bill and legs and bright rufous wings in flight. Duller southern race *atrifrons* has unpatterned underparts, but blackish forehead and red bill and legs are characteristic of the species. Does not overlap with Jackson's or Djibouti Francolins.

DESCRIPTION *F. c. castaneicollis.* Bill red. Irides brown. Legs pinkish-red. Sexes similar but female smaller and virtually unspurred, male has two spurs. **Adult (both sexes):** Forehead, lores and supercilium blackish; crown, nape and ear-coverts ginger-rufous, becoming whiter on throat, finely marked with grey; neck and upper breast rufous, intensely mottled dark grey. Breast and flanks striped blackish-grey and white, with chestnut outer edges to feathers, widest on upper flanks and breast (chestnut and black striping lacking in southern race *atrifrons*), central underparts whiter. Upperparts dull grey-brown with rump and uppertail-coverts unmarked and contrasting strongly with boldly-marked mantle, scapulars and wing-coverts, which have black and white V central marks and chestnut edges to each feather (latter absent in *atrifrons*). Flight feathers brownish-grey. Tail dark brown. **Juvenile:** Similar but duller, with fine buff barring on rump and uppertail-coverts (unmarked in adults) and duller red bill.

GEOGRAPHICAL VARIATION Two well-differentiated subspecies. Up to six races have been described

but variation appears clinal, with those from Somalia being palest and those west of Rift Valley darkest and most chestnut. Radically different *atrifrons* may already have attained species status.

F. c. *castaneicollis* Salvadori, 1888 (includes *bottegi*, *gofanus*, *ogoensis* and *kaffanus*) occurs over most of species range; described above.

F. c. *atrifrons* Conover, 1930 occurs around Mega, Sidamo Province of S Ethiopia (also one record from Moyale, N Kenya); compared to nominate it is much less marked, lacking chestnut markings on upper- or underparts, or blackish streaking below, the lower underparts being almost unmarked buffish-white, and is smaller (male wing 191–192, female 162–176).

MEASUREMENTS Length 38–43 cm. Male larger. *F. c. castaneicollis* given. Males: wing 191–226 (mean 210), tarsus 59–74 (mean 67), weight 915–1200. Females: wing 169–203 (mean 186), tarsus 48–67 (mean 56), weight 550–650.

HABITAT Shrubby thickets at edges and clearings of montane forest and above tree-line in shrubby heath zone, at 2500–4000 m, but chiefly 3100–3500 m. In Somalia, in arid juniper forest at 1200–2250 m.

VOICE Advertising call: apparently variable, basically a loud, strident *kawar-kawar* accompanied by a harsh *kek, kek, kek* that is presumably a duet between the sexes.

HABITS Generally in dense undergrowth in pairs or small parties; also feeds on roadsides and forest trails and grassy forest glades. Not particularly shy; in fact becomes remarkably confiding in national parks. Active throughout day, but in dry weather principally in early morning and evening. Roosts in trees and tall shrubs (e.g. giant heath). In wet weather reluctantly descends to ground or into wet undergrowth, remaining on roost perches until late in morning. If disturbed runs into cover, preferably uphill. Difficult to flush but often resorts to trees and tall shrubs, those in treeless open heath being easier to flush than in forest. Calls from dense cover, chiefly in early morning and evening.

BREEDING Probably monogamous. Nest a scrape under a bush or within undergrowth. Clutch 5–6. Eggs creamy and laid at various times, usually in drier months, principally October–March (also late May and late December in Somalia).

DISTRIBUTION From NW Somalia east through Ethiopian highlands south and east of Rift Valley. Also locally further west in upper Omo basin, Jimma and Kaffa. In Kenya, known only from a single 1975 sight record at Moyale, near Ethiopian border.

STATUS Common in Bale and Arussi Mts of S Ethiopia, less common in W Ethiopia and Somalia.

REFERENCE Urban *et al.* (1986).

---

55   HANDSOME FRANCOLIN
Francolinus nobilis Reichenow, 1908   Plate 15

Very shy francolin of highland forest undergrowth on border between Zaïre and Uganda.

IDENTIFICATION Dark rufous plumage, contrasting with greyer head and rump, and large size distinctive; over most of restricted range it is the only francolin in its montane forest habitat, but compare smaller, drabber brown Scaly Francolin, which is not strikingly rufous and lacks red bare skin around eye.

DESCRIPTION Bill red. Irides brown. Legs red. Extensive bare red skin around eye. Sexes similar, but female smaller and a little duller, with either one short spur or none (male has 1–2 spurs). **Adult (both sexes):** Head grey with darker centres and browner crown and neck; throat buffier grey. Breast and flanks rufous fringed greyish; belly grey becoming blacker on undertail-coverts, all feathers with buff or buffish-brown fringes. Mantle, back and wing-coverts bright rufous, those of back and mantle with greyish fringes and those of scapulars richest reddish-brown, contrasting with brownish-grey rump and uppertail-coverts. Primaries and outer secondaries grey-brown, inner secondaries rufous. **Juvenile:** Similar but duller and paler, with greyer breast centre and belly, and upperparts broadly fringed greyish-buff or brownish.

GEOGRAPHICAL VARIATION None recognised, although *chapini* described from Ruwenzori Mts is reportedly less grey and more reddish-brown than other populations, but individual variation appears to invalidate these distinctions.

MEASUREMENTS Length 33–35 cm. Male larger. Males: wing 191–210 (mean 198), tarsus 62–66 (mean 65), weight (n=2) 862 and 895. Females: wing 172–186 (mean 178), tarsus 53–57 (mean 55), weight (n=3) 600–670.

HABITAT Bamboo thickets and dense montane forest undergrowth, especially near water or in swampy patches, from lower edge of forest to alpine heath zone above tree-line, at 1850–3700 m.

VOICE Very noisy. Three call descriptions possibly all refer to one call type. Advertising call: a loud harsh crowing, *chuck-a-rick* repeated 4–5 times, or a squealing *cock-rack* repeated 6–8 times; another transcription of latter refers to a *kre-kar-kre-kar-kre-kor*.

HABITS Generally shy and elusive, remaining in dense undergrowth in pairs or small parties. Usually seen very early in morning or late afternoon when small parties occasionally noted feeding in open by forest tracks. Call is best indication of presence, especially noisy when going to roost in bushes and low trees. Prefers to escape by running through undergrowth, flushing with great reluctance, but if put-up only flies for very short distance before dropping into cover.

BREEDING Virtually unknown, nest and eggs undescribed. Considered to breed from late April to August or September.

DISTRIBUTION Highlands of Zaïre/Uganda border, from Bleus Mts of E Zaïre south to Itombwe Mts (South Kivu) and Mt Kabodo, into extreme SW Uganda (Ruwenzori Mts, the Impenetrable Forest and volcano region around Kisoro and Kabale), and adjacent Rwanda and Burundi.

STATUS Locally quite common, although few records from Uganda and presence usually indicated by voice rather than direct observation. In some areas significant numbers are reportedly snared by local people, which in view of its rather restricted range and forest habitat could pose a long-term threat to its future.

REFERENCE Chapin (1932), Urban *et al.* (1986).

---

56   JACKSON'S FRANCOLIN
Francolinus jacksoni Ogilvie-Grant, 1891   Plate 15

Replaces Chestnut-naped Francolin in montane W Kenya.

IDENTIFICATION Large size, chestnut-striped underparts, reddish-brown upperparts and red bill and legs distinctive within range. Overlaps with smaller Moorland Francolin, which has buff-streaked duller upperparts (rufous on wings in flight), black spotting on breast and dull yellowish bill and legs. Smaller Scaly Francolin is much less rufous overall, has almost unmarked underparts, and occurs at lower altitudes.

DESCRIPTION Bill red. Irides brown. Legs red. Sexes similar, but female smaller and virtually unspurred, male may have 1–2 spurs. **Adult (both sexes):** Lores, crown and nape reddish-brown, ear-coverts grey; head- and neck-sides whitish with chestnut feather centres; chin unstreaked whitish. Breast and underparts chestnut with white feather edges and sparse black vermiculations, feather edges becoming strongly vermiculated with grey and black on flanks and lower underparts. Upperparts rufous-brown with black and whitish edges to mantle feathers, lacking prominent dark streaking. Flight feathers grey-brown. **Juvenile:** Similar but paler below, with flanks and belly more barred black and white, the chestnut being most obvious on breast; upperparts duller, with extensive dark brown barring.

GEOGRAPHICAL VARIATION None recognised, although four races have been described: nominate from the Aberdares and Kinangopo Plateau, *gurae* from Mau escarpment and lower slopes of Aberdares, *patriciae* in the Cheranganis, and *pollenorum* on Mt Kenya. Only latter is perhaps worthy of recognition, it has narrower whitish edges to underparts feathering giving a much darker overall appearance.

MEASUREMENTS Length 39–48 cm. Male larger. Males: wing 203–234 (mean 218), tarsus 67–97 (mean 75), weight (n=2) 1064 and 1130. Females: wing 195–217 (mean 200), tarsus 59–79 (mean 66), weight, no data.

HABITAT Shrubby thickets on edges and in clearings of montane forest and above tree-line in shrubby giant heath and bamboo zones, chiefly at 2200–3700 m.

VOICE Advertising call: a very loud, high-pitched series of cackles, recalling Scaly or Hildebrandt's Francolins. Also a harsh repeated *grrr* that recalls a scythe being sharpened on a whetstone. While feeding, retains contact with a low, quiet, clucking.

HABITS Generally in dense undergrowth in pairs or small parties; also feeds on roadsides and forest trails, and in grassy forest glades. Not particularly shy, and may be remarkably confiding in some national parks, e.g. attends picnic tables and visits lodges in Aberdares and on Mt Kenya. Active throughout day, but in dry weather principally in early morning and evening. Roosts in trees and tall shrubs (e.g. giant heath). If disturbed runs into cover, being difficult to flush but often resorts to trees and tall shrubs when put-up. Freely dust-bathes in dry weather, favouring roadside banks and mole rat mounds.

BREEDING Monogamous. Only recorded nest was by a clump of bamboo. Clutch at least 3 pale brown eggs, but up to 7 chicks reported in brood sightings. Eggs laid December–February, also August–October. Those at very high altitudes probably only breed in dry season.

DISTRIBUTION Highlands of Kenya, from Mt Kenya and Aberdares to Mau Plateau and Cherangani Hills, with two records from isolated Mt Elgon, including one on the Ugandan side above Kapkwata Forest Station.

STATUS Locally quite common, being most abundant in Aberdares and on Mt Kenya. Subject to snaring by local people in some areas and is usually only numerous inside national parks.

REFERENCE Urban *et al.* (1986).

57   MOUNT CAMEROON FRANCOLIN
Francolinus camerunensis Alexander, 1909   Plate 12

Alternative name: Cameroon Mountain Francolin.

Apparently confined to southeast slopes of Mt Cameroon, it is one of the least known members of the genus.

IDENTIFICATION Very dark plumage and restricted range prevent confusion, but Scaly Francolin also occurs at same locality; Mount Cameroon Francolin has bare red skin around eye and sexual differences are visible if seen reasonably well, females having barred upperparts, whereas males are unmarked brown above.

DESCRIPTION Bill red. Irides brown. Legs red. Extensive bare red skin around eye. Sexes differ: female has one short or lacks spur (male has 1–2 spurs). **Adult male:** Upperparts unmarked dark brownish-grey, darker brown on crown and nape, and greyer on throat and neck, latter with paler feather fringes. Underparts dark grey, darkest on undertail-coverts, all feathers have darker centres and blackish shaft streaks. Flight feathers and tail dark brown. **Adult female:** Similar basal colour to plumage to male, but browner with upperparts mottled and barred black, buff and whitish, especially on uppertail-coverts. Head and neck feathers tipped buff, underparts streaked black and white, and undertail-coverts barred whitish. **Juvenile:** Like female but bill and legs dusky-red, bare red skin less extensive or absent, and underparts barred whitish from breast to belly, flank feathers have black and white tips.

GEOGRAPHICAL VARIATION Monotypic.

MEASUREMENTS Length 33 cm. Male slightly larger. Males: wing 167–175 (mean 171), tarsus 52–68 (mean 59). Females: wing 157–169 (mean 164), tarsus 56–61 (mean 59), weight (both sexes) c.510.

HABITAT Dense undergrowth in primary and secondary forest at 850–2100 m.

VOICE Only reported vocalisations refer to a high-pitched, musical, whistled note, repeated three times.

HABITS Generally shy and elusive, keeping to dense undergrowth in pairs or small parties. Will dust-bathe in open in sunshine. Prefers to escape by running through cover, although reported to fly up into trees if pursued by dogs.

BREEDING Virtually unknown. Probably breeds in the dry season, between October and December.

DISTRIBUTION Confined to the southern, especially southeastern, slopes of volcanic Mt Cameroon in Cameroon.

STATUS Vulnerable. Rarely seen, but considered not uncommon. An extensive area of suitable forest was destroyed by a volcanic eruption in 1982. Large tracts of forest high on eastern slope of mountain have been felled and there is some hunting pressure. Clearly very vulnerable to forest clearance, although it appears able to adapt to secondary forest. A conservation programme is being developed to secure most remaining forest inhabited by the species.

REFERENCES BirdLife International (2000), Collar & Stuart (1985), Urban *et al.* (1986).

58 SWIERSTRA'S FRANCOLIN
Francolinus swierstrai (Roberts, 1929)   Plate 16

A rare francolin of W Angolan highlands, deforestation has almost certainly brought the fragmented population to a seriously low level, although its present status is unknown.

IDENTIFICATION Restricted range (W Angola), whitish throat and foreneck, contrasting with blackish breast render this francolin unmistakable; only Red-necked Francolin overlaps and that occurs at lower altitudes and in more open habitats.

DESCRIPTION Bill red. Irides brown. Legs red. Sexes differ in upperparts coloration; female has one short or lacks spur (male has 1–2 spurs). **Adult male:** Crown and nape blackish-brown; eye-stripe and lores blackish; broad white supercilium continues on rear ear-coverts to join almost unmarked white throat, foreneck and chest. Band of black and white markings at sides and rear of lower neck, merges with broad blackish band on upper breast; rest of underparts streaked black and white. Upperparts grey-brown with pale feather centres and broken dark tips, rump and uppertail-coverts more uniform. Tail and flight feathers brownish-grey. **Adult female:** Similar to male, but upperparts more rufous-brown, each feather with pale buff shaft streaks, most apparent on mantle and scapulars. Underparts pattern similar to male, but markings browner and more irregular, with breast-band more mottled. **Juvenile:** Recalls female in distinctly rufous upperparts, but has pale buff supercilium and foreneck, and barred, rather than blotched, belly and flanks.

GEOGRAPHICAL VARIATION Monotypic.

MEASUREMENTS Length 33 cm. Male slightly larger. Males: wing 160–181 (mean 171), tarsus 49–58 (mean 53). Female (n=1): wing 167, tarsus 43, weight (both sexes) c.600.

HABITAT Highland evergreen forest and forest edges with dense undergrowth, also above tree-line on rocky and grassy slopes, gullies and grassy rolling peaks.

VOICE Advertising call: reportedly a shrill, harsh cry, recalling Jackson's Francolin. Otherwise undocumented.

HABITS Generally shy and elusive, keeping to dense undergrowth, where it scratches for food among leaves. Prefers to escape by running through cover, although one flushed from a bracken-covered stream bank perched in a tree.

BREEDING Nest and eggs undescribed. From specimen evidence and sightings of half-grown young it appears probable that the breeding season is March–September.

DISTRIBUTION W Angola, where known principally from scattered localities in Bailundu highlands and Mombolo plateau (Huambo district), with outlying records from further north at Cariango (Cuanza Sul) and south to the Chela escarpment and Tundavala (Huíla district).

STATUS Globally threatened (Vulnerable). Current status unknown due to Angola's unstable political situation during recent decades. Suspected to be severely threatened. Even in 1962 forest areas known to support this patchily distributed species had been reduced to a few hectares each, although remnants of suitable forest were known on some adjoining peaks. No recent information.

REFERENCES BirdLife International (2000), Collar & Stuart (1985), Dean (2000), King (1979), Urban *et al.* (1986).

Genus *PERDIX*: grey partridges

Small genus of three medium-sized partridges in open country across the Palearctic. All have dull-coloured bills and legs, streaked and barred dull brown upperparts, rufous tails and rusty flank barring. Sexes similar, although females drabber than males and both sexes lack tarsal spurs. Although all three are closely related, Grey and Daurian are particularly similar and form a species-pair, both have 18 tail feathers, while the third—Tibetan Partridge—differs not only in its head and breast pattern, but has only 16 tail feathers.

59   GREY PARTRIDGE
Perdix perdix (Linnaeus, 1758)   Plate 18

Alternative names: Common Partridge, Hungarian Partridge.

One of the most widespread Palearctic partridges, extending from Ireland to foothills of Altai Mts. Over most of this vast region it is declining, rapidly so in Europe, due to changes in farming practices.

IDENTIFICATION Widespread over Europe and W Siberia, introduced N America. A plump dull grey-brown partridge of open farmland. The only partridge over much of its range, but in S Europe, Crimea, parts of Turkey and N Caucasus it overlaps with members of genus *Alectoris*. Grey is easily distinguished from these by its finely barred and buff-streaked upperparts, orange face and less striking flank barring. Males, in particular, have a distinctive dark chestnut belly patch, usually concealed by their squat posture, but evident when standing upright. In flight all 'northern' partridges have rufous tails, but Grey has buff streaks on back and barred flight feathers, whereas plain-backed *Alectoris* have indistinct buff and dark wedges on primaries. Compare very similar Daurian Partridge in C and E Asia, which marginally overlaps in range.

DESCRIPTION *P. p. perdix*. Bill greenish-horn. Irides brown. Bare skin behind eye red. Legs greyish, yellower in juveniles. Sexes largely similar, female duller. Overall upperparts tone varies from grey to rufous-brown, even within populations. **Adult male:** Forehead, lores, crown-sides, chin and throat dull orange-rufous. Crown, nape and ear-coverts pale brown, mottled black and buff. Hindneck, neck-sides, breast and flanks vermiculated grey, purest on breast. Flank feathers have broad chestnut subterminal band, broken by narrow pale shaft streak. Large chestnut horseshoe-shaped patch on central lower breast and upper belly. Lower belly and vent whitish to dull pale buff, weakly vermiculated on undertail-coverts. Upperparts, including wings, dull grey to warm brown (even within populations), finely barred darker, with buff shaft streaks and fringes, scapulars finely vermiculated with chestnut on fringes. Flight feathers darker brown barred and mottled buff. Tail chestnut, finely mottled black with pale tips. In June–September male is duller, with buffish face and throat and is easily wrongly sexed, although minor differences in colour and pattern of scapulars are useful clues. **Adult female:** Similar pattern to male, but duller with less extensive and duller rufous on face, buffish wash to grey breast and obliterated or no chestnut belly patch. Upperparts less vermiculated, scapulars and wing-coverts lacking chestnut marks, being more coarsely barred black and buff. Pale shaft streaks on underparts larger and extend to breast-sides. **Juvenile:** Drabber than adult as lacks grey body colour and has no belly patch or rufous on face. Dull brownish overall, with pale shaft streaks both above and below. Much as adult when c.3–4 months old. **Variants:** Well known is '*montana*', a rare colour variant that is dark chestnut, with contrasting rufous-buff head and neck. Infrequent grey variant lacks dark belly patch but has whitish horseshoe on belly, otherwise almost entirely vermiculated grey.

GEOGRAPHICAL VARIATION Largely appears clinal. Isolated *hispaniensis* is more streaked, as is putative subspecies *italica*, which is, however, more often included within nominate. Western subspecies generally darker grey or rufous and smaller, while those in east are much paler and slightly larger. Considerable individual variation exists within subspecies and some features of certain native populations appear diluted by introductions from elsewhere. Racial taxonomy plainly requires revision.

P. p. hispaniensis Reichenow, 1892 occurs in Pyrenees and Cantabrian Mts in N Spain and NE Portugal; darker above than nominate, lacking chestnut below but extensively marked blackish above, belly patch larger and darker, and entire plumage more coarsely marked.

P. p. armoricana Hartert, 1917 occurs in Brittany, Normandy and C France; more rufous overall than nominate, even grey of breast is washed rufous.

P. p. sphagnetorum (Altum, 1894) occurs on heaths and peat moors of NE Netherlands and NW Germany; very dark with darker grey and closer barring on breast, almost blackish-rufous belly patch and heavy blackish upperparts markings (female especially dark).

P. p. perdix (Linnaeus, 1758) (includes *hilgerti* and *borkumensis = pallida*) occurs in British Is and Scandinavia east to Alps and Balkans; described above.

P. p. lucida (Altum, 1894) (includes *caucasica* and *rossica*) occurs in Finland east to Ural Mts and south to Black Sea and N Caucasus; paler and greyer above than nominate, with paler grey breast.

P. p. canescens Buturlin, 1906 (includes *furvescens*) occurs in Turkey, Caucasus, Transcaucasia and Iran; paler than *lucida*, with reduced brown upperparts markings, but intergrades in N Caucasus.

P. p. robusta Homeyer and Tancré, 1883 (includes *arenicola* and *buturlini*) occurs from Ural River east to W China; paler and greyer than *canescens*, lacking slight fulvescent tones of latter.

MEASUREMENTS Length 29–31 cm. Male rather larger. *P. p. perdix*. Males: wing 153–166, tail 76–83, tarsus 40–45, bill 12–14, weight 325–600. Females: wing 148–170, tail 68–76, tarsus 39–43, bill 11–13, weight 310–570.

HABITAT Open grassland in temperate and steppe zones of lowlands, but now largely occurs on arable farmland. It prefers large tracts of grass, which is not too high and contains patches of scrub and hedgerow cover. Also locally in east of range in grassy areas and *Saxaul* scrub within semi-desert biotopes, and montane meadows in N Spain and Caucasus, where recorded to 2600 m. Principally in and at margins of cereal and other crop fields, and meadows and pastures. Although it has adapted to less intensive agricultural systems, it disappears as land becomes increasingly intensively farmed.

VOICE Most common vocalisation, uttered by both sexes often from raised locations, is 'rusty-gate' call. This is a harsh metallic *skirl-sklERRRRRRek*, the last syllable often inaudible, typically given by male in advertisement and threat. When flushed, both sexes utter a sharp rapid *skip, skip...kip...kip...kipIPipIPipIP*. This can slow to the 'skirl call'. Variety of other vocalisations, including *guup, guup* when feeding, chick gathering calls, *chook-chee-erk* (final note rises sharply) and autumn dawn call of male, *churr-wit churr-wit*.

HABITS In non-breeding season usually in coveys of 5–15 and on occasion 20–25, while larger temporary flocks are not unknown. Family parties appear to constitute the majority of these groups, but can almost entirely comprise adults if chick survival is very low. Groups have overlapping home ranges within which each covey distances itself from others, especially when feeding at end of day. Forages at dawn and dusk, mostly picking items from ground, rather than scratching. Calls from raised positions, but not particularly conspicuous, even in breeding season. Roosts in pairs or groups of varying sizes in hollows, furrows and other ground that affords protection from wind and predators, such as near grass clumps or hay bales. Typical roost sites are ploughed fields with little cover for predators, and furrows provide some protection from wind.

BREEDING Variable mating pattern: usually monogamous, but males may rarely and briefly take two females from larger flock. Nest a shallow depression in ground lined with leaves and has internal diameter of 10–20 cm. Usually sited in dense vegetation, e.g. at base of hedgerow, in thick grass or crops. Clutch usually 15–17, but recorded range is 4–24 and second clutches are smaller; eggs typically broad, smooth and glossy olive-brown ovals. Season varies little on annual basis. Eggs late April–June, rarely early April and re-nests attempted August–September. Incubation 23–25 days by female alone, although male may assist with hatching period. Both sexes tend young, which are brooded while small.

DISTRIBUTION Throughout W Palearctic, from Ireland, British Is, N Iberia east across W and C Europe and W Asia, south to S Italy, N Greece, C Turkey and NW Iran. Northern limits are extreme SE Norway, S Sweden, S Finland, and north to 62°N in Siberia, extending south to N and SE Kazakhstan, reaching eastern limits in adjacent W Xinjiang Zizhiqu (China) and W Sayan Mts (Tuva). Although resident over most of range, Siberian populations depart in winter after heavy snowfall, when wanderers reach as far as west shore of Lake Baikal. Introduced W and N USA and adjacent S Canada, but feral New Zealand populations have died out.

STATUS Not globally threatened, but habitat now much reduced. Widely hunted, with 'bag' records over many years from several parts of its range all suggesting a large decline. It has been hypothesised that original numbers, against which population size is currently being compared, were artificially high due to stocking programmes. This appears impossible to confirm and it is inescapable that agricultural intensification has very seriously affected this species, bringing about an increasing number of local extinctions. Overall decline may be as high as 80% and is ongoing, although it probably still numbers in millions across its wide range. The British population, for example, decreased from 500,000 pairs in 1970 to 150,000 pairs by 1990. Critical is the reduction in insect food for chicks, which rely on invertebrates for up to 80% of their diet in the first two weeks of life. The drive for high crop yields, using pesticides to kill insects and herbicides to remove weeds (on which many insects breed and feed) has devastated chick food supply. Loss of nesting cover and increased predation are also problems.

REFERENCES Cramp & Simmons (1980), Dement'ev & Gladkov (1967), Potts (1986).

---

60 DAURIAN PARTRIDGE
Perdix dauurica (Pallas, 1811)   Plate 18

Alternative names: Mongolian Partridge, Bearded Partridge.

Closely related to Grey Partridge, which it replaces in the E Palearctic. Despite obvious similarities, the two overlap over a wide geographical area with only very limited hybridisation.

IDENTIFICATION Replaces Grey Partridge in China and Mongolia, but overlaps with pale grey *robusta* race of latter in C Siberia, extreme W China and E Kazakhstan. Habitat differences in the breeding season appear to separate the two species in these regions: in Kazakhstan Grey occurs on plains, whereas Daurian is found on shrubby slopes and in more wooded areas, notably foothills of the Tien Shan Mts. In winter, Daurian may also move onto plains and some mixed coveys have been reported. Daurian differs from *robusta* race of Grey in being darker grey, with extensive chestnut markings and bold pale shaft streaks on scapulars (like western forms of Grey), whereas *robusta* is paler grey overall, with weak upperparts markings. Daurian differs from all forms of Grey in having a blackish or sooty-brown, not chestnut, belly patch surrounded by ochre-buff (not whitish). Buff coloration, in many, extends over central breast to join orange-buff of throat, restricting grey of breast to sides, while others have narrow belt of grey on upper chest. Some merely have pale buff wash over grey of central breast. In autumn and winter, Daurian develops a 'beard' of stiff feathers on throat-sides, a feature never shown by Grey. Compare also Chukar, and Przevalski's and Tibetan Partridges, which also overlap with Daurian.

DESCRIPTION *P. d. dauurica*. Bill greyish-horn. Irides brown. Bare skin behind and below eye red (only obvious in male). Legs greyish-horn. Sexes generally similar, but female duller. In non-breeding season develops 'beard' of stiff feathers on throat-sides, a feature shared by Japanese Quail, which has a similar distribution. **Adult male:** Forehead, lores, crown-sides, chin and throat cinnamon-buff, often brighter orange-buff on supercilia area. Crown and ear-coverts dark brown, mottled and streaked whitish-buff. Hindneck, neck-sides, breast and fore flanks vermiculated grey, washed or wholly inundated ochre-buff on central breast. Flank feathers have broad chestnut subterminal band, broken by narrow pale shaft streak. Extensive large blackish-brown, or black, horseshoe-shaped patch on centre of lower breast and upper belly surrounded by ochre-buff wash. Lower belly and vent pale buff, weakly vermiculated on undertail-coverts. Upperparts, including wings, dull grey-brown, finely barred darker and with whitish-buff shaft streaks; scapulars have chestnut bands across each feather. Flight feathers darker brown, barred and mottled buff. Tail chestnut, finely mottled black with pale tips. In June–September duller and acquires stiff bristled feathers on sides of face. **Adult female:** Similar to male but duller, with less extensive and duller buff on face, fine whitish spotting on breast-sides and neck, and smaller or obscured blackish belly patch. Scapulars and wing-coverts have smaller chestnut marks, and mantle and back more coarsely barred black and brown. **Juvenile:** Featureless like juvenile Grey Partridge, but greyer brown overall.

GEOGRAPHICAL VARIATION Chiefly in overall colour saturation, with those in east darker and more rufous; differences obscured by clinal and individual variation. Two or three subspecies recognised, although several others have been described.

P. d. dauurica (Pallas, 1811) (includes *turcomana* and *occidentalis*) occurs east to Transbaikalia, intergrading with next form further east; described above.

P. d. suschkini Poliakov, 1915 (includes *castaneothorax*) occurs in E China, rarely into Russian Far East; darker and more rufous than nominate (similar to nominate Grey Partridge).

P. d. przewalski Sushkin, 1926 occurs in C China from SE Gansu to SW Qinghai; not usually separated from *suschkini* but pale, sandy tones suggest subspecific separation is valid.

MEASUREMENTS Length 28–30 cm. *P. d. suschkini.* Males: wing 137–141, tail 76–98, weight 294–300. Females: wing 133–145, tail 73–92, weight 200–340.

HABITAT Wide variety of habitats in plains and montane foothills to 3000 m. Exhibits marked preference for bushy or lightly wooded areas adjoining grassland. Also wooded steppe, grassy forest clearings,

shrubby meadows, riverine scrub, farmsteads and enclosed cultivation. Locally on semi-arid rocky hills, but usually shuns desert regions.

VOICE Much as Grey Partridge, but no comparative studies available.

HABITS Occurs in large groups, which in autumn may number 15–30 and apparently increase in winter to as many as 200. Virtually no other behavioural information is available, but habits assumed similar to other *Perdix*.

BREEDING Monogamous. Nest a depression lined with grasses, leaves, roots and soft feathers, concealed within, or adjacent to, cover. Clutch 18–20 (minimum 12) olive-brown eggs. Timing varies, with pair-formation during March in Altai Mts (eggs laid early April), but further south and east does not nest until late May in NC and NE China. Incubation occupies 25 days and both sexes tend chicks.

DISTRIBUTION China, Mongolia and adjacent regions, from northern edge of Fergana Basin in W Kyrgyzstan, through Tien Shan of SE Kazakhstan and adjacent foothills of Tien Shan in W China (west to Kashgar), with stragglers wandering to Tajikistan, thence north through western foothills of Russian Altai to Tuva and Sayan Mts, north and west to Krasnoyarsk (at c.55°N) in C Siberia (in winter west to Tomsk and has straggled in August to Baraba steppe), and east across Mongolia and Buryatia (north to Vitim plateau) to Chita. Widespread in N China, from W and N Xinjiang Zizhiqu, through Qinghai, Gansu, Shaanxi, Shanxi, Hebei and Nei Mongol to Heilongjiang in northeast. Also Russian Far East, where has occurred in winter around Khabarovsk and Lake Khanka. Resident in most areas but disperses to lower ground in winter after heavy snowfalls. Unsuccessfully introduced into Philippines and elsewhere.

STATUS Not globally threatened. Knowledge of status better developed in NE China than elsewhere and considered common in Jilin, Hebei and Heilongjiang. Few data from elsewhere, although numbers hunted are believed to have declined in Shanxi in NC China. Over-hunting perhaps significant in Jilin and given that hunting is reasonably common throughout most, if not all, of its range, further information on status and, especially, trends would be valuable. Whether it is susceptible to the same consequences of agricultural change that has had such a dramatic effect on Grey Partridge is also worthy of study.

REFERENCES Cheng (1987), Dement'ev & Gladkov (1967), Dolgushin *et al.* (1962), Lytoon & Flint (1993), Zhang & Wu (1992), Zhao *et al.* (1992).

---

61   TIBETAN PARTRIDGE
Perdix hodgsoniae (Hodgson, 1857)   Plate 18

Boldly patterned partridge of the Tibetan plateau; despite its striking head and neck pattern, its affinity to *Perdix* is demonstrated by its upperparts coloration, dark belly patch and chestnut flank barring.

IDENTIFICATION Grey-brown with streaked upperparts and boldly patterned head and chest. White face, throat and supercilium contrast with chestnut or rufous nape and black ear-patch, but despite gaudy appearance the head and breast pattern provides cryptic camouflage, rendering it difficult to locate in its rocky environment. Range almost certainly overlaps with Daurian Partridge in C Qinghai and Gansu, but if so it appears likely Tibetan replaces Daurian in more barren habitats at higher elevations. Compare also Chukar and Snow Partridge.

DESCRIPTION *P. h. hodgsoniae.* Bill pale greenish-horn. Irides brown or reddish-brown. Bare skin behind eye red (obvious only in breeding male). Legs greyish-horn. Sexes generally similar, but female duller. **Adult male:** Forehead, supercilium, chin, central throat and band extending partially around neck-sides white. Lores streaked black and white. Ear-coverts and throat-sides black. Band on forecrown and crown-sides above supercilium chestnut. Central crown mottled black and white. Nape and neck sides chestnut, forming collar. Ground colour of rest of underparts whitish, heavily scaled black and chestnut on breast-sides and lower fore flanks, rest of flanks boldly barred chestnut, interspersed with fine pale shaft streaks. Diffuse large blackish patch on central lower breast and upper belly. Lower belly and vent dull whitish. Upperparts, including wings, dull grey-brown, finely barred darker, with whitish-buff shaft streaks; scapulars and wing-coverts have rufous-brown bars on each feather. Flight feathers darker brown, barred and mottled buff. All but central feathers of tail chestnut. **Adult female:** Similar to male, but duller. **Juvenile:** Rather featureless, lacking both greyish and chestnut plumage tones. Crown and ear-coverts dark brown with white feather tips. Entire underparts brownish-buff, with fine pale streaks and weak vermiculations.

GEOGRAPHICAL VARIATION Clinal, becoming darker in east of range. Three intergrading subspecies recognised.

P. h. sifanica Przevalski, 1876 (includes *koslowi* = *occidentalis*) occurs in E Tibet to C Qinghai and Gansu, China; browner and more rufous than nominate and usually smaller.
P. h. hodgsoniae (Hodgson, 1857) occurs in border regions of N India (Kumaon) through Nepal to Bhutan and S Tibet; described above.
P. h. caraganae R. & A. Meinertzhagen, 1926 occurs in E Kashmir (India) to SW Tibet; paler and greyer above than nominate, with brighter chestnut markings.

MEASUREMENTS Length 28–31 cm. *P. h. hodgsoniae.* Both sexes: wing 149–165 (male above 155), tail 86–91, tarsus 40–43, bill c.15–17, weight 294–450.

HABITAT Mountain slopes and alpine meadows with some cover, usually at 3600–4250 m but occurs to snow-line at 5600 m in summer, and one winter record from just 2200 m in Nepal. Favours rocky country with *Caragana* scrub, and dwarf juniper and *Rhododendron* cover. Descends in winter to adjoining semi-desert plains. Locally also around basic cultivation.

VOICE Male call, often from an elevated rock perch, is a repeated rattling *scherrrrreck-scherrrrreck* given in early morning and evening. When flushed, utters a shrill *chee, chee, chee, chee, chee,* likened to the creaking of a wicker basket lid. If given as a contact call, after pair or covey separate, buzzing sound is apparently similar to a finger being drawn across teeth of a comb.

HABITS In non-breeding season occurs in groups of 10–15. Not overly wary and when disturbed usually runs rather than flies. On occasion, however, groups suddenly burst noisily into the air and scatter singly or in pairs in different directions with great commotion and shrill calls. When possible they glide downhill. Takes a variety of weed and grass seeds, and small invertebrates. Even recorded foraging in grasses and bushes near yak herder's camps.

BREEDING System unknown but presumably monogamous. Nest a grass-lined scrape on ground c.20–22 cm across, placed next to a boulder or other cover within *Caragana* scrub. Sometimes simply lays eggs on level ground. Clutch 8–10 (occasionally 6 in captivity) dark brownish-buff oval and elongated eggs, occasionally tinged olive, but pure white eggshells, apparently belonging to this species also reported. May form creches, given an observation of six adults 'herding' 15 chicks in Ladakh, where typical brood sizes appear to be 4–6. Breeds May–July, sometimes August. Incubation period unknown.

DISTRIBUTION W China and adjacent regions. Patchily distributed along Tibetan border with NW India (Ladakh in Himachal Pradesh and Kumaon in Uttar Pradesh), NC Nepal, N Sikkim and NW Bhutan, across Tibet to W Sichuan and north to Gansu in China.

STATUS Not globally threatened due to large range and apparent frequency in accessible parts. Considered fairly common in China and in NE India locally common, but few recent data. As it typically occurs in remote habitat, there is very little information on population sizes and trends, but this may also serve to ensure its relative population stability.

REFERENCES Ali & Ripley (1983), Cheng (1987), McGowan (1994), Pfister (2001).

Genus *RHIZOTHERA*: Long-billed Partridge

Monotypic genus containing an aberrant tropical Asian forest partridge. Relatively large and rather unmarked, with a long decurved stout bill and spurred tarsi (the latter shared by *Francolinus*). Like *Melanoperdix* it has 12 tail feathers, but tail is longer and stronger.

62 LONG-BILLED PARTRIDGE
Rhizothera longirostris (Temminck, 1815)   **Plate 19**

Alternative name: Long-billed Wood-partridge.

An elusive species of tropical jungle in the Malay Peninsula and Greater Sundas.

IDENTIFICATION Malaysia, Sumatra and Borneo. Partial to bamboo thickets within relatively dry forest. Combination of large size, unmarked rufous face and underparts (plus grey breast in male), and yellowish legs makes identification comparatively straightforward, even if rather long, thick bill is not seen. Flies very reluctantly but if flushed exhibits contrast between pale buffy wings and rump, and dark mantle and back. Forages chiefly in leaf litter of forest floor, but also readily perches in lower branches of trees. Smaller Ferruginous Partridge has extensive black and white barring on flanks and back, and black spotting on wings.

DESCRIPTION *R. l. longirostris*. Black bill is relatively long, heavy and slightly decurved. Irides pale brown. Small patch of bare red skin behind eye. Legs pale yellow. Both sexes possess short tarsal spurs. Sexes differ. **Adult male:** Supercilium, head-sides, and neck and throat rusty-rufous. Forehead, crown centre and nape dark chestnut-brown. A dusky line borders the crown-sides above supercilium, with another dusky line through eye. Breast, lower foreneck and mantle sides grey. Rest of underparts rusty-rufous becoming paler on belly and undertail-coverts. Mantle, back and scapulars mottled chestnut and black with some pale shaft streaks, contrasting with vermiculated buffy-grey rump, uppertail-coverts and tail (latter more strongly barred). Wing-coverts vermiculated buffy-grey and spotted yellowish-buff. Flight feathers barred grey and buffy-grey. **Adult female:** Similar but lacks grey breast, having entire face, throat and underparts uniform rusty-rufous. Upperparts, from back to uppertail, warmer and more brownish-buff. **Juvenile:** Both sexes resemble dull version of female, but with fine pale streaking on throat, breast and mantle, and weak dark spotting and barring on breast and flanks. Lacks tarsal spurs of adult and has brownish bill. Young male soon acquires grey breast patches.

GEOGRAPHICAL VARIATION Two subspecies recognised. The taxonomic position of *dulitensis* may repay investigation.

    R. l. longirostris (Temminck, 1815) occurs in the Malay Peninsula, Sumatra and lowlands of W and S Kalimantan, SW Sarawak and E Sabah (Borneo); described above.

    R. l. dulitensis Ogilvie-Grant, 1895 occurs in Sarawak (Mt Dulit and Mt Batu Song); greyer than nominate with greyish-white (not rufous) lower underparts.

MEASUREMENTS Length 30–35 cm. Sexes similar. Males: wing 189–212, tail 74–79, tarsus 54–61, bill 23–31. Females: wing 180–210, tail 73–90, tarsus 54–60, bill 21–26. No weight data, only estimates, male 800, female 700.

HABITAT Inhabits primary and well-grown secondary forest, dry forest and areas of bamboo. Occurs in low-land and montane forest to 1500 m in Malay Peninsula, but not above 1000 m in some other regions. Subspecies *dulitensis* is a highland form, unrecorded below 1000 m.

VOICE Most vocal in early morning and evening, but also occasionally at other times, such as after rain and even at night. A high-pitched duet, one gives a two-note call, which is followed or overlapped by a disyllabic whistle. The sequence is delivered in a seesaw rhythm, which can be transcribed as *ti-ooah-whee*, repeated over long periods; it has a rather bell-like (or tree-frog-like) quality. The duet's second part may be given separately. A soft whistle uttered as a contact call and a low *cluck-cluck*, the latter possibly in warning.

HABITS Probably remains paired throughout year and considered to be territorial. As they have been seen roosting separately 8–10 m above ground, duetting birds may be a few metres apart if they call from the roost. When flushed, flies into trees. No other information available, although it has been speculated that the upper-bill structure may be adapted for specialised feeding.

BREEDING Presumably monogamous as usually seen in pairs. Only one nest ever found, containing 2 eggs, on Borneo in February 1934. No information from the Thai-Malay Peninsula or Sumatra on nesting, although calling reported on the peninsula in February–May, August and November, but what relationship this bears to breeding activity is unknown. In captivity, clutch size is 2–5 long oval-shaped eggs of smooth texture and glossy appearance, the ground colour slightly tinged with rose-red spots. Incubation in captivity 18–19 days.

DISTRIBUTION Extreme S Myanmar (Tenasserim) and peninsular Thailand south through Malaysia to Sumatra and Borneo. Occurs patchily from c.14°S in the peninsula, with most of range in Malaysia (except northeast and extreme northwest). Few recent records from Sumatra. Considered patchy on Borneo where it occurs on Mt Dulit and Mt Batu Song (Sarawak) and at lower altitudes in SW Sarawak, Ulu Barito (Kalimantan) and Danum Valley (Sabah).

STATUS Near Threatened. Lowland rainforest clearance over much of its range has been such that, for example, it may be extinct in peninsular Thailand. Even hill forest is currently being logged, from the lower fringes upwards. The species' tolerance of habitat extremes is unclear, it being found in montane forest in some areas, which may offer its best prospects for long-term survival. Nonetheless, it appears that it may be unable to survive in hill forest in Thailand if still found there, whereas this habitat may become its main stronghold in peninsular Malaysia. Currently known from a number of protected areas, including Taman Negara National Park in peninsular Malaysia and Gunung Leuser National Park in N Sumatra.

REFERENCES BirdLife International (2000), Johnsgard (1988), MacKinnon & Phillipps (1993), van Marle & Voous (1988), Robbins (1998), Smythies (1981), Wells (1999).

Genus *MARGAROPERDIX*: Madagascar Partridge

Monotypic genus containing Madagascar's only endemic phasianid. Strongly sexually dimorphic, it has 12 feathers in its wedge-shaped tail and lacks tarsal spurs. In view of the primitive nature of Madagascar's wildlife, this species may be close to ancestral stock that gave rise to present-day partridges and quails.

63 MADAGASCAR PARTRIDGE
Margaroperdix madagarensis (Scopoli, 1786)   Plate 19

Richly coloured species of bushy grassland and forest clearings throughout Madagascar.

IDENTIFICATION Madagascar. Dark reddish-brown, with striking facial and underparts patterns. Male has black throat highlighted by white malar and supercilium, but more striking (if standing upright) is bold white spotting on black lower underparts. Female, by complete contrast, is distinctive in lacking any plumage features other than being wholly narrowly barred and freckled. Confusion unlikely on Madagascar (compare much smaller Harlequin Quail and Madagascar Buttonquail) but on Mauritius and Réunion compare female with larger Grey Francolin.

DESCRIPTION Bill black. Irides dark brown. Legs grey. Sexually dimorphic. **Adult male:** Forehead and crown dark brown, mottled black. Narrow white line on centre of crown. Lores, chin and throat black. Supercilium and malar white. Ear-coverts, neck-sides and breast-sides grey. Breast centre rich rufous. Lower breast and belly black with bold white spots on each feather. Flanks and vent rufous-brown, streaked white. Nape, mantle and scapulars rich dark rufous-brown with white shaft streaks. Rump and uppertail-coverts duller brown, streaked buff and finely vermiculated. Wings rufous-brown with duller brown primaries and narrowly black-barred secondaries. Tail dull brown, narrowly barred black. **Adult female:** Head, neck and underparts dull buff, finely scaled and barred black, forming scalloping on flanks; chin and upper throat virtually unmarked buff. Entire upperparts buff-brown, narrowly and closely barred black. Scapulars and mantle have fine whitish shaft streaks. Primaries unmarked brown. **Juvenile:** Poorly documented. Apparently very much like adult female but overall plumage duller.

GEOGRAPHICAL VARIATION Monotypic.

MEASUREMENTS Length 24–28 cm. Male slightly larger. Males: wing 119–131, tail 69. Females: wing 121–131, tail 69. No weight data, only estimates for both sexes, c.220.

HABITAT Variety of bushy and grassy habitats from dry fields to forest edges and clearings; recorded from sea level to 2700 m. Appears to favour secondary habitats and adjacent grassland.

VOICE Remarkably silent for a partridge, although the advertising call appears to be a loud *cou*, which is repeated and is audible over some distance. When flushed it gives a low-pitched *peet* or series of trilled notes.

HABITS In non-breeding season encountered singly, in pairs or trios, or groups of c.12. Shy and wary, preferring to run with erect carriage rather than fly when approached. Takes to wing only when hard-pressed or suddenly surprised, but even then only flies for a short distance before dropping and running on. Presumably fairly sedentary. No reliable information on feeding habits, but probably omnivorous, taking berries, seeds and insects.

BREEDING Mating pattern unknown. Breeds March–June (on High Plateau). Nest is a simple depression on ground well hidden under grass tuft or bush. In captivity clutch is 8–15 (15–20 claimed in wild); eggs brown to green-buff, with dark brown or black flecking and mottling. Incubation in captivity is 18–19 days.

DISTRIBUTION Widespread throughout Madagascar, although absent from extreme south. Introduced in Réunion (common) and Mauritius (uncommon).

STATUS Perhaps at risk. Extensively hunted and trapped, and while prime grassland habitat has been extensively degraded, it appears common in secondary habitats. If breeding can be confirmed in these human-altered habitats it may not be threatened. Clarification of its habitat requirements would constitute a major step towards a truer understanding of its status and prospects. Although it may have decreased markedly in recent decades the extant population must number several thousand. Known from many protected areas and proposed protected areas.

REFERENCES Dee (1986), Johnsgard (1988), Langrand (1990), McGowan *et al.* (1995).

Genus *MELANOPERDIX*: Black Wood-partridge

Monotypic genus containing an aberrant Asian tropical forest partridge. Strongly sexually dimorphic, this peculiar species has a remarkably stout bill and sports 12 soft tail feathers. It is probable that its nearest relatives are the hill-partridges.

Alternative name: Black Partridge.

A strange, rarely seen, unicoloured partridge of dense lowland jungle in the Greater Sundas and peninsular Malaysia.

IDENTIFICATION Malaysia, Sumatra and Borneo. Small all-black (male) or rusty-brown (female) partridge of the forest floor, especially fond of *Bertram* scrub. Unmistakable if seen well but in forest gloom other species (e.g. Crimson-headed Wood-partridge on Borneo or even Ferruginous Partridge) can appear equally dark or rusty-brown. Juvenile has white-spotted flanks like Bornean Hill-partridge, but latter has longer red legs and bill. No other partridge has such a thick bill, which also immediately separates females from larger Long-billed Partridge (which has a remarkably similar distribution). Compare also Crested Partridge.

DESCRIPTION Bill short and remarkably thick, black (male) or dark horn (female). Irides dark brown. Small patch of bare black skin behind eye. Legs blue-grey. Sexually dimorphic. **Adult male:** Entirely glossy black, with duller dark brown flight feathers. **Adult female:** Strikingly different. Tawny or chestnut-brown overall, becoming very pale buffish or whitish on chin and throat, belly and undertail-coverts. Pale ear-coverts barred chestnut, merging with pale throat. Some have blackish cheeks but significance unclear. Otherwise, only prominent black bars on scapulars relieve the near-plain plumage. **Juvenile:** Duller brown than female, with fine dark barring interspersed with bold white spotting on breast-sides and flanks, and whiter vent. Upperparts variably marked with pale spotting and vermiculated paler brown and darker brown, but scapulars less boldly marked with black than female; young male soon acquires blackish plumage.

GEOGRAPHICAL VARIATION Best considered monotypic, but the Borneo population has been separated (*M. n. borneensis*) on very minor differences.

MEASUREMENTS Length 24–27 cm. Female slightly smaller. Males: wing 140–149, tail 54–62, tarsus 44–47, bill 20–21, weight (n=1) 280. Females: wing 137–147, tail 56–58, tarsus 43–46, bill 18–21, weight (n=1) 281.

HABITAT Lowland rainforest in level areas of Thai-Malay Peninsula and hill slopes on Borneo, where also recorded in lower montane zone (perhaps to 1200 m). No altitude preferences noted on Sumatra, presumably due to paucity of reports. Apparently only occurs in primary and very well developed secondary forest with tall, closed canopies. On Sumatra also in peat swamp forest in Jambi. One feature of its habitat is a preference for *Bertram* (a spiny, stemless palm) undergrowth.

VOICE Quiet. Some dispute exists over a whistle call attributed to this species. MacKinnon & Phillipps (1993) describe a clear two-note whistle similar to Crested Partridge, but Wells (1999) considers that confirmation of this is required. Contact call apparently resembles a heavy old door, being low and creaking.

HABITS One of the least-known Galliformes, being very rarely seen and information on any aspect of its life history valuable. The lack of information may be partially attributable to its quietness, which means that it is rarely detected. Secondly, it typically sits tight and runs only when really pressed. Reliable observations have usually involved pairs, but also reported to occur singly. No dietary information, although its strong bill suggests an adaptation for crushing hard seeds or fruits.

BREEDING Mating pattern unknown. Five nests found on Borneo contained one clutch of 2 eggs (January), one of 3 (May) and three of 5 eggs (September). Downy young seen late October on the same island. At Perak on the Thai-Malay Peninsula downy young have been reported in late August and well-grown chicks in August–September. In captivity clutch size is 5–6 white eggs with a slightly rough chalky surface. Incubation in captivity is 18–19 days.

DISTRIBUTION Malaysia and Sumatra, from southern two-thirds of Malay Peninsula south to Sumatra and Borneo, except east of island. Formerly also on Singapore.

STATUS Vulnerable. No information on status changes primarily because it has only ever been recorded very sporadically. While known from lowland rainforest, its tolerance of other habitats is unclear. Widespread destruction of primary forest on level ground, to which it currently appears highly restricted, suggests that it could be at greater risk than presently understood. New records are urgently sought throughout its range, especially on Sumatra, where its contemporary distribution is very poorly known. Known from several protected areas, including Gunung Mulu National Park in Sarawak and Tanjung Puting National Park in Kalimantan. Long extinct on Singapore.

REFERENCES BirdLife International (2000), MacKinnon & Phillipps (1993), van Marle & Voous (1988), McGowan *et al.* (1995), Robbins (1998), Wells (1999).

Genus *COTURNIX*: Old World quails

One extinct and eight extant species, several of which are long-distance migrants (*Coturnix* contains the only migratory phasianids). Most form superspecies groups (Rain, Stubble and Harlequin; Common and Japanese; and Blue and King), between them covering most of the Old World. *Coturnix* have unspurred tarsi, tails of 8–12 insignificant feathers, concealed by the coverts, slender bills and markedly long outer primaries (an adaptation that aids long-distance flight).

Alternative names: Migratory Quail, Grey Quail, European Quail.

This and its close relatives (Japanese and Rain Quails) are the only strongly migratory phasianids and, as a result, have evolved relatively long wings.

IDENTIFICATION A tiny gamebird of open country, typically seen if suddenly flushed from underfoot, when it 'explodes' on whirring wings and flies swiftly away low, often for considerable distance. In flight, it appears relatively uniform brown (without striking pale covert-panel of some buttonquail). The only quail in Europe or W Asia (east to Lake Baikal), in parts of Africa and S Asia it overlaps with others of the genus and with buttonquails (which see for differences). The relatively long, pointed wing-tip in flight should help eliminate potentially confusing buttonquails and young partridges (which can fly when very young). Distinctive 'song' is usually best clue to its presence. See also Japanese, Rain and Harlequin Quails and Small Buttonquail.

DESCRIPTION *C. c. coturnix*. Bill grey, becoming brownish on culmen and fleshy on cutting edges. Irides red-brown to pale yellowish-brown. Legs pale yellowish to dull brownish-flesh. Sexually dimorphic, male variable (some have extensive rufous on face and throat). **Adult male:** Forehead and crown blackish obscured by extensive pale buff feather tips; pale creamy-buff, long and narrow central crown stripe and supercilium. Rather broad dull brownish band across lores and behind eye, reaches 'shoulder' and separates on lower neck-sides. Dusky malar stripe and anchor-shaped patch at centre of chin and throat hooks back nearly to malar. Lower ear-coverts, throat-sides and collar, below anchor, creamy-buff. Marked variation in facial pattern, some have rufous face and throat, with or without blackish throat anchor, sometimes with rufous extending onto breast. Breast and flanks dull rufous-buff, regularly marked with blackish and creamy-buff at sides, finely streaked whitish-buff central breast, flanks boldly streaked chestnut, and, more obviously, with pale buff (finely edged black), interspersed with irregular dark bars. Central and lower underparts pale buff. Upperparts dull brown (some distinctly rufous), with intense blackish blotching and buff barring and, except rump, bold pale buff shaft streaks (edged black). Wing-coverts dull brown with fine buff shaft streaks and buff (edged black) barring. Primaries and secondaries brownish, narrowly barred buff (except tips and inner webs of primaries, which are unmarked). Tail inconspicuous, dark brown cleanly barred buff. **Adult female:** Lacks black throat and has less marked facial bridle than male, with paler face and underparts and less chestnut on flanks. Not as variable as male, lacking rufous variants. **Juvenile:** Resembles adult female but has plainer head-sides (unstreaked), smaller dark spots at breast-sides, narrower shaft streaks on upperparts, but bolder whitish streaks on breast and stronger, more regular, dusky flank bars. Ground colour of breast richer buff in

young male. Much as adult by autumn, but young male pale throated until latter part of first winter.

GEOGRAPHICAL VARIATION Several races differ slightly in size or overall colour saturation; the precise relationship of some forms is controversial. The treatment here follows Vaurie (1965) and Cramp & Simmons (1980), except that *inopinata* is not recognised (see Hazevoet 1995). African forms are problematic, thus Urban *et al.* (1986) treats the migratory S African *africana* as synonymous with nominate. Melanistic individuals are typically rare but are oddly frequent in Malawi.

   C. c. coturnix (Linnaeus, 1758) (includes *inopinata, orientalis, corsicana, ragionierii* and *parisii*) breeds in Europe, N Africa, W Asia and Cape Verde Is, wintering south to equatorial Africa and east to India; described above.

   C. c. confisa Hartert, 1917 (includes *conturbans*) occurs in the Canaries, Madeira and Azores; darker than nominate, closer to *africana* but with paler upperparts.

   C. c. africana Temminck & Schlegel, 1849 occurs in South Africa and, presumably, Madagascar; paler than *erlangeri* and very close to nominate, but darker above.

   C. c. erlangeri Zedlitz, 1912 occurs in highlands of E Africa from Ethiopia south to E Zimbabwe; darker and more rufous than other forms, many males have rufous face, throat and underparts.

MEASUREMENTS Length 18–20 cm. Female slightly smaller. *C. c. coturnix* given. Males: wing 107–117, tail 34–40, tarsus 25–27, weight 70–140. Females: wing 109–118, tail 34–43, tarsus 25–28, weight 70–155.

HABITAT Open rolling grasslands and fields, preferably weedy, cornfields and relatively dry meadows; from lowland meadows (generally below 1000 m in Europe), through semi-desert grassland to montane plateaux (to 2400 m in E Zimbabwe, 3000 m in Kenyan highlands, 2990 m in Tajikistan, and once to 3600 m in Ladakh). Avoids trees and wetlands, favouring seasonally warm to hot regions, almost reaching the Arctic Circle in Russia (Yakutia), as well as equatorial Africa. On migration occurs in almost any weedy cover, especially on coasts.

VOICE Male advertising call very distinctive, most readily given near dawn or dusk, and often calls throughout night. A far-carrying series of rapid staccato, but liquid, notes *qwip-qwip, qwip, qw-qwip* or *whit-WHITtit, whit-WHITtit*, repeated 4–8 times (traditionally rendered as 'wet my lips'). Ventriloquial quality makes it difficult to pinpoint calls. Also a shrill, squealed *tree-tree* when flushed. Several other low or soft calls, but all are rather inconspicuous. Little vocal difference between nominate and *erlangeri*.

HABITS Shy and retiring, perhaps most often seen dust-bathing on tracks, or at migration watchpoints. Slips furtively through grasses in crouched ('quailing') posture, feeding unobtrusively on weed and grass seeds and small invertebrates. In many areas appears to require little water, but in hot climates regularly visits water source. Roosts alone in shallow hollows among grasses. If suddenly surprised, rises quickly in snipe *Gallinago*-like fashion, skimming low on mixture of rapid beats and short glides, before dropping back into cover and running on; rarely flushes twice. Typically solitary in breeding season, male defends defined territory, although noticeable aggregations form in prime habitat. After fledging, broods remain together and in autumn join other groups (bevies) prior to nocturnal migration, often in flocks. Periodic variations in abundance are due to nomadic nature of migratory arrivals.

BREEDING Pair-bond varies locally according to density and sex ratio—can be monogamous, bigamous, polygamous or even promiscuous. Nest a shallow scrape lined with sparse vegetation, usually in dense grass, constructed by female. Clutch 7–18 (mean 10), sometimes two females lay in same nest. Eggs whitish or pale buff, variably spotted and blotched chocolate-brown. Usually only female incubates, but male may do so rarely, for 17–20 days. Single-brooded but perhaps occasionally double brooded, with more southerly, early nesting, birds moving north to breed later in same calendar year. Eggs chiefly May–June and to lesser extent August (perhaps second broods from fresh inter-season influxes, or failed first broods) in Europe and C Asia. Elsewhere, March–April in India, March–May in Israel and N Africa, near end of rainy season in sub-Saharan Africa, but timing varies in E Africa (complex local rain patterns), and is September–December in W Cape, January in Zambia, January and May in Namibia, and October–January in Malawi. Chicks can flutter at 11 days and fledge at 19 days, remaining in family groups (bevies) until c.45 days old.

DISTRIBUTION Widespread in Eurasia and Africa in three main populations. Breeds over most of S and C Europe (uncommonly north to S Sweden and British Is), NW Africa (east to Tunisia) and W Asia (north to 64°N), including the Azores, Canary Is, Madeira and Cape Verde Is, south to N Egypt, Israel, N Iraq and N Iran, with an outlying resident population in E Saudi Arabia and perhaps UAE. Further north, it extends east to Lake Baikal and the Altai foothills in W Mongolia (east to Uvs Nuur), W China (W Xinjiang Zizhiqu east to Turfan Depression), C and N Afghanistan, Pakistan, Kashmir, east over N India (south to Maharashtra) through Nepal to Bhutan, W Assam and N Bangladesh (recent discovery of Japanese Quail in Bhutan suggests status of Common Quail in this part of the subcontinent requires review). Migrants arrive on Libyan and Egyptian coasts in huge 'waves', with massive build-up in numbers before overflying Sahara (comparatively scarce at desert oases) to winter in the Sahel, south to Cameroon and N Kenya. Some winter in S and SW Europe and C Asia, more rarely north to England, the Ukraine, the Aral Sea basin of Kazakhstan and even in S Tibet (Gyangtse). Many winter in Indian subcontinent, with large numbers migrating through Afghanistan and NW Pakistan. A separate, apparently resident, population inhabits eastern sub-Saharan Africa, isolated in highland grasslands of Ethiopia, Kenya, Uganda, E Zaïre, south through Tanzania to E Zimbabwe, extreme W Mozambique and, presumably this form, on Madagascar. The third population is principally migratory, breeding in South Africa, S Mozambique and possibly Namibia and Botswana (where recently nested), and moving north to winter in Angola, W Zambia and S Zaïre. Introduced Mauritius. Vagrant to Comoro Is, Seychelles (Aride), W and S Myanmar, Iceland and Faeroes (where has bred).

STATUS Locally common but numbers everywhere fluctuate markedly according to annual migratory influx. Overall marked decrease throughout range due to loss of natural grasslands is reflected in numbers trapped at key migration points (e.g. 1–3 million netted annually on Sinai coast in early 1900s, decreased to 600,000 by 1926 and 150,000–200,000 in 1960s). Status in India is intriguing, but apparently breeds in variable numbers according to extent of rains and even here is much scarcer than formerly.

REFERENCES Ali & Ripley (1969), Baker (1930), Bannerman (1963), Cramp & Simmons (1980), Urban *et al.* (1986), Witherby *et al.* (1941).

66 JAPANESE QUAIL
Coturnix japonica (Temminck and Schlegel, 1849)   Plate 20

Alternative name: Asian Migratory Quail.

Eastern counterpart of Common Quail that is superficially similar but vocally quite different; the two possibly overlap south of Lake Baikal and in NE India.

IDENTIFICATION Very similar to Common Quail, which it replaces in E Palearctic. The two perhaps marginally overlap in W Mongolia, Buryatia (Russia), Bhutan and Assam (India). Voice is unquestionably the best identification feature; Japanese uttering an abrupt chattering squawk while Common has a short rhythmic twitter. Taking account of variation within Common Quail, plumage differences are minor but Japanese is darker above than adjacent populations of Common Quail (often paler and greyer than those in Europe). Breeding males have rufous throat and head-sides (usually lacking dark throat patch), with rufous often extending over most of underparts. However, many Common Quail have almost as much rufous, especially *erlangeri* of E Africa. Females and non-breeding males are virtually inseparable from Common Quail on plumage coloration, although they are typically darker. However, non-breeders of both sexes develop curiously pointed elongated throat feathers, forming a short 'beard', which is lost during pre-breeding spring moult. In the hand, the two are separable on wing length: 90–105 mm in Japanese, 107–118 mm in Common. Shares buff barring on outer webs of outermost primaries with Common (*contra* Rain Quail, which see). Compare also buttonquails and female King Quail.

DESCRIPTION Bill greyish-horn. Irides brown. Legs pale yellowish to dull brownish-flesh. Sexually dimorphic, male variable in extent of rufous on face and throat. Non-breeders of both sexes have elongated spiked 'beard' on chin and throat. **Adult male breeding:** Forehead and crown blackish obscured by extensive pale buff feather tips. Long narrow central crown stripe and supercilium pale creamy-buff, tinged rufous. Dull brownish band across lores and behind eye. Head-sides, chin, throat and neck-sides brick-red, varying in extent and depth of colour; some have hint of blackish-brown throat centre. Breast and flanks dull to bright rufous, regularly marked with creamy-buff at breast-sides, finely streaked whitish-buff on breast, flanks boldly streaked chestnut and more obviously with pale buff, interspersed with irregular dark marks. Central and lower underparts pale buff. Upperparts blackish with rufous-brown blotching and buff barring, and bold buff shaft streaks. Wing-coverts rufous-brown with fine buff shaft streaks and buff barring. Primaries and secondaries brownish, narrowly barred buff (except tips and inner webs of primaries, which are unmarked). Tail inconspicuous, dark brown cleanly barred buff. **Adult male non-breeding:** Rufous of head and throat is lost or very obscured, being replaced by longer, more pointed whitish feathering on throat. Pattern and extent of markings variable, some have dark rusty-brown, or even blackish, central line on throat (like Common Quail), whereas others have rufous mottling, or broken dark face bridle and crescent (recalling Common Quail), or various combinations of same. **Adult female:** Lacks rufous or black on throat; generally much as female Common Quail, but black markings of breast and underparts often bolder than Common Quail and ground colour of breast and flanks richer rufous. Non-breeding female develops spiked feathers on chin and throat like male. **Juvenile:** Resembles adult female but has plainer head-sides; young male often attains rufous feathering at centre of throat.

GEOGRAPHICAL VARIATION Monotypic, but those in Siberia are slightly paler than Japanese birds and have been accorded subspecific status as *ussuriensis*. Japanese Quail is often considered a race of Common Quail, but differences in voice, migration strategy, throat feather structure and measurements suggest separation warranted. Small numbers collected in NE India (notably Manipur) in winter appear intermediate between the two species.

MEASUREMENTS Length 17–19 cm. Female slightly smaller. Males: wing 90–105 (mean 96), tail 35–49, tarsus c.25. Females: wing 90–101 (mean 96), tail 36–49, tarsus c.25. Weight (both sexes) mean c.90.

HABITAT Open rolling grasslands and cultivated fields, including steppe, montane foothills and forest clearings. Perhaps favours dry riverine meadows, but more tolerant of damp meadows than Common Quail. In breeding season ascends to 850 m in Japan, and up to 3200 m in Bhutan.

VOICE Male advertising call very distinctive, totally different to Common Quail: a sudden chattering squawk *chrr-churrk-chrr*, bearing a remarkable resemblance to the begging call of a recently fledged Blackbird *Turdus merula*. When flushed, a similar rippled call to Common Quail.

HABITS Like Common Quail, but while strongly migratory it is less given to fluctuations in abundance.

BREEDING Considered both polygamous and monogamous in the wild. Nest a shallow scrape lined with dried grasses, sometimes quite elaborately interwoven, constructed by female. Clutch 9–10 in Siberia and 5–8 (up to 13) in Japan. Eggs whitish to pale buff, variably spotted and blotched chocolate-brown (as Common Quail but slightly smaller). Incubation occupies 16–21 days, by female alone although male may occasionally share incubation duties. Single brooded but perhaps occasionally double brooded, as eggs reported until August (perhaps replacement clutches). Eggs chiefly late April–June but fresh clutches reported early August in Siberia, late May–August in Japan and March–July (if this species) in Bangladesh, while a nest with eggs (believed to be this species) was found in Myanmar on 30 October.

DISTRIBUTION Widespread summer migrant across E Palearctic, reaching its western limits at c.104°E around Ulan Bator in Mongolia and Romanovka (at 112°E) in Buryatia (Russia). Absent from mountains flanking Lake Baikal but recorded north to Vitim Valley at c.55°N (east of Baikal) and east across N Mongolia and S Siberia to Amurland, Ussuriland and Sakhalin. Also, north to Shantar Is and south to NE China (Heilongjiang, E Hebei and N Shandong), Korea and Japan (south to Kyushu). Further south, presumed breeders noted in SE Mongolia, China in Ordos (Nei Monggol Zizhiqu) and by Lake Qinghai (Sichuan), Vietnam (E Tonkin), Taiwan and Myanmar (nest reported in 1935). More recently, considerable numbers calling in suitable nesting habitat in C Bhutan (suggesting that quail breeding in adjacent Assam and Bangladesh may also prove to be Japanese). Main wintering grounds in S China, and Japan (chiefly EC Honshu to Kyushu), south to N Laos and N Vietnam, with smaller numbers in Thailand and NE India. Small numbers also winter as far north as Buryatia and Ussuriland (Russia) during mild winters. Vagrant to Cambodia and Philippines (one November record). Introduced Hawaii (established on all main islands except Oahu) and Réunion (Indian Ocean). Numerous introduction attempts in N America have met with little success.

STATUS Long-domesticated captives have developed into several colour varieties. Despite wide native range, the wild population is now distinctly uncommon overall having undergone a long period of decline through over-zealous trapping and habitat loss. In Japan it was considered abundant until the 1930s, when more than 500,000 were reportedly captured annually. It is now a very scarce breeder and an uncommon migrant and winter visitor; in consequence a captive-breeding programme has been established. There are few recent records from Taiwan, but in Russia it is apparently still locally frequent in meadows along the Amur and Ussuri Rivers, but was never numerous there. The discovery of an apparently healthy relict population in Bhutan indicates that the species should be searched for during the breeding season in adjacent areas. Introduced population on Hawaii is thriving and provides stock for the Japanese captive-breeding programme.

REFERENCES Ali & Ripley (1969), Baker (1930), Brazil (1991), Clements (1992), Dement'ev & Gladkov (1967), Eynon (1968), Inskipp & Inskipp (1995), Moreau & Wayre (1968), Taka-Tsukasa (1967).

67 STUBBLE QUAIL
Coturnix pectoralis Gould, 1837

Plate 20

Alternative names: Grey Quail, Pectoral Quail.

Australian representative of the 'grey' quail complex, which is perhaps closest to the ancestral form of the genus, sharing features with both Common/Japanese and Rain/Harlequin species-pairs.

IDENTIFICATION Dull brown quail of dry grasslands in much of E and SW Australia, with nomadic tendencies that have taken it to most parts of the country. Male distinctive in having plain rufous face and throat contrasting with boldly black and white striped underparts (the only Australian quail with streaked underparts). In all plumages, relatively easily distinguished from Brown Quail due to more slender bill, bolder creamy upperparts shaft streaks and relatively distinct long whitish supercilium. In flight, pale streaks on back form usually conspicuous whitish lines, whereas Brown Quail (and smaller female King) appear almost unmarked above (weakly streaked) and have blunter wing-tips than Stubble. Flushes on whirring wings, but is normally silent, although occasionally utters sharp chirps; Brown tends to rise with a more metallic whistling of wings, and a swift chatter. Range overlaps with several species of buttonquail, most of which are smaller and have blunter wingtips, and exhibit contrast between pale forewing panel and darker flight feathers. Compare also very localised Plains-wanderer *Pedionomus torquatus*.

DESCRIPTION Bill bluish or olive-grey, with browner culmen and tip. Irides red-brown to brown. Legs fleshy-white, pinkish or pinkish-brown. Sexually dimorphic. **Adult male:** Forehead and crown blackish-brown, obscured by grey-brown feather tips, long narrow whitish central crown stripe and supercilium, both reaching well down nape. Dull brownish lores and band behind eye extend to 'shoulder'. Chin, throat and lower ear-coverts unmarked cinnamon to rufous-buff. Breast, upper belly and flanks whitish, washed cinnamon on latter, the whole heavily streaked blackish, coalescing to form an irregular blackish blotch at centre of breast. Lower belly and undertail-coverts whitish. Upperparts grey-brown to dark brown, intensely blotched blackish with pale buff barring and bold creamy shaft streaks (edged black). Wing-coverts dull brown with fine pale shaft streaks and weak barring. Secondaries and primaries virtually plain brownish. Tail inconspicuous, grey-brown barred buff. **Adult female:** Lacks rufous throat of male, having whitish throat finely streaked black, a thin dark malar and whitish moustachial. Underparts more narrowly and sparsely streaked black than male, the streaks not forming a blackish breast patch. **Juvenile:** Resembles adult female but has spotted, rather than streaked,

dusky breast; young male attains rufous on throat at c.5 weeks of age.

GEOGRAPHICAL VARIATION Monotypic. Sometimes considered conspecific with extinct New Zealand Quail under *C. novaezeelandiae*.

MEASUREMENTS Length 16–20 cm. Female slightly larger. Males: wing 99–108 (mean 102), tail 28–37 (mean 34), tarsus 21–25 (mean 23), weight 82–120 (mean 100). Females: wing 100–110 (mean 104), tail 29–37 (mean 34), tarsus 22–26 (mean 24), weight 75–125 (mean 110).

HABITAT Open unimproved grasslands and well-drained riverine plains, including sparse cereal crops, weedy pastures, stubble fields, saltbush, *Spinifex* thickets and saltmarsh grassland. Generally in drier habitats than Brown Quail.

VOICE Male advertising call is a brisk liquid trisyllabic *two-to-weep* or an abbreviated two-note *two-weep* or *pippy-wheat* (possibly given by female); these may be repeated up to c.10 times per minute over a 15-minute period. Usually silent when flushed but may give 1–2 sharp chirps on rising.

HABITS Usually alone or in family parties. Most frequently recorded when accidentally flushed in open fields, but prefers to squat or run from danger, only flying when hard-pressed. Most groups are of 3–5 but gatherings of 12 or more occasionally reported, especially on dispersal, although no large migrating flocks or 'waves' occur as in larger African and Eurasian *Coturnix*. Feeds principally on grass seeds, and those of various weedy plants and fallen grain; a small percentage of invertebrates are also taken. Sometimes clambers up stems of low-growing plants to reach seed heads. A well-known dispersive migrant, local movements are associated with rainfall, but largest dispersals allied to build-up in numbers after a succession of good breeding seasons, followed by a sudden deterioration in food supply (through drought, mouse plague etc). Ringing recoveries indicate dispersal likely in all directions, with longest recorded distance being 1142 km.

BREEDING Monogamous, some remaining paired throughout year. Nest a shallow scrape, often under a shrub or grass tuft, lined with grasses, and constructed by female. Clutch 5–14 (mean 7) creamy-yellow eggs finely spotted and blotched red-brown and olive-green. Incubation, by female, occupies 18–21 days. Two or three broods raised in good seasons, exceptionally four successive broods following optimum conditions after drought. Timing varies according to rainfall and food availability. In Victoria in dry years, usually December (first clutch) and, following rains, a second clutch in March–April, but in years of early rainfall, commences in September, with second clutch from late November, and further broods later in winter; August–January in Western Australia. Male helps tend and defend chicks.

DISTRIBUTION Principally resident in SE Australia, in suitable habitats throughout New South Wales and Victoria, north over E Queensland to Atherton (colonised since 1960), west to SE South Australia at Streaky Bay. It is absent from the arid interior but has (since 1901) colonised SW Western Australia, with dispersal west to Goldfields and north to Shark Bay, while vagrants have reached the Kimberleys and Nullarbor Plain, and coastal N Territory, but more regular further south, e.g. Alice Springs. In Tasmania formerly widespread, but now virtually extinct. Introduced Hawaii and New Zealand (both unsuccessfully).

STATUS Locally common in Victoria and New South Wales. Generally increasing and spreading due to forest clearance, having spread north across E Queensland and colonised S Western Australia in last 50–100 years. However, agricultural changes in Tasmania have reduced numbers to a dangerously low level and it is clearly on the verge of extinction there.

REFERENCES Blakers *et al.* (1984), Cruise (1966), Frith *et al.* (1977), Frith & Carpenter (1980), Marchant & Higgins (1993), Pizzey & Knight (1997).

---

68   NEW ZEALAND QUAIL
Coturnix novaezeelandiae Quoy & Gaimard, 1830   Plate 20

Closely related to Stubble Quail, this New Zealand endemic is now extinct, the last reliable report being in 1876.

IDENTIFICATION Extinct. Formerly New Zealand's only native quail. Similar in many respects to Stubble Quail, but differed in being larger, plumper and darker, with intense black spotting, and scaled, rather than streaked, lower underparts on browner background. Males had rufous supercilia (white in Stubble) and the orange-rufous throat and face had a dark moustachial and dusky crescent on rear ear-coverts. Females had buff (not whitish) supercilia and unmarked whitish throats (speckled in Stubble) and were heavily scaled on lower underparts on browner background (female Stubble has almost unmarked belly on whitish background). Only introduced quail survive in New Zealand, the most widespread being California Quail but Northern Bobwhite survives patchily on North I., as does Brown Quail; only the latter could be momentarily mistaken for New Zealand Quail.

DESCRIPTION Bill blackish with a paler tip in adult, brownish in juvenile. Irides hazel-brown. Legs dull flesh to fleshy-brown. Sexually dimorphic. Bill slightly heavier and wings blunter tipped than Stubble Quail. **Adult male:** Forehead and crown blackish-brown obscured by grey-brown feather tips; long narrow whitish central crown stripe reaching well down nape. Lores, supercilium, chin, throat and lower ear-coverts orange-rufous with dark vertical crescent on ear-coverts not quite meeting short dark moustachial. Breast, upper belly and flanks whitish, washed pale brown on flanks, belly and undertail-coverts and heavily scaled with blackish U-shaped or V-shaped markings coalescing to form irregular blackish area on centre of breast and upper belly. Upperparts rich brown, with intense blackish fine wavy barring and blotching, and pale buff shaft streaks (edged black). Wing-coverts dark to olive-brown with fine pale shaft streaks and blackish-brown barring. Secondaries and primaries virtually plain brownish. Tail inconspicuous, dark brown marked with fine pale chevrons. **Adult female:** Lacked rufous on throat of male, having pale buff face and lores, marked black, unmarked whitish throat, dusky malar meeting dark crescent under eye. Underparts buff to pale brown, each feather with fine blackish subterminal mark and pale shaft streak, appearing as blackish scaling and lacking blackish breast patch of male. **Juvenile:** Resembled adult female, but underparts ground colour pale buff with blackish markings more pointed, less U-shaped, each feather having two converging black streaks separated by a whitish shaft streak at tip.

GEOGRAPHICAL VARIATION Those on North I. were possibly darker than South I. birds but marked individual variation and relative lack of specimens makes this difficult to evaluate. Sometimes considered conspecific with Stubble Quail, the latter being absorbed within an expanded *C. novaezeelandiae.*

MEASUREMENTS Length 22 cm. Female probably slightly larger. Males: wing (n=2) 118, 122, tail (n=2) 45, 47, tarsus (n=2) 23, weight c.220. Females: wing (n=1) 119, tail (n=2) 42, 43, tarsus (n=2) 23, 28, weight c.200.

HABITAT Grass-covered downs, presumably lowland tussock grassland and open fernlands.

VOICE Male advertising call was described as *twit-twit-twit-twee-twit,* repeated several times in quick succession.

HABITS Virtually unknown. Reference to a party of nine shot that consisted of a pair and seven young of the year. Found in open fernlands, where reportedly flushed in considerable numbers in cuts through vegetation. Stomach of one contained blades of green grass and some seeds. Apparently most vocal in damp or wet weather, taking shelter within grass tussocks during storms.

BREEDING Probably monogamous. Nest a shallow scrape lined with grasses. Clutch 10–12. Eggs reportedly variable, buff with darker brown blotches, or whitish-yellow covered in smudged brown spots. Incubation 21 days. Timing unrecorded, but young 'as late as April' on South I.

DISTRIBUTION Extinct. Formerly New Zealand, on Great Barrier I. and both North and South Is.

STATUS Extinct since c.1876. Formerly widespread on both major New Zealand islands. Reportedly abundant in parts of South I. until at least 1850, but extinct 20 years later. Its sudden disappearance has been attributed to several factors, including over-hunting, habitat destruction and introduction of mammalian predators. However, most populations had been extirpated by the time such introductions had been implemented. The most likely reason for its sudden disappearance was probably disease, possibly carried by introduced foreign birds.

REFERENCE Marchant & Higgins (1993).

69 RAIN QUAIL
Coturnix coromandelica (Gmelin, 1789)   Plate 20

Alternative name: Black-breasted Quail.

Oriental species, probably closest to Harlequin Quail of Africa, with which it forms a superspecies. Strongly dispersive, its presence in many areas is dependent on the extent of the monsoon (hence name).

IDENTIFICATION Nomadic and likely anywhere (apart from most arid parts of northwest) within the Indian subcontinent. Overlaps in range and habitats with Japanese and Common Quails and, like those species, most easily located by its distinctive call. Although slightly smaller than either, males are most distinctive, especially if seen head-on or standing alert, when Rain has an extensive blackish breast centre and a strikingly bold black and white facial pattern. Rain Quail never attains the rufous face of male Japanese or some Common. Amount of black on underparts variable and, in some males, may be restricted to blackish spotting at centre of chest. Female very similar to Common and Japanese and may only be safely separated by plain unbarred primaries (barred on outer webs in Japanese and Common), which are visible given optimum viewing conditions. Female King has similarly plain primaries but is smaller, has a very small bill, plainer and more rufous head-sides and scaled, rather than spotted, breast-sides. Compare also buttonquails.

DESCRIPTION Bill blackish (breeding male) or dusky-brown with paler base at other times. Irides brown. Legs fleshy (pinker in breeding condition) to greyish-flesh. Sexually dimorphic, male variable in extent of black on underparts. **Adult male:** Forehead and crown blackish, obscured by extensive pale buff feather tips; long, narrow buff central crown stripe and long whitish supercilium reaching well down neck-sides. Wide dark brownish band across lores and behind eye extends to 'shoulder'. Black malar and narrow stripe down throat centre, which hooks back towards ear-coverts. Lower ear-coverts, throat-sides and collar, below anchor, white, separated from breast by narrow black lower border. Neck-sides and breast pinkish-cinnamon, flanks cinnamon variably but often boldly striped blackish and with less obviously whitish shaft streaks. Centre of breast to upper belly blackish, extending as long blackish flank striping; extent of black extremely variable, the least marked just having blackish spotting at centre of breast. Lower central underparts whitish. Upperparts dull cinnamon-brown, intensely blotched blackish and barred buff with bold buff shaft streaks (edged black). Wing-coverts dull brown with fine buff shaft streaks and faint buff barring. Secondaries and primaries unbarred brownish. Tail inconspicuous, dark brown barred with buff. **Adult female:** Lacks black throat and has less marked facial bridle than male, with paler ground colour to face and underparts. Very similar to female Japanese and Common Quails, but breast often greyish, irregularly spotted, rather than streaked, blackish with fine whitish shaft streaks. Note unbarred primaries. **Juvenile:** Resembles adult female but has plainer head-sides and flanks (without spotting or streaking).

GEOGRAPHICAL VARIATION Monotypic.

MEASUREMENTS Length 16–18 cm. Female slightly smaller. Males: wing 93–96, tail 29–32, tarsus 23–26. Females: wing 90–97, tail 28–31, tarsus 23–27. Weight (both sexes) 64–85.

HABITAT Open grassland and cultivated fields, including dry rice fields, stubble, intermixed with scrub–jungle and even tea plantations and gardens. Recorded to 2500 m at some hill stations, with breeding reported as high as 1800 m.

VOICE Male advertising call very distinctive, a high-pitched musical double-noted phrase repeated 3–6 times, *whit-whit, whit-whit, whit-whit, whit-whit*. When flushed gives a similar squeaky whistle to Common Quail.

HABITS Like Common Quail, although it appears to feed principally on grass seeds and millet. Like Common and Japanese Quails is strongly migratory.

BREEDING Considered monogamous. Nest a shallow scrape lined with dried grasses, constructed by female in grass or standing crops, occasionally in scrubby cover. Clutch 4–6 but up to 18 recorded (perhaps the result of more than one female laying in same nest). Eggs whitish to pale buff, variably spotted and blotched chocolate-brown (as Common Quail but slightly smaller). Female alone incubates for 18–19 days. Single-brooded. Lays March–October (sometimes December) according to timing and extent of rains. Male apparently helps tend chicks.

DISTRIBUTION India and parts of SE Asia. Widespread in India, chiefly in eastern and southern areas, but dispersing over drier parts of the subcontinent at the onset of the southwest monsoon, regularly reaching the eastern plains and foothills of Pakistan and, in the northeast, Assam, Manipur and into Myanmar.

Thinly distributed over N and C Thailand, with recent reports from Cambodia and S Annam (Vietnam). A rare winter visitor to Sri Lanka, it is merely a vagrant to Nepal and Bangladesh.

STATUS Locally common in EC India but, despite wide range, appears distinctly uncommon and unpredictable in abundance elsewhere. The recent record in Vietnam and discovery that it is quite widespread in Thailand indicate how easily overlooked this dispersive species can be, unless observers are familiar with its distinctive call.

REFERENCES Ali & Ripley (1969), Baker (1930), Grimmett *et al.* (1998), Robertson (1989), Robson (2000).

70 HARLEQUIN QUAIL
Coturnix delegorguei Delegorgue, 1847 — Plate 21

Alternative name: African Harlequin Quail.

Closely related to Rain Quail of India, it should not be confused with the wholly unrelated 'Harlequin Quail' of C America, which is now better known as Montezuma Quail.

IDENTIFICATION Widespread in sub-Saharan Africa, where it is often the most frequently encountered *Coturnix*. Highly nomadic, it may appear suddenly in quite large numbers following rains. Male has rich chestnut and black underparts, contrasting with striking black and white facial pattern, a combination not shown by even darkest *erlangeri* Common Quail, which always has whitish belly and lower underparts, pale flank streaks and less bold facial pattern. If flushed, male Harlequin appears very dark overall and is slightly smaller than Common Quail, but larger than Blue Quail, the latter also differs in having chestnut forewing (male only). Female very similar to Common but underparts appreciably darker, with belly and undertail-coverts tawny-buff like breast and flanks; breast-sides more heavily spotted dusky than Common and, given optimum views, outer primaries plain brown (barred outer webs in Common). Compare also buttonquails and Blue Quail.

DESCRIPTION *C. d. delegorguei.* Bill blackish (male) or brownish (female) with yellowish base. Irides red-brown to brown. Legs fleshy-white, pinkish or pinkish-brown. Sexually dimorphic. **Adult male:** Forehead and crown blackish-brown obscured by extensive brownish-buff feather tips; long narrow whitish-buff central crown stripe and long whitish supercilium extend well down neck-sides. Broad dark brownish band on lores and behind eye extends to 'shoulder'. Black malar and narrow stripe down throat centre, which hooks back towards ear-coverts. Lower ear-coverts, throat-sides and collar, below anchor, white, separated from breast by narrow black lower border. Neck-sides and breast, flanks and lower underparts, including undertail-coverts, rich rufous-chestnut. Flank feathers have broad black central streaks that run back from solid blackish area at centre of breast and upper belly. Upperparts grey-brown to dark brown with intense blackish blotching, buff barring and bold creamy-buff shaft streaks (edged black). Wing-coverts dull brown with fine buff shaft streaks and buff barring. Secondaries and primaries unbarred brownish. Tail inconspicuous, dark brown barred with buff. **Adult female:** Lacks black throat and has less marked facial bridle than male, with paler ground colour to face and underparts. Very similar to female Common Quail, but underparts from breast almost uniform orange-buff, breast and flanks darker rufous, the latter weakly marked with creamy shaft streaks. Breast has dusky spotting and some weak scaling. Note unbarred primaries. **Juvenile:** Resembles adult female but paler brown crown and nape, and greyer, less rufous, underparts. Throat and breast boldly spotted and barred dark brown intermixed with white feather shafts.

GEOGRAPHICAL VARIATION Three races vary in overall colour saturation. Validity of *arabica* doubtful, as most records within this subspecies' range are probably migrants from Africa.

    C. d. delegorguei Delegorgue, 1847 occurs over most of species' range; described above.

    C. d. histrionica Hartlaub, 1849 occurs on São Tomé; darker than nominate.

    C. d. arabica Bannerman, 1929 occurs in SW Arabia; paler than nominate but validity doubtful.

MEASUREMENTS Length 17–19 cm. Female slightly larger. *C. d. delegorguei* given. Males: wing 91–100 (mean 96), tail 28–33, tarsus 24–27 (mean 25), weight 71–93 (mean 78). Females: wing 93–105 (mean 100), tail 28–33, tarsus 24–27 (mean 25), weight 68–95 (mean 81).

HABITAT Open grassland, damp pasture, lightly wooded savanna and lowland flood plains. Generally below 1500 m, being replaced at higher elevations by Common Quail.

VOICE Male advertising call faster, sharper and higher pitched than Common Quail, each note a near-metallic *wit* quickly repeated in various sequences, often in sets of three, or commences with two single notes, followed by two sets of three notes: *wit, wit, witwitwit, witwitwit.* Female occasionally answers with a soft *qwik-ik.* When flushed often utters a squeaky rolling *skreee.*

HABITS Like Common Quail, although much more gregarious, being found in bevies of 6–20 in non-breeding season. Like Rain Quail is nomadic, performing inter-regional movements following rains. Forms large flocks but numbers vary locally on annual basis, occasionally almost swarming over an area at onset of rainy season, with reports of up to 200 flushed during an exceptional influx. Breeds soon after arrival, forming small colonies with initial colonisation preceded by much intra-male aggression. Migrants are attracted to light at night, with mass kills recorded under certain conditions (e.g. misty nights). However, not all movements are associated with rainfall and it is resident in some areas, remaining throughout dry season. High percentage of invertebrates in diet, principally grasshoppers, beetles, bugs, ants, termites and their larvae, as well as small molluscs, seeds, shoots and leaves.

BREEDING Usually temporarily monogamous, but two females may use same nest, which is a shallow scrape in grass, lined and often domed with grasses, and constructed by female. Clutch 4–8 (mean 5), but up to 22 recorded (the product of more than one female laying in same nest). Eggs creamy-buff, finely spotted and blotched purplish-brown (rougher in texture than Common Quail). Female alone incubates for 14–18 days. Single-brooded. Lays at onset of local rains, which vary enormously over wide range: probably throughout the year on São Tomé, August–September in Zaïre, July in Sudan, April–June in Ethiopia, May–June and November–December in Kenya and Tanzania, January–March in Zimbabwe, October–June in Zambia, July–September in Namibia and October–March in South Africa. Male helps tend and defend chicks.

DISTRIBUTION Sub-Saharan Africa. Widespread intra-African migrant or nomad, which is absent from heavily forested, upland and desert regions. Occurs, locally, from S Sudan, Ethiopia and S Somalia south throughout E Africa to E and S South Africa, N Namibia, Angola and SE Zaïre. Over much of C and W Africa it is an erratic seasonal migrant, varying in annual abundance, but regular west to Nigeria and Chad and some records west and north to Mali and Côte d'Ivoire. Isolated populations on São Tomé in Gulf of Guinea (where resident) and in Yemen and adjacent Saudi Arabia, but it is unclear if those in Arabia are resident or follow large-scale dispersal from Africa. Uncommon but widespread seasonal visitor to E Madagascar. Vagrant to N Sénégal, The Gambia, Fernando Po, Gabon, Comoro Is (Anjouan) and Oman (Salalah). No firm evidence for occurrence on Socotra, although mentioned for the island by several authors.

STATUS Locally common or even abundant during periodic invasions, but numbers vary significantly in a given area on an annual basis. Temporary colonies may occupy relatively small areas within otherwise unused tracts of apparently suitable habitat.

REFERENCES del Hoyo *et al.* (1994), Mackworth-Praed & Grant (1957), Trollope (1966), Urban *et al.* (1986), Zimmerman *et al.* (1996).

---

71 BROWN QUAIL
Coturnix ypsilophora Bosc, 1792   Plate 21

Alternative names: Silver Quail, Swamp Quail, Tasmanian Quail.

Extremely variable, from buffy-rufous to slate black, within wide range. Formerly placed within the monotypic genus, *Synoicus*. The Tasmanian form has been accorded specific treatment as Swamp Quail; as its name pre-dates mainland forms, *ypsilophora* has priority over *australis* when the two are considered conspecific.

IDENTIFICATION Finely barred dull buffish, greyish or reddish-brown (even blackish in race *dogwa*) Australasian quail that extends north over New Guinea and west through the Lesser Sundas to Flores and Sumba. In Australia, it overlaps with Stubble Quail but is slightly larger and plumper, with a stouter bill, a relatively plain face (without distinct supercilium) relieved by a weak dusky ear-coverts smudge. Underparts unstreaked but close views should reveal fine wavy barring or narrow chevrons (varying in intensity according to subspecies), while the upperparts have fine pale shaft streaks (not bold streaks like Stubble). Polymorphic Australian populations consist of reddish-brown and (less frequently) grey variants at same localities. Appears uniformly dark above when flushed, the fine pale streaks being hardly noticeable; Brown rises with a more metallic whistling of wings than Stubble Quail and often utters a quick chatter or few chirps. Elsewhere, the main confusion is with buttonquails, which are smaller and show contrast between pale forewing panel and darker flight feathers, but in New Zealand compare very localised Northern Bobwhite and female of widespread California Quail. See also Snow Mountain Quail.

DESCRIPTION *C. y. australis*. Bill grey with blackish upper mandible. Irides dark brown to red-brown, becoming deep red in breeding condition. Legs pale greenish-yellow to orange-yellow. Sexes differ to a limited degree, with female less variable. Male has rufous, brown and blue-grey variants (latter very rare in Australia); female resembles brown phase male. **Adult male** (brown and rufous extremes, with intergrades): Crown and nape brown to reddish-brown, mottled blackish with narrow creamy central crown stripe. Forehead, crown-sides and ear-coverts paler, dull brown to reddish-brown, or grey, with almost circular dusky smudge on ear-coverts and hint of smudged malar. Chin and throat pale buff, underparts from breast buff, washed rufous or dull brown, sparsely marked with inconspicuous thin whitish shaft streaks, but intensely covered with wavy, blackish chevron-shaped bars. Upperparts, including wings, similar to underparts. Flight feathers plainer grey-brown, with rufous or paler brown marbling on outer webs. Tail inconspicuous, dark brown irregularly barred buff. Grey phase (very rare in Australia) variable, but extremes are largely blue-grey, with rufous or brown feather tips and some contrast due to blacker barring. **Adult female:** Similar to male but less variable, most are buffy-brown overall, with small black blotches on scapulars, back and rump. Both upper- and underparts have bolder and blacker chevrons, and more prominent white shaft streaks. Head-sides more heavily speckled, lacking pale-faced appearance of males. **Juvenile:** Resembles adult female but body markings broken into spotting, becoming barred on flanks (but weaker than in adult); all markings are dark brown, rather than black. Dusky ear-patch much fainter and sometimes almost absent. Both upper- and underparts have bolder, wider pale shaft streaks than adult.

GEOGRAPHICAL VARIATION Complex and requires review (especially New Guinea complex). Differences of size, overall colour saturation, strength of barring and shaft streaking, and eye colour, are most marked in males. Tasmanian form accorded specific status, as Swamp Quail, by some authorities, but not by Marchant & Higgins (1993). If the nominate is elevated to species status then a reappraisal of the taxonomy of the New Guinea forms is surely necessary. A recently discovered population on Yamdena (in Tanimbar Is—the easternmost of Lesser Sundas) may prove to be an undescribed form.

C. y. ypsilophora Bosc, 1792 (Swamp Quail) occurs in Tasmania (no proof of occurrence on Australian mainland); differs from *australis* in having yellow to orange-yellow irides (not brown or red), and is larger (male wing 103–112, weight (mean) 119) and less variable, lacking rufous or grey phases.

C. y. australis (Latham, 1801) (includes *queenslandica*, *cervina* and *sordida*) occurs in mainland Australia; described above.

C. y. raaltenii (Müller, 1842) (includes *castanea*) occurs on Lesser Sundas of Flores, Alor, Wetar, Dao, Doo, Roti, Timor, Kisar, Leti, Moa and Luang (Indonesia); grey and chestnut above and bright tawny chestnut below, with only weakly developed dark barring and pale shaft streaks.

C. y. pallidior (Hartert, 1897) occurs on Lesser Sundas of Sumba and Sawu (Indonesia); has blackish crown, bolder pale shaft streaks above and grey-toned underparts, with quite developed dark vermiculations on flanks.

C. y. saturatior (Hartert, 1930) occurs in N New Guinea lowlands; like *plumbeus*, but male darker with obscure barring below and pale shaft streaks on upper breast. Female much paler.

C. y. dogwa Mayr & Rand, 1937 occurs in S New Guinea lowlands; a uniform virtually unmarked blackish-slate form. Female much paler.

C. y. plumbeus (Salvadori, 1894) occurs in E New Guinea lowlands; like *dogwa*, but male darker below.

C. y. mafulu Mayr & Rand, 1937 occurs in southern slopes of SE New Guinea; underparts buffy-white washed with greyish-brown on breast, finely barred on sides and upperparts with conspicuous narrow white shaft streaks.

C. y. lamonti Mayr & Gilliard, 1954 occurs in highlands of C New Guinea; like *mafulu* but male with underparts washed pale chestnut; upperparts more richly coloured; irides pale yellow.

C. y. monticola Mayr & Rand, 1937 occurs in alpine regions of SE New Guinea; like *mafulu* but larger; male has more coarsely marked, buffy-brownish underparts; upperparts paler and more brownish with prominent whitish shaft streaks and coarser barring; irides pale yellow.

MEASUREMENTS Length 17–22 cm. Female slightly smaller. *C. y. australis* given. Males: wing 88–105 (mean 95), tarsus 20–24, tail 34–52, weight 75–123 (mean 90). Females: wing 87–106 (mean 95), tarsus 23–25, tail 34–48, weight 85–140 (mean 104).

HABITAT Rank grassland with shrubby cover, especially near wetlands or riverine flood plains, swampy hollows in coastal heathland, alpine tussock grassland, bracken-covered pasture, forest clearings, cereal crops, wide roadside verges, *Spinifex* savanna and salt-marsh (chiefly in New Zealand). Principally in lowlands but ascends to 1000 m on New Zealand and higher, to 3700 m, on New Guinea.

VOICE Advertising call distinctive, most readily given at dawn or dusk, a loud, rising two-note whistle, the first short and weak, variously rendered as *f-weeep*, *tu-eeeee*, or *be-quick*. Pitch varies, sometimes sharp and full, more plaintive at other times. When flushed may utter a series of sharp chirps, or short chatter. Tasmanian form (Swamp Quail) reportedly deeper pitched than mainland Australian populations.

HABITS Shy and retiring, most often seen dust-bathing on tracks or when flushed from underfoot. Usually alone or in family groups of 6–8, but coveys of 12–18 or more occasionally reported. Slips furtively through vegetation in crouched posture, feeding unobtrusively on weed and grass seeds, and small invertebrates, exceptionally small reptiles. Flushes very reluctantly, preferring to squat or run from danger. If suddenly surprised, rises vertically for c.2 m before commencing rapid horizontal flight, faster than Stubble Quail, and interspersed with glides before suddenly dropping into cover and running on; separated birds call and run towards each other after having initially 'exploded' in different directions.

BREEDING Monogamous. Nest a shallow scrape, lined and sometimes partially domed, with grasses; sheltered by grass tussock, fern, or low shrub. Clutch 7–12 (14 and 18 recorded) in Australia and 4–6 in New Guinea. Eggs pale bluish, yellowish or greenish-yellow, finely freckled brown, sometimes unmarked. Female alone incubates for 21–22 days. Two or three, rarely four, broods raised in seasons following optimum rainfall. Eggs reported December–June in New Zealand and November–February in Tasmania. In Western Australia and New South Wales, egg-laying starts in August and, in the latter state, continues until February, but in exceptional multi-brood years until May. In N Queensland breeds October–July, but throughout the year in S Queensland. In tropical regions of N Northern Territory nesting occurs January–May and in Lesser Sundas in February–April. Male helps tend and defend chicks, and takes charge of brood when two weeks old in order that female can incubate subsequent clutches.

DISTRIBUTION Australasia and Indonesia, throughout Lesser Sundas of Indonesia (west to Flores and Sumba, see Geographical Variation for full details) and New Guinea, with some dispersal possible across Torres Strait to N Australia. Bulk of Australian population resident in E Australia, throughout Tasmania, Victoria and most of New South Wales, west to extreme SE South Australia and north over E Queensland to Cape York. Absent from arid interior but reappears in coastal Northern Territory and extreme N and S Western Australia. Some dispersal evident following prolonged wet seasons and associated breeding success, but not as marked as Stubble Quail.

Introduced Fiji (Viti Levu and Vanua Levu) and New Zealand (North I.).

STATUS Locally common in Tasmania, Victoria and New South Wales but marked overall decline since late 19th century due to wetland drainage and inten-sification of farming. Conversely, forest clearance has permitted local range expansions, suggesting some degree of stability in populations.

REFERENCES Blakers *et al.* (1984), Frith *et al.* (1977), Marchant & Higgins (1993), Pizzey & Knight (1997).

---

72   BLUE QUAIL
Coturnix adansonii J. & E. Verreaux, 1851   Plate 21

Alternative name: African Blue Quail.

African relative of King Quail of Asia, with which it is often considered conspecific.

IDENTIFICATION Sparrow-sized blackish quail of African grasslands. Male has striking white throat patches against otherwise slaty plumage, a feature shared by commoner Harlequin Quail, but Blue Quail is markedly smaller, lacks white supercilium and has yellow (not fleshy) legs. In good light, the underparts are bluish-slate (with chestnut flanks), not extensively rufous with a black belly as in Harlequin. In tropical Asia and Australia it is replaced by similar King Quail, which differs in chestnut belly and vent (not flanks and forewing as in Blue). When flushed, tiny size and very dark appearance distinctive, only buttonquails are as small, but they have pale (not chestnut) panel on greater wing-coverts, contrasting with darker flight feathers. Beware confusing francolin chicks, which can fly at an early age. Female Blue differs from other quails in tiny size, barred (not streaked) underparts, yellowish legs and tiny bill. African buttonquails have longer stronger bills, pale (not dark) eyes and are either spotted or sparsely scaled at breast-sides, never extensively barred below. Female King Quail of Asia and Australia is very similar, but has unmarked wing-coverts (Blue has barred coverts) and thin dark line on cheeks.

DESCRIPTION Bill black with blue lower mandible (adult male), or brownish-horn with paler base (female). Irides dark brown (juvenile) to ruby-red (breeding male). Legs yellow to orange-yellow. Sexually dimorphic. **Adult male:** Forehead, crown, head-sides, ear-coverts, breast, belly and vent bluish-slate. Centre of crown and nape mottled blacker. Blackish facial bridle formed by malar stripe and throat centre joining and enclosing white malar patch; pure white chest patch below this is bordered by narrow blackish band. Flanks ruddy chestnut streaked bluish-slate. Mantle, back and rump dark bluish-slate, uppertail-coverts chestnut streaked bluish-slate, tail blackish. Scapulars and tertials chestnut streaked bluish-slate, wing-coverts chestnut, flight feathers brown. **Adult female:** Forehead, crown-sides, head-sides, ear-coverts, and neck-sides and flanks warm orange-buff, becoming whiter on throat. Crown and nape dull brown, mottled black, with clear pale central crown line. Breast and rest of underparts buff, barred blackish, boldest on rear flanks and undertail-coverts. Upperparts, including wings, mottled and streaked rufous and black, with fine pale shaft streaks; wing-coverts finely barred. **Juvenile:** Resembles adult female but shaft streaks bolder, particularly on rump and uppertail-coverts.

GEOGRAPHICAL VARIATION Monotypic. Often considered a subspecies of King Quail under *C. chinensis*.

MEASUREMENTS Length 12–15 cm. Sexes similar in size. Males: wing 78–82 (mean 80), tail 26–32 (mean 30), tarsus 18–20 (mean 19), weight 35–48 (mean 43). Females: wing 80–84 (mean 81), tail 26–32 (mean 30), tarsus 18–20 (mean 19), weight 44 (one).

HABITAT Damp grassland, grassy plains, rice fields, damp grassy areas in open woodland, margins of swamps etc. Chiefly in lowlands, ascending to 1800 m in E Africa, and mostly above 1400 m in Zimbabwe.

VOICE Very similar to King Quail. Male gives piping three-note whistle, likened to call of Little Bee-eater *Merops pusillus*, *ki-kew-yu*, the first note loud and shrill, the second and third softer and lower pitched. When flushed utters a weak squeaky triple whistle, *tir-tir-tir.*

HABITS Much as King Quail, but poorly studied by comparison.

BREEDING Monogamous, with strong pair bonds. Nest a shallow scrape, occasionally lined with grasses, well hidden in grass tussock. Clutch 3–9 pale olive-brown eggs that are finely freckled with minute reddish and purplish dots. Female incubates, although male suspected to assist occasionally, for c.16 days. Laying varies according to extent and timing of rains, usually at start of rainy season, which varies depending on location; December–April in South Africa, January–April in Zimbabwe, February–May in Malawi, May–July in E Africa and April–July in W Africa. Male helps tend and defend chicks.

DISTRIBUTION Sub-Saharan Africa. An intra-African migrant, arriving at onset of rains in many regions, departing again in early dry season. Ranges from Sierra Leone and Côte d'Ivoire very sparingly east through Nigeria, Cameroon, extreme S Chad and extreme S Sudan to extreme W Ethiopia, south in Uganda, SW Kenya (rare), S Zaïre, Angola and Tanzania to Zimbabwe (principally Mashonaland), C Mozambique and E South Africa (south to E Cape). Vagrant Mali (one record).

STATUS Precise details of movements poorly understood as local and uncommon throughout range. Easily overlooked due to weak and, in many areas, apparently brief vocalisation periods. It is one of Africa's least studied gamebirds (considering extensive range).

REFERENCES Clancey (1967), Mackworth-Praed & Grant (1957), Urban *et al.* (1986), Zimmerman *et al.* (1996).

Alternative names: Blue-breasted Quail, Asian Blue Quail, Chinese Quail, Painted Quail.

King and Blue Quails are often considered conspecific and were formerly placed within a separate genus, *Excalfactoria*. These minute colourful quails are the world's smallest phasianids and their ranges encompass most of the Old World tropics.

IDENTIFICATION Uncommon (although easily overlooked) sparrow-sized quail of tropical Asia and Australia. Male unmistakable if seen well, the gleaming white patterned throat contrasts with otherwise dark plumage and, in good light, the underparts appear blue with rufous-chestnut belly and vent (rufous sometimes extends over breast). Superficially similar Blue Quail, of Africa, has blue breast, belly and vent, with chestnut flanks and forewing (King has uniformly brownish forewing). If flushed, tiny size and very dark appearance are diagnostic, as few buttonquails are so small and most have pale panel on greater wing-coverts, which contrasts with darker flight feathers, and weaker fluttering flight. Beware chicks of partridges or francolins, which can fly at an early age and are quite bewildering. Female differs from other quail in combination of tiny size, barred (not streaked) underparts, yellowish legs and small bill. Buttonquails have longer, stronger bills, pale (not dark) eyes and are either plain or spotted, rarely barred, below (exception is widespread Barred Buttonquail, which has grey, not yellow, legs and scaly head-sides). Female Blue Quail is very similar, but has barred wing-coverts (King has plain coverts) and lacks thin dark bar from bill base, below eye, to ear-coverts of King.

DESCRIPTION *C. c. lineata*. Bill blackish-grey (blacker in adult male). Irides dark brown (juvenile) to brownish-red (male). Legs orange-yellow. Sexually dimorphic. **Adult male:** Crown and nape dull brown, mottled black, with weak narrow, pale central crown line. Blackish facial bridle formed by malar stripe and throat centre joining in loop, enclosing white malar patch; pure white horseshoe-shaped patch below this is bordered by narrow blackish band. Forehead, crown-sides (rarely entire crown), head-sides, ear-coverts, breast, neck-sides and flanks grey-blue. Belly, rear flanks and undertail-coverts rusty-rufous. Upperparts including hindneck, breast-sides and wings buff to warm brown, finely barred and blotched black, with indistinct fine buff shaft streaks, most obvious on inner scapulars. Wing-coverts grey-brown and weakly speckled; flight feathers dull grey-brown. Tail feathers soft and concealed, reddish-brown. **Adult female:** Forehead, crown-sides, head-sides, ear-coverts, neck-sides and flanks warm orange-buff, becoming whiter on throat. Thin black line extends from gape, below lores and eye across middle ear-coverts. Breast and rest of underparts, including undertail-coverts buff, barred with blackish crescents and bolder bars. Crown and nape dull brown, mottled black, with broader pale central crown line than male. Upperparts, including

wings, similar to male with larger black markings and bolder buff shaft streaks. **Juvenile:** Resembles adult female, but shaft streaks bolder and extend to underparts, breaking barring into spots except on flanks. Young male duller and greyer below than female, with traces of throat pattern at c.3 weeks of age.

GEOGRAPHICAL VARIATION At least ten subspecies described, differing in size, colour saturation and (females) extent of barring on underparts. Variation is minor and largely clinal, with supposed differences in urgent need of taxonomic review.

C. c. chinensis (Linnaeus, 1766) occurs in mainland Asia, Sri Lanka and Taiwan; both sexes less richly-coloured than *lineata*, with colder brown upperparts and less conspicuous pale shaft streaking; females less intensely barred below.

C. c. trinkutensis (Richmond, 1902) occurs on Nicobar Is (India); both sexes darker than nominate, male greyer above with virtually no pale shaft streaks and female wholly barred below.

C. c. palmeri (Riley, 1919) occurs on Sumatra and Java (Indonesia); male similar in colour tones to *lineata*, but female has obvious pale shaft streaks on upperparts and less heavily barred, and paler below.

C. c. lineata (Scopoli, 1786) (includes *manillensis, caerulescens, rostrata, lineatula, minima, colletti* and *victoriae*) occurs on Philippines, Borneo, Sulawesi, Lesser Sundas and Australia; described above.

C. c. novaeguineae Rand, 1942 occurs in montane New Guinea; central breast and abdomen chestnut-brown.

C. c. papuensis Mayr & Rand, 1937 occurs in SE New Guinea; like *novaeguineae* but central breast and abdomen darker, more deep maroon.

C. c. lepida (Hartlaub, 1879) occurs in Bismarck Archipelago (Papua New Guinea).

MEASUREMENTS Length 12–15 cm. Female slightly smaller. *C. c. lineata* (*'victoriae'* of Australia) given. Males: wing 68–78 (mean 72), tail c.26, tarsus 18–20, weight 35–48 (mean 41). Females: wing 68–74 (mean 72), tail c.26, tarsus 17–19, weight 31–41 (mean 36).

HABITAT Shrubby and swampy grasslands, paddy fields, coastal heathland, damp riverine scrub, scrubby wetland edges with mixed rank vegetation and fernlands. Principally in lowlands, but ascends to 2000 m in Sri Lanka and S India.

VOICE Male call is a piping musical two-note whistle, *ti-yu, ti-yu, ti-yu* or a three-note *ti-ti-yu*, the final note being lower pitched. Calls most readily at dusk, but in early breeding season may call all day and night. When flushed utters a series of sharp *cheeps* or a weak *tir-tir-tir.*

HABITS Shy, most often seen running or dust-bathing on tracks. Very difficult to flush (perhaps due to small size and its favouring rank vegetation), preferring to squat or run from danger. Usually in pairs or family parties of up to 6, but coveys of 40 and more reported in past. Progresses with mouse-like precision, running furtively before pausing and running again. Diet principally grass seeds and some small insects.

BREEDING Monogamous, with strong pair-bond. Nest a shallow, well-lined scrape, often domed with grasses and sedges, constructed by female with male offering some assistance collecting materials. Well hidden in grass tussock, sedges or weeds, even in a discarded tin. Clutch 4–8 pale olive-brown, buff or reddish-brown eggs, finely freckled dark brown, or sometimes unmarked. Female alone incubates for 18–19 days. Two broods raised in better seasons, while chicks become mature at eight weeks and are thus capable of breeding later in season of hatching. Laying season varies according to extent and timing of rains. Eggs reported December–January in Victoria, September–December in New South Wales, January–February and May in Northern Territory, April in Lesser Sundas (Lombok), January–August in Malaysia, November–February on Borneo, June–September in Philippines (Luzon), March–April in S India, May, August–September and December–January in Sri Lanka, and June–August in Assam. Male helps tend and defend chicks, subsequently taking charge of brood in order that female can incubate second clutch.

DISTRIBUTION SE Asia and Australia. Widespread but patchily distributed in India, chiefly in south, east and northeast, dispersing west at onset of rains, reaching Nepal and Bombay. Resident Sri Lanka and Nicobar Is, but now only vagrant to Bangladesh. Also east through Myanmar and Thailand to SE China, north to Fujian (also Shandong), including Taiwan and Hainan, south over Indochina and Malaysia, the Philippines, the entire length of Indonesia, including Sumatra, Borneo, the Moluccas, Lesser Sundas and New Guinea to Australia, where very local. Populations occur in the Kimberleys (Western Australia), coastal lowlands of Top End (Northern Territory), E coastal Queensland and New South Wales, with introductions in Victoria and (formerly) South Australia. Also introduced on Guam (W Pacific), Réunion (rare) and Mauritius (now extirpated).

STATUS Throughout most of range usually considered 'uncommon', and at least in India certainly appears to have declined during 20th century, doubtless due to drainage of favoured swampy grasslands. Always very localised in Australia.

REFERENCES Blakers *et al.* (1984), Grimmett *et al.* (1998), Marchant & Higgins (1993), Pizzey & Knight (1997).

Genus *ANUROPHASIS*: Snow Mountain Quail

Monotypic genus confined to the highest mountains of New Guinea. Some similarities to *Coturnix*, especially Brown Quail, but possesses several peculiar features; its plumage is boldly barred (approaching unrelated Snow Partridge of the Himalayas) and only weakly streaked, while its bill is markedly stout and tail feathers very soft (scarcely distinguishable from tail-coverts). It lacks tarsal spurs and has a strangely elongated, straight claw on the innermost toe.

74   SNOW MOUNTAIN QUAIL
Anurophasis monorthonyx van Oort, 1910   Plate 1

Alternative name: New Guinea Quail.

A little-known, rarely encountered quail of the Snow Mts of Irian Jaya; this unique species is probably not uncommon within its alpine environment.

IDENTIFICATION Unmistakable within its restricted range—alpine grassland above 3000 m in Snow Mts of New Guinea. A large dark partridge-sized quail, closely barred black and rufous (male) or black and buff (female). Smaller, more uniformly patterned Brown Quail is only similar species in range, but does not normally occur in high-altitude alpine zone inhabited by *Anurophasis* (Brown has exceptionally been found at 3700 m).

DESCRIPTION Bill horn. Legs yellowish. Irides brown. See genus introduction for peculiar structural features. Sexes differ. **Adult male:** Ground colour of almost entire plumage rufous-chestnut, clear and virtually unmarked on head-sides, throat and central underparts. Crown, ear-coverts, breast and flanks barred black, broadest and most angled on flanks. Entire upperparts, including wings and rump, close-barred black and rufous-chest-

nut, with very fine indistinct pale shaft streaks. **Adult female:** Ground colour of almost entire plumage pale buff, near whitish when worn. Body patterned as male, although barring less black, more brownish-black, and has wider and more prominent buff shaft streaks, making barring less defined and more broken. **Juvenile:** Differs from adult in more irregular, less distinct, barring.

GEOGRAPHICAL VARIATION Monotypic.

MEASUREMENTS Length 25–28 cm. Males: wing 157–161, tail 61–70. Females: wing 158, tail 65. Weight (both sexes) c.401.

HABITAT Alpine grassland on north-facing slopes and plateaus of Snow Mts, at 3100–4200 m, and recently discovered in the Star Mts.

VOICE Only described call is a noisy squeal or cackle when flushed, rendered as *quee-U* or *quee-ah*, repeated 4–5 times.

HABITS Poorly known. Apparently less sociable than most quail, being usually encountered singly or in pairs, rarely more than 3 together. Flies reluctantly, flushing only when hard-pressed and rarely flying far before landing and hiding among grass tussocks or bases of scrubby bushes. Food includes grass seeds, leaves, flower heads, caterpillars and invertebrates.

BREEDING Virtually unknown. A nest with 3 eggs was discovered beneath the edge of a grass tussock in late September.

DISTRIBUTION Endemic to Snow Mts of New Guinea, where it occurs on the Carstensz and Wilhelmina massifs and on Kemabu Plateau of Irian Jaya (Indonesia).

STATUS Near Threatened. Not protected by Indone-

sian law. Despite limited range and relative lack of recent observations (its population may be naturally low), the species is probably not at risk, and its threat category is more indicative of its restricted range than perceived decline. The remoteness of its habitat alone renders it safe from human interference, although the development of a mine is a problem in one area. Nevertheless this little-known species would greatly benefit from field research and ecological assessment.

REFERENCES Beehler *et al.* (1986), BirdLife International (2000), Collar *et al.* (1994), Iredale (1956), Johnsgard (1988), Rand & Gilliard (1967), Schodde *et al.* (1975).

Genus *PERDICULA*: bush-quails

Four small species, confined to the Indian subcontinent, with stouter bills, bristled forehead feathers and stiffer tail feathers (12) than *Coturnix*, while Jungle and Rock Bush-quails possess a short blunt tarsal spur (*Coturnix* are unspurred, have 8–12 soft tail feathers and relatively slender bills). Plumages of *asiatica* and *argoondah* are complex, differing not only between sexes and with age, but also quite markedly geographically. Although their ranges overlap widely they are reasonably separated ecologically.

75 JUNGLE BUSH-QUAIL
Perdicula asiatica (Latham, 1790)   Plate 22

The most widespread bush-quail, favouring scrubby grassland in dry hill country of C and S India and Sri Lanka.

IDENTIFICATION A sociable quail of dry grassy slopes with rocky and scrubby cover and grassy areas amidst scrub–jungle. Strongly sexually dimorphic, the boldly barred males suggest a miniature Grey Francolin in basic appearance, while females, with unmarked rusty underparts, are equally striking. Confusion unlikely with *Coturnix* or *Turnix* quails if seen reasonably well, but separation from very similar Rock Bush-quail more problematic, although latter prefers less bushy, more semi-arid, habitats. Given good views, male has dark brownish ear-coverts and long clear rufous and whitish supercilium, becoming whiter and more conspicuous at rear (producing 'masked' and 'capped' effects), variable whitish moustachial separating rusty throat from brown 'mask', and rufous vent (rusty ear-coverts and throat merge in male Rock, which has buffy-white vent—except *salimalii* with reddish vent). Buff streaks generally most conspicuous on dull-brown upperparts of Jungle (beware racial variation), whereas Rock has clearer dark and pale barring (like mini Grey Francolin). Females of both species pinkish-rufous, but Jungle has grey-brown crown, ear-coverts and upperparts, with variable buff streaking and black feather marks on scapulars (beware racial variation), long whitish supercilium and richer rufous throat. Rock has upper- and underparts almost uniform rufous without strong markings, pale chin and shorter whitish supercilium. Immatures confusing, juvenile Jungle of both sexes are female-like, with whitish streaking on throat and breast, whereas juvenile Rock is barred below (male-like). Older 'intermediate' stages also confusing as a Jungle with mixed-sex features is a young male, but in Rock is a young female. Distribution also a clue, e.g. Jungle has

most extensive range and is only bush-quail on Sri Lanka. Compare also Painted Bush-quail

DESCRIPTION *P. a. asiatica*. Bill blackish (adult males), paler at base, or dull brownish-horn (juvenile and female). Irides pale brown to orange-brown (darker brown in juvenile). Legs pinkish, dull orange or reddish (reddest in adult males). Sexually dimorphic, male has short tarsal spur. **Adult male:** Forehead, lores and narrow supercilium chestnut, upper and rear part of supercilium buffy-white becoming whiter behind eye and extending almost to nape. Crown and nape brown, mottled chestnut and blackish-brown. Ear-coverts dark brown. Chin and throat chestnut, separated from brown ear-coverts by mottled buffy-white moustachial. Breast, flanks and upper belly whitish, closely barred black, lower belly and undertail-coverts warm buffy-rufous. Mantle, back, scapulars and wings dull brown, with buff shaft streaks and blackish-brown blotches and vermiculations. Flight feathers barred on innermost, virtually unmarked on outer primaries (barred in juveniles). Rump and uppertail-coverts dull brown, barred buffish-brown. Tail pinkish-brown with buff, black-edged, cross-barring. **Adult female:** Head and throat pattern, and coloration similar to male, but moustachial stripe duller. Underparts dull pinkish-rufous, offering some contrast with richer rufous throat. Some (perhaps older) females attain weak dark and pale barring on breast. Upperparts as male although black blotching less bold and wings more uniform, less barred. **Juvenile:** Both sexes resemble female but have fine whitish shaft streaks on head-sides, throat and breast. Upperparts have more numerous buffy shaft streaks, black vermiculations and blotches than adult female, primaries mottled and barred. Young male gradually attains barring on underparts during first winter (c.3 months old).

GEOGRAPHICAL VARIATION Five intergrading subspecies generally recognised, differing in colour saturation.

P. a. asiatica (Latham, 1790) occurs in C India from Gujarat, Madhya Pradesh and Orissa south to N Karnataka and N Andhra Pradesh; described above.

P. a. punjaubi Whistler, 1939 occurs in NW India, from S Kashmir, Himachal Pradesh, Punjab, Haryana to Uttar Pradesh; paler than nominate, more sandy above with less conspicuous blotching, but more prominent barring on rump, and finer black barring on underparts of male.

P. a. vidali Whistler & Kinnear, 1936 occurs in coastal SW India from Bombay south; upperparts with marked reddish tone, especially crown, and underparts barring of male broader than nominate.

P. a. vellorei Abdulali & Reuben, 1964 occurs in interior of Tamil Nadu.

P. a. ceylonensis Whistler & Kinnear, 1936 occurs in Sri Lanka (dry zone); upperparts and chestnut throat much darker than other races, with reduced buff streaking and black blotching offering little contrast to upperparts.

MEASUREMENTS Length 17 cm. Female smaller. *P. a. asiatica* given. Males: wing 81–88, tail 34–41, tarsus 24–30. Females: wing 80–88, tail 32–41, tarsus 23–31. Weight (both sexes) 57–82.

HABITAT Dry grassy plains and hills with rocky and scrubby cover and grassy areas amidst scrub–jungle. Reaches 1200 m in Kashmir and 1500 m in S India.

VOICE Territorial call a harsh, grating *chee-chee-chuck, chee-chee-chuck*, likened to sound of Black Drongo *Dicrurus macrocercus* in dispute. Agitated and dispersed coveys reassemble using constant low, bubbling whistles, *tiri-tiri-tiri* or *whi-whi-whi-whi-whi*. Also a low chuckle when flushed (Henry 1971).

HABITS Typically encountered in coveys of 6–20 dust-bathing on tracks, or feeding in bushy grassland. Coveys walk to drink (morning and evening) at favoured water sources along well-trodden routes, creating 'tunnels' through taller grass. Tends to walk or run from potential danger, flying only as last resort. Coveys will squat in tight bunch at base of bush, facing outwards and 'explode' on whirring wings in different directions from almost underfoot, flying for short distance before dropping into cover and running on. They reassemble by running through grass towards each other, calling constantly. Roosts on ground. Feeds on grass and weed seeds, termites and other small insects and their larvae.

BREEDING Apparently monogamous. Nest a shallow scrape lined with grasses at the base of grassy tussock. Clutch 4–8 (mean 5–6) creamy-white to pale buff eggs. Female alone incubates for 16–18 days (21–22 days in captivity). Breeding reported at most times of year, chiefly in late rainy season, through dry season, e.g. August–April in C India, March–April in Sri Lanka. Male helps guard and tend brood after hatching.

DISTRIBUTION India. Throughout much of peninsular India north to Gujarat and Orissa, and foothills of Kashmir. Also dry zone of Sri Lanka. Recorded from lowland Nepal in 19th century but not subsequently. Introduced Réunion (Indian Ocean).

STATUS Locally common in India, where little direct contact with agricultural changes, but generally rare or uncommon in Kerala. Very local in Sri Lanka, being numerous only southeast of Uva Hills, and always scarce elsewhere. No recent information on introduced Réunion population.

REFERENCES Ali & Ripley (1969), Baker (1930), Henry (1971), Thornhill (1981), Wennrich (1983), Zacharias & Gaston (1999).

76 ROCK BUSH-QUAIL
Perdicula argoondah (Sykes, 1832)   Plate 22

Generally replaces Jungle in more arid, less wooded country but they have been much confused in the past.

IDENTIFICATION Very similar to Jungle Bush-quail, and like that species is strongly sexually dimorphic, boldly barred males appearing like miniature Grey Francolin while females are almost uniform pinkish-rufous. Rock prefers drier, more semi-arid habitats than Jungle, but some overlap exists. Given good views, male Rock has paler rusty-buff ear-coverts and throat joined (lacks whitish moustachial of Jungle) and has buffy-white vent (rusty in Jungle and race *salimalii* of Rock, which has restricted range). Although it has a distinct supercilium, it lacks the dark brownish 'mask' and 'capped' appearance of Jungle. The upperparts are more obviously barred pale and darker brown than Jungle, and the buff shaft streaks typical of Jungle are less apparent (see Geographical Variation for upperparts coloration). Females are

pinkish-rufous in both species, but Rock lacks grey-brown, slightly mottled and blotched upperparts, rich rufous throat and relatively long supercilium, instead having upper- and underparts almost uniform pinkish-rufous without strong markings, pale chin and vent and shorter whitish supercilium. Immatures confusing, juvenile Rock of both sexes is barred below (male-like), whereas juvenile Jungle is female-like. Older 'intermediate' stages also confusing as Rock with mixed-sex features is a young female, and that of Jungle a young male. Distribution useful in identification. Confusion unlikely with either *Coturnix* or *Turnix* quails, if seen well, but compare Painted Bush-quail.

DESCRIPTION *P. a. argoondah.* Bill blackish, paler at base, or dull brownish-horn. Irides pale brown to orange-brown. Legs dull yellowish or dusky-orange. Sexually dimorphic, male has short tarsal spur. **Adult male:** Forehead, forecrown, chin and throat, and ear-coverts buffy-rufous. Supercilium buffy-white, principally behind eye. Crown and nape brown, mottled blackish-brown. Breast, flanks and upper belly whitish, closely barred black, lower belly and undertail-coverts whitish-buff. Mantle, back, scapulars and wings dull brown, barred paler brownish-buff, with weak buff shaft streaks and indistinct blackish-brown blotches and vermiculations, flight feathers including outer primaries barred. Rump and uppertail-coverts dull brown, barred buffish-brown. Tail brown, with buff, black-edged cross-barring. **Adult female:** Underparts warm pinkish-rufous, paler on chin and lower underparts. Short whitish supercilium behind eye. Upperparts rufous-brown, weakly marbled and barred but lacking obvious markings. **Juvenile:** Both sexes resemble male in obviously barred underparts on buffy-whitish background. Upperparts have more numerous buffy shaft streaks and black vermiculations and blotches than adult. Young female gradually attains rufous underparts during first winter (at c.3 months).

GEOGRAPHICAL VARIATION Three intergrading subspecies generally recognised, differing in colour saturation.

   P. a. meinertzhageni Whistler, 1937 occurs in north of range, south to Kutch, Saurashtra and N and W Madhya Pradesh; the palest form, with pale brown upperparts, male has narrower dark barring on underparts.
   P. a. argoondah (Sykes, 1832) occurs in peninsular India from Madhya Pradesh south to Madras; described above.
   P. a. salimalii Whistler, 1943 occurs in red laterite

rocky terrain of Chitaldrug area of Karnataka and Wynaad district of Kerala; entire upperparts almost brick-red (but mottled and barred as nominate), flanks and vent of male strongly washed brick-red (like Jungle).

MEASUREMENTS Length 17 cm. Female smaller. *P. a. argoondah* given. Males: wing 82–89, tail 44–47, tarsus 25–27. Females: wing 82–86, tail 32–41, tarsus 24–25. Weight (both sexes) 59–74.

HABITAT Scrubby semi-desert plains and sparsely-vegetated, rocky hills, generally below 600 m.

VOICE Like Jungle Bush-quail, but no direct comparisons available.

HABITS Very similar to Jungle Bush-quail.

BREEDING Apparently monogamous. Nest a shallow scrape lined with grasses at the base of grassy tussock, bush or rock. Clutch 4–8 (mean 5–6) creamy-white eggs. Incubation, by female alone, occupies 16–18 days (21 days in captivity). Nesting reported at most times of year, chiefly August–November and March–April. Broods merge with other coveys soon after hatching.

DISTRIBUTION India. Throughout most drier parts of peninsular W India, north to Haryana and Gujarat, east to C Madhya Pradesh and C Andhra Pradesh, south to N Kerala. Possibly nomadic.

STATUS Locally common, having little direct contact with agricultural changes.

REFERENCES Ali & Ripley (1969), Baker (1930).

---

77   PAINTED BUSH-QUAIL
Perdicula erythrorhyncha (Sykes, 1832)   Plate 22

A beautifully marked bush-quail with two disjunct populations in peninsular India.

IDENTIFICATION Darker than previous two species, Painted Bush-quail favours grassy hillsides in lusher habitats. Both sexes rich rufous below; this and the combination of red bill and legs and, in the male, bright white throat and supercilium renders the species quite unmistakable. In many respects, the female recalls darker populations of female Jungle but is more richly coloured overall, with clearer white upperparts streaking, bold black flanks markings, and red bill and legs. Confusion unlikely with either *Coturnix* or *Turnix* quails, if seen reasonably well, but also compare male Blue-breasted Quail.

DESCRIPTION *P. e. erythrorhyncha.* Bill and legs bright coral-red (duller, more brownish-red in juveniles). Irides yellowish-brown to hazel-brown. Sexually dimorphic, both sexes lack obvious tarsal spur. **Adult male:** Forehead, chin, lores and surround to eye black extending as dark brown band behind eye down neck-sides. Broad white supercilium meets on upper forehead and extends to nape. Rest of crown and nape dark brown, becoming blackish along edge of supercilium. Throat and malar pure white narrowly edged black. Breast olive-brown with black-scaled feather

centres. Rest of underparts rufous-chestnut, flanks boldly marked with black scales and white tips; black markings extending onto undertail-coverts. Mantle, back, scapulars, rump, uppertail-coverts and wings olive-brown, barred paler brownish-buff and blotched and spotted with black. Clear white shaft streaks on scapulars and wing-coverts. **Adult female:** Lacks black and white head pattern of male, having rufous forehead, supercilium and throat. Black flanks markings less extensive than male. Rest of body and wing coloration much as male. **Juvenile:** Both sexes resemble female, but young male has throat and supercilium white, washed rufous and scattered white shaft streaks on breast and mantle.

GEOGRAPHICAL VARIATION Two reasonably well differentiated subspecies.

   P. e. erythrorhyncha (Sykes 1832) occurs in W Ghats; described above.
   P. e. blewitti (Hume, 1874) occurs in E Ghats; smaller (wing 76–84) and paler than nominate, more greyish-brown and less richly coloured overall, male has broader white frontal band, less black on forehead and little, or no, black on chin.

MEASUREMENTS Length 18 cm. Female smaller. *P. e. erythrorhyncha* given. Males: wing 81–87, tail 40–44, tarsus 23–25. Females: wing 81–86, tail 33–45, tarsus 24–25. Weight (both sexes) 50–85.

HABITAT Open grassy hillsides with sparse scrub, especially near forest edge or in broken moist-deciduous forest, at 600–2000 m. Tolerates patchy cultivation.

VOICE Territorial call of male a pleasant, triple note, rendered as a repeated *kirikee, kirikee, kirikee* (nominate). Race *blewitti* reported to utter a 'single loud note, often repeated' but difference perhaps in transcription rather than real (research required). Agitated and dispersed birds reassemble with repeated soft whistled *tu-tu-tu-tu-tu-tutu-tutu-tutu* rising in pitch, before fading away, and repeated after a few seconds. When flushed, reported to give a short, squeaky whistle like Common Quail.

HABITS Very similar to Jungle Bush-quail. Forages in coveys of 6–15. Typically found when dust-bathing by tracks in grassland or jungle clearings. Most active early morning and evening, but rarely wanders far from cover. Food includes grass and weed seeds, grain, shoots and small invertebrates, especially termites.

BREEDING Apparently monogamous. Nest a shallow scrape lined with grasses placed at base of grassy clump or bush. Clutch 4–7 (up to 10) creamy-buff eggs. Incubation, by female alone, occupies 16–18 days (but probably 21 days as other captive bush-quails). Apparently two breeding seasons per year, with eggs reported in most months, varying with location: chiefly December–February and July–September in Kerala, and January–March and August–November in the Nilgiri Hills (Tamil Nadu). Male helps tend chicks, which are capable of flight at an early age (when little bigger than a bumble-bee!).

DISTRIBUTION India. Two disjunct populations; the more southerly in the W Ghats from Khandala (W Maharashtra) south through Karnataka and Kerala, and adjacent Tamil Nadu (Nilgiri and Shevaroy Hills); and northern *blewitti* chiefly in E Ghats, from E Maharashtra through E Madyha Pradesh and Orissa, to Bihar and West Bengal.

STATUS Apparently locally common over wide range, but few specific data available.

REFERENCES Ali & Ripley (1969), Baker (1930), BirdLife International (2000), Grimmett *et al.* (1998).

---

78   MANIPUR BUSH-QUAIL
Perdicula manipurensis Hume, 1880   Plate 23

Alternative names: Manipur and Assam Painted Bush-quail.

Poorly-known bush-quail that is near-endemic to Assam and Manipur, has the most restricted range of the four species, and is threatened by habitat destruction.

IDENTIFICATION Very dark and rather featureless quail of extensive lowland grasslands in NE India. Likened to miniature female Black Francolin, but due to skulking nature and difficulty of exploring remaining elephant grassland (tiger country) presence more likely to be established aurally than visually. Given good views, dark olive-grey plumage is relieved by buffish lower underparts, rufous throat (male) and bold black markings (less obvious in northern *inglisi*). Uniform dark grey upperparts and sociable nature renders it unlikely to be confused with other quails, even if flushed.

DESCRIPTION *P. m. manipurensis.* Bill dark grey, paler and yellowish towards base. Legs orange-red. Irides dark brown or hazel-brown. Sexually dimorphic, both sexes lack obvious tarsal spur. **Adult male:** Forehead and supercilium rufous-chestnut, lores and patch behind eye, white, and chin, throat and malar rufous-chestnut. Rest of head, neck, breast and upperparts slate-grey (with olive tones), closely barred and spotted black and more boldly marked with black arrowheads on scapulars and breast. Lower breast, flanks and belly warm buff, becoming whitish on undertail-coverts, heavily marked black; flank feathers particularly boldly marked with black chevrons and shaft streaks. **Adult female:** Distinctly paler grey than male, with chestnut on head replaced by greyish-buff. Lower underparts paler buff and less intensely marked than male. **Juvenile:** Both sexes resemble female, but plumage browner and legs paler, more pinkish.

GEOGRAPHICAL VARIATION Two reasonably well-differentiated subspecies.
> *P. m. manipurensis* Hume, 1880 occurs in Manipur and Assam hills south of Brahmaputra River; described above.
> *P. m. inglisi* (Ogilvie-Grant, 1909) occurs in West Bengal and Assam, north of Brahmaputra River; paler and greyer than nominate, with both upper- and underparts less boldly marked black.

MEASUREMENTS Length 20 cm. Female slightly smaller. *P. m. manipurensis* given. Both sexes: wing 80–86, tail 45–52, tarsus 25–26, weight 50–85.

HABITAT Damp grassland and scrub–jungle, particularly tall elephant grass, up to 1000 m. Occasionally in bogs and swamps in Manipur Valley.

VOICE A captive female called a clear, softly-whistled *whit-it-it-it-it*, the notes becoming progressively higher pitched until running together. Repeated 3–4 times, louder and higher on each occasion (Ali & Ripley 1969). This is doubtless the rallying cry, given by members of a separated covey. No other calls described.

HABITS Apparently very similar to Jungle Bush-quail. Most active early morning and evening. Forages in coveys of 5–8, emerging from cover of tall grass to feed in open, being especially attracted to burnt grassland areas where fresh shoots are sprouting. Otherwise reputedly extremely hard to find. Foods include grass seeds, pods of wild lentils, ants and other small invertebrates.

BREEDING Almost unknown. Only nest found was of southern race, situated on a grassy plateau surrounded by forest. It was a shallow scrape among grass roots and contained 4 white eggs in May. One of the northern race was taken in breeding condition in March, and a fully-fledged chick was found in January.

DISTRIBUTION NE India. Two populations separated by Brahmaputra River; to the north it occurs from extreme NE West Bengal (Jalpaiguri) and Assam east to Sadiya; and south of the river the species ranges through the Assam hills, adjacent Meghalaya, perhaps Nagaland (specific details are lacking) and Manipur, and is possibly still extant in E Bangladesh.

STATUS Vulnerable. Rare and poorly known, with few records in recent years. Has presumably undergone a marked decline through the destruction of its grassland habitat, which is now heavily fragmented. It is extremely elusive and thus reasonable numbers may survive in grassland pockets of NE India. Its continued presence in Bangladesh is unlikely but it could survive in the Chittagong Hills, while its speculated presence in adjacent Myanmar is unproven.

REFERENCES Ali & Ripley (1969), Baker (1930), BirdLife International (2000, 2001), Choudhury (2001), Collar *et al.* (1994), Grimmett *et al.* (1998).

Genus *OPHRYSIA*: Himalayan Quail

A monotypic genus that is probably extinct. It exhibited a number of peculiar morphological features making its precise relationships unclear. More like a small partridge than a quail, it was strongly sexually dimorphic and had short stout legs (without tarsal spurs), long, lanceolate body feathers (reminiscent of Blood Pheasant), stiff bristle-shafted forehead feathers and a stout bill (like Blood Pheasant and bush-quails), plus a relatively long rounded tail of ten feathers (recalling spurfowls).

79   HIMALAYAN QUAIL
Ophrysia superciliosa (J. E. Gray, 1846)   Plate 23

Alternative name: Indian Mountain Quail.

An extraordinary bird of uncertain affinity known only from a few specimens collected in the W Himalayan foothills of India between 1836 and 1876.

IDENTIFICATION Probably extinct. Very dark and relatively large full-tailed quail or small partridge of the Kumaon Himalaya, although it is unlikely to survive in this region. Quite unmistakable given good views, when overall dark brownish-slate body plumage of male contrasts with whitish forehead, supercilium and facial marks, as well as red bill and legs. Female equally distinctive, being cinnamon-brown, paler on underparts, mottled black throughout, with red bill and legs but smaller white facial markings than male.

DESCRIPTION Bill and legs red (duller in female). Sexually dimorphic. See genus introduction for structural characteristics. **Adult male:** Forehead and supercilium white, bordered above and below with black. Head-sides, chin and throat black, with small white marks in front of and behind eye, and whitish band on neck-sides, separated from white of supercilium. Crown brownish-grey with small black streaks. Both upper- and underparts brownish-slate, evenly streaked black. Wings brown, appearing paler than body. Undertail-coverts black, broadly tipped white. **Adult female:** Forehead, supercilium, throat and ear-coverts pale greyish-cinnamon. Small white marks either side of eye. Blackish line along crown-sides and behind eye. Crown, nape and entire upperparts tawny-brown, boldly streaked with triangle-shaped black spots. Underparts similar but ground colour paler, more cinnamon-tawny, and has fine vermiculations on flanks and undertail-coverts. Tail barred. **Juvenile:** Young male differs from adult in having buff streaks and barring on tertials, and large black spots on back (like female).

GEOGRAPHICAL VARIATION Monotypic.

MEASUREMENTS Length 25 cm. Female slightly smaller. Males: wing 85–93, tail 76–78. Females: wing 87–91, tail 64–65. Tarsus (sex not stated) 29.

HABITAT Steep hillsides with long grass, and hollows with scrubby thickets. All specimens were collected at 1650–2100 m, but speculated to also have occurred at lower elevations (Rieger & Walzthöny 1992).

VOICE Only described call was 'low, short, quail-like', uttered while feeding. When alarmed, gave a shrill whistle (Ali & Ripley 1969).

HABITS Apparently occurred in coveys of 6–12, keeping to dense cover and favouring steep slopes. Shy and elusive, and very reluctant fliers, even if hard-pressed preferring to run from danger. Awkward and heavy fliers, even over very short distances. Only recorded food was grass seeds.

BREEDING Unknown.

DISTRIBUTION N India, where only known from three hill stations in N Uttar Pradesh and last recorded 1890.

STATUS Almost certainly extinct. Critical. Nine or ten specimens collected above hill stations of Mussoorie (Banog, Badhraj), nearby Dehra Dun (Jharipani) and Naini Tal (Sherka Danda) in 1836–1876, with the last confirmed report in 1890. Nearly all were taken in dry winter months (November–January),

HABITS Usually in coveys of 5–10 feeding amongst leaf-litter in dense forest undergrowth, especially on slopes by ravines and streams. When surprised, tends to run but often flies upwards on whirring wings following a short run, moving with great manoeuvrability between forest trees to perch on a leafy branch (in manner of some *Zoothera* thrushes), or return to ground. Once flushed is very difficult to relocate, tending to scuttle away under cover. Roosts in trees, the coveys huddling together on a branch in the manner of some babblers. Feeds on seeds, shoots, berries, insects and their larvae, and small snails.

BREEDING Apparently monogamous. Nest, constructed by male, a scrape sparsely lined or well padded with grasses, situated within a clump of ringal bamboo, amongst forest undergrowth, or a scraped-out hollow in a bank. Usually has a sparse grassy dome. Clutch 3–5, exceptionally 9 unmarked white eggs. Incubation

24 days (in captivity). Breeds April–June or July in India, slightly later at higher elevations. Reported February–May in China.

DISTRIBUTION S Himalayas, from NW India (at Chamba in Himachal Pradesh) east through Nepal, Sikkim, Bhutan and Arunachal Pradesh to N Myanmar, also adjacent China in SW Sichuan and NW Yunnan, and marginally Vietnam (NW Tonkin).

STATUS Still relatively numerous in India and Nepal, despite forest destruction that has adversely affected many local populations. Its elusive nature makes it easy to overlook, although its territorial calls betray its presence. Within its restricted range in China it has always been rare.

REFERENCES Ali (1949, 1962), Ali & Ripley (1968), Baker (1930).

---

82   SICHUAN HILL-PARTRIDGE
Arborophila rufipectus Boulton, 1932

Plate 27

Alternative names: Boulton's or Szechwan Hill-partridge or Partridge.

One of the most endangered hill-partridges, severely threatened by forest destruction throughout its limited range.

IDENTIFICATION Distinctive hill-partridge of SE Sichuan, where it is the only *Arborophila*. Like rest of genus, far more likely to be heard than seen. Given reasonable views, the white throat, supercilium and underparts, contrasting in males with broad chestnut breast-band, prevents confusion with other species.

DESCRIPTION Bill blackish. Irides brown. Bare skin around eye red. Legs grey. Sexually dimorphic. **Adult male:** Crown reddish-brown, streaked blackish; nape and neck-sides rusty-buff, streaked black; ear-coverts unmarked orange-buff. Supercilium white. Lores and eye-stripe black, streaked black and white behind eye. Chin, throat and chest white, streaked black. Broad rufous-chestnut breast-band with some grey feathering. Flanks blue-grey with white shaft streaks and chestnut edges. Belly whitish. Vent buffy with black feather centres. Mantle, back, rump and uppertail-coverts brownish-grey, feathers with narrow black fringes. Scapulars have broad chestnut edges. Wing feathers greyish to buffy-brown, tertials and wing-coverts prominently marked with black and edged rufous. **Adult female:** Differs from male principally in pale yellowish chin and throat bordered below by grey-brown breast-band; flanks grey with weak pale streaks. **Juvenile:** Apparently undescribed.

GEOGRAPHICAL VARIATION None. Similarities in upperparts pattern, leg colour and relatively strong sexual dimorphism indicate a close relationship with Necklaced. However, Davison (1982) aligned it with the Grey-breasted group, placed it closest to Brown-breasted.

MEASUREMENTS Length 29–31 cm. Female smaller. Males: wing 148–158, tail 68–74, tarsus c.45, weight 410–470: Females: wing 143–145, tail 64–71, tarsus c.42, weight 350–386.

HABITAT Subtropical broad-leaved forest, predominately oak with a significant understorey of bamboo and various shrubs. Altitudinal range 1100–2250 m, but chiefly found at 1400–1800 m.

VOICE Territorial call: a double-noted, rather slow, *ho-wo, ho-wo*, probably similar to far-carrying two-toned mournful whistle of Collared. Also a more complex whistle.

HABITS Much as Necklaced Hill-partridge, noted in pairs or family parties of 5–6, the coveys pair off during winter and early spring. Feeds on seeds and fruits of various shrubs, and some invertebrates.

BREEDING Few data. Apparently monogamous. Nest scrapes concealed amidst tree roots. Clutch 5–6. Breeds April–June.

DISTRIBUTION CS China. Endemic to area of less than 100 km² in SE Sichuan, encompassing Mabian, E'bian, Machuan, Ganluo, Pingshan, Leibo and, probably, Meigu counties. In 1997, its suspected presence in nearby Yunnan was confirmed from the adjacent counties of Suijiang and Yongshan.

STATUS Endangered. Until relatively recently, considered at least locally fairly common within its tiny range, but the logging industry is now decimating its native forests and replanting with conifers. Despite recent survey years, which identified key areas of remaining forest that could be declared reserves or protected by extending existing reserves, no protected areas exist to safeguard the species' future, and none are known in captivity. Fieldwork, in 1996–97, estimated the population at 612 territorial males (based on a mean density of 0.55 per km²) at ten sites, but subsequent work suggests the overall population may be significantly larger.

REFERENCES BirdLife International (2000, 2001), Cheng *et al.* (1978), Dai Bo (1997), Dai Bo *et al.* (1997, 1998), Collar *et al.* (1994), Davison (1982), Dowell (1998), He Fen-qi (1992), McGowan *et al.* (1995).

83 RUFOUS-THROATED HILL-PARTRIDGE
Arborophila rufogularis (Blyth, 1850)   Plate 27

Alternative name: Rufous-throated Partridge.

Widespread in montane forest throughout the Himalayas, and east to Vietnam. Unsurprisingly, for such a wide-ranging species, a number of races have been described.

IDENTIFICATION The only hill-partridge that lacks an intervening collar or belt of colour between the rufous throat and grey breast, but note that the throat is blackish in race *intermedia*, and may be boldly spotted in others. Banded wings merge into extensively chestnut (white-spotted) flanks, contrasting strikingly with almost unmarked plain brownish back and rump. Most likely to be confused with female Necklaced, but both sexes of Rufous-throated have plain or spotted (not barred) upperparts, spotted or blackish (not streaked) throat, reddish (not grey) legs and pure grey (rather than brownish) breast. Additionally, Rufous-throated is a mid-elevation species, most frequent at 1500–1800 m (recorded 600–2400 m), whereas Necklaced favours forest at 1500–4000 m. Confusion possible with little-known Chestnut-breasted Hill-partridge of E Himalayan foothills, but latter has chestnut (not grey) breast, separated from pale throat by narrow black and white collar.

DESCRIPTION *A. r. rufogularis.* Bill dusky-brown or blackish (blacker in male). Orbital skin, gular skin and legs, pinkish-red to crimson (reddest in breeding male); dull yellowish in juvenile. Irides brown to chestnut-brown. Sexes similar. **Adult male:** Forehead grey, central crown and nape olive-brown, heavily mottled black. Long whitish supercilium terminates at neck-sides. Whitish moustachial curves below mottled dusky ear-coverts. Chin, throat and neck-sides extensively orange-rufous, variably speckled black at sides, the orange neck-sides being only narrowly separated by dark central band down nape; very narrow black line divides orange of throat from rest of underparts. Breast, flanks and upper belly blue-grey, flank feathers with white shaft spot and wide chestnut edges. Central belly whitish. Vent buffy-brown spotted with black feather centres. Mantle, back, rump and uppertail-coverts olive-brown, almost unmarked apart from black spotting on rump and very weak barring on uppertail-coverts. Scapulars, tertials and wing-coverts chestnut on inner webs, with large black central mark and greyish outer webs, forming strong bands across folded wing. **Adult female:** Very similar to male but less spotting on chin and throat, and scattered whitish breast spots. **Juvenile:** Duller and paler orange on throat, dull grey below with whitish belly and breast centre; crown and flanks quite different, being marked with brown and black vermiculations.

GEOGRAPHICAL VARIATION Seven intergrading subspecies differ chiefly in colour saturation and extent and pattern of black on throat.

A. r. rufogularis (Blyth, 1850) occurs in Indian Himalayas, from Kumaon (in Uttar Pradesh) east through Nepal and Bhutan to Mishmi Hills of Assam; described above.

A. r. intermedia (Blyth, 1856) (includes *tenebrarum*) occurs from SE Assam east through Manipur (India) and Chittagong Hills (Bangladesh) to N Myanmar (Arakan Yoma, Chin and Kachin Hills) and extreme NW Yunnan (China); spotting on crown, nape, chin and upper throat intense, appearing blackish, contrasting with clear orange lower throat, which lacks thin black line bordering grey breast.

A. r. tickelli (Hume, 1880) occurs in S Myanmar (S Shan and Tenasserim), through Thailand to SW Laos; similar to *intermedia* but has rufous throat, extensive chestnut flanks and is richer in overall coloration.

A. r. euroa (Bangs & Phillips, 1914) occurs in SE Yunnan (China) and N Laos.

A. r. guttata Delacour & Jabouille, 1928 (includes *laotiana*) occurs in Laos and Vietnam.

A. r. annamensis (Robinson & Kloss, 1919) occurs on Lang Bian massif (S Vietnam); rufous throat paler than other forms and mixed with white, many have dusky line across upper breast delineating border with throat.

MEASUREMENTS Length 26–29 cm. Female smaller. *A. r. rufogularis.* Males: wing 144–161 (mean 154), tail (n=1) 70, tarsus (n=1) 45, weight 325–430. Females: wing 140–150, tail (n=1) 59, tarsus (n=1) 41, weight 261–386.

HABITAT Montane forest, primarily at 1800–3000 m, but known from 600 to 4000 m. Prefers oak forest, with laurel and rhododendron, chiefly where there is heavy undergrowth, such as stunted forest in ravines.

VOICE Territorial call: a far-carrying mournful double whistle, *wheeea-whu*, the first note prolonged and the second more abrupt. Some individual variation, occasionally the whistle is given in series of 2–3, repeated 3–4 times, on an ascending scale that abruptly ends. Occasionally a single whistle very similar to call of Necklaced Hill-partridge.

HABITS Usually in coveys of 5–10 feeding amongst leaf-litter in dense forest undergrowth, especially on slopes by ravines and streams. If surprised, tends to run but often flies up on whirring wings following a short run, moving with great manoeuvrability between the trees to perch on a leafy branch (in manner of some *Zoothera* thrushes), or returns to ground. Once flushed is very difficult to relocate, usually scuttling away under cover. Roosts in trees, the coveys huddling together on a branch like some babblers. Feeds on seeds, shoots, berries, insects and their larvae, and small snails.

BREEDING Apparently monogamous. Nest, constructed by male, is a scrape sparsely lined or well padded with grasses, situated within bamboo, amongst forest undergrowth, or a scraped out hollow in a bank.

Usually has a sparse grassy dome or tunnel of live grasses. Clutch 3–5, exceptionally 9 unmarked white eggs. Incubation 24 days (in captivity). Breeds April–June or July in India, usually slightly later at higher elevations. Reported February–May in China.

DISTRIBUTION S Himalayas, from NW India (Kumaon Hills of Uttar Pradesh) east through Nepal, Sikkim, Bhutan and NE Indian states to N Myanmar and Bangladesh (Sylhet and Chittagong Hills), and adjacent China in SE Yunnan, through N Thailand south through Laos and Vietnam (south to Lang Bian in S Annam).

STATUS Still considered numerous in India and common in Bhutan (especially in east) but scarce in Nepal.

Only one recent record from Bangladesh, in the northeast in 1991. Within its restricted range in China it has always been rare. Declining, and is now scarce but still widespread in N Thailand. Recently found to be common in parts of C Laos. Reports from S and C Vietnam and NW Myanmar indicate continued presence in these countries but its status in these areas is unknown. Forest destruction has adversely impacted its populations. Territorial calls are typically often the only clue to its presence.

REFERENCES Ali (1949, 1962), Ali & Ripley (1968), Baker (1930), Grimmett *et al.* (1998).

84   CHESTNUT-BREASTED HILL-PARTRIDGE
Arborophila mandellii Hume, 1874   Plate 27

Alternative names: Chestnut-breasted Partridge, Red-breasted or Mandell's Hill-partridge.

A beautifully marked hill-partridge of the E Himalayas that forms a species-pair with Collared of S China.

IDENTIFICATION This attractive and elusive partridge of E Himalayan forests is very little known. Chestnut-breasted generally favours lower elevations than Necklaced, and although its altitudinal range apparently overlaps that of the superficially similar Rufous-throated, Chestnut-breasted probably prefers more humid forests. Useful differences, given reasonable views, are the chestnut, not grey, breast and narrow black and bright white gorget (merely a black line in Rufous-throated). Flanks more boldly marked chestnut than Rufous-throated. Lack of knowledge of the vocal differences between these species hinders reliable identification using voice. Confusion less likely with White-cheeked, which has white cheeks, a black throat and lacks rufous on underparts.

DESCRIPTION Bill black. Irides brown or reddish-brown. Bare skin around eye red. Legs red. Sexes similar. **Adult (both sexes):** Forehead, crown and nape reddish-brown. Grey supercilia meet on hindneck. Lower nape and mantle chestnut, spotted black. Lores, ear-coverts, neck-sides, chin and throat pale rufous, tinged olive and finely mottled black on neck-sides. Narrow white moustachial borders lower ear-coverts. Breast deep chestnut, separated from pale chestnut throat by narrow black and white collar (white above black). Rest of underparts grey, becoming whitish in belly centre. Flank feathers have white central spot and prominent chestnut fringes. Undertail-coverts olive, spotted white and mottled rufous. Upperparts olive-brown, finely barred black on back and spotted black on rump, uppertail-coverts and scapulars. **Juvenile:** Undescribed.

GEOGRAPHICAL VARIATION Monotypic.

MEASUREMENTS Length 28–30 cm. Sexes combined. Wing 133–145, tail 56–58, tarsus 43–45, weight c.268.

HABITAT Evergreen (oak–rhododendron) forest in mountains and foothills. Recorded from 350 to 2450 m, but primarily at 900–1800 m. Prefers dense/secondary moist subtropical valley forest with thick undergrowth, especially bamboo, by streams and within ravines.

VOICE A repeated *prrreet* promptly followed by a series of ascending *prrr prrr-er-it* calls that reach a crescendo (Grimmett *et al.* 1998).

HABITS Undocumented, presumably similar to Necklaced.

BREEDING One authenticated nest, at 2400 m in Sikkim on 3 June. It contained 4 eggs and was described as a pad of grass under a rock within forest. Well-grown young reported in October and chicks accompanied by an adult in August (Bhutan).

DISTRIBUTION E Himalayas, from Sikkim east through Bhutan to Arunachal Pradesh (NE India) and adjacent SE Tibet (Xizang) close to the Myanmar border.

STATUS Vulnerable. Very few data or field observations. Historically known from a handful of widely scattered localities, with recent reports from two, possibly three, sites in Arunachal Pradesh and three in C Bhutan (considered 'fairly common' at one in Shemgang zone). No recent records from Tibet or Sikkim, but four probable sightings in 1992 at Buxa in NE West Bengal, close to the Bhutan border. Hunting and forest destruction are presumably important factors in its decline, but the lack of observations is indicative of a shy and retiring species.

REFERENCES Ali (1962), Ali & Ripley (1969), Baker (1930), BirdLife International (2000, 2001), Collar *et al.* (1994), Grimmett *et al.* (1998), Singh (1994), Tymstra *et al.* (1997).

85 COLLARED HILL-PARTRIDGE
Arborophila gingica (Gmelin, 1789)   Plate 27

Alternative names: Fukien, White-browed, White-necklaced or Rickett's Hill-partridge or Partridge.

Attractive hill-partridge of S China that forms a species-pair with Chestnut-breasted of the E Himalayas.

IDENTIFICATION Almost overlaps with Brown-breasted in Guangxi, but Collared is only hill-partridge within its range and is well separated from others of genus. It should be borne in mind that Hainan Hill-partridge is suspected to occur in S Guangxi, but would be easily distinguished by its blackish head and white ear spot. Collared has a prominent white forehead (usually quite striking in dark gloom of forest undergrowth) and almost plain grey underparts (chestnut flank edging not always obvious), and these features, plus the black, white and chestnut breast-bands, are its most salient field marks. Brown-breasted principally differs in its browner underparts, strongly piebald face pattern and boldly black and white spotted flanks.

DESCRIPTION Bill black. Irides brown. Bare skin around eye red. Legs red. Sexes similar, although male larger. Supposed sexual plumage differences disputed by Li *et al.* (1990). **Adult (both sexes):** Forehead white, long supercilium white or near-white, freckled black. Upperparts reddish-brown spotted black, spots largest on nape and back. Ear-coverts, neck-sides, chin and throat orange-rufous, mottled black on neck-sides. Black gorget borders lower throat, separated from chestnut upper-chest band by narrow white band (the three-banded pattern is bolder and brightest in mature male). Rest of underparts dark grey, becoming whitish in belly centre. Flank feathers fringed chestnut. Undertail-coverts barred black and white. Upperparts olive-brown, finely barred and spotted black on rump and uppertail-coverts. Scapulars have broad chestnut edges and black tips. Wing feathers greyish to buffy-brown, tertials and wing-coverts prominently marked black and edged rufous. **Juvenile:** Ageing process unclear, but those described as 'female' by earlier authors appear to be immatures of either sex (Li *et al.* 1990). Differ from adult in having duller breast pattern and chestnut undertail-coverts marked with white (little or no black).

GEOGRAPHICAL VARIATION Monotypic.

MEASUREMENTS Length 28–30 cm. Sex data combined, though female usually smaller with slimmer tarsus. Wing 137–147 (male 146–147; female, 137–143), tail 50–55. Weight (n=1) 253, mean in captivity 320.

HABITAT Dense forest in foothills and mountains at 500–1700 m, but primarily 700–900 m. Prefers dense or secondary moist subtropical valley forest with thick undergrowth by streams and ravines.

VOICE Territorial call: a far-carrying mournful whistle very similar to Necklaced, a plaintive rising *wooop*, repeated every 2–3 seconds, or a quickly repeated double-noted *co-qwee*. Variation probably linked to whether birds call in duet. Presumed male calls a series of ascending whistles that reach a crescendo (like a hawk-cuckoo *Cuculus* spp.). Most vocal in evening and early morning.

HABITS Undocumented, presumably similar to Necklaced. Feeds on seeds, berries, insects, etc.

BREEDING Clutch 5–7. Incubation 23 days (in captivity). Breeds April–May (but captive individuals in China laid February–August).

DISTRIBUTION SE China, from Yaoshan range in C Guangxi, east through N Guangdong, S Jiangxi, interior Fujian and SW Zhejiang. Also collected on Taiwan, but occurrence there considered to have resulted from introductions.

STATUS Vulnerable. Forest logging over much of its range together with widespread long-term hunting pressure has placed the remaining, now highly fragmented, populations at considerable risk. Although extirpated in many regions, it persists in NW Fujian (at Kuatan), at reserves in S Zhejiang and is still locally common in N Guangdong. In 1986, a captive-breeding programme was initiated at Guangzhou in Guangdong.

REFERENCES BirdLife International (2000, 2001), Carey, G. J. (tape recordings), Cheng *et al.* (1978), Collar *et al.* (1994), Kang (1969), Li *et al.* (1985, 1990, 1992), La Touche (1931).

86 WHITE-CHEEKED HILL-PARTRIDGE
Arborophila atrogularis (Blyth, 1850)   Plate 24

Alternative name: White-cheeked Partridge.

Attractive hill-partridge of E Himalayan foothills, occurring at lower elevations and tolerant of less dense forest than other members of genus with which it overlaps in range.

IDENTIFICATION Broadly overlaps with Necklaced and Rufous-throated, and marginally with Chestnut-breasted Hill-partridges, but White-cheeked favours lower elevations and more open habitats. Bold black and white head pattern prevents confusion with all of

these, particularly the white cheeks and whitish supercilium that contrast with black throat and 'bandit mask'. Coloration approaches that of Grey-breasted complex, particularly Malaysian, but latter has white forehead contrasting with blackish crown and nape (grey forehead and rufous crown in White-cheeked).

DESCRIPTION Bill black. Irides brown. Bare skin around eye pink or red (bright red in breeding season). Legs dull orange to bright red in male (brightest when breeding), dull yellow in female (but brighter, even tinged red, when breeding). Sexes similar, although male larger and has brighter bare-parts coloration. **Adult (both sexes):** Narrow whitish supercilium is yellow-tinged at rear where merges with nape. Forehead grey, becoming olive-brown on fore-crown; nape and neck-sides orange-yellow, streaked black. Cheeks and ear-coverts white, tinged buff on ear-coverts. Chin, throat and malar black, extending below ear-coverts to join black eye-stripe. Lores and eye-stripe black, encircling bare red skin around eye and extending narrowly on rear ear-coverts to join black of throat. Upper breast whitish streaked black, streaking extending to neck-sides and nape. Rest of underparts grey, becoming whitish in belly centre. Flank feathers have white central teardrop markings. Undertail-coverts rufous with white edges and black spotting. Mantle, back, rump and uppertail-coverts olive-brown, feathers with narrow black scale-like fringes. Scapulars similar, but with chestnut edging. Wing feathers golden-brown, tertials and wing-coverts prominently marked with black on inner vane, edged rufous on outer web. **Juvenile:** Apparently much as adult but poorly documented.

GEOGRAPHICAL VARIATION Monotypic. A western form, *rupchandi*, has been named but is not recognised by most authorities.

MEASUREMENTS Length 25–27 cm. Male larger. Wing male 135–147, female 126–130, tail (both sexes) 60–65. Weight (both sexes) 200–312, male mean 256, female mean 220.

HABITAT Favours bamboo and damp undergrowth in broad-leaved evergreen forest in foothills to 1700 m, but primarily below 750 m in India. Tolerates less dense forest than other hill-partridges, often occurring in tea-plantations, bushy grassland and scrub–jungle but usually near forest edge.

VOICE Apparently similar to Brown-breasted. Territorial call: a far-carrying series of 8–18 clear, but rather throaty, quavering *prrrer* notes, ascending and acceler-

ating, then ending abruptly. Similar number of emphatic *wi-chu* or *wa-hu* couplets often follows this series, the first syllable sharply stressed (Robson 2000). After flushing and scattering, the covey remains in contact by uttering a soft, mellow whistle (rally call).

HABITS Little documented, presumably similar to Necklaced. Forages in scattered coveys of 5–8, giving false impression of being solitary. Flushes suddenly, and invariably singly, from almost underfoot. Feeds on seeds, berries, shoots, insects, etc.

BREEDING Apparently monogamous. Nest a scrape, well padded with grasses and leaves, sheltered by a shrub in grassland or amongst bamboo. Clutch 3–7, usually 4–5 unmarked white eggs. Incubation period unknown. Breeds March–April at lower elevations (plains) and June–July at higher altitudes.

DISTRIBUTION E Himalayas, near Bhutan border (no Bhutanese records) east across NE India, in Arunachal Pradesh, Assam, Manipur, Meghalaya, Mizoram and Tripura, to adjoining E Bangladesh, Myanmar (Kachin Hills in north, and Arakan) and extreme S China (W Yunnan).

STATUS Near Threatened. Few precise data, and urgently requires study. Presumed reasonably widespread in NE India, but destruction of plains and foothill forests must have drastically affected numbers and has probably fragmented populations. Little known in Bangladesh, where formerly occasional in northeast, but believed still extant in southeast (Chittagong Hills). Always rare within its limited Chinese range, a pair seen in 1995 was the first report for many years. No recent information from Myanmar (with the exception of a record in November 1999, north west of Putao, at 980 m), where formerly (1940s) common in northern foothills to 1300 m.

REFERENCES Ali & Ripley (1968), Baker (1930), Collar *et al.* (1994), Grimmett *et al.* (1998), Johnsgard (1988), Robson (2000).

---

87 TAIWAN HILL-PARTRIDGE
Arborophila crudigularis (Swinhoe, 1864)   Plate 24

Alternative names: Formosan, Swinhoe's or White-throated Partridge or Hill-partridge.

Endemic to Taiwan, this and Hainan Hill-partridge are possibly isolates from ancestral White-cheeked, or even the more southerly *orientalis* complex.

IDENTIFICATION The sole hill-partridge on Taiwan, although Collared has been collected there in the past (presumably an introduced, rather than native, population). Chestnut crown, breast and flank markings, and striking white forecrown of Collared make confusion unlikely if seen reasonably well. Taiwan is, however, superficially similar to White-cheeked but both sexes have white (not black) throat and grey (not brown or rusty) mantle; the two species are also widely separated by range. Compare also Chinese Bamboo-partridge, which also occurs on Taiwan.

DESCRIPTION Bill black. Irides brown. Bare skin

around eye pink or red (presumably brighter during breeding season). Legs orange-red. Sexes differ in throat pattern and size, male larger with brighter bare-parts coloration. **Adult male:** Forehead grey becoming reddish-brown on rear crown and nape. Chin, throat and ear-coverts white, with extensive black and rufous streaking on neck-sides and lower throat, coalescing at centre of latter. Lores and eye-stripe black, encircling bare red skin around eye and broken by whitish streaking above rear ear-coverts. Rest of underparts grey, becoming whitish in belly centre. Flank feathers possess white central teardrop markings. Undertail-coverts whitish with dark centres producing scaled appearance. Mantle grey with blackish scaling, merging into olive-brown of back, rump and uppertail-coverts. Scapulars similar but have chestnut fringes. Wing feathers greyish-brown, tertials and wing-coverts prominently marked with black on inner vane, edged rufous on outer web. **Adult female:** Like male, but less dense black throat streaking and central throat is unmarked. **Juvenile:** Undescribed.

GEOGRAPHICAL VARIATION Monotypic.

MEASUREMENTS Length 27–28 cm. Male larger. Males: wing 141–143, tail 58–62, weight (n=1) 311. Females: wing 123–134, tail 47–51, weight c.212.

HABITAT Favours thickets and damp undergrowth in broad-leaved evergreen forest, principally at 1500–2000 m but ranges from 700–3000 m.

VOICE Poorly documented; presumed territorial call described as a 'soft whistle' (Cheng *et al.* 1978).

HABITS Presumably similar to Necklaced. Forages in coveys of 2–3 individuals. Roosts in trees. Feeds on earthworms, seeds, berries, seedlings, leaves and insects.

BREEDING Apparently monogamous. Nest sheltered in crevice between boulders or near base of tree. Clutch 6–8 (4–6 in captivity) unmarked white eggs. Incubation lasts 24 days (20–21 in captivity). Breeds March–August, according to elevation.

DISTRIBUTION Endemic to Taiwan.

STATUS Near Theatened. Formerly widespread in montane forest at 1500–2000 m but habitat degradation through logging must have dramatically affected numbers; there is a scarcity of recent reports away from protected areas. Considered extant in Taroko, Hsueh-Ba and Yushan National Parks and in following Wildlife Nature Reserves: Yu-Li, Chu-yun Shan, Nanao Lake and Hardwood and Tsuifeng Lake. Further study desirable.

REFERENCES Cheng (1987), Cheng *et al.* (1978), del Hoyo *et al.* (1994), Johnsgard (1988), McGowan *et al.* (1995).

88   HAINAN HILL-PARTRIDGE
Arborophila ardens (Styan, 1892)   Plate 24

Alternative names: White-eared Partridge or Hill-partridge.

Endemic to Hainan, where endangered due to extensive forest clearance.

IDENTIFICATION The only *Arborophila* on Hainan, making confusion unlikely. Combination of blackish head, gleaming white ear-patch, orange or red breast, and grey underparts is distinctive, but is approached by some forms of Grey-breasted complex, particularly Malaysian, although latter has white forecrown, lacks red or orange on breast and has more extensive white on cheeks.

DESCRIPTION Bill black. Irides brown. Bare skin around eye grey or dull pinkish. Legs dull reddish. Sexes principally differ in size, male is larger and is brighter overall (especially on breast). **Adult (both sexes):** Forehead, lores, throat and neck-sides blackish, with clear white ear-coverts patch. Diffuse mottled whitish supercilium extends from eye to rear of ear-coverts. Crown and nape dark brown, mottled black. Orange collar encircles lower neck, streaked and mottled black at sides and overlaid by a peculiar patch of stiff, hair-like and shiny, scarlet or orange feathers (usually orange in female, but fades to buffish on skins). Rest of underparts grey, becoming pale buffish on central belly. Flank feathers have narrow white central streak. Undertail-coverts virtually unmarked. Upperparts olive-brown with blackish scaling. Scapulars similar but have chestnut fringes. Wing feathers greyish-brown, tertials and wing-coverts prominently marked with black on inner vane, edged rufous on outer web. **Juvenile:** Apparently similar to adult, but clarification required.

GEOGRAPHICAL VARIATION Monotypic.

MEASUREMENTS Length 26–28 cm. Male larger. Males: wing 122–144, tail 42–55, weight (n=1) 300. Females: wing 112–120, tail 36, weight (n=1) 237.

HABITAT Understorey of primary broad-leaved evergreen tropical forest, and logged but well-recovered monsoon evergreen forest, at 650–1300 m.

VOICE Typical of genus. A repeated two-syllable whistle, the first note rising, the second falling, sometimes accelerating and rising in pitch; rendered as *kwe-ho, kwe-ho, kwe-ho...* Occasionally joined by a second bird, uttering a quicker series of single notes, with the ensuing duet speeding-up and rising in pitch (Jesper Hornskov).

HABITS Few data, presumably similar to others of genus. Reportedly occurs singly, in pairs, or coveys of up to five (in winter). Food includes snails and seeds of trees.

BREEDING No data.

DISTRIBUTION Endemic to Hainan, China. Suspected occurrence in S Guangxi on adjacent Chinese mainland requires confirmation.

STATUS Vulnerable. Range heavily fragmented, and some remaining populations perhaps inviable, following destruction of 70% of Hainan forests between 1949 and 1991. It survives in three (probably seven) areas, notably the Ba Wang Ling (still common, density 6–8 individuals per km² based on surveys in 1987–94) and Wu Zhi Shan National Nature Reserves. Whether these reserves provide adequate protection from logging is uncertain, and the species is also widely hunted. Clearly, a captive-breeding programme would be useful, but a complete halt to forest clearance is the only way to ensure its survival, along with several other species endemic to Hainan. Its possible occurrence in two mainland counties in S Guangxi requires confirmation.

REFERENCES Bird Life International (2000, 2001), Cheng (1987), Cheng *et al.* (1978), Collar *et al.* (1994), Gao (1998), del Hoyo *et al.* (1994), Johnsgard (1988), McGowan *et al.* (1995), Moroika (1957).

89   BROWN-BREASTED HILL-PARTRIDGE
Arborophila brunneopectus (Blyth, 1855)   Plate 26

Alternative names: Bar-backed, Bare-throated or Barred Partridge, or Hill-partridge.

Widespread in SE Asia, Brown-breasted forms a super-species with the more isolated Grey-breasted, Sumatran, Malaysian and Javan Hill-partridges. All share certain features, including sparse throat feathering, clearly barred mantle and rump and are, apparently, vocally similar.

IDENTIFICATION Combination of brownish underparts, black and white flank spotting and boldly banded wings distinctive within range. In Thailand, Brown-breasted usually replaces Rufous-throated below 1200 m. Despite striking similarity in wing patterns, confusion is unlikely as Brown-breasted has whitish or buff (not blackish or rich rufous) face and throat, brownish (not grey) underparts, chequerboard flank pattern and clearly barred, not plain, mantle. Separation from Scaly-breasted should also be unproblematic, due to latter's featureless flanks, wings and upperparts. Compare also Orange-necked, Siamese, Chestnut-necklaced and Annam Hill-partridges, Mountain Bamboo-partridge and Ferruginous Partridge.

DESCRIPTION *A. b. brunneopectus.* Bill black. Irides brown. Orbital and gular skin (usually concealed by sparse feathering) red. Legs pink to pinkish-red (brightest when breeding). Sexes similar, female slightly duller and smaller. **Adult (both sexes):** Forehead, crown and nape olive-brown, speckled darker. Prominent buffy-white supercilium, from base of bill to rear of ear-coverts where mottled. Throat and ear-coverts buffy-white. Lores, eye-stripe, lower throat and neck-sides black, becoming streaked and mottled black and buffy-white at neck-sides, and extending as necklace encircling lower neck. Rest of underparts warm olive-brown (sometimes washed rufous), becoming whitish on central belly, flanks boldly scalloped black and white (each feather has white subterminal patch and bold black tip). Mantle, back, rump and uppertail-coverts olive-brown, clearly barred dark brown. Scapulars, tertials and wing-coverts chestnut on inner webs, with large black central mark and greyish outer webs, forming prominent bands across folded wing. **Juvenile:** Inadequately documented.

GEOGRAPHICAL VARIATION Three well-marked races, varying in underparts coloration and head pattern. Racial identity of those in C and S Laos uncertain.
  A. b. brunneopectus (Blyth, 1855) occurs in E Myanmar, N and W Thailand, adjacent extreme S China (SW Yunnan) and N Laos; described above.
  A. b. henrici (Oustalet, 1896) occurs in Vietnam (except south) and, presumably, adjacent S China (W Guangxi); compared to nominate has more reddish-brown crown and underparts, warmer buff tone to more extensive whitish face and

throat, and less extensive blackish collar, while flank feathers have smaller black tips.
  A. b. albigula (Robinson & Kloss, 1919) occurs in SC Vietnam (S Annam); much purer white on face, throat, forehead and supercilium than other races, with restricted black.

MEASUREMENTS Length 26–29 cm. Female smaller. *A. b. brunneopectus.* Males: wing 135–159, tail 55–72, weight c.317. Females: wing 125–153, tail 50–68, weight c.268.

HABITAT Broad-leaf evergreen forest in foothills, at 500–1300 m in Thailand, but up to 1500 m in Myanmar and Laos, and rarely to 1850 m in S Annam (Vietnam).

VOICE Territorial call: a two-syllable whistled *ti-hu, ti-hu, ti-hu* varying little in pitch and volume but with see-saw rhythm. Usually preceded by series of measured, throaty, burring monotone whistles. Often duets, partner responding with repeated *kew-kew-kew.* Alarm a quiet, thin *wu-wirr wu-wirr wu-wirr.*

HABITS Little different to other hill-partridges. Usually in coveys of 4–9, presumably family parties, foraging in leaf-litter close to, or within, dense forest undergrowth.

BREEDING Only data is of a nest containing 4 white eggs, presumed to be of this species, near Rangoon (Myanmar) in early June, which consisted of a scrape, well padded with bamboo leaves and grasses, situated in open bamboo. In captivity, male builds a domed nest of long grasses and courts female by calling and exposing red gular skin.

DISTRIBUTION SE Asia, from S and E Myanmar through W and N Thailand to extreme S China (SW Yunnan) and N Laos. Indochinese forms range from W Guangxi (S China) south through Vietnam and adjacent Laos to S Annam. Recently discovered in Cambodia at Virachey National Park (Ratanakiri province).

STATUS Now uncommon or localised throughout its range due to forest destruction and hunting. No recent information from Myanmar but considered generally uncommon, although locally common in adjacent Thailand. Rare and poorly known in China. In Laos and Vietnam, logging has been severe and much concern was expressed concerning the status in Indochina, but recent surveys have demonstrated it to be locally frequent within several forest reserves in both countries.

REFERENCES Delacour & Jabouille (1931), Duckworth *et al.* (1998), Evans & Timmins (1998), del Hoyo *et al.* (1994), Lekagul & Round (1991), Robson (2000), Robson *et al.* (1989, 1993), Smythies (1953).

Arborophila davidi Delacour, 1927 **Plate 25**

Alternative names: David's Hill-partridge or Partridge.

Endemic to Vietnam, where it was relocated in 1991 having been 'lost' since its initial discovery in 1927.

IDENTIFICATION Rare endemic to E Cochinchina, Vietnam. Rusty throat and neck-sides broken by bold black collar, encircling throat and ear-coverts, which gives very distinctive pattern. In many respects it recalls Brown-breasted Hill-partridge, of which the race *albigula* occurs as close as S Annam but does not overlap. Another species, Scaly-breasted, replaces Orange-necked (which occurs in low hills) in flat lowland forest, but is unlikely to cause confusion due to its rather featureless plumage.

DESCRIPTION Bill black. Bare skin around eye pinkish (perhaps redder in breeding condition). Irides brown. Legs pinkish. Sexes apparently similar. **Adult (both sexes):** Forehead, lores, and centre of crown and nape dusky, mottled brown on nape. Broad blackish band from bill base, encloses eye to rear ear-coverts, extending on neck-sides to meet black breast-band. Whitish band from behind eye onto neck-sides becomes rusty-orange on neck. Chin and upper throat pale buff becoming rusty-orange on throat and cheeks. Breast olive-brown, becoming greyish and then whitish in central belly, flanks boldly scalloped black and white. Undertail-coverts whitish with dark feather bases. Mantle, back, rump and uppertail-coverts olive-brown, narrowly barred dark brown. Scapulars and wing-coverts have large black central mark and greyish outer webs, forming prominent bands across folded wing. **Juvenile:** Undescribed.

GEOGRAPHICAL VARIATION None. Closely related to Brown-breasted Hill-partridge, which it replaces in this area of Vietnam.

MEASUREMENTS Length 27 cm. One male specimen: wing 134, tail 49, weight c.241.

HABITAT Broad-leaf evergreen and semi-evergreen forest, in low hills at 140–250 m. Favours dense non-thorny bamboo forest (6–10 m high) with sparse undergrowth.

VOICE Territorial call: a repeated *prruu*, accelerating and becoming higher pitched, and a more plaintive *pwi* as tempo increases (70 notes, lasting c.23 seconds). Also a faster series of up to 60 plaintive piping *tu* notes, *tutututututututu* (lasting c.16 seconds). Often duets, the partner responding with a repeated *tchew-tchew-tchew*. Alarm a weak, thin *pher* or *phu* (J. C. Eames tape recordings).

HABITS Little information but recent observations indicate similarity to Brown-breasted Hill-partridge.

BREEDING Undocumented.

DISTRIBUTION Endemic to E Cochinchina, Vietnam. Known only from Nam Bai Cat Tien National Park, 37 km southeast of the type-locality, Bu Kroai, and Cat Loc Nature Reserve.

STATUS Endangered. Until recently, known only from the type-specimen taken at Bu Kroai in 1927. In late June 1991 two were briefly seen during surveys of Nam Bai Cat Tien National Park, and subsequent fieldwork, in 1997, revealed it to be not uncommon in suitable habitat within the park, as well as nearby Cat Loc Nature Reserve. Surveys of this extremely localised partridge are on-going.

REFERENCES Collar *et al.* (1994), King *et al.* (1975), McGowan *et al.* (1995), Robson (2000), Robson *et al.* (1993, 1997).

SIAMESE *Arborophila diversa* AND CAMBODIAN HILL-PARTRIDGES *A. cambodiana*

Previously treated as a single species, Chestnut-headed Hill-partridge. But, in view of their striking plumage differences, they are treated specifically here, a move that also highlights their highly restricted ranges and vulnerability as threatened species. Both are poorly known and virtually unstudied in the field. They are doubtless related to the bar-backed group, closest to Brown-breasted, especially Siamese, which is almost intermediate between Brown-breasted and Cambodian.

91 **SIAMESE HILL-PARTRIDGE**
Arborophila diversa Riley, 1930 **Plate 25**

Alternative name: Siamese Partridge, Chestnut-headed Hill Partridge.

Endemic to Thailand, this little-studied bird has one of the most restricted ranges of all mainland hill-partridges.

IDENTIFICATION Endemic to Khao Sabap Mts of SE Thailand, with a unique combination of buffy-brown supercilium and face, dusky foreneck, rusty breast and black and white spotted underparts. Boldly patterned

flanks shared by Brown-breasted, which in Thailand is confined to hill regions of the north and west, but in Siamese these markings extend onto the belly, and are not confined to the flanks. It also lacks the extensive blackish neck-sides of Brown-breasted and has chestnut, not olive-brown, breast. Scaly-breasted occurs in lowlands of this region, but is rather featureless, with plain brownish flanks and greenish legs. Compare Cambodian Hill-partridge.

STATUS Considered Vulnerable according to Mace-Lande threat criteria. Sparsely distributed in suitable hill forest throughout highlands, including Cameron Highlands and Bukit Fraser (Fraser's Hill) Wildlife Sanctuaries. Technically all remaining forest above 750 m in Malaysia is 'Protection Forest'.

REFERENCES Glenister (1951), McGowan *et al.* (1995), Medway & Wells (1976), Robinson & Chasen (1936), Robson (2000).

94   SUMATRAN HILL-PARTRIDGE
Arborophila sumatrana Ogilvie-Grant, 1891   Plate 26

One of two hill-partridges endemic to Sumatra. Closely related to Malaysian and Grey-breasted Hill-partridges, with which it is usually treated as conspecific.

IDENTIFICATION This and Red-billed Hill-partridge are endemic to Sumatra, and while both occur at similar elevations they are easily distinguished given reasonable views. The grey head and underparts of Sumatran (brownish-grey in northern *rolli*) are relieved by bold black and white flank bands and small white ear-patch. Red-billed differs not only in bill colour (black in Sumatran) but has brighter red legs and browner overall plumage, becoming reddish-brown on breast with blackish head (most in north have varying amounts of white on face and throat) and flanks (only very narrowly barred white). A third species, Chestnut-necklaced, also occurs on Sumatra, but is a rare and little-known lowland species; it is relatively featureless with brownish flanks and greenish legs. Compare also Long-billed and Ferruginous Partridges.

DESCRIPTION *A. s. sumatrana.* Bill black. Irides dark brown. Bare skin around eye and throat grey, pinkish, or red (perhaps grey in male, red in female but significance of age unclear). Legs greyish to reddish-pink (perhaps redder when breeding). Sexes similar, female slightly duller and smaller. **Adult (both sexes):** Forehead, crown and nape dull brown, speckled darker. Head-sides and neck dull bluish-grey with clear white patch on rear ear-coverts; throat greyish-white. Rest of underparts bluish-grey, becoming white on belly, flanks broadly banded black and white, undertail-coverts whitish with dark bases. Entire upperparts dull brown, clearly barred blackish. Scapulars, tertials and wing-coverts chestnut on inner webs with large black central mark and greyish outer webs. **Juvenile:** Inadequately documented, but perhaps has greyish bare parts.

GEOGRAPHICAL VARIATION Two reasonably well marked races.
   A. s. sumatrana Ogilvie-Grant, 1891 occurs in C and S Sumatra (Indonesia); described above.
   A. s. rolli (Rothschild, 1909) occurs in N Sumatra (Indonesia); compared to nominate has blacker throat, usually a whitish loral spot, and breast and flanks buffy-grey rather than pure bluish-grey.

MEASUREMENTS Length 28 cm. Female smaller. *A. s. sumatrana.* Males: (n=3) wing 137–147, tail (n=1) 56. Females: (n=1) wing 131.

HABITAT Dense undergrowth of broad-leaved forest in mountains and foothills, at 500–2000 m.

VOICE Territorial call apparently similar to Brown-breasted, a double chirruping whistle, increasing in volume *wut-wut, wut-wut, wut-wut* and usually preceded by a series of measured single whistles. Often calls in duet. These transcriptions may apply to Grey-breasted of Java, but all forms are reported to be vocally similar.

HABITS Little known, presumably as other hill-partridges.

BREEDING No information.

DISTRIBUTION Endemic to Sumatra (Indonesia), where it occurs in Barisan Mts.

STATUS Considered Vulnerable according to Mace-Lande threat criteria. Assumed to be still common in suitable hill forest on Sumatra, but very few recent sightings. Forest destruction and hunting must have fragmented the remaining population.

REFERENCES van Balen (1992), MacKinnon & Phillipps (1993), Ogilvie-Grant (1896–1897), Robinson & Kloss (1924)

95   GREY-BREASTED HILL-PARTRIDGE
Arborophila orientalis Horsfield, 1821   Plate 26

Endemic to E Java. A close relative of Sumatran and Malaysian Hill-partridges with which it is usually treated as conspecific.

IDENTIFICATION Extensive white face and throat could give impression of a wholly white head in the field, which would be particularly striking in gloom of forest undergrowth. This, combined with otherwise grey underparts render it unmistakable, especially in its very limited range (montane E Java). No overlap with

other hill-partridges, although Javan, which has chestnut flanks and belly contrasting with grey breast and rufous (not white) face, occurs in montane forest in W and C Java. No other partridges occur on the island.

DESCRIPTION Bill reddish-brown. Irides pale reddish-yellow. Bare skin around eye and throat red (latter normally concealed by sparse feathering). Legs reddish-yellow. Sexes similar, female slightly duller and smaller, perhaps with duller bare parts. **Adult** (both sexes): Crown and nape blackish. Head and throat almost entirely white, extending over forehead, lores, superciliary and neck-sides, with dusky-brown line from bill base through eye and on neck-sides, becoming diffuse on lower neck. Breast brownish-grey, slightly mottled blackish, breast-sides and flanks grey with broad and irregular black and white barring, and rufous fringes on rear flanks, undertail-coverts whitish with black 'feather bases. Entire upperparts dull brown, narrowly barred blackish. Scapulars, tertials and wing-coverts have chestnut outer webs and large black central marks. **Juvenile:** Inadequately described, but perhaps has greyish bare parts.

GEOGRAPHICAL VARIATION Monotypic, but *A. orientalis* usually includes *A. sumatrana* and *A. campbelli.*

MEASUREMENTS Length 28 cm. Female probably smaller. Wing (n=1 male) 149, tail 64. Weight unrecorded.

HABITAT Undergrowth of primary montane forest, at 500–2200 m.

VOICE Territorial call apparently similar to Brown-breasted: a double chirruping whistle, increasing in volume *wut-wut, wut-wut, wut-wut* and usually preceded by a series of measured single whistles. Often calls in duet.

HABITS Little known, presumably as other hill-partridges.

BREEDING Undocumented in wild, but captive male builds domed nests of long grasses and courts female by calling and exposing red gular skin (normally concealed by sparse feathering).

DISTRIBUTION Endemic to montane forest in extreme E Java (Indonesia).

STATUS Vulnerable due to its very limited range (c.2500 km²). Until recently, only one report in last 50 years but presence confirmed in Yang Highlands, the Ijen Crater, Meru Betiri and Baluran. Logging and hunting pose serious threats to this localised species, but c.100 are known in captivity and captive breeding could play a role in the future conservation of the species.

REFERENCES van Balen (1992), BirdLife International (2000, 2001), MacKinnon & Phillipps (1993), McGowan *et al.* (1995), Ogilvie-Grant (1896–1897).

96 JAVAN HILL-PARTRIDGE
Arborophila javanica (Gmelin, 1789)   Plate 26

Alternative names: Chestnut-bellied Hill-partridge or Partridge.

Endemic to Java. This and the closely related *A. orientalis* are the only partridges on Java.

IDENTIFICATION Chestnut flanks and belly contrasting with grey breast and rufous, rather than white, face easily distinguish this species from Grey-breasted, if seen well. As they are very difficult to observe, distribution is perhaps the most useful identification aid. Javan occurs in montane forest over W and C Java (east to Mt Semeru and Mt Tennger), being replaced in extreme E Java by Grey-breasted (no overlap, see map on p.76). No other partridges occur on the island.

DESCRIPTION *A. j. javanica.* Bill black (reddish-brown in juvenile). Irides grey. Bare skin around eye and throat red (latter normally concealed by sparse feathering). Legs red. Sexes similar, female slightly duller and smaller, perhaps with duller bare-parts coloration. **Adult (both sexes):** Crown and nape orange-rufous, streaked and mottled dark grey and brown in centre. Lores, band through eye, neck-sides and throat blackish, providing clear black border to lower throat, central throat streaked rusty-orange. Unmarked rufous-orange chin and cheeks extending as band across ear-coverts. Breast bluish-grey. Lower breast and flanks rufous-chestnut; central belly whitish, undertail-coverts rusty-buff with black bases giving scaled effect. Back, rump and uppertail-coverts bluish-grey, closely barred black. Wing feathers browner, with chestnut outer webs and black terminal marks. **Juvenile:** Rufous and blackish pattern on face and throat replaced by whitish, has whitish shaft streaks on reddish-brown scapulars and duller, overall more brownish, breast and flanks.

GEOGRAPHICAL VARIATION Three subspecies differ in amount of black on throat and neck. Extent of individual variation requires clarification and investigation.

A. j. javanica (Gmelin, 1789) occurs in W Java; described above.

A. j. bartelsi Siebers, 1929 occurs on Mt Ciremai, WC Java; much less black than other forms, with throat and chest almost unmarked rufous.

A. j. lawuana Bartels 1938 occurs on Mt Lawu, EC Java; throat rufous, but more extensive blackish on nape and neck-sides than *bartelsi.*

MEASUREMENTS Length 28 cm. Female probably smaller. *A. j. javanica.* Males: (n=1) wing 142, tail 56, weight c.286. Females: (n=1) wing 137, tail 51, weight c.257.

HABITAT Hill and montane forests, at 300–3000 m.

VOICE Territorial call: apparently similar to other group members. Van Balen (1992) considered it most like Grey-breasted. One or more individuals give a monotonous series of far-carrying double cries increasing in both tempo and volume. Vocal throughout year, except December.

HABITS Little known, apparently as other hill-partridges.

BREEDING Lays up to 4 eggs. Breeding season prolonged, January–April and July–November. In captivity, male builds a domed nest of long grasses like others in this complex.

DISTRIBUTION Endemic to montane forest in W and C Java (Indonesia), east to Mt Semeru and Mt Tennger.

STATUS As access to hill forest on Java improves, logging and hunting could pose considerable threats to this poorly-known species. Prior to 1989 there had been only two reports in recent decades, but presence recently confirmed in most montane forests above 1200 m that have been investigated. Strangely, still unreported from central mountains of Dieng plateau, where could occur. Survives well in captivity, c.250 are thought to be held worldwide. A captive-breeding programme may be an option within a species conservation programme, but care should be taken to retain each subspecies' 'purity'.

REFERENCES van Balen (1992), MacKinnon & Phillipps (1993), McGowan et al. (1995), Ogilvie-Grant (1896–1897).

---

97 BORNEAN HILL-PARTRIDGE
Arborophila hyperythra (Sharpe, 1879)   Plate 25

Alternative names: Borneo or Red-breasted Hill-partridge or Partridge.

Endemic to Borneo. As with Javan Hill-partridge, we have revived an older English name to emphasise its endemic importance. Although the widely used alternative, Red-breasted, is descriptive it offers confusion with the E Himalayan *A. mandellii*, which was formerly known by this name.

IDENTIFICATION Boldly black and white spotted flanks contrast with dull reddish-brown rest of plumage. Superficially most similar to Ferruginous Partridge, but latter has greenish (not red) legs, less boldly patterned flanks and black and white scaled upperparts. The two overlap to some degree, especially in the Kelabit highlands, but Ferruginous is absent from Mt Kinabalu. Chestnut-necklaced also occurs on Borneo, but is a little-known species of the Sabah lowlands (Bornean replaces it in hills west of Kinabalu) best separated by its dull coloration, especially the featureless brownish flanks, and greenish legs. Compare also Long-billed Partridge.

DESCRIPTION *A. h. hyperythra*. Bill black. Irides grey. Bare skin around eye and throat red (latter normally concealed by sparse feathering). Legs salmon-pink. Sexes similar, female slightly duller and smaller, with smaller white flank spots. Adult (both sexes): Crown and nape blackish mottled brown. Lores and supercilium ash-grey or dull rufous. Blackish-brown band through eye extends onto ear-coverts. Chin, throat and cheeks rufous, upper cheeks sometimes greyish. Breast and fore-flanks bright reddish-chestnut, becoming whitish on belly, some have browner breast. Flanks black with large white spot on each feather, forming chequerboard pattern. Undertail-coverts whitish. Entire upperparts dull brown, narrowly barred blackish. Scapulars, tertials and wing-coverts have large black central spots. Juvenile: Inadequately described.

GEOGRAPHICAL VARIATION Two subspecies differ in head pattern. The Kinabalu population may be specifically distinct, but individual variation within the Sarawak population confuses the issue.
    A. h. hyperythra (Sharpe, 1879) occurs in N Borneo to W Sabah; described above.

A. h. erythrophrys Sharpe 1890 occurs on Mt Kinabalu, Sabah; much brighter rusty-rufous supercilium, face and throat than nominate, male also has blackish chin and central upper throat.

MEASUREMENTS Length 27 cm. Sexes combined, but female probably smaller. *A. h. hyperythra*. Wing 132–147, tail 45–56, weight c.270.

HABITAT Bamboo and other thickets in understorey of secondary and primary hill and montane forests, at 600–1800 m, but principally above 1200 m.

VOICE Territorial call usually given in duet: a clear, rising, ringing abrupt *chu* (repeated three times per second) increasing in volume and tempo, answered by a loud double note, transcribed as *cuckoo*, falling in pitch, at a rate of one per second. A captive uttered soft, sweet bubbling musical calls and a louder, fluty warbling, also a rising *kuwar* quickly repeated in series of 12 notes.

HABITS Apparently as other hill-partridges but little recorded. Groups forage within thickets, or on forest tracks and river 'flats'. Food includes acorns, seeds, fruits, grubs, termites, beetles, crickets and ants. Roosts in bushes close to ground.

BREEDING Unknown in wild. Reported to build a domed nest, with a hole at one side c.3 cm above ground level.

DISTRIBUTION Endemic to hill and montane forests in N Borneo, centred on Kelabit highlands, south to upper Kayan Valley (NE Kalimantan, Indonesia) and Usun Apau (C Sarawak), and with apparently isolated populations on Mt Kinabalu (Sabah) and at Ulu Barito (C Kalimantan, Indonesia).

STATUS Poorly known, with few recent records, although one of these was from Ulu Barito, c.150 km from previously known sites, suggesting that it is more widespread than previously considered. Protected by several reserves in Sarawak and on Kinabalu in Sabah, but in Kalimantan its habitat is potentially threatened by logging and it is doubtless hunted for food. Nonetheless, it was notably described as 'common' in the Kelabit highlands of Kalimantan.

REFERENCES van Balen (1992), MacKinnon & Phillipps (1993), McGowan et al. (1995), Ogilvie-Grant (1896–1897), Smythies (1981).

RED-BILLED HILL-PARTRIDGE
Arborophila rubrirostris (Salvadori, 1879)   Plate 25

Alternative names: Red-billed Partridge.

Endemic to Sumatra. Very distinctive, with striking red bill and legs and variable head pattern.

IDENTIFICATION Easily separated from other partridges in range by bright red bill and legs, blackish head (with or without white on face) and overall reddish-brown breast and flanks (only very narrow white bars). Range and altitude overlap with Sumatran Hill-partridge, but latter has black bill and grey head and underparts, bolder black and white flank bars and a small white ear-patch. Chestnut-necklaced, a rare and little-known species of lowland N Sumatra, is rather featureless with brownish flanks and greenish legs. Compare also Long-billed and Ferruginous Partridges.

DESCRIPTION Bill bright red. Irides brown. Bare skin around eye and legs red. Sexes similar, female slightly duller and smaller, with heavier and more extensive black upperparts markings, and reportedly has more white on lores and throat, but this requires verification as Robinson & Kloss (1924) claim that the foreneck is largely white in males, black in females. **Adult (both sexes):** Crown, nape, head-sides and neck blackish, finely mottled white. Throat white, intensely marked black, and in many appears all blackish, but others have extensive white on face and throat, most apparent in northern populations. Breast ruddy brown with small white spots, belly greyish-white variably marked black. Flanks black with white fringes, giving scaly appearance. Undertail-coverts whitish with dark bases. Entire upperparts dull brown, narrowly barred blackish. Scapulars, tertials and wing-coverts have larger black spots. **Juvenile:** Inadequately described.

GEOGRAPHICAL VARIATION Monotypic. Northernmost populations tend to have more extensive white on head than those in south, but individual variation and perhaps sexual differences make this difficult to interpret.

MEASUREMENTS Length 29 cm. Female smaller. Males: wing 128–143, tail (n=1) 43, weight c.243. Females: wing 127–138, tail (n=1) 41, weight c.209.

HABITAT Lower and upper montane forests (including scrub in pines), at 900–2500 m, but principally above 1200 m.

VOICE Territorial call: a series of loud whistled couplets *keow*, rising in pitch and increasing in volume.

HABITS Apparently as other hill-partridges but little recorded. Considered unobtrusive, occurring in small groups within steep mossy gullies or dense undergrowth on ridges. Roosts in low trees and bushes.

BREEDING Undocumented. Chicks reported in late August.

DISTRIBUTION Endemic to N and W Sumatra (Indonesia), in Barisan Mts.

STATUS Population believed stable. Recent reports come from two areas in N Sumatra—Mt Sibayak (in Aceh) and Mt Brestagi—and one in west, Mt Kerinci. As suitable habitat is widespread in the Barisan Mts it appears probable that the species inhabits intervening areas and is locally quite numerous. Further field research is clearly required. Unknown in captivity.

REFERENCES van Balen (1992), MacKinnon & Phillipps (1993), McGowan *et al.* (1995), Ogilvie-Grant (1896–1897), Robinson & Kloss (1924).

Subgenus *TROPICOPERDIX*: scaly-breasted hill-partridges

Members of this group differ from other hill-partridges in being primarily lowland species, with overall scaly or mottled plumages without strong patterning, and yellowish or greenish legs. Their relationships are extremely confused; some authorities treat all taxa within *A. charltonii* (e.g. Johnsgard 1988, Inskipp *et al.* 1996), and others consider them to involve two species (*merlini* being included within *chloropus*, e.g. Peters 1934 and Davison 1982). A move to recognise three species was promulgated by del Hoyo *et al.* (1994), although the intermediate nature of *tonkinensis* is a major stumbling block to this treatment. The latter has been considered a form of *A. chloropus*, primarily on geography, or within *A. charltonii* on morphological features. In view of the already disjunct distribution of *A. charltonii* it appears logical to align *tonkinensis* with that form (C. Robson in *litt.*).

99   CHESTNUT-NECKLACED HILL-PARTRIDGE
Arborophila charltonii (Eyton, 1845)   Plate 28

Alternative names: Chestnut-breasted Hill-partridge or Partridge, Tonkin Hill-partridge or Partridge (*tonkinensis*).

Four disjunct populations are included in this, the most colourful member of the *Tropicoperdix* group.

IDENTIFICATION A lowland forest species represented by four well-separated subspecies, in the Malay Peninsula, N Sumatra, NE Borneo and N Vietnam. All are distinguished from other members of this complex by their unmarked chestnut breast-band bordered above by a blackish collar (except *tonkinensis*), rusty ear-coverts patch (obscured in *tonkinensis*), red orbital skin and yellowish legs (see Scaly-breasted and Annam Hill-partridges for fuller discussion). Does not overlap with others in group but its range (or former range) approaches Scaly-breasted in S Thailand (where Chestnut-necklaced now virtually extinct) and Annam Hill-partridge in Vietnam. From other hill-partridges, the yellowish legs, weakly patterned buffish flanks and lowland haunts provide relatively easy distinctions.

DESCRIPTION *A. c. charltonii.* Bill greenish, with reddish at base of both mandibles. Irides brown. Bare skin around eye red. Legs yellowish. Sexes similar, female slightly duller and smaller. **Adult (both sexes):** Forehead, crown and nape dull brown, speckled darker. Supercilium, chin, throat, head-sides and neck whitish, streaked dark brown; mottled dusky eye-stripe, from base of bill through eye and onto neck-sides, broken by rusty-chestnut patch on upper ear-coverts behind eye. Narrow blackish lower border to whitish throat forms inconspicuous collar and borders otherwise unmarked chestnut upper breast. Lower breast brown, scaled darker. Rest of underparts buff, becoming orange-buff on upper belly and fore flanks, scaled dark brown on flanks. Upperparts and wings dull brown, closely marked with narrow dark brown bars, and tertials have large dark brown bases. **Juvenile:** Inadequately described, but reportedly has duller bare parts, white shafts and tips to breast and flanks feathers and more boldly barred upperparts.

GEOGRAPHICAL VARIATION Three similar subspecies, with a fourth (*tonkinensis* in Vietnam), which is markedly duller and may deserve species status.
  A. c. charltonii (Eyton, 1845) occurs in S Thailand and Malay Peninsula; described above.
  A. c. atjenensis Meyer de Schauensee & Ripley, 1940 occurs in N and, formerly, S Sumatra (Indonesia); very similar to nominate but brighter, a poorly differentiated form.
  A. c. graydoni (Sharpe & Chubb, 1906) occurs in NE Borneo (Sabah); slightly duller than previous race with greenish-yellow (rather than yellow) legs and brown (rather than rusty) ear-coverts.
  A. c. tonkinensis (Delacour, 1927) occurs in Tonkin (Vietnam); duller with greenish-yellow (rather than yellow) legs, obscured and speckled ear-coverts patch, chestnut of breast does not extend

so far onto neck-sides, richer spotted lower breast and lacks dark collar and eye-stripe.

MEASUREMENTS Length 26–32 cm. Female smaller. *A. c. charltonii.* Males: wing (mean) 160, tail c.70–80, weight c.290. Females: wing (mean) 155, weight c.250.

HABITAT Dense lowland jungle and foothills with dense evergreen forest, also locally common in secondary or logged forest. Recorded to 300 m on Borneo and 500 m in Tonkin.

VOICE Territorial call: a series of clear melodious whistles, even in pitch and volume, uttered in couplets or triplets, and often given in duet. Also a wilder fuller series of calls, commencing with a number of monosyllabic notes that reach a crescendo of double and triple notes (perhaps the product of more than one individual).

HABITS Little known. Reportedly shy and perhaps most likely to be found in small parties foraging at forest edge. Food includes seeds, berries and termites.

BREEDING No information.

DISTRIBUTION Four disjunct populations; one in peninsular S Thailand south to peninsular Malaysia; another in lowland N Sumatra; a third in lowlands of Sabah in NE Borneo; and the fourth in Tonkin and N Annam in N Vietnam.

STATUS Near Threatened. Like all lowland forest species has become very scarce through logging. The nominate form is estimated to number less than 1000, the vast majority in Malaysia, it being on the verge of extinction in S Thailand (known only from a tiny area in Khlong Phraya National Park). Very rare on Sumatra, where unrecorded for several years and has almost certainly disappeared from the south (with the forest), but small numbers probably persist in northern lowlands. On Borneo, a few hundred probably survive in partially logged forest, but the only recent reports are from Danum Valley. Reportedly still locally common in Indochina, where occurs in three protected areas in N Vietnam. Clearly, remaining lowland forest must be protected in order to save this vulnerable species. None are known in captivity.

REFERENCES van Balen (1992), BirdLife International (2000, 2001), Collar *et al.* (1994), MacKinnon & Phillipps (1993), Ogilvie-Grant (1896–1897), Robinson & Kloss (1924), Smythies (1981).

---

100 ANNAM HILL-PARTRIDGE
Arborophila merlini (Delacour & Jabouille, 1924)   Plate 28

Alternative names: Annamese Hill-partridge or Partridge.

Intermediate in several respects between Scaly-breasted and Chestnut-necklaced, and replaces them in a small area of C Vietnam, it may be one of the world's rarest gamebirds.

IDENTIFICATION Endemic to Vietnam, where isolated in C Annam. Replaced further north by *tonki-*

nensis form of Chestnut-necklaced, which principally differs in its unmarked chestnut breast-band. South and west, it is well isolated from the subspecies *cognacqi* and *olivacea* of Scaly-breasted, from which Annam differs in having yellowish (not green) legs and bold dark scaling and spotting on lower breast and flanks. The otherwise relatively speckled and finely barred plumage, lacking bold patterning, distinguishes this species from other forest partridges.

DESCRIPTION Bill greenish with reddish base to both mandibles. Irides brown. Bare skin around eye red. Legs olive-yellow or yellowish. Sexes similar. **Adult (both sexes):** Forehead, crown and nape dull brown, speckled darker. Supercilium, lores, chin, upper throat, head-sides and neck whitish, streaked and mottled dark brown; dull brown, mottled upper earcoverts patch. Lower throat and upper breast rufous-buff, spotted blackish; lower breast brown, scaled dark brown. Rest of underparts warm buff, whiter on belly, flanks strongly spotted and boldly scaled blackish-brown. Upperparts and wings dull brown, closely marked with narrow dark bars. **Juvenile:** Undescribed.

GEOGRAPHICAL VARIATION Slight. Southern population (*vivida*) described as brighter but differences minor and not recognised by Robson (2000) who considered the species monotypic.

MEASUREMENTS Length 29 cm. Female smaller. Males: wing 150–162, tail 70–80, weight c.290. Females: wing 141–150, tail 70–75, weight c.250.

HABITAT Lowland broad-leaf evergreen forest and secondary growth, on plains and in low hills, at 90–600 m.

VOICE Very similar to Scaly-breasted and Chestnut-necklaced (C. Robson pers. comm.).

HABITS Very similar to Scaly-breasted and Chestnut-necklaced (C. Robson pers. comm.).

BREEDING No information.

DISTRIBUTION Endemic to two small areas of NC Annam, Vietnam: northern population inland from Quang Tri, and southern population in Bach Ma National Park.

STATUS Endangered. Like all lowland forest species it has become very scarce through forest destruction. Its extremely limited range makes the species particularly vulnerable. Persists in Bach Ma National Park, where considered common in 1990, but no recent reports from elsewhere. Field surveys continue. Unknown in captivity.

REFERENCES Collar *et al.* (1994), del Hoyo *et al.* (1994), McGowan *et al.* (1995), Robson (2000), Robson *et al.* (1993).

101 SCALY-BREASTED HILL-PARTRIDGE
Arborophila chloropus (Blyth, 1859)   Plate 28

Alternative name: Green-legged Hill-partridge or Partridge.

Four races recognised in this group, which inhabits much of the remnant lowland forest of mainland SE Asia.

IDENTIFICATION Widespread in lowlands and foothills of mainland SE Asia. A dull brown to rufous-brown partridge, differing from equally widespread and similarly distributed Brown-breasted by indistinct face pattern, plainer wings, green (not reddish) legs and insignificant flank pattern. Scaly-breasted favours lower elevations (Brown-breasted is usually above 750 m) but there is some overlap. Scaly-breasted is distinguished from other members of this complex by its green (not yellowish) legs and weak flanks scaling. The otherwise relatively speckled and finely barred plumage, without bold patterning, distinguishes it from other forest partridges.

DESCRIPTION *A. c. chloropus*. Bill greenish, with reddish base to both mandibles. Irides brown. Bare skin around eye red. Legs green. Sexes similar, female slightly duller and smaller. **Adult (both sexes):** Forehead, crown and nape dull brown, speckled darker. Supercilium, lores, chin, upper throat, head-sides and neck whitish, streaked and mottled dark brown; dull brown, mottled upper ear-coverts patch. Lower throat and upper breast rufous, spotted blackish; lower breast brown, with narrow black scales. Rest of underparts rusty-buff, whiter on belly, flanks dull brownish, weakly and narrowly scaled dark on flanks. Upperparts and wings dull brown, closely marked with narrow dark bars. **Juvenile:** Inadequately documented.

GEOGRAPHICAL VARIATION Four similar subspecies differ mainly in colour saturation.

A. c. chloropus (Blyth, 1859) occurs in Myanmar, W Thailand and Yunnan (China); described above.
A. c. peninsularis Meyer de Schauensee, 1941 occurs in SW Thailand; warm-toned upperparts (as nominate) but dull buff underparts (like cognacqi).
A. c. olivacea (Delacour & Jabouille, 1928) occurs in Cambodia, Laos and W Tonkin (Vietnam).
A. c. cognacqi (Delacour & Jabouille, 1924) occurs in Cochinchina (Vietnam); duller and colder plumage, with whiter foreneck and drabber buff underparts.

MEASUREMENTS Length 26–31 cm. Female smaller. *A. c. chloropus*. Males: wing (mean) 140–146, tail 70–84, weight 280–300. Females: (n=1) wing 146, weight 250.

HABITAT Dense evergreen and mixed deciduous primary and secondary forest, with bamboo thickets, from plains to 1400 m.

VOICE Territorial call (15–70 seconds): a variable series of 20–90 variably spaced, often double, plaintive notes repeated at an increasing tempo, terminating in a series of wildly ascending and descending harsh shrill couplets that come to an abrupt end *tu-tu...tu-tu...tu-tu...tu tu tu tu tutututututututu CHIRRA-CHEW-CHIRRA-CHEW-CHRRA-CHEW*. Voices of Annam and Chestnut-necklaced similar.

HABITS Poorly documented. Food includes seeds, berries and termites.

BREEDING Few data. Three eggs obtained in May in Thailand is the only documentation.

DISTRIBUTION SE Asia, from Myanmar through foothills of W and N Thailand to extreme S China (SW

Yunnan), south through Cambodia and Laos to Vietnam in Cochinchina.

STATUS Declining and locally scarce over much of its range. Always rare and little known in China, and no recent information from Myanmar or Cambodia. However, it is still locally relatively common in parts of Thailand and Laos, and has recently proved to be common at Nam Bai Cat Tien National Park in Vietnam (the only recent report of *cognacqi*). Unknown in captivity.

REFERENCES Delacour & Jabouille (1931), Duckworth *et al.* (1998), del Hoyo *et al.* (1994), Evans & Timmins (1998), Johnsgard (1988), Lekagul & Round (1991), Ogilvie-Grant (1896–1897), Robson *et al.* (1989, 1993), Smythies (1953)

Genus *CALOPERDIX*: Ferruginous Partridge

Forest partridge of the Indo-Malay region that has been allocated to a monotypic genus. Superficially similar to hill-partridges (and also has 14 tail feathers), *Caloperdix* principally differs in lacking bare skin behind eye, having a stronger tail and strong tarsal spurs (the latter feature suggests an affinity with *Francolinus*).

102 FERRUGINOUS PARTRIDGE
Caloperdix oculea (Temminck, 1815)   Plate 29

Alternative name: Ferruginous Wood-partridge.

A beautifully marked species, with a remarkably similar distribution pattern to little-known Black Wood-partridge.

IDENTIFICATION Malaysia, Sumatra and Borneo. Bright rusty forest partridge with distinctive round black spots on pale brown wings. Latter provides an easy distinction from all other partridges in range, which either have plain or barred wings. Blackish upperparts and flanks clearly scaled rufous, white or buff (according to subspecies) that contrast with pale wings, especially if flushed, which it only does with great reluctance. Compare female Black Wood-partridge and larger Long-billed Partridge, which are equally rusty in coloration.

DESCRIPTION *C. o. oculea*. Bill relatively long, black or brownish-black. Irides sepia-brown. Legs olive-green to yellowish-green with 1–2 tarsal spurs. Sexes similar, although female usually has only one, and sometimes no tarsal spurs. **Adult (both sexes):** Head, neck, breast, lower and rear flanks rusty-rufous, throat and head-sides paler and buffier. Dusky line through, but chiefly behind, eye. Central belly whitish. Fore flanks, breast-sides and mantle black, each feather cleanly, but narrowly, edged white. Rear flanks sparsely spotted black, becoming barred on undertail-coverts. Wings entirely olive-brown, each feather with a drop-shaped or rounded black subterminal spot, largest on tertials, smallest on wing-coverts. Back, rump and uppertail-coverts black, clearly marked with rufous V-shaped bars on each feather. Tail black. **Juvenile:** Resembles adult, but duller and greyer brownish-rufous, all pale feather edges buffish, rather than white, irregular blackish barring and spotting almost forms chest-band, and has blackish scaling on nape.

GEOGRAPHICAL VARIATION Three subspecies vary in colour of pale fringes to mantle and flanks, and extent of spotting on lower flanks.

    C. o. oculea (Temminck, 1815) occurs in Thai-Malay Peninsula; described above.

    C. o. ocellata (Raffles, 1822) (=*sumatrana*) occurs in Sumatra; pale fringes to blackish mantle feathers and flanks mostly buff, rather than white, but variable.

    C. o. borneensis Ogilvie-Grant, 1892 occurs in NE and NC Borneo; most extensive black spotting on rear flanks, with buff and white fringes to black flanks and mantle feathers.

MEASUREMENTS Length 23–27 cm. *C. o. oculea* given. Males: wing 141–148; tail 59–67, tarsus 43–48, bill 20–22, weight (n=1) 191. Females: wing 134–142, tail 54–60, tarsus 39–42, weight (n=1) c.230.

HABITAT Evergreen and semi-evergreen rainforests, including swampy areas, dry hill forest and secondary forest with sufficient bamboo. Secondary scrub considered principal habitat in Sumatra. Recorded to 1200 m in peninsular Thailand and c.1000 m elsewhere. In peninsular Malaysia all recent records are from hill slopes, presumably because its lowland habitat is everywhere under exceptional pressure.

VOICE Distinctive. Male advertising call: a rising series that becomes progressively quicker *pi-pi-pi-pipipipipipipi*, repeated 8–9 times, after which it breaks into four trisyllabic notes *ee-ter-rang* or *dit-duit, dit-duit* with a very clanging quality. Female replies with up to 20 rapidly whistled notes rising swiftly up the scale. Neighbouring pairs often counter call.

HABITS Poorly known. Reliable encounters in peninsular Malaysia are with singles or pairs, although unconfirmed reports of small groups exist. Reported taking berries, seeds, grasses and beetles, implying that it picks items from forest floor and low vegetation, rather than scratching sufficiently extensively to leave signs.

BREEDING Sole information from Thai-Malay Peninsula is a half-grown chick in Surat Thani in September. On Borneo the nest is reportedly domed and has a hole 2–3 cm off the ground. Laying reported December–January. A downy young was collected in Padang

Highlands of W Sumatra in August–September. In captivity, clutch is 8–10 pure white and glossy eggs. Incubation (in captivity) 18–20 days.

DISTRIBUTION SE Asia, from extreme S Myanmar (S Tenasserim) and S peninsular Thailand through peninsular Malaysia to Sumatra (Indonesia) and Borneo, where known from Mt Magdalena (Sabah), and Kelabit uplands to Usuan Apau plateau, as well as Mt Dulit (Sarawak).

STATUS Near Threatened. Lowland rainforest has been logged within much of its range, such that in peninsular Thailand it is now very rare and its future uncertain. In peninsular Malaysia lowland forest clearance has left only patches (some quite large) on hill slopes, where viable populations are believed to persist. Secondary scrub, e.g. bamboo, is the principal habitat on Sumatra, although this may be a function of the species' increased detectability in such areas. Like all lowland rainforest specialists in SE Asia, the species' tolerance of habitat extremes is unclear and if it can breed in hill-slope forest and secondary scrub these habitats may offer the best prospects for long-term survival. Known from a number of protected areas, including Taman Negara National Park in peninsular Malaysia and Gunung Leuser National Park in N Sumatra.

REFERENCES BirdLife International (2000, 2001), MacKinnon & Phillipps (1993), McGowan *et al.* (1995), Robbins (1998), Robson (2000), Smythies (1981), Wells (1999).

Genus *HAEMATORTYX*: Crimson-headed Partridge

Distinctive forest partridge, endemic to hill forest on Borneo. Both sexes' black and red plumage renders it unique among partridges. Males sport up to three tarsal spurs, and the rounded tail has 12 feathers.

103 CRIMSON-HEADED PARTRIDGE
Haematortyx sanguiniceps Sharpe, 1879   Plate 29

Alternative name: Crimson-headed Wood-partridge.

A striking black and crimson jungle partridge, confined to hill forest on Borneo.

IDENTIFICATION Endemic to Borneo. Its crimson head, breast and vent and otherwise black plumage make it entirely unmistakable. Plumage coloration is only approached by male (especially patchy immature male) Black Wood-partridge, which has a much broader black bill. Although latter occurs on Borneo, it has only been found in lowlands of south and west, whereas Crimson-headed occurs in the north and central highlands.

DESCRIPTION Bill yellow or yellowish-white (male), or brownish-horn (female). Irides brown. Orbital ring yellow. Legs grey, male has up to three tarsal spurs. Sexes similar, although female duller and lacks tarsal spurs. **Adult male:** Head, neck and breast crimson-red. Rest of plumage dull sooty-black, except terminal portion of longest undertail-coverts, which are also crimson-red. **Adult female:** Duller and browner than male but pattern similar, red of head and breast duller, more brownish-rufous. **Juvenile:** Mostly dull blackish, with brownish-orange head and mottled black crown. Breast blackish-brown, with rusty markings on many feathers. Wing-coverts have small red tips.

GEOGRAPHICAL VARIATION Monotypic.

MEASUREMENTS Length 25 cm. Both sexes: wing 149–168, tail 40–50, weight (one male) 330.

HABITAT Lower montane forests, including heath forest and poor quality forest on sandy soils in valley bottoms. Mostly at 1000–1500 m, rarely down to 200 m.

VOICE Advertising call: a distinctly harsh, high-pitched *KRO-krang, KRO-krang, KRO-krang,* repeated several times. Also a harsh clucking *kak-kak-kak, ok-ak-ok, krak-krak.*

HABITS One of the more regularly encountered Bornean galliformes, although less common than formerly, it probably still occurs at reasonable density in suitable habitat. Smythies (1981) reported that it would run along trails in front of humans looking back periodically, making them extremely easy to shoot! Reportedly eats berries, insects and even small crustaceans implying that it takes these from forest floor and low vegetation, and does not scratch sufficiently extensively to leave any signs.

BREEDING Largely unknown. Nest of dry leaves raised on a tussock of grass or lichen, in which earliest reported eggs were laid in mid-January. Clutch 8–9 coffee-milk-coloured eggs, streaked with umber. Incubation (in captivity) is 18–19 days.

DISTRIBUTION Montane NC Borneo, and reported from Sabah and Sarawak–Kalimantan border region.

STATUS Near threatened and certainly at risk due to habitat loss. Not uncommon in certain areas, the extent of its known habitat is now much smaller than historically, suggesting a large decline in the species' population size. No recent records from C Kalimantan. Still occurs in Gunung Mulu National Park in Sarawak.

REFERENCES MacKinnon & Phillipps (1993), Smythies (1981).

Genus *ROLLULUS*: Crested Partridge

Monotypic genus containing a unique Indo-Malay forest partridge. *Rollulus* is a superbly ornate rotund bird, males having a bushy crest, while both sexes possess elongated frontal bristles. Short stubby bill and short downturned tail with 12 feathers. The hind toes lack claws and the legs are spurless.

104 CRESTED PARTRIDGE
Rollulus rouloul (Scopoli, 1786)   Plate 29

Alternative names: Crested Wood-partridge, Green Wood-partridge, Rouloul Partridge.

One of the most attractive partridges, both sexes being uniquely striking.

IDENTIFICATION Malay Peninsula, Sumatra and Borneo. Rotund little partridge of forest floors that appears blackish or all-dark in gloom, but in ideal light male is a shining metallic blue-green, with a remarkable red 'shaving brush' crest and surprisingly obvious white forecrown spot. Female can appear equally dark and lacks obvious crest, but is distinctively pea-green with rufous wings and slate-grey head. Unlikely to be confused, but compare male of rarer Black Wood-partridge.

DESCRIPTION Bill short and stubby, black, male has scarlet-red over gape of upper, and basal half of lower, mandibles. Irides dark brown. Bare skin surrounding and extending back from eye, scarlet. Legs scarlet. Sexually dimorphic. **Adult male:** Glossy blue-black, becoming metallic green on back and uppertail-coverts. White patch on forecrown between small projection of elongated black bristles just ahead of massive brush-like chestnut-red crest. Tail blackish. Wings dark brown with paler outer webs to primaries forming brown panel on folded wing. **Adult female:** Lacks brush-like crest of male but possesses some long forehead bristles. Head and throat slate-grey, becoming blackish on nape. Rest of body plumage green, except rufous scapulars and wings, the latter finely vermiculated. **Juvenile:** Resembles dull version of female, but wings less rufous, each feather having buff spot at tip. Body plumage greyer-green and has less extensive, duller bare skin around eye. Young male soon visibly acquires adult features.

GEOGRAPHICAL VARIATION Monotypic.

MEASUREMENTS Length c.25 cm. Male marginally larger. Males: wing 139–146, tail 58–67, tarsus 42–47, bill 17–19, weight 225–300. Females: wing 133–143, tail 51–62, tarsus 40–47, bill 17–18, weight 225–275.

HABITAT Lowland rainforest in level lowlands and hill slopes to 1200 m. Persists in well-developed forest that has been selectively logged.

VOICE Long series of mournful disyllabic whistles, *si-ul* with higher-pitched second note. Most commonly heard in early morning and late evening.

HABITS One of the most frequently encountered Asian forest partridges, usually singly or in pairs, but also frequently in mixed-sex and age groups up to 15, which presumably consist of 2–3 family parties. Gait a brisk jerky walk. When alarmed scatters noisily, before emitting a contact call that serves to reassemble the group—individuals often dash across paths to rejoin others. Prefers to escape potential danger by running, only flying low and for a very short distance as a last resort. Pairs forage in close proximity, with female following male closely; the two retaining contact using soft whistles. Feeds by scratching, scuffling and picking in leaf litter for fruits, seeds, and a broad mix of invertebrates; often in association with wild pigs, or below fruiting trees on discarded items dropped by arboreal feeding monkeys or birds. Family parties roost a few metres above ground.

BREEDING Monogamous. Nest a leaf-lined scrape, c.15–20 cm across, on forest floor beneath a loose pile of leaf-litter through which parent burrows. Very difficult to locate unless birds seen entering or emerging. In peninsular Malaysia males typically call from January, but eggs found in December–June and August, and chicks in late November. Clutch 5–6 matt white eggs (6–8 dull yellow-white eggs in captivity). Incubation occupies 18 days (sometimes 19 in captivity). Both sexes tend chicks, passing food items from bill to bill (most galliform chicks pick own food from ground). Strangely, among partridges, they roost in the nest while small. Self-sufficient at c.3 months.

DISTRIBUTION Thai-Malay Peninsula from S Myanmar (S Tenasserim) and S Thailand through Malay Peninsula to Sumatra and Borneo. Formerly on Bangka and Beli tung Is, off SE Sumatra, but apparently now extinct there.

STATUS Near Threatened. One of the most commonly detected SE Asian galliformes and almost certainly the most frequently seen, giving rise to the impression that it is still common. However, it shares the same lowland rainforest habitat as a number of threatened species, including a number of pheasants. There is some evidence that it is more resistant to habitat changes in this region, but it is unknown whether the species breeds well in logged and otherwise modified areas. Records of nests or adults with young are therefore especially welcome. No recent reports from Myanmar or Kalimantan (Borneo), but still known from a number of protected areas, including Taman Negara National Park in peninsular Malaysia, Gunung Mulu in Sarawak and Gunung Leuser National Park in N Sumatra.

REFERENCES BirdLife International (2000, 2001), Chasen (1939), Davison (1986), Medway & Wells (1976), Ogilvie (1949), Wells (1999).

Genus *PTILOPACHUS*: Stone Partridge

This monospecific species differs from other African galliformes in that both sexes are similarly drab, possess unspurred tarsi, reddish legs and bill, and a prominent cocked tail of 14 feathers. Its nearest relatives are probably Asian spurfowls and bamboo-partridges, and in common with these taxa may more appropriately be included in the subfamily Phasianinae, rather than within partridges.

105 STONE PARTRIDGE
Ptilopachus petrosus (Gmelin, 1789)

Plate 6

Alternative name: Stone Bantam.

Widespread in rocky scrub and wooded areas of C Africa; with its small size and habitually cocked tail, this peculiar partridge superficially resembles a female 'bantam'.

IDENTIFICATION A social partridge of dry woodland thickets and bushy country with rocky outcrops. In field, appears dark brownish with slightly paler, almost mealy head but darker, almost blackish-brown vent and tail. Closely barred and mottled body plumage, and pale lower breast usually invisible unless close. Readily identified by combination of uniform brownish plumage, small size (with tiny bill), and very prominent and invariably cocked 'bantam'-like tail. Crested Francolin also carries tail cocked, but has striking head pattern, clear whitish upperparts streaks and contrasting paler underparts. In W Africa also compare very localised Ahanta Francolin.

DESCRIPTION *P. p. petrosus.* Bill small, reddish at base, greyish-yellow at tip. Irides brown. Bare skin around eye red. Legs dark red. Sexes similar, both lack tarsal spurs. Tail relatively broad and ridge-shaped. Rear crown feathers slightly elongated and may be raised in a short ruffled crest. **Adult male:** Forehead and crown almost whitish, with blackish feather centres. Throat and head-sides almost whitish, freckled dark brown. Foreneck dull grey-brown, with whitish feather edges, each with a black shaft and chestnut central streak. Mantle and upperwing-coverts dull brown, with whitish edges and chestnut streaks. Central lower breast and belly clear buff. Rest of upperparts and underparts dull brown, vermiculated buff and whitish; flanks have broad chestnut streaks. Primaries and secondaries brown, vermiculated chestnut. Tail blackish-brown. **Adult female:** Very similar to male, but pale area on lower breast whitish, rather than buff. **Juvenile:** Much as adult but has clearly barred body plumage, secondaries and tail.

GEOGRAPHICAL VARIATION Several forms described, but most exhibit evidence of intergradation and can be considered to represent clinal variation. Populations inhabiting drier areas are overall usually paler and more rufous. Two subspecies admitted by Urban *et al.* (1986).
  P. p. petrosus (Gmelin, 1789) (includes *brehmi, florentiae, saturation, emini* and *butleri*) occurs over most of range; described above.
  P. p. major Neumann, 1908 occurs in Eritrea; larger (wing 130–133) and paler than other populations, with broader chestnut streaking below.

MEASUREMENTS Length 23–28 cm. Sexes similar. *P. p. petrosus* given. Wing (male) 115–128 (mean 123), wing (female) 116–126 (mean 122), tail (both sexes) 63–76, tarsus (both sexes) 29–33, weight (n2) 190.

HABITAT Dry, rocky country at 600–1500 m, in dry thornbush on rocks and cliffs, most frequently in dense scrub at base of cliffs and on hillsides littered with boulders. Also tops of level laterite hills, dry watercourses with trees, and patchy woodland interspersed with cultivation and grassland. Occasionally found away from scrubby or woody cover.

VOICE Listening for calling birds at dawn and dusk is easiest method of detecting this difficult-to-observe species' presence. During rainy season, calls throughout day, a shrill and repetitive *ouit-ouit-ouit* or *weet-weet-weet*, also described as liquid piping *rrr-weet, rrr-weet, rrr-weet,* or *we've been weetin-weetin-weetin* and *will-we-weet, will we weet.* Higher pitched and more whistle-like than a francolin call.

HABITS Most easily detected in rocky areas where it roosts, vocalises and to which it retreats if disturbed. Elsewhere, very shy and easily overlooked, most often encountered dust-bathing on tracks, or feeding under bushes and thickets in pairs or groups of 3–4, sometimes coveys of 15–20. Takes seeds and small berries in morning and evening, resting in middle of day within shady cover. May occur far from permanent water. Rapidly scales cliffs on foot, sometimes perching and clambering on low tree branches. Prefers to run when disturbed, but takes to wing in fast direct flight, uttering high-pitched calls, if hard-pressed.

BREEDING Monogamy claimed in captivity, but polygyny reported in wild. Nest is a well-hidden scrape at base of a rock or tree, sometimes lined with grass. Clutch 4–6 matt dull pale stone to buff eggs. Breeding perhaps stimulated by start of rains, especially in drier areas: it breeds during wet season in dry areas and in dry season in wetter areas. Incubation period unknown, even in captivity. Families remain together until start of subsequent nesting season.

DISTRIBUTION C Africa, between 7°N and 17°N, from coastal Gambia and Sénégal, Guinea-Bissau, Guinea, and Sierra Leone east through S Mali, Burkina Faso, SW Niger, S Chad, N Côte d'Ivoire, N Ghana, Togo, Bénin, interior Nigeria, N Cameroon and Central African Republic and extreme NE Zaïre, to C Sudan, N Uganda and W Kenya, with isolated populations in W and S Ethiopia and N Eritrea.

STATUS Locally and patchily distributed in suitable

habitat throughout C Africa. Though not subject to detailed assessment, it appears locally common to abundant over most of its extensive (albeit relatively patchy) range, which suggests that no immediate concern need be raised for its conservation prospects.

REFERENCES Bannerman (1930, 1953), Crowe *et al.* (1986), McGowan (1994), Urban *et al.* (1986).

Genus *BAMBUSICOLA*: bamboo-partridges

Two, possibly three, species of forest partridge in E Asia, with relatively long wedge-shaped tails of 14 feathers and sexes similar, though only males sport a tarsal spur. Like their relatives, the spurfowls, they have occasionally been included within the subfamily Phasianinae, rather than with partridges.

106 MOUNTAIN BAMBOO-PARTRIDGE
Bambusicola fytchii (Anderson, 1871)   Plate 23

Distinctive long-tailed partridge of E Himalayan foothills, from India to Vietnam.

IDENTIFICATION Rather large, long-tailed rufous partridge of second growth and forest edge in hills of S Asia. Buff face and throat contrast with pale supercilium and blackish or rufous eye-stripe, while chestnut breast markings and bold black flank spotting are all salient features. Found in similar habitats to Black Francolin but confusion unlikely, as even when flushed easily identified by rufous primaries and rufous sides to rather long tail. Overlaps with several hill-partridges, which are all smaller, dumpier and have short tails. Range does not overlap with Chinese Bamboo-partridge, which see for differences.

DESCRIPTION *B. f. hopkinsonii.* Bill blackish-brown (male) or dark horn-brown, paler at tip and on lower mandible (female). Irides brown or pale yellowish-brown. Legs olive-brown. Sexes similar, male has one strong tarsal spur, female unspurred. Tail relatively long and graduated. **Adult male:** Crown, nape and upper mantle rufous-brown. Supercilium buffish-white, with blackish band behind eye. Throat, lower ear-coverts and foreneck rich buff, broadly spotted and streaked dark rufous on breast. Flanks whitish, boldly marked with large black heart-shaped spots. Central belly and vent virtually unmarked buff. Upperparts greyish olive-brown, with bold black and chestnut spots on mantle, scapulars and wing-coverts. Rump, back and uppertail-coverts vermiculated grey. Primaries and secondaries rufous. Outer tail feathers rufous, barred brown; central tail barred buff and brown. **Adult female:** Like male but band behind eye rufous, not blackish. **Juvenile:** Differs from female in paler rufous crown, more buff-grey, less rufous upperparts, and greyer breast with some dark barring.

GEOGRAPHICAL VARIATION Two subspecies recognised.

B. f. hopkinsonii Godwin-Austen, 1874 (includes *rincheni* occurs in NE India and Bangladesh east to N Myanmar; described above.

B. f. fytchii Anderson, 1871 occurs in SC China south to EC Myanmar and east to N Vietnam; averages smaller than *hopkinsonii* with whiter underparts ground colour and less grey-toned upperparts.

MEASUREMENTS Length 25–30 cm. Male larger. *B. f. hopkinsonii* given. Males: wing 140–156, tail 105–130, weight 278–400. Females: wing 129–143, tail 90–115, weight 256–340. Both sexes: tarsus 44–47, bill 18–20.

HABITAT Variety of open and scrubby habitats at 500–3000 m, including tall grassland in damp areas, bamboo patches, open scrub and woodland with oak and willow, and mixed thickets. Often near villages, in nearby scrub and in patches of scrubby woodland on largely cleared hillsides.

VOICE A rapidly repeated, loud resonant two-note cackle likened to Black Francolin but less shrill: *che-chirree-che-chirree, chirree, chirree, chirree.* Also rendered as a continuous chattering *pishup, pishup, pishup.* Cumulative effect is of entire covey 'shouting'. When flushed birds 'scream'. Female reportedly 'crows', giving 'discordant squawks'.

HABITS Usually in groups of 5–6, which are thought to be family parties. Emerges from scrub, e.g. near villages, into patches of shifting cultivation within forest or other village lands and cultivated areas in morning and evening to scratch for buds, shoots, seeds, grain, berries and a wide variety of insects, rarely far from permanent water. Sits very tight, before flushing short distance and 'tumbling' back into cover, usually grass, but sometimes trees.

BREEDING Mating pattern unclear, but groups are assumed to be family parties. In NE India these remain together throughout winter before disbanding around March. Males then very vocal, flying to call from raised positions, before jumping down. Season usually from April in China and May in Myanmar, rarely extending beyond July. Nest a scrape on ground amid scrub, bamboo or grassland and lined with grass and leaves. Clutch 4–6 (8 in captivity) finely textured eggs, creamy buff to deep buff and unspotted. Incubation occupies 18–19 days, by female alone, but male believed to help tend young.

DISTRIBUTION NE India in Assam (south of the Brahmaputra), Meghalaya, Manipur Mizoram, Nagaland and E Arunachal Pradesh, south to E Bangladesh and north to Sichuan and Yunnan in SC China; also east through N Myanmar, NW Thailand and N Laos to west Tonkin (Vietnam).

STATUS Not considered threatened. McGowan *et al.* (1995), however, considered that its future is uncertain, principally because its habitat is now probably fragmented and due to hunting. But, in Thailand it may even be increasing, although this is a relatively small part of its global range. Uncommon in China, but considered common in N Myanmar during last regular fieldwork prior to 1948. Virtually extirpated from Bangladesh, but despite lack of recent records, may persist in eastern hills. Its use of second growth and scrub suggest that it is not immediately at risk, although the increasingly extreme degree to which habitats are being altered should be noted. For example, while it occupies cultivated areas, as agricultural development intensifies, the species is likely to decrease.

REFERENCES Ali & Ripley (1983), Johnsgard (1988), McGowan (1994), McGowan *et al.* (1995), Robson (2000), Smythies (1986).

107 CHINESE BAMBOO-PARTRIDGE
Bambusicola thoracica (Temminck, 1815)   Plate 23

Alternative name: Taiwan Bamboo-partridge (*sonorivox*).

An attractive partridge of E China and Taiwan, the latter population differs markedly from that in mainland China and may be specifically distinct.

IDENTIFICATION A distinctive long-tailed partridge, unlikely to be confused within its native range. The Chinese form has bright rufous face, throat and neck-sides, bordered by a grey supercilium and breast-band; underparts very pale buff with scaly black spots. In Taiwan has blue-grey head, neck and breast with an inconspicuous small rusty area in centre of throat, and richer buff flanks spotted chestnut. Sexes similar in both populations. Mountain Bamboo-partridge is easily separated by its buff throat and rusty-streaked breast, lacking grey on head and breast of Chinese, and their ranges do not overlap.

DESCRIPTION *B. t. thoracica*. Bill grey with blackish tip. Irides dark brown. Legs greyish-olive. Sexes similar, male has one strong tarsal spur, female unspurred. Tail relatively long and graduated. **Adult (both sexes):** Crown and nape brown, with reddish feather tips. Forehead, lores and supercilium bluish-grey. Throat, lower ear-coverts, neck-sides and foreneck rusty-rufous. Breast bluish-grey, bordered below with narrow band of rusty-rufous. Rest of underparts cinnamon-buff, with large black, or chestnut and black, heart-shaped spots. Upperparts warm olive-brown, vermiculated grey, boldly marked with large black and chestnut spots, and small white spots on mantle, scapulars and wing-coverts. Rump, back and uppertail-coverts brown, with scattered small black spots. Primaries and secondaries grey-brown. Tail rufous, barred cinnamon and dark brown. **Juvenile:** Duller than adult, less bright rufous, with brownish head and buffish supercilium, underparts have fine buff shaft streaks.

GEOGRAPHICAL VARIATION Two subspecies distinctly differ in coloration; the Taiwan form may arguably warrant specific status.

B. t. thoracica (Temminck, 1815) occurs in S China, introduced Japan; described above.
B. t. sonorivox Gould, 1863 occurs in Taiwan and introduced to Japan (perhaps extirpated in latter); darker than nominate, finely vermiculated with black on grey breast-band, chestnut (not blackish) spots on richer buff flanks and less extensive rufous on throat (restricted to centre).

MEASUREMENTS Length 30–32 cm. Male larger. Nominate race given. Males: wing 124–140, tail 91–106, weight 242–297. Females: wing 125–134, tail 90–97, weight 200–342.

HABITAT Dense bushes in low hills to 2000 m, but rarely higher than 1000 m. Inhabits, but does not prefer bamboo forest, and is also common in shrubs and grassy areas, even in parks (Japan).

VOICE Male advertising call is a loud and resonant *gi-gi-gi-gi-gi-gi-gigeroi-gigeroi*. In non-breeding season emits a *sih-mo-kuai, sih-mo-kuai* (rendered as 'people pray'), but as breeding season approaches, pairs duet, giving a *killy-killy* that soon becomes *e-put-kwai*. Males usually initiate calling, the repeated sequences rising to a crescendo.

HABITS Encountered in pairs or groups of up to 20, with up to 40 frequent during winter in Japan. Each group reportedly has an exclusive fixed home range, foraging area and roost site, but this requires confirmation as it implies group territoriality. Feeds in cultivation with weeds and some cover, and noted foraging with domestic fowl near habitations. Reported to move from lower areas used in winter to hilltops in summer, where small groups roost in trees.

BREEDING Mating pattern unknown; given frequency of records of pairs and duetting behaviour, monogamy is likely. Large groups begin to disperse in spring. Nest situated at base of a tree, under a shrub or in grass. Clutch 3–7 (up to 15 in Japan) dark creamy to pale brown eggs. Incubation period 17–19 days. Lays from mid-April in Japan.

DISTRIBUTION S China, from Red Basin of E Sichuan and Guizhou east through Hunan, E Jiangxi and N Guangdong to Fujian and S Zhejiang. Also Taiwan. Introduced in Japan (Honshu, Sado, Shikoku, Kyushu, O-Shima, Nii-Jima, Shikine-Jima, Miyake-Jima, Hachijo-Jima and Iwo-Jima) and reportedly Hawaii (but not included in Pratt *et al.* 1987).

STATUS Apparently common over much of large range, although uncommon in other areas. Declining in China due to hunting, as well as habitat loss and degradation, but not sufficiently to warrant concern. Probably stable on Taiwan, despite some pressures on its habitat. Introduced populations (Chinese form) in Japan are common and widely hunted.

REFERENCES Brazil (1991), Johnsgard (1988), McGowan (1994).

275

Alternative name: Ceylon Spurfowl.

An elusive endemic to Sri Lanka, where it is the only spurfowl.

IDENTIFICATION Very distinctive endemic to Sri Lanka, where it favours (but is not restricted to) rainforest in the wet zone in the south of the island. Like other spurfowls it is extremely shy and reclusive, although its loud, ringing cackles betray the species' presence. Combination of chestnut rear-body and wings, and boldly white-spotted foreparts of male renders it unmistakable; better views should reveal the red legs and facial skin. Female overall ruddy-brown but its whitish throat offers some contrast. Only female Sri Lanka Junglefowl is confusable, but latter is dumpier, with barred wings and streaked body plumage.

DESCRIPTION Bill red (paler in female). Irides yellow-brown to red-brown. Bare skin around eye red (paler in female). Legs red (paler in female), male has 2–3 prominent spurs, female one (sometimes two). Sexes differ. Tail relatively broad and ridged. Forecrown feathers smooth and unruffled. **Adult male:** Head and neck black, intensely marked with white shaft streaks. Throat and head-sides white, streaked black. Breast and flanks black, heavily spotted/ streaked white. Belly centre white. Vent blackish, spotted white. Upperparts, including wings, black and chestnut with white streaks and spots. Rump and uppertail-coverts chestnut, vermiculated black. Tail and terminal tail-coverts blackish. **Adult female:** Head and neck dark brown, paler on head-sides, darkest on crown, contrasting with whitish throat. Rest of plumage dull chestnut-brown, weakly vermiculated black, except breast, which is narrowly scaled black. **Juvenile:** Resembles appropriate sex, but young male has fewer, but relatively larger, white spots than adult.

GEOGRAPHICAL VARIATION Monotypic.

MEASUREMENTS Length c.30–34 cm. Male slightly larger. Males: wing 157–174, tail 121–130, tarsus 54–57, bill 25–27, weight 312–368. Females: wing 143–150, weight 200–312.

HABITAT Forests throughout wetter parts of island and occasionally in drier areas. Inhabits tall, dense undisturbed forest in both lowlands and hills to 2000 m.

VOICE Male has ringing call, comprising a rising series of three notes, each with three syllables: *yuhuhu, yuhuhu, yuhuhu, yuhuhu, yuhuhu, yuhuheeyu,* the last note on the same pitch as the first. Given periodically throughout morning and provoking bouts of calling from neighbouring males.

HABITS Invariably occurs in pairs or family parties. Like congeners, very secretive and presence usually betrayed only by distinctive call. When disturbed, escapes on foot, only flying when very hard-pressed and over short distances before alighting within cover. Walks with high-stepping strut, but capable of running very swiftly if alarmed. Scratches in leaf-litter for various foods, including seeds, berries and insects.

BREEDING Probably monogamous. Nest a shallow depression in ground under rock or other cover. Clutch usually 2 eggs, but up to 5 recorded; cream or warm buff and very similar to, but smaller than, village chicken's eggs. Breeds mostly during northwest monsoon, in November–March, and sometimes again in July–September. Incubation period unknown.

DISTRIBUTION Endemic to Sri Lanka, where local, predominantly in south of island, but also north towards Trincomalee on east coast.

STATUS Not threatened, although considered at risk (McGowan *et al.* 1995). Its localised distribution may augur ill in the long term if populations are small and isolated. Frequently encountered in some commonly visited areas, e.g. Horton Plains, Uda Walawe and Wasgomuwa National Parks, and Sinharaja Man and Biosphere Reserve. Information from sites outside protected areas, which are less frequently visited, would be valuable.

REFERENCES Ali & Ripley (1983), Grimmett *et al.* (1998), Henry (1971), McGowan *et al.* (1995).

SUBFAMILY PHASIANINAE
Pheasants

The 67 species, within 20 genera, of the pheasant subfamily include some of the most colourful and exotic of birds. Many have developed extraordinary displays (Bulwer's Pheasant, peacock-pheasants, arguses, peafowl and tragopans) to exhibit their apparently cumbersome feathers to maximum effect. Due to striking differences in male plumage, many additional genera were erected in the past, but intergeneric relationships are more easily appreciated by comparing females. Pheasants are currently treated within the same family as partridges and quails, but are usually clearly differentiated, males tending to be large and long tailed, with iridescent plumages. Partridges largely moult their tails centrifugally (the reverse in pheasants), but their close affinity is reflected in genera such as the spurfowls, Blood Pheasant and tragopans that effectively 'bridge the gap'. Because of their large size and striking plumage they have long been popular with aviculturists, indeed some are virtually unstudied in the wild, but comparatively well known in captivity. Their often restricted ranges and dependence on forest habitats render pheasants particularly vulnerable, and no fewer than 23 species are considered globally threatened (BirdLife International, 2000).

Genus *ITHAGINIS*: Blood Pheasant

Monotypic genus supporting a peculiar soft-plumaged Sino-Himalayan pheasant. In some respects, i.e. tail moult sequence (centrifugal), it is partridge-like, but the striking sexual dimorphism alone indicates that it is a pheasant. The small bill and lanceolate-shaped feathers are shared by Koklass Pheasant, which is perhaps its closest relative. Like Koklass it is highly variable, with many forms named. Spurred (male) or knobbed (female) strong tarsi and 14 feathers in tail.

111 BLOOD PHEASANT
Ithaginis cruentus (Hardwicke, 1821)   Plate 31

A plump, partridge-shaped montane pheasant, remarkably variable in coloration from drab greyish-olive forms to those with extensive crimson.

IDENTIFICATION A rotund, relatively short-tailed pheasant of the Himalayas and Chinese mountains, usually in small parties at edge of upper levels of forest in close proximity to stands of bamboo. Loose mop-crested appearance and relatively short tail in both sexes distinctive, but males show striking variation in presence or absence of red on head and breast, and some races appear dull greyish in the field unless seen well. Crested appearance and relatively unmarked (although finely vermiculated) body plumage of female prevents confusion with female tragopans and Koklass.

DESCRIPTION *I. c. cruentus.* Plumage relatively soft, with short crest in both sexes (shorter in female); body feathers lanceolate in male. Tail moderately short (for a pheasant), rather graduated, with 14 feathers. Bill short and strongly decurved, black with bright red base and cere (paler in winter). Bare skin around eye red (brightest in breeding male). Irides brown. Tarsi rather long and strong, in male with up to three variable-length spurs; female with blunt knobs; bright red (duller in winter). Sexes differ. **Adult male:** Blackish forehead, lores, crown-sides and surround to red ocular skin. Central crown buffy-grey, with white shaft streaks, forming floppy crest. Chin blackish-red, throat speckled crimson, with black feather bases and yellow tips. Sides of head, neck and upper breast pale yellowish, with blackish feather bases and fringes; sometimes a hint of crimson on upper breast. Underparts from lower breast apple green, with dark fringes, becoming buffish on central belly and crimson on undertail-coverts. Mantle, back, rump, uppertail-coverts, scapulars and wing-coverts grey, tinged green on greater coverts and tertials, with whitish or greenish-white, black-fringed shaft streaks. Longest uppertail-coverts extensively edged crimson. Primaries and secondaries brownish. Tail pale grey becoming whitish at tip, central feathers and base fringed crimson. **Adult female:** Forehead, face and throat cinnamon-rufous, contrasting with ash-grey short floppy crest. Nape ash-grey. Rest of head, neck and underparts almost plain rufous-brown, with weakly vermiculated flanks and belly. Upperparts brown, more clearly vermiculated dusky-brown, especially on wings and tail. **Juvenile:** Resembles dull version of female, but crest shorter, and entire body plumage intensely mottled dark brown and pale buff. Young male resembles dull version of adult male at four months.

GEOGRAPHICAL VARIATION Intergradation between many subspecies suggests that most variation is clinal. Two (perhaps three) subspecies clusters are identifiable, each containing considerable variation. Across the species, males vary in the extent of red and black on head and breast, and green in wing-coverts. Western males typically possess some red on head and breast, increasing east through Himalayas to NE India and Myanmar, north and east of which there is no red on head or breast. Latter group also has ear tufts. Himalayan populations have greater wing-coverts at least partially green, whereas to the north and east they are more rufous-brown. Females less variable, but more reddish-brown in Himalayas, and paler and greyer to the north and east.

The green-winged *cruentus* group
I. c. cruentus (Hardwicke, 1822) (includes *affinis*) occurs in Nepal and Sikkim; described above.
I. c tibetanus Baker, 1914 occurs in E Bhutan and SE Tibet; male more crimson on head and breast, and female darker than nominate.
I. c. kuseri Beebe, 1912 occurs in Upper Assam to SE Tibet; even more extensive and darker crimson than *tibetanus*, with blackish ear-coverts and collar, and darker green on wings and breast; female slightly darker than *tibetanus*.
I. c. marionae Mayr, 1941 (perhaps a synonym of *kuseri*) occurs on Myanmar–Yunnan (China) border; similar to *kuseri* but blackish on head and neck more broken with crimson, and upperparts more narrowly streaked white.
I. c. rocki Riley, 1925 (includes *holoptilus*) occurs between the Salween and Yangtze rivers, NW Yunnan, China; less crimson on breast and longer crest than *kuseri*, less blackish on head and neck, but has black lores.
I. c. clarkei Rothschild, 1920 (perhaps a synonym of *geoffroyi*) occurs in Lichiang Mountains, NW Yunnan, China; much less (or no) crimson on head and breast than preceding forms, with black forehead but grey, rather than black, head-sides and throat and longer, straggly, crest. Female greyer brown.
I. c. geoffroyi Verreaux, 1867 occurs in SE Tibet; lacks crimson, having very uniform grey throat and breast, and much shorter crest and hackles than *clarkei*. Female duller and more coarsely marked with white spots.

279

The red-winged *sinensis* group

I. c. berezowskii Bianchi, 1908 (includes *annae*) occurs in S Gansu and N and W Sichuan, China; lacks crimson on head and breast, but wing-coverts reddish-brown (not green or greenish) and has marked ear tufts.

I. c. beicki Mayr & Birckhead, 1937 occurs in N Gansu, China; wing-coverts paler brown than *berezowskii*, with some green. Female paler and greyer brown.

I. c. michaelis Bianchi, 1903 occurs in NW Gansu, China; paler than *beicki*, with greenish shaft streaks on rump and uppertail-coverts.

I. c. sinensis David, 1873 occurs in Tsinling Mountains, Shaanxi, China; darker grey above than other forms, with black-edged white shaft streaks and lacks any green in wings. Female paler brown, less greyish in tone, with more extensive whitish vermiculated uppertail-coverts.

MEASUREMENTS Length: 44–48 cm (male), 40–42 cm (female). Male larger. *I. c. cruentus* given. Males: wing 193–214, tail 164–178, tarsus 72–77, weight 482–655. Females: wing 190–195, tail 140–155, tarsus 72–77, weight (three individuals of *berezowskii*) 410–620.

HABITAT Woodland and scrub at mid or high altitudes. In summer on alpine meadows above tree-line and subalpine scrub and forest below it, including bamboo, rhododendron, juniper and pine. In winter descends to lower elevations owing to snow cover; occurs in fir, juniper and other open forests. Slope, aspect and location all influence altitude at which its favoured habitats occur, as well as seasonal weather extremes. Consequently, it has been recorded between 2500 m (presumably in winter), in Myanmar, to 4500 m in summer in Indian Himalayas and Yunnan.

VOICE Variety of largely typical galliform calls, including a repeated *chuck* or *chic*, which is quite strident and seems associated with alarm, and a high-pitched repetitive *sree* during foraging. Also a long drawn-out high-pitched trill (similar to a kite *Milvus* spp.), given by both sexes, and serving to maintain contact and regroup a scattered covey. A loud *sree cheeu cheeu cheeu* (with 2–6 *cheeu* notes) may also rally dispersed flocks.

HABITS Typically occurs in groups of 5–30, sometimes larger, which also roost together in trees or thickets, or on the ground. It is unknown whether, or how, group size changes prior to breeding, and how quickly coveys re-form in post-breeding season (up to 60–70 recorded), but flock size is significantly larger in early, as opposed to late, winter. Spends most of day foraging, by scratching in leaf-litter with their feet, sometimes feeding on moss on branches of trees. Rarely flies, even in alarm. Often very confiding around Buddhist monasteries where unmolested. Some altitudinal movement enforced by snowfall within high-altitude summer areas, although it is known to dig through snow to feed. Home range size increases during breeding season, declining marginally while the female is brooding.

BREEDING Mating system probably monogamy, but unclear and perhaps variable as polygamy and polyandry are claimed. Rough nest is scrape in ground under shrubs or bamboo and lined with grass and leaves. Clutch 2–7 pinkish-buff eggs, variably speckled and blotched reddish and dark brown. Season mid-April to late June, with most nests in May. Incubation in captivity by female alone, 26–29 days. Both sexes take care of chicks.

DISTRIBUTION From W Nepal (Rara and Jumla) east through NE India, Bhutan and NW Myanmar, thence north through Tibet, Yunnan and Gansu to Sichuan and Shaanxi, China.

STATUS Not globally threatened across large range, but probably inhabits an area much smaller than geographical limits suggest as its habitat is naturally restricted and increasingly fragmented. Few population data, but considered common and widespread in suitable areas. Known from many localities, which suggests a reasonably healthy global population. Occurs in several protected areas, including Sagarmatha and Langtang National Parks in Nepal, and Foping (Shaanxi) and Wolong (Sichuan) Panda Reserves in China. Many sites are reasonably remote and unlikely to be lost completely, but continued habitat degradation is a major concern. Removal of timber, overgrazing of understorey shrubs and increasing cultivation all pose threats. Those subspecies in the E Himalayas and deep valleys of the Myanmar/Yunnan border region (Mekong and Salween) may be threatened. Apparently protected in Buddhist areas, due to religious beliefs, including Bhutan where it is relatively common.

REFERENCES Delacour (1977), Grahame (1971, 1976), Grimmett *et al.* (1998), Johnsgard (1986), McGowan (1994), McGowan & Garson (1995), Vaurie (1965).

Genus *TRAGOPAN*: tragopans (horned pheasants)

Distinctive genus of five rather stocky, blunt-tailed pheasants of Himalayan and Chinese montane forests. Like Blood Pheasant, tail moult sequence (centrifugal) is partridge-like. Tragopans have very short, stout bills and rather compressed tails of 18 feathers. Males have intensely white-spotted plumage, remarkable bare fleshy erectile 'horns' and bare facial and throat skin that is extremely colourful and bizarre-looking when inflated during courtship display. Females difficult to separate, except on range. Males have one tarsal spur, females unspurred. Tragopans, unusually among pheasants, nest in trees, either in holes or the old nest of another large bird. Most species probably occur sympatrically with a congeneric at one periphery of their range, but climatic, habitat or altitudinal differences presumably exist in potential overlap zones.

Tragopan melanocephala (Gray, 1829)   **Plate 32**

Alternative name: Western Horned Pheasant.

The darkest tragopan, now largely confined to the politically volatile border regions of Pakistan and India.

IDENTIFICATION The darkest tragopan is the only species in Pakistan and NW India, where it occurs east to the Great Himalayan National Park in Himachal Pradesh and formerly further east. Male easily distinguished from Satyr in having blackish body plumage contrasting with scarlet nape and orange breast, and red facial and blue gular skin. Male Satyr has blue facial and gular skins, bright red underparts and brownish upperparts. Female Western is duller, overall more grey-brown than corresponding plumage of Satyr, with reddish or orange (not bluish) orbital skin, whiter spotting and streaking, and exhibits contrast between darker breast and paler lower underparts. Satyr is rufous-brown in comparison, especially on underparts, and has pale markings distinctly buff, rather than white. Compare female with females of Koklass Pheasant and Himalayan Monal.

DESCRIPTION Bill black, with paler tip in male; horn-brown in female. Bare skin around eyes and head-sides orange-red, with tiny blue spots below eye; bare throat skin blue, becoming blue-green on cheeks; inflatable throat bib or lappet pink at sides, purple-blue at centre; inflatable horns blue (male). Irides brown. Legs pinkish, paler in non-breeding season and female. Sexes differ. **Adult male:** Head black, slightly elongated crest feathers tipped dark red. Hindneck and neck-sides deep red. Breast rusty-orange, with fine, bristle-like feathers. Rest of underparts black, vermiculated brownish on flanks, belly and vent, each feather red at base, with round white spot, edged black. Entire upperparts, including wings, finely vermiculated buffy-grey and black, with round white spot, edged black, at feather tip; spots on wings more olive than white. Longest uppertail-coverts large and blunt, whitish, terminally edged black, subterminally rufous. Tail mottled buff and black, with irregular black barring and dark tip. **First-year male:** Intermediate between sexes. Larger and longer legged than female, with variable black on head and red on neck, and bolder white-spotted body plumage. **Adult female:** Plumage largely uniform dull brown, finely vermiculated and spotted dark. Head and neck tinged rufous, rest of plumage duller, greyish-brown, darkest on breast, contrasting with paler lower underparts, which have whitish feather centres and subterminal round white spots, edged black. Upperwing-coverts streaked white. Tail vermiculated grey-brown, with blackish terminal band on outer feathers. Orbital skin reddish or orange. **Juvenile:** Apparently very similar to female.

GEOGRAPHICAL VARIATION Monotypic.

MEASUREMENTS Length: male 69–73 cm, female c.60 cm. Male markedly larger. Males: wing 255–290, tail 220–250, tarsus 78–97, weight c.1800–2150. Females: wing 225–250, tail 190–200, tarsus 65, weight c.1250–1400.

HABITAT Mid-altitude moist to dry Himalayan forests, typically dominated by oak, most often *Quercus baloot* at lower elevations, and conifers, with a dense understorey. Seasonal movements dictated by snowfall and descends from summer altitudes, as high as 3600 m, to 1735 m and even claimed at 1350 m. Movements and habitat influenced by slope, aspect and severity of climatic extremes, and thus variable throughout its range.

VOICE Principally a nasal bleating *khuwah*, uttered by both sexes and often described as being akin to the wailing of a lost goat or child. Usually given from tree roosts or other positions above ground, at dawn and dusk, and repeated 7–15 times, up to 5 seconds apart. Males, which are apparently relatively silent for much of the year, call more frequently at the onset of breeding and even during the day, although principally in early morning and evening. Alarm rather similar, *waa, waa, waa* (or *quoink, quoink, quoink*), but much quicker and shorter, and accelerates with increasing anxiety. Low clucking calls given by female in vicinity of nest.

HABITS Extremely difficult to see as it is very wary and skulks among undergrowth, remaining hidden from view even when very close in bamboo etc.; when disturbed sometimes escapes into branches of nearby tree. Usually encountered singly or in pairs, but family parties occasionally seen in post-breeding season. Foraging behaviour poorly known, other than it feeds in early morning and late afternoon, often with other pheasants, e.g. Himalayan Monal, sometimes in relatively open forest glades. Actively selects fresh green shoots. However, given behaviour of other tragopans and its presumed vegetarian diet, it probably also feeds in trees, on leaves (such as oak), as well as on ground. Selects more open and exposed areas for preening and resting. Some altitudinal movement is precipitated by snowfall.

BREEDING Mating system unknown, owing to lack of breeding information, both in the wild and captivity. Assumed to be monogamous, with males apparently assisting in raising the young. Nests found on ground, in a tree hollow 3 m above ground and 13 m up in what appeared to be an old crow *Corvus* sp. nest, to which the hen brought a new lining of fresh leaves and shoots, principally oak. Clutch 2–6 dull reddish-brown eggs with faint dark brown dots. Breeding season uncertain, but calling commences in March, pairing apparently takes place in April and nests discovered in late May and June.

DISTRIBUTION NW Himalayas, from Swat in North-West Frontier Province (N Pakistan) east through Kashmir and Ladakh (NW India), as far as the Kattor and Bhilling valleys of Garwhal (Himachal Pradesh). Former occurrence further east in India, in Kumaon district, is based on the type-locality being stated as Almora, but the precise origin of the type-specimen is unclear. Also reported from one locality in SW Tibet, close to the border with the Spiti region of India.

STATUS Globally threatened (Vulnerable). Very local.
Considerable attention, over the last 15 years, has
revealed it to be not as seriously at risk as once thought.
STATUS Globally threatened (Vulnerable). Very local.
Considerable attention, over the last 15 years, has
revealed it to be not as seriously at risk as once thought.
Minimum population perhaps 5000, based on
encounter rates in some areas (and estimated population sizes) extrapolated across its entire remaining
habitat. Several sizeable populations have been found,
but widespread loss of mid-altitude forest is the most
significant threat. Still common in a very small number
of localities; the Palas Valley, in Pakistan, may hold the
most important population (estimated at 325 pairs in
mid 1990s), but is at risk from timber extraction and
other forms of habitat disturbance. Known from several protected areas, including Machiara National
Park in Pakistan and the Great Himalayan National
Park in India. Ongoing captive breeding projects are
underway in India and Pakistan.

REFERENCES Ali & Ripley (1983), BirdLife International
(2000, 2001), Delacour (1977), Gaston et al. (1983), Grimmett et al. (1998), McGowan & Garson (1995), Mirza et al.
(1978), Whale (1997).

113 SATYR TRAGOPAN
Tragopan satyra (Linnaeus, 1829)

Plate 32

Alternative names: Crimson Horned Pheasant, Crimson Tragopan.

A beautiful pheasant, closely related to Temminck's
Tragopan, which it replaces across Bhutan and Nepal.

IDENTIFICATION The only tragopan over most of
its range, but almost meets Blyth's in C Bhutan and
comes close to Western in Uttar Pradesh (NW India).
Males distinctive with gorgeous red underparts, with
round white spots, edged black, which become grey
on lower underparts (behind legs). Red underparts
shared only by similar Temminck's, which has much
redder (not brown) upperparts, more extensive flaming orange neck and pale grey streak-spots (not black-
rimmed white eye-spots) from breast downwards.
Temminck's conceivably occurs in E Bhutan but is
unknown west of Arunachal Pradesh in NE India. All
female tragopans are similar, but Satyr has bluish
orbital skin (like Temminck's), is usually overall more
rufous-brown and lacks Temminck's clear white
underparts spotting. Females prone to variation,
many quite dull grey-brown, but even these typically
have warm brown tail. Compare also Western
Tragopan, female Koklass Pheasant and female
Himalayan Monal.

DESCRIPTION Less extensive bare facial skin and
relatively longer tailed than other tragopans. Bill
black, with pinkish tip in male; horn-brown in female.
Bare throat skin and around eye bluish-purple, inflatable throat bib, or lappet, blue in centre, pale green
at edges, with 4–5 triangular red patches on each side;
inflatable horns blue (male). Irides brown. Legs pinkish, paler in non-breeding season and female. Sexes
differ. Adult male: Head black, slightly crested, with
red stripe on crown-sides. Black surround to bare
gular skin. Neck, breast and underparts crimson-red.
From breast down each feather has black-rimmed
white eye-spot, which become progressively larger on
flanks; black border to spotting disintegrates and
spots become pearl-grey and more angular on belly
and thighs. Scapulars and wing-coverts crimson, mottled black and vermiculated buffy-brown; primaries
and secondaries brown. Rest of upperparts olive-
brown, with black-rimmed white eye-spots, scattered
red feathering and weak vermiculations. Longest
uppertail-coverts large and blunt, brown, terminally
edged black. Tail mottled buff and black at base, terminally black. First-year male: Intermediate between
sexes. Larger and longer legged than female, with
variable black on head, and some red and white spotting on body plumage. Adult female: Entire plumage
uniform brown, individually variable in tone; usually
quite rufous-brown but many distinctly dull grey-
brown. Overall finely vermiculated and spotted dark,
with buff shaft streaks. Tail distinctly rufous-brown,
often contrasting with body plumage, with irregular
buff and black barring. Orbital skin blue. Juvenile:
Apparently very similar to female.

GEOGRAPHICAL VARIATION Monotypic.

MEASUREMENTS Length: male 67–72 cm, female
c.57–59 cm. Male larger. Males: wing 245–285, tail
250–345, tarsus 85–95, weight 1600–2100. Females:
wing 215–245, tail 195, tarsus 66, weight c.1000–1200.

HABITAT Varies according to geography: seemingly
occurs at lower elevations in west of range where tree-
line apparently lower. Prefers oak forest with dense
understorey of ringal bamboo and rhododendron in
Nepal, and mixed conifer and broad-leaf forest in
Bhutan. Found at 1800–4300 m, according to season,
available habitat and extent of altitudinal movements.

VOICE Most notable call is a repeated deep wailing,
rendered as wah waah oo-ah oo-aaaaa (from distance of
c.50 m), given 12–14 times, becoming louder as series
progresses and emitted mainly during breeding season, principally in early morning and peaking in
April. Calling commences pre-dawn and lasts c.30
minutes during peak calling period. A quieter wak wak
appears to serve as an alarm call, being given by either
sex when disturbed, e.g. when flushed. During spring
and autumn, a repeated wah is given by either sex at
any time of day.

HABITS Usually very difficult to see as typically
extremely wary, skulking amidst undergrowth and
bamboo; can remain hidden from view even when
observer very close. When disturbed often escapes
into branches of nearby tree where disappears from
view. However, sometimes remarkably confiding in
areas where not persecuted, such as in parts of
Bhutan. Usually encountered in pairs during summer
and small groups in post-breeding season, but is principally solitary the rest of the year. Little is known concerning foraging behaviour, other than it feeds in

282

early morning and is thought to gradually move uphill, returning in mid-morning and late afternoon. Often forages in moist areas, even by streams, but also clambers about in trees and bushes, including *Rhododendron* and *Berberis*, feeding on petals, berries, buds, leaves and invertebrates. Some degree of altitudinal movement engendered by snowfall.

BREEDING Mating system unknown, owing to paucity of breeding information from the wild. Male may remain with female until onset of incubation, but this requires clarification. Nest a crudely assembled structure of sticks among tree branches, up to 6 m or more above ground, sometimes the old nest of another large bird, but may also be placed in long tussock grass near forest edge. Clutch 2–3 (4–6 in captivity) buff eggs with reddish-brown dots and blotches. Incubation in captivity usually 28 days. Breeding season May–June, occasionally into July.

DISTRIBUTION C and E Himalayas, from the Kattar and Alakanda Valleys in Uttar Pradesh (NW India) east through Nepal, Sikkim and Bhutan to extreme W Arunachal Pradesh in NE India. Also in SE Tibet from the Chumbi Valley (89°E) east to the Lo La (93°E).

STATUS Near Threatened. Now patchy over most of its range. Previously considered widespread but populations now fragmented, apart from in Bhutan where there is still significant forest cover and Buddhist beliefs afford it protection. Its total range may comprise c.100,000 km², but habitat within this area is much reduced and the population perhaps numbers fewer than 20,000 individuals. It occurs in approximately ten protected areas, including Sagarmatha and Langtang in Nepal, Black Mountains in Bhutan and Singhalila (Darjeeling) in India, all of which are national parks. Mean density estimates, of groups, in the latter varied from 4.52/km² to 6.19/km² in 1995–97 surveys. Based on spring call counts, numbers appear stable in Pipar Reserve, WC Nepal. Principal threats are further habitat loss, with attendant increasing fragmentation, and progressive deterioration in quality of extant forest due to overgrazing, fodder and firewood collection etc.

REFERENCES Ali & Ripley (1983), BirdLife International (2000, 2001), Beebe (1918–22), Grimmett *et al.* (1998), Johnsgard (1986), Kaul & Shakya (2001), Khaling *et al.* (1998), McGowan & Garson (1995).

---

114 TEMMINCK'S TRAGOPAN
Tragopan temminckii (Gray, 1831)   Plate 31

Alternative names: Chinese Crimson or Temminck's Horned Pheasant.

Eastern counterpart of Satyr Tragopan and the most widespread of the genus, ranging over most forested mountains of China, from the Indian border to that with Vietnam.

IDENTIFICATION Over most of its range the only tragopan, although known to overlap with Cabot's in NE Guangxi Zizhiqui (C China) and with Blyth's, northwest of Putao, N Myanmar (where aggressive interaction between the two has been noted), and virtually meets Satyr at 93°E, in SE Tibet, and perhaps on border with NE Bhutan. The two apparently fail to meet in the watershed of the Manas and Subsaniri rivers, which separates them. Even males are similar, but Temminck's is readily distinguished (even in flight) by having red not brown upperparts. Male's red underparts shared only by similar Satyr, but Temminck's has a flame orange collar and pale grey streak-spots (not black-rimmed white eye-spots) from the breast downwards; the red upperparts are covered in white eye-spots. All female tragopans are similar, but Temminck's has bluish orbital skin (like Satyr), is usually overall dull brown, lacking rufous tones to tail typical of female Satyr, and has clearer white underparts spotting than other species. See also Cabot's and Blyth's Tragopans, female Koklass Pheasant and female monals.

DESCRIPTION More extensive bare facial skin and relatively shorter tailed than Satyr. Bill black, with pinkish tip in male; horn-brown in female. Bare facial skin and around eye blue; inflatable throat bib or lappet dark blue, spotted pale blue, with eight scarlet triangular patches on each side; inflatable horns greenish-blue (male). Irides brown. Legs pinkish-red, paler in non-breeding season and female. Sexes differ. **Adult male:** Head black, slightly crested, with red stripe on crown-sides. Black surround to bare gular skin. Neck, upper breast and mantle bright rusty-orange, becoming darker red over entire body. Underparts from breast downwards dark red, covered in pearl-grey spots that become progressively larger on flanks. Wing-coverts, back, rump and uppertail-coverts covered in black-rimmed white eye-spots, which become larger on uppertail-coverts. Longest uppertail-coverts large and blunt, pale grey, terminally edged red. Tail mottled buff and black at base, terminally black. **First-year male:** Intermediate between sexes. Larger and longer legged than female, with variable black on head, and red and white spotting appearing on body plumage. **Adult female:** Entire plumage uniform brown, individually variable in overall tone; usually quite rufous-brown but never as rufous as some Satyr or as grey as Cabot's; many are distinctly dull grey-brown. Plumage overall finely vermiculated and spotted dark, with pale buff or whitish shaft streaks and spots. Tail dull brown, marked irregularly with buff and black barring. Orbital skin blue. **Juvenile:** Apparently very similar to female.

GEOGRAPHICAL VARIATION Monotypic. Those from Vietnam have been named *tonkinensis*, but this now considered invalid, confusion having occurred when comparing fresh skins with older, faded material.

MEASUREMENTS Length: male c.64 cm, female c.58 cm. Male larger. Males: wing 210–265, tail 185–232, tarsus 70–80, weight 980–1600. Females: wing 202–225, tail 158–178, tarsus 70, weight 970–1100.

stripe on crown-sides. Black surround to bare gular skin. Neck, head-sides and often narrow band below throat orange-red. Breast and underparts pale buff, with flanks, thighs and vent marked red and black. Upperparts maroon-red, very heavily marked with large pale buff spots, bordered below by black and maroon-red. Wings mottled and barred brown and buff. Longest uppertail-coverts large and blunt, pale buff, terminally edged red and black. Tail mottled buff and black at base, terminally black. **First-year male:** Intermediate between sexes. Larger and longer legged than female, with variable red and black on head and buff spotting on upperparts apparent. **Adult female:** Entire plumage dark grey-brown, overall finely vermiculated and spotted black and rufous, with whitish wedge-shaped shaft streaks. Underparts very heavily patterned with lines of large pale spots. Tail dull brown, with irregular buff and black barring. Orbital skin orange. **Juvenile:** Apparently very similar to female.

GEOGRAPHICAL VARIATION Until recently considered monotypic, but a second subspecies was described in 1979.

T. c. caboti (Gould, 1857) occurs in Zhejiang east to Guangdong in SE China; described above.

T. c. guangxiensis Cheng, 1979 occurs in NE Guangxi Zizhiqui, CS China; male overall darker maroon-red, with more extensive maroon-red on back and rump than nominate, and yellowish-white rather than buff spots near feather tips. Female generally darker brown, with heavier black streaking and better developed white spots than nominate.

MEASUREMENTS Length: male c.61 cm, female c.50 cm. Male larger. *T. c. caboti* given. Males: wing 210–233, tail 207–230, weight c.1400. Females: wing 192–214, tail 151–171, weight c.900.

HABITAT Both evergreen and mixed forests; utilises areas with a plentiful supply of nuts of *Lithocarpus* and *Cyclobalanopsis* in winter. At same study site, in Zhejiang Province, there was little evidence of altitudinal movements, with individuals encountered at 800–1000 m in winter and 800–1400 m in summer. No data from elsewhere. Also reported from open country above tree-line in summer.

VOICE Territorial calls in breeding season comprise two notes, commencing with a *wa-r*, like a baby's cry, followed by 3–5 *gua* notes. Also during breeding season, a rapid and continuous *chi-chi-chi, chi-chi-chi* often heard—made by a rapid beating of the wings, rather than vocally. When disturbed or alarmed, emits a loud *gua-gua-gua* for several minutes or more.

HABITS General behaviour much as other tragopans. Often seen in trees. Spring home range is larger than that used in winter, and females often forage with territorial males. Home range expands with onset of breeding, and females use larger areas than males before season intensifies. Forages, sometimes in small groups, in early morning and late afternoon on favoured diet of nuts and seed capsules of specific trees.

BREEDING Both monogamous and polygamous. Males remain with a single female early in the breeding season, but as incubation progresses either feed alone or with other males, or mate with additional females that enter their home range. Nests in pine *Pinus taiwanensis* and *Cryptomeria* woodland, depending on local conditions, often at the forest edge, one being found in an old squirrel drey. Clutch 3–5 (rarely 2 or 6); eggs similar to Temminck's, but even shorter and broader. Season March–May, with nests found as early as 1 April. Incubation occupies 28 days. Female raises brood.

DISTRIBUTION SE China, from NE Guangxi Zizhiqui east through N Guangdong and SE Hunan to C and NW Fujian and S Zhejiang. Probably now restricted to small, isolated forests.

STATUS Vulnerable. Not uncommon, but suitable habitat is increasingly reduced and fragmented. Extant populations known from much of its historical range, but extirpated from some areas, including several counties in Fujian. Range has always been small and this, together with the scale of ongoing habitat fragmentation, may have reduced its numbers to fewer than 5,000 individuals. Occurs in several protected areas, including Nanling, Wuyanling and Wuyishan reserves. Main pressures, in this densely populated part of China, are habitat loss for timber and land conversion to agriculture.

REFERENCES Beebe (1918–22), BirdLife International (2000, 2001), Cheng (1987), Ding (1995), Johnsgard (1986), McGowan & Garson (1995).

Genus *PUCRASIA*: Koklass Pheasant

Monotypic genus consisting of a peculiar point-tailed, crested and long-tufted pheasant of Sino-Himalayan montane forests. Both sexes have lanceolate-shaped feathers (unlike Blood Pheasant). Koklass is extensively distributed, but peculiarly absent from the E Himalayas. As a result, considerable subspecific variation has arisen, principally expressed in male coloration and pattern. Females, in contrast, are largely similar throughout and superficially similar in plumage to female monals. Like Blood Pheasant and tragopans, Koklass commences tail moult with the central feathers (a trait commoner in partridges than in pheasants). Among pheasants, it is remarkably long winged, the primaries projecting beyond the secondaries on the closed wing. The long, graduated tail has 16 feathers, but is largely concealed by very long uppertail-coverts. Males have a single tarsal spur; females are unspurred.

Alternative name: Koklas.

Its oddly discontinuous distribution has given rise to a large number of subspecies; it is apparently similar to Blood Pheasant and monals in several respects.

IDENTIFICATION Variable pheasant, with a moderately long tail, of montane forests in the W Himalayas and China. Male has distinctive, elongated straggly crest, projecting like quills from rear of crown, and striking white patch on neck-sides. Basic coloration varies from dark mahogany in NW Pakistan to silver-grey in E China (see Geographical Variation). Female has whitish throat and buffy-brown, barred and streaked body plumage, recalling female monal, but is smaller, lacks pale surround to eye and has pale supercilium, boldly streaked underparts, rusty undertail-coverts and more pointed tail.

DESCRIPTION *P. m. macrolopha.* Elongated spike-like crest in both sexes (c.10 cm in male) and male also has greatly elongated (c.12 cm) feather tufts behind eye (elevated like erect 'ears' in display). No bare facial or gular skin. Most body feathers lanceolate in both sexes. The moderately long, graduated tail has 16 feathers, but is virtually concealed by very long uppertail-coverts. Bill brown or black (darkest in males). Irides dark brown. Tarsus dark bluish-grey and rather long; male has single, relatively long spur, but female unspurred. Sexes differ. **Adult male:** Head and elongated 'ear' tufts glossy blackish-green, contrasting with white patch on neck-side. Crest rufous-brown, with longest feathers black. Lower neck, breast and most of body plumage silver-grey, washed warm buff on rump, with black shaft streaks. Foreneck, breast centre, belly and vent chestnut, darkest on undertail-coverts, which have narrow white tips. Wings buffish-brown to rufous-brown, with black shaft streaks and subterminal mottling (on secondaries). Elongated uppertail-coverts chestnut, tipped grey, with broken black shaft streaks. Tail chestnut, blackish on inner webs of outer feathers; each with black tip and white subterminal bar. **Adult female:** Buff crown and short crest, barred black, and crest whitish at tip. Supercilium short and broad, unmarked buffy-white. Lower ear-coverts and throat whitish, separated by mottled malar. Rest of head, neck and underparts buff, mottled black and brown, becoming streaked on whitish lower underparts; undertail-coverts chestnut, tipped white. Upperparts, including wings, buffy-brown, with broken black barring and blotching, and buff shaft streaks. Tail chestnut, blackish on inner webs of outer feathers; each with black tip and white subterminal bar. **Juvenile:** Largely as female; male attains dimorphic features in first year.

GEOGRAPHICAL VARIATION Intergradation suggests that variation is largely clinal. Males vary in amount of chestnut, black and yellow-orange in the upperparts and tail. Those with darker upperparts, breast and flanks occur in the west; a partial yellowish or orange collar and upperparts feathers with two

black streaks are indicative of central and northern populations; and those in the southeast lack a collar and have four black streaks on upperparts feathering. Tail chestnut in west and black/silver-grey in other subspecies. Three geographically isolated subspecies groups, each encompassing considerable variation.

Himalayan *macrolopha* group
Feathers of upperparts, breast and flanks possess a single, broad black shaft streak. Hindneck chestnut to silver-grey.

    P. m. castanea Gould, 1854 occurs in E Afghanistan east to Chitral (Pakistan); darker, more maroon underparts than nominate and blacker tail. Female also darker, with blackish tail.

    P. m. biddulphi Marshall, 1879 (includes *bethelae*) occurs in Kashmir east to the Kulu Valley; intermediate, with maroon on hindneck and underparts, often grey mantle and brownish tail. Female darker than nominate.

    P. m. macrolopha (Lesson, 1829) occurs in Kumaon (Uttar Pradesh); reddish-chestnut neck and underparts; (described above).

    P. m. nipalensis Gould, 1854 occurs in W Nepal; very dark, rich chestnut and black overall, relieved by grey fringes to wing-coverts.

Golden-collared *xanthospila* group
Populations in W and N China possess a golden collar, while the upperparts, breast and flanks feathering have two black streaks and a central grey shaft streak.

    P. m. meyeri Madaràsz, 1886 occurs in W and SW Sichuan, south and east to NW Yunnan, extinct in SE Tibet; tail rufous, while other features are those of the group as a whole (see above).

    P. m. ruficollis David & Oustalet, 1877 occurs in W Sichuan, north to S Gansu and Shaanxi; very dark, with almost orange neck and maroon underparts, becoming blackish on undertail-coverts, tail black and grey.

    P. m. xanthospila Gray, 1864 occurs in SE Nei Mongol, Shaanxi northeast to W Hebei and SW Manchuria; paler and duller than *ruficollis*, with golden collar and reddish undertail-coverts, tail grey and black, fringed rufous.

Eastern *darwini* group
Populations in E China lack a golden collar, while *darwini* has two colour phases, plus intermediates.

    P. m. joretiana Heude, 1883 occurs in Anhui; crest dense and blunt, not pointed, rich chestnut on central neck and breast, feather centres to upperparts and flanks greyish, with two black streaks, no rufous fringing to central tail.

    P. m. darwini Swinhoe, 1872 (includes *styani*) occurs in Hubei, SW Sichuan, Zhejiang and Fujian, now extinct in NW Fujian and N Guangdong; variable, but all males have upperparts feathers with four black streaks, tail grey and black, fringed rufous, reddish-chestnut central neck and breast, and buffy wash to underparts. Black-and-grey phase ('*styani*') lacks chestnut in plumage and occurs throughout range; intermediates known.

MEASUREMENTS Length: male 58–64 cm, female 52.5–56.0 cm. Male larger. *P. m. macrolopha*. Males: wing 215–244, tail 221–277, crest up to 104, tarsus 63–69, weight 1135–1415. Females: wing 180–218, tail 172–195, tarsus 55, weight 1025–1135.

HABITAT Coniferous and mixed forests, on steep to precipitous slopes, from 1600 m in winter, to 4000 m in summer. Like other temperate forest species, it prefers areas with a well-developed understorey of rhododendron, bamboo or other scrub, but is also recorded in forest heavily grazed by domestic goats.

VOICE Dawn call a loud, far-carrying *kok* repeated at up to one-minute intervals. This note has been rendered in many different ways, probably reflecting some variation (principally geographic, but perhaps also individual) as well as, possibly, acoustic conditions under which they are heard. Examples include *kok kok kok*; *kok-ras*, *kok kark kuk*; *kukuk* and *ka ka kaaah kah*. When flushed, often gives a harsh *kwak kwak kwak* while disappearing downslope, and females have a rapid and more musical two-note alarm call, *qui-quik qui-quik qui quik*.

HABITS Difficult to see well, as it is wary and, when disturbed, runs through the undergrowth or explodes into flight, disappearing downslope alarm calling. Usually seen singly or in pairs, but loose parties occasionally form in winter. Forages during early morning and late afternoon, in grassy areas, but dug-over patches found in a variety of places, presumably searching for roots and tubers. Roosts in trees, from where males call at dawn in November–June, but especially vocal in spring, from before sunrise for up to 50 minutes. In suitable forest, up to a dozen may be heard from one point. In display, male erects long 'ear' tufts and crest, fluffs out body plumage and struts around female. Descends up to 1000 m or more in winter if snowfall dictates.

BREEDING Considered monogamous, as males and females often found in close proximity. Nest a scrape in the ground, under dense bushes, lined to some extent with twigs and leaves. Clutch typically 5–7 (up to 9 recorded) variably coloured eggs, from pale yellowish to rich deep buff, always with reddish-brown markings. Season April–June, but one nest found in mid-July. Incubation in captivity 26–27 days, although 21–22 days also reported.

DISTRIBUTION W and C Himalayan range widely separated from that in China, and may represent several discrete populations. In the west, found from E Afghanistan (the Kunar Valley) through the Himalayas of Pakistan and Kashmir across NW India to C Nepal (east to Annapurna). Also, from Tibet and Yunnan north through Guizhou and Sichuan to Ningxia and Gansu. In C and E China it occurs from Jiangxi and Zhejiang north through Anhui and Hubei to Henan and Shaanxi.

STATUS Widespread and reasonably common in suitable habitat. Forest within its large range is increasingly disturbed and fragmented, isolating many subpopulations. Not considered threatened, it is known from many localities, including the Ayubia (Pakistan), Great Himalayan (India) and Khaptad (Nepal) National Parks, and Fanjingshan and Mazong reserves in China and numbers appear stable, based on spring call counts, in Pipar Reserve, WC Nepal. Still common over much of its historical range, but now extinct in SE Tibet, NW Fujian and N Guangdong, and perhaps in Afghanistan. The two Chinese subspecies groups may be at greater risk than that in the W and C Himalayas, especially *joretiana* and *darwini*, which inhabit densely populated SE China and may number fewer than 10,000. It appears to prefer a significant understorey and where this is being degraded through grazing or collection of fodder for domestic stock or firewood, the species is probably under pressure.

REFERENCES Ali & Ripley (1983), Cheng (1987), McGowan & Garson (1995).

Genus *LOPHOPHORUS*: monals

Three distinctive, very large and stocky pheasants of alpine meadows in the Himalayas and W China. Blackish males exhibit highly refulgent coloration in strong light. Both sexes have bare skin around eye and moderate-length, flat, rather broad tails of 18 feathers. Bills strong and markedly decurved, the upper mandible conspicuously overlapping the lower. Legs stout and strong, males having a single short spur and females usually unspurred. Over most of the genus' range only one species occurs, but the situation is less clear in NE India/China border regions, where Sclater's and Himalayan are found in close proximity.

118 HIMALAYAN MONAL
Lophophorus impejanus (Latham, 1790) Plate 33

Alternative names: Impeyan Pheasant, Impeian Monal.

Considered by many to be one of the beautiful and magnificent pheasants, it is the National Bird of Nepal.

IDENTIFICATION Typically found at forest edges, on grassy slopes at or just above tree-line. Male unmistakable with its black but very glossy plumage and chestnut tail, often with a white rump (latter may be obscured, wholly lacking or only evident in flight). The peacock-like crest and all-rufous tail are unique to this monal, although it is only in extreme NE India (and adjacent Tibet and Myanmar) that confusion could arise with congenerics. The smaller brown female is boldly streaked and vermiculated pale buff on dark brown underparts, has a slight crest on the rear crown, and a striking, clean white throat and bare bluish skin around eye. Additionally, the dark tail is narrowly barred buff and the uppertail-coverts and tail are tipped white, which can appear as a narrow white horseshoe and tip when flushed. Compare with female Koklass, tragopans and other female monals, particularly Sclater's.

DESCRIPTION Male has elongated tuft of bare-shafted, racket-like feathers immediately behind mid-crown, female a scruffy tuft on rear crown. Bill greyish-horn (paler in female), with enlarged and de-curved upper mandible, overlapping lower mandible. Bare skin around eye turquoise-blue (both sexes). Irides brown. Legs dark grey (male) to yellowish-green (female). Male has single short spur, female un-spurred. Sexes differ. **Adult male:** Head, including crest, metallic green; chin and throat black (sometimes glossed green). Rest of underparts velvety black. Neck (except black foreneck) iridescent copper. Mantle brilliant yellow-green, becoming purple on scapulars. Lower back white (but sometimes obscured by black streaking or even appears wholly blackish). Lower rump and shorter uppertail-coverts purple; longer uppertail-coverts metallic green. Upperwing-coverts metallic green, becoming purple-blue on inner greater coverts and inner secondaries. Primaries and inner webs of secondaries dark brownish. Tail rufous, darker (very rarely blackish) at tip. **First-year male:** Intermediate between sexes. Larger than female, with variable amounts of black on foreneck and metallic purple feathers on upperparts. **Adult female:** Chin and throat clean white or buffish-white, otherwise entire plumage dark brown, each feather centre blackish-brown, with vermiculated buff fringes, and buff and white streaks. Lower back buffish, weakly scaled dark brown (thus obviously paler than upper-tail-coverts). Longest uppertail-coverts tipped white, forming narrow white band at base of tail. Tail blackish-brown with narrow rufous-buff bars and shallow white tips. Orbital skin bluish. **Juvenile:** Very similar to female, but markings less distinct.

GEOGRAPHICAL VARIATION None currently recognised, but marked individual variation in extent and colour of iridescence, and extent of white on the back exists. Some males in Himachal Pradesh (NW India) lack any white and have quite extensive green on breast (sometimes named *chambanus*), others have the green replaced by purple (*mantoui*), while some have mostly black body feathers, with gloss confined to the wings (*obscura*). Females usually more rufous and richly toned in east of range.

MEASUREMENTS Length: male 70–72 cm, female 64 cm. Male larger. Males: wing 289–320, tail 215–235, crest 75–88, tarsus c.70–80, weight 1980–2380. Females: wing 259–287, tail 182–200, weight c.1800–2150.

HABITAT Coniferous and mixed forests with well-developed bamboo, rhododendron and other under-storey scrub. Usually in meadows and forest clearings on steep Himalayan slopes, it is the only pheasant for which much information on altitudinal movements exists. In NW India, predominantly above 3000 m in December–January, descending in February to c.2300 m, returning upslope in March (above 2500 m), reaching the tree-line (c.3500 m) in April, and emerging periodically onto alpine meadows in May. In Nepal reported as high as 4350 m in summer, and in NW Pakistan at 2300–3500 m in spring and 2000–2500 m in winter. Recorded to 1900 m in Arunachal Pradesh. Occasionally forages close to cultivation.

VOICE When alarmed, a ringing two-note whistle, rendered as *kleeh-wick kleeh-wick*, interspersed with several *kwick kwick* calls. Breeding season call (mostly males), given dawn to mid-morning and at dusk from roost site, is not dissimilar to alarm and also likened to that of Eurasian Curlew *Numenius arquata*, being upwardly inflected and sounding like *kur-lieu*, or *kleeh-wick*, each whistle separated by a single high-pitched note.

HABITS Perhaps the easiest of the predominantly forest-dependent Himalayan pheasants to observe. Slightly less wary than other species and occasionally flushes noisily from forest on steep slopes, flying around spur of a hill or into a side valley. Usually encountered singly or in loose groups of up to four, even during breeding season (usually with only one male). Appears to forage throughout day, using stout bill to search for insects and their larvae and tubers, as well as smaller quantities of seeds, shoots and berries, leaving characteristic patches of dug-over soil up to 25 cm deep. In summer feeds on alpine pastures and, in exceptional circumstances, within cultivated fields. Calls at dawn in January–June and infrequently during other months. In courtship, male fans chestnut tail, droops wings and struts around female, parading brilliant iridescent plumage. Rarely seen display flight involves male gliding on spread tail, with wings held above the body, while uttering piping call.

BREEDING Mating pattern uncertain, polygamy suspected. Nest a scrape in grasses, often sheltered by a rock or fallen tree, among bushes on relatively steep hillsides and usually unlined. Nests recorded at 2100–4500 m, but usually at higher elevations. Clutch typically 3–6 variable eggs (2–8 reported, but largest clutches dubious), being pale yellowish or reddish-buff, with reddish-brown markings. Season mid-April to mid-July.

DISTRIBUTION Forested Himalayas, from E Afghanistan (Nuristan and apparently formerly the Afghani Safed Koh range), N Pakistan, Kashmir and NW India through Nepal, Sikkim and Bhutan to W Arunachal Pradesh, reaching as far east as extreme S Tibet (west to c.85°E, east to 95°E). An apparent gap in its range occurs in N Arunachal Pradesh, where it is only known from the extreme west and northeast, although it may prove contiguous on the Tibetan side of the border. Also known from NE Myanmar (around Putao).

STATUS Widespread and common in suitable habitat. Its still fairly extensive range is suffering increasing encroachment and fragmentation, and concern has been raised that the species is undergoing a moderate decline. Not considered threatened, being known from many localities, including several protected areas, e.g. the Machiara Wildlife Sanctuary in Pakistan and Great Himalayan and Khangchendzonga (India), and Khaptad and Langtang (Nepal) National Parks. In the Kulu Valley, more than 70 individuals were encountered per 100 hours of fieldwork in some areas, and also common in Nanda Devi National Park, where it has obviously benefited from increased protection in recent years. It appears to use forest with significant understorey growth and where this is being lost and/or degraded through grazing or collection of fodder for domestic stock or firewood, it is probably under pressure. Hunting appears to be a threat in some regions, and it may already be extinct in Afghanistan.

REFERENCES Ali & Ripley (1983), Delacour (1977), Grimmett *et al.* (1988), McGowan (1994).

119 SCLATER'S MONAL
Lophophorus sclateri Jerdon, 1870

Plate 33

Alternative names: Crestless Monal, White-tailed Monal (status of latter uncertain).

Confined to the E Himalayas, this distinctive monal appears to be sandwiched between two populations of Himalayan Monal.

IDENTIFICATION Unmistakable monal of the poorly explored Tibet/Yunnan/Myanmar/Arunachal Pradesh border regions in the E Himalayas. Male easily separated from Himalayan Monal (marginal overlap at least in Myanmar, where Sclater's usually occurs at lower elevations) in having much more white on rear body and tail (with a chestnut subterminal band), but lacking an obvious crest (it has a short curly one). Himalayan, in contrast, has a small white back patch separated from the chestnut tail by blackish rump and uppertail-coverts, and a much longer, peacock-like crest. In flight, Sclater's has white back, rump, uppertail-coverts and most of tail (entire tail in presumed western population). Female differs from Himalayan in its relatively shorter tail with whiter barring and broader white tip, and much paler (greyish) rump and uppertail-coverts, contrasting (rather than appearing uniform) with mantle and wings. Female Himalayan lacks large white throat and streaking on closely barred underparts, although has bolder upperparts streaking than Sclater's. See also Chinese Monal.

DESCRIPTION *L. s. sclateri.* Male has curly crown feathers (curving forwards) forming short ruffled crest; female has slightly ruffled rear crown. Tail marginally shorter than in other monals. Bill pale orange-yellow (paler yellow in female), with enlarged and decurved upper mandible, overlapping lower mandible. Bare skin around eye and lores bright blue (both sexes). Irides brown. Legs olive-brown (male) to brown (female). Male has single short spur, female also often has a short spur. Sexes differ. Adult male: Crown and curly tuft metallic green. Nape and neck-sides iridescent copper. Chin and throat glossy purple-black. Rest of underparts velvety black. Mantle, scapulars and inner wing shining purple, becoming green; outer wing brilliant green, with purple and copper iridescence; lesser and median coverts bronze-green. Primaries and secondaries blackish. Back, rump and shorter uppertail-coverts white, with inconspicuous fine dark shaft streaks; longer uppertail-coverts pure white. Tail white with broad chestnut subterminal band, mottled chestnut and black at base (concealed by white uppertail-coverts). First-year male: Intermediate between sexes. Larger than female, with variable black on foreneck and metallic green feathers on upperparts. Adult female: Chin and throat buffish-white, rest of head and neck brownish-black, with buff subterminal marks to each feather (producing freckled appearance). Underparts closely and finely barred, or vermiculated, dark brown and buff (lacking pale streaking of other monals). Nape, mantle, scapulars and wing-coverts dark brown with bold pale buff shaft streaks and brown barring. Back, rump and uppertail-coverts pale ash-grey, closely and finely barred, or vermiculated, dark brown, with fine white shaft streaks. Tail blackish-brown, narrowly barred buffy-white, with a bold, broad white tip. Orbital skin bluish. Juvenile: Very similar to female, but poorly known. A young male had the upperparts barred cinnamon, rather than freckled.

GEOGRAPHICAL VARIATION Perhaps monotypic, but recent discovery of tiny numbers of an undescribed 'white-tailed' monal in a remote area of Arunachal Pradesh (Suresh Kumar & Singh 1999) suggests that revision is necessary. Given differences in tail-band width between the two described (but not widely accepted) subspecies, this white-tailed population may prove to be a third, rather than a new species or a hybrid between Himalayan and Sclater's. Research continues, but until further results are published we tentatively treat it as a form of Sclater's.

L. s. orientalis Davidson, 1974 occurs in NE Myanmar and W Yunnan (China); males differ from nominate in having a narrower tail band (10.5–20 mm versus 20–28 mm in nominate). Female has rump and uppertail-coverts greyish, inconspicuously barred white (nominate has narrow dark barring).

L. s. sclateri Jerdon, 1929 occurs in SE Tibet, N Arunachal Pradesh (India) and N Myanmar (Myanmar); described above.

Lophophorus sp. (taxon *incerta*) occurs in W (Subsaniri, Kameng and Tawang districts) Arunachal Pradesh (India); male has all-white tail, lacking chestnut band. Female appears to have rump and uppertail-coverts as nominate.

MEASUREMENTS Length: male 64–68 cm, female 62–64 cm. Male larger. *L. s. sclateri.* Males: wing 298–317, tail 195–223, tarsus c.73, weight c.2267–2948. Females: wing 266–302, tail 180–185, tarsus 71, weight 2126–2267.

HABITAT Montane coniferous forest with bamboo understorey and subalpine rhododendron scrub on rocky slopes. In Myanmar (Burma) it may remain entirely above the tree-line, never descending below c.2600 m. In China found at 2500–4200 m but extent of altitudinal movement uncertain. Reported to descend, in winter, to forests dominated by *Abies densa*, in Arunachal Pradesh.

VOICE In alarm utters a repeated shrill, but rather harsh, plaintive call. Far-carrying call of male is a loud whistled *go-li*, similar to that of Himalayan Monal, and described as 'part owl and part curlew'.

HABITS Little known but thought similar to Himalayan Monal. In summer, encountered in flocks among scrub and cliffs above the tree-line where they blend into the surroundings. Appears quite gregarious, even when breeding. Forages in early morning and late evening, in forest openings, presumably largely by digging, judging from the bill size and shape. Tubers of *Arisaema* sp. taken in Arunachal Pradesh.

BREEDING No information other than specimens taken in mid-May in breeding condition and a pair with two young seen in early June, in W Yunnan; reliable data on nest, clutch size or incubation is entirely lacking. In captivity clutch is 3–5, but no description of the eggs is available.

DISTRIBUTION E Himalayas, from border regions of W or C Arunachal Pradesh (India) and SE Tibet (west to the Lo La at 93°E) east through N Myanmar (Burma) and W Yunnan (west of the Salween River) in SC China.

STATUS Vulnerable. Abundance difficult to assess, but apparently rare over much of its small range, although it may be reasonably common in suitable areas. Little current information available, owing to the difficulty of travel within its physically remote and politically sensitive range, but it is known from a small number of sites in China and recently also from NE India. It occurs in Gaoligongshan and Lujian reserves, in Yunnan, China. Recent fieldwork in its increasingly fragmented range suggests a population of fewer than 10,000. Pressures, primarily habitat loss and hunting, appear quite localised and small scale, which is perhaps unsurprising given the remoteness of its habitat.

REFERENCES Ali & Ripley (1983), Bird Life International (2000, 2001), Grimmett *et al.* (1998), King *et al.* (2001), McGowan & Garson (1995), Smythies (1986), Kumar and Singh (1999, 2000).

120 CHINESE MONAL
Lophophorus lhuysii Geoffrey St. Hilaire and Verreaux, 1866   Plate 33

The largest and most highly glossed of the monals, restricted to montane WC China, where it is the only *Lophophorus*.

IDENTIFICATION A large crested monal of high-altitude forests in montane WC China, which does not overlap with the other two species. Male has extensive white on the rump and shorter uppertail-coverts (concealed by the folded wings when perched). Rather long shining blue-black tail contrasts strikingly with white rump if flushed. As well as being markedly larger, female differs from other monals in the relatively longer, more evenly barred tail (dark bars broader in other species), which lacks a white tip. Rump and uppertail-coverts very pale (recalling Sclater's), while both upper- and underparts are clearly streaked pale (like Himalayan). Females also possess a distinct rear crown tuft and whitish throat, albeit less extensive than in Himalayan.

DESCRIPTION Male has drooping, elongated crest just behind mid-crown; female a scruffy tuft on rear crown. Tail relatively longer than other monals. Bill long with enlarged and decurved upper mandible, overlapping lower mandible; greyish-horn (paler in female). Bare skin around eyes bright blue (paler and greyer in female). Irides brown. Legs greyish-horn (both sexes). Male has single short spur, female unspurred. Sexes differ. **Adult male:** Drooping purple-bronze crest. Head metallic green; chin, throat and foreneck black (occasionally glossed green). Rest of underparts velvety black, longer feathers fringed shining blue-green. Neck (except black foreneck) and mantle, brilliant golden-copper. Scapulars and inner wing blue fringed copper-bronze. Wing-coverts metallic blue, becoming purple-blue on inner greater

coverts and inner secondaries. Primaries and inner webs of secondaries dark brownish. Back, rump and shorter uppertail-coverts white, the latter with black wedge-shaped spots. Longer uppertail-coverts brilliant blue-green. Tail shining blue-green, with faint white shaft spots on outermost feathers. **First-year male:** No information. Assumed to possess a first-year plumage like other monals. **Adult female:** Chin and throat creamy-white, rest of head, neck and entire underparts, mantle and wings brownish-black, the feathers narrowly and evenly barred rufous-brown, and with buffish-white shaft streaks. Undertail-coverts have large buffish-white blotches. Back almost white, grading to pale grey on shorter uppertail-coverts; longer uppertail-coverts barred rufous-brown and blackish. Tail narrowly and evenly barred blackish-brown and rufous-brown. Orbital skin pale bluish. **Juvenile:** Undocumented; probably very similar to female.

GEOGRAPHICAL VARIATION Monotypic.

MEASUREMENTS Length: male 76–80 cm, female 72–75 cm. Male larger. Males: wing 345, tail 305, tarsus 72, weight 2837. Females: wing 285–320, tail 185–270, tarsus 71, weight 3178.

HABITAT Higher elevation coniferous and *Rhododendron* forest, and adjacent alpine meadows. Occurs at 3000–4900 m, with movements to below tree-line noted only in winter, but degree of altitudinal movement, if any, unknown.

VOICE Male call is a whistled series of three or four *guo-guo-guo* notes, given every few minutes, commencing on a high pitch, but after 3–4 minutes drops to a more mournful tone and then fades. In winter a dull

291

a...awu, a...awu heard. Alarm is a loud gabbled series of whistled *gee* notes upon taking flight.

HABITS Single- and mixed-sex flocks noted during breeding season, in areas with more than one pair. Groups, typically 2–8 individuals, observed more frequently in winter. Unearths bulbs, mosses and tubers, takes leaves and flowers in open areas, and some insects. Assumed to descend little, or not at all during winter, presumably implying that it can find snow-free areas, or is capable of digging through snow to feed. Males call on spring and summer mornings.

BREEDING Mating system unknown and very little information on breeding in the wild is available. Nests beside crags at 3800–4000 m. Clutch in captivity 3–5; eggs undescribed. Incubation, by female alone, occupies 28 days. May perhaps not breed every year. In captivity, males reach maturity at three years old and females at two.

DISTRIBUTION C China, centred on Sichuan Province, extending from W Sichuan, marginally into adjacent SE Qinghai, S Gansu, NE Tibet and NW Yunnan.

STATUS Vulnerable. Its range covers less than 50,000 km². Locally common, there are recent records from 25 sites in Sichuan, Gansu and Yunnan, but none from Qinghai, NW Sichuan or Tibet. The total population perhaps numbers 5,000–20,000. Mean density in Mia Mts (Sichuan) estimated at six per 1 km² in winter, declining to four in summer. It occurs in at least seven protected areas, including Wolong and Bai Shui Jang reserves, and it may also inhabit some recently established Giant Panda (*Ailuropoda melanoleuca*) reserves. A successful, USA–China cooperative captive-breeding programme was initiated in the 1980s. Perhaps in slight decline, owing to habitat degradation brought about by yak grazing and collection of herbs, and also through hunting in some areas.

REFERENCES BirdLife International (2000, 2001), Cheng (1987), Johnsgard (1986), McGowan & Garson (1995), MacKinnon & Phillips (2000), Rimlinger *et al.* (1998).

Genus *GALLUS*: junglefowls

Junglefowl form a very familiar and distinctive genus, indeed they are sufficiently distinct that it is difficult to consider them 'pheasants' at all. They have no close relatives and almost form their own subgroup. Cocks have a prominent fleshy coronal comb, throat wattles and ear lappets, and extensive bare facial skin. Tails are laterally compressed, of 14–16 feathers, those of cocks with elongated, rather soft-shafted, decurving central feathers which fall either side of the supporting shorter feathers of the ridged tail. Neck, back and rump feathers are elongated and usually pointed, forming hackles in cocks (these are shed following breeding in some species). Legs are relatively long, those of cocks bearing a single spur, hens usually unspurred.

121 RED JUNGLEFOWL
Gallus gallus (Linnaeus, 1758)   Plate 34

This very colourful inhabitant of tropical Asian forests is the wild ancestor of the domestic chicken. Precisely when junglefowls were first domesticated is uncertain, but they were certainly kept by ancient civilisations in the Indus Valley 5000 years ago, a habit which had spread to Europe by 1500 BC.

IDENTIFICATION Widespread in tropical Asian lowland forests, their presence indicated by the well-known *cockadoodle* call of the cockerel. Handsome male resembles domestic bantam cock, with fiery golden neck and back hackles, and is virtually unmistakable, though in parts of C India it overlaps with Grey Junglefowl, which has blunt, spangled neck hackles, grey body plumage and lacks whitish patch on uppertail-coverts (latter conspicuous when either running or flying away). Male assumes 'eclipse' plumage post-breeding, shedding neck hackles and elongated tail feathers; blackish head and neck then suggest Green Junglefowl but Red retains rufous in wing and Green has very limited range. Female differs from other junglefowls in combination of greyish legs, weakly streaked underparts (*contra* Grey and Sri Lanka Junglefowls) and noticeable golden fringes to neck feathers forming a shawl. Compare female with Red Spurfowl, female *Lophura* pheasants and female

Black Francolin, the latter being most easily confused when flushed as both have dark tails. Junglefowl tend to rise almost vertically and drop back to cover quite quickly, whereas Black Francolin favours more open country and flies at a shallower angle over a greater distance when flushed.

DESCRIPTION *G. g. murghi*. Male has extensive bare reddish skin on face and throat, dominated by large, deeply toothed, red fleshy coronal comb, single red wattles either side of throat and small lappets of whitish skin develop by ear-coverts (sometimes red in other subspecies). See genus introduction for general structural features. Neck hackles and elongated tail feathers lost after breeding. Though male plumage is acquired by first-winter it is not fully assumed until second year. Female has reduced or almost lacks comb, throat wattles and ear lappets but has bare pinkish facial and throat skin. Bill horn, almost pale pinkish in breeding season. Irides pale orange to reddish-brown (cock) or brown (hen). Tarsi grey or brownish-grey, rather long, cock with a single, long sharp spur, hen usually unspurred. Sexes differ. **Adult male breeding:** Extensive shawl of narrowly elongated, pointed, black-shafted shining straw-yellow to golden- and orange-yellow hackles over rear crown, neck and mantle. Back glossy black, with green and blue sheen. Rump hackles long and pointed, orange-red becoming maroon-red on back. Uppertail-coverts slightly elongated, metallic green-black. Tail metallic green-black, central feathers greatly elongated, with white feather bases visible as striking white patch on lower rump. Upperwing glossy green-black, with contrasting orange-red lesser and median coverts, flight feathers dull black edged rufous, forming rusty wing panel. Entire underparts black, only slightly glossed. **Adult male non-breeding (June–September):** Sheds golden hackles of upperparts and elongated tail feathers. Feathers of head and neck short, blunt and dull black. Retains rufous in wing. Comb reduced in size and paler in coloration. **First-year male:** Hackles shorter than adult, overall coloration duller and spurs shorter. **Adult female:** Feathers of head and neck slightly elongated and pointed, dark brown broadly edged straw-yellow. Upperparts, including wing-coverts, reddish-brown with narrow dark shaft streaks, vermiculated dark brown. Flight feathers dark brown, edged rufous. Tail dark brown, mottled rufous on all but outermost feathers. Underparts have indistinct pale shaft streaks, reddish-brown, vermiculated brown and becoming paler rufous on belly centre. Rear underparts blackish-brown on undertail-coverts. **Juvenile:** Similar to hen, but darker, especially on underparts; young males soon develop reddish-yellow neck hackles and feathering on back, and have blacker tails than female.

GEOGRAPHICAL VARIATION Distinctly clinal, with intergradation between four of the five recognised subspecies. Differ chiefly in size of facial lappets, and colour and shape of neck hackles of breeding cocks. Neck hackles of hens vary in similar manner, but are much shorter than in cock.
  G. g. gallus (Linnaeus, 1758) (includes *philippensis* and *robinsoni*) occurs in Cambodia, C and S Vietnam, C and S Laos and E Thailand; neck hackles of cock long and golden-orange to bright red, and ear lappets large and white. Philippine populations often regarded as introduced, but Dickinson *et al.* (1991) regarded *philippensis* as valid.
  G. g. spadiceus (Bonnatere, 1791) occurs in SW Yunnan (China) and adjacent extreme E Arunachal Pradesh (India), Myanmar, Thailand (except east), Peninsular Malaysia and N Sumatra (Indonesia); neck hackles of cock shorter than nominate and golden-yellow, and ear lappets small and red.
  G. g. jabouillei Delacour & Kinnear, 1928 occurs in N Vietnam, SE Yunnan and Hainan (China); darker and redder than nominate, with all hackles of cock shorter and less pointed, those of neck more golden-yellow, facial lappets and comb shorter, and all red. Hen darker than most other races.
  G. g. murghi Robinson & Kloss, 1920 (includes *gallina*) occurs in India, Nepal, Bhutan and Bangladesh; described above, like *spadiceus* but neck hackles yellower, the longer ones with black shaft-streaks, rump hackles paler orange, ear-lappets white and much smaller, and hen paler than other races.

  G. g. bankiva Temminck, 1813 occurs in S Sumatra, Java and Bali; like *spadiceus* but neck hackles even shorter and more rounded, golden-yellow.

MEASUREMENTS Length male 65–78 cm, female 41–46 cm. *G. g. gallus.* Male wing 203–250, tail 260–275 (300–380 *murghi*, 167–340 *jabouillei*), tarsus c.70–80, spur c.25 sometimes up to 50, weight 672–1450; female wing 177–200, tail 145–165, small spur sometimes present, weight 485–1050.

HABITAT Broad variety of habitats throughout range, especially lightly wooded areas such as forest edges and secondary forest, though in some areas (e.g. Java) occurs within forest. Recorded to c.2000 m in Malaysia and Yunnan. Where overlaps with Green Junglefowl, habitat segregation is clear, with latter occupying more open areas, e.g. meadows. In India it is closely associated with moister sal *Shorea* forest, as opposed to drier teak *Tectona* forest favoured by Grey Junglefowl.

VOICE Typical call of male very reminiscent of the *cock-a-doodle-do* of farmyard or village chicken, though usually more shrill and with strangulated finale. Mainly given from roost at dawn and prior to roosting in evening. A considerable number of different calls (c.30) have been described, including various clucks and cackling calls used in alarm and while feeding, as well as other contact and 'contentment' calls.

HABITS Wary, quickly disappearing into cover beside scrub-forest tracks and field edges, where it is often encountered. Usually in groups, typically a male and several females, particularly in winter. Emerges in open in early morning and late afternoon to feed, which it does by scratching ground and picking items from floor. Spends rest of day in cover. During dry periods, visits to water sources become part of daily routine. Roosts socially in trees and bushes from which males crow in early morning. If flushed, escapes very noisily into surrounding trees where sits on perch and can be very difficult to locate.

BREEDING Mating pattern variable and both monogamy and polygamy considered reasonably common. The number of males a female is associated with appears to vary as season advances. Nest typically a scrape on ground lined with dry grass, palm fronds and bamboo leaves below bush or within clump of bamboo in dense second growth and bamboo forest. Clutch usually 5–6, though 4–12 reported. Eggs very similar to domestic chicken, varying from pale buff to pale reddish-brown. Breeds in most months over broad range, typically March–May during dry season in India, March–June in Bangladesh, year-round (peak January–February) on Malay Peninsula, and February–May in China. Incubation by female alone lasts 18–21 days. Chicks able to fly at one week.

DISTRIBUTION Throughout much of SE Asia, from Java and Bali north through Sumatra, and Malay Peninsula north to S Yunnan, Guangxi and Hainan (China), and west through Myanmar and Bangladesh to NC India (west to low-lying areas of C Madhya Pradesh and south to Godaveri River in NE Andhra Pradesh). Sporadic older records from further west correspond to former range, which extended to S Gujarat and almost Bombay. In north it extends through *terai* at foot of Himalayas, through Bhutan and Nepal to Jammu and Kashmir in NW India. Introduced populations occur in many parts of world, including many Pacific islands and it may even be an ancient introduction to both Java and Bali. Those in Philippines and Sundas east of Bali (where it occurs east to Timor and Wetar) are also thought to have been introduced. Also introduced elsewhere in world, e.g. in West Indies, where occurs in Dominican Republic, Puerto Rico and the Grenadines.

STATUS Widespread and common in some areas and in others more patchily distributed. Fairly common within protected areas in India, locally common in lowland forests of Nepal and Bhutan, whereas in Bangladesh it is much more sparsely distributed. In Thailand it is common and widespread, despite continued hunting and it is more or less common throughout the Malay Peninsula. In Indonesia it is still widespread but declining, being now scarce on Java (with most recent reports in the montane west)

and not very common on Sulawesi or in the Lesser Sundas (where it is probably feral, see above). Known from more than 100 protected areas throughout its range. Intriguingly, it has been suggested that hybridisation with domestic stock around villages has resulted in genetic contamination of wild populations and that it may be more threatened than thought, but through loss of the wild genotype rather than reduction in overall numbers. The usual threats are, however, much in evidence, it being especially heavily hunted in Sulawesi and Thailand and in parts of Nepal. Habitat loss and degradation are problems in many areas, though it persists mainly in human-modified habitats in several areas, e.g. the Malay Peninsula, where probably most at risk from hybridization with domestic stock.

REFERENCES Ali & Ripley (1983), Arshad & Zakaria (1998), Baker (1930), Collias & Collias (1967), Collias & Saichuae (1967), Delacour (1977), Grimmett *et al.* (1998), Morejohn (1968), Parkes (1962), Wells (1999).

122 GREY JUNGLEFOWL
Gallus sonneratii Temminck, 1813

Plate 34

Alternative name: Sonnerat's Junglefowl.

An elegant and distinctive junglefowl, replacing Red Junglefowl in S India, having adapted to drier forests. This is particularly noticeable within limited contact zones in C India, where the two are segregated ecologically.

IDENTIFICATION Endemic to C and S India. Distinctive over most of range where it is the only junglefowl, but it marginally meets Red Junglefowl in C Madyha Pradesh, NE Andhra Pradesh and at least formerly on northern fringe of Western Ghats. Cocks readily distinguished from those of Red in boldly spotted dark and whitish, blunt neck hackles instead of golden-orange hair-like 'cape' of Red. Body plumage overall much greyer, finely streaked (visible if seen well), and though the orange-yellow elongated scapulars are conspicuous they hardly compare with the extensive fiery-orange hackles sported by Red. Additionally Grey lacks whitish patch at base of the tail shown by Red and has brighter, yellowish to reddish, legs (greyish in Red). Female most easily distinguished from female Red by boldly spotted breast and underparts, plain wings and reddish or yellowish legs. Occasional hybridisation between the two recorded in narrow zone of overlap.

DESCRIPTION Male facial skin configuration similar to Red Junglefowl but comb only slightly and shallowly indented. Bare skin of face and throat, including various adornments, red except whitish patch by ear-coverts. See genus introduction for general structural features. Neck hackles elongated and blunt, these and central tail feathers lost post-breeding. Though male plumage is acquired by first-winter it is not fully assumed until second year. Female has reduced or almost lacks comb, throat wattles and ear lappets but has bare reddish facial and throat skin. Bill yellowish-flesh with dark brownish culmen. Irides yellow to orange-brown (both sexes). Tarsi (both sexes) yellow

to red (brightest when breeding); cock has single, long sharp spur, hen usually unspurred. Sexes differ. **Adult male breeding:** Extensive shawl of blunt, but elongated, blackish, boldly spotted hackles conceal rear crown, neck and upper mantle (each feather has 2–3 white spots and a waxy yellow spangle at tip). Back and rump purplish-black, with broad grey feather fringes and whitish shaft streaks. Hackles at rump-sides and scapulars long and pointed, orange-red, spotted white and yellow. Wing-coverts grey, median coverts edged rufous and tipped with waxy orange-yellow spangles. Greater coverts and flight feathers blackish-brown. Uppertail-coverts and tail purplish-black. Underparts grey with darker feather centres and whitish shaft streaks, fringed rufous on rear flanks and belly and darkening to blackish on vent and tibia. **Adult male non-breeding:** Sheds spotted neck hackles and elongated tail feathers. Head and neck feathers short and dull black. Comb reduced in size and paler. **First-year male:** Hackles, spurs and central tail feathers shorter than in adult, overall coloration duller, with retained female-like wing. **Adult female:** Feathers of head and neck buffy-brown narrowly edged darker brown, and pale centres marked with black lines. Upperparts, including wing-coverts brown, narrowly mottled black and with fine pale shaft streaking. Flight feathers dark brown. Tail very dark brown, weakly mottled rufous on fringes of central feathers. Throat unmarked whitish or buffy-white, rest of underparts buffy-whitish, with bold dark brown scaling, most prominently scalloped on flanks. **Juvenile:** Similar to hen, but darker, especially on underparts; young males soon develop reddish-yellow neck hackles and feathering on back, and have blacker tails than females.

GEOGRAPHICAL VARIATION Monotypic. Gradual radiating cline evident, from darkest individuals in southwest to paler populations in southeast, northeast and north. In view of this it appears unwise to recognise *wangyeli*, which has been described from Mt. Abu at northernmost limit of range. See also comment under Voice.

MEASUREMENTS Length: male 70–80 cm, female c.38 cm. Males: wing 220–255, tail 314–390, tarsus 70–80, weight 790–1136. Females: wing 190–215, tail 100–170, tarsus 60–67, weight 700–790.

HABITAT Favours drier forest types than Red, especially where teak *Tectona* is dominant. Known from a variety of wooded habitats with reasonably dense understorey, including *Lantana* thickets and secondary areas of mixed bamboo and other scrub in various forest types. Also forages around cultivation and in overgrown and abandoned tea, coffee and rubber plantations. Found to 1700 m in Eastern and Western Ghats and 2400 m in the Nilgiris.

VOICE Male 'crow' is loud, staccato and distinctive, being slightly grating and not particularly musical. Rendered as *kuk ka kuruk ka* or *kuck kaya kaya kuck* repeated up to five times per minute. Often preceded by wing flapping, which gives loud clapping sound. Males also occasionally heard to monotonously intone a loud, aggressive *klick...kluck kluck*. Significance of variation in vocalisations poorly understood, i.e. there is reported to be a distinct difference in timbre of cock's 'crow' between those in far north of range (Mt. Abu) and those of Kerala (Ali & Ripley 1983).

HABITS Similar in many respects to Red Junglefowl. Very wary, never far from cover into which it quickly disappears at slightest disturbance, though in some areas where it is not hunted it is quite tame. Usually seen singly, but occasionally in groups of up to 5–6 of one or both sexes. Large numbers recorded in areas where food seasonally or periodically abundant, such as seeding bamboo. Emerges in open in early morning and again either around noon or in late afternoon to feed, scratching with their feet and digging with their bills, often pecking at dung of large mammals (cattle, elephants etc.). Roosts socially in small trees, including

Acacia, and bamboo clumps where several perch side by side at 7–8 m. Males call in most months, but seemingly less during monsoon.

BREEDING Mating pattern unclear and perhaps variable, including both monogamy and polygamy depending upon situation. Nest as Red Junglefowl, often at base of a tree. Clutch typically 3–5, but sometimes 2 and can be up to 10 (perhaps resulting from two females laying in same nest); eggs similar to those of Red Junglefowl, being white to rosy and buff and usually unspotted. Breeds mainly February–May, but some activity throughout its range in most months, probably slightly later in north. Incubation by female alone lasts 20–21 days.

DISTRIBUTION India, over much of peninsula, south and west of Godaveri River watershed. In the west it ranges north through E Gujarat, where it reaches extreme S Rajasthan in vicinity of Mt. Abu.

STATUS Locally common through much, if not entire range. Formerly considered Near Threatened. Few detailed data, but no longer occurs in coastal plains of Kerala (if indeed it ever occurred there in any more than relict populations) and though it may be found in a variety of wooded habitats (including plantations), strong populations are now largely confined to protected areas, such as Periyar Tiger Reserve and Satpura National Park. Thus its extensive range may offer a deceptive picture of its true status and more detailed information from much of its range would be valuable. Thought to have suffered both from habitat loss and hunting, which may have commenced in the 1870s (aggravated by the gorgeous neck hackles being much in demand for making artificial flies for trout fishing in the USA). Currently, it suffers from trapping and collection of eggs in some areas, such as Periyar Tiger Reserve, where fuelwood collectors also remove understorey that the species uses extensively. Hybridisation with Red Junglefowl and domestic chickens reported in some areas.

REFERENCES Ali & Ripley (1983), Baker (1930), Grimmett *et al.* (1998), Morejohn (1968), Zacharias (1997).

---

123 SRI LANKA JUNGLEFOWL
Gallus lafayetii Lesson, 1831   Plate 34

Alternative names: La Fayette's Junglefowl, Ceylon Junglefowl.

A gorgeous junglefowl, endemic to Sri Lanka, sharing features of both Red and Green Junglefowls but quite distinct nevertheless.

IDENTIFICATION Endemic to Sri Lanka where it is the only junglefowl, though confusion could arise with wandering domestic poultry (which can be very similar to Red Junglefowl). Cocks readily differentiated from superficially similar Red in having rusty-orange (not black) breast and belly, so that entire body appears rusty-orange, contrasting with glossy black wings (which lack rufous panel on secondaries) and tail. Yellow centre to red-tipped comb and brighter, yellow or

reddish, legs are also distinctive. Hen has browner breast than female Grey and lacks shawl of golden feather edges of Red, and differs from both in clearly barred (not plain) wings and tail.

DESCRIPTION Male facial skin similar to Red Junglefowl but comb only slightly and shallowly indented. Bare skin of face and throat, including various adornments, red except elongate bright yellow patch on interior portion of comb. See genus introduction for general structural features. Narrow lanceolate, elongated hackles cover not only neck, but extend over much of body plumage. Like Green, but unlike both Red and Grey, there is no distinct 'eclipse' plumage after breeding. Though male plumage is acquired by first-winter it is not fully assumed until second year. Female has reduced or almost lacks comb, throat wattles and ear lappets but has bare pinkish facial and throat skin. Bill yellowish-flesh with dark brownish culmen. Irides yellow to orange-yellow (cock), or brown (hen). Tarsi (both sexes) brownish-yellow to red (brightest in breeding males). Cock has single, sharp spur, hen usually unspurred. Sexes differ. **Adult male:** Extensive cape of narrowly elongated, pointed, shining orange-yellow, rusty-red or golden-yellow hackles over rear crown, neck, breast, mantle, rump and wing-coverts, partially concealing wings. These become orange-red on back. Yellowest hackles have narrow black central streak, redder feathers with maroon central streak. Lower back and rump coppery becoming glossy blue-black on longer uppertail-coverts; tail glossy blue-black. Upperwing glossy blue-black, with contrasting orange-red elongated lesser and median coverts. Belly, thighs and vent black. **First-year male:** Duller, with partially-feathered throat and lacking elongated central tail feathers. Feathers of neck short and blunt, blackish with yellow-brown fringes. Hackles shorter than adult, overall coloration duller and spurs shorter. **Adult female:** Feathers of head and neck dull rufous. Mantle blackish-brown, with whitish shaft streaks; rest of upperparts reddish-brown with fine vermiculations. Wings, both flight feathers and coverts, boldly barred buff, reddish-brown and blackish-brown. Tail rufous-brown, narrowly barred black. Throat buff-brown becoming darker rufous-brown on breast and flanks, each feather vermiculated black, but with large whitish central mark and fringe. Whitish on central belly, thighs and vent; each feather fringed black and finely barred at base. **Juvenile:** Similar to hen, but darker, especially on underparts; young males soon develop reddish-yellow neck hackles and rufous on underparts.

GEOGRAPHICAL VARIATION Monotypic. Race *xanthimaculatus* from the dry Northern Province, described on basis of minor differences, is rarely recognised.

MEASUREMENTS Length: male 66–72 cm, female c.36 cm. Males: wing 216–240, tail 230–400, tarsus 69–82, weight 790–1140. Females: wing 170–180, tail 108–118, tarsus 57–63, weight 510–625.

HABITAT Variety of wooded habitats, favouring dry forest, but including primary and montane rainforest, plantations and scrub–jungle from sea level to c.2300 m.

VOICE Male call typically loud, staccato and distinctive, comprising three separate notes and slightly more musical than Grey Junglefowl. Rendered as *chick chow-chik* with final *ik* higher than rest. This 'crow' also rendered as *tsek* (G. Joyce). In some contexts, these calls are preceded by a loud clapping sound produced by wing flapping. Females have a high-pitched, metallic *kwikukk kwikkukkuk* and both sexes give harsh *clock clock*.

HABITS Basically similar to Red Junglefowl. Shy and wary near habitation, such as by villages and roads, but rather tamer where it is not hunted. In some areas there is a distinct altitudinal migration from lowlands into hills to take advantage of abundant food available when the montane shrub, nillu *Strobilanthes*, seeds. Usually singly, but sometimes in groups of up to 5–6 of one or both sexes, and non-breeding males may feed in large groups. Emerges in open areas such as forest tracks in early morning and late afternoon to feed. Seeks cover during middle of day. Roosts socially in trees and bamboo clumps where several perch side by side, and from where males call to some degree through much of year.

BREEDING No reliable information on mating pattern, though pairs and trios observed. Nest of dry leaves sometimes in scrape on ground among buttress roots of large tree, or under logs etc., but usually slightly above ground in tree stump or branches up to 4 m above ground in dense growth. Clutch usually 2, but perhaps up to 5, even larger numbers probably result of two females laying in same nest. Eggs pale cream with very fine pale brown and purple spots. Breeds principally February–May, but perhaps also most other months depending on conditions. Incubation in captivity 20–21 days.

DISTRIBUTION Endemic to Sri Lanka, where occurs over much of the island, but is most abundant in more remote regions of the dry zone.

STATUS Locally plentiful in protected areas and more remote sites. Not considered globally threatened and appears tolerant of habitat modification and human disturbance, though there is no detailed recent information. Formerly reported to occur throughout the island, but apparently commoner in the drier east. There are recent records from much of the island, with most from the south, which receives greater ornithological coverage.

REFERENCES Ali & Ripley (1983), Grimmett *et al.* (1998), Henry (1971), Morejohn (1968), da Silva *et al.* (1993).

---

124 GREEN JUNGLEFOWL
Gallus varius (Shaw, 1798)

Plate 34

Alternative name: Javan Junglefowl.

A striking junglefowl, with multi-coloured facial and coronal skin, endemic to Java, Bali and adjacent islands, where it overlaps with the larger Red Junglefowl.

IDENTIFICATION Endemic to Indonesia, overlapping with Red Junglefowl on Java and Lombok. However, on Java, Green is very much restricted to more open lowland habitats, being replaced by much scarcer Red in montane forests. In contrast, on Lombok, Green has been recorded to 2400 m, but Red only to 1200 m. Except occasional hybrids (perhaps chiefly of feral origin), cocks unlikely to be confused as Green is distinctive in its highly glossed blackish-green plumage, contrasting with pale fringes to back hackles, straight-edged purplish comb and pinkish legs. Hen has barred wings and tail and pinkish legs (recalling female Sri Lanka Junglefowl), the upperparts are quite strongly scaled with blackish feather centres, whereas the underparts are only indistinctly patterned except rather contrasting white throat.

DESCRIPTION Male differs from Red Junglefowl in shape and colour of facial adornments. Comb green at base, becoming mauve and finally red at outer edge, latter not toothed. Single large throat lappet, red at base becoming pale yellow, and blue and purple at outer edge. Bare skin of face and throat red. See genus introduction for general structural features. Feathers of neck and mantle broad, almost square tipped. Narrow lanceolate, elongated hackles on back and rump, droop over wings. Like Sri Lanka, and unlike both Red and Grey, there is no distinct 'eclipse' plumage post breeding. Adult male plumage is acquired by first-winter. Female has reduced or almost lacks comb and throat wattle, has bare pinkish-red facial and throat skin. Bill yellowish with dark brownish culmen. Irides yellow (both sexes). Tarsi (both sexes) whitish, through pale yellow to pinkish-red (brightest in breeding males). Cock has single, sharp spur, hen usually unspurred. Sexes differ. **Adult male:** Head, neck and mantle black with square-tipped feathers subterminally fringed green and blue. Back and rump glossy blue-black with elongate, narrow, yellow-edged hackles. Tail glossy blue-black. Wings glossy blue-black, with contrasting orange-red edges to elongated lesser and median coverts. Underparts dull black. **First-year male:** Much as adult male but comb and throat wattle smaller, tail shorter and spurs less developed. **Adult female:** Feathers of head and neck dull brown. Upperparts blackish-brown, with pale buff shaft streaks and feather fringes, giving scaly appearance. Wings, both flight feathers and coverts, blackish-brown, feathers boldly edged pale buff. Tail blackish-brown, with metallic green and pale buff edges to feathers. Throat whitish, contrasting slightly with pale brown foreneck and breast, feathers narrowly edged black. Rear underparts greyish or warm buff, finely scaled darker, on central belly, thighs and vent. **Juvenile:** Similar to hen; young males soon develop adult male feathering.

GEOGRAPHICAL VARIATION Monotypic.

MEASUREMENTS Length male 65–75 cm, female 42–46 cm. Males: wing 220–245, tail 320–330, tarsus 70–75, weight 672–1450. Females: wing 180–195, tail 115–126, tarsus c.63–72, weight 485–1050.

HABITAT Typically in more open habitats than Red Junglefowl, e.g. savanna, grassland and woodland edge, but also lowland woodland and plantations. Occurs near settlements in some heavily populated areas. Though often considered to favour coastal lowlands, in the Lesser Sundas it inhabits montane areas. Recorded to 1500 m in W Java, 3000 m in E Java, 1500 m in Bali and 2400 m in Lesser Sundas.

VOICE 'Crow' of male is a crisp and shrill three-noted *cha-aw-awk* or *chow-a-aaaar*, the two terminal notes only slightly higher pitched than first; sometimes a short extra note precedes the phrase. Male also gives a slow cackling *wok-wok-wok...* and, when alarmed, a brisk *chop chop chop...*, whereas the female utters a rapid *kok kok kok...*

HABITS Wary close to habitation, e.g. near villages and roads, but generally rather tamer than Red Junglefowl, especially where it is not hunted. Usually singly, but sometimes in groups of 5–6, which may be family groups, and parties of up to 12 recorded. Emerges in open areas such as tracks and grain fields in very early morning and late afternoon to feed, where it often forages near grazing ungulates, preying on insects disturbed by the animals or feeding on latter's droppings. For most of day confined to undergrowth, though rarely found in dense forest.

BREEDING Assumed monogamous, based on sightings only of pairs and not males with two or more females. Nest a scrape among dense undergrowth, but occasionally in elevated situations. No reliable data on clutch size, but probably 3–4 (up to 10 claimed). Eggs unmarked buff-white. Breeds earlier in east than west and apparently subject to annual variation, thus seasonal delimitation difficult but perhaps largely June–November. Incubation in captivity 21 days.

DISTRIBUTION Endemic to Indonesia, where occurs on Java, Madura, Bawean, Bali and Kangean east through Lesser Sundas, on Lombok, Sumbawa, Komodo, Rinca, Flores, Besar, Paloe, Alor and Sumba.

STATUS Locally common in suitable habitat throughout range. Inhabits a broad range of open and lightly-wooded habitats (including secondary vegetation and plantations, such as coffee). Occurs close to densely populated areas in parts of Java. Given tolerance of altered habitats, protected areas may be unnecessary for its long-term survival, but it is found in several, including Ujong Kulon and Baluran National Parks in Java, and Bali Barat National Park. It hybridises with domestic chickens and this has been exploited in some areas, such as along the north coast of Bali, where the species is trapped and crossed with domestic stock to produce male offspring used in vocal competitions and known locally as 'bekisar'. This practice threatens to seriously affect wild populations in some areas through over-trapping.

REFERENCES Coates & Bishop (1997), Delacour (1977), Johnsgard (1986), Mackinnon & Phillips (1993), McGowan (1994), Morejohn (1968).

Genus *LOPHURA*: gallopheasants and firebacks

A large, complex genus encompassing at least nine medium-sized pheasant species of subtropical and tropical forests. In several respects they superficially recall junglefowls, though the two genera are probably not very closely related. Males of most species have long, graduated, tails, composed of 16 feathers, which are quite strongly arched and sometimes very elongated. Their rather long legs sport a single white spur in males, females are normally unspurred. *Lophura* contains a peculiar range of pheasants, most species were formerly allocated monotypic genera. Such clumsy treatment was revised by Delacour (1949) who united several genera and species.

Subgenus *GENNAEUS*: Kalij and Silver Pheasants

These pheasants replace each other geographically across vast stretches of hill and montane forests from Kashmir to Vietnam and E China. Currently 23 subspecies are recognised in this superspecies complex, which have been considered to form as many as six species in the past. Delacour's 1949 revision reduced this to two polymorphic species, placing emphasis on male leg coloration and the fact that western races (i.e. Kalij) become adult as first-years, whereas Silver Pheasants mature in their second year. Though Himalayan Kalij and northern races of Silver bear little resemblance to each other, there is a large area centred on the Yunnan/Myanmar/Thai border regions where differences are far from clear. McGowan & Panchen (1994) deduced that, based on a number of male features, the two species appear well separated by the lower Irrawaddy River, with Kalij extending slightly further east above the junction with the Chindwin, and the two extensively intermingling above the upper reaches of the Irrawaddy. In NE Myanmar, Kalij meets *occidentalis* Silver, a number of intermediate variations from this region have been named in the past, but Silver mainly tends to replace Kalij at higher elevations. By taking the lower Irrawaddy as the division between the two, McGowan & Panchen (1994) recommended treating all populations to the east as Silver Pheasant, those to the west being Kalij, and this is adopted here. The complex is in great need of taxonomic reassessment, and a study of female plumages may provide some interesting alternative interpretations.

125 KALIJ PHEASANT
Lophura leucomelanos (Latham, 1790)   Plate 36

Alternative name: Kaleej. See Geographical Variation for other names.

A dark, crested pheasant of Himalayan forests, widespread in its various forms which become particularly complex in the E Himalayas.

IDENTIFICATION Rather small dark pheasant of Himalayan forests, distinctive (particularly males) in having full arched tail, prominent crest and bare red facial skin in both sexes. It is the only *Lophura* present west of Myanmar. All races appear very dark in the field, indeed E Himalayan populations often look all black (little-known *moffitti* of C Bhutan is just that), but most have whitish scaling on rump (often hidden by folded wings), or on underparts (difficult to see if walking away from observer). Range does not overlap with other all-black *Lophura* pheasants in Vietnam and Sumatra. Western Kalij males (*hamiltoni*) have distinctive whitish crests and pale chest and flanks. Easternmost *williamsi* (W Myanmar) and *oatesi* (SW Myanmar) are very similar to westernmost forms of Silver Pheasant (*lineata* of E Myanmar and NW Thailand, *crawfurdii* of Tenasserim and SW Thailand). Though some interbreeding, between *williamsi* and *occidentalis* Silver, occurs in N Myanmar, further south the two species are separated by the Irrawaddy River. Most similar are males of *williamsi* Kalij and *lineata* Silver, but *williamsi* is darker and longer legged, with narrow white barring on rump, and entire tail is narrower and evenly obscured by linear markings (longest, arching feathers extensively clear buffy-white in *lineata*). Also close are *oatesi* Kalij and *crawfurdii* Silver: though *oatesi* virtually lacks white barring on rump, it does have greyish legs (as in all forms of Kalij) and a coarsely barred tail. Females vary from almost uniform pale brown (*hamiltoni*) to uniform dark rufous-brown,

most races have pale tips to body feathers giving slightly scaled effect but this is far less apparent than boldly patterned underparts of some forms of Silver Pheasant, which see for comparison.

DESCRIPTION *L. l. leucomelanos*. Bill greenish-horn. Bare skin around eyes red. Irides orange-brown. Legs greyish to purplish-brown. Sexes differ but both have prominent loose crest at rear crown. Tail elongated, slightly ridged, male with central tail feathers broad and long, tapering to point. **Adult male:** Forehead, crown, throat, neck and upperparts glossy blue-black, latter with indistinct whitish shaft streaks. Feathers of lower back, rump and uppertail-coverts broadly tipped white. Wings and tail blackish-brown, glossed greenish-blue. Underparts dull blackish, lanceolate feathers of breast and flanks edged whitish. **First-year male:** Attains adult male plumage as first-year. **Adult female:** Entire plumage quite uniformly dull brown, finely vermiculated blackish, contour feathers have pale shaft streak and pale fringe. Tail dark brown, with paler central feathers vermiculated black and buff. **Juvenile:** Similar to female but feathers of underparts have white spot at tip, and those of upperparts have dark subterminal bar and buff fringe.

GEOGRAPHICAL VARIATION Very variable. Broadly speaking, males in the Himalayas have blue-black upperparts with pale-coloured breasts, whereas in lower areas to the south, they have closely vermiculated upperparts with blackish underparts. Other traits also vary in some subspecies. For example, males of the western subspecies (*hamiltoni*) have a white or pale crest, in all others it is blue-black, and males of the Bhutanese *moffitti* are entirely black, lacking white terminal band to rump feathers. Females vary in saturation and colour tones, being typically paler in west.

Subspecies *lathami* and *williamsi* have blunt, not lance-olate tips to breast feathers, which may indicate more distant relationships than other forms, perhaps even to species level as *L. lathami*. Note that *oatesi* is sometimes treated within Silver Pheasant, but as its range lies west of the Irrawaddy and males have narrow white scaling on the rump, it is perhaps better considered an extreme form of Kalij.

L. l. hamiltoni (J. E. Gray, 1829) (White-crested Kalij) occurs in the W Himalayas from Indus River in N Pakistan east to W Nepal; male has whitish or very pale crest, broad whitish barring on rump and brownish-white edges to lanceolate under-parts feathering; female almost uniformly medium brown, only weakly marked, tail darker.

L. l. leucomelanos (Latham, 1790) (Nepal Kalij) (includes *fockelmanni*) occurs in W to EC Nepal; male has shorter blackish crest, less extensive pale fringes on underparts and narrower whitish barring on rump than *hamiltoni*; female darker brown than *hamiltoni* with broader greyish fringes to underparts feathers.

L. l. melanota (Hutton, 1848) (Black-backed Kalij) occurs in extreme E Nepal (Mai Valley), through Sikkim to W Bhutan (east to Mo Chu); male has upperparts wholly blue-black, lacking whitish barring, but sometimes has whitish edging to wing-coverts; underparts as nominate but less distinct whitish feather edging; female darker than nominate, with whitish throat, more distinct pale scaling to body plumage and slightly shorter crest.

L. l. moffitti (Hachisuka, 1938) (Black Kalij) occurs in C Bhutan (recent sightings in Black Mountains National Park); male wholly glossy blue-black above and below; female like *melanota* but throat buffier and central tail peppered, rather than vermiculated.

L. l. lathami (J. E. Gray, 1829) (Black-breasted Kalij) (includes *horsfieldi*) occurs in E Bhutan, Arunachal Pradesh and Manipur (India), E Bangladesh and extreme SE Tibet (Pome) and NW Yunnan (those from W Myanmar are perhaps better included in *williamsi*); crest more erect and underparts feathers blunter (not lanceolate) than in previous forms, with shorter, straighter tail and relatively longer legs; male glossy-black except broad white barring on rump and uppertail-coverts; female much more uniformly rufous-brown than previous forms, with only faint pale tips and very indistinct tail markings.

L. l. williamsi (Oates, 1896) (Williams's Kalij) occurs in W Myanmar and perhaps extreme E Manipur (India); shape and feather structure as *lathami*; male glossy blue-black, but hindneck and entire upperparts, including tail, vermiculated with fine white lines (looks grey at distance); rump and uppertail-coverts have narrow white scaly tips; and female paler brown than *lathami*, with unmarked paler brown central tail feathers.

L. l. oatesi (Ogilvie-Grant, 1898) (Oates's Kalij) occurs in Arakan Yomas in SW Myanmar; male similar to *williamsi* but breast-side feathers lanceolate and have narrow whitish shaft streaks; over-all dull, not glossy black and with no, or very narrow and indistinct, white scaling on rump and

uppertail-coverts; central tail feathers may be less intensely vermiculated on inner web (thus approaches *crawfurdii* Silver in some respects); and female rufous-brown, with fine buff shaft streaks on breast and flanks, tail reddish-brown, with irregular coarse dark markings.

MEASUREMENTS Length male 63–74 cm, female 50–60 cm. Considerable overlap among subspecies. Subtle differences between *oatesi*, *lathami–williamsi* and others are indicated (notably longer tarsus of eastern birds). There are no meaningful data available for *moffitti*. Western races (*hamiltoni*, *leucomelanos*, *melanota*): male wing 215–250, tail 230–305, tarsus 75–80, weight 800–1150; female wing 198–222, tail 186–215, tarsus 65–70, weight 848–1025. Eastern races (*lathami*, *williamsi*): male wing 210–247, tail 210–265, tarsus 76–96, weight 1025–1700; female wing 205–230, tail 190–225, tarsus 68–76, weight 715–750. Arakan race *oatesi*: male wing 235–295, tail 275–300; female wing 206–220, tail 191–202.

HABITAT Wide range, from secondary vegetation and abandoned cultivation to all types of forest (including sal, oak, spruce and rhododendron, and other evergreen and deciduous forests) with dense undergrowth. Recorded from 35 m, in Bangladesh, and to 3700 m in Nepal.

VOICE Varied repertoire, but can be virtually silent during day, though often quite noisy in areas where undisturbed. At dawn and dusk gives a call described as a loud whistling chuckle or chirrup. During breeding season male makes a drumming sound by flapping half-open wings against body while displaying to female, typically in deep cover. When disturbed emits a series of guinea-pig like squeaks and chuckles, or a rapid *koorchi koorchi koorchi* or, if forced to fly, a whistling *psee psee psee*.

HABITS Quite wary, spending much time in secondary and scrubby undergrowth. Group size varies during year; usually encountered in groups of 2–10 or more, disbanding as pairs or trios in January onwards. Larger groups probably represent family parties after breeding. Emerges in early morning and late afternoon onto tracks and in fields to feed, which it does mostly by pecking and scratching ground, but also by digging. Makes excursions to water sources. Roosts socially with several on same branch, to c.15 m above ground in medium-sized trees; generally used on consecutive nights.

BREEDING Mating pattern uncertain, but variation in number of females accompanying males suggests both monogamy and polygamy occur. Nest a scrape in undergrowth, with plenty of cover and close proximity to water apparently important. Clutch usually 6–9; eggs similar to domestic chicken and vary from creamy-white to reddish-buff. Incubation, from 20 days (in warmer climes) to 22 days at higher altitudes, by female alone.

DISTRIBUTION Broad range, from Indus River in Pakistan east, in India along front ranges of the Himalayas, through Nepal and Bhutan and W Myanmar, extending into E Bangladesh, SE Tibet and NW Yunnan (SC China). Introduced to Hawaiian Is.

STATUS Variable, being scarce and local in Pakistan, fairly common and widespread in Nepal, common in India and Bhutan, and rare in Bangladesh. Few recent data from Myanmar, where it was regarded as common 50 years ago. It inhabits a wide variety of habitats, including second growth and plantations, such as teak. One subspecies, *moffitti*, is especially poorly known and its conservation status is unknown. The species occurs in many protected areas, including Ayubia and Marghalla Hills National Parks, Chail, Kalesar and Maenam Wildlife Sanctuaries in India, and the Black Mountains National Park in Bhutan. While Kalij occur mostly in secondary habitats and close to villages, there are limits to the extent of habitat alteration it can tolerate—excessive habitat degradation is a concern, as is hunting in some areas.

REFERENCES Ali & Ripley (1980), Grimmett *et al.* (1998), McGowan & Garson (1995), McGowan & Panchen (1994), Roberts (1991), Robson (2000), Smythies (1986).

126 SILVER PHEASANT
Lophura nycthemera (Linnaeus, 1758)   Plate 36

Alternative names: see Geographical Variation.

Northern, whitest populations are stunningly lovely, however, even the darker, less fancy southern races are beautifully patterned. Some of these, however, are often considered to belong with its sister species, Kalij Pheasant.

IDENTIFICATION Combination of red legs, black underparts and white or close-barred (appearing grey) upperparts, with long arching or very long tail, renders male unmistakable in most of range. Southern and southwestern races, notably *lineata* (E Myanmar) and *crawfurdii* (Tenasserim and SW Thailand), however, are shorter tailed, have intensely vermiculated upperparts and appear very similar to easternmost races of Kalij (which see). Interbreeding between *williamsi* Kalij and *occidentalis* Silver occurs in N Myanmar, producing a number of intermediates. Females vary according to population, from almost uniform olive-brown, through chestnut to uniform dark brown, some races have pale shaft streaks to body feathers while others have blackish underparts with bold white streaks or spots (see Geographical Variation). Apart from range, it is basically the reddish legs which is the most useful distinction from female Kalij. In Vietnam (and perhaps E Laos) be aware of the possibility of confusion with females of other, much rarer, *Lophura* pheasants, notably Imperial, Vietnamese and Edwards's (which see).

DESCRIPTION *L. n. nycthemera*. Bill greenish-horn. Bare facial skin scarlet. Irides orange (adult male) or brown (female). Legs reddish to bright red, greyish in *lineata* and variable, usually greyish-pink, in *crawfurdii*. Sexes differ but both have prominent loose crest on rear crown. Tail elongated, slightly ridged, male with central tail feathers broad and very long, tapering to a point. Adult male plumage not attained until second year (unlike Kalij). **Adult male:** Forehead, crown and mop-like crest glossy blue-black. Head-sides, neck and nape virtually unmarked white, and rest of upperparts including wings and tail white, each feather pencilled with several narrow black lines, loops or chevrons. Tail has many fine irregular black bars over basal portion of each feather. Chin, throat, foreneck and rest of underparts glossy black; feathers at breast-sides and fore flanks with white streaks. **First-year male:** Upperparts closely mottled buff and black, and crest black. Tail longer than female, with more prominent barring on outer feathers. Underparts dull blackish, with irregular whitish chevrons. **Adult female:** Entire plumage quite uniformly dull olive-brown, finely peppered blackish, contour feathers with pale shaft streaks. Crest has black tip. Tail olive-brown, with outer feathers mottled black, brown and white. **Juvenile:** Similar to female but wing-covert feathers have narrow buff and black tips.

GEOGRAPHICAL VARIATION Very variable, with c.15 subspecies recognised. Some male characters, such as tail length and whiteness of upperparts, are clinal, increasing northeastwards from Myanmar. There may be a case for lumping the larger, longer tailed, whitest subspecies as clinal variants of the nominate, though more work on female plumages could place a different perspective on Silver Pheasant taxonomy. Some isolated subspecies (including those in the south) also vary in relative thickness of the black-and-white V markings on upperparts, which affects how pale or dark they appear in the field. Races *lineata* and *crawfurdii* are often included in Kalij Pheasant.

L. n. lineata (Vigors, 1831) (Lineated Kalij/Pheasant) occurs in E Myanmar and NW Thailand; male has upperparts very finely and closely vermiculated (appears grey in field), whitish streaking on breast-sides, rather long, broad tail coarsely vermiculated becoming unmarked buffy-white on arch and at tip, and legs greyish or brownish; female buffy-brown, with darker brown crest, becoming rich rufous below, underparts with bold white streaks, upperparts with white chevrons and dark feather edges to nape and mantle. Tail buffish, the outer feathers barred rufous, black and white.

L. n. crawfurdii (J. E. Gray, 1829) (includes *sharpei*) (Crawfurd's Kalij/Pheasant) occurs in SE Myanmar (Tenasserim) and SW Thailand; male resembles *lineata* but legs often reddish, vermiculations on upperparts coarser and tail rather shorter; female darker, with almost blackish underparts, more boldly streaked white below and often has reddish legs.

L. n. lewisi (Delacour & Jabouille, 1928) occurs in Elephant and Cardamom Hills of SW Cambodia and SE Thailand; male similar to *crawfurdii* but crest and tail slightly longer, markings of upperparts coarser and in the form of chevrons (not lines); female quite different to *crawfurdii*, having rufous-brown upperparts and tail, and greyish-buff underparts, with weak whitish shaft streaks.

L. n. annamensis (Ogilvie-Grant, 1906) occurs in S Annam (Vietnam); male differs from preceding forms in white band on neck-sides and narrower, straighter tail; female has quite long crest and is uniform dull brown, with rufous tail, and mantle and underparts have faint pale shaft streaks.

L. n. engelbachi Delacour, 1948 occurs on Bolovens Plateau, S Laos; male resembles *annamensis* but has narrower, irregular, white band on neck-side and upperparts have broader white markings; female has entire upperparts chestnut-brown, brighter on tail, and paler rufous underparts vary from virtually plain to being streaked and peppered white.

L. n. beli (Oustalet, 1898) occurs in C Annam (Vietnam), at higher elevations in E Annamitic Mts; male like *engelbachi* but white band on neck-side broken or absent, white markings on upperparts finer, and has narrower, more arching tail, which is whiter, less buffy, on central feathers; female bright rufous-brown overall, brightest on tail, and has white-streaked underparts.

L. n. berliozi (Delacour & Jabouille, 1928) occurs in C Annam (Vietnam), in W Annamitic Mts; male has whiter upperparts and longer tail than previous forms, with mantle and most of neck white (except front), central tail mostly white (but wholly vermiculated in some); female like female *beli* but vermiculated white on vent and belly.

L. n. rufipes (Oates, 1898) occurs in N Myanmar in Northern Shan States between Irrawaddy and Salween Rivers; male resembles *engelbachi* but larger and with longer tail, but lacks white at neck-sides; female resembles female *ripponi* or *occidentalis* rather than *engelbachi*.

L. n. ripponi (Sharpe, 1902) (includes *jonesi*) occurs in N and C Thailand, SW Yunnan (China) and N Myanmar in Southern Shan States; male has full black crest, and compared to *berliozi* has even whiter upperparts and much longer tail; female dark dull brown above, with dark chestnut tail, underparts dark brown to blackish, with pale buff or white chevrons.

L. n. occidentalis Delacour, 1948 occurs in NW Yunnan (China) and NE Myanmar; male similar to *ripponi* but tail longer; female quite different, having underparts closely mottled rich buff and dark brown, and brighter dark chestnut tail, which is finely vermiculated.

L. n. beaulieui Delacour, 1948 occurs in SE Yunnan (China), N Laos and N Vietnam; male similar to previous two races but tail slightly shorter; female dark brown, underparts with broken pale buff or whitish bands, sometimes forming reticulated pattern, and outer tail mottled and barred black, brown and white.

L. n. fokiensis Delacour, 1948 occurs in NW Fujian (and possibly Zhejiang) (China); male similar to *beaulieui* but tail longer, with wavy lines over basal half of inner webs; female dark olive-brown, often lightly peppered or vermiculated greyish-white on underparts.

L. n. nycthemera (Linnaeus, 1758) occurs in Guangdong and Guangxi in S China and N Vietnam; male larger and whiter than all other forms; see Description.

L. n. whiteheadi (Ogilvie-Grant, 1899) occurs on Hainan (China); male similar to nominate but black markings on upperparts much bolder, tail very long, with white central feathers and boldly barred lateral feathers; female very distinctive, having chestnut upperparts and short dark chestnut crest, with mantle and underparts boldly patterned: each feather white at centre with black border.

L. n. omeiensis Cheng, Chang & Tang, 1964 occurs in C Sichuan (China); another distinctive form, male similar to nominate but has most tail feathers (except long white central pair) extensively black at base; female overall dark brown with blackish lateral tail feathers.

L. n. rongjiangensis Tan & Wu, 1981 occurs in SE Guizhou (China); few data available, reported to resemble both *beaulieui* and nominate in basic appearance.

MEASUREMENTS Length: male 80–125 cm, female 56–71 cm. Considerable overlap among subspecies. In general, northern forms are larger and have strikingly longer tails. For example, males of the most northerly subspecies, *omeiensis*, have wing 276–299 and tail 765–800, while those of one of the most southerly, *crawfurdii*, have wing 240–250 and tail only 270–290. Western races (*lineata, crawfurdii*): male wing 220–260, tail 230–345, tarsus 72–76; female wing 203–235, tail 202–272. Southern races (*lewisi, engelbachi, annamensis*): male wing 220–260, tail 230–345, tarsus 75–89; female wing 203–235, tail 220–238. Northern races (the remaining 10 subspecies): male wing 230–305, tail 340–800, tarsus 95–105, weight (*occidentalis*) 1425–1725; female wing 150–270, tail 225–353, weight (*occidentalis*) 1150 (n=1).

HABITAT Variety of forested, scrub and open habitats to 2200 m. In China in open scattered forests and alpine meadows and in Thailand inhabits both semi-evergreen and hill-evergreen forests. In Laos, Vietnam and Cambodia reportedly widespread in montane evergreen forest and also in submontane forest, in places down to 300 m (but higher in others, such as on Bolovens Plateau in S Laos).

VOICE During breeding season, male call likened to both Common Pheasant (but shorter and deeper) and Kalij. Male displays to female by wing-whirring and uttering a quiet, trill-like *koo koo*. Soft whistles uttered while feeding. A shrill whistle if disturbed.

HABITS Little information, but apparently similar to Kalij Pheasant, spending much time in secondary growth and scrub. Encountered in groups of up to at least 7–8. Emerges in early morning and late afternoon on tracks and in grassy areas and fields to feed, which it does mostly by pecking and scratching ground, but also by digging. When disturbed typically escapes by running.

BREEDING Observations of single males with several females suggest polygamy. Nest poorly described. Clutch averages 7, but can be up to 12; eggs of *nycthemera* pale to dark rosy buff. Breeding season appears to vary across range, in China being mid-March in the southeast and from April elsewhere, and March–May in N Myanmar and Thailand. Incubation in captivity is 25–26 days.

DISTRIBUTION From E Myanmar (east of the Irrawaddy), including Tenasserim, adjacent W, N and C Thailand, through much of E Laos and Vietnam (south to C Annam), with isolated populations in Elephant and Cardamom Mountains on Thai–Cambodia border, on Bolovens Plateau in S Laos and S Vietnam (Dong Nai, Lam Dong and Ninh Thuan Provinces). Also across S China, from Yunnan north to Guizhou and Sichuan, and northeast through Guangxi and Guangdong to Fujian, Zhejian and Anhui, with an isolated population on Hainan.

STATUS Variable across range, being generally common to very common in China, but at risk in Thailand and sparingly recorded in Laos. Considered

common in Myanmar 50 years ago. Some subspecies, typically isolated ones, such as *annamensis* in C Vietnam, *engelbachi* in Laos and *whiteheadi* on Hainan are probably threatened. Like the Kalij, it inhabits a variety of wooded habitats, including secondary vegetation, but is possibly less inclined to venture into open and may be more restricted in degree of open vegetation it tolerates. Occurs in many protected areas, including Bach Ma and Cuc Phuong National Parks in Vietnam, Tianmushan and Ba Wang Ling and many other Natural Reserves in China, and Khao Soi Dao, Kaeng Krachen and Khao Sam Roi Yot Wildlife Sanctuaries in Thailand. Excessive habitat degradation is a concern, as is hunting in some areas.

REFERENCES Johnsgard (1986), McGowan (1994), McGowan & Garson (1995), McGowan & Panchen (1994), Robson (2000), Smythies (1986).

Subgenus *HIEROPHASIS*: vietnamese pheasants

The three taxa in this group are very rare, little known and of uncertain taxonomic status. Initial genetic studies have revealed little difference in DNA and consequently Edwards's and Vietnamese are perhaps better treated as conspecific, while Imperial may have originated as a rare hybrid between Vietnamese Pheasant and *annamensis* Silver Pheasant. The rediscovery in the past decade of both Edwards's and Imperial, after having been feared extinct in the wild for over 60 years, indicates the great conservation importance of remaining lowland forest in Vietnam. Perhaps then, detailed study may reveal the true relationships between these enigmatic pheasants.

127 IMPERIAL PHEASANT
Lophura imperialis (Delacour & Jabouille, 1924)   Plate 35

This dark blue pheasant is known from fewer than a handful of wild individuals. Following nearly 70 years of mystery one was trapped in 1990, and another, 10 years later. The recent rediscovery indicates that it must be one of the world's rarest birds, although it now appears certain that it is just a rare hybrid between Silver and Vietnamese Pheasants.

IDENTIFICATION Lowland forests of C Vietnam, where very rare. Confusion most likely with female and first-year male Vietnamese Pheasant (latter has all-dark tail), which is known from the site that produced the 1990 record of Imperial; such individuals differ in much the same way as Edwards's. Male Imperial is wholly dark blue-black (including short, ruffled crest), with red legs and facial skin. Larger, with rather more downcurving, longer tail than Vietnamese and Edwards's, and lacks white in crest. Fortunate observers should check for less highly glossed plumage (notably less green in wings). Female pale grey-brown on head becoming pale brown overall, with chestnut and greyish fringes and pale shaft streaks to upperparts feathers; tail blackish-brown, more rufous on central feathers. Presumably also overlaps with *annamensis* Silver Pheasant, females of which are similar, but Imperial has darker tail and dull brown, ruffled rear crown, whereas *annamensis* Silver has a longer, almost blackish-brown crest, reddish

(not blackish) outer tail and is overall more rufous-brown. Larger than Edwards's, with more distinct crest, paler underparts and chestnut feather centres which give a more rufous and mottled appearance to body plumage.

DESCRIPTION Crown has short, ruffled crest. Tail broadly pointed, narrowly tapering and curving central feathers. Bill pale yellowish-green with blackish at very base (adult) or pale whitish or greyish-horn (immature). Irides reddish-orange (adult male) or olive-ochre (immature male). Extensive scarlet bare facial skin. Legs crimson (adult male) or pinkish-red (immature male). Claws and spurs whitish (immature male). Sexes differ. Male assumes adult plumage during second year at c.18 months old. **Adult male:** Short crest blue-black. Plumage wholly dark blue, each feather blackish at base, with broad blue terminal fringe. Fringes of back, rump, uppertail-coverts and wing-coverts brighter and more metallic blue, with deeper black base. Tail bluish-black, inconspicuously spotted brown. **First-year male:** Almost wholly dark brown with bluish fringes to feathers of upperparts. Crest, spurs and tail all shorter than adult. **Adult female:** Crest even shorter than male. Head pale greyish-brown becoming even paler on chin and throat. Underparts pale greyish-chestnut, slightly mottled. Upperparts chestnut-brown, brightest on uppertail-coverts, with weak dark vermiculations and pale shaft streaks. Primaries black, with grey vermiculations along shaft, secondaries black edged chestnut. Tail blackish, the central feathers chestnut-brown, vermiculated black. **Juvenile:** Like female but more olive-brown, with slightly stronger vermiculations. Subterminal black marks to feathers of upperparts give a more scaly appearance. Tail pale chestnut.

GEOGRAPHICAL VARIATION None, but taxonomy uncertain.

MEASUREMENTS Length: Male c.75 cm, female c.60 cm. Males: wing 248–252, tail 241–303, tarsus 87–103, weight, no data. Females: wing 194–234, tail 176–290, tarsus 67, weight, no data.

HABITAT The 1990 individual was trapped in lowland broad-leaf secondary evergreen forest, at 50–100 m. Originally collected in rugged limestone mountains covered in dense forest and brush.

VOICE No information, but Kalij-like wing whirring reported.

HABITS No information on its habits in the wild.

BREEDING No information from the wild. Captive clutch size 5–7; eggs creamy to rosy-buff 'with small white pit marks' and incubation lasts 25 days.

DISTRIBUTION Known only from Dong Hoi/Quang Tri provincial border and Ke Go, 12 km west of Cat Bin in Ha Tinh Province, both in southern N Annam (Vietnam).

STATUS Data Deficient. Extremely rare, for many years being only known from a pair taken alive in 1923 and brought to Europe. From this pair a captive stock was established in both Europe and the USA, which eventually had to be maintained by selective cross-breeding with female Silver Pheasants. In 1990, an immature male was trapped by rattan collectors at a quite different site, but died a few days later. It was taken in Ke Go Forest, part of which was subsequently declared a reserve. In February 2000 another immature male was trapped by rattan collectors, this time in the proposed Dakrong Nature Reserve in Quang Tri Province. Presumably exceptionally rare due to habitat loss, but lack of historical information makes this difficult to confirm. The only recent records were trapped, suggesting that this may be a major threat. Occurrence in adjacent C Laos is unproven, though local hunters have reported an all-dark, black-crested pheasant around Savanakhet and Nakai-Nam Theun National Biodiversity Conservation Area, which requires investigation.

REFERENCES BirdLife International (2000, 2001), Collar *et al.* (1994), David-Beaulieu (1949), Delacour (1977), Garson (2001), McGowan (1994), McGowan & Garson (1995), Rasmussen (1998), Robson *et al.* (1993).

128A EDWARDS'S PHEASANT
Lophura (edwardsi) edwardsi (Oustalet,1896)   Plate 35

Another mysterious Vietnamese endemic, which re-appeared in 1996 after having been 'lost' in the wild since 1928, though there had been probable reports in 1988. Like Imperial Pheasant it must be considered one of the most threatened species in the world.

IDENTIFICATION Lowland wet forests of C Vietnam, where very rare. Male almost wholly shining blue-black, with exception of short snow-white crest, red legs and facial skin. Smaller, with shorter, blunter tail than Im-perial, and white crest and glossy green edges to wing-coverts. Very similar to first-year male Vietnamese Pheasant, distinctions from which require investigation (the two may well be conspecific). Range not known to overlap with either, as currently both Vietnamese and Imperial are known only from sites close to southern border in N Annam, whereas reports of Edwards's are from further south in C Annam. Female smaller and darker than female Imperial, with almost unmarked chestnut-brown upperparts and duller, but quite dark, underparts; the blackish outer tail feathers contrast slightly with the dark brown central feathers. See Vietnamese Pheasant for further discussion. Female *annamensis* Silver Pheasant is larger, has a longer, pointed tail, longer, almost blackish-brown crest, reddish (not blackish) outer tail and is overall more rufous-brown.

DESCRIPTION Crown has short, tufted crest. Tail rather elongated, the central three pairs of feathers blunt and virtually equal in length. Bill whitish-green, blackish at very base (horn-brown in female). Irides reddish-brown (browner in female). Extensive scarlet bare facial skin. Legs crimson (adult male) or scarlet (female). Sexes differ. Male assumes adult plumage during first year. **Adult male:** Central crown and crest white, with a few black feathers admixed. Plumage wholly dark blue, each body feather fringed silky blue. Feathers of back, rump and uppertail-coverts with subterminal black band, terminally edged metallic blue. Wing-coverts similar but tipped shining green. Secondaries dark blue, primaries dull blackish. Tail blue. **First-year male:** Virtually as adult male, though plumage less bright and shiny. **Adult female:** Crest virtually absent. Head, neck and underparts quite dark greyish-brown. Upperparts dark reddish-brown, reddest on mantle. Entire body plumage finely and inconspicuously vermiculated. Primaries and outer tail feathers black, three pairs of central tail feathers dark brown, tinged rufous. **Juvenile:** Like female but has slightly stronger vermiculations and subterminal black marks to feathers of mantle and wing-coverts.

GEOGRAPHICAL VARIATION None, but possibly conspecific with Vietnamese Pheasant.

MEASUREMENTS Length 58–65 cm. Male larger. Males: wing 220–240, tail 240–260, tarsus 75, weight 1115 (n=1). Females: wing 210–220, tail 200–220, tarsus c.65, weight 1050 (n=1).

HABITAT Forested habitats on level and gently rolling hills of eastern slopes of the Annamitic chain and coastal plains. Recently recorded at 300–400 m in secondary lowland evergreen forest with well-developed understorey of rattan and other palms, and bamboo, on relatively flat land.

VOICE Seemingly simple low guttural *uk uk uk uk uk...*, calls uttered by male during breeding season. Male also whirrs wings.

HABITS Being largely only known from specimens and captive individuals, there is no information on its habits in the wild. Early observations report its wariness and fondness for keeping strictly to dense cover of underbrush and liana-covered hillsides.

BREEDING No information from wild. Captive clutch size 4–7; eggs similar to those of Imperial but smaller, and incubation lasts 21–22 days.

DISTRIBUTION Known only from Quang Tri and Thua Thien Hue Provinces in C Annam (Vietnam).

STATUS Endangered. Extremely rare, having been recently rediscovered, and population placed at 1000–2949 individuals. Historical forest sites where the species was originally collected are now largely cleared, indicating that habitat loss is the main cause for its decline, but trapping is also a problem. Until recently known only from 20–30 individuals sent to Europe in 1924–28. From this stock an extensive captive population exists worldwide, though some may be genetically impure. Following reports by hunters in 1988 of the species' presence in Thua Thien Hue Province, the survival of this enigmatic bird was finally confirmed in late August 1996, in nearby Phong Dien district, when a pair was captured. Unfortunately both died, but 3–4 months later a male was trapped to the north of Bach Ma National Park, in Dakrong District, Quang Tri Province, and eventually taken to Hanoi Zoo, where it is hoped that the genetic pool of captive birds can be improved.

REFERENCES BirdLife International (2000, 2001), Dang (1997), Delacour (1977), Eames (1996, 1997), Johnsgard (1986), McGowan & Garson (1995), Robson *et al.* (1989).

128B VIETNAMESE PHEASANT
Lophura (edwardsi) hatinhensis Vo Quy, 1975   Plate 35

Alternative name: Vo Quy's Pheasant.

Vietnam's third enigmatic *Lophura* was discovered as recently as 1964 and described in 1975. We now know rather more about this species than its two congeners, but even so a great deal of its lifestyle is mysterious, and the possibility has recently emerged that this 'form' is actually the product of inbreeding within local populations of Edwards's Pheasants (a DNA analysis is currently ongoing, which should confirm or disprove this hypothesis).

IDENTIFICATION Lowland forests of C Vietnam, where very rare but has been found alongside even rarer, larger and longer tailed Imperial Pheasant. Adult male easily distinguished from other pheasants in area by its pure white central tail feathers and crest, otherwise it is almost wholly blue-black, with the exception of red legs and facial skin. It appears that only older individuals acquire white central tail feathers, and that first-year males have an all-dark tail like Edwards's (but recent captive studies have revealed that the number of white tail feathers is variable and asymmetrical). Subtle differences in structure include rather slimmer and longer legs, and slightly more elongated and more pointed central tail feathers of Vietnamese. Females also very similar but Vietnamese has rufous-chestnut, not dark brown, central tail feathers. Indeed older females variably develop white tail feathers (generally second and/or third pair from centre); these white feathers are apparently never shown by Edwards's, which in any case is thought not to overlap with Vietnamese. Female *annamensis* Silver Pheasant is larger, has a longer, pointed tail, longer and almost blackish-brown crest, and reddish (not blackish) outer tail.

DESCRIPTION Crown has tufted crest. Tail slightly elongated, the central pair of feathers rather pointed and slightly longer than next pair. Bill whitish-green, blackish at very base (horn-brown in female). Irides reddish-brown (browner in female). Extensive scarlet bare facial skin. Legs crimson (both sexes, but duller in female). Sexes differ. Male does not assume full adult plumage until second year. **Adult male:** Central crown and crest white. Plumage wholly dark blue, each body feather being fringed silky blue. Feathers of back, rump and uppertail-coverts have subterminal black band, terminally edged metallic blue. Wing-coverts similar but tipped shining green and reddish-purple. Secondaries dark blue, primaries dull blackish. Tail blue, with up to six central feathers white in older individuals. **First-year male:** Similar to adult male, though plumage less bright and shiny, and tail does not develop white feathers until second year (17–20 months, but one captive individual did not attain its first white tail feather until 30 months). Those with six white feathers are at least three years of age. **Adult female:** Crest virtually absent. Head and neck quite dark greyish-chestnut. Entire body plumage and wings reddish-chestnut. Primaries grey. Central tail feathers reddish-chestnut, rest blue-black on outer webs, rufous on inner webs, with outermost pair blackest; tail develops up to four white feathers when older, though unlike males, the central pair are always rufous. **Juvenile:** Not documented.

GEOGRAPHICAL VARIATION None, treated as monotypic here but often considered conspecific with Edwards's Pheasant.

MEASUREMENTS Length 60–67 cm. Male larger. Males: wing 230, tail 263–270, tarsus 94, weight 1100 (n=1). Females: wing 219, tail 220, tarsus 83, weight, no data.

HABITAT In secondary and logged lowland (50–200 m) evergreen forest on level and gently sloping ground, with well-developed understorey of palms (including rattans) and bamboo clumps. Specifically, close to streams where there is denser cover.

VOICE Alarm call described as a subdued, hard *puk puk puk puk...*, which is probably virtually identical to that of Edwards's.

HABITS No information other than being shy and wary, keeping close to forest undergrowth.

BREEDING No information, but presumably similar to Edwards's.

DISTRIBUTION Endemic to Annam (Vietnam). Known only from Ha Tinh, Qunag Binh and possibly Nghe Tinh Provinces in southern N Annam and northern border of C Annam.

STATUS Globally threatened (Endangered), with population placed at 250–999 individuals. Rare, being infrequently recorded since its initial discovery in 1964 but known to survive in Ke Go area, which is now a reserve. The only recent information derives from this site where current threats are habitat loss and trapping.

REFERENCES BirdLife International (2000, 2001), Corder (1996), Dang & Le (1996), Davison (1996), Garson (2001), Lambert *et al.* (1994), Robson *et al.* (1993), Rozendaal *et al.* (1991).

129 SWINHOE'S PHEASANT
Lophura swinhoii (Gould, 1862)   Plate 35

Alternative names: Formosan or Taiwan Blue Pheasant.

One of Taiwan's two endemic pheasants, the white central tail feathers giving the male a superficial resemblance to Vietnamese Pheasant; females, however, suggest a more distant relationship.

IDENTIFICATION Hill forests of Taiwan, where, though locally numerous, their shy and wary nature makes them elusive. Male unmistakable: glossy blue-black, with white crown, mantle and central tail feathers, and easily distinguished from male Vietnamese by white mantle and nape, and maroon-red scapulars. Female separated from other pheasants on Taiwan (Mikado and Common) by blunt tail, spotted upperparts and reddish legs; the boldly spotted upperparts, barred central tail and rufous outer tail being quite unlike Edwards's and Vietnamese females, and closer to Siamese Fireback (which see).

DESCRIPTION Crown has short, tufted crest (virtually absent in female). Tail slightly elongated, the central feathers strongly elongated and broadly tapering to point. Bill horn-yellow, blackish at very base (duller in female). Irides reddish-brown (brown in female). Very extensive scarlet bare facial skin (smaller area in female). Legs crimson. Sexes differ. Male assumes adult plumage during second year. **Adult male:** Central crown and crest white, with a few black feathers admixed. Plumage chiefly dark blue, each body feather being fringed silky blue. Feathers of back, rump and uppertail-coverts have narrow subterminal black band and broad shining metallic blue tip. Lower nape and mantle white. Scapulars shining crimson-maroon. Wing-coverts black, feathers tipped shining green. Secondaries and primaries greyish-black. Tail dark blue, with pure white central feathers. **First-year male:** Apparently individually variable. Similar to adult male but plumage less bright and shiny, often dull black rather than blue. Crest has mixed black and white feathers. Upperparts mottled brown and black, with brown feathering among white of mantle and maroon of scapulars. Central tail feathers chestnut, mottled black, often with variable amounts of white on inner webs. **Adult female:** Crown chestnut-brown, finely barred black. Upperparts, including wing-coverts dark reddish-brown, vermiculated black; each feather with prominent buff and black arrowheads forming striking pattern. Tail reddish-chestnut, the central feathers mottled black and brown and with irregular buff barring. Face, throat and foreneck pale grey becoming cinnamon-buff on breast and paler on rear underparts; underparts with numerous black chevrons, most prominent on breast. **Juvenile:** Like female but duller and browner, and with slightly stronger vermiculations. Feathers of wing-coverts patterned with two subterminal black spots, separated by whitish and fringed rufous-buff.

GEOGRAPHICAL VARIATION Monotypic.

MEASUREMENTS Length: male c.79 cm and female c.50 cm, the difference almost entirely due to differing tail lengths. Males: wing 250–260, tail 410–500, tarsus 90. Females: wing 240–245, tail 200–220, tarsus 75. Two unsexed had mean weight of 1100.

HABITAT Hardwood forest, where it is encountered in primary and secondary stands with dense undergrowth at 300–2000 m, with reports to 2300 m.

VOICE Though several calls are given, the species is notably quiet for much of the time, even when escaping after being disturbed. When undisturbed is virtually silent. A very soft liquid murmuring is emitted, seemingly while foraging. Two calls, which may be more or less indicative of alarm, are a rather high and sharp, incisive sucking sound accompanying a loud and plaintive call, sometimes given as short quick syllables: *oot-oot, oot-oot.*

HABITS Shy, but can be seen early morning, especially around dawn, on trails in suitable habitat. Most easily seen in dry season, appearing to remain more inside forest during wetter winter months. Usually encountered singly, but pairs and small groups also seen. Feeds in early morning and late afternoon, in open areas of forest floor and among ground cover at road edges, and sometimes in second growth. Though clears leaves with one foot, it doesn't really scrape ground and usually feeds by digging and by walking slowly and pecking. During day retreats into forest, where may continue to feed among leaf-litter, and where often exceptionally difficult to see. Uses regular paths in and out of forest. Roosts from shortly after sunset to just after dawn, usually alone, but up to eight observed in a single roost tree.

BREEDING Mating pattern unclear and though polygamy suspected, pairs often seen. Nest previously thought to be quite spartan, or eggs laid directly on ground at base of tree or below an overhang, but recently nests of grass lined with leaves and feathers have been found. All are in locations sheltered from rain and are exceptionally difficult to detect. Clutch usually 4–8; eggs reddish to creamy-buff. Breeds mostly March–May, but rarely February and to October. Incubation in captivity lasts 25 days and is by female alone.

DISTRIBUTION Endemic to Taiwan, where it occurs in the central mountains.

STATUS Near Threatened. Locally common but extirpated from several areas, such as Kenting and Mt. Kuan Teng and Mt. Chen Chung. Although in 1958 it was estimated that only c.120 remained in the wild, through protection and a successful reintroduction programme this number has increased to c.10,000 individuals. Even this may be too low if the estimate of c.6500 for Yushan National Park is correct. It is also known from other protected areas where it seems stable, but is probably declining where its habitat is not protected. In the long term this suggests that each protected area will hold an isolated population.

REFERENCES McGowan (1994), Severinghaus, L.L. (1996), Severinghaus, S.R. (1980).

Subgenus *ACOMUS*: Sumatran firebacks

Four taxa of the genus *Lophura* are known from Sumatra: Crestless Fireback and Crested Fireback are quite distinct, but the other two, Hoogerwerf's Pheasant and Salvadori's Pheasant are more problematic. Both are poorly studied and male Hoogerwerf's awaits formal description. As females do appear to differ to a reasonable degree the two are tentatively treated separately to highlight this situation.

130A SALVADORI'S PHEASANT
Lophura (inornata) inornata (Salvadori, 1879)   Plate 37

Alternative name: Sumatran Pheasant.

A rather dull member of this normally extravagantly plumaged genus, which is nonetheless interesting as males bear a superficial resemblance to female Crestless Fireback, which also occurs on Sumatra.

IDENTIFICATION A little-studied species of montane forest in S Sumatra. Glossy blue-black male has scarlet facial skin, near-white bill, and pale grey eyering and legs. As range does not meet Hoogerwerf's (which see), the most likely confusion is with strangely similar female Crestless Fireback, which is a lowland species and probably does not occur alongside Salvadori's. Latter is rather longer bodied and holds tail depressed whereas stockier Crestless Fireback tends to carry its tail cocked. Closer views should reveal the black (not pale) bill, the less glossed plumage and greyer head of Crestless Fireback. Female Salvadori's is distinctive within its range, being overall chestnut-brown with contrasting dusky tail, each body and wing-covert feather with a prominent buff shaft streak, giving mottled appearance. See further discussion under Hoogerwerf's Pheasant.

DESCRIPTION Crestless. Tail relatively short and rounded, slightly graduated; 14 feathers. Bill pale greenish-white. Irides orange-red (browner in female). Bare skin around eye pale yellowish-green or greyish-green, with tiny yellow spot behind eye. Bare facial skin scarlet. Legs greenish-grey. Sexes differ. Male has prominent spur. **Adult male:** Plumage almost wholly blue-black. Most body and neck feathers black with broad metallic blue fringe. Belly, vent, flight feathers and tail dull black. **Adult female:** Plumage almost wholly reddish-chestnut, each feather finely peppered black, with pale shaft and buff streak. Throat paler brown. Tail blackish-brown. **Juvenile:** Poorly documented. Like female but feathers fringed pale buff, giving scaled as well as streaked effect.

GEOGRAPHICAL VARIATION Almost certainly conspecific with Hoogerwerf's Pheasant, but as both are so little known, and females do appear to be quite distinct, tentatively afforded separate treatment here.

MEASUREMENTS Length 46–55 cm. Male only slightly larger than female. Males: wing 213–230, tail 152–170, tarsus 70–75, weight, no data. Females: wing 208–228, tail 145–150, weight, no data.

HABITAT Montane forest, often with dense understorey, at 1000–2200 m.

VOICE Males cluck in early morning during breeding season. Wing-whirring forms part of display.

HABITS Extremely poorly known. Virtually nothing is known of its habits in the wild, other than a relatively recent sighting of a pair walking on a trail before disappearing into undergrowth.

BREEDING No information from wild. Captive clutch 2. Eggs chocolate-brown and incubated for 22 days.

DISTRIBUTION Endemic to S and C Barisan Mountains of SW Sumatra. There are few known localities for Salvadori's Pheasant, but these include Gunung

Kerinci and Gunung Kaba in C Sumatra, and Gunung Dempu in the south.

STATUS Vulnerable. Considered uncommon to rare, with estimated population of 2500–10,000 individuals, but this perhaps due to secretive nature and lack of surveys in relevant regions. Only rediscovered after nearly 70 years in 1986. Precise distribution within its range unknown, but probably more widespread in montane forest than the recently known sites on Gunung Kerinci and Gunung Kaba may suggest. Further survey effort in C and S Sumatran montane forests is desirable, especially at the historical locality of Gunung Dempu in the south. Though the huge Kerinci-Seblat National Park holds the species, it is under considerable human pressure and it is the prospect of substantial expansion of human activities to higher altitudes that is responsible for its conservation status. Indeed, there is already some logging encroachment at lower reaches of its altitude zone.

REFERENCES BirdLife International (2000, 2001), Delacour (1977), Johnsgard (1986), Lambert & Howes (1989), MacKinnon & Phillips (1993), van Marle & Voous (1988), McGowan (1994), McGowan & Garson (1995).

130B HOOGERWERF'S PHEASANT
Lophura (inornata) hoogerwerfi (Chasen, 1939)   **Plate 37**

Alternative name: Atjeh Pheasant.

Probably conspecific with Salvadori's Pheasant, which it replaces in extreme N Sumatra, but this form is virtually unstudied.

IDENTIFICATION Known only from N Sumatra, where it overlaps with no similar species. Known from only two female specimens and a few sight observations. Though male is formally undescribed, field photographs suggest it closely resembes male Salvadori's, but if dark blue-grey leg colour described for female is correct, and also applies to male, then this would be a useful distinction (male Salvadori's has pale grey legs). Females differ significantly from Salvadori's in being plainer, darker and duller brown, less chestnut, lacking prominent buff streaking and mottling which is such a feature of Salvadori's. See also Salvadori's for comments on Crestless Fireback.

DESCRIPTION Crestless. Tail relatively short and rounded, slightly graduated. All comments refer to female only (male is undescribed): bill blue-grey, irides amber, bare facial skin red, legs dark blue. **Adult male:** Undescribed but field sightings indicate that it is similar to Salvadori's and a description is in preparation based on a new captive specimen (see below). **Adult female:** Plumage almost wholly dull brown, edged reddish only at sides of feathers of rump, wings and flanks. Overall finely vermiculated black, with vermiculations coarsest and most apparent on wing-coverts. Throat whitish, rest of underparts washed yellowish-brown. Tail black. **Juvenile:** Undescribed.

GEOGRAPHICAL VARIATION None, though perhaps best treated as conspecific with Salvadori's Pheasant.

MEASUREMENTS Length 40–50 cm. No other published data, but unlikely to be significantly different from Salvadori's.

HABITAT Montane forest with dense understorey at 600–2000 m.

VOICE Not described, but presumably similar to Salvadori's Pheasant.

HABITS Almost nothing is known of this taxon's habits due to the paucity of sightings. Further information is much needed.

BREEDING No information, other than a single nest with 2 eggs was found in February 1979, at 1800 m. Neither nest nor eggs were described.

DISTRIBUTION Endemic to Gayo Highlands of N Sumatra, but known only from Gunung Leuser National Park in Aceh Province. Its precise distribution is unknown, but it is probably more widespread in montane forest than present observations suggest.

STATUS No threat listing, as not considered specific by BirdLife International, but the IUCN/WPA/-BirdLife Pheasant Specialist Group consider it threatened. Very few records, but this is probably due to secretive nature and because relatively little survey work has been undertaken in N Sumatra. Indeed, the taxon is known only from two female specimens and a few photographs and sightings from Mamas Valley in Gunung Leuser National Park. Further ornithological effort throughout the park's forests is desirable. Six individuals, including an unknown number of males, were recently discovered in a market in N Sumatra (of which the only two that survived are currently in an aviary in W Java). Though the National Park is large, the prospect of substantial expansion of human activities into higher altitude areas is significant. Indeed, there is already some agricultural encroachment at lower reaches of the relevant altitude zone.

REFERENCES Delacour (1977), MacKinnon & Phillips (1993), van Marle & Voous (1988), McGowan (1994), McGowan & Garson (1995).

Another distinctive species, particularly interesting in that, unlike all other pheasants, the female is almost entirely black, and was considered a different species for some years before its relationship was realised. The female bears a peculiar similarity to male Salvadori's Pheasant.

IDENTIFICATION Lowland tropical forests of Malaysia, Sumatra and Borneo. Male uncrested and unmistakable: appears dark greyish (with white streaks) in race *pyronota* (Borneo), or blackish in nominate (Malay Peninsula and Sumatra) in the field, with stunning cinnamon-buff full tail and copper-maroon rump. On Borneo note that Crested Fireback has similarly coloured tail, but is unlikely to be mistaken as it has blue (not red) facial skin, a peacock-like crest and copper-chestnut central underparts. Female almost wholly blue-black with bare red facial skin, recalling male Salvadori's or Hoogerwerf's (of Sumatra), but is stockier, lacks strong metallic blue reflections, has whitish chin and dusky-brownish head, blackish (not whitish) bill and carries tail cocked in bantam-like fashion.

DESCRIPTION *L. e. erythrophthalma*. Crestless. Tail slightly rounded or graduated, central pair of feathers a little shorter than next, and all relatively short and broad 14 or 16 in number. Bill whitish-green, blackish at very base (male), or black, becoming paler at very base (female). Irides reddish-brown (brown in female). Extensive scarlet bare facial skin. Legs bluish-grey. Sexes differ. Male has prominent and rather long spur, female a shorter spur. Male assumes adult plumage during first year, at c.4 months. **Adult male:** Plumage almost wholly purplish-black, virtually unmarked over most of underparts but finely vermiculated whitish on mantle, back, wings and breast-sides; latter have indistinct silver shaft streaks. Lower back bright rufous-chestnut, richer on rump and glossy purple with maroon fringes on uppertail-coverts. Tail warm cinnamon-buff, blackish at very base. **Adult female:** Plumage almost wholly blackish, with blue and green gloss on body and wings, head brownish, becoming whitish on throat. Rear underparts, flight feathers and tail dull black. **Juvenile:** Like female but feathers fringed rusty-buff. Young male soon acquires male rump and tail colour.

GEOGRAPHICAL VARIATION Quite marked, but less striking than differences between Bornean and Sumatran Crested Firebacks. Two well-marked subspecies recognised.

L. e. erythrophthalma (Raffles, 1822) occurs in Peninsular Malaysia and Sumatra; described above.
L. e. pyronota (G. R. Gray, 1841) occurs on Borneo; male has neck, breast, mantle and wings grey, vermiculated black and white and with whitish shaft streaks, breast-sides with lanceolate purplish-black feathers and clear white shaft streaks, and uppertail-coverts steel-blue; female as nominate.

MEASUREMENTS Length: male 47–50 cm, female 42–44 cm. Nominate race given. Males: wing 240–250, tail 150–180, tarsus 75–85, weight mean 1043 (n=2). Females: wing 200–220, tail 140–160, tarsus 70–75, weight 837 (n=1).

HABITAT Perhaps restricted to primary lowland rainforest on Sumatra and Borneo, but found in secondary forest in Malaysia, where encountered up to 300 m. It is unknown whether it can survive in peat-swamp forest and given extent of such forest on Sumatra, this may have important conservation implications.

VOICE When alarmed gives a loud *kak*. Also a vibrating throaty *purr* and a repeated, low croaking, rendered *tak-takrau* or *tooktaroo*. Males also wing-whirr in display.

HABITS Wary, inhabiting undergrowth in rainforest and rarely seen sufficiently well to permit study of its habits. Usually in pairs and groups of 5–6 also encountered, though group size may be difficult to gauge given poor visibility in understorey. Appears to feed throughout day by scratching and picking animal items as well as plant material, and pecking at fallen fruit.

BREEDING Mating pattern unknown. A single wild nest of twigs was placed between buttress roots. Clutch 4–5 rosy or buffy-white eggs. Breeds April–June. Incubation in captivity 24 days.

DISTRIBUTION Occurs in suitable habitat throughout Sunda region, from N Peninsular Malaysia through Sumatra to Borneo, including Sarawak, Brunei, Sabah and Kalimantan, though there are very few recent records from Sumatra or Kalimantan.

STATUS Vulnerable. Generally relatively scarce and uncommon and probably fewer than 10,000 individuals persist. Appears quite sparsely distributed in Peninsular and E Malaysia, and scarce on Sumatra and in Kalimantan, where it occurs at low densities. Relative paucity of records and its possible dependence upon a quite restricted habitat (valley-bottom forest), in at least some of its range, suggests that it may be under considerable pressure. Its future seems likely to rely on maintaining tracts of plains forest in protected areas, and the species is known only from a few, including Krau Wildlife Reserve (and probably in Taman Negara National Park) in Malaysia, and Way Kambas National Park on Sumatra. On Borneo it occurs in Gunung Mulu National Park, but not in any protected area in Kalimantan. The main pressures are habitat loss through logging and conversion of land to agriculture.

REFERENCES BirdLife International (2000, 2001), Delacour (1977), Johnsgard (1986), King *et al.* (1975), McGowan & Garson (1995), Medway & Wells (1976), Wells (1999).

Alternative names: Bornean Crested Fireback (nominate and *nobilis*), Vieillot's Crested Fireback (*rufa*).

A beautiful forest pheasant, with striking plumage variation indicating that the process of speciation is well underway.

IDENTIFICATION Lowland and foothill forests of Sumatra, Malay Peninsula and Borneo. Males unmistakable if seen well, though varies according to subspecies: all are blue-black, with blue facial-skin, coppery-red rump, black outer tail feathers and peacock-like crest, but leg colour, underparts and central tail colour varies according to race. Those of Borneo (Bornean Crested Fireback) have chestnut-red central underparts (without white streaks), cinnamon-buff central tail and very pale pink or greenish-white legs. Populations of Sumatra and Malay Peninsula have white central tail, white streaks on blackish underparts and red legs. Females also crested and have blue facial skin, spotted black and white underparts and plain brown upperparts, with legs whitish and tail blacker on Bornean birds, whereas those elsewhere are reddish with rufous tail. Compare also Crestless Fireback.

DESCRIPTION *L. i. ignita*. Peacock-like crest of stiff, bare-shafted and racket-tipped feathers projects from crown (but is flatter, less stiff and not so eye-catching in female). Tail of male rather graduated, becoming increasingly elongated towards central pair, which form an arching 'bustle'. Bill whitish (brownish at base in female). Extensive bare facial skin cobalt blue (concealing most of head-sides, as in Silver Pheasant) forming small fleshy lobes at 'corners'. Irides red. Legs whitish (pale flesh or pale greenish) to pale brownish (female); male has long spurs, usually lacking in female. Sexes differ. Male attains adult plumage at 5–6 months. **Adult male:** Plumage mostly shining dark purplish-blue, including rump and uppertail-coverts, feathers of lower back have broad shining copper-maroon fringes, rump and uppertail-coverts metallic blue fringes. Wing-coverts dark blue with shining blue fringes, flight feathers duller bluish-black. Lower breast and flanks copper-chestnut, with lower underparts black. Two or three pairs of central tail feathers warm cinnamon-buff, outermost five pairs bluish-black. **Adult female:** Head, neck and most of upperparts rufous-chestnut, finely vermiculated black on wing-coverts and uppertail-coverts. Tail blackish, vermiculated chestnut along feather edges. Chin and throat whitish, lower foreneck and breast chestnut-brown, with white fringes, becoming darker brown on lower breast and flanks, each feather with scaly white border, and vent whitish. **Juvenile:** Like female, but wing-coverts with large black spots, young male darker, becoming much like dull adult at c.4 months.

GEOGRAPHICAL VARIATION Males vary to some degree in size and more markedly in coloration of tail and underparts. Differences between Bornean birds and other populations are so striking that it is difficult

to imagine them as the same species; however, the variable intermediate features of *mcartneyi* are difficult to ignore.

L. i. ignita (Shaw & Nodder, 1797) (Bornean Crested Fireback) occurs in S Borneo and formerly Banka I. (off Sumatra); described above.

L. i. nobilis (Sclater, 1863) occurs in N Borneo; plumage as nominate, but larger (male wing 280–293, tail 254–285).

L. i. rufa (Raffles, 1822) (Vieillot's Crested Fireback) occurs on Malay Peninsula and Sumatra (except southeast); male has white (not cinnamon) central tail feathers, black underparts with white streaks and four lobes to facial wattles, the female an entirely chestnut tail, and both sexes have red legs; this form is larger, with relatively shorter legs, but longer and fuller tail than nominate, male wing 270–300, tail 265–295.

L. i. macartneyi (Temminck, 1813) (includes *delacouri* and *albipennis*) occurs in SE Sumatra (Palembang Province and parts of Lampongs); variable form between *rufa* and *ignita*, with various combinations even at same locality, which is perhaps better treated as an intermediate population rather than as a subspecies.

MEASUREMENTS Length: male 65–70 cm, female 56–57 cm. *L. i. ignita* given. Males: wing 270–280, tail 245–260, tarsus 110–120, weight 1800–2605. Females: wing 234–254, tail 156–177, tarsus 76, weight c.1600.

HABITAT Lowland forest specialist, with upper limites varying according to locality: up to 1000 m or more in both Peninsular and E Malaysia, but upper altitude limit unknown in Peninsular Thailand, Sumatra and Kalimantan. Recorded from logged forest (e.g. in Way Kambas National Park in S Sumatra and part of E Malaysia), but tolerance of secondary habitats unclear and it would be surprising if it survived in forest that was extensively and recently modified.

VOICE Male and female emit a sharp *chukun, chunkun* when disturbed, which sounds very similar to call of Black-backed Squirrel *Sciurus bicolor*. Male wing-whirrs quite loudly, often in combination with a subdued *woonk-k woonk-k*. Also a questioning croak followed by a shrill whistle or chirp.

HABITS Wary, inhabiting undergrowth in rainforest and rarely observed for sufficiently long to permit close study of its habits. Apparently found more often close to rivers and streams. Sometimes betrayed by groups making (presumably) contact calls while moving through forest, and presence may be given away by wing-whirring sound of male. Group size difficult to gauge given poor visibility in understorey, but quite large groups observed and 5–6 common, often (but not always) with just one male. Appears to feed throughout day by scratching and picking animal items as well as plant material, and pecking at fallen fruit. If disturbed runs swiftly, usually together rather than scattering, but will take to air in noisy, fussy flight for a short distance if hard-pressed.

BREEDING Mating pattern unknown. Single wild nest was made of dead leaves, grass and bamboo in dense undergrowth. Clutch usually 4–8 creamy-white to creamy-buff and relatively round eggs. Apparently breeds April–June. Incubation in captivity 24 days.

DISTRIBUTION Occurs in suitable habitat throughout Sunda region, from S Peninsular Thailand to Sumatra and Borneo. Population on Bangka I., off SE Sumatra, may be extirpated.

STATUS Near Threatened. Local and sparse to reasonably common. Appears quite sparsely distributed in Peninsular and E Malaysia, but reasonably common on Sumatra and in Kalimantan. Recorded from logged and secondary forest in some areas, but not on Malay Peninsula and considered a lowland forest specialist, probably reliant on valley-bottom forest and hence especially restricted in its habitat use. This habitat is under considerable pressure throughout its range. It is almost certainly restricted to boundary strips of lowland forest in protected areas of S Thailand, which are mainly on mountains, and where it is hunted. Like other species in the same habitat, its future appears reliant on maintaining tracts of plains forest in protected areas: it is known from a number, including Krau Wildlife Reserve and Taman Negara National Park (Malaysia), Way Kambas (Sumatra) and Tanjung Putting National Parks (Kalimantan), and Khao Luang National Park (Thailand).

REFERENCES McGowan & Garson (1995), Medway & Wells (1976), Smythies (1981), Wells (1999).

133 SIAMESE FIREBACK
Lophura diardi (Bonaparte, 1856)   Plate 38

Alternative name: Diard's Fireback.

An elegant forest pheasant of mainland tropical Asia, the male sharing features that link Silver Pheasants with the firebacks, while the female is surprisingly similar to female Swinhoe's Pheasant of Taiwan.

IDENTIFICATION Lowland and foothill forests of SE Asia. Male unmistakable if seen well: a rather long-legged, slender grey pheasant, with long blackish tail, long red legs and very extensive red facial skin topped by a prominent coronal tuft. Female lacks crest, has rufous mantle and underparts, and contrastingly strongly banded wings and tail, quite unlike other female Lophura in the region, though compare Swinhoe's Pheasant of Taiwan, which although superficially similar has shorter legs and spotted upperparts.

DESCRIPTION Male has usually drooping crest of bare-shafted, racket-tipped feathers, which can be erected when alarmed; female lacks obvious crest. Tail of male long, curving outwards and tapering to falcate tip, central pair of feathers actually shorter than next two pairs; female has shorter, broadly pointed tail feathers. Bill whitish-green (dusky in female). Extensive bare facial skin red (concealing most of head-sides), forming small fleshy wattles at throat-sides; less extensive in female. Irides red or brown. Legs crimson; male has long spurs, usually lacking in female. Sexes differ. Male attains adult plumage during first year, though plumage duller and tail shorter than in older individuals. Adult male: Plumage mostly grey, finely vermiculated black, underparts from lower breast down blackish, the feathers broadly edged blue. Visible parts of head also black. Deep yellow patch on back enhanced by golden feather fringes and contrasts with crimson-edged metallic blue feathers of rump and uppertail-coverts. Larger uppertail-coverts and tail metallic black, with blue and green sheen. Adult female: Head and neck dull brown, becoming paler on throat, while mantle, breast and lower underparts are bright rufous-chestnut, belly pale grey. Feathers of mantle finely vermiculated black, breast and flanks feathers edged whitish.

Rump, uppertail-coverts, wings and two central pairs of tail feathers barred blackish and pale buff, variably tinged rufous. Outer tail feathers unmarked rufous-chestnut. Juvenile: Like female, but duller; young males soon possess patches of grey feathering.

GEOGRAPHICAL VARIATION Monotypic.

MEASUREMENTS Length: male c.80 cm, female c.60 cm, the difference principally due to tail length. Males: wing 220–240, tail 330–360, tarsus 75–85, weight 1420 (n=1). Females: wing 220–240, tail 220–260, tarsus 75–85, weight 680–1025 (n=3).

HABITAT Inhabits lowland evergreen, semi-evergreen and bamboo forests (both primary and secondary) mainly in plains, but to c.800 m. Appears able to tolerate some disturbance, as often found along roads and tracks through forest. Considered a lowland resident in Cambodia.

VOICE Male gives a loud whistling call and often emits a continual pee-yu pee-yu. Like other Lophura, male also wing-whirrs.

HABITS Not especially well known, being difficult to see except when it emerges into open to feed or cross roads and tracks. All additional information valuable. Encountered either singly or in groups, which are presumed to be family parties. Forages in morning and late afternoon when observed on forest tracks. Reasonably approachable in areas where not hunted.

BREEDING Mating pattern unknown. A single nest was placed in hollow tree on ground. Clutch 4–8 pale rosy-buff and quite round eggs. Breeds April–June. In captivity incubation 24–25 days.

DISTRIBUTION From E Myanmar, where formerly considered rare in Southern Shan States, through NE and SE Thailand to Laos, C and S Vietnam and Cambodia.

STATUS Near Threatened. Thought to be scarce to locally common. Population estimated at 5000 individuals in Thailand, which, together with calculation of extant habitat elsewhere in its range, led to an over-all population estimate of c.10,000 individuals. In Laos and Vietnam rarely encountered, but it is unclear whether this reflects a genuine scarcity, or the thickness of undergrowth beside roads. It occurs in several protected areas, including Nam Cat Tien National Park and Mom Ray Nature Reserve in Vietnam, and Phou Xang He and Xe Pian National Biodiversity Conservation Areas in Laos. Fieldwork in Laos has indicated that it is locally very common in some places: for example, hundreds are probably snared each year in Xe Pian National Biodiversity Conservation Area in the south. Pressures from hunting appear significant in some areas, perhaps especially in Laos, and also habitat degradation. Some uncertainty exists over habitat specificity, as the species has been observed in disturbed forest-edge habitat in some areas, but is thought to be a lowland forest specialist elsewhere. Clarification would be valuable for conservation assessment and planning.

REFERENCES BirdLife International (2000, 2001), Delacour (1977), McGowan (1994), McGowan & Garson (1995), Thewlis *et al.* (1996).

134 BULWER'S PHEASANT
Lophura bulweri (Sharpe, 1874)   Plate 38

Alternative names: Wattled Pheasant, White-tailed Pheasant.

An extraordinary pheasant, the male indulging in an almost grotesque and strangely silent display. This rarely-seen species is endemic to forests of interior Borneo.

IDENTIFICATION Hill and montane forests of Borneo. The remarkable white bustle of a tail and blue facial skin of this otherwise blackish pheasant renders the male quite unmistakable, its appearance being approached only by Malay Peninsula and Sumatran populations of Crested Fireback, as Bornean races have warm buff bustle and whitish (not red) legs. Young males, however, have a straighter reddish tail. Smaller, drab brown female has blue facial skin like female Bornean Crested Fireback, but differs in being uncrested, with plain brownish (not spotted) underparts and reddish (not whitish) legs.

DESCRIPTION No crest. Tail feathers of male remarkable in that outermost seven pairs have few barbs and consist primarily of long stiffened shafts, the remaining 8–9 pairs broadly elongated and arching; female has 13 pairs of 'normal' straight feathers, though tail is relatively long. Bill black with pale tip. Extensive bare facial skin cobalt-blue (in male concealing most of head-sides and pumped up into remarkable hammer shape in display, see Habits). Irides crimson. Legs crimson. Sexes differ. Male has small spur and does not attain full adult plumage until second year. **Adult male:** Plumage mostly blackish, but breast and foreneck shining maroon-red, each feather with narrow blue fringe, lower breast to undertail-coverts black, each feather with fringe of blue spots on lower breast. Upperparts black with shining blue spangles at feather tips and subterminal crimson iridescence. Secondaries black. Primaries brown. Uppertail-coverts and tail (of 30–32 feathers) pure white. **First-year male:** Body plumage similar to adult male but blue feather fringes narrower and reddish-maroon colour more extensive, tail rather short, chestnut, of 24 'normal' feathers. Blue facial skin less extensive, but more so than female. **Adult female:** Plumage overall chestnut-brown, finely vermiculated black, fractionally paler on underparts and becoming whitish on throat. Wings richer and darker, with coarser vermiculations. Tail chestnut, with some vermiculations, of 26 feathers.

Juvenile: Like female, but wing-covert feathers have V-shaped black subterminal marks and warm buff tips.

GEOGRAPHICAL VARIATION Monotypic.

MEASUREMENTS Length: male 77–80 cm, female c.55 cm. Males: wing 255–260, tail 450–460, tarsus 68–72, weight 1470–1800. Females: wing 225–235, tail 175–190, weight (n=2) 916 and 1004.

HABITAT Primary hill and sub-montane forest from 300 m to 1500–1600 m, though recently reported as low as 150–250 m at Ulu Barito.

VOICE Poorly known in wild, but a relatively recent sighting was accompanied by a call very reminiscent of a squirrel. A shrill, piercing cry has been heard from male during breeding season in captivity, where a soft monotonous *gack* was also uttered when aviary was intruded upon, which appears the same as sharp *kak kak* of mild alarm given in wild. A sharp metallic and quite penetrating *kook kook* appears to be a contact call. The Iban people report a distinctive *bek-kia* call, clarification of this would be very useful.

HABITS Few data and most largely anecdotal as species rarely seen in wild. Thought to prefer drier forest on ridges and hills, descending twice per day into wet gullies where feed around streams on worms and insects. The only information on group size is that pairs with two young have been seen. It is speculated that the species may be nomadic, with movements possibly linked to food supply, i.e. fruiting trees in season. Male display is spectacular, with white tail feathers spread in vertical plane forming a large white disc shape, the facial skin engorged with blood to a remarkable extent, forming a blue hammerhead shape at each side of head, with red eye at centre adding to grotesque face while strutting about, occasionally wing-whirring and scraping ground with stiff quills of outer tail feathers.

BREEDING Mating pattern unknown, though elaborate display of male suggests polygyny, while monogamous pair bonds indicated by sightings of pairs with young. A single wild nest was placed between buttress roots. Clutch size perhaps 2, but more suspected; eggs pale pinky-cream. Breeding season unclear, but may be quite long, or alternatively in different months in different years. Incubation in captivity 24–25 days.

311

DISTRIBUTION C Borneo, where it occurs in adjacent montane areas of Sarawak, Brunei, Sabah and Kalimantan. A relatively recent record from Ulu Barito in C Kalimantan considerably extended known range to the south.

STATUS Vulnerable. Probably locally not uncommon but increasingly rare. Poorly known and very few reliable data. If the species is reasonably nomadic, following fruiting trees, then assessing its status and conservation requirements will be difficult. Historically considered very common in Bornean interior and this may still hold true in those areas with little disturbance. Now thought to be locally common in parts of Sabah and Sarawak, but some assessments may be due to encounters with nomadic individuals that may have moved into areas with fruiting trees. It occurs in few protected areas, namely Gunung Mlu and Lanjak-Entimau National Parks in Sarawak, and Bukit Raya Nature Reserve in Kalimantan. Also recently recorded for the first time in Danum Valley Conservation Area in Sabah. It is considered a forest specialist and is threatened by loss of hill forest, and hunting which seems widespread in much of its range.

REFERENCES Beebe (1918–1922), BirdLife International (2000, 2001), Delacour (1977), Johnsgard (1986), MacKinnon & Phillips (1993), McGowan & Garson (1995), Smythies (1986).

Genus *CROSSOPTILON*: eared-pheasants

A small, very distinct genus of large, rather long-bodied, short-legged Chinese pheasants, with brush-like tails and rather soft, almost hair-like, relatively unpatterned plumages, lacking not only iridescence and cryptic patterning but also sexual dimorphism. That females are similar to males is unusual among ground-nesting birds, as cryptic patterning is important for concealment. Two species have prominent 'ears' of stiffened feathers that form pointed tufts or 'horns' rising from the head-sides like a 'handle-bar moustache'. Tails are vaulted, medium-long and rather graduated, of 20–24 feathers; the central pairs are particularly broad, soft vaned and arching, forming a 'bustle'. Their distributions are largely mutually exclusive and clearly arose from a common ancestor.

135 WHITE EARED-PHEASANT
Crossoptilon crossoptilon (Hodgson, 1838)   Plate 39

A variable, almost earless eared-pheasant, which has both grey and white populations bridging the gap between Tibetan (with which it may be conspecific) and Blue Eared-pheasants.

IDENTIFICATION Subalpine meadows and alpine scrub of SW China. A distinctive whitish, or ashy-grey and white pheasant, with contrasting black cap and blackish drooping bushy tail. Whitest populations also have blackish wings. Only likely to be confused with darker (and possibly conspecific) Tibetan Eared-pheasant which is much darker slate-grey on neck, breast and upperparts, contrasting strongly with white 'chinstrap' and whitish belly and uppertail-coverts; they meet in the vicinity of the Salween River in SE Tibet where they interbreed. Indeed the variable subspecies *drouynii* of White probably reflects the influence of Tibetan, as some have slate-grey upperparts. See also Tibetan and Blue Eared-pheasants, which White meets, or nearly meets, in distribution.

DESCRIPTION *C. c. crossoptilon.* Crown of short, dense velvet-like feathers. Ear-tufts short, not projecting as 'horns'. Bill reddish-horn. Bare facial skin red. Irides orange-yellow. Legs scarlet. Uppertail-coverts long, loose and hair-like. Tail drooping and elongated, of 20 feathers, margins soft and loose. Sexes similar, though male has short spur, absent in female. **Adult male:** Forehead and crown velvet black. Chin and ear-coverts pure white. Most of rest of neck and body plumage off-white, tinged grey on longer feathers of wings and uppertail-coverts. Primaries dark brown, secondaries brownish-black, with purple sheen. Tail dull blackish, becoming purplish-bronze at base and through greenish-blue to purple towards tips. **Adult female:** Slightly smaller and duller than male, becoming brownish not greyish; lacks spurs. **Juvenile:** Grey-brown, with rusty-buff shaft streaks and feather edges, rump and belly greyer. Tail grey. Soon acquires adult feathering and much as adult at 8–10 weeks.

GEOGRAPHICAL VARIATION Chiefly concerns darkness of wings and breast, which is pale grey in *dolani* and white in the other three subspecies. These latter are separable by wing colour: dark grey in *crossoptilon*, pale grey in *lichiangense*, and almost pure white in *drouynii*. Variability at a single site noted in *drouynii*, which suggests instability and casts some doubt on its taxonomic validity. Tibetan Eared-pheasant is probably the westernmost and darkest form of the complex and may be conspecific with White.

C. c. crossoptilon (Hodgson, 1838) occurs in SE Tibet and W Sichuan; described above.

C. c. dolani Meyer de Schauensee, 1938 occurs in Yushu and Lamdo regions of S Qinghai; pale ashy-grey above and below, including wings, but foreneck and belly white.

C. c. drouynii Verreaux, 1838 (includes *leucurum*) occurs in SE Tibet (between Yangtze and Salween Rivers). Variable, perhaps invalid and merely a population of intergrading forms. Some are slate-blue on mantle, others pale grey or white above; some have white basal portions of tail, others a dark tail base.

312

C. c. *lichiangense* Delacour, 1945 occurs in NW Yunnan; another poorly differentiated form, similar to nominate but with pale grey wings and tail base.

MEASUREMENTS Length 86–96 cm. Male larger. *C. c. drouynii* given. Males: wing 300–340, tail 310–365, tarsus 74–100 (both sexes), weight 2350–2750. Females: wing 271–308, tail 280–319, weight 1400–2050.

HABITAT Higher hillsides, where it occurs in coniferous (pine and spruce) and mixed forests in winter, and in subalpine birch and rhododendron scrub above the tree-line in summer. Normally encountered at 3000–4300 m, but occasionally to 2800 m.

VOICE Advertising call a far-carrying raucous grating, virtually identical to Tibetan Eared-pheasant though perhaps delivered at slightly faster tempo: *gag, gag, gagerah, gagerah, gagerah, gagerah, gagerah*. Audible at considerable distance.

HABITS Large groups of up to 30 are often encountered in winter although in the past, at least, flocks of up to 230 have been recorded. At other times, smaller groups are more likely as with similar Tibetan Eared-pheasant. Forages by pecking at ground and also by digging, presumably for bulbs and tubers, in early morning and late afternoon when also seeks water at streams.

BREEDING Presumed monogamous. No reliable information from the wild, but thought to breed May–June. Captive clutch usually 4–7 pale stone to buff eggs. Incubation in captivity lasts 24 days and is by female alone.

DISTRIBUTION China. From northern limit in S Qinghai, south through Sichuan and Tibet (largely to east of *C. harmani*) to NW Yunnan.

STATUS Near Threatened. Probably locally common within some of its large range, though much scarcer where persecuted. No systematic surveys for the species have been undertaken, but it is known from at least 20 localities throughout its range, including several reserves, such as Wolong Panda Reserve. It has been estimated, principally on the basis of range size and presumed fragmentation of populations, to number 10,000–50,000 and is declining due to habitat loss and hunting.

REFERENCES BirdLife International (2000, 2001), Cheng (1987), Delacour (1977), Johnsgard (1986), McGowan & Garson (1995).

136 TIBETAN EARED-PHEASANT
Crossoptilon harmani Elwes, 1881

Plate 39

Alternative names: Harman's or Elwes's Eared-pheasant.

The westernmost of the eared-pheasants, sharing short 'ears' and droopy tail of White. In view of structural and vocal similarities, and the occurrence of intermediates within the overlap zone, the two are perhaps best treated as conspecific.

IDENTIFICATION Subalpine meadows and alpine scrub of SE Tibet. The dark slate-grey plumage contrasting strongly with white 'chinstrap' is shared only by Blue Eared-pheasant, but their ranges do not overlap. Tibetan is smaller and lacks white bases to more droopy all-dark tail feathers, lacks obvious 'horns', has whitish chin and belly centre and paler greyish-white rump and uppertail-coverts. At northeastern limits of range meets *drouynii* subspecies of White in the Salween Valley, where there is some interbreeding. This and both vocal and structural similarities lend support to their being conspecific.

DESCRIPTION Crown of short, dense velvet-like feathers. Ear-tufts short, not projecting as 'horns'. Bill reddish-horn. Bare facial skin red. Irides orange-yellow. Legs scarlet. Uppertail-coverts long, loose and hair-like. Tail drooping and elongated, of 20 feathers, margins soft and loose. Sexes similar, though male has short spur, absent in female. **Adult:** Forehead and crown velvet black. Chin, ear-coverts, upper nape and line on foreneck pure white. Most of rest of neck and body plumage blue-grey, darkest and tinged brown on neck, breast and mantle. Lower back, rump, uppertail-coverts and rear underparts very pale, almost whitish-grey.

Primaries blackish-brown, rest of wing blackish-brown, feathers greyer on outer webs. Tail shining blue-black, greyer towards base. **Juvenile:** Short-lived juvenile plumage is presumably similar to that of White.

GEOGRAPHICAL VARIATION Monotypic. Often treated as conspecific with White Eared-pheasant.

MEASUREMENTS Length 75–85 cm. Male rather larger than female. Males: wing 272–306, tail 457–559, tarsus 87–94 (both sexes), weight, no data. Females: wing 265–282, weight, no data.

HABITAT Subalpine meadows and alpine scrub at upper limits of forest, including tall dense riverine scrub in valleys and clearings in both mixed and coniferous forests. Ranges from 3000 m to 5000 m, rarely recorded to 2280 m in winter.

VOICE Very similar to White Eared-pheasant. Advertising call a far-carrying, raucous grating, the first 1–2 notes starting slowly, then quickly running together in short bursts: *gag, gag, gagerah, gagerah, gagerah, gagerah, gagerah.*

HABITS Generally encountered in parties of 3–10, digging and foraging in grassy clearings near cover of rhododendron or *Juniperus* scrub at forest edge. In areas where unmolested may be remarkably confiding, even feeding close to human encampments with little fear. Elsewhere shy and wary, even taking to the wing if hard-pressed and capable of flying considerable distances downhill.

BREEDING Presumed monogamous, as both sexes reported caring for chicks. One nest was placed under a fallen tree, and constructed of bark and pulp, lined with moss. In the wild thought to breed May–July. Captive clutch usually 4–7 grey-green eggs. Incubation in captivity lasts 24 days and is by female alone.

DISTRIBUTION SE Tibet, north of the main Himalayan ranges and extending west to c.91°E in the Tsangpo valley and east to the Yigrong Range at c.95°E reaching its northern limit 80 km north of Lhasa. Reputed occurrence in India, along northeast border with Tibet disputed but very recently proven at Towang in extreme NE Arunachal Pradesh.

STATUS Little known but probably locally numerous in areas where not persecuted. Deforestation and hunting are significant pressures on the overall population. In urgent need of population assessment as previously considered within more widespread White Eared-pheasant. If treated specifically, would probably be classified as threatened.

REFERENCES Cheng (1987), Delacour (1977), Grimmett *et al.* (1998), McGowan & Garson (1995), Vaurie (1965).

137 BROWN EARED-PHEASANT
Crossoptilon mantchuricum Swinhoe, 1863   Plate 39

The rarest and most easterly of the genus, being even found close to Beijing. Its sooty-brown plumage is enhanced by the striking white uppertail-coverts and long white 'horns'.

IDENTIFICATION Montane forests of NE China, where now confined to a handful of sites. Range approaches, but does not overlap or meet that of Blue Eared-pheasant. Despite sharing long 'horns', white tail base and arching 'bustle' of a tail with Blue, confusion unlikely as Brown is dark brown with stunning white rump and uppertail-coverts.

DESCRIPTION Crown of short, dense velvet-like feathers. Ear-tufts long, projecting as 'horns'. Bill reddish-horn. Bare facial skin red. Irides reddish-brown. Legs crimson. Uppertail-coverts long, loose and hair-like. Tail of 22 feathers, the central two pairs with soft, drooping vanes (reminiscent of Ostrich plumes). Sexes similar, though male has short spur, absent in female. **Adult:** Forehead and crown velvet black. Chin, upper nape and ear-coverts pure white, the latter appear as long horns like a 'handle-bar moustache'. Most of rest of body plumage and wings dull darkish brown, becoming blackish on neck, the feathers with hair-like fringes. Lower back, rump and uppertail-coverts silvery-white. Primaries brown, secondaries brownish-black with a purple sheen. Tail feathers white but brownish-black on terminal third, darkening and glossed purple at tip. **Juvenile:** Dark grey-brown, mottled due to buff shaft-streaks and edges to feathers. Tail relatively short. Soon acquires adult feathering and much as adult at eight weeks.

GEOGRAPHICAL VARIATION Monotypic.

MEASUREMENTS Length 96–100 cm. Sexes very similar in size. Males: wing 270–312, tail 518–582, tarsus (both sexes) c.100, weight 1650–2475. Females: wing 265–290, tail 447–576; weight 1450–2025.

HABITAT Montane forests, both mixed coniferous and deciduous with shrub understorey, at 1100–2600 m

VOICE During breeding season male utters call that commences softly, but quickly increases in volume, lasting on occasion up to a minute. It has been ren-

dered as *trip crrrr ah*. Possibly this and other calls are similar to those of Blue Eared-pheasant.

HABITS Found in moderate to large groups, of 10–30, in non-breeding season, but pairs within these groups sometimes evident. Forages mostly on plants and can be observed in small groups digging around clumps of grass in search of roots, bulbs, tubers etc.

BREEDING Presumed monogamous. Nest a scrape in larch and spruce forest. Clutch probably 5–8, though 4–20 reported (mean 8.8) and once even 22. Smaller clutches may be laid by first-years or be replacements. Eggs pale stone green. Breeds April–June. Incubation in captivity lasts 26–27 days and is by female alone.

DISTRIBUTION NE China. Range now very small and fragmented, surviving at a few places in Luya Shan and Luliang Shan, in Shanxi, and on Xiao-wutai Shan in adjacent Hebei. There is a small population in the Dongling Shan on west edge of Beijing municipality.

STATUS Vulnerable. Locally common in suitable habitat, but this is now drastically reduced and probably concentrated in 5–6 areas. Apparently widespread until the 1930s, since when a combination of forest loss and hunting has wrought a dramatic decline within its small range, and the total population probably numbers just 5000–17,000 individuals. Forest loss is probably the major factor, but hunting may have had an increasingly disproportionate effect as habitat is reduced. Much of the population is now found in protected areas, such as Pangquangou National Natural Reserve, and Luya Shan and Wulu Shan Natural Reserves. Outside these areas, populations are still under pressure from a variety of human activities, including habitat encroachment for development and agriculture. Within protected areas, disturbance to nesting birds caused by seasonal mushroom collectors is a major problem, as is egg collection by farmers; nest failure rates reach 78% in some areas.

REFERENCES BirdLife International (2000, 2001), Cheng (1987), Delacour (1977), Johnsgard (1986), McGowan & Garson (1995).

The most numerous, and arguably the most attractive of the eared-pheasants.

IDENTIFICATION Montane forests and meadows of C China, with range virtually meeting that of White Eared-pheasant in C Sichuan (Songpan district). Confusion unlikely as White Eared-pheasant really is white in W Sichuan, with greyer populations much further west. Superficially similar in coloration to Tibetan Eared-pheasant, but Blue is much larger, with a high 'bustle' of a tail and white bases to outer feathers, prominent long white 'horns' and more uniformly darker grey uppertail-coverts and rear underparts. Compare also Brown Eared-pheasant.

DESCRIPTION Crown of short, dense velvet-like feathers. Ear-tufts long, projecting as 'horns'. Bill reddish-horn. Bare facial skin red. Irides yellow. Legs crimson. Uppertail-coverts long, loose and hair-like. Tail of 24 feathers, the central two pairs with soft and drooping vanes (reminiscent of Ostrich plumes). Sexes similar, though male a little larger and has short spur, absent in female. **Adult:** Forehead and crown velvet black. Chin, upper nape and ear-coverts pure white, the latter appear as long horns like a 'handle-bar moustache'. Most of rest of neck and body plumage bluish-grey, the feathers with hair-like fringes. Primaries dull brown, secondaries brownish-black with purple sheen. Tail bluish-grey, darkening and glossed green at tip, which is purple; the outermost 5–6 feather pairs are white on basal third or half. **Juvenile:** Dark grey-brown, mottled with buff shaft streaks and edges to feathers. Tail relatively short. Soon acquires adult feathering and much as adult at eight weeks.

GEOGRAPHICAL VARIATION Monotypic.

MEASUREMENTS Length c.96 cm. Male slightly larger. Males: wing 285–314, tail 447–570, tarsus (both sexes) c.100, weight 1735–2110. Females: wing 283–311, tail 470–510, weight 1820–1880.

HABITAT Both coniferous and mixed forests, at 2700–4400 m. Often on rocky slopes with juniper scrub and alpine meadows. Descends in winter, but still usually above 3000 m.

VOICE During breeding season males give loud and hoarse calls similar to other eared-pheasants and rendered as *ka ka...la* or *krip krraah krraah*. Calls usually in early morning, sometimes at other times of the day, but repeats call perhaps only 5–6 times.

HABITS Presumably similar to other eared-pheasants. Encountered in large flocks of up to 50–60 outside breeding period and these are thought to comprise a number of family groups. Flocks disband in spring. Forages in early morning and late afternoon, feeding on buds, leaves, stems and roots of various plants, including grasses, sedges, herbs, spruce and other trees, and also some animal matter, such as beetles. Feeds by digging during warmer months, and on leaf buds and berries in late autumn and winter.

BREEDING Assumed monogamous. Nest a scrape under trees or shrubs. Clutch usually c.8 but can be 6–12; eggs pale greyish-brown. Breeds April–June. Incubation in captivity 24–28 days by female alone.

DISTRIBUTION C China. From northern limit in NE and E Qinghai, south over S Gansu, reaching extreme NE Tibet (Tanggula range) and N Sichuan (south to Songpan). There is an apparently isolated population in the Helan Shan of Ningxhia Nei Mongol.

STATUS Apparently locally not uncommon throughout much of range. No obvious conservation problems and it is considered unthreatened. Perhaps partially due to the lack of conservation concern, it has not been formally surveyed, but anecdotally overall population is thought to number hundreds of thousands and is possibly not declining. Probably particularly well protected within panda reserves.

REFERENCES Cheng (1987), Delacour (1977), Johnsgard (1986), McGowan (1994), McGowan & Garson (1995).

Genus *CATREUS*: Cheer Pheasant

A monotypic genus created for this peculiar W Himalayan pheasant. Though clearly resembling *Syrmaticus* and *Phasianus* in its long tail, the lack of strong sexual plumage dimorphism, its hair-like crest, rather short legs and several behavioural traits indicate a closer affinity to eared-pheasants.

139 **CHEER PHEASANT**
Catreus wallichii (Hardwicke, 1827) **Plate 40**

Alternative name: Chir Pheasant.

A unique pheasant, sharing features of several other genera, yet retaining a number of distinctive features.

IDENTIFICATION Grassy Himalayan slopes with crags and stunted forest in W India and W Nepal; now rare and very localised. Large, distinctive, long-tailed pheasant, characterised by habitat and calls, and lack of strong plumage features other than barred tail and hairy crest. Confusion unlikely within range as it is the only pheasant with a long barred tail in the W Himalayas, though compare female Koklass and Kalij Pheasants for clarification of their features.

DESCRIPTION Crest of long hair-like feathers projects from rear crown (longest in male). Bill strong, pale yellowish-brown to pale bluish-horn. Bare skin around eye crimson-red (duller in female). Irides golden-brown. Legs relatively short, greyish-brown to fleshy-brown. Tail of 18 feathers, long and pointed, with graduated outer feathers. Sexes similar in plumage, but female smaller and has shorter tail. Male has single spur, female unspurred. **Adult male:** Lores, head-sides, crown and crest blackish-brown. Neck, throat and breast pale grey, becoming buff on lower breast and flanks, each feather with black subterminal bar, largest and boldest on breast-sides and flanks. Belly centre blackish. Vent greyish-buff. Upperparts pale buff, feathers with black bars and grey fringes; mantle with bolder bars and reddish tips. Rump and uppertail-coverts buff, rustier on rump where feathers have dark subterminal bars. Tail brownish-buff, broadly barred blackish-brown throughout. **Adult female:** Crown, face and shorter crest, brown. Chin and throat whitish-buff, neck and upper breast feathers blackish, with bold whitish borders. Lower breast and flanks chestnut-buff, with narrow white borders, blackish markings and bars. Belly centre whitish, flanks and vent buff with blackish spotting and barring. Upperparts vermiculated rusty-buff and black, with buff shaft streaks, bold black subterminal bar and broad buff tips. Rump and uppertail-coverts unbarred. Tail shorter and more vermiculated than male, with narrower buff barring and overall less strongly patterned. **Juvenile:** Duller than female, with less distinct markings and no crest.

GEOGRAPHICAL VARIATION Monotypic.

MEASUREMENTS Length: male 90–118 cm, female 61–76 cm. Males: wing 235–270, tail 450–580, tarsus 74–78, weight 1475–1700. Females: wing 225–245, tail 320–470, tarsus 60–63, weight 900–1360.

HABITAT Grassland on mid-altitude slopes as low as 1200 m in winter and to 3050 m. Slopes usually dissected by ravines and containing pockets of 0.5-1 m-tall scrub and trees, oak, pine and rhododendron being particularly favoured, with rocky outcrops. Typically, in early successional habitats and disappears if scrub cover becomes too dense.

VOICE Apparently remarkably similar to calls of eared-pheasants. A distinctive raucous, grating series, often accelerating to crescendo of staccato whistles, rendered as *chir-a-pir, chir-a-pir, chir, chir chirwa, chirwa.* Both sexes chorus at dawn and dusk with series of high-pitched *chewewoo* whistles, interspersed by short *chut* calls and harsh staccato notes.

HABITS Generally encountered in pairs or family groups, but parties of up to 15 recorded formerly. Digs for roots and tubers with strong bill in manner of monals and eared-pheasants, even digging quite deep pits that almost conceal it from view. Around dawn emerges onto village lands and grassy slopes to feed. Roosts on high rocky outcrops or in wooded gullies, usually on stunted trees but also reported on ground. Noisy at roost times, particularly when assembling in late afternoon and again soon after dawn. Despite occupying relatively open habitat is difficult to observe as often remains close to available cover. If disturbed prefers to crouch or run upslope, but will take off and 'rocket' down hillside for some distance at great speed.

BREEDING Monogamous. Nest at base of structure, such as rock or cliff, in undergrowth; no real scrape made, but usually lays amid grasses. Clutch usually 9–10, but up to 14 reported. Eggs pale yellowish-grey with reddish-brown speckles. Breeds late April–June. Incubation in captivity lasts 26 days and is by female alone, though male remains close by and helps tend and protect young after hatching.

DISTRIBUTION W Himalayas. Historically from NW Pakistan along Himalayan front ranges through NW India to WC Nepal. It appears to be extinct in Pakistan, though there are occasional reports from parts of North-West Frontier Province and Azad Kashmir. Few recent sites in Nepal. The stronghold is probably in Himachal Pradesh in India. Statements referring to its former occurrence in E Afghanistan and Sikkim are in error.

STATUS Vulnerable. Very locally distributed and approximately 20 years ago it was considered to be on the verge of extinction, being known only from a few sites. Surveys, mostly in the Indian Himalayas, since then have demonstrated that it persists in a number of areas and is more widespread than previously thought. Typically appears to survive as small relict populations, rarely numbering tens of pairs (sometimes just a handful), but clarification of this would greatly assist long-term conservation planning. Outside India, it is very rare (if it still occurs) in Pakistan and has been recently recorded from only a few localities in Nepal. Inhabiting early successional grassy habitats, it always occurs near habitation and cultivation, and striking a balance between the disturbance necessary to prevent sites scrubbing over, but avoiding overgrazing and hunting, is likely to be the key to the species' survival. Consequently, though now known to be more widespread than previously thought, each site is potentially very fragile. It occurs in a number of protected areas, including the Great Himalayan National Park and Chail Sanctuary in India, and Rara Lake National Park in Nepal.

REFERENCES Ali & Ripley (1983), BirdLife International (2000, 2001), Garson (1983), Grimmett *et al.* (1998), Lelliot (1981), McGowan & Garson (1995).

Genus *SYRMATICUS*: long-tailed pheasants

Males of this genus of primarily Chinese and Japanese pheasants have red facial skin (very restricted in Reeves's), rather short spurs, lack head adornments, have very long barred tails of 16–20 feathers and differ markedly from the cryptically patterned females. Though close to *Phasianus* they differ in having 'normal' rump and uppertail-covert feathering and in lacking head tufts. Shared behavioural (including display postures) and vocal differences of the genus also differ from *Phasianus*, as do patterns of downy chicks.

140 ELLIOT'S PHEASANT
Syrmaticus ellioti (Swinhoe, 1872)

Plate 41

Alternative names: Bar-backed Pheasant, White-necked Long-tailed Pheasant.

This localised pheasant of hill and coastal forest in SE China forms a species group with Mrs Hume's in the E Himalayas and Mikado on nearby Taiwan.

IDENTIFICATION Forested hills in SE China, where unlikely to be mistaken. Male a fancy pheasant with long rusty-barred whitish tail, and striking blackish throat, chestnut breast and wings, contrasting with whitish nape, wingbars and belly. Female completely mottled above, with relatively short and white-tipped tail, less buffy-brown than female Common and has contrasting whitish belly and dusky face and throat. Range overlaps with Common Pheasant but latter avoids dense forest.

DESCRIPTION Bill yellowish-horn. Bare facial skin red. Irides orange to brown (brownest in female). Legs grey. Tail elongated and pointed, of 16 feathers, the outer feathers graduated; tail shorter with blunter tip in female. Sexes differ. Male has short spur, absent in female. **Adult male:** Crown mixed grey and chestnut. Cheeks and ear-coverts grey-brown. Neck-sides whitish-grey, hindneck darker grey. Chin, throat and foreneck black. Mantle and breast rufous-chestnut, each feather with subterminal black bar and metallic copper fringe. Lower breast and belly white, flanks chestnut with broad white tips, and vent marked black and chestnut. Scapulars black with broad white tips, forming white band either side of back. Rump and uppertail-coverts blue-black with white scaling. Wings basically chestnut, lesser coverts steel-blue, greater coverts and secondaries chestnut with blue-black subterminal bar and white tips forming double white wingbar, primaries brown. Tail greyish-white, narrowly barred chestnut. **Adult female:** Crown rufous, with blackish feather tips. Head-sides, and rear and sides of neck greyish-buff, chin and foreneck blackish. Mantle and breast rufous, each feather with black subterminal bar, those of mantle also have whitish shaft. Lower breast and belly brown, each feather tipped white, those of belly appearing white due to concealed brown bases, vent marked black and chestnut. Scapulars dull rufous, tipped grey-brown. Rump and uppertail-coverts rufous, vermiculated dark brown, brightest rufous on uppertail-coverts. Wings vermiculated brown and black, each feather with subterminal black patch and greyish tip, primaries brownish-black. Tail rufous-brown, central feathers tipped rufous; others with black subterminal bar and white tip. **Juvenile:** Resembles dull version of female, but whiter throat; young male soon acquires male-like tail pattern.

GEOGRAPHICAL VARIATION Monotypic.

MEASUREMENTS Length: male c.80 cm, female c.50 cm, much of difference accounted for by tail length. Males: wing 230–257, tail 390–470, tarsus 70, weight (captive) 1044–1317 (mean 1156). Females: wing 197–200, tail 176–180, tarsus 63, weight (captive) 726–1090 (mean 878).

HABITAT Evergreen broad-leaf and conifer forests, bamboo and other dense scrub in mountains at 300–1500 m.

VOICE Fairly simple, principally comprising low clucks and chuckles. Both sexes also give shrill squeal, which is not especially loud. Though males do wing-whirr this appears to be rather quiet and is usually followed by a repeated, rather low-pitched, *ge-ge-ge-ge-ge-ge* call.

HABITS Shy and elusive. Forages mostly in morning and late afternoon in small groups of 3–4, probably family parties. Feeds predominantly on seeds, berries, leaves etc., and presumably also scratches at ground and digs in manner of Reeves's Pheasant. During breeding season, males display, including wing-whirring, which is audible at some distance, in morning and early afternoon.

BREEDING Mating pattern unclear. Nest a simple scrape. Clutch 5–8 creamy to rosy-white eggs. Breeds at least mid-March to late May. Incubation in captivity lasts 26 days and is by female alone.

DISTRIBUTION SE China, from Guangxi and E and S Guizhou east through Hunan and E Jiangxi to W Zhejiang. Also recorded from N Guangdong, N Fujian and S Anhui.

STATUS Vulnerable. Until c.10 years ago regarded as rare in most areas, but now considered possibly locally common in suitable habitat, though population is probably still fewer than 10,000 individuals. Sites include a number of protected areas, including Jinggan Shan and Leigong Shan Natural Reserves in Guizhou, and Gutian Shan Nature Reserve in Zhejiang, where the population was estimated at 500–600 individuals in July–September 1999, with a density of 0.88 individuals/ha within the reserve and 0.335/ha outside the protected area. However, its habitat is now limited to increasingly isolated blocks of forest within large tracts of cultivation. It is also hunted for food

REFERENCES Cheng (1987), Ding Ping & Zhuge Yang (1990), McGowan & Garson (1995).

Alternative names: Hume's Pheasant, Bar-tailed Pheasant, Black-necked Long-tailed Pheasant.

Little-studied and rather elusive forest pheasant of E Himalayas; though clearly closely related to Elliot's Pheasant, the rich chestnut underparts and blue neck render males quite distinctive.

IDENTIFICATION Montane forests of E Himalayas. Distinctive male has red face within dark head and metallic blue neck, chestnut body and very long almost whitish, but barred, tail. Prominent white scapular and wingbars, and whitish-scaled rump (whitest in eastern race *burmanicus*) provide striking highlights. Rather drab but heavily marked female differs from female Elliot's in whitish throat, buffier belly and overall warmer plumage tones. Forest habitat and rather blunt, white-tipped tail provide easy distinctions from other female pheasants of the region.

DESCRIPTION *S. h. humiae*. Bill yellowish-horn. Bare facial skin red. Irides orange to brown (brownest in female). Legs grey. Tail elongated and pointed, of 16 feathers, the outer feathers graduated; tail shorter and blunter tipped in female. Sexes differ. Male has short spur, absent in female. **Adult male:** Crown, cheeks and ear-coverts dark grey-brown. Chin, throat, neck, upper mantle and upper breast rich metallic blue. Back, most of wings and rest of underparts, rufous-chestnut, each feather with subterminal black bar and metallic copper fringe. Scapulars black with broad white tips, forming white band either side of back. Rump and uppertail-coverts blue-black with white scaling. Wings basically chestnut, lesser coverts steel-blue, greater coverts and secondaries chestnut with blue-black subterminal bar and white tips forming double white wingbar, primaries brown. Tail very long and greyish, some almost whitish, narrowly barred black and chestnut. **Adult female:** Crown rufous-brown, with chestnut feather tips. Head-sides, entire neck and upper breast virtually unmarked, or weakly spotted, buffy-brown. Upperparts and breast vermiculated greyish-brown, each feather with black subterminal bar, those of mantle also have whitish shaft. Lower breast and belly buffy-brown with whitish barring. Wings basically vermiculated brown and black, each feather with subterminal black patch and greyish tip, forming indistinct wingbars; primaries brownish-black. Central tail feathers dull brown, with narrow bars and blunt buff tips, other feathers tinged rufous near shaft with black subterminal bar and white tip. **Juvenile:** Resembles dull version of female, but young male soon acquires adult male-like tail pattern.

GEOGRAPHICAL VARIATION Two subspecies recognised, differing chiefly in colour saturation of males. Their ranges are separated by the Irrawaddy River in Myanmar.

    S. h. humiae (Hume, 1881) occurs in NE India, east to the Irrawaddy in Myanmar; described above.

    S. h. burmanicus (Oates, 1898) occurs in SW Yunnan and Guangxi (China), E Myanmar and N

Thailand; male has blue of upperparts slightly deeper and more purplish, and more restricted on upper breast and back than *humiae*. Lower back and rump black, not bluish, but has broader whitebars giving whiter-rumped appearance.

MEASUREMENTS Length: male 90 cm, female c.60 cm, much of difference being due to long tail of male. *S. h. humiae* given. Males: wing 206–225, tail 400–535, tarsus 58–66, weight 975–1080. Females: wing 198–210, tail 195–200, tarsus 55–60, weight 650–850.

HABITAT Variety of open forested habitats, such as evergreen, broad-leaf and mixed forest with patches of grass and bracken on steep and rocky hillsides in China and Myanmar, and oak–pine forest with scattered clearings in Thailand. Also scrubby areas in some places and has even been found in conifer plantations in China. Altitude varies according to location, but mostly at 1200–2400 m, being recorded to 3000 m and as low as 780 m (in Guangxi).

VOICE Like Elliot's, vocabulary appears limited to low clucks and chuckles in the main. Contact note a loud *chuck*, also a low, muttering, repeated *buk-buk-buk-buk* when feeding in group. Louder versions of these calls apparently given in alarm; also gives vent to a loud screech in such circumstances. Males wing-whirr in display, but this is not accompanied by significant calling. Finally, if hard-pressed, takes flight with a low chuckle on rising. The oft-repeated statement that this species gives a loud crowing in the manner of Cheer Pheasant (*cher-a-per cher-a-per cher cher cheria cheria*) is in striking contrast to other *Syrmaticus*, which are remarkably quiet, and it is probable that this is an error perpetuated from Beebe (1922).

HABITS Poorly known. At northern edge of range in China, feeds mainly on ground in groups of up to five; generally only one male is present suggesting that these may be family units. Foraging individuals keep close to, or within, dense grasses and bushes at forest-edge. Roosts usually singly in bushes and trees in winter, but sometimes in small groups.

BREEDING Mating pattern unclear, but group composition suggests polygamy. Nest fairly simple, of dried leaves, pine twigs etc. and body feathers. Clutch 3–12 creamy to rosy-white eggs. Breeds mid-March–May. Incubation in captivity 27–28 days by female alone.

DISTRIBUTION E Himalayas, historically from Manipur, Mizoram and Nagaland (no recent records in latter), in extreme NE India through N Myanmar to NW Thailand and S China. In China it is known from several localities in SW Yunnan and Guangxi.

STATUS Vulnerable. Rare throughout except possibly in heart of range, in Myanmar, from where there are no recent data, except two sightings in the Chin States. Subspecies *humiae* may number as few as 1000 individuals, in India there have been recent reports only from Mizoram. In Thailand, there are perhaps only 200–500 *burmanicus*. No estimates from China, but it is known from more than 20 sites. Based on these data, a total population not exceeding 10,000 has been suggested, and is presumed to be declining due to habitat loss. It is known from few protected areas, including Doi Chaing Dao National Park in Thailand and Ailao Shan Natural Reserve in China. Principal threats are habitat degradation, abetted by annual burning of wooded slopes in Thailand, the intensification of agriculture and hunting.

REFERENCES Ali & Ripley (1983), BirdLife International (2000, 2001), Davison (1979), Grimmett *et al.* (1998), King *et al.* (1975), McGowan & Garson (1995), Smythies (1986).

---

142 MIKADO PHEASANT
Syrmaticus mikado (Ogilvie-Grant, 1906)   Plate 41

Alternative name: Taiwan Long-tailed Pheasant.

This very elegant dark pheasant of high wet forest on Taiwan appears most closely related to Mrs Hume's of the Himalayas, females being especially similar.

IDENTIFICATION Endemic to montane forests on Taiwan. Male unmistakable: wholly blackish (scaled purplish-blue), with contrasting white wingbars and very long, slender, pointed tail, crossed by narrow white bars. Female darker than congeners, resembles dark version of female Mrs Hume's but scaled with overall blacker markings, is more boldly streaked and spotted white on upperparts and has bolder tail markings. Only other pheasants on Taiwan are Common and Swinhoe's, neither of which are likely to be confused. Though there is some overlap with Swinhoe's, Mikado favours wetter forests at higher elevations.

DESCRIPTION Bill has black upper mandible, pale yellowish-horn on lower (duller in female). Bare facial skin red. Irides reddish-brown (brownest in female). Legs dark grey. Tail very elongated and pointed, of 16 feathers, the outer feathers graduated; shorter and blunter tipped in female. Sexes differ. Male has short spur, absent in female. **Adult male:** Most of plumage rich bluish-purple, each feather with concealed black base. Breast and mantle feathers with blue fringe broken by subterminal black spot, some feathers of rump and uppertail-coverts with variable white fringes. Wings black, greater coverts and, more narrowly, secondaries tipped white, forming two white wingbars; primaries brownish-black. Belly and undertail-coverts black, latter have white fringes. Tail very long, also black, but crossed by numerous well-spaced narrow white bars. **Adult female:** Crown and nape dull olive-brown. Head-sides and foreneck olive-grey, spotted white. Upperparts greyish-olive brown, vermiculated black and reddish, contour feathers have white shaft streaks (fewer on rump and uppertail-coverts). Wings vermiculated olive-brown and black, each feather with subterminal black patch and whitish tip, forming indistinct wingbars, primaries brownish-black. Tail feathers rufous, with narrow black and buff bars, and tipped buffy-white. Rear underparts olive-grey, mottled and barred black and white, central belly unmarked greyish-olive. **Juvenile:** Resembles female, but head and neck heavily spotted buffy-white; may be sexed after a few weeks, as young male soon acquires adult male tail feathers.

GEOGRAPHICAL VARIATION Monotypic.

MEASUREMENTS Length: male c.87 cm and female 53 cm, much of difference due to long tail of male. Males: wing 210–230, tail 490–530, tarsus 66–67, weight (captive) 1300. Females: wing 187–215, tail 172–225, tarsus 57–61, weight (captive) 1015.

HABITAT Inhabits dense undergrowth of rhododendron and bamboo in primary forest in mountains at 1600–3300 m. Also occurs in some secondary habitats.

VOICE Apparently quiet much of time, though male gives repeated short rising plaintive squeal, preceded by mellow clucked *chup chup* in breeding season. Quiet, high-pitched *wok, wok, wok* in alarm uttered when disturbed and, on rare occasion that is flushed, bursts into flight amid loud calls. Female has quiet *cluck* that keeps chicks close by.

HABITS Typically shy and elusive, an impression enhanced by its quiet habits. More often seen at dawn and dusk than at other times. Males are usually observed alone or with a female, whereas female is often encountered in company of males, other females or young. Female appears to have much larger home range than male, and size appears to vary being larger in spring and autumn, and smallest in winter. During heavy rain perches above ground, a group of nine was observed in such circumstances, but apparently easier to see and for longer periods during light rain or immediately after heavy rain. It has been suggested that most sightings are in April–July when wild fruits and seeds are ripe. Quietly slips into undergrowth if disturbed.

BREEDING Mating pattern unclear and very few breeding data from wild. Nest, at least occasionally, is apparently constructed of bamboo stalks on fallen tree c.1 m above ground. Apparently breeds from late April. Captive clutch 5; eggs creamy-white. Incubation in captivity lasts 28 days and is apparently by female alone.

DISTRIBUTION Endemic to Taiwan where occurs in central mountains.

STATUS Near Threatened. Probably reasonably common in suitable habitat, which is increasingly restricted to protected areas, the most notable being Yushan National Park which may hold c.10,000 individuals. It has probably undergone a substantial decline in the past due to hunting, but this practice has probably decreased now (possibly because the species is not as widespread as formerly), and the current main threat is habitat loss. It is probably less affected by this than Swinhoe's Pheasant, as it occurs at higher altitudes in the central mountains. Given that much of its habitat is now protected, it is hoped that the population may now be stable.

REFERENCES BirdLife International (2000, 2001), Bridgman (1993), Johnsgard (1986), Poltack (1972), Severinghaus (1977, 1978).

143 COPPER PHEASANT
Syrmaticus soemmerringii (Temminck, 1830)   Plate 41

Alternative name: Soemmerring's Pheasant.

Considering that its range is centred on Honshu, the largest of the Japanese islands, surprisingly little research appears to have been undertaken on this interesting pheasant. Like Mikado Pheasant of Taiwan, females bear a similarity to those of Mrs Hume's and Elliot's Pheasants in mainland Asia.

IDENTIFICATION Hill and montane forests of Japan. Wary and elusive, both sexes being distinctive in their native range. Male a large, rich copper-chestnut pheasant with a very long barred tail. Variation exists in overall colour tones and in prominence of white or buff scaling on rump and rear underparts; some appear white-rumped in the field (especially *ijimae*). Overlaps with Green Pheasant, though latter favours second growth or more open country shunned by Copper. Female rather intermediate between female Elliot's and Mrs Hume's but tail more rufous and almost unbarred. Female Green has longer, more pointed and clearly barred tail, lacking rufous tones or white feather tips of Copper. Compare female with Chinese Bamboo-partridge.

DESCRIPTION *S. s scintillans*. Bill yellowish-horn. Bare facial skin red. Irides brown. Legs grey. Tail elongated and almost ribbon-like, of 18 or 20 feathers, the outermost very short; tail much shorter and blunter tipped in female. Sexes differ. Male has very short spur, absent in female. **Adult male:** Head rich reddish-chestnut, neck and mantle rather paler and have black feather bases and bright coppery-purple fringes to feathers. Rump and uppertail-coverts similar, but with broad pale buff or white scaling at feather tips. Scapulars dark chestnut with black centres and white tips. Wing-coverts similar, flight feathers barred blackish-brown and buff. Breast pale chestnut, feathers with black central marks and pale buffy-grey fringes, becoming even paler on flanks and belly, undertail-coverts dark chestnut, with black spots and bars. Tail very long, cinnamon, crossed by numerous narrow black bars, which are edged buff and chestnut. **Adult female:** Crown dark brown, with buff feather tips. Head-sides, entire neck and upper breast buff, heavily marked blackish-brown forming irregular dark collar on lower throat. Upperparts vermiculated greyish-brown, each feather with black subterminal bar, those of mantle also have buff shaft streaks. Lower breast and flanks dark brown with buff barring. Wings basically vermiculated brown and black, each feather with subterminal black patch and buff tip, forming weak wingbars; primaries brownish-black. Central tail feathers banded rufous and grey, vermiculated throughout (less strongly barred than other *Syrmaticus*), outer tail feathers rufous with black subterminal bar and white

tip. **Juvenile:** Resembles female, but young male soon acquires adult male-like tail pattern.

GEOGRAPHICAL VARIATION Generally paler and less richly coloured males occur in north. Much individual variation throughout range and intergrades occur, suggesting that some subspecies are invalid. Particularly dubious is the distinction between the first three subspecies.

  S. s. scintillans (Gould, 1866) (includes *septentrionalis*) occurs in N and C Honshu; described above, males paler and relatively shorter tailed than other races.
  S. s. intermedius (Kuroda, 1919) (includes *inabaensis*) occurs in SW Honshu and Shikoku; male has longer and redder tail than *scintillans* (male tail 676–845), overall richer and slightly darker red, with belly and breast concolorous, golden fringes to mantle and scapular feathers.
  S. s. subrufus (Kuroda, 1919) occurs in SE and SW Honshu and SW Shikoku; males even darker red overall, with very little white on fringes of upperparts, feathers of mantle and back have shining golden-orange fringes.
  S. s. soemmerringii (Temminck, 1830) occurs in N and C Kyushu; the darkest and reddest-chestnut race, with golden-carmine fringes to upperparts, intergrading with following race in SW Kyushu.
  S. s. ijimae (Dresser, 1902) occurs in SE Kyushu; similar in darkness of red to nominate, but has broad white fringes to feathers of back and rump, some appearing completely white-backed in the field, others bar-backed.

MEASUREMENTS Length: male 87–136 cm and female 51–54 cm, some of difference due to long tail of male. *S. s. scintillans* given. Males: wing 205–230, tail 484–752, tarsus 59–69. Females: wing 197–217, tail 164–196, tarsus 54–59. Weight 907 (an unsexed captive).

HABITAT Predominantly in gullies, within broad-leaf forest, which are well vegetated and shaded, and in dense deciduous or coniferous (especially *Cryptomeria* and cypress) forests. Also occurs in adjoining areas with dense undergrowth. From sea level to c.1800 m, most frequent at higher altitudes.

VOICE Not especially vocal, the call being a hoarse and indistinct *ko ko ko*. Males also wing-whirr, usually in mornings and sometimes without calling.

HABITS Difficult to locate, it usually occurs singly or in pairs, sometimes in family parties and rarely flocks of six. Usually within deep forest, where most common around gullies and streams, but also at forest edge and sometimes in villages. Roosts in trees, often on steep slopes and typically in pines. During breeding season wing-whirring male may be audible over some distance.

BREEDING Mating pattern unclear and both monogamy and polygyny claimed, though sightings of pairs and family parties suggest former. Nest on ground, usually among tussocky grass or next to tree trunk or fallen tree. Clutch usually 6–7, but sometimes up to 13, relatively small cream eggs. Breeds from March in south and April–May in north. Incubation in captivity 24–25 days.

DISTRIBUTION Endemic to Japan, on main island of Honshu and adjacent Shikoku and Kyushu.

STATUS Near Threatened. Once common, if not abundant, but now considered uncommon and is difficult to find. Undoubtedly the main reason for the decline is over-hunting as annual bags of 500,000 (if not almost a million) were made in 1925–1975. Following awareness of decline, it was declared illegal to hunt females in 1976. Since then, there is surprisingly little information on status of this Japanese endemic, though until 1991, at least, it was still extensively hunted, despite its rarity. Any data on encounter rates at various sites, presence in protected areas etc. would be valuable.

REFERENCES BirdLife International (2000, 2001), Brazil (1991), Delacour (1977), Johnsgard (1986), McGowan & Garson (1995), Yamashina (1976).

144 REEVES'S PHEASANT
Syrmaticus reevesii (J. E. Gray, 1829)   Plate 38

Alternative name: White-crowned Long-tailed Pheasant.

Males of this spectacular pheasant have uniquely scaled golden body plumage and the longest tail among typical pheasants.

IDENTIFICATION Hill and montane forests, especially in steep-sided valleys, of C China. Male unmistakable with black-and-white patterned head, scaly golden body plumage and extremely long barred tail. Female less striking, having a longer and more pointed tail than congeners, but rufous in outer tail and striking pattern created by dusky crown and cheek bar, contrasting with otherwise unmarked whitish or pale buff head and throat, distinctive.

DESCRIPTION Bill greenish-horn. Bare skin around eye red (obscured by black plumes, which are very extensive in female). Irides brown. Legs grey. Tail very long (central feathers up to 1600 mm in males), graduated (outermost feathers only 65 mm) and tapering, of 20 feathers. Sexes differ. Male has very short spur, absent in female **Adult male:** Crown white. Forehead, lores, head-sides and occiput black. Patch on ear-coverts, throat and upper neck white, bordered below by black collar. Rest of neck and most of upperparts golden-yellow, each feather with neat black border giving very scaly appearance. Scapulars and wing-coverts white, feathers bordered black or chestnut. Secondaries buffy-yellow, barred black, white and chestnut. Primaries dark brown, barred rufous-buff. Foreneck and breast blackish-chestnut, marked with white, becoming tawny-rufous on rear flanks and deep black on thighs and vent. Tail silvery-white, crossed by numerous black and chestnut bars, with cinnamon-buff at edges, outer feathers progressively shorter, more broadly edged cinnamon-yellow. **Adult female:** Crown blackish, with reddish feather tips. Eyebrow, head-sides and front and sides of neck clear warm buff, face with blackish eye-stripe and cheek bar. Hindneck and upperparts grey-brown, vermiculated with buff and black shaft streaks, mantle blacker, with chestnut and white marks. Breast and flanks chestnut, with whitish and grey mottling,

upper breast has some black mottling, central belly whitish and vent buff, with chestnut markings. Wings grey-brown vermiculated black, each feather with subterminal black patch and buff streak, primaries and secondaries barred rufous and dark brown. Central tail feathers grey-brown, vermiculated black, irregularly barred pale buff and dark brown, outer feathers with extensive rufous and black-and-white tips. **Juvenile:** Resembles female, but paler and duller, with whiter foreneck and whitish streaking on pale brown breast; young male soon acquires adult male-like tail pattern.

GEOGRAPHICAL VARIATION Monotypic.

MEASUREMENTS Length: male 210 cm and female 150 cm, much of difference accounted for by very long tail of male. Males: wing 260–300, tail 1000–1600, tarsus 80, weight 1529 (captive mean). Females: wing 218–250, tail 330–450, tarsus 57–61, weight 949 (captive mean).

HABITAT Evergreen and deciduous (especially oak-dominated) forests, with tall grasses and bushes. Altitudinal range 300–2000 m.

VOICE Generally quiet, a soft contact *pu pu pu* call uttered by members of a flock. During breeding season males wing-whirr and then give series of high-pitched chirping calls audible over c.200 m.

HABITS Appears at forest edge or emerges onto adjacent farmland in early morning and late afternoon to forage. At other times retreats into forest and is largely quiet. Often in small groups, but up to 10 or more congregate in winter. Forages by scratching ground, but also digs using stout bill. Typically escapes by running, but if pressed will fly swiftly, with quick strong wingbeats, making a very impressive appearance. Roosts in trees within forest.

BREEDING Mating pattern unclear. Nest a deep scrape lined with needles, leaves and herbs among grass and undergrowth in forest. Clutch 6–9, but up to 15 reported; eggs olive-brown to olive-cream. Breeds mid-April–mid-July.

DISTRIBUTION C China. Recently extirpated from Hebei and Shanxi in north. Presently occurs from NE Yunnan north through Sichuan, Guizhou and Hunan to S Gansu, Shaanxi, Hubei, Henan, Anhui and Jiangxi. This spectacular pheasant has been introduced into several areas worldwide, including the Czech Republic, France, Germany, Austria, England and the USA (including Hawaii), but only those in parts of E Czech Republic and N France appear to be self-sustaining.

STATUS Vulnerable. Local and probably scarce to reasonably common. Approximately 10 years ago it was considered one of China's most threatened birds and a range contraction of c.50% was estimated. Subsequent surveys have found it at a number of localities, but many are small and isolated. The number of sites and fragmented nature of its range suggest that there may be fewer than 10,000 individuals, and it is almost certainly continuing to decline through further habitat degradation. Known from a few protected areas, including Fanjingshan and Badagongshan National Nature Reserves. As well as loss of its hill forest habitat, it is still under pressure from hunters, both for food and for majestic tail feathers of male, which can reach up to 1.5 m and are sometimes used in head dresses in opera productions, though plastic feathers are now used in some Beijing Opera costumes. Introduced population in Czech Republic numbered c.2500 individuals in 1985, but just 200–400 estimated by Kren (2000).

REFERENCES BirdLife International (2000, 2001), Johnsgard (1986), McGowan & Garson (1995), Xu Wei-shu *et al.* (1990).

Genus *PHASIANUS*: northern pheasants

Phasianus is close to *Syrmaticus* but differs in having hair-like feathering on rump and 'feathery' tail fringes, while males possess a short tuft of feathers either side of the rear crown. Significant differences also exist in the patterns of the downy chicks and in display behaviour. The two pheasants included here form a species-pair, and there is strong rationale for treating them as conspecific within a monotypic genus. However, despite broad geographic variation within Common Pheasant, the native Japanese taxa constitute a very distinctive, significantly differentiated group, maintained at species level here.

145 COMMON PHEASANT
Phasianus colchicus Linnaeus, 1758   Plate 42

Alternative name: Ring-necked Pheasant.

Familiar species of farmland in most temperate zones having been widely introduced for shooting purposes—the archetypal 'game' bird. Its native range extends over much of temperate Asia and perhaps west to extreme SE Europe.

IDENTIFICATION The most widespread pheasant, with a range almost worldwide due to introductions, e.g. in Chile, New Zealand, Tasmania, North America, Japan and Europe. The only phasianid likely to be encountered in most of its range, as it shuns dense forests and high montane zones inhabited by others. Male unmistakable: bottle-green head, short 'ears', 'goggles' of bare red skin, long barred tail and highly glossed, colourful golden or often purplish-copper plumage. With c.30 subspecies recognised in its native range, colour tones vary and introduced populations may combine a host of features through racial mixing; some have white collars or pale forewings, and rumps vary from bluish-grey to reddish. Melanic variant ('*tenebrosus*') with blackish-green body frequently encountered among introduced populations (perhaps most frequent in UK); though similar to Green Pheasant it is easily distinguished by the dark rump, dark grey wings and blackish underparts (Green has blue-grey forewings and rump, and greener underparts), while the female is dark chestnut, closely marked buff and black. Females of wild populations vary in colour saturation but are less variable than males. Their scale-spotted underparts and partial tail bars distinguish them from similar-sized females of Golden, Lady Amherst's and Copper Pheasants (which see).

DESCRIPTION *P. c. colchicus*. Bill greenish-horn to yellowish-horn (brownish-horn in female). Bare facial skin bright red (male). Irides brownish-yellow to orange-brown or brown (brownest in females). Legs greyish (browner when very young). Male has small erectile tuft at each side of rear of head. Rump feathers loose and disintegrated (male). Tail of 18 feathers, graduated, with central pair longest and tapering at tip, and feathers disintegrated at sides towards base. Sexes differ. Male has short spur, absent in female. **Adult male:** Head, throat and upper neck blackish, glossed green, with bronze tone to crown and purple sheen on throat. Lower neck, breast and underparts coppery-orange, with purple-pink reflections and blackish (glossed purplish-blue) scaling. Central belly and vent glossy blackish, undertail-coverts rich chestnut. Upperparts coppery-red, each feather with black fringe and terminal central spot, becoming buff-centred on back and scapulars. Rump feathers dense and hair-like, coppery-red; uppertail-coverts buffy-brown with chestnut tips. Wing-coverts buff, greater coverts with purple-rufous edges and some blackish marks; flight feathers dark brown mottled and barred buff. Tail buffy-brown, reddish-violet at sides, with numerous dark brown bars across central part of feathers. **First-year male:** Much as adult.

Adult female: Entire plumage uniformly dull sandy-brown, indistinctly mottled darker brown on neck- and breast-sides. Throat, head-sides, central breast and belly almost unmarked, and flanks with strong blackish-brown V markings. Crown intensely mottled black. Lower nape and mantle feathers have chestnut centres and buff subterminal U; most of remaining upperparts have black feather bases. Wing-coverts buffy-cinnamon, dotted black; flight feathers dark brown barred buff. Tail buffy-brown, with numerous dark brown and buff bars across central portion of feathers. **Juvenile/immature:** Like female but mantle feathers duller and with buff shaft streaks; rump and uppertail-coverts browner, scaled buff; flank markings irregular and broken. Males swiftly moult to immature plumage (at 6–8 weeks), prior to fully attaining male features at c.5 months—thus they appear constantly patchy during first few months of life.

GEOGRAPHICAL VARIATION Considerable, especially among males. Where ranges are contiguous, variation often appears clinal (including presence of white collar, intensity of plumage coloration, and body size), but differences can be more abrupt between slightly isolated populations and the striking Japanese forms demand specific rank as Green Pheasant. The 30 generally recognised subspecies form five groups, which have been occasionally afforded specific status, but the two principal groups meet in the Tarim Basin of extreme W China. Within each group there is a degree of plumage variation, casting substantial doubt on the validity of many subspecies. Introduced populations may be unassignable to one subspecies as, in many parts of the world, released stock are of several, often mixed, origins.

Black-necked Pheasants (*colchicus* group)
Western group with pale brown to buff wing-coverts and well-developed purplish tones, lacking white on neck.

P. c. septentrionalis Lorenz, 1888 occurs in N Caucasus from Dagestan north to the Volga Delta (Russia); paler, less spotted and barred, and has more golden plumage tones than nominate.

P. c. colchicus Linnaeus, 1758 (includes *lorenzi* and *europaeus*) occurs in E Georgia, NE Azerbaijan, S Armenia and NW Iran. Those in European Turkey, NE Greece and SE Bulgaria appear to be of this form and are probably native, though purity threatened by mixed-race introductions. Described above.

P. c. talischensis Lorenz, 1888 occurs in SE Transcaucasia and Caspian lowlands of N Iran; poorly differentiated from nominate but reportedly has narrower purplish-blue borders to breast feathers and females usually darker.

P. c. persicus Severtzov, 1875 occurs in SW Turkmenistan and NE Iran; paler than previous forms, with more buffy wing-coverts and paler golden body plumage.

White-winged Pheasants (*principalis–chrysomelas* group)
C Asia, redder, less purplish than nominate group with whitish wing-coverts, and often a partial white collar.

P. c. principalis P. L. Sclater, 1885 (includes *bogdanowi* and *komarowii*) occurs in S Turkmenistan, extreme NE Iran and NW Afghanistan; see group features.

P. c. zarudnyi Buturlin, 1904 (includes *tschardjuensis*, *medius* and *gordius*) occurs in C Amu Darya on Turkmenistan–Uzbekistan border between Kerki and Darganata; paler and brighter than previous form, with variable amount of white on nape.

P. c. bianchii Buturlin, 1904 (includes *jabae* and *michailowskii*) occurs in upper Amu Darya in S Uzbekistan, SW Tajikistan and extreme N Afghanistan; darker below than previous two subspecies, with blackish markings merging on breast, and upperparts duller and browner, less reddish, than others.

P. c. chrysomelas Severtzov, 1875 (includes *dorandti* and *oxianus*) occurs in Amu Darya Delta, Uzbekistan and adjacent N Turkmenistan; brighter than previous form, with breast markings not merging, darker, tinged copper and bronze above, and has distinct, but broken and irregular white collar.

P. c. zerafschanicus Tarnovski, 1893 (includes *tarnowskii* and *klossovskii*) in Zerafshan Valley and Kaska Daya near Samarkand in Uzbekistan; differs from rest of group in having well-developed white collar, but similar to *zarudnyi* in being overall rather pale, buff and golden.

Kirghiz Pheasants (*mongolicus* group)
The *mongolicus* group differs from the last in having iridescent coppery-maroon and green upperparts and a partial white collar.

P. c. mongolicus J. F. Brandt, 1844 (includes *brandti* and *semitorquatus*) occurs from N Tien Shan (N Kyrgyzstan) north through E Kazakhstan to Lake Balkash and east to NW Xinjiang and Urumchi (W China); features as above for the group.

P. c. turcestanicus Lorenz, 1896 (includes *triznae*, *kvaskovskii* and *bergii*) occurs in SE Kazakhstan, from the east shore of the Aral Sea along the Syr Darya to the W Fergana Valley in E Uzbekistan and borders of Kyrgyzstan; differs from the previous form in being more purplish, less bronzy-green above, with bolder, more regular markings below and in having a bolder white collar.

Tarim Basin Pheasants (*tarimensis* group)
Two rather different forms, though *shawii* has some features associated with the C Asian group and was included therein by Delacour (1977). It is, however, separated from these by the massive Tien Shan, and is best grouped with *tarimensis* (Vaurie 1965).

P. c. tarimensis Pleske, 1888 occurs in E and S Tarim Basin, Xinjiang (W China); no white collar and olive-yellow on lower back and rump.

P. c. shawii Elliot, 1870 occurs in W Tarim Basin, Xinjiang (W China); differs in having whitish wing-coverts, reddish rump and uppertail-coverts.

Grey-rumped Pheasants (*torquatus* group)
In most forms of this large group, males have a conspicuous white eyebrow and collar, the lower back and rump greenish-grey, and bluish-grey wing-coverts. Many forms intergrade.

P. c. hagenbecki Rothschild, 1901 is isolated in the

Kobdo Valley of W Mongolia; the largest and palest form, with complete white collar, pale crown and straw-yellow ground colour to body plumage.

P. c. pallasi Rothschild, 1903 (includes *alpherakyi* and *ussuriensis*) occurs in Ussuriland and S Amurland in Russian Far East, adjacent NE North Korea and NE China (N Heilongjiang); darker than previous form, with a browner crown and more golden-yellow body plumage.

P. c. karpowi Buturlin, 1904 occurs in Korea and NE China (C Heilongiiang, south to N Hebei to the suburbs of Beijing); darker and more richly coloured than *pallasi*, and intermediate with the following taxon.

P. c. kiangsuensis Buturlin, 1904 (includes *pewzowi* and *schensinensis*) occurs in NE China (W Hebei and adjacent Nei Mongol, N Shanxi and Shaanxi); darker and more richly coloured than previous forms in the group, with a dark crown and narrower white collar.

P. c. alaschanicus Alphéraky & Bianchi, 1908 occurs in N China (isolated in Ningxia north to Nan Shan and east to Lang Shan); paler than the previous form with whiter 'eyebrows' and a narrow collar broken at the front.

P. c. edzinensis Sushkin, 1926 is isolated in the valley of the Edzin Gol in N Gansu (China); like the following form but with more contrastingly marked scapulars (darker borders and purer white centres) and paler underparts.

P. c. satscheuensis Pleske, 1892 is isolated in extreme NW Gansu (China); very pale and sandy above but dark coppery-red and golden-yellow below, crown pale, collar narrow and broken.

P. c. vlangalli Przhevalski, 1876 is isolated in W Zaidam basin of N Qinghai (China); darker than the previous form, relatively rufous above and lacking pale centres to scapulars, crown quite dark and collar vestigial.

P. c. strauchi Przhevalski, 1876 (includes *holdereri*, *berezowskyi* and *chonensis*) occurs in S Shaanxi and S Gansu (China); resembles *kiangsuensis* but even darker and more richly coloured, collar narrow and broken, and virtually absent in some.

P. c. sohokhotensis Buturlin, 1908 is isolated in the Soho-Khoto oasis in E Gansu (N China); like the previous form but paler and duller.

P. c. suehschanensis Bianchi, 1906 occurs from Songpan south to Kwansien in W Sichuan (China); strongly patterned, dark and richly coloured race, with no collar, coppery and maroon above, glossed bronze-green, copper-brown below, glossed green, becoming purple-blue on lower foreneck, and tail purplish-brown.

P. c. elegans Elliot, 1870 (includes *sladeni*) occurs in extreme E Tibet (Xizang) and adjacent W Sichuan, south to NW Yunnan (China), reaching N Myanmar; similar to previous form but blacker below, with more extensive purple-blue on breast, and more reddish, less maroon, on scapulars.

P. c. rothschildi La Touche, 1921 occurs in SE Yunnan (China) and adjacent extreme N Tonkin (Vietnam); like *elegans* but blue of breast more restricted, flanks and mantle paler and more

golden, and sometimes has vestigial collar.

P. c. decollatus Swinhoe, 1870 occurs from W Hubei west to the Red Basin of E Sichuan, south to NE Yunnan and Guizhou (C China); paler above and below than the previous form, with more boldly spotted scapulars; tail virtually identical to *suehchanensis*.

P. c. takatsukasae Delacour, 1927 occurs in S Guangxi (China) and extreme NE Tonkin (Vietnam); darker and more richly coloured than *torquatus*.

P. c. torquatus Gmelin, 1789 (includes *gmelini* and *hemptinnii*) occurs from Shandong and Henan south to S Guangdong (E China); golden-yellow mantle and flanks, purplish-red breast centre, bluish belly centre, and collar prominent but broken at front.

P. c. formosanus Elliot, 1870 occurs in Taiwan; paler than the previous form, with flanks almost whitish-buff and mantle straw coloured.

MEASUREMENTS Length: male 75–89 cm, female 53–62 cm. Northern populations typically larger than southern races, i.e. wing length of male *hagenbecki* of W Mongolia is 260–265, whereas *rothschildi* of Yunnan has wing 210–230. *P. c. colchicus*. Males: wing 250–266, tail 490–590, tarsus 69–74, mean weight 1150. Females: wing 210–220, tail 290–310, tarsus 62–70, mean weight 850.

HABITAT Throughout its natural range occurs in a broad variety of temperate habitats in mountains and foothills near cover: riverine scrub and lakeside reeds, woodland edge, steppe and open country, usually scrub and woods near cultivation, but tends to avoid dense forest, highest mountains and very dry areas. Also subtropical plateaux, in cold valleys and oases surrounded by deserts and high mountains. Where introduced its habitat use is similar, but occurs especially in agricultural landscapes.

VOICE Most conspicuous call is the loud and distinctive crow of males, given especially during breeding season. Call is harsh and only slightly variable, being typically rendered as *korkk korkk, KO, OK korkk-kok* or similar. It is often followed by wing-whirring. Up to a dozen other calls have been described, but most are much quieter. Alarm a loud and strangled *gogOK gogOK gogOK* or *kuttUK kuttUK kuttUK*.

HABITS Encountered in a wide variety of group sizes and compositions according to season and, probably, local conditions. Occurs singly, in pairs, in groups containing a male and several females, and, in winter, in single-sex flocks in some areas, or flocks in which males outnumber females. Emerges from cover to feed in early mornings and late afternoons at forest edges, in woodland rides and cultivation, plantations, secluded parks and gardens etc. close to cover. Water sought either in morning or evening and seeks cover in middle of day. When disturbed walks quickly or runs for cover with tail cocked and head high, but if pressed will fly short distance to escape, before walking or running on alighting. If flushed 'explodes' from underfoot, though most prefer to run rather than fly from danger. After noisy initial rise, may tower to clear hedge and continue with speedy flap-flap-glide action over short distance. Roosts usually in bushes, but also uses trees.

BREEDING Where introduced it is polygamous with male defending harem of two or more females. This system can be assumed to also occur in its native range and harems of five females have been reported. Nest usually on ground in grass tussocks or beneath cover such as a bush, occasionally above ground. Coarse grass appears to be favoured for nest building. The lining is of finer grasses and feathers. Clutch 8–14 in native range, but 1–28 reported; eggs small and unmarked olive-brown, but sometimes greenish, bluish or pale greyish-olive. Breeding season apparently variable within native range and where introduced, presumably due to local conditions; from approximately late February in Jiangsu (C China), April in Turkmenistan and May–June in Amurland (Russia). Incubation 22–25 days.

DISTRIBUTION From the Korean Peninsula through much of China south to N Vietnam, but absent from highest areas of Tibetan Plateau. Local in extreme NW, SC and SE Mongolia and Ussuriland in Russian Far East. West of China distribution appears patchy and not well known (see Geographical Variation). From N Afghanistan and N Iran through Turkmenistan and Uzbekistan (including islands within Aral Sea) to Kyrgyzstan, Tajikistan and E and S Kazakhstan. Also Caucasus republics and adjacent Russia west of the Caspian Sea, and patchily west to the Black Sea. Possibly also native in extreme SE Bulgaria, NE Greece (Nestos Delta) and adjacent European Turkey. Widely introduced, most notably to North America, West Indies (on Eleuthera, in the Bahamas, Cuba, especially Isladela Juventud, and perhaps Puerto Rico), Europe, Morocco, Tasmania, New Zealand, Chile (marginally established in Cautín and Valdivia) and Hawaii. In Japan long established as an introduction in S Hokkaido and on

Tsushima (in Korean Strait), where native Green Pheasant is absent, but introductions elsewhere in Japan apparently less successful, seemingly due to low fertility of hybrid offspring with Green.

STATUS Where introduced it is generally common to superabundant as resident populations are regularly supplemented by game-reared birds in advance of shooting seasons. Status of many native populations largely unknown, or show precipitous decrease through hunting or habitat destruction. It is the commonest galliform in China, being frequent throughout except on Hainan and most of the Tibetan plateau. There are no formal estimates of density other than one from Pangquangou, a reserve created to protect Brown Eared-pheasant in Shanxi, where there was an autumn density of 64/km² in 1989, which is similar to autumnal densities on managed estates in the UK. Additional data from elsewhere and in different habitats would be valuable. On Taiwan it is declining but still common in the south and east. Elsewhere the only recent information is from Azerbaijan where the nominate subspecies is locally common, but *talischensis* is now very rare. Certain restricted-range subspecies may be endangered (i.e. *hagenbecki* and *edzinensis*). Given its apparent tolerance of considerable habitat alteration (see Habitat) and its broad distribution, its overall population probably numbers millions, if not tens of millions within its native range. Given the relative stability of the overall population, it is not considered globally threatened. Provided suitable habitat remains it is likely to be safe, despite heavy hunting in some areas, both for food and sport. It does, however, suffer from conversion of its habitat for agriculture.

REFERENCES Bannerman (1963), Cramp & Simmons (1980), Delacour (1977), Hill & Robertson (1988), Johnsgard (1986), King *et al.* (1975), Robertson & Carroll (1989), Smythies (1986), Vaurie (1965).

---

146 GREEN PHEASANT
Phasianus versicolor Vieillot, 1825

Plate 42

Alternative name: Japanese Pheasant. The national bird of Japan, it is widespread and common throughout the major islands of the archipelago, where Common Pheasant is only a localised introduction.

IDENTIFICATION Endemic to Japan, favouring farmland and generally more open country at lower elevations than Copper Pheasant. Male unmistakable with dark green plumage, appearing black at distance, though paler bluish-grey wing-coverts and rump provide some contrast if unconcealed by body feathering or folded wings. In Japan only darkest populations of Copper Pheasant approach male colour saturation, though that species often appears white-rumped and lacks small ear-tufts of Green, but if these are visible then colour differences should be apparent. As well as being a much shyer forest species, female Copper has shorter, virtually unbarred tail with whitish tips to the rufous sides, a whiter belly and less heavily spotted body plumage

than female Green. Outside Japan, particularly in UK, beware confusing frequent melanic variant ('*tenebrosus*') of Common Pheasant, which has a blackish-green body and dark tail, but lacks bluish-grey wing-coverts and rump of Green and has blacker underparts. Female '*tenebrosus*' is mottled rich chestnut and black, much darker and redder than female Green, which resembles a heavily blotched, slightly darker, and shorter tailed, female Common Pheasant.

DESCRIPTION *P. v. versicolor.* Bill greenish-horn to yellowish-horn (brownish-horn in female). Bare facial skin bright red (male). Irides brownish-yellow to orange-brown or brown (brownest in females). Legs greyish (browner when very young). Male has small erectile tufts at each side of rear of head. Rump feathers loose and disintegrated (male). Tail slightly shorter than Common Pheasant, has 18 feathers, graduated, with central pair longest and tapering at tip; feathers

325

disintegrated at sides near base. Sexes differ. Male has short spur, absent in female. **Adult male:** Head, throat and upper neck blackish, glossed purplish, with green sheen to crown. Neck, breast and underparts dark green, with purple and blue reflections. Mantle dark green, with some buff subterminal markings. Back and rump green, tinged grey, uppertail-coverts greenish-grey. Scapulars black with buff streaks and subterminal markings, bordered black, with chestnut fringes. Wing-coverts bluish-grey, with some chestnut and buff edgings and markings to greater coverts. Flight feathers dark brown, barred and mottled buff. Tail dark olive-brown, crossed by clear dark bars, tinged pink at sides near base. **First-year male:** Much as adult. **Adult female:** Differs from female Common Pheasant in being much more heavily spotted and blotched black. Upperpart feathers black with brownish-buff streaks and subterminal borders, narrowly tipped green. Sides of head, neck and breast well marked with dark spotting. Ear-coverts have darker bar below pale crescent under eye; very weak in most forms of Common. Flanks have stronger blackish scalloping than Common Pheasant. **Juvenile:** Like female but tail shorter.

GEOGRAPHICAL VARIATION Some variation in degree of colour saturation, apparent in crown and rump of males. Three subspecies recognised here.

P. v. **versicolor** Vieillot, 1825 (includes *kiusiuensis*) occurs in SE Honshu and Kyushu; largest and darkest with dark green rump and bluish-green underparts; described above.

P. v. **tanensis** Kuroda, 1919 (includes *affinis*) occurs on Izu and Miura Peninsulas of E Honshu, Seven Is of Izu, and Tanega-shima and Yaku-shima Is; male has back and rump greyer, and is more purplish and bluish below than nominate.

P. v. **robustipes** Kuroda, 1919 (includes *tohkaidi*, *maedius*, *nankaidi* and *kigis*) occurs on Sado and most of Honshu; rather smaller (male wing 215–225) and paler in overall coloration than previous races, with underparts greener, rump bluer-grey, bronze tones on mantle and greyish bronzy-green crown. Female distinctly paler than nominate.

MEASUREMENTS Length: male 75–89 cm, female 53–62 cm. *P. v. versicolor*. Males: wing 225–243, tail 270–425, tarsus 64–78, weight c.900–1100. Females: wing 200–220, tail 207–275, tarsus 55-64, weight c.800–900.

HABITAT Broad variety of lowland and foothill habitats, reaching 1100 m in hills. Favours bushy hillsides, areas of sparse woodland with nearby cultivation, tea plantations and secluded parks and gardens, and riverine thickets. Southern populations also in more luxuriant broad-leaf woodland.

VOICE Similar to Common Pheasant, but male call reportedly distinctly shorter than latter species (at least with experience). Also confusingly similar to Copper Pheasant.

HABITS Found singly, in pairs or groups, with larger gatherings in winter at good food sources. Single-sex flocks often form in winter. In cold weather visits farms and feeds with domestic hens. Most active in early mornings and late afternoons when descends to more open lower ground to feed on woodland rides and in cultivation, plantations and parks. Seeks cover in middle of day, resting on grassy hilltops, or on bushy slopes; especially favouring sandy areas for dust-bathing. Roosts on ground and in bushes and trees.

BREEDING Apparently differs little from Common Pheasant, but is seemingly both monogamous and polygamous, perhaps depending on local sex ratios and population densities. Nests usually on ground near low bushes, or occasionally near base of a tree. Clutch 6–15, usually 7–9; eggs small, unmarked and greyish-olive in colour. Lays mid-March in S Kyushu but later, generally April–May, on Honshu. Incubation 23–28 days.

DISTRIBUTION Endemic to Japan: on Honshu (including Sado and Izu Is of Oshima and Niijima), Shikoku and Kyushu (and adjacent Goto Is, Tanega-shima and Yaku-shima). Introduced North America (Delaware and Virginia and probably elsewhere) and main island of Hawaii.

STATUS Widespread and not uncommon throughout native range. An estimated 500,000 are shot annually (though shooting of females is prohibited), thus to help maintain a reasonable population, large numbers have been released (i.e. 100,000 annually in the 1980s). There are indications that the overall population may be affected by conversion of its habitat to agricultural land.

REFERENCES Bohl (1964), Brazil (1991), Delacour (1977), Johnsgard (1986), Kuroda (1981).

Genus *CHRYSOLOPHUS*: ruffed pheasants

Small genus containing two very distinctive Chinese pheasants. Though females possess obvious similarities, males are so stunningly different that initially it may appear odd to place them together; however, they share a number of peculiar features. Both are small-bodied pheasants with very long tails and possess a ruff or cape of large squared feathers at the head-sides, which may be fanned in display. Body feathers are disintegrated and hairy, especially those of the uppertail-coverts, which are very long and stiffened at tips. Legs rather slim and spur only weakly developed. Their close relationship is also manifest in captivity, where they readily hybridise and first-generation offspring are usually fertile.

147 GOLDEN PHEASANT
Chrysolophus pictus (Linnaeus, 1758)

Plate 42

Being popular in ornamental collections this beautiful species is one of the most familiar of all pheasants. Despite this it is remarkably little studied in the wild.

IDENTIFICATION Hill forest (chiefly 800–1600 m) in C China, introduced UK. A small, slender, shy forest pheasant, often revealing presence by distinctive loud rasping call of male (see Voice). Male unmistakable, with red underparts, yellow face, crown and rump, golden cape and long, coarsely marked brownish tail; in display golden cape is fanned forwards and upwards, concealing the face. Female very similar to female Lady Amherst's but has plainer head and lacks contrasting white throat and belly of latter; bill and legs yellowish (not grey). Small size and closely barred, unspotted, body plumage and longer, more boldly barred tail are useful distinctions from Common Pheasant.

DESCRIPTION Male has greatly elongated crest of fine silky feathers, female slightly elongated feathers, visible as a 'bump' on rear crown. Male has ruff of large square-ended feathers from nape, forming a cape when relaxed. Feathers of both upper- and underparts rather disintegrated and hair-like in texture, especially on rump and uppertail-coverts (which are elongated and rather stiff). Tail greatly elongated, consists of 18 feathers, tapering to a point; central feathers broader and vaulted; female has tail unremarkably elongated. Bill yellowish-horn. Bare skin around eye and small wattle deep yellow. Irides whitish or pale yellow (brown in female). Legs yellowish-horn, rather long and slender. Sexes differ. Male has very small spur, often hardly visible, female unspurred. **Adult male:** Crown crested, shining golden-yellow. Head-sides buffy-yellow, becoming orange-buff on throat and almost whitish on cheeks. Elongated square-ended feathers from nape, orange with blue-black edges, forming cape. Neck, breast and underparts scarlet, becoming brownish on vent and undertail-coverts. Mantle dark green, feathers black edged. Back and rump bright golden-yellow. Uppertail-coverts stiff and elongated, scarlet. Scapulars and wing-coverts rich cinnamon, with some black mottling, flight feathers brownish-black, with cinnamon or pinkish-buff outer edges. Central tail feathers cinnamon-brown, freckled with buffy-white spots, each with narrow blackish highlight; rest of long tail feathers closely wavy-barred or almost vermiculated brown and whitish. **First-year male:** Mix of male and female plumage features, but with more 'female' features than male. **Second-year male:** Similar to adult male, but ruff not fully developed, with more round-tipped feathers; wing-coverts more mottled black and buff, less clear. **Adult female:** Head and neck cinnamon-buff, closely barred blackish-brown on crown and neck, throat unmarked. Head-sides silvery-grey, barred blackish. Most of rest of plumage (including belly and undertail-coverts) barred rufous-buff and blackish-brown, very noticeable on breast, flanks and wings. Back, rump and uppertail-coverts almost plain but finely peppered and streaked. Tail buffy-brown, broadly barred blackish-brown on central feathers, narrowly on outermost ones, and becoming paler at tip. **Juvenile:** Very similar to female, but has warmer plumage tones and is less heavily and regularly barred on breast and flanks.

GEOGRAPHICAL VARIATION Monotypic.

MEASUREMENTS Length: male 100–115 cm, female 61–70 cm, largely differ due to longer tail of male. Males: wing 190–209, tail 630–790, tarsus 75, weight 575–710. Females: wing 165–193, tail 340–375, tarsus 70, weight 550–665.

HABITAT Inhabits bamboo and scrub on rocky hills and slopes at mid-altitudes (800–1600 m), occasionally at edges of terraced cultivation or scrubby tea plantations. Habitat use may vary seasonally. Those in UK inhabit dense lowland half-grown coniferous plantations, usually with rhododendron thickets.

VOICE Far more often heard than seen, male calls February–May, with a loud, strident *ka-cheek*, the second note louder and higher pitched (compare Lady Amherst's). Other courtship calls not as far carrying, though males do utter a loud hiss often audible 25 m distant and sometimes up to 50 m away.

HABITS Very difficult to observe as it keeps to cover of dense, dark forest or bamboo thickets; most likely to be encountered feeding on tracks or in clearings in early morning or late afternoon. Usually in groups during much of year, though also seen singly. In larger flocks during winter when males and females roost together. Flocks disband in spring (from late March), when males begin to defend territories. Female has much larger home range than male. Roosts in trees and large bushes. Feeds in deciduous forest, edges of farmland and scrubby grassy areas in winter, deciduous forest in spring and both deciduous and mixed coniferous/broad-leaf forest in summer, especially relatively open woodland. Shy nature makes observation difficult, and probably best located by tracking down calling male. Runs rapidly from danger, slipping through dense cover with great agility, aided by its slender body and relatively long legs. Hardly ever flies.

BREEDING Mating pattern unclear, evidence for both monogamy and polygamy based on scant anecdotal information. One nest was situated within a bamboo thicket surrounded by tall herbs interspersed by rocky outcrops. Clutch 5–12 pale buff to cream eggs. Breeding thought to commence in April. Incubation in captivity lasts 22 days and is by female alone, which sits motionless throughout this period.

DISTRIBUTION China. Distributed through much of centre of country in suitable habitat. From SE Qinghai in the northwest, east through W and S Gansu, S Shaanxi to W Hubei and W and S Hunan. South from Qinghai to NW Yunnan and Giuzhou to Wuzhou in E Guangxi. Introduced to France, New Zealand and UK, but only in latter has it become very locally established (see Status).

STATUS Fairly common in suitable habitat. Little formal assessment of its status until recently and results of an ongoing study awaited. Frequency of observations in some areas, together with size of range and density estimates from some areas, suggests a population in the tens of thousands. Though this appears secure, declines were formerly sufficient for it to be considered globally Near Threatened (it has recently been removed from the Red Data List). Occurs in a number of protected areas, including Foping Panda Reserve and Taibaishan Nature Reserve. Its prominence in Chinese traditional culture may be to the species' disadvantage as it is considered a delicacy and is expensive, when available, in restaurants. It is principally threatened by loss of its wooded habitat, though some direct exploitation exists. Introduced to the UK, where a small number of very localised populations (totalling 1000–2000 individuals) survive, most notably in SW Scotland, East Anglia, the South Downs and Gloucestershire.

REFERENCES Beebe (1931), Cramp & Simmons (1980), McGowan (1994).

148 LADY AMHERST'S PHEASANT
Chrysolophus amherstiae (Leadbeater, 1829)   Plate 42

Another stunning pheasant, arguably even more exquisite than Golden.

IDENTIFICATION Hill forest (chiefly 1800–4600 m) in NE Myanmar and SW China (also very locally introduced to England). Like Golden this is a shy forest pheasant, its presence often only revealed by distinctive loud rasping call of male, or discarded tail feather. Male unmistakable, generally appearing black and white in brief view, with white belly, blackish throat, breast and upperparts, highlighted by scaly white nape and incredibly long white tail with narrow black bars. Female similar to Golden but slightly larger, warmer brown, more strongly barred, with darker rufous crown contrasting with whiter throat, paler belly and with paler but more boldly barred, blunter tipped tail and blue-grey (not yellowish) bill and legs. Hybrids with Golden may occur in feral English population; these resemble Lady Amherst's but have extensive red below. In China Lady Amherst's inhabits forests at higher altitudes than Golden, and though ranges almost meet they are not known to overlap. Smaller size and closely barred, unspotted, body plumage and broader dark barring on longer tail are useful distinctions from Common Pheasant.

DESCRIPTION Male has an elongated but inconspicuous stiff crest on rear crown, and ruff of large round-tipped feathers from nape, forming a cape when relaxed, which are fanned forwards, concealing bill and head-sides, in display. Feathers of lower breast, lower neck, mantle and scapulars large and broad. Rump and uppertail-covert feathers rather disintegrated and hair-like in texture. Tail greatly elongated, of 18 feathers, tapering to point; central feathers rather broader and vaulted; female has tail unremarkably elongated. Bill, bare skin around eye and small wattle, and legs, pale grey to blue-grey. Irides whitish or pale yellow (brown in female). Legs rather long and slender. Sexes differ. Male has very small spur, often hardly visible, but female unspurred. Adult male: Crown glossy green, with flaming orange-red droopy crest at rear. Forehead, lores, throat, head-sides and neck black, each feather with glossy green spot. Elongated rounded feathers from nape, white with black edge, forming scaled cape. Breast, lower neck, mantle and scapulars glossy blue-green, each feather with black border. Lower back and rump bright yellow, with dark feather bases often visible; uppertail-coverts barred black and white, with greatly elongated bright orange-red tips. Wings glossy purple-blue, each feather with black border. Primaries blackish, with white edging to outer webs. Underparts from breast white, unmarked (except concealed dark grey feather bases) until legs; rear flanks and vent barred dark; undertail-coverts greenish-black with white barring. Central tail feathers white, crossed by numerous narrow black bars, the intervening white portions with fine wavy pencilling; outer feathers marbled black and white, admixed buff on outer webs. First-year male: Mix of male and female plumage features, but with more 'female' features than male. Second-year male: Like adult male, but ruff not fully developed, appearing as smaller feathers, wing-coverts more mottled black and buff, and red 'extensions' to uppertail-coverts less developed. Adult female: Head and neck cinnamon-rufous, closely barred blackish-brown on crown and neck; throat unmarked white. Sides of neck and breast rufous-chestnut, narrowly barred blackish. Underparts from breast buffy-white, with broad blackish barring on flanks and vent. Upperparts, including wings, barred rufous-cinnamon and blackish-brown. Tail rufous-cinnamon, broadly barred blackish-brown on central feathers, narrowly on outers; barring bolder than on female Golden, and feathers with blunter, less pointed, tips. Juvenile: Like female, but overall has much duller, indistinct barring, with virtually unmarked crown, weaker flank and tail bars and duller, less rufous, plumage tones.

GEOGRAPHICAL VARIATION Monotypic.

MEASUREMENTS Length: male 130–173 cm, female 66–68 cm, largely differ due to longer tail of male. Males: wing 205–235, tail 830–1150, tarsus 75–85, weight 675–850. Females: wing 183–203, tail 286–375, tarsus 66–74, weight 624–804.

HABITAT Dense forest, bamboo and dense scrub on hills and rugged mountains at 1800–4600 m, but usually 2100–3600 m. In UK, however, occurs in lowland wooded parkland with rhododendron shrubbery, and in half-grown or mixed forestry plantations; as trees mature in forestry monocultures understorey disappears and habitat becomes unsuitable.

VOICE During breeding season strident, harsh call of male is similar to that of Golden Pheasant, but typically has three components (not two), with emphasis on first note (not the last): *cheek ker-chek*. One- and two-note calls are also given occasionally.

HABITS Typically very skulking, strictly keeping to cover of dense shrubbery at forest edge and is rarely seen; typically it is the long, barred white tail that attracts attention as it disappears off a forest trail. Large groups occur in late autumn and winter when as many as 20–30 congregate at good feeding areas. Otherwise usually encountered singly, in pairs or trios. In C Yunnan (S China), males display in small glades within coniferous and other evergreen secondary forest from about mid-March. Some altitudinal movements reported.

BREEDING Mating pattern unclear, males seen with either single, two or, rarely, more females. Nest a scrape lined with leaves, placed under thick bushes or fallen branches. Clutch 6–7 buff to cream eggs. Breeds from mid-April. Incubation in captivity lasts 24 days and is by female alone.

DISTRIBUTION From NE Myanmar, near the eastern border with China, east through Yunnan to W and C Guizhou, and north through SE Tibet to C Sichuan (including Emei Shan). Small numbers of introduced birds survive in the UK.

STATUS Fairly common in suitable habitat. Little formal assessment of its status, but some intensive fieldwork (though more concerning behaviour than ecology) suggests a population in the tens of thousands when extrapolated across its range. Formerly considered globally Near Threatened. Surprisingly it is only noted from Jinzhongshan Nature Reserve, but must surely occur in other protected areas and such information would be very useful. It is mainly threatened by habitat loss and increasing fragmentation, which seems a likely consequence. Introduced to England, where the population was estimated to be fewer than 200 individuals in 1991 (principally in Bedfordshire).

REFERENCES Cramp & Simmons (1980), Han *et al.* (1988), McGowan (1994).

Genus *POLYPLECTRON*: peacock-pheasants

A distinctive group of small, relatively sombre forest pheasants of tropical mainland Asia and adjoining larger islands. Shy and elusive, they inhabit dense undergrowth and are rarely seen, but most species can be detected by their distinctive calls. Generic characters include slender legs with 2–3 (sometimes more) short sharp spurs (males only)—in this respect they recall spurfowls of India. Some have elongated crown feathers and neck ruffles, which can be raised as forward-pointing bushy crests, and peacock-like ocelli on the wing and tail feathers. Several have spectacular display postures and, strangely among phasianids, produce only two eggs in a full clutch.

149 SUMATRAN PEACOCK-PHEASANT
Polyplectron chalcurum Lesson, 1831

Plate 43

Alternative names: Lesson's/Bronze-tailed Peacock-pheasant.

Strikingly different from all congeners in lacking ocelli in its plumage; perhaps most closely related to Mountain Peacock-pheasant, which has both the narrow-tailed appearance of Sumatran and ocelli of the others.

IDENTIFICATION Endemic to montane forests of Sumatra. An elegant and rather small, dark rusty-brown elusive forest pheasant, which lacks a crest and has a long, graduated, barred tail, which lacks ocelli, these being replaced by diagnostic metallic violet-blue panels on the outermost feathers (much reduced in shorter-tailed female). Unmistakable in range, but small size and skulking nature renders it little known and its presence is probably best indicated by the distinctive far-carrying call of the male.

DESCRIPTION *P. c. chalcurum.* Head rather small and uncrested. Uppertail-coverts long, concealing basal third or more of tail. Tail very elongated, graduated and pointed, consists of 16 feathers, adorned by metallic panels. Bill and legs greyish-black. Irides yellow in

male, dark brown in female. Sexes similar. Legs slender, male has two spurs; female unspurred. **Adult male:** Head, neck and underparts dark brown, with whitish spotting on throat and faint blackish barring from breast downwards; bolder barring on undertail-coverts. Upperparts chestnut-brown, with narrow and irregular dark barring throughout, apart from primaries, which are unmarked dark brown. Tail chestnut, barred black, becoming metallic violet-purple, fusing to form extensive areas of metallic purple over much of inner webs, less extensively on outer webs; tip mottled brown and buff. **First-year male:** Like female in plumage, in that metallic patches often reach tail tip but larger and with indication of developing spurs. **Adult female:** Much as male, though metallic purple areas of tail extend further towards tip; smaller and relatively shorter tailed. **Juvenile:** Differs from adult in having shorter tail, with little or no metallic blue; plumage rather paler and redder brown, less earthy.

GEOGRAPHICAL VARIATION Slight, though two subspecies generally recognised, they intergrade and their separation may be invalid.

329

P. c. chalcurum Lesson, 1831 occurs in montane S Sumatra (south of the equator); described above. *P. c. scutulatum* Chasen & Hoogerwerf, 1941 occurs in montane N Sumatra; upperparts more strongly marked than nominate, with broader and more distinct barring.

MEASUREMENTS Length: male c.56 cm, female c.40 cm; female obviously smaller due, in part, to longer tail of male. *P. c. chalcurum.* Males: wing 162–190, tail 260–380, tarsus 65, weight (two captives) 425 and 590. Females: wing 150, tail 180–220, tarsus 55, weight (four captives) 238–269.

HABITAT Found in both undisturbed and logged lower montane forest, including pine plantations and other lower montane forest types at 800–1700 m.

VOICE Relatively quiet: male reported to give a loud, far-carrying harsh *karau-karau-karau* with emphasis on slightly higher pitched second note. But this not noted in captive birds, which utter twittering sequences, a repeated *pitt* call and various clucks.

HABITS Shy and skulking; rarely seen and thus its habits remain virtually unknown. Very wary and liable to slink away through undergrowth at least sign of disturbance. Captive birds display by wing-spreading, but tail at most only partially opened, twisted to vertical plane and tilted toward female.

BREEDING Presumed monogamous due to limited sexual dimorphism, but no information from wild. Clutch 2 buffy-white eggs. Incubation in captivity lasts 22 days.

DISTRIBUTION Endemic to Barisan Mountains of W Sumatra (Indonesia).

STATUS Locally not uncommon, with recent records from several areas across much of its historical range in montane Sumatra. A very tentative assessment suggested a population size in tens of thousands based on anecdotal information (encounter rates) and extent of suitable habitat, which is overall reasonably secure, though some encroachment is evident and this may well expand rapidly in some areas. It has been recorded from the two large montane National Parks on Sumatra, Gunung Leuser in the north and Kerinci-Sebalt in the south, which cover probably 50% of its habitat. A clearer idea of its distribution in these parks would be of great value, especially away from the better visited areas. It is hunted in some parts of its range.

REFERENCES Delacour (1977), Johnsgard (1986), MacKinnon & Phillips (1993), McGowan & Garson (1995).

---

150 MOUNTAIN PEACOCK-PHEASANT
Polyplectron inopinatum (Rothschild, 1903)   Plate 43

Alternative name: Rothschild's Peacock-pheasant.

Similar to the Sumatran species, including its partiality for montane forests, but this species possesses numerous small ocelli on the upperparts.

IDENTIFICATION Endemic to montane forests of Peninsular Malaysia, being replaced in lowlands by Malayan Peacock-pheasant. A long-bodied uncrested pheasant, almost blackish-grey on head, neck and underparts, with rusty-brown upperparts marked by small blue ocelli. Long graduated, vermiculated dark grey tail, sporting large green ocelli. Female smaller with shorter browner tail and upperparts spotted by black ocelli. Easily separated from Malayan Peacock-pheasant in being much darker on head and underparts, having reddish-brown upperparts, a longer narrower tail and lacks ruffled crest; also habitats and elevations differ. Compare female Crested and Great Argus, which are both much larger and have distinctive head patterns

DESCRIPTION Head rather small, uncrested but has slight ruffle on upper nape. Uppertail-coverts long, concealing basal quarter or more of tail. Tail greatly elongated, graduated and pointed, consists of 20 feathers (18 grey in female) adorned by metallic ocelli. Bill and legs grey. Irides brown. Sexes similar. Legs slender, male has two spurs; female unspurred. **Adult male:** Head and neck dark grey, finely spotted and freckled white, most intensely on throat. Underparts from breast blackish, vermiculated pale grey; undertail-coverts browner. Upperparts chestnut-brown, with narrow blackish vermiculations and small blue ocelli (with buffy-white spot at base of each) and concealed grey feather bases. Primaries unmarked dull black. Uppertail-coverts chestnut-brown, more coarsely barred black; the outermost feathers have large blue ocelli on both webs. Tail freckled buff and black, with metallic green subterminal ocelli on each web, except for central pair of feathers. **First-year male:** Smaller and duller than adult male. **Adult female:** Smaller and has relatively shorter and less strongly graduated tail than male. Much like male in plumage, but ocelli of upperparts replaced by black spots and has virtually none on tail. **Juvenile:** Very similar to female.

GEOGRAPHICAL VARIATION Monotypic.

MEASUREMENTS Length: male c.65 cm, female c.46 cm; female smaller and relatively shorter tailed. Males: wing 230–255, tail 320–400, tarsus 65. Females: wing 175–190, tail 220–275, tarsus 55. No weight data.

HABITAT Rugged montane forest, including dipterocarp, on upper slopes at 820–1800 m, with one record of a feather at c.600 m.

VOICE Male gives 1–4 (usually 2) quite loud harsh clucks or squawks in bouts 5–6 seconds apart. When alarmed, clucks not unlike domestic chicken. Also a quiet burbling descending whistle. Considered less vocal than congeners.

HABITS Encountered in parties of 4–5, but like congeners is very wary and liable to slink into undergrowth at least sign of disturbance. Favours overgrown gullies in mountainous terrain but most frequently seen on trails on or close to ridges. Takes grubs, beetles, ants and especially berries (particularly *Calamus*). Display postures intermediate between Sumatran and other congeners, but closer to former.

BREEDING Presumed monogamous because of limited sexual dimorphism, but no categorical data. One nest described from wild was between two fallen trees among rocks and another was a virtually unlined scrape under a rhododendron within dense elfin forest. Clutch 2 buffy-white, quite elongated eggs. Season apparently from February, at least occasionally earlier (e.g. female on eggs in January in Malaysia) and probably weather dependent. Incubation in captivity lasts 19–21 days.

DISTRIBUTION Endemic to montane C Peninsular Malaysia, from the Cameron Highlands south to the Genting Highlands, northwest to the Larut Range and the outlying peaks of Gunung Tahan and Gunung Benom.

STATUS Vulnerable. Locally uncommon to reasonably common, with stable or slightly declining population estimated at 2500–10,000 individuals, based on anecdotal information (encounter rates) and extent of suitable habitat. Recent records from 12 areas and concentrated at Fraser's Hill and Cameron Highlands, making its overall status unclear. Its montane forests have been very little impacted upon as yet, but its small range and the very real prospect of development expanding from existing hill stations, together with the possibility of a road linking these, could have serious consequences for this fragile habitat. Known from three protected areas: Krau Wildlife Reserve, Taman Negara National Park and the small Fraser's Hill Wildlife Sanctuary. A clearer image of its distribution along the main range and in these protected areas would be of great value.

REFERENCES BirdLife International (2000, 2001), Johnsgard (1986), King *et al.* (1975), McGowan & Garson (1995), Wells (1999).

151 GERMAIN'S PEACOCK-PHEASANT
Polyplectron germaini Elliot, 1866
Plate 44

A distinctive small dark peacock-pheasant, lacking crest of other similar species, with a range almost confined to southern Vietnam.

IDENTIFICATION Lowland and hill forests of S Vietnam where it is the only peacock-pheasant. Unlike Grey (where male is considerably the larger), the sexes differ little in overall size. Germain's lacks crest and ruff of Grey and is markedly smaller and darker, with finer and closer pale vermiculations and more, purplish-blue (rather than green) ocelli. Bare facial skin dull red (pale yellowish to pinkish in Grey) and the relatively smaller and darker head only exhibits whitish on chin (pale area extends over cheeks on Grey, which appears to have a relatively large pale head exaggerated by the bushy forecrown). Compare females of larger *Lophura* pheasants.

DESCRIPTION Lacks prominent crest and ruffed collar of other members of group. Uppertail-coverts long, some greatly elongated and concealing up to half of tail, with subterminal pairs of ocelli. Tail consists of 20 feathers (18 in female), greatly elongated and graduated, with rather broad, blunt-tipped feathers, adorned with subterminal pairs of metallic ocelli. Bill and legs blackish-brown. Bare skin around eye dull red. Irides brown. Sexes similar. Legs slender, male has two spurs; female unspurred. **Adult male:** Head and most of neck blackish, finely barred greyish-white, becoming whitish on chin and upper throat. Entire underparts blackish, closely and irregularly barred buffy-brown. Upperparts, including wings and tail dark brown, finely spotted buff. Feathers of mantle, scapulars, wing-coverts and tertials have single terminal ocellus, purple-blue with green reflections, bordered by black and buff rings; primaries unmarked dull black. Central pair of elongated uppertail-coverts lack ocelli, but rest have pair of subterminal ocelli, one on each web. Tail has pair of subterminal metallic green ocelli on each feather. **First-year male:** Smaller and duller than adult male, with blackish ocelli, shorter tail and spurs only weakly developed. **Adult female:** Smaller, with relatively shorter and less strongly graduated tail than male. Much like male in plumage, but has fine buffish streaking and speckling above, not spotting of male. Ocelli of mantle and wings triangular (not rounded), metallic blue with black base. Tail finely barred with prominent green ocelli, but these lack defined border, especially on outer feathers where markings tend to merge. **Juvenile:** Very similar to female, but ocelli blackish.

GEOGRAPHICAL VARIATION Monotypic.

MEASUREMENTS Length: male 56–60 cm, female c.48cm. Male larger (but less disparity between sexes than in Grey). Males: wing 180–200, tail 250–320, tarsus 65, weight (one captive) 510. Females: wing 160–185, tail 220–250, tarsus 55, weight (one captive) 397.

HABITAT Confined to lowland and submontane evergreen and semi-evergreen forest to at least 1400 m (and perhaps 1800 m). Recorded in modified habitats such as logged, secondary, swampy and bamboo forest.

VOICE During breeding season male gives chuckling call, similar to Grey but louder and harsher. It also appears to vary in intensity, being a loud swift cackle, or a repeated (4–7 times) low purring rattle, which becomes more rapid with increasing agitation when responding to rival: *erraarrrrakak aarrr-akh-akh-akh-akh AKH-AKH-AKH...* (lower pitched and faster than in Grey).

HABITS Wary and can be difficult to observe, but common and often encountered in suitable areas, such as in parts of Nam Bai Cat Tien National Park, where it occurs in logged forest and patches of thorny bamboo. Loud calls belie its presence, and often given in response to neighbouring males. Usually escapes on foot, but if pressed will fly low and fast. Food probably similar to Grey Peacock-pheasant, but no data from wild. In display, tail is less raised and not as fully fanned as in Grey.

BREEDING No reliable information on mating pattern in wild. Season is February–April at least. One wild nest contained a single egg placed in a shallow hollow lined with down, and a pair with one fledgling was observed in April. Eggs creamy-white. In captivity, breeds year-round and 1–2 egg clutches take 21 days to incubate.

DISTRIBUTION S Vietnam where historically known from c.14°N south through S Annam and Cochinchina. Recent records are from Lam Dong, Dong Nai, Song Be, Gia Lai and Dak Lak provinces. Recently discovered in adjacent extreme E Cambodia in Mondulkiri province, but unconfirmed reports from Laos appear almost certainly incorrect.

STATUS Vulnerable. Locally common (e.g. in Cambodian range, where occurs in Snoul Wildlife Sanctuary, and at six sites in Dak Lak province during 1998

surveys) to uncommon. Of concern is the paucity of recent localities, especially given that it was considered widespread throughout S Vietnam in the mid-1960s. Anecdotal information and an estimate of the amount of habitat thought likely to remain within its range suggests a current population estimate of fewer than 10,000 individuals. Declining as a result of habitat loss and fragmentation through commercial logging and resettlement programmes, combined with clearance for subsistence agriculture and commercial crops. Known from at least five protected areas, including Nam Cat Tien National Park and the integrated and adjacent Cat Loc Nature Reserve, where a five-year research and development programme commenced in 1998. More detailed information from other sites is required, as is the establishment of additional protected areas. It is also under pressure from hunting, even within protected areas due to staff shortages and resources.

REFERENCES BirdLife International (2000, 2001), Delacour (1977), McGowan & Garson (1995), Robson (2000), Robson *et al.* (1993), Wildash (1968).

---

152 GREY PEACOCK-PHEASANT
Polyplectron bicalcaratum (Linnaeus, 1758)   Plate 44

Alternative name: Chinquis Peacock-pheasant.

The most widespread peacock-pheasant, inhabiting most of SE Asia except Indochina.

IDENTIFICATION Lowland and hill forest of mainland SE Asia, west to Sikkim but excluding most of Indochina. Male markedly larger, with contrast between relatively darker grey (but pale-barred) forward-pointing bushy crest and whitish throat and cheeks. Rest of plumage relatively uniform vermiculated and barred grey-brown, with numerous ocelli on upperparts, each spot chiefly green, with buffish or whitish surround. Some variation in colour saturation, with those in the west being greyest and browner populations in the east. Bare facial skin varies from pinkish to yellowish. Female smaller and darker, especially head, with less obvious blackish ocelli, which are virtually absent on tail. See congeners for comparative distinctions, especially Germain's, Hainan and Malayan Peacock-pheasants, none of which overlap in range.

DESCRIPTION *P. b. bicalcaratum.* Male has elongated hair-like feathers on crown, which can be elevated forwards to form bushy crest reaching over bill. Nape feathers distinctly elongated, broad and fluffy, and can be fanned into short ruff in display. Crest and ruff of female shorter and less 'hairy'. Uppertail-coverts long, some greatly elongated and covering up to half of tail, with subterminal pairs of ocelli. Tail consists of 22–24 feathers, greatly elongated and graduated, with rather broad, blunt-tipped feathers, adorned by subterminal pairs of metallic ocelli. Bill and legs dark grey. Bare skin around eye pale yellow to dull pinkish (exceptionally reddish in male). Irides whitish or pale grey. Sexes similar. Legs slender, male has up to five spurs; female unspurred. **Adult male:** Head and most of neck dark

grey-brown, finely barred pale buff or greyish-white, becoming whitish on chin and throat. Rest of body brownish-black, closely and irregularly barred and speckled buff. Upperparts, including wings and tail dark brown, finely spotted buff. Feathers of mantle, scapulars, wing-coverts and tertials marked with single terminal ocellus, purple-blue with green reflections, bordered by black and buff rings; primaries unmarked dull black. Elongated uppertail-coverts have pair of subterminal ocelli, one on each web. Tail has pair of subterminal metallic green ocelli on each feather. **First-year male:** Smaller and duller with relatively shorter crest and ruff than adult male, blackish ocelli, shorter tail and spurs absent or only weakly developed. **Adult female:** Smaller, with relatively shorter crest, ruff and legs than male. Plumage duller, having smaller blackish ocelli (which are virtually absent on tail) and has more irregular fine buffish streaking and speckling above. **Juvenile:** Very similar to female, but young male can have larger, metallic violet ocelli after a few weeks.

GEOGRAPHICAL VARIATION Varies in general coloration, with browner birds in east and greyest populations in west. Hainan Peacock-pheasant is often treated as conspecific with Grey, but is given specific status here. Four subspecies recognised but perhaps require revision, especially in view of apparent variation in Assamese birds.

    P. b. bakeri Lowe, 1925 occurs in NE India (Sikkim to Assam and Arunachal Pradesh) and Bhutan; the palest and greyest form, intergrading with nominate.

    P. b. bailyi Lowe, 1925 occurs in E Himalayas (probably NE India but locality of specimens uncertain); very dark grey form, with almost pure white markings.

P. b. bicalcaratum (Linnaeus, 1758) occurs in S China, Myanmar and E Bangladesh east to N Laos; described above; dark brown and buff specimens from NE Assam also perhaps belong here.

P. b. ghigii Delacour & Jabouille, 1924 occurs in C Laos and N and C Vietnam; browner than nominate, with buff surrounds to tail ocelli neat and complete, not broken by tip of ocelli. Intermediates with previous form have been reported in Laos.

MEASUREMENTS Length: male 56–76 cm, female 48–55 cm; difference partially due to longer tail of male. *P. b. bakeri.* Males: wing 210–240, tail 350–400, tarsus 75–80, weight 568–910. Females: wing 175–215, tail 230–255, tarsus 65–70, weight (two birds) 460–500.

HABITAT Lush lowland evergreen and semi-evergreen forest with dense understorey, including bamboo, to 1800 m in Thailand and 2000 m in Yunnan, but typically lower.

VOICE Male has both a loud whistle and harsh chuckling call. Shrill whistle is rendered *trew-tree, taa-pwi* or *phee-hoi* (the second note longer and rising) and is repeated up to five times at various intervals. The other loud call is a guttural and raucous *qua qua qua* or *wak wak wak*, which may serve as an alarm, as it is sometimes heard when disturbed.

HABITS Virtually unknown due to relative lack of observations. Very wary and likely to slink away through undergrowth at least sign of disturbance, rather than flushing. Usually alone or in pairs, though it is possible that others may be close by within understorey, and during breeding season family parties sometimes encountered. Presence usually belied by call, which can often be heard erratically throughout the day in breeding season and at dawn and dusk at other times. Feeds principally on seeds, berries, fruits and invertebrates, with a particular liking for termites. Foraging appears deliberate and slow, birds gently scratching with little sound. Males have spectacular display, crouching with wings and tail fully fanned to reveal ocelli in peacock fashion.

BREEDING Considered monogamous in wild as pairs observed, but mating system requires clarification given that polygamy has been recently observed in captivity. Nest a scrape or natural depression among tangled vegetation, or in a bamboo clump, thick bushes etc. Clutch usually 2, but rarely up to 5 pale cream to rich chocolate-buff, white-stippled eggs. Season varies across range, but essentially March–June and mainly April–May. Incubation in captivity lasts 21 days.

DISTRIBUTION From western limit in Sikkim, in E Himalayan foothills, it occurs east through NE India, Bhutan, E Bangladesh, Myanmar and into S China (extreme W Yunnan and S Guangxi; reports from E Tibet are probably erroneous). Southward it extends through much of Thailand to S Laos and C Vietnam (Tonkin and N Annam).

STATUS Variously considered common to rare and local over broad range. Locally not uncommon in undisturbed forest in NE India (though perhaps no longer in Sikkim) and frequent in Bhutan, but rare and local in Thailand. In China it is very localised, but perhaps expanding (merely as a result of more intensive searching in Yunnan). No recent information from Myanmar, but formerly considered very common in north and Tenasserim and common elsewhere (except the Pegu Yomas). In Thailand it is widespread and fairly common in the largest and best-protected areas. Considered reasonably common in several areas of Laos, where overall population appears healthy. Known from some protected areas, including Bach Ma (Vietnam) and Thung Salaeng Luang (Thailand) National Parks. The vagueness of population assessments and inter-country variations precludes any overall assessment of numbers. It is principally at risk from habitat loss, but hunting is also a serious problem in some areas.

REFERENCES Cairns (2000), Delacour (1977), Johnsgard (1986), King *et al.* (1975), Robson (2000), Thewlis *et al.* (1998), Wildash (1968).

---

153 HAINAN PEACOCK-PHEASANT
Polyplectron katsumatae Rothschild, 1906   Plate 44

A veritable miniature of the Grey Peacock-pheasant (with which it is often considered conspecific), confined to the island of Hainan where it is probably endangered through habitat loss.

IDENTIFICATION Endemic to Hainan (S China) where it is the only peacock-pheasant. Very similar to darkest and brownest populations of Grey Peacock-pheasant, but smaller, with a shorter crest. Differs also in colour of ocelli, with those of mantle and wings being blue and green (rather than blue and purplish-pink) with a clear white surround that broadens at tip. Tail ocelli have a complete greyish-buff border as in *ghigii* form of Grey. Female distinguished from female Grey in having steel-blue, not black ocelli.

DESCRIPTION Male has elongated hair-like feathers on forecrown, which can be fanned over bill. Feathers of nape somewhat elongated and can be fanned into a short ruff in display. Crest and ruff of female vestigial. Uppertail-coverts long, some greatly elongated and covering up to half of tail, with subterminal pairs of ocelli. Tail greatly elongated and graduated, with rather broad, blunt-tipped feathers, adorned by subterminal pairs of metallic ocelli. Bill and legs dark grey. Bare skin around eye pale fleshy-yellow. Irides pale grey. Sexes similar. Legs slender, male usually has at least one spur; female unspurred. **Adult male:** Head and most of neck dark brown, finely barred pale buff. Chin and throat whitish. Rest of body brownish-black, closely and irregularly barred and speckled buff. Feathers of mantle, scapulars, wing-coverts and tertials marked by a single terminal blue-green ocellus, edged black and bordered by a complete whitish ring, which broadens at tip. Primaries unmarked dull black.

Elongated uppertail-coverts have pair of subterminal ocelli, one on each web. Tail has pair of subterminal metallic ocelli on each feather, the spots clearly and completely outlined whitish. **First-year male:** Presumably smaller and duller than adult male. **Adult female:** Smaller and has vestigial crest. Plumage duller than adult male, having smaller, steel-blue ocelli. **Juvenile:** Probably very similar to female, but poorly described.

GEOGRAPHICAL VARIATION Monotypic, though often treated as conspecific with Grey Peacock-pheasant.

MEASUREMENTS Length: male 53–65 cm, female 40–45 cm; difference in part due to longer tail of male. Males: wing 195–198, tail 285–300, tarsus 60, weight (n=1) 456. Females: wing 160–165, tail 170–190, tarsus 53.

HABITAT Evergreen and semi-evergreen forests at 600–1200 m. Apparently persists in mature secondary forest.

VOICE Male gives a relatively loud and melodious *guang-gui, guang-gui, guang-gui* with the first note being more prolonged. Females utter a more rapid *ga, ga, ga.*

HABITS Rarely seen and poorly known. Presumably much as other peacock-pheasants.

BREEDING Seemingly undocumented.

DISTRIBUTION Endemic to SW Hainan, China.

STATUS Considered Endangered under Mace-Lande criteria and poorly known. Severely threatened by habitat loss, Hainan having lost some 75% of its native forests in recent decades. Logging of primary forest on the island was declared illegal in 1994, but secondary forests may still be cut. Scarce or uncommon in remaining undisturbed forest, of which over half of the 740 km² remaining in the late 1980s/early 1990s was in reserves. Known from at least six sites, including Ba Wang Ling (where population estimated at 3.75 individuals per 1 km²) and Jian Feng Ling National Nature Reserves, in recent years. Its overall population was estimated at 2775 individuals in the early 1990s. This taxon has suffered from neglect, having long been considered conspecific with the widespread mainland Grey Peacock-pheasant. It is in great need of further conservation research, as despite being protected by Chinese law it is still hunted for food.

REFERENCES Cheng (1978), Delacour (1977), Johnsgard (1986), MacKinnon & Phillips (2000), Yu-Ren (1998).

---

154 MALAYAN PEACOCK-PHEASANT
Polyplectron malacense (Scopoli, 1786)   Plate 44

Alternative names: Malaysian/Crested Peacock-pheasant.

A close relative of the Bornean Peacock-pheasant, with which it has sometimes been considered conspecific.

IDENTIFICATION A rather small, brownish peacock-pheasant now known only from lowland forests of Peninsular Malaysia. Recalls larger Grey in its prominent crest, but their ranges no longer overlap (both formerly occurred in W Thailand), with Grey inhabiting foothill forest further north and, until recently, Malayan was rarely encountered in lowland forest in the now largely deforested extreme south. Male Malayan has glossy blue-green crest, which reaches forward over bill when erect, and blackish ear-coverts framing reddish-orange facial skin giving dark-headed appearance quite different to pale face and crest of Grey. Female duller, with vestigial crest and reddish facial skin. In Malaysia it is replaced in central highlands by Mountain Peacock-pheasant, both sexes of which are much darker, almost sooty, on breast and underparts, have a longer narrower tail and lack both crest or reddish facial skin.

DESCRIPTION Male has elongated hair-like feathers on crown, which can be elevated to form bushy crest reaching over bill. Nape feathers distinctly elongated, broad and fluffy, and can be fanned into short ruff in display. Crest and ruff of female shorter, almost vestigial. Uppertail-coverts long, some greatly elongated and covering almost half of tail, with subterminal pairs of ocelli. Tail consists of 22 feathers, greatly elongated and somewhat graduated (the four central pairs of feathers almost equal), rather broad and blunt tipped, adorned by a subterminal metallic ocellus on outer web of each, only central pair with two ocelli. Bill dark grey, with fleshy-yellow lower mandible. Legs dark grey. Bare skin around eye reddish-orange. Irides bluish-white (brown in female). Sexes similar. Legs slender, male has up to three, perhaps more, spurs; female unspurred. **Adult male:** Crown, including crest, metallic greenish-blue. Ruff feathers have violet fringes. Forehead and head-sides streaked pale grey and black. Lower and rear ear-coverts purplish-black bordering reddish facial skin. Throat pale greyish. Underparts vermiculated brown and black, centre of breast paler (vermiculated buff and black). Upperparts, including wings and tail buffy-brown, spotted black. Feathers of mantle, scapulars, wing-coverts and tertials marked by terminal blue ocelli, bordered by black and buff rings; primaries unmarked dull black. Elongated uppertail-coverts and tail have subterminal metallic green ocelli edged black and buff. **First-year male:** Similar to female but larger and brighter. **Adult female:** Smaller and duller with relatively shorter tail than male; crest vestigial. Plumage duller, having smaller, triangular blackish ocelli on mantle and wings, and blue ocelli on longest tail-coverts and tail. **Juvenile:** Very similar to female, but young male can possess larger, metallic ocelli after a few weeks.

GEOGRAPHICAL VARIATION Monotypic.

MEASUREMENTS Length: male 50–53 cm, female 40–45 cm. Males: wing 200–215, tail 240–250, tarsus 65. Females: wing 180–185, tail 180–190, tarsus 60. Weight (both sexes) 455–680.

HABITAT Primary lowland dipterocarp forest, though also recorded from mature secondary forest that was not extensively cut. Apparently largely restricted to forest on level or gently undulating terrain, but not slopes. Prefers dense understorey, particularly that rich in small palms. Usually at 15–80 m, but recorded at 300 m.

VOICE Three loud calls, two of which show some gradation. During unpredictable breeding period, male gives melancholy two-note whistles, the second being higher. Another loud call is a harsh *tchorr*. Both predominantly given from roost at dawn and dusk, and sometimes audible over up to c.250 m. Given in bouts of just one call type, or in a mixed bout in which the whistle follows the *tchorr* call, but not vice versa. Final loud call is an explosive cackle that is clearly identifiable as a peacock-pheasant call, rendered as *kwok-kwok* or *gwak-gwak* and typically seems to be given when disturbed. Sometimes a few such calls may be given or a bout may continue for several minutes, before tailing off. In some cases the calls become progressively shorter and more strained, until they turn into a short series of *tchorr* notes.

HABITS Very wary and elusive, slinks away into undergrowth at slightest disturbance rather than flushing. Presence most reliably indicated by calls during apparent breeding periods, but occasionally heard in most months. Presence also indicated by cleared areas on ground from where leaf-litter is removed, which are made by males for display purposes. Maintenance of such 'scrapes' is unpredictable, though it appears likely that males are close by while 'scrapes' are clean. Female tends to occupy much smaller home range than male. Digs or scratches for insects and their larvae. Roosts alone up to c.3–4 m above ground, moving site on nightly basis.

BREEDING Mating pattern almost certainly polygynous, males probably mating serially with females. Male maintains a breeding territory, into which female enters when ready to breed. Latter insigates own mutual-preening display at this time. Nest a slight scrape or eggs laid directly onto leaf-litter. Breeding perhaps linked to food availability, which varies both within and between years: nests found in March, April and August, with one situated within a slight hollow atop a 1.4 m-high termitarium, two on open ground among dead leaves and a fourth against a recent tree-fall. This is the only pheasant species to lay a single-egg clutch; eggs buffy with white pit marks. Incubation in captivity lasts 22–23 days.

DISTRIBUTION Endemic to lowlands of Malay Peninsula (except south). Formerly also S Thailand. Historical claims from S Myanmar (where it was never widely reported) and from Sumatra are probably erroneous.

STATUS Vulnerable. Very local, but common in a few remaining areas. Formerly it was probably patchily, but well distributed throughout lowlands of the peninsula. Ongoing forest loss has confined it to a few isolated blocks and may ultimately restrict it to only a handful of protected areas: its habitat currently stands at 25% of that available in 1970 and in Malaysia, by 1997, it remained at just 54% of previously known localities. Intensive fieldwork at one site (where 10.5–11.6 males/km²) extrapolated through amount of estimated extant habitat within its historical range suggest a population of 2500–10,000 individuals. Almost certainly extinct in Thailand from where there have been no definite records for over ten years (though a report of peacock-pheasants at Tong Yang in Narathiwat should be investigated). Known from Taman Negara National Park and Krau Wildlife Reserve, and a handful of other quite small forest reserves, but the continual loss of forest on level plains place this lowland forest specialist at significant risk.

REFERENCES BirdLife International (2000, 2001), Davison (1983), Johnsgard (1986), McGowan & Garson (1995), Robson (2000), Wells (1999).

---

155 BORNEAN PEACOCK-PHEASANT
Polyplectron schleiermacheri Bruggemann, 1877   Plate 43

This mysterious bird is the least known of all peacock-pheasants; few of the reports throughout much of Borneo have been in recent years.

IDENTIFICATION A rather small, relatively short-tailed peacock-pheasant known only from lowland forests of Borneo. Little known and endangered it is closely related to Malayan, but male has distinctively patterned underparts, which are blackish, becoming iridescent blue-green on breast-sides, contrasting with white throat and stripe on breast centre (latter perhaps only evident in display). Female very similar to female Malayan but smaller, somewhat shorter tailed, with smaller ocelli and more rufous-brown overall, becoming almost blackish-brown on underparts.

DESCRIPTION Male has somewhat elongated hair-like feathers on crown, which can be elevated to form small bushy crest reaching over bill. Nape feathers distinctly elongated, broad and fluffy, and can be fanned into short ruff in display. Crest and ruff of female shorter, almost vestigial. Uppertail-coverts long, some greatly elongated and covering almost half of tail, with subterminal pairs of ocelli. Tail consists of 22 feathers, greatly elongated, somewhat graduated (the four central pairs of feathers almost equal), rather broad and blunt tipped, adorned by a subterminal metallic ocellus on outer web of each, only central pair with two ocelli; the inner webs of lateral rectrices have a blackish subterminal spot. Bill and legs dark grey. Bare skin around eye reddish. Irides pale bluish (brown in female). Sexes differ. Legs slender, male has spurs; female unspurred. **Adult male:** Crown, including crest, barred grey and black, glossed green at centre. Ruff feathers similarly barred, with violet-blue tips. Forehead and head-sides black, bordering red facial skin. Throat pure white, the white extending onto upper breast and as stripe on central underparts (becoming most conspicuous in display). Breast-sides metallic blue-green; rest of underparts black (with weak whitish vermiculations and shaft streaks), becoming brown with black spotting on undertail-coverts. Upperparts, including wings and tail almost rufous-brown, spotted black. Feathers of mantle, scapulars, wing-coverts and tertials marked by small terminal green ocelli, bordered black; primaries unmarked dull black. Elongated uppertail-coverts and tail have subterminal blue-green ocelli edged black and buff; the inner webs of lateral rectrices with a blackish subterminal spot rather than ocelli. **First-year male:** Like female but larger and brighter, and also differs from adults in having outer webs of flight feathers mottled and barred rufous and buff. Underparts more vermiculated. **Adult female:** Smaller and duller, lacking areas of black and pure white, almost without gloss compared to male. Tail relatively shorter and dull crest vestigial. Plumage duller, having smaller, blackish ocelli on mantle and wings and often lack (perhaps first-years) blue-green ocelli on longest tail-coverts and on irregularly and coarsely barred tail. Underparts finely vermiculated sooty brown. **Juvenile:** Apparently undescribed; presumably much as female.

GEOGRAPHICAL VARIATION Monotypic.

MEASUREMENTS Length: male c.50 cm, female 35.5 cm . Males: wing 200, tail 190–200, tarsus 70. Females: wing 165, tail 155–180. No weight data.

HABITAT Primary lowland rainforest, possibly restricted to riverine alluvial forest and local people report it at 300–1000 m in the Danum–Linau area.

VOICE Unknown, though a vocalisation recorded in Borneo that greatly resembled the Malayan Peacock-pheasant may have been this species.

HABITS Unknown due to extreme paucity of wild observations.

BREEDING Mating pattern unknown, but presumably polygamous. Nest unknown in wild, but constructs no nest in captivity. Observations of juveniles in wild suggest season is late October–mid-March (year-round in captivity). A captive female laid three one-egg clutches, but eggs undescribed. Incubation in captivity lasts 20–22 days.

DISTRIBUTION Endemic to Borneo, with records across much of the island. Exact distribution, however, remains uncertain, though C Kalimantan may contain a large proportion of remaining population.

STATUS Endangered. Extreme paucity and scatter of records suggest that it is either very unusual in its habits, or exceedingly rare and locally distributed. It has recently been recorded through hunter interview surveys in C Kalimantan, where firm evidence (feathers) was also found at four localities, but wild sightings remain elusive and most respondents considered it to have declined within living memory. Given habitat use by closely-related Malayan Peacock-pheasant, it has been thought that if the Bornean species is confined to alluvial terraces then it is probably at serious risk, as this forest is often the first to be logged along main river drainages. If it demonstrates the same ability to ascend slopes as the Palawan Peacock-pheasant, it may be in rather better shape. At present there is much scope for speculation; the only facts are the lack of confirmed recent records, with none in protected areas or from some historical localities, such as Paitan in Sabah and the type-locality at Muara Tewe in Kalimantan.

REFERENCES BirdLife International (2000, 2001), MacKinnon & Phillips (1993), McGowan & Garson (1995), O'Brien *et al.* (1998), Smythies (1981).

156 PALAWAN PEACOCK-PHEASANT
Polyplectron emphanum Temminck, 1831

Plate 43

With its upstanding crest, black underparts and highly developed upperparts iridescence this is the most 'peacock-like' of the peacock-pheasants.

IDENTIFICATION A very distinctive peacock-pheasant, endemic to Palawan in the S Philippines. Male has a prominent crest, which may be erected to a point in display, and coupled with white cheeks, blackish underparts and wings, the latter with extremely glossy blue-green reflections, makes identification straightforward. Female also distinctive, being almost uniform dark brown with buffy-white cheeks and throat, and often a whitish eyebrow, the crest shorter than in male, but longer than in other peacock-pheasants, and invariably carried flat. Compare female Red Junglefowl, which also occurs on Palawan.

DESCRIPTION Male has long pointed crest, which can be vertically erected; female has shorter, but quite prominent crest. Uppertail-coverts long, some greatly elongated and covering almost half of tail, with subterminal pairs of ocelli. Tail consists of 22–24

feathers, greatly elongated and somewhat graduated. Rectrices rather broad and blunt tipped, adorned by a subterminal metallic ocellus on outer web of each, the central pair with two ocelli; inner webs of lateral rectrices have ocelli becoming progressively smaller, absent on inner web of outermost feathers. Bill blackish with pale horn tip. Bare skin around eye reddish. Irides brown. Legs dark grey. Sexes differ. Legs slender, male has two spurs; female unspurred. **Adult male:** Crown, including crest, metallic green-black. Ear-coverts and often also stripe over eye to nape white (stripe variable, often absent). Rest of head, neck and underparts black. Mantle, scapular and wing feathers velvet black at base, with most of exposed part of each feather bright iridescent violet or blue-green; flight feathers dull black. Rump and back vermiculated black and rufous-brown. Uppertail-coverts and tail finely peppered buff and blackish-brown; larger tail-coverts and tail feathers tipped buff and barred blackish-brown. Elongated uppertail-coverts and tail have subterminal metallic green ocelli edged black and buff; ocelli on inner webs of lateral rectrices becoming progressively smaller, absent on inner web of outermost feathers. **First-year male:** Mixture of male and female plumage features, having extensive metallic blue-green or black feathers on wings and underparts; tail similar to adult male; spurs absent or very short. **Adult female:** Head and neck dusky-brown, with prominent backward-curving short crest; short supercilium, lower ear-coverts and throat brownish-white. Body plumage almost uniform dull brown, warmer on upperparts, which are finely freckled buff. Wing feathers and uppertail-coverts have blackish patches and tawny-buff bars. Tail dull brown with blackish subterminal patches replacing ocelli, though those on outer webs glossed blue. **Juvenile:** Basically similar to female, though young male soon acquires black spotting on wings.

GEOGRAPHICAL VARIATION Monotypic, but variation in extent or absence of white in supercilium of male (birds with white supercilia have been termed '*nehrkornae*'), but significance of this yet to be resolved.

MEASUREMENTS Length: male c.50 cm, female, c.40 cm; much of difference due to longer tail of male. Males: wing 190–195, tail 240–250, tarsus 66, weight 436 (mean of two captive males). Females: wing 170–175, tail 165–170, tarsus 55, weight 322 (mean of two captive females).

HABITAT Though historically claimed to be restricted to coastal lowland forests, it has been recorded up to c.800 m. It appears probable that it is now mainly found on forested slopes and is probably intolerant of much habitat disturbance.

VOICE Call a harsh, rasped screech *auukk, kratt, krotch* and *ka reeeetch*, each note lasting up to one second and repeated approximately every 5 seconds. Also a two-note *krotchh-kritchh* in seesaw rhythm, which may be repeated for several minutes. Each call ends with a metallic ringing, likened to hitting a metal pipe with a piece of wood. When disturbed, distinctive peacock-pheasant-like clucks are given.

HABITS Like all peacock-pheasants, wary and elusive, slinking away in undergrowth at slightest disturbance rather than flushing. Presence most reliably indicated by calls during apparent breeding periods and by cleared areas on ground, from where leaf-litter is removed, made by males for display purposes. Maintenance of such 'scrapes' is unpredictable, though it appears likely that males are close by while 'scrapes' are clean.

BREEDING Mating system unknown and suggestions that it is monogamous are unsubstantiated. No wild nest has been found. In captivity clutch is 2; eggs rosy to buff-white. Season also unclear (December–January or February–April). Incubation in captivity lasts 18–20 days and is by female alone.

DISTRIBUTION Endemic to Palawan in the Philippines, where it occurs at least as far north as Danlig.

STATUS Vulnerable. Locally common, but patchily distributed being known from c.20 localities, 11 of these with records since 1980. Formerly thought confined to coastal strip in southern two-thirds of island and loss of forest in this zone was a cause of great concern. While forest loss remains a major concern (all remaining forest on the island is under logging or mining concession), the species is now known to occur in the central mountains and has been recorded up to 800 m, suggesting that a more or less continuous population may persist to the north. It is unknown how optimal this habitat is and concerns exist that birds may have retreated to marginal habitat as plains forest has been felled. Firm evidence of successful breeding (i.e. sightings of chicks) would be very valuable. The highly restricted nature of available habitat allied to encounter rates (34 males/km² at one forest-edge site) suggest a population in the low thousands. In addition to forest loss, both for timber and conversion of land to agriculture, hunting has been a serious problem since the 1960s as access to dwindling forest has increased.

REFERENCES BirdLife International (2000, 2001), Jeggo (1975), Johnsgard (1986), Kennedy *et al.* (2000), McGowan *et al.* (1989), McGowan & Garson (1995).

Genus *RHEINARDIA*: Crested Argus

A monotypic genus reserved for this spectacular pheasant, which has a compressed tail of 12 long, broad-based, tapering feathers. In males, the central rectrices can be as much as five times the length of the outermost. Sexes differ chiefly in tail structure, but neither sports tarsal spurs. Additional structural features are discussed below.

157 CRESTED ARGUS
Rheinardia ocellata (Elliot, 1871)   Plate 45

Alternative name: Ocellated Pheasant.

A remarkable bird, which despite the spectacular plumage of the male is notoriously shy and difficult to see within its dense forest habitat.

IDENTIFICATION A large dark pheasant, with a 'full'

(female) or fantastically elongated (adult male) tail. Found in dense hill and montane forest in Annam (Vietnam) and C Malaysia, it is locally not uncommon but best detected by the distinctive far-carrying call of the male. Prominent black-and-white or black-and-buffy crest, pale surround to dark cheek and dull brown legs are useful identification pointers. Replaced in lowland Malaysia by superficially similar Great Argus, but latter has prominent bare blue skin on head and throat, stubbly black crest and redder legs, though vocalisations are surprisingly similar (see Voice). Compare female with female *Lophura* pheasants and female peacock-pheasants.

DESCRIPTION *R. o. ocellata.* Head rather small, with stiff upcurved feathers on rear crown and upper nape, which may be expanded to form striking white 'puff' crest (much less conspicuous on female). Wing structure unremarkable, but tail compressed and greatly elongated, consisting of 12 long, broad-based tapering feathers. Central feathers can be up to five times length of the outermost in male, but do not reach maximum length until fifth or sixth year. Uppertail-coverts also much enlarged. Sexes differ chiefly in tail structure, but female also has shorter crest and is duller. Legs relatively short and slim; neither sex usually sports tarsal spurs, but a faint indication of one occasionally appears. Bill pink, paler at tip (browner in female). Head-sides quite sparsely covered, revealing slate-blue skin. Irides brown. Legs brownish-pink. **Adult male:** Central crown, including central portion of crest, and ear-coverts blackish-brown. Broad and long whitish or buffy-white supercilium, extending onto nape where underside of crest pure white. Chin and throat grey, becoming whitish on malar region. Neck chestnut. Body and wing feathers dull darkish brown, intensely spotted buff and black; these being whiter on back and tertials. Massive tail has four central pairs of feathers pale grey, washed chestnut on sides, profusely speckled white and intensely and irregularly spotted chestnut, many with black central dots. Remaining tail feathers progressively darker towards shorter outermost. **First- and second-year male:** Similar to adult male, but tail much shorter; maximum tail length may not be fully attained until fifth year (based on captive observations). **Adult female:** Differs from male in having browner and duller head pattern, with shorter crest. Body plumage warm brown, vermiculated black, with some fine buff markings. Upperparts, particularly wings and tail distinctively barred blackish; tail considerably shorter than in male. **Juvenile:** Resembles female, but young male soon acquires male features at first moult, although they may not become fully mature until second-year or older.

GEOGRAPHICAL VARIATION Two well-differentiated subspecies recognised.

   R. o. ocellata (Elliot, 1871) occurs in Vietnam and adjacent Laos; described above, male has crest of c.60 mm.

   R. o. nigrescens Rothschild, 1902 occurs in the Malay Peninsula; male has longer and whiter crest (of c.85 mm), is darker especially on breast and more regularly spotted, with pale buffy eyebrows and throat (rather than white and pale grey respectively), and female marginally brighter, with finer black markings and paler underparts.

MEASUREMENTS Length: male 190–235 cm, female 74–75 cm; much of difference due to extremely long tail of male, which may contain longest feathers of any bird. *R. o. ocellata.* Males: wing 350–400, tail 1500–1700

(first- and second-year males much shorter), central rectrices up to 130 wide, tarsus 88–92. Females: wing 320–350, tail 350–430, tarsus 78–82. No weight data.

HABITAT In Laos it occurs in wetter forests of the Annamitic Chain to 1500 m, whereas in Vietnam it inhabits primary, logged and secondary evergreen forests (including those damaged by herbicides) at 100–700 m, but also at 1700–1900 m on the Da Lat Plateau. Encountered principally in tall forest at transition between upper dipterocarp and montane forest in Peninsular Malaysia (which occurs at 600–1200 m on Gunung Rabong, with most records at 800–1000 m).

VOICE Far-carrying calls of territorial male resemble those of Great Argus. Loud, resonant *WOO-KIA'WAU* (first part rising, second part louder and more resonant) has three components and is usually uttered singly from dancing ground. More frequently heard is series of up to eight loud, far-carrying disyllabic *oowaaa* or *oowaau* calls, which vary in volume and length (often have humming quality, or given as terminally rising *waaaauu*). A repeated, yelping *pook* or *puwoo* may be given in distress or alarm.

HABITS Very wary and elusive, slinks into undergrowth at slightest disturbance rather than flushing. Probably forages in manner similar to Great Argus. Presence most reliably indicated by calls during apparent breeding periods and by cleared areas ('dancing grounds') where the leaf-litter is removed, made by males. It appears likely that males are close by when 'scrapes' are clean. Diet consists of berries, grubs, insects, leaves, fruits and occasionally amphibians. In display, male raises crown feathers to reveal white 'powder-puff' nape and may partially open tail and droop wings as it circles female.

BREEDING Believed polygamous in wild, but no nest has been found. In captivity clutch consists of 2 deep pinkish-buff, finely spotted purplish-brown eggs. Season thought to commence during March in both subspecies. Incubation in captivity lasts 24–25 days.

DISTRIBUTION Two widely separated populations. Nominate *ocellata* occurs in Annamitic Chain of N, C and S Annam (Vietnam) and adjacent extreme EC Laos. The other subspecies, *nigrescens*, has a very small range, almost entirely contained within Taman Negara National Park in Peninsular Malaysia.

STATUS Vulnerable. In Malaysia considered very localised but common, and in Vietnam appears local and uncommon to common. Malaysian race *nigrescens* historically known to occur on just two mountains in Taman Negara National Park, but has now been confirmed from five other peaks within the park. Each appears likely to hold isolated populations, unless birds are remarkably dispersive, and some may be extremely small. The only assessment of density is eight calling males per 1 km² on Gunung Rabung in the mid-1970s. The nominate form appears quite common in suitable areas of Vietnam, such as in Bach Ma National Park (75 individuals recorded in 34 km²) in early 1990, and it was judged numerous in Nakai-Nam Theun National Biodiversity Conservation Area in Laos in 1994, and overall no evidence for any major decline in latter country. These assessments, extrapolated through extent of remaining habitat suggest that *ocellata* numbers in the thousands, and *nigrescens* probably in the low thousands. Most of *nigrescens* is contained within the park, but there is some habitat loss at the fringes. In Laos and Vietnam *ocellata* is not only under pressure from habitat loss and degradation, but from hunting as well.

REFERENCES BirdLife International (2000, 2001), Davison (1977, 1978, 1979), Johnsgard (1986), King *et al.* (1975), Mamat & Yasak (1998), McGowan & Garson (1995), Robson (2000), Thewlis *et al.* (1998), Wells (1999).

Genus *ARGUSIANUS*: Great Argus

Today this spectacular pheasant enjoys a monotypic genus. Like the Crested Argus there are 12 tail feathers, however, males of this peculiar bird have a greatly elongated central pair which can be up to 4 times the length of the outermost. The secondaries are strangely elongated, being markedly longer than the primaries, sporting a row of ocelli. Much of the head and neck is naked. Sexes differ chiefly in tail structure. Neither sex sports tarsal spurs.

158 GREAT ARGUS
Argusianus argus (Linnaeus, 1766)   Plate 45

Alternative name: Argus Pheasant.

Another spectacular pheasant, widespread in the Sunda region and perhaps marginally meeting Crested Argus in C Malaysia.

IDENTIFICATION This large dark pheasant inhabits dense lowland forest (chiefly below 1000 m) in the Malay Peninsula, Sumatra and Borneo. Both sexes are unmistakable having a 'full' (female) or very long (male) tail. Only in C Malaysia is there a chance of confusion with superficially similar Crested Argus, but Great easily distinguished in lacking long white crest and patterned face of Crested, instead having bare blue skin on head and an inconspicuous stubbly black crest and redder legs. The rows of ocelli on the secondaries are usually concealed by folded wing, but become obvious in display.

DESCRIPTION *A. a. argus.* Head and neck relatively small and almost naked, with a few scattered hair-like feathers; crown centre has band of short velvety feathers and nape a central mane of hair-like feathers. Secondaries square-ended and strangely elongated, being considerably longer than primaries; inner portion of outer webs sport a row of ocelli on feather shafts. Primaries also peculiarly formed, relatively stiff, with outermost the shortest and becoming progressively longer towards secondaries (these features less exaggerated in females). Tail greatly elongated, consists of 12 long tapering and somewhat graduated feathers, in male central pair can be up to four times length of outermost and twisted at tip. Sexes differ chiefly in tail structure, female also lacks ocelli and is duller. Legs relatively short and slim; neither sex usually sports tarsal spurs but an indication of one sometimes appears. Bill yellowish-white. Bare skin of head and neck cobalt-blue. Irides greyish-brown. Legs dull crimson-pink to deep red (duller in female). **Adult male:** Most of head and upper neck naked cobalt-blue, with scattered grey hair-like feathers. Central crown has band of velvety black feathers forming small tuft on rear crown. Hindneck has short mane of barred black-and-white feathers. Rest of underparts rufous-chestnut, dotted black and white

on foreneck and mottled and barred black below, becoming grey-brown on central vent. Mantle and wing-coverts dark brown, irregularly spotted buff. Back, rump and shorter uppertail-coverts yellowish-ochre spotted black. Larger uppertail-coverts grey and brown, marbled white. Secondaries and tertials intricately patterned with dark brown, buff and grey shading and reticulations. Rows of large but non-metallic ocelli are present close to pink and white shaft on inner part of outer web of secondaries. Primaries greyish-buff, shafts blue, vanes very intricately patterned with dark brown, black, yellow, rufous and white spotting. Tail feathers grey, becoming dark chestnut on edges; finely spotted white (each spot encircled by black). **First- and second-year male:** Similar to adult male, but tail much shorter; maximum tail length may not be fully attained until sixth or seventh year (based on captive observations). **Adult female:** Differs from male in having browner crown and rather longer 'mane'; tail and secondaries considerably shorter and latter lack ocelli. Entire plumage less finely spotted, but more vermiculated. Primaries rufous, with black spots. Coloration of bare skin on head and legs duller than male. **Juvenile:** Resembles female, but young male soon acquires male features at first moult, even though they may not become fully mature until second-year or older.

GEOGRAPHICAL VARIATION Two quite well-differentiated subspecies recognised.
   A. a. argus (Linnaeus, 1766) occurs in Sumatra and the Malay Peninsula; described above.
   A. a. grayi (Elliot, 1865) occurs in Borneo; male slightly smaller and greyer than nominate, with back pinky-buff (not yellowish), upper breast chestnut-orange (not dark chestnut) and spots on upperparts almost all white (not whitish, brownish and buff), while female has brighter reddish-orange neck and breast and paler brown underparts.

MEASUREMENTS Length: male 160–200 cm, female 74–75 cm; much of difference due to extremely long tail of male. *A. a. argus.* Males: wing attains 430–500 (secondaries), tail 1050–1430 (central rectrices up to 130 wide), tarsus 100–120, weight 2040–2605 (up to 2725 in captivity). Females: wing 300–350 (secondaries 350–400), tail 300–360, tarsus 82–90, weight 1700 (two captives: mean 1590).

HABITAT Inhabits lowland dipterocarp forest, including that on hill slopes up to maximum of 500 m (Sumatra), 1000 m (Malay Peninsula) and 1300 m (Kalimantan), though altitude further varies according to location. Also tolerates secondary forest (typically tall, mature forest).

VOICE Most conspicuous and recognisable are two loud calls, which are among the most distinctive and evocative sounds of these forests. The first is a disyllabic *kwow-wow*, which is repeated up to c.12 times, given from ground during day and also from nocturnal roost in some places. The second is, initially, a monosyllabic musical *wow*, but as series of up to 70 or more calls progresses, pitch becomes higher and last few calls audibly rise in tone, giving impression of increasing excitement, before stopping abruptly.

HABITS Very wary and elusive, slinks into undergrowth at slightest disturbance rather than flushing. Usually encountered singly. Presence most reliably indicated by far-carrying calls and by cleared areas ('dancing grounds') from where leaf-litter is removed, made by males, usually during first half of year. Occasional calls heard most months. Male indulges in spectacular display postures in which wings are elevated and fanned to reveal ocelli of long secondaries in similar manner to peacocks. Maintenance of dancing grounds implies that males are close by while they are clean. Forages by pecking at items on surface of leaf-litter and by scratching to expose food. After foraging in early morning, males, at least, spend much of day perched before feeding again in evening. Roosts in trees from where nighttime calls given during part of year in some areas, probably according to local conditions.

BREEDING Polygamous. One wild nest was a scrape between buttress roots lined with grass stems. Clutch 2

pale reddish-buff eggs with brown freckles. Season unclear, but perhaps linked to food availability and varies both within and between years, but typically early March–July. Incubation in captivity lasts 24–25 days.

DISTRIBUTION Occurs in suitable habitat throughout Sunda region, from extreme S Tenasserim (Myanmar) and adjacent SW Thailand south through Malay Peninsula (including Pangkor I.) to Sumatra and Borneo.

STATUS Near Threatened. Uncommon to common and in some areas now local. Thought to be now uncommon in Thailand, where it is confined to marginal submontane forest, tolerably common in Malaysia, but also increasingly confined to hill dipterocarp forest. Still apparently widespread in Indonesia, but alarming forest fragmentation, especially in Sumatra, can have resulted only in a substantial decline in numbers. It occurs in a number of protected areas, including Khao Luang National Park in Thailand, Taman Negara National Park in Malaysia, Way Kambas National Park on Sumatra and Pleihari-Martapura Wildlife Reserve in Kalimantan. Impressions of its abundance are invariably biased by its vocal nature: because it is far more easily detected than other galliformes, which share its habitat, it is perceived as more common. While principally a lowland forest resident, it is also found on hill slopes and so may have fared slightly better than those species restricted to level lowlands such as Malayan Peacock-pheasant. However, as logging reaches the hill–plains boundary, it is likely to be at greater risk than it has been in the past. Consequently, while more than 100,000 individuals may persist, the human onslaught on its habitat throughout its range implies a marked decline. In addition to habitat loss and degradation, it also suffers from excessive hunting in some areas.

REFERENCES BirdLife International (2000, 2001) Davison (1981, 1987), Johnsgard (1986), McGowan & Garson (1995), Robson (2000), Wells (1999).

159 DOUBLE-BANDED ARGUS
Argusianus bipunctatus Wood, 1871   not illustrated

Described from the portion of a single primary feather found among a bundle of feathers of Great Argus, which are assumed to have been collected for the plume trade and bought in London. Its natural origin is quite unknown, but Delacour (1977) speculated that it might have come from Java. However, Davison (1983) considered a more likely point of origin to be the island of Tioman off Malaysia. The structure and

pattern of the feather are too different for it to be a variant Great Argus. Davison considered that the feather structure indicated that the bird was probably incapable of flight, which would explain its apparent extirpation prior to discovery. This tantalising feather is housed in the Natural History Museum (Tring).

REFERENCES Davison (1983), Delacour (1977).

Genus *PAVO*: peafowl

These two species require little introduction. Both are quite spectacularly plumaged and are the largest of the pheasants. Males have colourful 'trains' in which the uppertail-coverts are enormously elongated and elaborately colourful, adorned by metallic ocelli. Tails are relatively short in comparison and flattened, formed of 20 feathers in males, 18 in females, and act as a support to the 'train'. Sexes differ markedly in plumage, though both have coronal tufts and iridescent plumages. Their legs are relatively long and slender and males have well-developed tarsal spurs.

160 INDIAN PEAFOWL
Pavo cristatus Linnaeus, 1758 Plate 46

Alternative names: Blue/Common Peafowl/Peacock.

Loud in more ways than one, the peacock produces one of the most elaborate and perhaps the most stunning of all avian displays. It is little wonder that it is the national bird of India, as it plays an important role in both Hindu and Buddhist mythology.

IDENTIFICATION Quite unmistakable, this is the only peafowl to be found in the Indian subcontinent. The shining blue and black neck and breast of the male and white underparts of the female are diagnostic when compared with superficially similar Green Peafowl of SE Asia (which could conceivably still occur in NE India). Being so well known, identification presents little problem, though glimpses of flying birds moving through tree cover can be quite baffling when only apparent colour can be rufous primaries. Immature and non-breeding males have shorter, or may even lack 'train' but have more colourful neck and breast than female. Compare Green Peafowl, especially of westernmost race *spicifer* (which may be extinct).

DESCRIPTION Head rather small, with fan-shaped crest atop wire-like feather shafts. Neck slender. In male, feathers of longer uppertail-coverts much elongated forming 'train'. Tail of moderate length, rather graduated and flattened, formed by 20 feathers in male, 18 in female, and acts as support to 'train'. Primaries well developed but wing structure unremarkable. Sexes differ. Legs relatively long and slender, male and some females have well-developed tarsal spurs. Bill whitish (greyer in females). Bare skin below eye and stripe in front of eye white. Irides brown (darker in female). Legs grey (brownish-grey in female). **Adult male:** Crown, neck and breast metallic blue, with green and mauve reflections, including tips of bare-shafted fan-like coronal tuft. Throat and head-sides black, broken by bands of bare whitish skin. Lower breast, flanks and belly blackish-blue, tinged green, becoming brown on vent. Mantle, back and rump metallic golden-green, each feather with narrow black border, imparting scaled appearance. Uppertail-coverts tremendously elongated, disintegrating at sides and tip, bronzed golden-green with white shafts and large tricoloured subterminal ocelli, forming 'train'. Scapulars, lesser and median wing-coverts and tertials closely barred dark brown and buffy-whitish. Greater coverts and secondaries black. Primaries rufous. Tail brown. **First-year male:** Similar to female, but crest and patches of blue feathering more strongly developed, and primaries dull rufous. **Second-year**

male: Similar to adult male, but 'train' much shorter; maximum length may not be fully attained until fifth or sixth year. **Adult female:** Crown and nape chestnut-brown, with feathers edged green. Throat and head-sides whitish. Neck, upper breast and mantle bronze-green, barred blackish. Lower breast barred dark brown and buffy-white. Rest of underparts buffy-white becoming dark brown on vent. Upperparts earth-brown, vermiculated pale brown. Flight feathers and tail dark brown, mottled whitish. **Juvenile:** Resembles female, but head buffy and breast brownish, lacking iridescence or notable crest of female; young male acquires rufous primaries after first moult.

GEOGRAPHICAL VARIATION Monotypic. Having been long kept as an ornamental curiosity, a number of colour variants have developed, most notable being white and pied 'breeds'. One captive mutation is interesting because it 'breeds true', *nigripennis* (Black-winged Peacock), which differs in having scapulars, wing-coverts and tertials glossy black rather than barred.

MEASUREMENTS Length: male 180–230 cm, female 90–100 cm; much of difference due to long 'train' of male. Males: wing 440–500, tail 400–450, 'train' (uppertail-coverts) reaches 1400–1600 by fifth/sixth year, tarsus 140–155, weight c.4000–6000. Females: wing 400–420, tail 325–375, tarsus 120–130, weight c.2750–4000.

HABITAT Scrub–jungle and forest edges. Also human-modified habitats, even feeding in crop fields in places where tolerated by people (on religious or sentimental grounds) and can almost be considered semi-feral around many villages. Away from human settlements, inhabits open moist and dry deciduous forest with an understorey and near to watercourses. Reaches 1800 m in Himalayas, and occasionally encountered to 2000 m.

VOICE Variety of calls, of which probably the most characteristic is a far-carrying, mournful piercing wail *may-awe may-awe may-awe*, also rendered as *kee-ow kee-ow kee-ow* and repeated several times at various pitch. Other loud calls include somewhat more urgent *ka-an ka-an ka-an*, likened to a braying donkey, which is typically repeated 6–8 times. When alarmed a *kok-kok* or *cain-kok* is uttered.

HABITS Typically encountered in small groups, often with just a single male, though after young hatch it is common to see flocks of males and females with young. Emerges from cover in early morning and late afternoon to drink at water holes or streams, and to forage in open areas such as forest clearings and cultivated land, where they scratch ground and peck at food. Spends much of rest of day in dense thickets. Displaying male raises and fans open train, elevated and supported by stiff tail, periodically rustling feathers into shimmering mass of colourful ocelli. Though peafowl can be wary in some areas, disappearing into cover when disturbed, they are typically treated sympathetically because of their religious significance and are thus mostly very confiding. Typically roosts at considerable height above ground in tall trees, accessed by short flights. Call given from roost is far carrying and very distinctive. When disturbed, escapes on foot into cover and only flies with loud wingbeats when hard-pressed, often only alighting some distance away after passing a prominent feature, such as a wall, hedge or thicket.

BREEDING Polygamous with males having harems of two or more females. Leks also observed at which males gather to display to females; this is sole contact between sexes as female is responsible for all nest and chick-rearing duties. Nest a scrape, sometimes roughly lined with grasses etc. and well hidden under thick bushes such as *Lantana* and *Zizyphus*, but sometimes above ground if flooding is a problem. Clutch size usually 3–6, but up to 8 pale cream or coffee-coloured to buff eggs, rarely with spots. Breeding starts after onset of rains in June in N and C India, but may be earlier at moderate altitudes in Himalayas; October–December in S India and apparently January–April in Sri Lanka. Incubation lasts 28–30 days.

DISTRIBUTION Indian subcontinent, from River Indus in Pakistan east through most of India, parts of Bangladesh and Sri Lanka. Eastern limit is thought to be c.95°E, but no recent information from NE India or Bangladesh, where it may be extinct. Being a popular ornamental species, numerous attempts have been made to introduce it elsewhere. Most have failed or been rather short lived, but small populations are currently established in the USA (SE California), Hawaii (Maui, Niihau, Oahu and Hawaii), the West Indies (now only on Little Exuma in the Bahamas), South Africa (Robben I. in the Cape), New Zealand (possibly still established in parts of North I.) and Australia (a few tiny mainland populations and on islands in Bass Strait).

STATUS India encompasses vast majority of range. Here it is widespread and often very common (though largely scarce or absent in northeast) wherever it is not persecuted; a similar situation applies in Sri Lanka, where it is locally common in protected areas of the dry zone. No detailed information available on population densities as species is so widespread that, despite its religious importance and status as the national bird, it is rarely studied. It occurs in many protected areas, though formal protection is unlikely to be important to its survival. Only two populations survive in Pakistan, it being numerous in both: one in extreme NE Punjab and the other in extreme SE Sind. It is locally common in the Nepal terai, whereas in Bhutan it is uncommon and very local in the southern lowlands, and in Bangladesh it may now be extinct (though one was heard in 1986).

REFERENCES Ali & Ripley (1980), Baker (1930), Delacour (1977), Grimmett *et al.* (1998), King *et al.* (1975).

---

161 GREEN PEAFOWL
Pavo muticus Linnaeus, 1766

Plate 46

Alternative names: Burmese Peafowl/Peacock.

In contrast to the Indian species, the Green Peafowl is now very rare and much fragmented over its formerly quite extensive range.

IDENTIFICATION The only peacock over its present range in SE Asia and on Java, but now very rare almost throughout. Even larger and taller than Indian Peafowl, male easily distinguished in having scapulars and tertials as dark (green or black depending on race) as rest of upperparts (not closely barred whitish), green (not steely-blue) neck, breast and flanks (but see *spicifer* below) and narrowly erect spike-like coronal tuft (bare-shafted fan in Indian). Apart from absence of a 'train', female remarkably similar to male in basic coloration and has dark underparts (white in Indian Peafowl), being most readily sexed in comparison to 'train'-less male by barred tail and uppertail-coverts. Western race *spicifer* of NE India and NW Myanmar (probably now extinct) resembles Indian Peafowl in blue foreneck, but shape of coronal tuft and blackish (not whitish-barred) scapulars and tertials provide easy distinctions.

DESCRIPTION *P. m. imperator.* Head rather small, with slender, erect spike-like crest. Neck slender. In male, feathers of longer uppertail-coverts much elongated, forming 'train'. Tail of moderate length, rather graduated and flattened, consisting of 20 feathers in male, 18 in female, and acts as support to 'train'. Primaries well developed but wing structure unremarkable. Sexes differ, but less so than in Indian Peafowl. Legs relatively long and slender, male has well-developed tarsal spurs. Bill dark grey. Bare skin around eye pale blue; bare skin from ear-coverts to base of bill chrome-yellow (duller in female). Irides brown. Legs brownish-black. **Adult male:** Crown, neck and breast metallic blue-green, becoming bluer on foreneck and breast and greenest on crown; feathers have blue bases shading green, scaled golden-copper on fringes and black at tip. Except blue-black loral-stripe, head-sides naked. Lower breast, flanks and belly dark brown and green, becoming dark grey on vent. Mantle, back and rump metallic golden-copper, each feather with thin black border, giving scaled appearance. Uppertail-coverts tremendously elongated, disintegrating at sides and tip, bronzed golden-green with white shafts and large tricoloured subterminal ocelli, forming 'train'. Wing-coverts metallic blue. Tertials blackish-brown, freckled buff and edged blue. Secondaries blue and green, but dull blackish-brown on concealed inner webs. Primaries rufous. Tail brown. **First-year**

male: Like female, sharing barred rump, uppertail-coverts and tail but has blackish loral-stripe, almost clean dull rufous primaries and longer legs. **Second year male:** Similar to adult male, but 'train' much shorter and lacks ocelli; maximum length may not be fully attained until about fifth year. **Adult female:** Remarkably similar to male in basic coloration, but overall duller, especially on back and rump, which are barred buffish and blackish-brown, the longer tail-coverts extend almost to tip of tail, and are green barred buff. Graduated tail barred buff and blackish-brown. Underparts similar to male, but somewhat duller. Primaries dull pale rufous, mottled and tipped black. Bare facial skin duller than in male and notably the loral-stripe is reddish-brown, not black. **Juvenile:** Resembles female, but much duller and has some white feathering, especially on face and foreneck; young male acquires brighter rufous, plainer primaries after first moult.

GEOGRAPHICAL VARIATION Three subspecies recognised, differing in shade of green plumage and coloration of wings, the westernmost form being dullest and most blue-toned, whereas those on Java are brightest and most golden-toned. Racial differences often difficult to interpret unless specimens are mature males, and may require review. Those in Yunnan not recognised taxonomically, but may differ sufficiently substantially to warrant recognition.

P. m. spicifer (Shaw & Nodder, 1804) occurs in NE India and NW Myanmar (west of the Irrawaddy), but perhaps now extinct; duller and bluer on neck and breast than *imperator*, with almost black secondaries and wing-coverts, and facial skin duller.

P. m. imperator Delacour, 1949 occurs in SE Asia including N Myanmar and Yunnan; described above.

P. m. muticus Linnaeus, 1766 occurs only on Java; brighter and overall more golden-green, less coppery, with greenest underparts compared to others.

MEASUREMENTS Length: male 180–300 cm, female 100–110 cm; much of difference due to long 'train' of male. Males: wing 460–540, tail 400–475, 'train' (uppertail-coverts) reaches 1400–1600 when fully grown, tarsus 160–170, weight 3850–5000. Females: wing 420–450, tail 400–450, tarsus 135–145, weight 1060–1160.

HABITAT Inhabits riverine forest and adjacent open country in much of range, even foraging in farmland. Typically in lightly wooded and forest-edge habitats, such as open woodland and teak plantations in Java, and mixed deciduous forest and rocky savannas often with patches of semi-evergreen forest in Laos (where some localities have limited supplies of water).

VOICE Male gives very loud far-carrying trumpeting *ki-wao* or *yee-ow*, which is repeated; compared to Indian Peafowl the cry is less harsh and piercing. Female also gives loud *AOW-aa*, with emphasis on first syllable and repeated quickly. An alarmed *tak tak ker-r-r-r oo oo, ker-r-r-roo* also reported.

HABITS Broadly similar to Indian Peafowl, but more timid and retiring. Because of this and widespread persecution throughout range, it can be very difficult to observe in many areas. Presence usually revealed by calls from roost sites. Apparently quite reliant on water at most remaining localities and normally encountered near water sources, such as streams and rivers.

BREEDING Believed polygamous, with male having harems of as many as five females. Nests on ground, usually in areas afforded some degree of protection and with good visibility. Clutch 3–6 pale cream or coffee-coloured to buff eggs, very similar to those of Indian Peafowl but usually slightly larger. Season in NE India and Bangladesh (if it survives) apparently January–May, though July–September also reported; on Java in August–October. Incubation lasts 26–28 days and is by female alone.

DISTRIBUTION SE Asia. Once distributed continuously in suitable habitat from NE India and Bangladesh east through Myanmar and S China (W and SW Yunnan and perhaps SE Tibet; formerly many other provinces) to Vietnam, and south through Malaysia to Java. Now restricted to isolated populations, most of which are widely scattered and small.

STATUS Vulnerable. Very local throughout extensive range, but once considered among the most easily seen phasianids in Asia. Now typically rather difficult to see even in places where populations of more than a few birds exist. Extinct in Peninsular Malaysia by the mid-1960s and extirpated across much of its Chinese range, and probably so in Bangladesh and NE India. A single (large and perhaps expanding) population survives in Hua Kha Khaeng Wildlife Sanctuary in W Thailand and very fragmented pockets persist in Laos (chiefly in the extreme south and further north in Phou Khao Khouay National Biodiversity Conservation Area). In Vietnam there has also been a massive decline, but it occurs in Nam Cat Tien National Park and Yok Don Reserve and perhaps elsewhere in the western highlands. There are at least 30 small, scattered populations in Yunnan (China) and on Java (Indonesia) it is known from a number of sites, with the bulk in two national parks, Ujong Kulon and Baluran. It persists in at least three localities in N Myanmar, and records from eight sites, including three protected areas, in Cambodia raises hopes that E Cambodia could hold the species' largest populations. There are unlikely to be more than a handful of populations elsewhere holding more than c.100 birds. The only reasonably reliable population estimates are c.1000 for Java, 500–1100 in China and more than 300 for the Thai population in Hua Kha Khaeng. The massive decline in numbers is mainly a result of hunting, both for food and in some places for sport. Its 'train' feathers are used for decorative costumes in traditional dances in Java, are sought for decoration elsewhere and are traded on the Thai–Lao border.

REFERENCES van Balen (1997), BirdLife International (2000, 2001), Delacour (1977), Evans & Timmins (1996), Grimmett *et al.* (1998), Le Trong Trai (1997), McGowan *et al.* (1998).

Genus *AFROPAVO*: Congo Peacock

The sole member of this Afrotropical genus shares certain affinities with the peafowls, including the presence of a vertical crest, iridescent plumage and tarsal spurs in both sexes. Clearly, few other features are shared, but various studies do indicate that its origins are closer to peafowls than to any other group.

162 CONGO PEACOCK
Afropavo congensis Chapin, 1936   Plate 46

There has been much speculation on the relationships of this peculiar bird, but it appears to share with Udzungwa Partridge the distinction of being an ancestral African galliform, with links to what are now Asiatic genera.

IDENTIFICATION A rare and little-known peacock restricted to lowland rainforest of the Congo basin. Both sexes quite unmistakable if fortunate to be encountered. Though birds can appear very dark in forest gloom, both sexes are iridescent green above. Male's remarkable vertical white coronal tuft can be striking; better views should reveal bare red skin on neck, while rest of underparts basically shining violet-black or greenish-black. Female equally distinctive, having head, neck, underparts and most of wings rufous-chestnut. The only likely confusion would be with poorly seen Black Guineafowl, with which it sometimes associates when feeding under fruiting trees.

DESCRIPTION Head small on slender neck and covered by very short downy feathers, becoming almost naked on foreneck (female has more feathering). Prominent tuft of vertical white bristles rises from crown centre, with shorter tuft of naked black bristles; female has indistinct shorter crest. Feathers of upperparts almost hair-like, disintegrating at edges, upper-tail-coverts somewhat elongated but do not reach tail tip. Tail flattened, somewhat rounded and moderately long; it comprises 18 feathers. Sexes differ markedly. Bill pale blue-grey. Irides brown. Bare skin of face blue and that of neck red (brightest in male). Legs pale blue-grey. Tarsal spurs whitish and can be present in both sexes. **Adult male:** Head black (covering of short downy feathers), with tuft of long, upstanding white bristles on crown centre, backed by somewhat shorter, thicker tuft of black feathers. Throat and upper foreneck sparsely feathered with black down. Lower neck and breast black, each feather broadly tipped iridescent blue or violet. Rest of underparts black, feathers broadly edged green on flanks and thighs. Entire upperparts shining green, with bronze reflections; some long uppertail-coverts have violet fringes. Wings brownish-black, lesser coverts green with broad violet tips; tertials fringed green. Tail black, feathers with some green gloss and disintegrating violet edges. **First-year male:** Duller than adult male, with brown tones on back and dull black underparts, and only very narrow violet fringes to neck and breast feathers. Coronal tufts and bristles much shorter than adult and lacks tarsal spurs. Full adult plumage attained in second year. **Adult female:** Head, including short crest, neck and entire underparts rufous-chestnut, mottled and barred

dark brown at breast-sides, flanks and undertail-coverts; central belly dull black. Back, scapulars, wing-coverts and tertials shining green, barred fulvous; feather bases blackish-brown with buffy chevrons and broad disintegrating green fringes. Flight feathers fulvous-chestnut, boldly barred and spotted black. Long uppertail-coverts soft and disintegrated, broadly tipped green, but blackish-brown at base. Tail fulvous-chestnut, barred and spotted black, with green tip. First-year female duller than adult. **Juvenile:** Overall mottled cinnamon and black; young male soon acquires a few green feathers on mantle and wing-coverts, and can be sexed when only seven weeks old.

GEOGRAPHICAL VARIATION Monotypic.

MEASUREMENTS Length: male 64–70 cm, female 60–63 cm. Males: wing 306–330, tail 206–260, tarsus 96–106, weight (two captives) 1361 and 1475. Females: wing 270–295, tail 169–205, tarsus 85–90, weight (two captives) 1135 and 1154.

HABITAT Lowland rainforest to 1200 m.

VOICE Duets most commonly heard. One starts with a resounding *rro-ho-ho-o-a*, reaching a crescendo and followed by male emitting a high-pitched *gowe* and female a lower *gowah*; repeated 20–30 times. In second duet, male utters *ko-ko-wa* and female a higher *hi-ho-hi-ho*. Other typical gallinaceous calls are given, and also a snore-like call which males give when disturbed around nest.

HABITS Very wary and rarely seen, so knowledge of habits very patchy. Usually encountered in pairs or small family parties. More likely to be detected by calls, which are often heard throughout night, especially when moon is full. Pairs sometimes duet and males will respond to calls of others, but calling apparently does not occur more than c.3 nights per week. Claimed to be fairly nomadic, but origin of this statement unknown. Takes fruits *Celtis adolfi-friderici* and seemingly of various other fruiting trees. Invertebrates also eaten, presumably by pecking at ground and possibly scratching among leaf-litter.

BREEDING Thought monogamous, though information from wild required. Nest apparently placed between buttress roots or close to fallen trees, but in captivity eggs often laid on a concave platform up to 3 m above ground, not in a typical nest. Captive clutch usually 2–3, but up to 9 unspotted rufous-buff eggs reported. Season unclear, but perhaps year-round depending upon local rainfall. In captivity incubation lasts 27–28 days.

DISTRIBUTION Endemic to Congo River Basin of C and E Democratic Republic of the Congo (former Zaïre). Southern limit is presumably boundary of equatorial forest, whereas in north it may be Aruwimi River in east and Lopori River in west. In the east it reaches mid-altitudes of the Albertine Rift Mountains.

STATUS Vulnerable. Generally uncommon, but rarely detected by any means in wild and even less frequently seen by ornithologists. Population placed at fewer than 10,000 individuals. Known to local people in Kahuzi-Biega National Park and its extension, from Okapi Wildlife Reserve and at several localities in and around Maiko National Park, which is thought to be its stronghold. Indeed, while tolerably secure in these two areas, elsewhere it is thought to be in serious decline.

Historically, its range has never been well known because of the difficulty in obtaining reliable locality information. The extent of forest loss within its range cannot therefore be gauged with certainty, but its presumed range (see above) is seriously affected by deforestation and habitat degradation caused by mining, logging and subsistence agriculture. As it is thought to require largely undisturbed forest, these activities may have great effect. It also appears to have been locally extirpated by hunting in some areas, despite the high esteem in which some tribal cultures seem to hold it.

REFERENCES BirdLife International (2000), Collar & Stuart (1985), Crowe & Kemp (1986), Hart & Upoki (1997), Lovel (1976), McGowan & Garson (1995), Urban *et al.* (1986).

Genus *AGELASTES*: spurred guineafowl

Two species of red-headed and unspotted forest guineafowl from central and west Africa. Unlike all other guineafowl, members of this genus have rather full tails, tarsal spurs and high-pitched calls. Their tarsal scaling and spur positioning resemble those of the francolins. It may well be that these are the most primitive of guineafowl.

163 WHITE-BREASTED GUINEAFOWL
Agelastes meleagrides Bonaparte, 1850 Plate 54

A rare and distinctive guineafowl of W African forests, little studied and now the most endangered of its family; rainforest destruction having reduced it to a small number of fragmented sites.

IDENTIFICATION Relatively small, full-tailed guineafowl of W African forests, easily identified by combination of white fore body (breast and collar) contrasting with blackish body plumage and naked red head (adult), or being sooty with white belly (juvenile). Though it shares forest haunts with larger Crested Guineafowl confusion is unlikely if seen well. Latter has tufted crest, bluish facial skin and more conventional guineafowl spotted plumage.

DESCRIPTION Legs greyish-brown or greyish-black, relatively long. Bill greenish-brown. Irides brown. Sexes generally similar, male has 1–2 spurs, absent in female and juvenile. Tail relatively long. **Adult (both sexes):** Head and upper neck naked; rose-red bare skin becoming pinker on lower neck (with sparse white filaments). Lower neck, mantle and upper breast white. Rest of plumage, including wing-coverts, dull black, finely and inconspicuously vermiculated white. Secondaries brown, vermiculated white on outer webs. Primaries dark brown, fringed grey on outer webs. **Juvenile:** Head and neck pattern unclear, reported as either covered by blackish down (Urban *et al.* 1986) or having brown and tawny crown-stripes (Gatter 1997), has no white on breast or collar, but does have pure white belly. Plumage otherwise sooty-black, with reddish-brown wash and scattered rufous feather tips.

GEOGRAPHICAL VARIATION Monotypic.

MEASUREMENTS Length 40–45 cm. Male larger. Males: wing 204–214, tail 148–157, tarsus 79–89, weight c.815. Females: wing 197–205, tail 135–142, tarsus 76–82, weight (one captive) 815.

HABITAT Tall, dense primary and mature secondary forest of Upper Guinea forest block, favouring drier stretches with sparse undergrowth. May persist in logged forest where no hunting pressure.

VOICE Little information available. Feeding flock keeps in contact using deep *kok-kok*. If scattered by potential predator, flock reassembles, keeping in contact with cheeping calls. Also reported to give 'loud, ringing melodious' call (Bechinger 1964).

HABITS Generally roams forest in bands of 15–20, covering quite extensive area. Less frequently in pairs or small (family?) parties. Very shy and elusive, as traditionally hunted by man. Forages on forest floor; scattered flock walks slowly, scratching leaf-litter with feet, especially under fruiting trees. Flock converges in squabble when one discovers a good food source. Feeds on fallen berries and seeds of forest trees; also large number of invertebrates from worms and small molluscs, to termites and beetle larvae. Roosts in spindly trees of forest understorey.

BREEDING Virtually undocumented. Nests on ground in patch of dense undergrowth. Clutch c.12 eggs, reddish-buff with white pores. Season October–May, probably peaking in wet season, November–January. Possibly nests year-round (e.g., in Liberia, recently hatched chicks recorded early April and sub-adults in February, May and November).

N. m. marungensis Schalow, 1884 (includes, '*maxima*', '*frommi*', '*rikwae*' and '*bodalyae*') occurs from S Zaïre basin south to C Angola, east to Luangwa Valley in Zambia; like *mitrata* but larger, and has broader, squatter yellow-ochre casque (wing 270–302, casque 13–23, weight 1200–1822, mean 1612).

N. m. damarensis Roberts, 1917 (includes '*papillosa*') occurs in arid regions of Namibia and Botswana; like *mitrata* but casque taller and more back-arching, withered somewhat at base, cere more covered with papilli, and body and wing spotting larger and even more dense (wing 265–283, casque 17–27, weight 1150–1600).

N. m. coronata Gurney, 1868 (includes '*transvaalensis*' and '*limpopoensis*') occurs in humid regions of E South Africa (Natal, Kwazulu-Natal, Mpumalanga and E Cape, also introduced W Cape); like *mitrata* but casque taller and larger, and mantle streaked, rather than barred white (wing 263–283, casque 19–31, weight 1135–1823).

MEASUREMENTS Length 53–63 cm. Male larger. *N. m. meleagris*. Males: wing 253–276 (mean 269), tail 164–176 (mean 172), tarsus 74–89 (mean 84). Females: wing 247–268 (mean 259), tail 160–179 (mean 170), tarsus 69–82 (mean 79). Casque (both sexes) 4–22. Weight (both sexes) 1150–1600 (mean 1300).

HABITAT Grassy plains and hills, often with nearby cultivation. Favours patches of bushy cover, such as along riversides or other water sources, and most favours mosaic of fragmented habitats, including maize and fallow fields. Locally inhabits semi-arid country, forest edge or ascends to 3000 m. Shuns extensively grazed areas, or large grassland biomes.

VOICE All calls raucous or cackling. Typically a loud, nasal, staccato *kek-kek-kek-kek-kek-kek-kek...* in alarm; varying somewhat in intensity and length of delivery; also given when gathering at roost. Female has far-carrying two-note call, *ka-bak* (also rendered as *buck-wheat*), the first note nasal and clear, the second higher pitched and more rasping. Male often responds with single harsh grating note. Flocks maintain contact while foraging or walking with an inconspicuous, metallic *chenk-chenk-chenk*. Various other calls, including a plaintive far-carrying *CHER-cheeng, CHER-cheeng...* from flocks.

HABITS Highly sociable, generally in flocks of 20–25 but groups may number hundreds or even thousands, especially when gathering at waterholes in dry season. At onset of wet season many flocks disband into smaller units or pairs to breed. Forages at first light, moving slowly in single file toward water source, before spending early part of day feeding, dust-bathing and preening. Rests in shade of trees or bushy cover during middle of day, feeding again in late afternoon. Flies to roost in large trees and even on telegraph poles and wires; roost sites may be used for many years. Home-range size typically 11.4 ha, but in areas of low-density populations may reach 252.7 ha. Escapes ground predators by running, taking to wing over short distances, sometimes flying into trees. Sometimes flock chases ground predators. In-flock skirmishes frequent, with birds chasing each other on ground. Feeds on roots, tubers, seeds and grain, plus wide range of invertebrates in breeding season, e.g. grasshoppers, locusts, snails and others. Reported taking ticks from backs of warthogs.

BREEDING Chiefly monogamous, sometimes bigamous. Single-brooded. Nest constructed by female; shallow scrape sparsely lined with feathers and grass stems, well hidden amid bushy cover or tall grass, often at ecotone of grassland and bushy country. Eggs creamy-buff to pale brown, usually speckled darker, sometimes white. Clutch 6–12 (sometimes 20 or even 50 recorded, these being result of two or more females laying in same nest). Dates vary over wide range, but usually commences at onset of rainy season, reaching peak at height of rains. September–October in Cape Verde Is, March–May in Morocco, May–July in much of W Africa, Sudan, Tanzania and Somalia, chiefly July–September in C Ethiopia, March–December in Uganda, peak November–February in Zambia and Zimbabwe, January–February in Namibia, and in South Africa, September–December in Cape, and December–January in Natal and Transvaal. Incubation 24–27 days by female alone, but male broods chicks for most of first two weeks after hatching.

DISTRIBUTION Africa. Isolated population in Middle Atlas of Morocco, otherwise native range extends over most of sub-Saharan Africa, north to Sénégal, The Gambia, S Mali, C Niger, C Chad, C Sudan and Eritrea. Absent from lush equatorial rainforest belt (most of Zaïre, Congo and Gabon), but widespread over most of E and S Africa, being absent elsewhere only from most arid parts of Namibia (Namib Desert) and W Cape of South Africa. Introduced populations thrive in Cape Verde Is (Santiago, Fogo, São Nicolau, Maio and perhaps Boa Vista), Yemen, the Comoros and Madagascar. Also widely introduced or temporarily feral in various parts of world, with varying degrees of success. Established in Dominican Republic, but elsewhere in West Indies (Cuba, Puerto Rico, Virgin Is, Barbuda and St Martin), as well as New Zealand, Australia and Hawaii introduction attempts appear not to have persisted for very long.

STATUS Numerous and widespread over most of range. However, local threats through over-zealous hunting or egg collecting have affected some populations. Overall population estimated at well over 1 million birds and regarded as stable. The only exception being race *sabyi* of Morocco, which may already be extinct (just three sightings since 1970, all within tiny area of Middle Atlas). This distinct race is in desperate need of conservation (e.g., if possible, instigation of a captive-breeding programme). Local declines noted elsewhere, e.g. in parts of South Africa, due to increases in crop agriculture and indirect effects of pesticides.

REFERENCES Ayeni (1981, 1983), Bannerman (1953), Cramp & Simmons (1983), Crowe (1978), Mackworth-Praed & Grant (1970), van Niekerk (1979), Siegfried (1966), Skead (1962), Snow (1978), Urban *et al.* (1986).

Genus *GUTTERA*: crested guineafowl

Two or three species of large and spotted forest guinefowl, bearing a crested topknot of black feathers.

166 PLUMED GUINEAFOWL
Guttera plumifera (Cassin, 1857)

Plate 55

Shy guineafowl of equatorial forests, forming superspecies with Crested Guineafowl, which it replaces in denser forest.

IDENTIFICATION Prominent topknot of stiff black feathers makes it unlikely to be confused with any species other than closely related Crested Guineafowl. Plumed has longer and stiffer crest than Crested, much more prominent gape wattles, boldly spotted (not plain black) collar, lacks red on slate-grey bare skin of head and neck (but eastern race *schubotzi* of Plumed has patches of orange-yellow, and red on throat often difficult to discern on overlapping *verreauxi* Crested), is slightly smaller and has pure white (not bluish-white) body spotting. Plumed tends to inhabit dense forest, whereas Crested favours forest edge and second growth in narrow contact zone in parts of former Zaïre. Sympatric with smaller, red-headed Black Guineafowl, which lacks white wing flash (formed by outer webs of secondaries) of both Plumed and Crested (which see).

DESCRIPTION *G. p. plumifera*. Legs bluish-grey, moderately long, unspurred. Bill bluish-grey. Irides brown. Sexes similar, but male larger. Tail unremarkable, short but sometimes held elevated. **Adult (both sexes):** Prominent topknot of stiff black feathers (c.30 mm tall) on length of crown; rest of head and upper neck naked, with grey-blue bare skin, and relatively long gape wattles. Entire body and wings black, intensely covered by small white spots, largest on collar. Tail black, closely spotted white. Flight feathers dark brown, darker on secondaries, which are weakly spotted white. Outermost three secondaries white on outer webs, forming white stripe on folded wing. **Juvenile:** Black downy feathers conceal skin of head and neck, and shorter coronal tuft; upperparts, including flight feathers grey, barred blackish, and breast blackish-grey, finely spotted and barred white.

GEOGRAPHICAL VARIATION Two races, differ in coloration of bare skin on head, intergrading in E Congo.
 G. p. plumifera (Cassin, 1857) occurs in Cameroon, Gabon and Congo (west of 16°E); described above.
 G. p. schubotzi Reichenow, 1912 occurs in E Congo and Zaïre; has orange-yellow patches in front of ear and on hindneck, otherwise as nominate.

MEASUREMENTS Length 45–50 cm. Male larger. *G. p. plumifera*. Males: wing 223–232 (mean 228), tail 127–135 (mean 83) tarsus 78–87 (mean 131). Females: wing 216–227 (mean 222), tail 118–128 (mean 124), tarsus 73–83 (mean 77). Weight (both sexes) c.750–1000.

HABITAT Dense and humid primary and mature secondary rainforest, with sparse undergrowth.

VOICE Typically a nasal *kak* in alarm, repeated in discordant cackling chorus *Ka-Ka-Ka-Ka-Ka-Ka-Ka-Ka...* Foraging flock maintains contact using rather far-carrying, curious quacking.

HABITS Highly sociable, foraging in dense forest in flocks of 20–40, generally avoiding clearings or cultivation. Forages at first light, flock scratching up large areas of forest floor in search of food. Feeds on seeds, fruits, leaves and variety of invertebrates. At dusk flock flies to roost in large trees, using different trees each night. Flocks scatters, running in various directions, when disturbed by potential predator; only flies to dense tree canopy if hard-pressed.

BREEDING Virtually undocumented. Probably monogamous and single-brooded. Nest a basic scrape on ground amid dry leaf-litter. Eggs pale buff, but stain easily, pores becoming soiled as if speckled. Clutches of 9–10 recorded. Eggs recorded March and September in Zaïre, but probably also other months, no doubt chiefly in wetter season.

DISTRIBUTION Equatorial Africa, from S Cameroon, Equatorial Guinea, Gabon and Loango coast of Congo, east through extreme S Central African Republic, N Congo and N Zaïre in forests of Congo Basin, to W Rift Valley and forests to west of N tip of Lake Tanganyika.

STATUS Despite large range, seemingly uncommon throughout, with somewhat patchy distribution limited by extent of extant primary rainforest. Lack of basic information makes it difficult to give more than vague estimate of overall population but it is likely to be 10,000–100,000 birds.

REFERENCES Bannerman (1930), Chapin (1932), Mackworth-Praed & Grant (1970), van Niekerk (1979), Urban *et al.* (1986).

Genus *ACRYLLIUM*: Vulturine Guineafowl

A monotypic genus containing a long-necked, long-tailed, long-legged spotted guineafowl, remarkable for its metallic blue and white elongated hackles and plush-like cheek patches.

168 VULTURINE GUINEAFOWL
Acryllium vulturinum (Hardwicke, 1834)   Plate 55

The largest and most colourful guineafowl, which despite its rather scrawny neck must rank as one of Africa's most spectacular birds.

IDENTIFICATION Strikingly elegant guineafowl of dry bushy savanna in NE Africa. Relatively small bluish head with diagnostic dark chestnut 'handlebar moustaches', which meet on back of head, making identification straightforward even if bird largely hidden by grass. Long, slender neck projects from cape of metallic blue and white-striped lanceolate hackles; this and relatively long legs and long drooping, pointed tail emphasise its elegance and render it quite unmistakable. Helmeted shares its grassy habitat, but locally also invades forest edge and meets Kenya Crested, both of which are unlikely to be confused with Vulturine.

DESCRIPTION Legs greyish-black, relatively long, with several spur-like lumps (less prominent in female). Bill relatively stout, grey becoming paler at tip. Irides red. Sexes similar, male larger. Tail long, with elongated central feathers forming long drooping point to tip. **Adult (both sexes):** Relatively dense, velvety band of dark chestnut feathers extends from below eye to join on back of head; rest of head and neck naked, rather thin and scrawny, bare skin greyblue. Feathers of lower neck, mantle and chest extremely elongated, forming cape of long, lanceolate hackles; each is cobalt-blue with broad white shaft stripe highlighted by black edging. Breast and fore flanks bright cobalt-blue. Belly and vent unmarked black. Rest of body, including flanks and wing-coverts black, intensely and finely covered with small white spots. Primaries and secondaries dark brown; primaries have whitish edges to outer webs and secondaries edged pinkish-lilac. **Juvenile:** Striped downy feathers conceal skin of head and neck. Plumage overall greybrown, mottled and barred rufous, black and buff. Hackles less developed than in adult; blue of underparts duller. Attains adult plumage at c.9–11 months.

GEOGRAPHICAL VARIATION Monotypic.

MEASUREMENTS Length 61–71 cm. Male larger. Males: wing 290–311 (mean 298), tail 265–280 (mean 272), tarsus 100–117 (mean 109), weight (n=2) 1026, 1645. Females: wing 285–296 (mean 290), tail 251–274 (mean 260), tarsus 94–103 (mean 99), weight (n=2) 1135, 1523.

HABITAT Dry savanna, semi-arid grasslands with *Acacia* and *Commiphora* scrub. Locally in dense riverine thickets and, exceptionally, even montane forest (e.g. Mt Marsabit, Kenya).

VOICE Relatively quieter than Helmeted Guineafowl. Typical call higher pitched than Helmeted, a strident, metallic, rattled *chink-chink-chink-chink-chinka-cheek-cheek-chickerrr-chickerrr*, given at roost and in alarm. Foraging birds maintain contact with an occasional lower pitched *chink*.

HABITS Highly sociable, typically encountered in flocks of 20–30 but several hundred recorded at favoured waterholes in dry season. Flocks disband at start of breeding season when rains commence. Despite being a bird of semi-arid conditions it rarely wanders far from cover; flocks prefer to forage within relatively easy reach of bushy thickets to which they resort if danger threatens, or to seek shade in heat of day. Feeds from dawn, the birds digging more vigorously than Helmeted, taking roots and tubers, whereas Helmeted tends to pick from ground between bouts of scratching. Vulturine also has broader diet, including berries, shoots and leaves, molluscs, spiders, scorpions, small lizards and frogs. Clambers into bushes or low trees in search of berries. In some areas it appears to survive without drinking, but in other areas waterholes are visited each evening prior to roost. Roosts in large trees, typically a very large *Acacia* near water, with surrounding bushy thickets. In midday heat rests in dense cover under bushes. If disturbed by potential predator prefers to walk or run into thickets, only flying if particularly hard-pressed.

BREEDING Monogamous. Nest a scrape on ground among grasses, usually under shade of an *Acacia* or boulder; sometimes sparsely lined with grass. Eggs creamy-white or very pale brown; clutch 4–8, sometimes up to 13–15 (doubtless due to 2–3 females laying in same nest). Incubation 23–32 days, presumably by female alone. Lays from start of wet season: June in Ethiopia, June, August and December in Somalia, whereas in Kenya recorded most months, with peaks in June and December–January. Both parents tend young; family joins flock when less than one month old.

DISTRIBUTION NE Africa, from S Ethiopia and W Somalia over most of E Kenyan lowlands (west to Lake Turkana and Tsavo West) and just entering N Tanzania (from Kilimanjaro to Mkomazi Game Reserve). Formerly occurred in NE Uganda (north Karamojo district), but no recent records.

STATUS Given quite extensive range and preference for semi-arid, thorn-bush habitat there is little to threaten its survival. Some localised decreases have been reported, including apparent extinction in Uganda. Overall estimate of c.1 million birds suggested as measure of relative abundance.

REFERENCES Grahame (1969), Mackworth-Praed & Grant (1957), Martínez (1994), Urban *et al.* (1986), Zimmerman *et al.* (1996).

FAMILY MELEAGRIDIDAE
Turkeys

The name turkey was originally bestowed upon guineafowl brought to Europe from Africa via the Turkish Empire. Meanwhile the Aztecs had long domesticated what we now know as the turkey; it duly impressed the first Europeans to reach Mexico in the 16th century. Soon the turkey arrived in Europe and spread in popularity as a table bird, but presumably because of its naked head and neck was somewhat confused with guineafowl. Being much larger and meatier than the African 'turkey' the American version carried the name, as it still does today.

The two turkeys form a distinctive American family of galliformes, characterised by naked heads, with colourful wattles, massive size, glossy blackish or dark plumage and large tails (which are elevated and fanned in display). The two species are here both treated in *Meleagris*, although Ocellated Turkey is sometimes elevated to the monotypic genus *Agriocharis*.

169 WILD TURKEY
Meleagris gallopavo Linnaeus, 1758   Plate 53

Well known as a wild bird in North America, and among the most familiar domesticated birds worldwide (attains colours and shapes that bear little resemblance to the true wild bird).

IDENTIFICATION The native American Wild Turkey is considerably sleeker and more agile than its overweight domestic cousin. Large dark bronzy-brown forest birds with relatively long bodies and long pinkish legs; bare bluish-grey and rose-pink wrinkled heads and necks relatively small compared to bulk of body. Long-bodied impression enhanced by large, broad tail tipped rufous (eastern races) or whitish (southern and western races), often evident in flight, and certainly so when fanned in display. Widely reintroduced in areas where previously extirpated by over-zealous hunting. Unfortunately, in many cases, the 'wrong' subspecies has been released, therefore it can be difficult to establish what is a pure wild turkey as opposed to one having feral influences (but overall body bulk and colour of terminal tail bar helps). In spring presence indicated by displaying males 'gobbling' in forest; a sound that can carry over a considerable distance.

DESCRIPTION *M. g. gallopavo.* Legs reddish-pink, relatively long, male has well-developed tarsal spur; greyer, becoming almost silvery in older birds. Bill insignificant, yellowish-horn, becoming bluish with pinkish tip when breeding. Irides brown. Sexes generally similar, but larger and brighter male has prominent tarsal spur, absent in smaller and duller female and juvenile. Tail relatively long and broad. **Adult male:** Head and upper neck have some sparse black bristles but otherwise naked and wrinkled, grey-blue, becoming almost whitish on forehead, with red caruncles and long somewhat inflatable wobbly red 'snood' which hangs on side of bill from forehead. Rose-red dewlap under chin and throat. Intensity of colour of head and neck varies seasonally. Elongated black bristly tuft ('beard') hangs from chest. Lower neck and entire body metallic dark bronzed brown (with gold, green and red reflections), each feather with terminal black scaled bar. Rump metallic blue-black, with black scaling. Lower rump and uppertail-coverts broadly tipped whitish. Tail rufous closely barred black, with broader subterminal black band and broad whitish tip. Primaries and secondaries dark brown, closely barred whitish. **Adult female:** Similar but smaller and duller, browner (less glossy), normally lacks 'beard' (but may develop in those over three years old) and lacks forehead 'snood'. **Juvenile:** Head and neck have dark down. Smaller than adult, lacking metallic reflections; overall dark brown, with buff streaks, black subterminal marks and rufous- or buff-tipped body and wing-covert feathers. Flight feathers and tail much as adult.

GEOGRAPHICAL VARIATION At least six races, differing chiefly in colour of rump and tips to uppertail-coverts and tail. Differences somewhat obscured by artificial releases.

M. g. gallopavo Linnaeus, 1758 occurs in S Mexico (north to Veracruz and Jalisco); described above (characterised by white tail tip and tips to uppertail-coverts). This form gave rise to domestic turkeys.

M. g. mexicana Gould, 1856 (Gould's Turkey) occurs in Sierra Madre range, NW Mexico.

M. g. silvestris Vieillot, 1817 (Eastern Turkey) occurs in E USA, from Pennsylvania, E Kentucky and SE Montana south to N Florida and Gulf of Mexico; chestnut-brown uppertail-coverts and rusty-buff tips to tail feathers.

M. g. osceola Scott, 1890 (Florida Turkey) occurs in peninsular Florida; smallest race, similar to *silvestris* in coloration.

M. g. intermedia Sennett, 1879 (Rio Grande Turkey) (includes *onusta*) occurs on Central plains from Kansas south to Mexico, and introduced Hawaii, California, Oregon and Washington; glossy blackish rump, buff tips to uppertail-coverts.

M. g. merriami Nelson, 1900 (Merriam's Turkey) occurs in Western Great Plains and Rocky Mountains, and introduced Wyoming, Idaho, Oregon and Washington; buffy-white tips to tail and uppertail-coverts.

MEASUREMENTS Length: male 100–125 cm, female 76–95 cm. Male c.30% larger. *M.g. silvestris.* Males: wing 204–214, tail 245–505 (mean 343), tarsus 97–191 (mean 127), weight 5000–11,000 (mean 8000). Females: wing 197–205, tail 135–142, tarsus 76–82, weight 3000–5000 (mean 4000).

HABITAT Open deciduous and mixed woodland, forest with extensive clearings and meadows, and prairie brush, mixed with some cultivation. Mostly in lowlands, but locally ascends to 2100 m.

VOICE Well known: displaying male struts with elevated, fanned tail and drooped wings, uttering liquid, gobbling call, an unmistakable sound that may carry for well over 1 km. Other calls include a liquid *cluk-cluk* when flock reassembles after being disturbed, a trilled, repeated *putt* or *perk* in alarm and yelping *keeow, keeow, keeow*, which maintains contact between group members. Also variety of short barks, low purrs, high screams, croaks, hisses and whining sounds.

HABITS Sociable unless breeding, with some populations gathering into large flocks in winter; in parts of Texas and Oklahoma gatherings of race *intermedia* can reach 500 at this season, but in contrast those of eastern race *silvestris* rarely exceed 40–50. Flocks usually single sex. Older males begin gobbling displays as early as February, attracting females by intensity of gobbling. Male gathers harem of 4–5 females. Gobbling of rival males incites antagonistic responses, but do not defend defined territories. Sudden noises can stimulate gobbling, be it a car back-firing, an aeroplane or even a barking dog. Males gobble incessantly at height of breeding season, having little time for eating or roosting. In late summer, males either remain alone or form small flocks for winter. Females remain with young until following spring, joining other families to forage as winter flock. Feeds chiefly by picking at ground, with occasional scratching. Takes variety of weed and grass seeds, berries, fruits, shoots, leaves and acorns, as well as many invertebrates, especially grasshoppers, but also small crabs and even some vertebrates (lizards, frogs, small snakes etc.); over 350 plant and 300 animal species have been identified as prey. Gait slow while feeding but when suspicious of danger runs quickly into cover, only flying as a last resort, though strongly when required.

Typically only flies when going to roost, favouring large stands of sheltered trees (especially big pines). Roost is centre of flock's feeding range; from here they may range over 5–8 km².

BREEDING Polygamous; male takes no part in incubation or rearing young. Nest a scratched depression, sparsely lined with grass and leaves, and situated at edge of clearing, usually below fallen branch or bush. Clutch 8–20 (usually 10–12) pale buff or whitish eggs, with reddish-brown and mauve spotting. Incubation by female alone, for 27–28 days. Female also tends young, the family (without male) remaining together until following spring. Will lay replacement clutch if first fails and also known to attempt (unsuccessfully) a second brood. Eggs laid late February–May.

DISTRIBUTION Mexico and USA. In latter widespread as native and introduced bird from S Vermont and SE Massachusetts, south to Florida, west to SE Arizona, SC California, EC Utah, parts of Washington, Oregon, Wyoming and Montana, east to North Dakota, Wisconsin, Michigan, south through Nebraska and Kansas, to Texas and east along Gulf coast. It extends just into Canada (where introduced) in S Ontario and probably also still in SE Quebec. In Mexico it ranges south to N Jalisco and San Luis Potosí, but formerly occurred south to Oaxaca. Widely introduced around world, with feral 'wild' populations marginally established in Hawaii (Niihau, Lanai, Maui and Hawaii), New Zealand (North I.), Australia (islands in Bass Strait) and, at least formerly, in Austria and Germany.

STATUS Locally not uncommon, but North American population suffered prolonged decline through excessive hunting until mid-20th century (in 1940s overall population estimated at fewer than 300,000 birds). Following field research, hunting management and comprehensive reintroduction programmes, increased to c.3.5 million birds by 1990. In Mexico, very local and rare throughout, but true situation unclear; it has been exterminated from several areas.

REFERENCES Aldrich (1965), Hewitt (1967), Harper & Exum (1999), Howell & Webb (1995), Lewis (1973), Porter (1994), Schorger (1966).

170 OCELLATED TURKEY
Meleagris ocellata Cuvier, 1820

Plate 53

Even more colourful than its more widespread relative, the Ocellated Turkey is a scarce endemic of the Yucatán Peninsula of Central America.

IDENTIFICATION Endemic to Yucatán Peninsula, where the only native turkey, but even here beware wandering domestic 'wild turkeys'. Ocellated is slightly smaller than Wild Turkey and brighter in plumage, being basically glossed green and copper (rather than dark bronzy-brown), notably on neck, shoulders and wings, which have wide panel of shining copper across greater coverts, contrasting with whitish secondary panel and the much whiter remiges than in Wild Turkey. Bright cobalt-blue head has supercilia of bright orange 'warts', and lacks reddish dewlap of Wild

Turkey. Bright blue ocelli (which give bird its name) are situated subterminally near tips of uppertail-coverts and tail, forming bands of blue eye-spots when tail fanned in display, with copper bars distal to the ocelli on the terminal tail coverts and rectrices. Blackish chest 'beard' of Wild Turkey is absent.

DESCRIPTION Legs reddish-pink, relatively long, male with well-developed tarsal spurs (female may have enlarged dark scutes, but never exhibits real spurs). Bill insignificant, black with horn-coloured tip in male; fleshy, becoming greyer at base in female. Irides brown. Orbital ring red (male) or orange (female). Sexes generally similar, but male larger and brighter than female or juvenile. Tail relatively long and broad. **Adult male:**

Head and upper neck, including small dewlap, naked and bright cobalt-blue, with orange-red caruncles scattered on neck-sides, or more intensely forming super-cilium. Long inflatable blue rostral appendage, with orange warts, hangs on side of bill from forehead, while inflatable lump on crown swells into yellow-tipped blue 'horn'. Lower neck and entire body metallic blue-black, feathers tipped copper and green, and subterminally barred black. Median coverts metallic green, with gold reflections, tipped with narrow black bar; greater coverts shining copper. Primaries noticably white and secondaries closely barred dark brown and whitish; latter unmarked whitish on outer webs creating whitish panel that contrasts with copper greater coverts. Tail, rump and uppertail-coverts have shining-blue subterminal ocelli and copper tips. Tail otherwise vermiculated grey. **Adult female:** Similar but smaller and duller, with greyer blue skin on head, fewer 'warts' and lacks both forehead 'snood' and coronal 'horn'. **Juvenile:** Head and neck initially covered in down. Smaller than adult, lacking metallic reflections; overall grey-brown with whitish feather tips. Flight feathers and tail much as adult, but lacks blue ocelli, instead has blackish subterminal band.

GEOGRAPHICAL VARIATION Monotypic.

MEASUREMENTS Length: male 92–102 cm, female 66–84 cm. Male c.30% larger. Males: wing 348–412 (mean 388.5), tail 284–347 (mean 328), tarsus 131–139 (mean 136) weight c.4000. Females: wing 313–357 (mean 340), tail 244–281 (mean 262.5), tarsus 109–115 (mean 113), weight c.3000.

HABITAT Humid oak and mixed pine–oak woodland, forest with extensive clearings, humid broadleaf, savanna-scrub forests, small open wetlands within forest mosaic and abandoned cultivation with bushy cover. Lowlands to 300 m.

VOICE Quite different to gobble of Wild Turkey but vocabulary not fully documented. Displaying male elevates and fans tail, and droops wings, uttering peculiarly nasal pumping sequence, somewhat hesitant, then accelerating into gobble *puhk, puhk-puhk, puhk-puhk...* or *wump-wump-wump pum-pum-pum-peedle-glunk* (final note having bell-like quality), likened to motor scooter starting up. Female gives low, clucking notes.

HABITS Poorly studied. Often attracted to clearings near forest edge, and frequently seen near/on roads, in areas where not heavily persecuted. Annual flocking behaviour similar to Wild Turkey: Flocks largest (10+ birds) in November–January. Females and yearlings may be seen together, usually associated with groups of 2–5 adult males, though not always together during day. Females begin separating from flocks in early spring (presumably to search for nest sites), and adult males commence battle for dominance of flock. Adult males sing from roosts shortly before dawn, and on ground, sometimes in morning and at midday, increasing frequency of calls in early evening before and after roosting. Many small flocks of first-year males, with some first-year females, are observed at this period. Male singing can commence as early as mid-February, and often continues until late May/early June. Adult females/broods rarely seen in open habitats during spring/summer. Females remain with their broods and sometimes form brooding flocks (1–3 hens with their collective poults) until September–October. Usually in small parties within dense forest. In autumn often vacates tree cover to forage in adjacent open country, especially bushy cultivation. Shy and wary, but where protected may become remarkably confiding (e.g. in Tikal National Park in Guatemala). Feeds chiefly by picking at ground, taking variety of weed and grass seeds, corn grain, berries, fruits, shoots, leaves and selection of invertebrates. Typically only flies when going to roost, favouring large groups of trees. Emergents that have a view over an open canopy are favoured. Often entire flock will roost in same tree, sometimes in 2–3 smaller trees.

BREEDING Presumably polygamous. Male takes no part in incubation or rearing young. Nest a shallow scrape, often within buttress roots of canopy trees, or in areas of dense ground cover. Clutch 8–15 (usually 12). Incubation by female alone, for 28 days. Only female tends young. Eggs laid late April–May. Poults observed June–August.

DISTRIBUTION Chiefly Mexico, just extending into Guatemala and Belize. In Mexico widely recorded in Yucatán Peninsula (extreme E Tabasco, Yucatán, Quintana Roo and Campeche); its supposed occurrence in NE Chiapas has been questioned. Also occurs in adjacent N Guatemala (Petén) and NW and WC Belize.

STATUS Near Threatened, but true status unclear. Widely hunted in past, which has resulted in elusive behaviour. This, combined with forest environment, makes it hard to assess population and no overall estimates appear to have been made, but densities of 1.5-4.0 birds/km² in Mayan Biosphere Reserve. Remains locally abundant in reserves, especially in Belize, but probably extirpated from N Yucatan, W Campeche and E Tabasco. Main threats appear to be uncontrolled subsidence hunting, live animal trade and continued hunting for food (and occasionally sport), combined with large-scale clear-cutting and agricultural conversion, which is heavily fragmenting suitable habitat. In addition breeding season survival rates for females and young are reported to be very low in some areas, e.g. Tikal National Park, due to high abundance and diversity of natural predators.

REFERENCES BirdLife International (2000), Blake (1977), Gonzalez *et al.* (1998), Howell & Webb (1995), Porter (1994), Steadman *et al* (1979), Sugihara & Heston (1981).

FAMILY TETRAONIDAE
Grouse

Small family of 18 species, often treated as a subfamily of the Phasianidae. However, grouse form a very distinct group, and though clearly closely allied to pheasants, they share a number of features. Grouse have feathers covering their nostrils, their tarsi are short and often feathered to base of toes, and some even have toes feathered as well. They lack tarsal spurs, but their toes are pectinate to enable them to grip when walking along branches. Another feature is the presence of a fleshy wattle or 'comb' above the eye, most marked in breeding males when it becomes engorged with blood. Grouse inhabit cooler climates than most pheasants, with most distributed in the N Holarctic. Males of most species indulge in elaborate courtship displays, using both plumage adornments and inflatable, often coloured neck sacs to draw attention. Displaying males may join communal leks. Opinions differ as to the number of genera. Short (1967) reduced these to only six, a move followed by Johnsgard (1983) in his monograph. The situation was further reviewed in a more recent monograph by Potapov (1989), who recognised nine genera (which is followed here).

Genus *FALCIPENNIS*: spruce grouse

These two congeners form a species-pair and are clearly closely related, despite today being separated by the N Pacific. Both are relatively small, cryptically patterned forest grouse, related to Blue Grouse but differing markedly in pattern of the downy chicks, the absence of inflatable air-sacs and generally smaller size.

171 SIBERIAN SPRUCE GROUSE
Falcipennis falcipennis (Hartlaub, 1855)   Plate 47

Alternative names: Siberian Grouse, Sharp-winged Grouse.

A remarkably fearless forest grouse of the far-east Siberian taiga, forming a super-species with American Spruce Grouse.

IDENTIFICATION Coniferous forests of E Siberia, where overlaps with superficially similar Hazel Grouse. Both sexes differ from Hazel Grouse (Plate 51) in lacking scruffy frontal crest (which is generally visible on wary birds) and in having a more uniformly patterned head and neck, becoming especially dark, almost blackish-brown on throat and breast in male. Underparts have bold white triangular spotting on brown flanks, merging to form white barring on dark lower breast and belly. In comparison, Hazel Grouse has more scalloped pattern of rufous and black blunt-tipped markings on pale ground colour. Male has far less white on throat-sides than Hazel Grouse, having a thin white broken border, which hardly reaches base of bill, whereas male Hazel has a broad white malar, which meets above base of bill. Both sexes of Hazel Grouse have variable whitish band on lower neck-sides, almost to mantle and whitish tips to scapulars forming 'braces' (Siberian Spruce has a few scattered spots on scapulars rather than a continuous pale stripe). In flight rising Siberian Spruce has warm brown rump contrasting with distinct white terminal band at tip of dark tail (in male), whereas Hazel Grouse (especially overlapping race *amurensis*) appears distinctly grey on rump and tail, and has pale grey terminal-band, highlighted by dark subterminal bar. Closely related American Spruce rather smaller, lacks white tail tip (or narrow in some populations), has underparts less intensely marked white, with flanks more streaked than spotted. Female resembles rufous phase of American but has underparts much more boldly spotted white.

DESCRIPTION Plump, rather short-tailed small grouse, with little size dimorphism. Male has ruffled forecrown when feathers erect; neck feathers somewhat enlarged. Tarsi feathered to base of toes. Middle toe distinctly elongated and slender. Larger uppertail-coverts conceal basal half of tail. Tail graduated, usually of 16 feathers. Primaries distinctly narrower and more sharply pointed than American Spruce Grouse, particularly attenuated on outermost three. Comb (conspicuous only in male) bright red. Bill very short, black. Irides dark brown. Feet greyish-black. Sexes differ. **Adult male:** Crown, neck, nape and mantle dull black, each feather barred grey; feathers in front and behind eye have white tips. Throat black, bordered by irregular line of white-tipped feathers. Breast black. Lower breast and underparts dark warm brown, vermiculated black but obscured by feathers being heavily marked with white bands, which appear as larger triangular spots on flanks and undertail-coverts. Upperparts, including wings, dark olive-brown, vermiculated black; scapulars and uppertail-coverts with irregular white spots and shaft streaks. Flight feathers dull dark brown. Tail blackish, but vermiculated brown at base and on central feathers; all but central feathers broadly tipped white. **First-winter male:** Like adult male but upperparts less boldly marked black and has conspicuous pale shaft streaks. **Adult female:** Head and neck rather uniformly and finely mottled and speckled buff, brown and black; ground colour of throat paler. Breast and mantle ochre-buff with larger blackish-brown scalloping. Underparts from lower breast vermiculated ochre-buff and black, but almost completely obscured by large white triangular markings on feathers, making central belly and undertail-coverts appear almost white. Entire upperparts vermiculated buff and blackish-brown, feathers with large dark central marks and tiny fine pale shaft streaks. Scapulars have irregular white spots. Flight feathers grey-brown. Tail barred and vermiculated, lacking obvious white tip of male. **Juvenile:** Resembles brighter, warmer buff version of female, but has larger, longer and brighter buff streaks on upperparts and dark feather markings smaller and more barred, rather than blotched.

GEOGRAPHICAL VARIATION Monotypic. Sakhalin birds named '*muratai*' but this not generally recognised.

MEASUREMENTS Length 38–43 cm. Male averages slightly larger. Males: wing 185–200, tail 105–137, weight 625–735. Females: wing 175–195, tail 88–95, weight 650–740.

HABITAT Coniferous forests, mostly those dominating taiga in far E Russia, namely spruce *Picea jezoensis* and *P. abies*, fir *Abies nephrolepsis*, larch *Larix dahurica* and pine *Pinus koraiensis*. Apparently uses mixed forests with at least some spruce and where denser, moist areas of understorey are interspersed with more open areas. May also use young forests with very little spruce, which is notable as spruce needles are thought to be sole winter food. Does not use open areas, earliest successional stages of forest or pure deciduous forest.

VOICE During advertising display, male emits drawn-out 'whistling-cooing', which is followed by a click or double click as male jumps into air, the latter sound can be heard up to 100 m away; it has been transcribed as a rising *Vuuuuuuuuuiiiii* immediately followed by *klpp-klakllp*. Female gives quiet coarse calls when alarmed.

HABITS Almost fearless of man, permitting remarkably close approach. Encountered singly or in groups according to season. During breeding season, males dispersed on territories, where they display alone. Display likened to miniature capercaillie in postures and clicking sounds; it starts with male cocking and fanning tail to reveal white rim and boldly spotted undertail-coverts, simultaneously stretching neck upwards before uttering cooing-whistle, and jumps into air, uttering clicking sounds. Often initial part of display is given from tree or stump, before jumping to ground. In autumn may gather in parties of up to ten to feed on berries. Largely sedentary, but some seasonal movements, such as to take advantage of berry-rich areas in autumn in lower Amur and upper Tetyukhe and Iodyzh valleys. May return to dense forest to winter, where forage and roost in tunnels under snow. Following coldest part of winter, roost in trees. Adept at foraging both on ground and in trees, and is remarkably agile when walking on quite small branches. In winter appears to take entirely spruce *Picea* needles and perhaps fir *Abies*, but some insects taken, especially by females in spring and young in summer, switching to primarily berry diet in autumn

BREEDING Promiscuous, with males occupying dispersed territories. Nests on ground at base of tree; simple depression with scant lining of conifer needles and twigs. Clutch 6–12 (usually 6–7) rusty-buff eggs, freckled and spotted dark rusty-brown. Incubation by female alone for 23–24 days. Eggs incubated from mid-May to mid-June, with apparently little regional variation.

DISTRIBUTION E Siberia (Russia) from E Transbaikalia (west to S Stanovoi range at c.120°W) and S Yakutia, south over Amurland and Ussuriland (except extreme south) to 44°S, east to Sea of Okhotsk and in N Sakhalin, reaching as far north as 60°N. Also NE China, in extreme N Heliongjiang, within Amur Valley and Xiao Hinggan Ling range, where apparently extirpated.

STATUS Near Threatened. Little information available on population changes. It is assumed that increasing human land use and exploitation of forest products in its range has led to a decline since 1970s, if not before. Vulnerable to forestry related habitat change, especially large-scale operations that destroy its apparent preferred patchwork of habitats. Due to sensitivity to change in forest structure, it has been considered an indicator for forest ecosystem that dominates and is characteristic of Okhotsk taiga. Population in extreme NE China apparently always small, and surveys in 1965, 1988 and 1992–1997 failed to locate it.

REFERENCES Andreev (1990), Andreev & Hafner (1998), Flint (1995), Johnsgard (1983), Nechaev (1991), Potapov & Flint (1989), Storch (2000).

172 AMERICAN SPRUCE GROUSE
Falcipennis canadensis (Linnaeus, 1758)   Plate 47

Alternative names: Taiga Grouse, Franklin's Grouse (*franklinii*).

Small grouse of boreal forests, remarkably confiding towards humans, which contributed to a former decline. Despite its tameness and extensive range it remains remarkably difficult to find. The two readily differentiated populations could arguably be treated as species.

IDENTIFICATION Rather small, plump short-tailed grouse of North American coniferous forests. Male greyish above, contrasting slightly with blackish throat and underparts, latter barred and streaked/spotted white. Smaller and shorter tailed than Blue Grouse, with which it overlaps in west of range: male Spruce more strikingly patterned below, with prominent white chest barring and no bare neck patches in display. Male over most of range has distinct dull rufous terminal tail-band, obvious when tail fanned in display or if flushed, but this absent in plain, or narrowly white-tipped tail of southwestern subspecies *franklinii* (Franklin's Grouse), which also differs in having conspicuous white tips to long uppertail-coverts (particularly noticeable in display), whereas other forms of American Spruce have, at most, small greyish-white tips. Female relatively uniformly mottled brownish, apart from quite boldly spotted black-and-white underparts and rufous tail tip (latter absent in female *franklinii*), which help separate it from larger female Blue Grouse. Females of all races occur in two colour phases (grey and rufous). See also very similar Siberian Spruce Grouse and Ruffed Grouse (Plate 51).

DESCRIPTION *F. c. canadensis.* Plump, rather short-tailed small grouse, with little size dimorphism. Male has neck feathers somewhat enlarged. Tarsi feathered to base of toes. Middle toe distinctly elongated and slender. Larger uppertail-coverts conceal basal half of tail. Tail graduated, usually of 16 feathers. Primaries unremarkable in shape. Comb (conspicuous only in male) bright red. Bill very short, black. Irides dark brown. Feet greyish-black. Sexes differ. **Adult male:** Head, neck, nape and mantle dull black, each feather with broad grey fringe; several small white feathers in front of and behind eye. Nostril covering, throat, foreneck and upper breast black. Larger neck feathers have white tips; narrow and often broken whitish border to black throat. Central underparts blackish, feathers becoming narrowly barred grey-brown and black on flanks. Lower breast and central underparts obscured by white markings, forming streaked spots on flanks; undertail-coverts blackish, each feather with large white tip. Upperparts, including wings, dark olive-brown, vermiculated black; scapulars and rump with some irregular white spots and shaft streaks. Longer uppertail-coverts dull blackish-brown, narrowly tipped pale grey. Flight feathers dull dark brown, primaries mottled on outer webs. Tail blackish-brown, all but central feathers broadly tipped rufous, but tips very narrow on central pair. **First-winter male:** Like adult male but duller, with retained mottled juvenile outer primaries. **Adult female:** Two colour morphs throughout range: grey morph and rufous morph reflect degree of warmth in plumage tones. Head and neck rather uniformly and finely mottled and speckled buff, whitish, brown and black; ground colour of throat paler. Breast and mantle warm buff or grey-brown with larger blackish-brown scalloping. Underparts from lower breast vermiculated buffy-brown and black, obscured by broad white bars on feathers, becoming more sparsely spotted/streaked on flanks. Entire upperparts vermiculated buff and blackish-brown, feathers with large dark central marks and fine pale shaft streaks. Flight feathers grey-brown. Tail barred and vermiculated, usually with rufous-buff terminal bar. **Juvenile:** Resembles rufous morph female, but has buff or whitish spots at tips of wing-coverts and mottled primaries; feathers with dark markings smaller and more barred, rather than blotched.

GEOGRAPHICAL VARIATION Apart from very obvious differences between two groups of races indicated below, there is surprisingly little variation across large range. Indeed a more sensible treatment might be to treat the two groups as different species, despite significant intergradation where their ranges meet.

Taiga Grouse *F. (canadensis) canadensis*
Characterised by both sexes having rufous tail tip and

males no or very narrow pale grey tips to uppertail-coverts. Status in need of revision.
 F. c. atratus (Grinnell, 1910) occurs in coastal S Alaska.
 F. c. canadensis (Linnaeus, 1758) (includes '*osgoodi*') occurs in C Alaska east to Labrador (Canada).
 F. c. canace (Linnaeus, 1766) (includes '*torridus*') occurs in SE Canada (including Nova Scotia) and NE USA.

Franklin's Grouse *F. (canadensis) franklinii*
Population in Rocky Mountains and Cascades rather different as both sexes lack rufous terminal tail-band, but may have narrow whitish tip; male also has conspicuous white tips to larger uppertail-coverts. Both features are conspicuous in displaying birds and, as aspects of male display also appear to differ, this suggests that speciation may be near complete. However, it apparently interbreeds with nominate form in N Rockies.
 F. c. franklinii (Douglas, 1829) occurs in SE Alaska and British Columbia (Canada) south to C Idaho and NW Wyoming (USA).

MEASUREMENTS Length 38–43 cm. *F. c. canadensis.* Males: wing 161–192, tail 107–144, weight 550–650. Females: wing 159–191, tail 94–119, weight 450–550.

HABITAT Typically early successional coniferous habitats, usually dominated by spruce and pine, and indeed, its distribution is largely governed by these species. Occurs from sea level to over 3600 m. Fairly young forests (less than 30 years old) are usually preferred, with dense understorey between 2 to 8 m tall. In western mountains during breeding, also use open subalpine areas with widely scattered trees. During dispersal and in those populations that perform seasonal movements, appear less reliant on conifers while on move and can be found quite some distance from them.

VOICE Among the quietest grouse. At least ten distinct calls, and one song given by males in SW Alberta on spring territory. Known as the 'cantus' it is uttered spontaneously when light levels are low, e.g. at dawn. Territorial males also 'trill' when attacking intruders. Both sexes give alarm calls. Males of some populations also wing-clap during display, which can be heard up to 150 m away. Other non-vocal sounds do not travel very far, e.g. drumming in which male thumps ground while displaying.

HABITS Largely sedentary, though some populations may move slightly in spring and autumn. Usually encountered either feeding along roadsides or perched in trees. Remarkably confiding, often showing little concern even if approached to within a few metres. Typically, displaying male attracts attention, strutting with tail fanned and neck erect, enlarged by fluffed feathers; various other display postures, including tail swishing in time with alternate stepping and 'flutter-jumps'. Some regional variation evident, as *franklinii* also indulges in wing-clapping during flutter-jumps. Forages throughout day, especially in early morning and late afternoon, on ground and individually or in family parties. If there is snow cover it forms loose flocks of up to 30 and also spends considerable time foraging in conifers, typically at mid-crown level. Feeds primarily on needles and buds of spruces, firs, pines and larches; only chicks appear to rely on invertebrates. In autumn berries are favoured. Predominantly on ground, but will fly to trees to feed and climbs among branches. Otherwise, rarely flies and even when hard-pressed only takes to wing as last resort.

BREEDING Promiscuous with males occupying dispersed territories, preferentially under good canopy cover. Female nests on ground and always below overhead cover, often a conifer (such as black spruce, spruce pine or jack pine). Simple depression on ground, lined with dead needles and leaves. Female incubates eggs, which like other grouse starts when last egg is laid. Clutch size usually 5–6. Eggs tawny-olive with umber and brown markings. Lays from late May, but mainly June, though in SW Alberta can vary by more than two weeks between years. Onset of laying closely linked to more than half of ground being snow free, and starting c.2.5 weeks later. Incubation usually lasts 21–24 days, as a consequence of differing degrees of female attention.

DISTRIBUTION Distributed throughout much of mainland Canada into N USA. Extends from Yukon of Alaska, south through Rockies to NE Oregon and C Idaho east to NW Montana, and also east across Canadian forests, south into NE USA in Maine, N New York and New Hampshire. Introduced and well established on Newfoundland. Distribution is closely linked to northern conifer forests.

STATUS Still occurs in reasonable numbers throughout much of range. Some populations have suffered from habitat loss, such as at southern and eastern extremities of range, and others, principally in Alaska, are seemingly isolated and low density. Like Blue Grouse some populations may fluctuate considerably between years. Though up to 0.5 million birds were shot each year in late 1970s, the impact of hunting is thought to be marginal. Major threat is habitat change, as patchwork of mature and regenerating coniferous blocks is altered by changing land practices, such as more widespread logging or prevention of natural burning regimes. Developments, such as road-building programmes may exacerbate the genetically isolating effects of typically scattered populations occurring at low density.

REFERENCES Boag & Schroeder (1992), Johnsgard (1983), de Juana (1994), Storch (2000).

Genus *DENDRAGAPUS*: Blue Grouse

This monotypic genus is sometimes expanded to include *Falcipennis*, which although admittedly similar lacks naked neck sacs and differs significantly in pattern of downy chicks. Other features are mentioned under Description below.

173 BLUE GROUSE
Dendragapus obscurus (Say, 1823) Plate 47

Alternative names: Dusky Grouse, Richardson's Grouse, Sooty Grouse.

This large grey forest grouse of the Rockies and Pacific forests of North America comprises eight races, which fall quite neatly into two groups that may even merit species status.

IDENTIFICATION Relatively large dark grey grouse of both deciduous and coniferous forests in W North America, only likely to be confused with American Spruce Grouse, with which it widely overlaps in north of range. Both sexes distinctly larger, longer necked and longer tailed than spruce grouses. In display male inflates colourful sacs, which part neck feathers to expose white feather bases that form white surround to neck-sides. Male quite uniform bluish-grey to blackish-grey (darkest in Pacific forests), with orange-yellow comb (red in display) and yellowish or purplish (varies with race) cervical sacs. Lacks clear black-and-white pattern to throat and breast, or whitish spotting on uppertail and has greyish (or lacks) terminal tail-band (not rufous as northern races of American Spruce). Female resembles dullest males, but distinctly mottled on upperparts; plainer and greyer than female American Spruce, with less defined and sparser white markings on underparts and has plainer, greyer belly. Compare also Ruffed Grouse (Plate 51).

DESCRIPTION *D. o. fuliginosus.* Plump, but relatively long-bodied and long-tailed grouse. Crown slightly ruffled when feathers erect. Male has well-developed neck feathers, spread in display. Tarsi feathered to base of toes. Middle toe distinctly elongated. Larger uppertail-coverts conceal basal third/half of tail. Tail relatively square ended, usually of 18 feathers. Comb (conspicuous only in male) deep yellow, becoming orange or even red in full display. Bare skin at neck-sides (insignificant in female but clearly revealed in male display) deep yellow and strongly caruncled. Bill very short, black. Irides dark brown. Feet greyish-black. Sexes differ little. **Adult male:** Almost entire plumage dark grey, indistinctly vermiculated brown over entire upperparts. Neck feathers white, broadly tipped dark grey. Belly and vent have darker feather centres and white streaks and edges, the latter abrading to make underparts appear almost unmarked, though white marks always visible on undertail-coverts. Tail dark grey, subterminally darker with pale grey terminal-band. **Adult female:** Basically rather drab greyish-brown, with head, neck, scapulars and flanks barred darker and have browner feather edging. Neck feathers wholly grey-brown (no white bases). Underparts vermiculated grey-brown, with darker feather centres and sparse white tips on flanks and uppertail-coverts. Tail similar to male, though more vermiculated and has narrower grey tip. **First-winter:** Both sexes much as adult female, but pale buffy or even whitish, less grey, ground colour to central underparts. Tail shorter than adult and lacks grey terminal bar. **Juvenile:** Resembles female, but feathers of upperparts, including wings, have fine pale shaft streaks. Tail mottled brown, narrowly barred and lacking grey tip.

GEOGRAPHICAL VARIATION Surprisingly variable, with eight recognised forms varying in basic size, colour saturation, colour of neck sacs of male, tail pattern and to certain degree display. They form two reasonably well-defined groups, a coastal group (Sooty Grouse) and an interior group (Dusky Grouse), and were formerly considered to be two separate species.

Dusky Grouse D. (obscurus) obscurus
Males of interior populations have purplish and smoother bare skin on neck-sides, with very extensive white surround. Tails squarer, less graduated, with individual feathers more square tipped and comprised of 20 feathers. Usually display from ground and have greyish downy chicks. Hoots softer and lower pitched than coastal forms (see Voice). The two northeastern races (Richardson's Grouse), richardsonii and pallidus lack or virtually lack grey terminal tail-band.
    D. o. richardsonii (Douglas, 1829) (includes 'flemingi') occurs in S Yukon and N British Columbia to N Idaho and NW Wyoming.
    D. o. pallidus Swarth, 1921 occurs in S British Columbia to NE Oregon.
    D. o. obscurus (Say, 1823) occurs in the Rocky Mountains from C Wyoming to N Arizona and W New Mexico.
    D. o. oreinus Behle & Selander, 1951 occurs in NE Nevada.

Sooty Grouse D. (obscurus) fuliginosus
Males of coastal populations tend to be darker than interior birds, have yellow and deeply caruncled bare skin on neck-sides and tend to have more graduated tails of 18 rounder tipped feathers. Usually display from trees and have yellowish chicks. Voices louder and higher pitched than those of interior (see Voice).
    D. o. sitkensis Swarth, 1921 occurs in Alexander Archipelago (SE Alaska) to Queen Charlotte I in British Columbia.
    D. o. fuliginosus (Ridgway, 1873) occurs in SE Alaska and S Yukon to NW California; also Vancouver I.
    D. o. sierrae Chapman, 1904 occurs in C Washington to Sierra Nevada in California.
    D. o. howardi Dickey & van Rossem, 1923 occurs in S Sierra Nevada to Tehachapi and Pinto mountains in California.

MEASUREMENTS Length: male 47–57 cm, female 44–48 cm. Males: wing 196–248, tail 131–201, weight (mean) 1273. Females: wing 178–235, tail 111–159, weight (mean) 839.

HABITAT Inhabits great variety of habitats from wet forest in coastal lowlands to alpine tundra, including forests ranging from closed canopy at lower altitudes to relatively open canopy in montane forests, though generally becomes rarer with increasing canopy cover. Found in grassland at forest edge and even at considerable distance from forest, though usually close to tree cover. Appears to require Douglas fir and other firs as part of breeding habitat, interspersed with a well-developed herb, grass, and shrub layer, and montane coniferous winter habitats. Occurs from sea level to above 3600 m.

VOICE Male possesses one song and two calls, whereas female has as many as 11 calls. Male song is a 'hoot', quite different in coastal populations from those of interior. On coast, song typically has six syllables (rather than five) and is higher pitched and louder than in interior. Also a pre-copulation 'hoot' (higher pitched than in song) and a 'growl' given in aggressive situations. Female utters a 'hard cluck' in aggressive contexts and variety of other calls in a wide range of situations, including loud high-pitched calls during differing types and stages of disturbance: e.g. *kweer kweer* when separated from brood, *kwa kwa* or *skree* on being disturbed.

HABITS Displaying males often draw attention with their far-carrying hooting cries, either given from tree canopy in coastal populations, or ground (e.g. rocky outcrop) in interior birds, but such differences not always absolute. Displays with tail fanned and twisted, wings dragging, and struts with inflated neck sacs. Also flutters into air and may make short circular flights. Males begin to display when females arrive in breeding areas, and do so throughout day, with only short periods devoted to feeding, resting etc. Singing may commence before sunrise and some bursts may be given after dark. Though adults sometimes encountered together, it is more usual to find solitary birds in summer, apart from females with young. Some broods gather into loose associations in late summer. In winter, adult males remain solitary or band as small groups. For the most part, males, in particular, move upslope from breeding grounds to wintering areas in higher forests, though some populations do not migrate. Feeds during day, primarily in evening and will even forage extensively after dark. Almost entirely takes conifer needles, primarily of firs *Abies* spp. but in summer a proportion of invertebrates, notably grasshoppers and ants; seasonally varies diet with variety of seeds, leaves and buds, and particularly berries.

BREEDING Most likely promiscuous, though it has been suggested that pairs form for duration of breeding season. Male territories dispersed and females appear on breeding grounds from late March, though this varies regionally, probably according to climate. Female nests on ground in great variety of situations. Typically some cover for nest, such as small conifers or shrubs. Simple depression, with sparse lining of plant material and some body feathers. Female alone constructs nest and incubates eggs. Clutch size usually 6–8. Eggs somewhat elliptical and smooth, generally buff with some brown markings. Earliest laid in late April–early May and most during mid-May. Some variation across range, with peak appearing to vary by one month according to locality. Incubation lasts 25–28 days.

DISTRIBUTION W North America. Inhabits hill and mountain ranges of coastal and inland W Canada and USA. From extreme SE Alaska, southern Yukon and SW Mackenzie south (including several offshore islands) to coastal N California and in Rockies to SE California and N Arizona and C New Mexico.

STATUS Still common throughout most of range, though some populations have disappeared as suitable habitat has been developed. Densities can be very high, though typically low, and extirpated from some areas. Apparently coastal populations fluctuate far more than those of interior. Habitat alteration that results in more open canopy leads to an increase in numbers, which then decline as canopy matures. Subspecies *howardi* has disappeared from several areas and may be in overall decline. In general, the species' remote range has protected it and implies that many populations have good survival prospects. Others may be at risk as pressures on habitat (e.g. for logging) increase annually.

REFERENCES Johnsgard (1983), Storch (2000), Zwickel (1992).

Genus: *LAGOPUS*: ptarmigans

Three species of relatively small grouse that occur in open habitats from heather moorland to tundra and mountain slopes. All are very similar in basic shape, having short tails of 16 feathers, toes and tarsi thickly clothed with dense white feathering and cryptically patterned 'breeding' plumages. With the exception of Red Grouse, they attain an all-white winter plumage. Moult sequence and geographical variation complex.

174 WILLOW GROUSE AND RED GROUSE

Together these grouse complete a circumpolar distribution making them the most widespread species of grouse. Though Red Grouse differs strikingly in some aspects of plumage from the other subspecies of Willow it is otherwise very similar and is clearly a geographical replacement. However, it differs markedly in its specialised habitat choice of heather moorland, to a certain degree in the timing of pair formation and number of moults, thereby warranting separate treatment.

174A WILLOW GROUSE
Lagopus (lagopus) lagopus (Linnaeus, 1758)   Plate 48

Alternative name: Willow Ptarmigan.

The most widespread grouse, inhabiting a variety of open and scrubby habitats across both North America and Eurasia, being represented in the British Isles by the well-known Red Grouse.

IDENTIFICATION Relatively easily identified in spring and summer by its combination of white wings and belly (and dorsal upperparts in spring males) and chestnut-brown or buffy-brown body. The other two ptarmigans share a similar pattern, but confusion is most likely with Rock, which has a similar distribution. However, be aware that for a few weeks in late summer juveniles have dark brownish wings (as in the British form, Red Grouse), but soon acquire white primaries as moult to winter plumage commences. Willow best distinguished from Rock by voice and habitat, with Willow ascending quite high in mountains but restricted to lusher regions, whereas Rock occurs on barren screes and crags. Situation more complex in the Aleutians (Alaska), where Rock favours grassy habitats on islands where Willow is absent. Plumage differences vary according to subspecies but Willow is much browner, lacking grey tones of many populations of Rock. In white winter plumage male (sexed by presence of red comb) lacks black eye-stripe of Rock, but shares latter's black tail, though this may be concealed by white tail-coverts unless spread upon flushing. Winter females of the two identical in plumage, but Willow is larger and has a markedly stouter bill. See also White-tailed Ptarmigan with which it also overlaps.

DESCRIPTION *L. l. lagopus*. Plump, short-tailed small grouse, with little sexual size difference. Bill short and stout. Tarsi and toes feathered, feathering longer in winter. Central toe lacks claw. Longest uppertail-coverts reach tip of tail in centre (some authorities consider these to be the real central tail feathers). Tail short, slightly rounded, consisting of 16 feathers. Comb (conspicuous only in male) bright red. Bill short and stout, dark brown. Irides dark brown. Feet concealed by whitish feathering. Sexes differ but plumage sequences complicated by three gradual moults during year. **Adult male breeding** (April–June): Head, neck and breast chestnut-brown, barred and mottled black, sometimes almost all black on breast. Rest of underparts white. Tail black. Mantle blackish-brown, tipped chestnut. Rest of upperparts, including wings white, though primary shafts black. **Adult male non-breeding** (July–September): Duller non-breeding plumage acquired through gradual moult. Head, neck and upperparts have buff, rufous-brown and blackish barring, and buff feather tips; feathers of lower underparts white, variably spotted and barred. Scapulars, uppertail-coverts, rump and innermost wing-coverts barred black and buffy-brown. Rest of wings white, with black primary shafts. Tail black. **Adult female breeding** (April–June): Similar to male non-breeding, but more buffy-yellowish, less rufous and pattern more coarsely barred black than male, and covering entire upperparts. Breast and underparts have both older white and fresh barred feathers. **Adult female non-breeding** (July–September): Very much as male non-breeding, but plumage possesses more retained old breeding feathers than male. **Adult male and female winter** (October–March): Almost all white, except black primary shafts and tail. **Juvenile:** Ephemeral juvenile stage, with moult commencing soon after hatching, overall heavily barred black and yellowish-buff, including tail and wings. At 3–4 weeks white primaries develop, and wings gradually moult to white during first autumn. First-winter becomes as white as adult, but has dull worn outer two primaries, which are retained throughout winter.

GEOGRAPHICAL VARIATION Considerable variation, mainly in breeding plumage (both colour and pattern), but complicated by sex and moult, hampering clear analysis. Variation complex and subspecific taxonomy probably in need of reassessment. Number of recognised forms varies widely according to authority. Due to complexity of situation, clearly defined race *scoticus* (Red Grouse) is treated separately, whereas rest of generally accepted subspecies merely listed below.

L. l. variegatus Salomonsen, 1936 occurs on islands off Trondheim Fjord, SW Norway.
L. l. lagopus (Linnaeus, 1758) occurs in Scandinavia east to N European Russia.
L. l . rossicus Serebrovsky, 1926 occurs from the Baltic Sea east to C Russia in the Kama Basin.
L. l. birulai Serebrovsky, 1926 occurs on the New Siberia Is.
L. l. koreni Thayer & Bangs, 1914 (including ‘*septentrionalis*’) occurs in N Russia, from the Urals to the Sea of Okhotsk.
L. l. brevirostris Hesse, 1912 occurs in the Altai Mountains in E Kazakhstan and Mongolia, and the Sayan Mountains of Buryatia.
L. l. kozlowae Portenko, 1931 occurs in montane W Mongolia.
L. l. sserebrowsky Domaniewski, 1933 (including ‘*dybowsii*’) occurs in E Siberia, from Lake Baikal to the Sea of Okhotsk and coastal montane Ussuri-land.
L. l. kamtschatkensis Momiyama, 1928 occurs in Kamchatka and N Kuril Is in extreme E Russia.
L. l. okadai Momiyama, 1928 occurs on Sakhalin I. (Russia).
L. l. muriei Gabrielson & Lincoln, 1959 occurs in the Aleutian Is (Atka to Unimak) and Kodiak I. (Alaska).
L. l. alexandrae Grinnell, 1909 occurs on islands off SE Alaska (USA) and W British Columbia (Canada).
L. l. alascensis Swarth, 1926 occurs in mainland Alaska (USA).
L. l. leucopterus Taverner, 1932 occurs on Banks,

Victoria, Southampton and Baffin islands (Canada).
L. l. albus (Gmelin, 1789) occurs in mainland Canada, from N Yukon south and east to the Gulf of Lawrence.
L. l. ungavus Riley, 1911 occurs in N Quebec and Labrador (Canada).
L. l. alleni Stejneger, 1884 occurs in Newfoundland (Canada).

MEASUREMENTS Length 36–43 cm. Male rather larger. *L. l. lagopus*. Males: wing 197–218, tail 111–135, weight 405–795. Females: wing 187–203, tail 101–116, weight 405–700.

HABITAT Mainly cold, treeless Arctic tundra and other open boreal habitats, such as bogs, heaths and moors in Arctic, subarctic and northern temperate zones, where its food plants occur. Typically prefers fairly damp places with well-developed cover of dwarf willow and birch, but varies between subspecies. For example, the British form *scoticus*, is now largely confined to moorland above the lower tree-line, whereas in N Russia prefers damper areas with shrubs, small willows and birches. Uses lower areas in winter, even sometimes occurring on farmland, but still tends to avoid taller trees. In areas where Rock Ptarmigan also occurs, Willow Grouse utilises moister, well-vegetated areas, leaving bare, lichen-covered rocks to the former species.

VOICE Many calls given in variety of contexts. Male noisy, uttering range of barked nasal calls, including an angry (‘grousing’) guttural *go-bak, go-bak, go-bak-AK-AK-AK*. In display flight, male gives distinct three-part call: a loud rising *aa*, followed by a *ka-ka-ka*, repeated 8–12 times as returns to ground, and finally *kohWA-a kohWA*, also repeated, when on ground. Second advertisement call a rapid clucking *ko-ko-ko* uttered above ground, which speeds-up to *-krrrr*. Calls given in either aggressive (or sexual) situations, or in alarm, typically harsh and loud. These include *kohway* given just before chasing another bird and single loud *kok* in general warning. Female calls at higher frequencies than those of male.

HABITS Encountered singly or in groups. Explodes from cover with whirring wings, uttering cackling series of calls. Flight rapid, interrupted by brief glides on bowed wings, banking to drop down when just out of sight. In spring, male has swollen red wattles and utters territorial calls from posts, stunted trees and rocks, and in flight. When coveys disband in autumn, groups form, which in much of range persist throughout season. Composition can be very variable, probably depending upon location and potential movements. For example, large mixed flocks of up to 300 have been recorded on migration in Russia, whereas in Alaska roving flocks are typically single sex. Male highly territorial throughout range and usually uses conspicuous sentry posts. Largely sedentary, but movements of 200–300 km recorded in N Siberia, where moves south from exposed Arctic habitats in winter.

BREEDING Monogamous, with males competing for territories and females visiting these in spring. Female nests on ground amid low cover, such as heather or rushes. Simple depression, lined with plant material, constructed by female alone, who also incubates eggs. Clutch size usually 8–11. Eggs oval, glossy and pale yellow, sometimes reddish, with various dark brown or red-brown markings. Given extensive distribution, season variable: earliest eggs from mid-April in west of range (i.e. Scandinavia), but later in east, even late June in N Siberia, presumably because birds must return to open Arctic tundra prior to territory establishment. Incubation lasts 19–25 days and eggs hatch synchronously. Willow and Red Grouse are only grouse in which both sexes raise brood.

DISTRIBUTION Largest range among grouse: circumpolar in North America, Europe and Asia. Excluding Red Grouse (treated separately and confined to British Isles), range extends south to N Lithuania, N Belarus, N Kazakhstan, N Mongolia and mountains of Amurland, Ussuriland and Sakhalin in extreme E Siberia (Russia). Its presence in N Heilongjiang (NE China) apparently requires confirmation, but considered very rare along Amur River there by MacKinnon & Phillips (2000). In North America, it is widespread across Alaska (including Aleutians west to Unimak), Arctic and subarctic regions of Canada south to Gulf of St. Lawrence and Newfoundland. Northernmost populations move south in winter. Populations in extreme N Siberia,

especially Arctic islands, and those of Canadian Arctic islands undertake long-distance migrations to avoid harsh winter conditions. At such periods birds occasionally reach N USA as stragglers.

STATUS Common, if not abundant, throughout much of range, though local extirpations have occurred, usually at southern edge of distribution. For example, it formerly bred further south in Finland and parts of Russia than at present. Numbers subject to (often considerable) natural fluctuations, and length of such cycles varies according to locality, being generally 3–4 years in Palearctic and ten years in Nearctic. Hunted everywhere, except Baltic countries, Belarus and China, where fully protected. Such shooting is often of considerable socio-economic importance, with an estimated 1.2 million individuals shot annually in the Russian tundra and well over 0.5 million in Scandinavia. Overall, it appears able to withstand such harvests, at least while there are no other adverse pressures, such as reductions in habitat quality or extent. Due to remoteness of its habitat, most populations do not suffer from habitat pressure or disturbance, except locally. Like Western Capercaillie, high-tension power lines and deer fences kill many birds that collide with them in flight.

REFERENCES Cramp & Simmons (1980), Hannon & Eason (1994), de Juana (1994), MacKinnon & Phillips (2000), Potapov (1985), Storch (2000).

174B RED GROUSE
Lagopus (lagopus) scoticus (Latham, 1787)   Plate 48

Long considered the only bird species endemic to the British Isles, but this accolade was lost when it was 'lumped' with the circumpolar Willow Grouse. There is perhaps a case for reinstating its position, at least as an allospecies.

IDENTIFICATION Britain and Ireland, where it is familiar on heather moorland. Differs from all other forms of Willow Grouse in lacking a white winter plumage and in having dark wings (except whitish underwing-coverts) at all seasons (Willow Grouse has dark wings for only week or two in juvenile plumage). Often heard before seen, male particularly noisy in spring when a variety of gruff, barking calls betray presence. Male utters territorial calls from posts and rocks among heather, showing-off swollen red combs. When flushed 'explode' from heather with whirring wings, uttering cackling calls; they appear dark reddish-brown, but may bank to reveal whitish underwing-coverts. Vary, with some being particularly dark, almost purplish-chestnut, whereas others have quite extensive white spotting on belly. Female and young in particular have extensive buff feather markings, which lighten shade of brown and offer greater contrast with blackish tail. Compare female Black Grouse and particularly Rock Ptarmigan, which occur almost alongside Red Grouse in Scotland, but in very different habitats.

DESCRIPTION Structure as Willow Grouse, though bill and tail relatively shorter than nominate *lagopus*.

Sexes differ but plumage differences arising from moult sequences complicate issue. Unlike nominate *lagopus* has two, not three, moults per year. **Adult male non-breeding** (August–March): Head, neck, body plumage and upperwing-coverts chestnut-brown, barred and mottled black, many also have a few greyish or whitish feather tips on malar, scapulars and uppertail-coverts. Belly and flanks have variable number of white feather tips, most obvious when fresh, indeed some can have belly heavily mottled white. Basic colour saturation varies individually, with occasional birds being sufficiently dark purplish-brown to appear blackish in field. Flight feathers dark grey-brown, with primaries darker. Tail blackish-brown, central feathers vermiculated rufous. **Adult male breeding** (April–July): Duller than non-breeding plumage, and acquired through gradual moult. Head, neck and upperparts have buff and yellowish barring and feather tips; feathers of rear underparts retained, but any pale tipping usually abraded through feather wear. **Adult female non-breeding** (June–March) Similar to male breeding, but more closely spotted, rather than barred, with buff as feathers have larger buffish wedge-shaped spot at tip. Breast more clearly barred black (often unmarked in male). **Adult female breeding** (March–June): Even more clearly and closely barred black, buffish and yellowish, making pattern extremely cryptic. Scapulars and rump often also barred whitish. **Juvenile:** Both sexes resemble non-breeding male, but feathers of upperparts marked with concentric buff lines, rather than tipped buff. Breast and underparts yellowish-buff, more boldly marked with black scaling.

GEOGRAPHICAL VARIATION Complexity of plumage stages, various colour morphs and very gradual moult makes analysis of variation difficult. Irish populations have been separated as '*hibernicus*' on basis of female being paler, but this perhaps a result of more prolonged moult than British birds. Willow Grouse of form *variegatus* (Trondheim, Norway) approach Red Grouse in having brownish in flight feathers, retained even in very short white winter plumage.

MEASUREMENTS Length 37–42 cm. Male slightly larger. Males: wing 199–216, tail 105–122, mean weight 680. Females: wing 188–205, tail 93–110, mean weight 586.

HABITAT Open moorland, peat bogs and mosses, more specifically moors with extensive stands of ling *Calluna vulgaris*. Large tracts of these are carefully managed by rotational burning to ensure mosaic of different-age heather, thus providing nutritious young shoots, and older stands for shelter. Prefers taller heather in autumn/winter, but increasingly uses heterogenean grass/heather mixtures in spring, at which season females show strong preference for boundaries between different-age heather stands. Broods are largely raised in areas with taller and older heather, with significant edge habitats. From sea level to 900 m.

VOICE Very similar to Willow Grouse.

HABITS Very like Willow Grouse, but diet primarily consists of shoots of ling *Calluna*, though a small percentage of shoots and berries of associated plants are also taken.

BREEDING Monogamous, with males competing for territories and pair forming in autumn (spring pairing is norm in other races of Willow Grouse). Nest a simple depression, lined with plant material, constructed by female alone; on ground amid low cover, such as heather or rushes. Clutch usually 6–9. Eggs oval and pale yellowish-white, blotched throughout with dark brown or red-brown markings. Incubation lasts 19–25 days and eggs hatch synchronously. Generally laid early–late May. Unusually among grouse, male accompanies family and helps guard chicks.

DISTRIBUTION Britain and Ireland. Widespread in Wales and Scotland, including both Inner and Outer Hebrides, Isle of Man and Orkney. Also upland areas of N England, with isolated outposts, resulting from introductions, on Shetland and in Devon. Less numerous in Ireland but widespread in western bogs and mountains. Attempts to introduce it elsewhere have met with little success, though small populations briefly persisted in Belgium and Germany.

STATUS Locally common, even abundant on managed grouse moors. Marked decline apparent in recent decades as extensive areas of moorland have been 'lost' to forestry plantations and less intensive 'keepering' of grouse moors. British population estimated at c.500,000 pairs in 1970s, but had halved by 1990. Irish population, considered less than 5000 pairs, and has declined by c.50% since 1960s.

REFERENCES Bannerman (1963), Watson & Miller (1976), Witherby *et al.* (1941).

---

175 ROCK PTARMIGAN
Lagopus mutus (Montin, 1776)

Plate 48

Alternative name: Ptarmigan.

Almost as widespread as Willow Grouse, its preference for rugged mountains has fragmented its range and permitted a remarkable degree of variation to develop with more than 30 described subspecies—more than any other galliform. It is notable in being virtually the only bird able to survive the rigours of a high-Arctic winter, being recorded as far north as 75°N at this season, when this region receives three months of 24-hour darkness.

IDENTIFICATION Almost exclusively in rocky tundra and alpine zone of mountains, in many areas overlapping with Willow Grouse, but ecologically separated by habitat preference (though see comments under Habitat). Slightly smaller than Willow, with an even smaller bill and relatively slimmer winged. Like Willow, plumage varies both with complex seasonal moults and geographically, but never as rich or dark chestnut as Willow (some races distinctly rufous but most closely barred yellowish-buff or greyish on body; yellowish birds very difficult to separate from female Willow on plumage alone). In general, spring male much greyer than Willow and utters distinctive dry rattling belch when flushed. In winter, male has black eye stripe (absent in female and other *Lagopus*). Black tail an easy distinction from White-tailed at all seasons but often not visible until flushed. Juvenile has mottled brownish upperwing and tail until first autumn, and may then suggest Red Grouse (which see) of British Isles. See White-tailed Ptarmigan for further discussion.

DESCRIPTION *L. m mutus.* Plump, short-tailed small grouse, distinctly sleeker and neater, with relatively smaller bill, slightly narrower wings and even shorter legs than Willow Grouse, but otherwise basic structure similar. Comb (conspicuous only in breeding male) bright red. Bill short, black. Irides dark brown. Feet concealed by whitish feathering. Sexes differ but plumage sequences complicated by three gradual moults during year. **Adult male breeding** (April–June): Head, hindneck and neck-sides barred blackish-brown and rufous-buff; chin and scattered feathers on head white; throat, foreneck and breast dark grey-brown, with sparse buff fringes, becoming almost blackish on centre of lower breast. Flanks dark grey-brown, mottled and barred buff. Central underparts and vent chiefly white (retained from winter). Upperparts, including tertials and innermost wing-coverts, uppertail-coverts and scapulars dark grey-brown, feathers edged buff or whitish. Mantle darker. Rest of wing white. Tail black (except concealed whitish central feathers). **Adult male non-breeding** (July–September): Paler buffy-grey or olive-grey, more finely barred and vermiculated than breeding plumage, with whitish edging to feathers of head and neck. Extent of white on rear underparts and wings as breeding. **Adult female breeding** (April–June): Similar to male non-breeding, but more clearly barred buffy-yellowish, less dark grey; pattern more coarsely barred black than male. Extent of white in wings similar. Underparts more extensively barred buffy-yellow and black than male. **Adult female non-breeding** (July–September): Very much as male non-breeding but markings coarser and plumage more mixed with buff-and-black breeding feathers than male. **Adult male and female winter** (October–March): Almost all white except black primary shafts and tail, the latter tipped white (unlike Willow Grouse) and male has black loral-stripe, which extends to just behind eye (absent in female and congeners). Individuals of some southern races often retain scattered dark feathers throughout winter. **Juvenile:** Ephemeral juvenile stage begins soon after hatching, overall heavily barred black and yellowish-buff, including wings and tail. At 3–4 weeks white primaries develop and wings gradually moult to white during first autumn. First-winter as white as adult, but has dull worn outer two primaries, which are retained throughout winter.

GEOGRAPHICAL VARIATION Considerable variation across massive range, some of which is clinal and related to size, with larger birds in far north. Variation largely concerns relative amounts of brown and grey in non-breeding plumage, and amount of black in breeding and non-breeding plumages. Also individual variation, partially due to variable moult progression ,which hinders understanding of geographical variation. Additionally, it was recently reported that Rock Ptarmigan on some Aleutian islands is not only somewhat larger and heavier billed than congeners, but also favours lowland grassy habitats and seemingly differs in its display postures from mainland forms; the significance of this is intriguing, considering the complexity of subspecies inhabiting the islands. The plethora of named forms requires complete revision. The recently discovered relict population in Tajikistan has yet to be formally named. Vaurie (1965) divided the forms into two groups, though this approach is not entirely satisfactory. Because of the complex situation, the generally accepted subspecies are merely listed below.

Nominate group: four European races, largely isolated from one another. Males all tend to be greyer and less brownish in autumn, while in breeding plumage they become distinctly unmarked blackish on breast.

    L. m. mutus (Montin, 1776) occurs in Norway and N Sweden east to the Kola Peninsula in extreme NW Russia.

    L. m. millaisi Hartert,1923 (=*'cinereus'*) occurs in Scotland.

    L. m. pyrenaicus Hartert, 1921 occurs in the Pyrenees on the France–Spain border.

    L. m. helveticus (Thienemann, 1829) (=*'montanus'*) occurs in the Alps from the France–Swiss border to C Austria.

The *rupestris* group: the remainder of races.

    L. m. hyperboreus Sundevall 1845 (=*'alpina'*) occurs on Bear I, Svalbard and Franz Josef Land.

    L. m. komensis Serebrovsky, 1926 occurs in N Ural Mts in E European Russia.

    L. m. pleskei Serebrovsky, 1926 occurs in CN Siberia east to the Bering Strait.

    L. m. macrorhynchus Serebrovsky, 1926 occurs in the Tarbagatay Mts on the Kazakhstan–Mongolia border.

    L. m. nadezdae Serebrovsky, 1926 occurs in mountain ranges of S Siberia and N Mongolia.

    L. m. transbaicalicus Serebrovsky ,1926 (includes *'barguzinensis'*) occurs from Lake Baikal east to the Sea of Okhotsk in SE Russia.

    L. m. krascheninnikovi Potapov, 1985 occurs on the Kamchatka Peninsula in far E Russia.

    L. m. ridgwayi Stejneger, 1884 occurs on the Commander Is off Kamchatka (Russia).

    L. m. kurilensis Kuroda, 1924 occurs on the Kuril Is (Russia).

    L. m. japonicus Clark, 1907 occurs on C Honshu (Japan).

    L. m. evermanni Elliot, 1896 occurs on Attu, in the W Aleutians (USA).

    L. m. townsendi Elliot 1896 occurs on Kiska, in the Aleutians (USA).

    L. m. gabrielsoni Murie, 1944 occurs on Amchitka, in the Aleutians (USA).

    L. m. sanfordi Bent, 1912 occurs on Tanaga and Kanaga, in the C Aleutians (USA).

    L. m. chamberlaini Clark, 1907 occurs on Adak, in the C Aleutians (USA).

    L. m. atkhensis Turner, 1882 occurs on Atka, in the EC Aleutians (USA).

    L. m. yunaskensis Gabrielson & Lincoln, 1959 occurs on Yunaska, in the E Aleutians (USA).

    L. m. nelsoni Stejneger, 1884 occurs on Unimal, Unalaska and Amaknak, in the E Aleutians (USA).

    L. m. dixoni Grinnell, 1909 occurs on islands in Glacier Bay and adjacent mainland SE Alaska (USA).

    L. m. kellogae Grinnell, 1910 occurs in Alaska (USA) and Yukon (Canada).

    L. m. rupestris (Gmelin, 1789) occurs in N Canada, from Melville and the Ellesmere Is south to C British Columbia.

    L. m. captus Peters, 1934 (=*'groenlandicus'*) occurs in E Greenland.

    L. m. saturatus Salomonsen, 1950 occurs in NW Greenland.

    L. m. reinhardti (Brehm, 1824) occurs in SW Greenland.

    L. m. welchi Brewster, 1885 occurs in Newfoundland (Canada).

    L. m. islandorum (Faber, 1822) occurs on Iceland.

MEASUREMENTS Length c.33–38 cm. Male averaging larger. *L. m. mutus.* Males: wing 195–215, tail

104–117, weight 375–515. Females: wing 187–193, tail 91–104, weight 347–471.

HABITAT Inhabits cold, bleak rocky slopes at high latitude and altitude, usually further north and higher than congeneric Willow Grouse. Typically at lower altitudes further north than in south, where occurs solely in alpine areas. Usually in areas of comparatively sparse vegetation and prefers patchwork of bare rocks and boulders interspersed by moss, lichens, heath shrubs and dwarf trees. Some winter movement as feeds predominantly on ground and must have access to areas where snow does not lie deeply. An interesting situation arises on some Aleutian islands, where Rock Ptarmigan favour grassy areas, presumably where Willow Grouse is absent.

VOICE Calls typically not as loud as those of Willow Grouse. A low-frequency *kar-r-rk* is often described as a rattle, grating cackle or guttural belch. Another common call is a low harsh croak *aar-aar-ka-ka-ka* used in advertisement. Display call resembles that of Willow Grouse, with a *AA-ka-ka* emitted as it lifts into air, becoming a cackling *ka-ka-ka* as it descends, with a gentle *kwa-kwa* given on ground. Female has a high-pitched call, recalling a barking puppy or mewing cat.

HABITS In pairs, family parties and groups for much of year and in many areas absurdly confiding, showing little fear of humans. In Scotland, winter flocks disperse in spring when male establishes territory, though some gather in groups late in day. Males usually pair, though some may have 2–3 females. Following breeding, coveys disband and flocks form, their size varying across range: usually 3–6 in Russia (but up to 35), whereas hundreds recorded in Scotland. Inclement weather results in larger flocks. Solitary birds encountered, but these usually very quiet. Prefers to escape by walking fast or running, and easily moves across craggy landscape. Movements normally restricted to descending (either in latitude or altitude) in winter to find food, returning in spring. In winter, flocks often roam over large areas. Eruptive movements occasional in northernmost regions, with immense flocks sometimes reported on move in Greenland during exceptionally severe weather; longest ringing recovery is 1000 km. Feeds primarily on buds and leaf shoots of various low-growing plants, supplemented by berries in autumn.

BREEDING Largely monogamous, but some males polygynous. Territories established in spring when males move to higher altitudes and latitudes prior to females. Female nests on ground in open and though may be slightly sheltered, most sites are exposed. Simple depression, lined with a little plant material (sometimes unlined), constructed by both sexes. Female incubates, while male stands guard. Clutch size usually 5–8, but sometimes up to 12. Eggs oval and glossy, brownish-red with dark brown markings. Colour fades during incubation to yellow-buff, and markings become black. Lays in May in southern areas (at least in Europe), but mostly June in Spitsbergen and N Russia. Incubation usually 21–23 days and eggs hatch synchronously.

DISTRIBUTION Circumpolar. Breeds across most northerly parts of Europe, Asia and North America. In Europe, isolated populations in Pyrenees and Alps, as well as Scotland, Scandinavia, Kola Peninsula (Russia), Iceland and Svalbard. It reappears across a wide sweep of the Arctic, from the Urals east to N Pacific, chiefly above Arctic Circle. E and C Siberia populations inhabit mountains around Lake Baikal, south into Altai of Mongolia, just entering extreme NW China on border with NE Kazakhstan. In 1992, a (presumably) very isolated population was discovered much further south, in the Pamirs of Tajikistan. Its citation for montane Ussuriland (Far East Russia) appears in error. Widespread across E Siberia, including Kamchatka and related islands, with an isolated population on C Honshu (Japan). Across Bering Strait, it is widespread in Alaska and Aleutian chain, and virtually entire Arctic Canada and Greenland. Found on many coastal and offshore islands in northern seas and Arctic Ocean. Most northerly populations breed at 83°N, wintering further south where suitable food available, escaping worst of Arctic winter. Introduced on Faeroe Is but apparently now extirpated. Recently reported (vagrant?) in Bulgaria.

STATUS Inhabits most northerly and remote areas possible; thus its distribution has contracted relatively little and populations remain fairly healthy. The few local extinctions known are of little importance at global level. Local extirpations reported from parts of Scotland and England, and near habitation in Siberia. Recent discovery as far south as Bulgaria extends known range. Locally faces some pressures, such as habitat degradation and over-hunting.

REFERENCES Cramp & Simmons (1980), Holder & Montgomerie (1993), Potapov (1985), Storch (2000), Watson (1972).

---

176 WHITE-TAILED PTARMIGAN
Lagopus leucurus (Richardson, 1831)

Plate 48

The smallest ptarmigan, with a relatively restricted range in Rocky Mountains of W North America.

IDENTIFICATION Mountains of W North America, where it overlaps with other two *Lagopus*, but is the only ptarmigan likely to be encountered south of the Canadian border. Almost exclusively a bird of rocky alpine tundra, above tree-line in Rockies and associated ranges. In all plumages, resembles Rock Ptarmigan very closely, though its white, not black, tail is diagnostic. However, when at rest, ptarmigans keep their tails tightly closed and concealed below their well-developed tail-coverts. As they tend to escape by walking, it is by no means easy to observe the tail unless they are flushed. In breeding and non-breeding plumages, White-tailed (particularly male) has much more finely barred or merely faintly vermiculated upperparts, contrasting with more boldly spotted head, neck and breast than Rock Ptarmigan. White-tailed is smaller than other two ptarmigans and tends to replace them at highest elevations. In winter both sexes are wholly white, lacking both black eye-stripe and tail of Rock.

DESCRIPTION *L. l. leucurus.* Plump, short-tailed small grouse, very close to Rock Ptarmigan in structure but smaller, with even smaller bill (at least in overlap zone). Comb, present in both sexes in spring (but most conspicuous in male), bright red. Bill short, black. Irides dark brown. Feet concealed by whitish feathering. Sexes differ but plumage sequences complicated by three gradual moults during year. **Adult male breeding** (May–July): Head, neck and breast whitish, boldly spotted with blackish markings, which become large irregular blotches on lower breast and flanks; rest of underparts white. Upperparts, including scapulars, tertials and innermost wing-coverts, white with increasing numbers of irregular dark feathers as season progresses; these are buffy-brown, barred black, with black central mark. Uppertail-coverts similar, generally concealing white tail. Rest of wings white. Tail all white. **Adult male non-breeding** (July–October): Head and neck finely speckled black and white. Breast and upperparts greyish or cinnamon-buff over back, rump, scapulars, tertials, inner-wing-coverts and uppertail-coverts, all very finely barred with blackish vermiculations, lacking coarse black markings. Rest of wings, rear underparts and tail white. **Adult female breeding** (May–July): Much more evenly patterned than male, having head, neck, breast, flanks and entire upperparts clearly barred buffy-yellowish and black. Extent of white in wings and tail as male. **Adult female non-breeding** (July–October): Like male non-breeding but several scattered coarser black markings from retained breeding plumage. **Adult male and female winter** (October–April): Almost all white except black primary shafts. **Juvenile:** Ephemeral juvenile stage commences soon after hatching, overall heavily barred black and yellowish-buff, including wings and tail. At 3–4 weeks white primaries develop and wings gradually moult to white during first autumn. First-winter becomes as white as adult, but has dull worn outer two primaries, which are retained throughout winter.

GEOGRAPHICAL VARIATION Slight, but some variation in size, with smaller and darker populations in north and larger greyer birds in south of range. Validity of subspecies questioned, as much variation appears largely clinal.

    L. l. peninsularis Chapman, 1902 occurs in montane Alaska to the Kenai Peninsula (south of Anchorage) and east to Yukon and Mackenzie (W Canada).
    L. l. leucurus (Richardson, 1831) occurs in the Rocky Mountains in British Columbia and adjacent Alberta (Canada).
    L. l. saxatilis Cowan, 1939 occurs on Vancouver I. (Canada).
    L. l. rainierensis Taylor, 1929 occurs in the Cascade Range in Washington (USA).
    L .l. altipetens Osgood, 1901 occurs in the Rocky Mountains, from Montana south to New Mexico (USA).

MEASUREMENTS Length 31–34 cm. Male rather larger. Males: wing 164–194, tail 85–109, weight c.1300. Females: wing 155–192, tail 83–98, weight c.840.

HABITAT At or above tree-line in relatively dry open areas, so although stays near streams, does not usually venture onto montane peatland. Both willow and alder influence its distribution year-round. In winter it feeds on catkins of these trees and those of birch, whereas in summer it feeds on ground vegetation uncovered by snow, namely grasses and herbs etc. The three ptarmigan are sympatric in some parts of North America, with White-tailed generally encountered at higher altitudes.

VOICE Male has a variety of calls, including a 'flight scream' that is a series of four distinct syllables *ku-ku-KII KIIER* uttered during display. The 'ground challenge call' is a series of notes interspersed by clucking sounds *duk-duk-DAAAk-duk-duk* etc. Also a high-pitched chirp when alert, and other calls given as threat (e.g. *buc buc buc*) and softer calls. Female has call similar to 'flight scream' of male and a low-pitched 'growl' *girr*. The alert call comprises high frequency *cucks*.

HABITS Usually in pairs or loose flocks. In pairs during breeding season when both sexes defend own territory: that of male overlaps that of female to large degree. Moves from high-altitude breeding grounds to winter at lower elevations around mid-October, returning mid–late April, though exact timing affected by weather and females tend to arrive in late April or May either alone or in small groups. Males depart their territories in late summer to form loose flocks, though they remain around breeding areas until females have completed incubating. Not territorial in winter, when forms loose single-sex flocks, juveniles more commonly with adult females than adult males. These may contain up to 80 birds. In winter may roost in snow burrows. Feeds predominantly on buds, shoots and catkins of dwarf willow and alder.

BREEDING Predominantly monogamous, with pairs staying close together during breeding season, though some males polygynous. Pair-bonds survive for up to three years. Nest on ground, but situation varies considerably (e.g. in degree of exposure); almost always in snow-free areas. Shallow scrape either among vegetation or in rocky landscape, lined with some plant material and feathers. Clutch size usually 5–6, though up to 9 recorded. Eggs cinnamon with dark brown spots and laid in late May–July. Incubation by female alone lasts 24–26 days.

DISTRIBUTION W North America from C Alaska and Yukon south through Rocky Mountains and coastal British Columbia (including Vancouver) to Washington (south to Mount St Helens) and Montana, south in Wyoming and Colorado to N New Mexico. In north distribution largely continuous, but in Rockies is highly fragmented. Introduced populations in California, Colorado, New Mexico, Oregon and Utah.

STATUS Largely remains numerous and widespread throughout range. Numbers vary, often considerably, over time and between areas, but overall species is thought stable and not to have contracted in range. Probably reasonably secure because its remote habitat is largely undisturbed. Local pressures result from human activities, mainly at lower altitudes, and thus mostly in wintering areas. Developments, including roads and tourist resorts, alter habitat and permit greater human access to previously remote areas. Hunting is not a major problem, but may be an issue in those areas where densities are particularly low.

REFERENCES Braun *et al.* (1993), Johnsgard (1983), Storch (2000).

Genus *LYRURUS*: Black Grouse

Though often absorbed within *Tetrao*, the two species of black grouse form a distinctive pair. Like *Tetrao*, they have quite long, feathered tarsi, but bare toes, and males have extensively black plumage, plus elongated tails of 18 feathers. However, both *Lyrurus* have quite ornate, peculiarly twisted tail feathers and indulge in communal lekking, which differs considerably from the often solitary 'popping' of forest-living capercaillies.

177 BLACK GROUSE
Lyrurus tetrix (Linnaeus, 1758)

Plate 49

Alternative names: Eurasian Black Grouse, Blackcock (male), Greyhen (female).

Now more localised throughout its vast range, this lovely grouse is most readily seen by visiting a communal lek in spring, which makes for a memorable experience.

IDENTIFICATION Usually encountered at open-country borders, such as between heaths and mixed forests, this attractive and distinctive grouse is widespread, though becoming more local across N Eurasia. Breeding male quite unmistakable with white vent, underwing and wing-bar (latter obvious in flight), contrasting with otherwise black plumage and lyre-shaped tail; moults into plumage showing number of female features for short period in late summer. Female brown, vermiculated and barred over entire plumage, and recalls small compact female capercaillie, but underparts evenly barred black and rufous, has distinctly notched tail, and usually quite distinct pale wing-bars in flight. Compare also Caucasian Grouse.

DESCRIPTION *L. t. tetrix*. Medium-sized grouse, male with distinctive long, outwardly curving, blunt-tipped, lyre-shaped tail of 18 feathers that become progressively shorter towards centre. Female has shallow-forked tail of blunt-tipped feathers. Tarsi feathered, but toes bare. Undertail-coverts of male well developed and in both sexes longer than tail centre. Comb (conspicuous only in male) bright red. Bill short and stout, black. Irides dark brown. Toes dark brown; tarsi concealed by brownish feathering. Sexes differ. **Adult male breeding:** Largely black, deepest on neck and breast, glossed blue, becoming more bluish-green on head. Undertail-coverts strikingly white. Belly and flanks dull black, with white feather tips on belly. Wings brownish-black, with white bases to greater coverts; secondaries white with black subterminal band, giving effect of double white bar on closed wing. Underwing-coverts white, often visible at 'shoulder' of closed wing. Tail distinctively lyre-shaped, black with slight gloss; shorter central feathers have white tips. **Adult male 'eclipse'** (June–August): Partial moult in late summer, with newly acquired brownish feathers appearing among black on head and neck, and whitish on throat. Similarly, brownish feathering may also appear on mantle and wing-coverts at this season. **First-winter male:** Resembles adult male but has varying amounts of rufous vermiculations on head, neck and upperparts. Tail feathers not fully developed until late winter. **Adult female:** Crown, nape and ear-coverts rufous, barred blue-black. Chin, throat and rest of underparts rufous-buff, richer rufous on breast; entire underparts barred blackish, these smallest on head- and neck-sides, most spaced on breast, and broadest on flanks and undertail-coverts, the latter with long white tips. Upperparts including wing-coverts blackish, barred rufous and tipped grey; larger wing-coverts have whitish tips. Flight feathers mottled brown, with white bases to inner webs of primaries and white basal halves and tips to secondaries. Tail blackish, closely barred and vermiculated rufous; narrowly tipped grey. A few, presumably old, females may acquire male characteristics. **Juvenile:** Short-lived plumage resembling small version of female, but barred buff (less rufous) and black below, with buff shaft streaks to scapulars and wing-coverts. Lacks whitish bar on mottled brown secondaries and has short, narrow tail feathers. Rapidly moults to first-winter plumage.

GEOGRAPHICAL VARIATION Rather slight and distinctly clinal, with males having blue sheen in west, becoming green sheen in east. Western birds average slightly smaller than those in east and ground colour of female also varies.

L. t. britannicus (Witherby & Lönnberg, 1913) occurs in the British Isles, now chiefly Scotland, Wales and N England; male has slightly bluer gloss than nominate, but female distinctly darker and warmer brown.

L. t. tetrix (Linnaeus, 1758) (includes '*tetrix-fedjuschini*') occurs in continental Europe from

Scandinavia and Alps to N Siberia; described above.
L. t. viridanus (Lorenz, 1891) occurs in SE Russia east to the River Irtysh on W Siberian Plain; male has large white wing patch and greener plumage gloss, while female is paler than other forms.

L. t. tschusii (Johansen, 1898) (includes '*jenissensis*') occurs in S Siberia east of River Irtysh to Lake Baikal; male has brighter azure-blue gloss and darker leg feathering than *mongolicus*, female more boldly mottled and barred.

L. t. mongolicus (Lönnberg, 1891) occurs in C Tien Shan and slopes of Altai north to W Mongolia; male has purplish-blue gloss and larger white wing patch than nominate, while female is buffier, less rufous, and often lacks white edging to wing-coverts.

L. t. ussuriensis (Kohts, 1911) (includes '*baikalensis*' and '*korensis*') occurs from Lake Baikal east to extreme NE China, and adjacent SE Siberia and North Korea; dull, quite oily green tone to male, with white in wing well developed, while female is relatively dull and quite dark brown.

MEASUREMENTS Length: male c.60 cm, female c.45 cm. *L. t. tetrix*. Males: wing 246–291, tail 173–219, weight 1050–1750. Females: wing 214–263, tail 113–131, weight 750–1120.

HABITAT Broad variety of boreal, subarctic and arctic habitats, mainly confined to forest edge, such as ecotone with heath, peatland or land that is not intensively managed. Habitat requirements more generalised than most grouse. Open woodland interspersed with glades and other clearings, or early successional stages most used, with numbers lower, or is absent where canopy becomes closed or tree cover dense. Younger, more open stands often preferred to denser, older ones. In general, any habitat that resembles forest edge or young forest is used.

VOICE Both sexes give loud calls; male advertisement being described as a musical and resonant dove-like bubbling, transcribed as *rrooo-oo-rroo-rroo*. Audible at quite some distance and can be difficult to pinpoint. Loudest female call a harsh repetitive *tchuk tchuk*, often given from a perch. Both are mainly given in spring, but can be heard in many other months. Male also emits variety of hissing calls: a harsh *tsshuu-IIISH* or *whush-EE*; a more drawn-out version of same made in flight, *tchu-u-u* or *chorrrrr*; a long 'call-hiss' given mainly at lek, but also elsewhere and throughout year; and a hiss that appears to indicate apprehension, such as when fighting. Several different calls given from territories on lek, including 'soft nasal' *kok* or *ka* when squaring-up to another male, which varies considerably during confrontation. Also calls to warn of predators etc., including a *guck guck* when predator approaching on ground and a *tuett-tuett-tuett-tuett* when from air.

HABITS Usually in groups year-round; flock size varying throughout range, often related to habitat, but males typically in larger groups than females, as overall, flocks largely single sex. Up to 1000 recorded in birch woods in Russia and 200–500 apparently not unusual in cold months. Flocks form in autumn, when broods band together, and in some areas females and young males flock together, while older males flock separately. Some are encountered singly, either most of time, or for at least part of day throughout year. Predominantly sedentary, though occasional long movements reported and, in some areas, birds undertake short regular migrations. Most striking behavioural trait is that males gather at dawn leks in spring; uttering low bubbling and whooshing cries, they jump and spar with drooped wings and tail elevated to expose white undertail-coverts. Females visit lek to select mate. Many leks persist year-round and number of males varies from a mean of less than ten in some areas in west of the range to more than 150 in parts of Russia. Leks nearly always sited in same place year after year. Lekking activity most pronounced in spring and autumn. Forages usually on ground in spring, summer and autumn, but in trees and shrubs during winter. Readily perches in trees and on walls. Usually shy and wary. Flushes with rather silent wingbeats, often flying quite high when well underway. Hybridisation frequently recorded between Black Grouse and capercaillies, the resultant male offspring being known as 'Rackelhens'. Hybridisation also recorded with Red and Willow Grouse, and even Common Pheasant.

BREEDING Promiscuous, with females visiting leks at which males display for at least part of each day. Female mostly nests on ground amid low cover. Slight lined depression constructed by female alone, which also assumes all incubation duties. Clutch size usually 6–11, with more than 15 eggs thought to be result of two females laying in same nest. Eggs oval and glossy, usually buffy with pale red-/yellow-brown spots. Given broad distribution, season variable, with earliest eggs laid in late April and latest in June. Incubation lasts 25–27 days and eggs hatch synchronously.

DISTRIBUTION Widely distributed in forest regions of N Palearctic. Range extends from British Isles (chiefly Scotland and Wales), Scandinavia and E France east through Europe, south to N Italy, Austria, Slovenia and Slovakia (plus relict populations just persisting in N Romania and perhaps Albania), N Ukraine, N Kazakhstan, through Siberia, N Mongolia, N China to Amurland (Far East Russia) and North Korea. At both eastern and western extremes considerable range contraction has left fragmented and declining populations. Extinct now in Turkey (formerly Istanbul area) and Hungary and on verge of extinction in Netherlands, Belgium, Denmark and North Korea.

STATUS Overall population thought stable, though locally may vary considerably on annual basis. For example, in some northern areas, 4–10-year cycles are commonly observed. However, where populations are fragmented, such as in W and C Europe (where it is listed in several national Red Data books), numbers have declined in 20th century and many lowland populations have been lost during last 30 years. Major threat, at least in European range, is changing land use, as heaths and moors are 'improved' by drainage for agricultural purposes. Abandonment of other 'extensive' practices, such as low-intensity summer grazing and grass cutting has seen other suitable areas become less suitable for Black Grouse. Situation less clear in Siberian part of range, but it appears that most cause for concern is in Amurland and adjacent North Korea where declining habitat quality or outright loss is leaving surviving populations small and fragmented as in W Europe; such small populations are inherently at risk.

REFERENCES Bannerman (1963), Cramp & Simmons (1980), Dement'ev & Gladkov (1952), de Juana (1994), Potapov (1985), Storch (2000).

178 CAUCASIAN GROUSE
Lyrurus mlokosiewiczi (Taczanowski, 1875)   Plate 49

Alternative name: Caucasian Black Grouse.

Distinctive grouse of the Caucasus mountains, with one of the most restricted ranges of all grouse species.

IDENTIFICATION Confined to the Caucasus region, where it is quite unmistakable. Generally encountered in alpine scrub and meadows above tree-line in summer, lower into forest in winter. Almost all-black male distinctive in range. Differs from Black in lacking white wing-bar and vent and in having longer, more slender tail. In flight, white underwing-coverts can be striking, and often appear as a white 'shoulder' spot on ground. Female lacks wing-bars of Black, has slightly longer and more square-ended tail and more finely vermiculated underparts, becoming brownish on belly and under-tail-coverts. Displaying birds, with erect tail look like black 'hoovers' moving about lekking site.

DESCRIPTION Medium-sized grouse, but relatively smaller bodied than Black Grouse. Male has distinctive long tail (feathers longer, narrower and have more pointed tips than Black Grouse), the outermost feathers curving downward and outwards toward tip, the innermost much shorter but longer than undertail-coverts. Female has longer and more shallow-forked tail than Black Grouse. Tarsi feathered, but toes bare. Comb (conspicuous only in male) bright red. Bill short and stout, black (weaker than in Black Grouse). Irides dark brown. Toes dark brown; tarsi concealed by brownish feathering. Sexes differ. **Adult male** (apparently similar year-round): Largely dull black, feather tips slightly glossed bluish-green. Wings dark brown; flight feathers greyer brown. Underwing-coverts strikingly white, often showing as tiny white spot at 'shoulder' of closed wing. Tail distinctively shaped, black with slightly browner inner webs on underside. **First-winter male:** Resembles female (unlike Black Grouse at this stage, which is more like adult male), but differs in more rufous-brown upperparts, including wing-coverts, with smaller and finer black feather markings and whitish feather tips. Tail dark brown, irregularly barred and vermiculated rufous, narrowly tipped white. Underparts darker brownish, vermiculated rufous and grey, especially dark brown on central underparts. Has more pronounced whitish edges to flight feathers than adult female. Adult male feathers appear from November, by first spring much as adult male but some brownish feathering scattered over head, neck and wing-coverts. **Adult female:** Crown, nape and ear-coverts dark brown, barred rufous-buff, and tipped whitish. Chin and throat whitish, freckled darker, becoming brownish on rest of underparts, but closely vermiculated grey and irregularly spotted and scaled dark brown; belly centre darker brown. Upperparts including wing-coverts blackish-brown, barred rufous and vermiculated grey. Flight feathers mottled brown, with secondaries tipped whitish, but lacking extensive pale bar often shown by Black Grouse. Tail warm brown, closely barred darker brown and weakly tipped whitish. **Juvenile:** Short-lived plumage resembling small version of female but more rufous-brown, less greyish. Pale tips to greater coverts form whitish wing-bar. Rapidly moults to first-winter plumage. First-winter female very similar to adult female, though tail has broader dark bars, and markings on upperparts finer and more regular.

GEOGRAPHICAL VARIATION Monotypic.

MEASUREMENTS Length: male c.53 cm, female 38 cm. Males: wing 180–220, tail 199–222, weight 820–1005. Females: wing 170–210, tail 147, weight 712–820.

HABITAT Forests and meadows of Caucasus and transition between two habitats at 1500–3000 m. In winter, descends lower (reported as low as 700 m), due to snow cover, and in summer emerges from forest onto alpine and subalpine meadows above treeline, where it occurs within shrubby vegetation (dwarf willow, birch and rhododendron).

VOICE Unlike Black Grouse, remarkably silent; wingbeats of male audible in display and male also snaps bill during confrontations. Female reported to utter an excited cackle.

HABITS Usually in groups in autumn and winter, which tend to be much smaller than Black Grouse flocks. Few quantitative data on flock-size changes during year; other than when breeding, more than three are rarely seen together away from lek. Leks of up to 30 recorded but norm is 6–12 males, which display with flutter jumps, exposing white underwing and walk with tail raised high. Almost entirely sedentary, though some altitudinal migration as snow forces birds to lower altitudes in autumn and winter, when roosts under bushes or among rocks, and even in hollows in snow, flying directly to them to avoid leaving tell-tale footprints. Unlike Black Grouse, rarely perches high in trees. Tends to feed in early morning and late afternoon; favoured diet includes shoots and buds of willow and birch, catkins and juniper berries and needles; very few insects taken by adults, though young feed almost exclusively on them for first two weeks of life.

BREEDING Promiscuous, with females visiting leks, where males display for at least part of each day, though solitary males encountered away from these sites. Leks typically in open on south-facing slopes above montane forests; males display in spring and autumn. Larger leks comprise 10–15 males, but up to 30 reported. Leks nearly always sited in same place each year. Female mostly nests on ground under cover, making shallow hollow lined with feathers and grass. Lays in May and clutch size usually 6, though as many as 12 eggs recorded. Eggs oval and glossy, usually pale buff, spotted red-brown. Incubation 20–25 days and eggs hatch synchronously.

DISTRIBUTION Restricted to Caucasus, chiefly within Great Caucasus range of Georgia and adjacent extreme S Russia. Also Lesser Caucasus, extending through Armenia, Azerbaijan, into NE Turkey and just entering NW Iran.

STATUS Compared to other grouse, current status and recent trends poorly understood. Listed in Red Data books of all range states and may be at risk: its rather small range suggests it should be carefully watched. Though still locally numerous and reason-ably widespread, it is thought to have dramatically declined at lower elevations since 1930s. Some areas have been lost at fringes of its range and increasing habitat degradation, especially of lower montane slopes, through intensive and higher sheep grazing, in summer pastures, has left large areas unsuitable. In addition to deteriorating habitat quality, the disturbance associated with these human activities is cause for concern. Feral dogs are now common around some larger settlements and may even predate grouse. Sheepdogs belonging to graziers are also reported to take young birds. Overall population estimated at c.70,000 birds in the Greater Caucasus in 1984, and 500 in Lesser Caucasus in 1974, but considered to have declined since. Recent fieldwork in NE Turkey has indicated a quite healthy extant population, with 138 males counted at 33 leks in 1993; c.100 birds are thought present in Iran, with 1500–2000 in Azerbaijan.

REFERENCES Cramp & Simmons (1980), Johnsgard (1983), Potapov (1985), Tucker & Heath (1994), Storch (2000).

Genus *Tetrao*: capercaillies

A genus of two species of huge forest grouse, males being the largest members of the entire family, though females are considerably smaller than males. Like black grouse they have quite long, feathered tarsi and bare toes, while males have 18 long, broad tail feathers, which are erected and fanned in display. Though the two capercaillies replace each other geographically across the Palearctic there is considerable overlap between them in C Siberia; however, they are largely ecologically separated and direct competition between them is probably minimal.

179 WESTERN CAPERCAILLIE
Tetrao urogallus Linnaeus, 1758
Plate 50

Alternative names: Capercaillie, Eurasian Capercaillie.

The largest grouse, a huge bird of mature forests. Its interesting common name derives from Gaelic, but opinions differ as to whether it translates as 'horse of the woods', accounted for by the clip-clop or popping sounds produced in display, or 'old man of the woods', with reference to its great size and ragged beard!

IDENTIFICATION Huge grouse of ancient, especially coniferous, forests. Male a massive turkey-like bird, 30% larger than female, dark in plumage (some populations have whitish flanks and belly), with ivory bill, shaggy throat and broad tail. Old males larger, with broader tails than younger birds. Female resembles larger version of female Black Grouse, but has more contrastingly marked underparts, varying in colour according to subspecies, but typically bright rufous breast contrasts with whitish ground colour to rest of underparts; tail also relatively longer, more boldly barred, and rounded, not cleft, at tip; in flight it lacks pale wing-bar often shown by female Black Grouse. Even massive males fly through trees in dense forest with remarkable agility, and sometimes high above forest when moving between valleys or crossing lakes; at such times appear very dark, with contrasting white underwing (and sometimes belly) and long thick neck and tail; pale bill can be surprisingly obvious when viewed against dark background. In far east of range it overlaps with similar Black-billed Capercaillie (which see).

DESCRIPTION *T. u. urogallus.* Very large (male) or large (female) grouse, male with somewhat elongated neck hackles and throat feathers; latter form ragged 'beard'. Male has long, rather broad, rounded tail of 18 (sometimes up to 24) square-tipped feathers (that become progressively broader with age). Female has shorter, narrower tail feathers. Tarsi feathered, but toes bare. Tail-coverts of male well developed, especially upper, which conceal basal two-thirds of tail, even more in female. Comb (conspicuous only in male) bright red. Bill large and stout, especially in male, yellowish-white to pale yellow (male), or grey-brown (female). Irides dark brown. Toes dark brown; tarsi concealed by brownish feathering. Sexes differ. **Adult male:** Head and neck slate-grey, darker on throat and foreneck; weakly vermiculated paler grey. Throat hackles tipped green. Breast metallic green or blue, according to light. Underparts below breast blackish-brown, some feathers with green tips, others, on belly and lower flanks, have variable white flecking. Wings dull dark brown, primaries with whitish shaft streaks. Underwing-coverts white, appearing as patch on shoulder by closed wing. Mantle, rump and uppertail-coverts brownish-grey, greyest on uppertail-coverts; longest tail-coverts have narrow whitish tips. Tail greyish-black, basal three-quarters vermiculated grey, and subterminal band of white marbling. For short period in late summer, head and throat feathers more vermiculated pale grey and throat-sides have shorter dark brown feathers. **First-winter male:** Resembles adult male but smaller, and has narrower and more uniform tail. Throat hackles undeveloped and lacks metallic blue-green gloss on breast. Varying rufous vermiculations on feathers of head, neck and upperparts. Tail feathers not fully developed until late winter. **Adult female:** Crown, nape, neck-sides and mantle orange-buff, barred blue-black, feathers finely edged whitish. Throat and chest bright rusty-buff, with sparse black scaling on breast of some, and rear underparts paler orange-buff, barred black, feathers with broad whitish tips. Mantle, back, scapulars and wing-coverts blackish, with orange-buff barring, and some scapulars and median coverts have white terminal spots. Uppertail-coverts orange-buff, irregularly barred black and tipped whitish. Flight feathers dark brown, mottled rufous, secondaries with narrow white tips. Tail rufous, narrowly barred black, tipped white. Some, presumably old, females may acquire male characteristics. First-winter female similar but buff of head and neck paler, more yellowish; tail feathers narrower and less bright than adult. **Juvenile:** Short-lived stage resembling small version of female, but upperparts and wing-coverts have buff shaft streaks and triangular spot at feather tip. Tail shorter and dull rufous, with buff tip. Juvenile female more coarsely barred black than juvenile male, which is washed grey on uppertail-coverts. Rapidly moults to first-winter plumage, but down often remains on head while rest of bird is as first-winter.

GEOGRAPHICAL VARIATION Like several other grouse there is considerable individual and clinal variation, especially in colour saturation and extent of white on belly of males, and degree of pale spotting on upperparts and colour tones of females. Interpreting these variations has raised much discussion: Vaurie (1965) considered only three races valid, a dark western nominate form, a paler southern and eastern form *taczanowskii*, linked by a very extensive intergradation zone, and *aquitanicus* (the Cantabrian population was not separated until later), but Potapov (1985) recognised 12 subspecies, a treatment amended slightly by Stepanyan (1990), which is basis for that followed here.

T. u. cantabricus Castroviejo, 1967 occurs in the Cantabrian Mountains (Spain); smaller than most populations, except next, and in its limited range favours broad-leaf woodland, with holly as evergreen component.

T. u. aquitanicus Ingram, 1915 occurs in the Pyrenees (France/Spain); smaller than most other western birds, and females overall much darker and more heavily barred, also has buff, rather than whitish underparts.

T. u. major Brehm, 1831 (includes *rudolfi* and *hiomanus*) occurs in Germany and the Alps east to the E Carpathian Mountains and W Belarus and south through Balkans to Macedonia and Bulgaria; extensively dark on underparts and upperparts, with warm brown tone to male wings.

T. u. urogallus Linnaeus, 1758 (includes *lonnbergi*, *karelicus*, *pleskei* and *lugens*) occurs in Scotland, Scandinavia, Belarus, and east over W Siberia; described above.

T. u. kureikensis Buturlin, 1927 (includes *obsoletus*) occurs in N Russia from River Onega at c.38°E in west, east to River Lena at east end of C Siberian Plain; rather dark with extensive white patches on belly.

T. u. volgensis Buturlin, 1907 occurs in C and SE Russia; male quite pale grey on head, neck and rump and has extensive grey-and-white marbling on rear underparts.

T. u. uralensis Menzbier, 1887 (includes *grisescens*) occurs in WC Russia, from S Urals to Barnaul on south edge of W Siberian Plain; similar to *taczanowskii* but even paler.

T. u. taczanowskii Stejneger, 1885 occurs in C Siberia in Russia south to the Altai in E Kazakhstan and NW Mongolia; male quite pale grey on head, neck and rump, with extensive white on belly, and ground colour of female yellowish-brown above and whitish below.

MEASUREMENTS Length: male 83–90 cm, 59–64 cm female. Large male can be up to 40% larger than female. *T. u. urogallus.* Males; wing 350–420, tail 291–322, weight 3300–6500. Females: wing 286–320, tail 167–194, weight 1500–2500.

HABITAT Primarily mature coniferous forest and woodland, but also mixed coniferous–deciduous woodland and, in some areas (e.g. Cantabria), deciduous woodlands. Ideally, prefers extensive forests, forming mosaic with peatlands supporting typical bog plants, such as bilberry and heather, and young stands of trees. Old shady forest is most used, preferably with neither very open nor wholly closed canopy, and undergrowth not very dense. Altitudinal band varies through range, but ascends to 2000 m in Pyrenees.

VOICE Male emits several calls. Song is rather complex series of sounds (see Cramp & Simmons 1980 for details). Briefly, this commences with a low-intensity 'tapping-phase' (disyllabic clicks *TE-lip*, *Kikop* etc.), followed by 'drum-roll phase', when clicks uttered rapidly and finally a quick gurgling 'whetting-phase', which sounds like a strangled squealing *tzjiTHEthethe tzjiTHEthethe*. Males of western populations also emit popping sound during 'drum-roll'. Harsh and loud *koor KRERK koroor* given when challenged or otherwise agitated, and some hissing towards rivals and predators. Female most vocal in spring before emerging from roost. When arriving at male display areas gives a weak bray and while observing displays emits a chuckling cackle *kok-kok* (recalling Common Pheasant). Variety of other calls given at display ground and also to young.

HABITS Generally shy and elusive, most easily found in early spring when males lekking. Encountered singly or in groups. Adult male usually alone, whereas as broods disband in autumn, females and young form flocks of up to ten, which may persist through winter. In display, male struts like turkey-cock with broad dark tail fanned like turkey, head and neck erect, uttering peculiar 'popping' sound. Some solitary individuals known to become very aggressive, even attacking humans and cars in full display! Though males often display alone, they also do so collectively and are perhaps slightly less territorial at such sites than typical lek species. Females visit leks for only short time and peak activity may last only 3–4 weeks. However, less intense male display may persist for several months from midwinter to late summer. Predominantly sedentary, though patchy food supplies may enforce local movements in winter. When provoked to flight, rarely flies very high, just above canopy being usual maximum, but in instances of occasional (possibly irruptive) long flights, may fly quite high. Forages usually on ground in spring to autumn and in tree canopy during winter; females even walking among small branches. Feeds almost entirely on needles and seeds of various conifers, but summer and autumn diet varied by leaves and shoots of other plants, and when available of berries. Occasionally hybridises with Black Grouse.

BREEDING Promiscuous (or briefly polygynous when male may obtain harem). Female nests on ground amid dense vegetation or under other shelter. Shallow depression barely lined with plant material, constructed by female alone, which also assumes sole incubation duties. Clutch usually 7–11, but up to 16 or more probably result of two females laying in same nest. Eggs oval and glossy, off-yellow with some buff marks. Onset of laying varies with both latitude and altitude, starting in mid- to late April in Scotland and C Europe, but May over much of range and may continue until June in most northerly populations. Incubation 24–26 days and eggs hatch synchronously.

DISTRIBUTION Northern forests of Eurasia, to tree limit of taiga of Scandinavia and Siberia. Except isolated populations in Scotland (where reintroduced following extinction of native population), Cantabrian Mountains (Spain) and Pyrenees, more or less continuously distributed through montane and hill forests of C and E Europe, west to French Alps, south to Italian Alps, and SE Europe, south and east to Romania, Albania, Macedonia and Bulgaria. Extends from S Poland (also present extreme north) and Belarus through N Ukraine and south to limit of forest in C Siberia, reaching N Kazakhstan, W Mongolia and extreme NW China. Extends east to beyond Lake Baikal, reaching c.120°E.

STATUS Occupies bulk of huge historical distribution and, in many places, probably still common. However, at eastern and western extremes considerable range contraction has occurred, resulting in local extinctions and remaining populations being increasingly fragmented. For example, extirpations in W and C Europe (Portugal, Ireland, Belgium, Hungary and Denmark), leaving remnant populations in adjoining countries. Further north, in Scandinavia, extensive tree clearance has brought decrease in numbers. East of there numbers currently healthy through bulk of range. Given its reasonably specific habitat requirements, it is at risk from forestry practices that affect its habitat either within forest (e.g. alteration of structure), or at larger scales in which mosaic of preferred habitats altered (Storch 2000). Where Man is active in capercaillie landscapes, effects many and varied, ranging from birds striking deer fences (possibly largest cause of mortality in Scotland) and high-tension power lines to increased disturbance as habitats opened for tourism.

REFERENCES Bannerman (1963), Cramp & Simmons (1980), Potapov (1985), Storch (2000).

---

180 BLACK-BILLED CAPERCAILLIE
Tetrao parvirostris Bonaparte, 1856   Plate 50

Alternative names: Small-billed/Spotted/Rock Capercaillie.

The eastern cousin of the well-known Western Capercaillie; despite their similarity the two are sympatric over a large area of C Siberia.

IDENTIFICATION Larch and birch forests of E Siberia, where it replaces Western Capercaillie, but the two overlap in EC Siberia. Male easily distinguished from Western in being much darker (particularly in south of overlap zone, where Western has whitish underparts), with smaller black bill and has bold white spots at tips of uppertail-coverts and on wings. Female close to female Western, but greyer above and has more uniformly scaled underparts, lacking unmarked rusty breast area, and bolder white spots on wings. Hybridisation probably not infrequent in overlap region, particularly where habitat zones meet. Isolated populations on Kamchatka distinctly less heavy, darker grey than 'mainland' forms, but specific differences between these and Western exaggerated by even larger white markings in both sexes of Kamchatka subspecies, though confusion with Western not an issue, as it is the only capercaillie in this region.

DESCRIPTION *T. p. parvirostris.* Compared to Western Capercaillie, male Black-billed slightly smaller, with relatively smaller bill, slightly longer tail and shorter 'beard'. Females of the two similar in structure. Comb (conspicuous only in male) bright red. Bill black, or blackish (female). Irides dark brown. Toes dark brown; tarsi concealed by brownish feathering. Sexes differ. **Adult male:** Head, neck and breast-sides black, glossed purplish-blue, becoming glossed blue-green on chest and upper breast. Rear underparts blackish-brown, with scattered white spots and feather edges. Undertail-coverts blackish with large white tips. Wings dull dark brown, scapulars and larger wing-coverts patterned with large white spots. Secondaries have narrow whitish tips and primaries whitish shaft streaks. Underwing-coverts white, appearing as patch on shoulder by closed wing. Mantle, rump and upper-tail-coverts dark brownish-grey; longest tail-coverts with large white tips. Tail blackish, with even blacker terminal band. **First-winter male:** Poorly documented, but presumably differs much like Western Capercaillie of same age. **Adult female:** Crown, nape, neck-sides and mantle cinnamon-buff, barred black, feathers finely edged whitish. Throat buff, speckled black; rest of underparts barred black and cinnamon-buff, with whitish feather edges. Mantle, back, scapulars and wing-coverts blackish, with buff barring and greyish-white edges; scapulars and median coverts have relatively conspicuous white terminal spots. Rump and uppertail-coverts buff, irregularly barred black and tipped greyish-white. Flight feathers dark brown, mottled rufous, secondaries with narrow white tips. Central feathers chiefly blackish, the rest of tail rufous, narrowly barred black and tipped white. **Juvenile:** Poorly documented, but apparently much as Western Capercaillie.

GEOGRAPHICAL VARIATION Several races described, differing in size, strength of white markings and colour saturation. Much of this due to individual and clinal variation. Potapov (1985) recognised only three forms, while Stepanyan (1990) permitted just two (absorbing *stegmanni* within nominate); certainly the Kamchatka form is strikingly different from the nominate.

T. p. parvirostris 6 Bonaparte, 1856 (includes *kolymensis, sachalinensis, macrurus, janensis* and *turensis*) occurs over most of the range; described above.

T. p. stegmanni Potapov, 1985 occurs over southwest part of range including environs of Lake Baikal, south to Mongolia); male slimmer and longer tailed than nominate, with relatively larger white spots on uppertail-coverts.

T. p. kamschaticus Kittlitz, 1878 occurs on Kamchatka Peninsula; both sexes average smaller than nominate and are considerably paler, above and below, with much larger white markings on wings and uppertail-coverts, and male less glossy blackish, more dark grey, on head, neck and underparts.

MEASUREMENTS Length: male 89–97 cm, female 69–75 cm. *T. p. kamschaticus.* Males: wing 382–402, tail 248–345, weight c.3350–4580. Females: wing 298–324, tail 210–235, weight 1700–2200.

HABITAT Largely confined to larch woodlands in riverine lowlands and mountains of E Asian taiga, from open birch woods of northern taiga to forest–steppe in south. In east, on Kamchatka Peninsula, occurs predominantly in birch stands.

VOICE Song louder than Western Capercaillie and consists of rhythmic clicks, some similar to those of former and others that are resonant. Together, sounds like *tack-tack-tack*, rolling into a climactic *tr-r-rack*, usually lasting 5–7 seconds, sometimes up to 12. In good weather, song audible over up to 0.5 km. In aggressive situations less rhythmic.

HABITS Much as Western Capercaillie based on available information. Males form leks, though these are rather loose aggregations compared to other species. In some areas forms winter flocks, but these considered relatively temporary. Movements between seasons recorded, presumably in response to food availability. Interestingly, 'prunes' young trees at certain times of year, which results in trees growing outwards rather than upwards, turning surrounding area into 'capercaillie garden'. Habitat use varies seasonally according to food supply, more open areas favoured in warmer months and trees and shrubs favoured in winter. Larch needles and buds form important component of diet, which also includes birch buds and leaves and, especially in autumn, variety of berries.

BREEDING Promiscuous, with males gathering in leks, visited by females. Eggs laid May–June in shallow scrape lined with any available material, such as conifer needles and feathers. Clutch 6–7 eggs. Incubation c.20–25 days, young noted as late as the end of July.

DISTRIBUTION E Siberia. Reaches western limit in vicinity of Yenisey Basin, at 85–90°E, but extends across entire taiga belt of E Siberia, north to limit of forest (approximately the Arctic Circle), east to Anadyr River (E Siberia) and Kamchatka. South it reaches western environs of Lake Baikal, the Khangai and Kentei ranges of N Mongolia, the Great Khingan range of Heilongjiang (NE China) and Russian Far East (including Sakhalin). Distribution largely defined by the larch *Larix gmelinii.*

STATUS Like many taiga species, generally sparsely distributed throughout range. Global-scale trends largely unknown, though presumably its fate is intricately bound to that of larch forests of E Asia taiga. In some areas, increasing human pressure is causing problems, principally in opening-up forested areas, leading to greater access to its habitat. Unsurprisingly, this is a more significant problem at the southern fringe of its range than in more inhospitable northern areas. One consequence is increased hunting pressure; it has been suggested that concentrations of males at leks provide opportunities for hunting that may be implicated in some sharp population declines.

REFERENCES Andreev (1979), Dement'ev & Gladkov (1967), Johnsgard (1983), Storch (2000).

Genus *TETRASTES*: hazel grouse

Both *Tetrastes* are among the smallest grouse; they have short ruffled forecrowns, tiny bills, lack a prominent comb, have cryptically patterned plumages, barred graduated tails of 16 feathers and relatively small feet, with bare slender toes. These two Old World forest species are often included in *Bonasa*, with the similar but larger Ruffed Grouse of North America. Despite superficial similarities, members of the two genera differ strongly in behaviour, *Tetrastes* forming monogamous pair-bonds and lacking elaborate plumage adornments or indulging in the outlandish displays for which *Bonasa* is renowned.

Alternative name: Hazelhen.

One of the most widespread grouse, inhabiting forests from France to Japan, but an extremely frustrating bird to observe well in its densely-wooded environment.

IDENTIFICATION Coniferous and mixed forests with undergrowth of N and E Europe and Siberia east to the Pacific. This shy forest grouse is difficult to observe, being generally first seen, when flushed, as a partridge-like bird with pale grey rim to barred tail whirring away between trunks of close-growing forest trees. Sometimes perches in trees following short flight. Best located by listening for distinctive, very high-pitched thin whistle (not unlike dog-whistle) and then patiently tracking source. Over most of huge range no comparable species, but in E Siberia beware superficially similar Siberian Spruce Grouse (which see for differences), but latter lacks slight crest and broad white malar stripe extending onto forehead, clear whitish shoulder stripe and whitish ground colour to irregularly scalloped flank pattern, all typical of Hazel Grouse. See also Severtzov's Grouse.

DESCRIPTION *T. b. bonasia.* Plump, rather short-tailed small grouse, with little difference in size between sexes. Crown feathers somewhat elongated, forming obvious crest when alarmed. Tarsi feathered to base of toes. Middle toe distinctly elongated and slender. Larger uppertail-coverts conceal basal half of tail. Tail graduated, usually of 16 feathers. Comb inconspicuous (most visible in male) and red. Bill very short, black. Irides dark brown. Feet greyish-black. Sexes differ. **Adult male:** Crown, ear-coverts, neck, nape and mantle greyish-brown, barred black. Small white streak behind eye. Bold white malar stripe on throat-sides, almost encircling black throat, crossing lores to meet on forehead. Less-defined whitish line extends from lower malar towards mantle-sides. Chin and throat black. Lower breast and underparts whitish, irregularly scaled black and rufous. Undertail-coverts brownish, with long white tips. Scapulars grey, tipped white and patterned rufous and black on inner webs. Wing-coverts grey, larger feathers have white spot at tip, others edged buff or mottled rufous, black and buff. Flight feathers grey-brown, secondaries narrowly tipped white. Rump and uppertail-coverts grey, with dark shaft streaks. Tail vermiculated brownish-grey, with blackish subterminal band and whitish tip to all but central pair of feathers, which are vermiculated greyish throughout. In summer (July–September) assumes drabber 'eclipse' plumage, with duller head pattern and black throat obscured by whitish feather edges. **Adult female:** Dull version of male, having black of throat and white malar stripe obscured by buffy feather fringes. Underparts more closely patterned than male. **Juvenile:** Short-lived stage that resembles small version of female but has throat whitish and upperparts more rufous in tone, with buffy shaft streaks. Lacks white spots on scapulars and blackish subterminal tail band of adult. By first-autumn, plumage almost inseparable from adult in field.

GEOGRAPHICAL VARIATION Complexity compounded by two colour morphs, grey and rufous, over much of range. Some variation clinal, but not throughout range. Examples of clinal variation include those from N Scandinavia and Russia, which are larger and greyer than populations to south, and tawny-coloured birds becoming richer from east to west. Overall, these characters appear to vary most: size and depth of brown and grey tones. In some areas, e.g. SE Europe, considerable individual variation also exists. As in other widespread grouse, opinions differ as to number of subspecies. Various patterns have produced differing interpretations as to number and composition, e.g. contrast W Palearctic subspecies listed below, based on Potapov (1985) with those admitted by Cramp and Simmons (1980).

T. b. styriacus (von Jordan & Schiebel, 1944) (includes *horicei* and *carpathicus*) occurs in Jura Mountains on Swiss–French border (perhaps also Pyrenees) through Alps and Hungary to Slovakia and S Poland.

T. b. rhenana (Kleinschmidt, 1917) occurs in NE France and Luxembourg to Belgium and W Germany.

T. b. rupestris (Brehm, 1831) occurs in Germany to mountains on Polish–Czech border.

T. b. schiebeli (Kleinschmidt, 1943) occurs in the Balkans (Slovenia south to Greece and Bulgaria).

T. b. volgensis Buturlin, 1916 occurs in parts of Poland and Ukraine east to mid-Russia.

T. b. bonasia (Linnaeus, 1758) (includes *gryseiventris* and *grassmanni*) occurs in S Scandinavia east to the Urals.

T. b. griseonota Salomonsen, 1947 occurs in N Sweden.

T. b. sibiricus Buturlin, 1916 (*septentrionalis* is synonym) occurs from the Urals east to E Siberia and Mongolia, with one record from Nei Mongol (China).

T. b. kolymensis Buturlin, 1916 occurs in E Siberia, from the Verkhoyanskiy Mountains to the Sea of Okhotsk.

T. b. amurensis Riley, 1916 (*gilacorum* is a synonym, includes *ussuriensis* and *coreensis*) occurs in Amurland and Ussuriland (extreme SE Russia), Nei Mongol (rarely also Hebei) in China and North Korea.

T. b. yamashinai Momiyama, 1928 occurs on Sakhalin (Russia).

T. b. vicinitas Riley, 1916 occurs on Hokkaido (Japan).

MEASUREMENTS Length 35–40 cm, female only slightly smaller. *T. b. bonasia.* Males: wing 160–176, tail 112–128, weight 305–470. Females: wing 159–168, tail 107–114, weight 307–422.

HABITAT Usually in mixed deciduous–coniferous forest in boreal, temperate and montane zones. Appears to have very specific requirements for habitat structure, requiring relatively dense cover up to c.2 m tall. Given this, it occurs in habitats as diverse as ancient forests and managed deciduous or coniferous forests of varying stages. Avoids open areas.

VOICE Male advertisement call a high-pitched sound usually audible only at close range: a whistled *(t)seeeeee-(t)see-(t)see* repeated up to nine times. Varies in length of notes and pitch of each. Also whirrs wings, audible up to 100 m away. If another male appears in territory, male emits a 'challenge call', usually from perch, which is a sharp *srit srit*. Female gives a few low-pitched calls, including a distraction call, which is a melodious *piih-tettettettett*. Both sexes call *plit plit* or *pitt pitt pitt* in alarm.

HABITS Forms monogamous pair-bonds and thus typically encountered alone, in pairs or family groups. Male gives territorial whistles from prominent stump or rock, with tail spread and wings drooped; indulges in wing-whirring and short jumps in display. Occasional winter flocks reported. Coveys disband in autumn. Tends to roost in trees, not far above ground, except on coldest nights when roosts within cover on ground, or in holes dug in snow. In winter, when snow is deepest, feeds mainly in trees and close proximity to food trees, e.g. alder, birch and hazel, very important. In summer, forages mostly on ground, feeding on buds, shoots, seeds and berries of broad range of ground plants. Though almost entirely sedentary, some local movements recorded, probably related to food availability.

BREEDING Monogamous. Male claims territories in autumn when covey disbands and pairs form, though some females may spend winter roaming. In spring male territorial activity increases. Lays between late March and May in C Europe and slightly later in Scandinavia and N Siberia, where extends into June. Female alone responsible for constructing nest, which is a shallow hollow in ground, lined with grass and leaves. Usually sited in cover or under shelter, such as at foot of tree or under fallen log, and is not easily found. Clutch usually 7–11 glossy oval eggs, yellow-brown and usually lightly speckled with red-brown. Incubation 23–27 days, usually 25, and male often leaves territory during this period.

DISTRIBUTION Throughout much of Palearctic. From E France (with tiny relict population in Pyrenees) and S Belgium east through C and SE Europe (south to Italian Alps, Macedonia and marginally Greece). Main population from Norway east across taiga of Scandinavia and Siberia to Kolyma Basin and Sea of Okhotsk, including Sakhalin. Also Japan (Hokkaido) and reaches south to C Korea, NE China, N Mongolia and extreme NE Kazakhstan. Range has contracted in some areas, perhaps best documented in C and W Europe, including historically.

STATUS Despite some reverses, still occurs throughout vast majority of recently occupied range and is generally common. In areas where human population encroaching on forests, e.g. C Europe, is retreating to upper montane slopes. In C Europe many populations now scattered and small; thus while globally not at risk, local concerns exist (e.g. long extinct in Spain but recently rediscovered in French Pyrenees). Elsewhere, large-scale forest loss has wrought local extinctions in parts of China and Mongolia. Presumably its strict habitat structure requirement makes it sensitive to changes in forest practices, let alone clear-cutting. In Japan, sharp fall in numbers during 1970s, which coincided with rapid increase in number of Red Foxes *Vulpes vulpes*. Overall, major problem is change in forest habitat. Due to its very specific habitat structure requirements, any changes in management practices almost inevitably impact upon the species.

REFERENCES Bergmann *et al.* (1996), Cramp & Simmons (1980), Fujimaki (1995), Johnsgard (1983), Nechaev (1991), Potapov (1985), Potapov & Flint (1989), Storch (2000).

---

182 SEVERTZOV'S GROUSE
Tetrastes sewerzowi Przhevalski, 1876   Plate 51

Alternative names: Black-breasted or Severtzov's Hazel Grouse, Chinese Grouse.

Restricted to forested mountains of C China; this is not only the smallest grouse but also has the most restricted range.

IDENTIFICATION Being the only hazel grouse in C China identification is relatively straightforward given reasonable views. Severtzov's Grouse resembles some dark populations of Hazel Grouse but overall is less vermiculated and streaked, having bolder, closer black-and-rufous barring (rather than irregular scalloping) on both underparts and upperparts; male also has bold chestnut feather centres with narrow white borders on breast. Most important is tail pattern: four (not two) central feathers almost unmarked brown, the rest blackish with narrow whitish bars and narrow whitish tip. Spread tail appears quite blackish in brief flight view. Most frequently found under streamside willow thickets in forest clearings.

DESCRIPTION *T. s. sewerzowi*. Overall structural features much as Hazel Grouse, but averages even smaller and has less feathering on tarsus. Comb inconspicuous (most visible in male), red. Bill very short, black. Irides dark brown. Feet greyish-black. Sexes differ. **Adult male :**Crown, ear-coverts and nape reddish-brown; mantle, back, rump and uppertail-coverts boldly barred black and greyish-brown. Small white streak behind eye. Bold white malar stripe on throat-sides, almost encircling black throat and crossing lores to meet on forehead. Less-defined whitish line extends from lower malar towards mantle. Chin and throat black. Breast chestnut, feathers with neat white borders. Rest of underparts boldly barred chestnut, black and white. Scapulars tipped white and patterned rufous and black on inner webs. Wing-coverts brown, larger feathers with white spot at tip, others edged buff or mottled rufous, black and buff. Tail has two pairs of central feathers brown, weakly barred darker; rest blackish crossed by three whitish bars, with narrow whitish tip. **Adult female:** Resembles dull version of male, with more mottled duller head, black of throat obscured by whitish feather fringes and buffier underparts, with less intense black barring. **Juvenile:** Unknown.

GEOGRAPHICAL VARIATION Slight. Southernmost population separated but distinctions perhaps rather clinal.

T. s. sewerzowi Taczanowski, 1876 occurs over most of range; described above.

T. s. secunda Riley, 1925 occurs in S Sichuan; more rufous than nominate.

MEASUREMENTS Length 33–36 cm, female only slightly smaller. *T. s. sewerzowi.* Males: wing 169–183, tail 115–153, weight 290–375. Females: wing 167–176, tail 88–136, weight 270–310.

HABITAT Montane forests dominated by conifers from valley bottoms to tree-line; recorded at 1000–4000 m depending on habitat and latitude. Typically, such habitats occur at higher altitudes on south-facing slopes and mainly comprise pines and firs. Favour stretches of riverside willow thickets, or areas of birch and other deciduous species among conifers. In summer, emerge into less forested habitats amid *Rhododendron* scrub above treeline.

VOICE Little documentation, other than that female gives typical galliform alarm call when accompanied by chicks, *ze ze ze-dackdack.* Recently, studies in Gansu have revealed that male gives hoarse *en er en er en* etc. when confronting another male and that during 'flutter jumps' wings make *pu pu pu pu* sound.

HABITS Poorly known. In winter, flocks form in valley bottoms and these persist until early spring, apparently disbanding by mid-March. They form in mid-October and initially usually comprise 4–5 birds, increasing to 13–14, depending upon habitat. For example, larger flocks feed in sea buckthorn thickets. Dispersal usually followed by birds being seen singly, thereafter in pairs, with some pairs forming as early as March. Forages both on ground and in trees and bushes, feeding principally on buds and shoots of willows and birches, switching to seeds and flowers of *Polygonum* later in season, with various berries in late summer and autumn.

BREEDING Apparently monogamous but polyandry occasionally suspected. Locally occurs at very high densities, e.g. 15 occupied territories in 1km² in Lianhuashan Reserve, Gansu. Though individuals spend time with more than one mate during pair formation, female accompanies one particular male when most receptive. Territories established in late winter as males perform 'flutter jumps' from ground, but also from tree to ground, and vice versa, which also serve to attract females and occur throughout most of day. Noisy territorial flights in crowns of trees as noted. Nests amidst rocks in coniferous and birch woodland, the scrape being lined with moss and pine needles, and a few feathers, located at the foot of a small birch or stump. Clutch 5–8 yellowish-brown eggs, with diffuse dark chestnut markings. Lays late May–mid-June; incubation c.25 days.

DISTRIBUTION Endemic to C China. From C Gansu and S Qinghai Provinces to E Tibet (Xizang Autonomous Region), NW Yunnan and N and W Sichuan. Western boundary unclear.

STATUS Near Threatened. It has been suggested that its range has declined significantly since the onset of large-scale forest clearance in historical times, but this is by no means clear. It is certain that its distribution has recently become more fragmented, with increasing habitat loss, a pressure that appears set to continue. Total population estimated at 5000–10,000 birds, but clarification urgently required. While fragmentation of forest habitat as a result of timber demand is main threat, direct exploitation is also a problem in some areas. Increasing access to previously remote areas may open its habitat to human disturbance. Nests appear to be quite heavily predated by Largebilled Crows *Corvus macrorhynchos*, with c.50% being destroyed in one study area.

REFERENCES Johnsgard (1983), de Juana (1994), Potapov (1985), Storch (2000), Sun Yue-hua & Fang Yun (1997).

Genus *BONASA*: **Ruffed Grouse**

Monotypic North American genus as treated here, but often includes the two species of *Tetrastes*, with which it shares a number of plumage characteristics. Plumages of both genera are cryptic, but considerably larger Ruffed Grouse has well-developed elongated neck plumes, lacks black-and-white throat and facial patterns of other two, and indulges in elaborate drumming displays to attract females.

183 RUFFED GROUSE
Bonasa umbellus (Linnaeus, 1766)   Plate 51

One of the most familiar North American grouse, the sound of drumming males being a peculiar feature of spring in most northern forests.

IDENTIFICATION Deciduous and mixed forests of N USA and Canada. Typically first seen in flight; a large reddish-brown or grey grouse, rising with a roar of wings, exhibiting distinctive prominent blackish subterminal band to weakly barred rufous or grey fanned tail, which provides easy distinction from American Spruce (Plate 47) and Sharp-tailed (Plate 52), with which it widely overlaps. Most easily found in early spring when males displaying. Sexes similar but male has unbroken black tail band, whereas band is broken by unmarked central feathers in female. Rufous and grey colour phases occur, which complicates racial variation.

DESCRIPTION *B. u. umbellus*. Medium-sized grouse with relatively long, somewhat round-tipped tail. Crown feathers elongated, forming obvious crest when alarmed. Feathers of neck-sides greatly elongated, forming shawl, which can be erected into circular ruff in display. Tarsi relatively slender, feathered but lower tarsus naked, like toes. In winter develops horny pectinations at sides of toes, which act as 'snow-shoes'. Larger uppertail-coverts conceal basal third of tail. Comb inconspicuous (only just visible in male), orange. Bill very short, black. Irides dark brown. Feet greyish-black. Sexes similar. **Adult male:** Head, neck and upperparts, including wings, vermiculated warm brown to grey-brown depending on colour variant. Crown, ear-coverts, neck, nape and mantle flecked and streaked white, the feathers also barred black. Elongated, broad neck feathers form blackish-brown ruff when spread in display, visible as dark patch when relaxed. Small white streak behind eye. Chin, throat and entire underparts buffy-white, barred and scaled darkish brown, the bars darkest and longest on flanks. Scapulars have relatively large buffy-white marks, wing-coverts small whitish shaft-streaks. Primaries uniform dark brown on inner webs, whitish with brown markings on outer webs. Secondaries vermiculated brown, becoming paler at tips. Rump and uppertail-coverts heavily marked with pearl-white arrowhead spots. Tail vermiculated grey or rufous, crossed by many fine back bars and a broad black subterminal band, sometimes preceded by narrow whitish band, and terminal pale grey tip. **Adult female:** Resembles dull version of male, most easily sexed by central tail feathers lacking black subterminal band. Neck feathers less elongated and whitish spotting on rump and uppertail-coverts less intense. **Juvenile:** Short-lived stage, resembles small version of female but tail shorter and lacks broad subterminal band. By first-autumn almost inseparable from adult in field.

GEOGRAPHICAL VARIATION Complex, to some extent dependent on size and, like Hazel Grouse, compounded by grey and brown morphs, and intermediates. Some variation clinal, both in size and colour saturation. In E North America grey birds predominate in north and browner birds towards south, whereas Pacific coast populations are mostly reddish, but those in Rockies are primarily grey phase. Different subspecies and colour phases linked to both climatic factors and specific vegetation zones. Variation occurs in nearly all populations. Like other widespread grouse, opinions differ as to number of subspecies: 14 usually recognised.

B. u. yukonensis Grinnell, 1916 occurs in Alaska through Yukon to NW Saskatchewan in C Canada.
B. u. umbelloides (Douglas, 1829) occurs in C Canada, from N British Columbia in the west to Quebec in the east.
B. u. labradorensis Ouellet, 1990 occurs on the Labrador Peninsula (Canada).
B. u. sabini (Douglas, 1829) occurs in SW British Columbia (Canada) south through USA to NW California.

B. u. brunnescens Conover, 1935 occurs on Vancouver I. (Canada).
B. u. castanea Aldrich & Friedmann, 1943 occurs on the Olympic Peninsula in extreme NW Washington (USA).
B. u. affinis Aldrich & Friedmann, 1943 occurs in C British Columbia (Canada) south to Oregon (USA).
B. u. phaia Aldrich & Friedmann, 1943 occurs in S British Columbia (Canada) to Oregon and SC Idaho (USA).
B. u. incana Aldrich & Friedmann, 1943 occurs in SE Idaho and W Wyoming south to Utah (WC USA).
B. u. mediana Todd, 1940 occurs in Minnesota and S Wisconsin (NC USA).
B. u. togata (Linnaeus, 1766) occurs on the USA–Canada border from S Ontario and S Quebec to parts of Minnesota, Wyoming and New York.
B. u. thayeri Bangs, 1912 occurs in Nova Scotia.
B. u. umbellus (Linnaeus, 1766) occurs in C New York, Massachusetts, New Jersey and Pennsylvania.
B. u. monticola Todd, 1940 occurs in S Michigan east to Pennsylvania and south along the Appalachians to N Georgia.

MEASUREMENTS Length 43–48 cm, male slightly larger. Males: wing 171–193, tail 130–181, weight c.600–650. Females: wing 165–190, tail 119–159, weight c.500–590.

HABITAT Various dense woodland habitats, including boreal forest, Pacific coast rainforest and relatively dry deciduous forests, where dependent on early successional stages. Some deciduous trees always present, especially aspen *Populus* spp. Over most of range, inhabits quaking and big-tooth aspen, which are typical of disturbed vegetation, but in west (west of the Cascade Mountains and those of north coast) it occurs in riverine habitats that contain black cottonwood. In general favours brushwood clearings and open areas in forest and forest edge.

VOICE Perhaps the most conspicuous sound produced by male is non-vocal 'drumming' of wings (see Habits). While drumming, several calls may be given by male and a *queet*, as well as hissing and whining have also been recorded. Also a quiet *psst*. Female also hisses and, if distracting an intruder, may squeal.

HABITS Almost entirely sedentary. When coveys disband, young move relatively short distances: 15 km apparently exceptional, and even in winter there is very little movement. Winter roosts are principally in conifers, several gathering together during particularly cold weather; if windy conditions persist forsake trees and resort to snow-holes, where may remain for several days in bad weather. Well known for its drumming activities, which occur year-round but are most evident in March–June; male adopts upright posture on favoured log or stump, leaning back to brace body against spread tail and forcefully beats opened wings in forward and upward motion to produce throbbing sound (beats begin slowly and suddenly accelerate into muffled roar). Typically 3–5 minutes between drumming. Most drumming occurs at dawn, beginning before daybreak, and again in evening. Often best way to observe Ruffed Grouse is to stalk drumming male, walking towards sound when drumming, pausing during breaks. Male also 'struts', with elongated neck feathers puffed into ruff, and tail erect and fanned, while walking slowly towards intruder. In some areas drumming males cluster, which suggests an approach towards lekking behaviour. Forages chiefly on ground, taking wide variety of plant materials, including buds and shoots of birches, aspens and cherries, augmented by variety of fruits, seeds and berries in late summer and autumn; young thrive on richer diet of various small insects in first few weeks.

BREEDING Promiscuous; males occupy dispersed territories, though some territories are clustered. Nest a depression in leaf-litter on forest floor, typically at base of tree, but also under log, bush or similar place, and often relatively close to forest gap. Most lay in May. Eggs creamy to pinkish-buff, sometimes with fine brown spotting. Clutch usually 10–12. Incubation 23–25 days. If nest is at base of aspen tree, then female will forage there during incubation.

DISTRIBUTION Throughout forested N North America, from Alaska across S Canada to Labrador and Nova Scotia. In W North America ranges south to NW California and C Utah, while in east ranges south through Appalachians to extreme N Georgia. Introduced Newfoundland and Nevada.

STATUS Still occurs through much of historical range and is common in most areas, though declining in E USA. Densities vary according to habitat type and, therefore, numbers vary, being lower in the southern part of the range. Distribution has contracted in some areas, but there have been attempts to translocate birds from areas where it is common. Efforts to restock areas where species has declined or disappeared are probably due to high levels of interest in hunting the species: it is the most hunted grouse in North America. Overall, high level of hunting is considered to have had relatively little impact, though locally there may be cause for concern. Numbers at any one place vary over time, fluctuating even annually in some areas, but over c.10-year cycles in north of range.

REFERENCE de Juana (1994).

Genus *CENTROCERCUS*: sage grouse

Large grouse of sagebrush plains in North America, until recently believed to be a monotypic genus. Male's massive air sacs are inflated during spectacular display, reminiscent of some Old World bustards. Long pointed tail feathers unique to genus. See description for other important features.

184 GREATER SAGE GROUSE
Centrocercus urophasianus (Bonaparte, 1827)   Plate 49

Alternative names: Sage Hen, Northern Sage Grouse.

The largest North American grouse, a specialised inhabitant of dwindling aromatic sagebrush plains of America's Great Basin.

IDENTIFICATION Distinctive large grouse, with peculiarly long tapering tail, found in small parties on rolling western plains of North America. In usual posture, long tail and dark mottled plumage momentarily suggest bulky, dark and rather squat female Common Pheasant; blackish underparts may be concealed due to squat, low-slung posture. Male considerably larger than female and some white visible at breast-sides even when feeding. In flight, white underwing contrasts strongly with blackish body; sexual differences readily apparent as larger, bulkier male rises heavily and flies with head and neck horizontal, whereas flying female more agile, and lighter body moves from side to side. Much more conspicuous when lekking as male inflates neck sacs to expose massive area of white, and raises and fans tail of long spiked feathers; they gather at favoured lekking sites to 'pop' and strut, offering a wonderful spectacle in their Wild West surroundings. Quite unmistakable in range; newly described Gunnison Sage Grouse is almost identical (which see for discussion), but ranges do not overlap.

DESCRIPTION Very large, with long tapering tail of 20 feathers (tips attenuated as long spikes in male). In male, neck-sides have two large sacs, which can be inflated at front exposing areas of bare olive-yellow skin. Feathers immediately surrounding bare skin short and stiff, but gradually become absorbed within longer, softer white feathers; several very long black hair-like feathers are erected from this area in display (but are shed after breeding). These features not present in female. Tarsi strong, feathered to base of toes. Longest upper- and undertail-coverts conceal basal half of tail. Comb (conspicuous only in male) yellow. Bill short and stout, dark brown. Irides dark brown. Feet dark green in adult, paler green when younger (tarsi feathered pale grey-brown). Sexes differ but basic plumage patterns similar. **Adult male:** Crown, head-sides and nape dull brown, mottled black; forehead and ear-covert patches blacker. Chin and throat brownish-black, with narrow whitish border reaching base of bill, joining narrow whitish line from bill base to just behind eye. Lower neck blackish, forming bib, becoming mottled at neck-sides, extending to ear-coverts. Breast white, often sagging due to deflated air sacs (see above). Rear underparts blackish, mottled brown and white, but solid blackish belly and vent; flanks whitish, mottled and scaled brown and blackish. Longer undertail-coverts have prominent triangular white tips. Upper-parts, including wing-coverts, closely marked ochre, brown and black; secondaries finely mottled buff on brown; primary-coverts and primaries uniform brown. Tail dark brown with narrow, uneven buff markings and quite long dark spike-like tips. **First-year male:** Resembles female, but gradually acquires clear whitish breast as winter progresses; primary-coverts have whitish tips (plain in adult); and tail feathers blunter than in adult male, with whitish tips. **Adult female:** Similar to male, but markedly smaller, lacking solid blackish areas on throat and bib, or clean white breast. Throat and bib freckled brown and whitish, having 'ghost' of pattern of male, with whiter border to throat and whitish eyestripe. Breast mottled dark brown and whitish, but has paler lower breast and blackish belly. Undertail-coverts have longer, less triangular, white tips than male. **Juvenile:** Ephemeral juvenile stage resembles small version of female but feathers of upperparts, including shorter tail, have whitish shaft streaks.

GEOGRAPHICAL VARIATION Monotypic. Some authors consider populations in northwest of range (parts of Washington and Oregon) to be subspecifically distinct as *C. u. phaios*, but differences small and its validity doubtful.

MEASUREMENTS Length: male 66–76 cm, female 48–58 cm. Males: wing 282–323, tail 297–332, weight 2300–3200. Females: wing 248–279, tail 188–213, weight 1350–1750.

HABITAT Dry grassland where sagebrush *Artemisia* spp. (especially *A. tridenta*) occurs on plains and low hills. Sagebrush habitats used include tall sagebrush, short sagebrush, forb-rich mosaics of low and tall sage-brush, riparian meadows, sagebrush savannas, and small areas of cropland and planted grasses. *Artemisia* spp. crucial for many life-history requirements, including nesting habitat and substantial part of adult diet throughout year.

VOICE During 'strutting' display, male emits *wa-um-poo*, the first two parts very quiet, with series of audible non-vocal sounds, including brushing of wings against body-sides, like a 'resonant squeaking, swishing noise followed by two plopping sounds'. In aggressive contexts, male calls *kerr* 8–12 times. High-frequency *wut* repeated in alarm. Female gives 'quaking call' when approaching display grounds. Flushed birds give an abrupt cackling *kek-kek-kek* upon rising.

HABITS In winter moves to areas of tall sagebrush visible above snow: these plants form virtually entire winter diet and principal means of escape. In summer takes a greater variety of plants, notably dandelions, vetches and clovers. Young feed principally on insects

in early weeks. Largely sedentary, but where snow covers all sagebrush, especially in more hilly areas, descends to lower altitudes with first snow. In some areas, such as parts of Idaho, movements of up to 160 km reported and more than 100 km in parts of Wyoming. Return to summer grounds as snow recedes, typically walking in small groups, though short distances may be flown. In winter, spend day foraging, resting and preening. Male arrives on display grounds before dawn and remains part of morning before leaving to feed. Female rarely returns to display grounds in afternoon. Displaying male adopts remarkable appearance: elevating and spreading tail into spiked fan, backed by ball of white spots on black undertail-coverts. With head drawn back and chest inflated into white 'horse-collar', stringy black filoplumes erect and bare chest patches pumping double-hooting and popping sounds, male moves forward, brushing drooped wings against stiffened breast feathers to produce double swishing sounds. Within group of lekking males, there are 1–2 dominant birds that mate with most females; the others appear to be merely a supporting cast.

BREEDING Promiscuous, with males forming leks. Males appear on breeding grounds before females, typically as soon as snow melts, which in N USA is in late February–early March. Female constructs shallow depression in ground, among sagebrush, sparsely lined with grass and sage leaves, though sometimes unlined. Clutches of 7–8 most common, but up to 15 recorded in a nest. Eggs olive to olive-buff, profusely speckled reddish-brown. Incubation occupies 25–27 days.

DISTRIBUTION W North America. In Canada now only in SE Alberta and SW Saskatchewan; formerly also British Columbia. Extends south across western plains of USA from C Washington south to E California and east to SW North Dakota, Nevada, Utah and W Colorado. Extinct in Arizona, New Mexico, Nebraska and Oklahoma, though some of these populations may have been of Gunnison Sage Grouse (which see for comment).

STATUS Declined across much of range during 20th century. Extensive hunting by early settlers is thought to have reduced some populations, though currently has generally minimal impact. Much of decline in last 100 years due to habitat loss and degradation, which has affected populations throughout range, though those at edges of range have declined most. Only central populations of California, Colorado, North and South Dakota, Utah and Washington thought reasonably secure.

REFERENCES Johnsgard (1983), Patterson (1952), Potapov (1985), Storch (2000), Young *et al.* (1998).

185 GUNNISON SAGE GROUSE
Centrocercus minimus Young, Braun, Oyler-McCance,
Hupp & Quinn, 2000   Plate 49

One of the most surprising ornithological discoveries of recent years was this newly described species from the USA heartland. Its range is restricted to SW Colorado and SE Utah, but is suspected to have formerly been more widespread.

IDENTIFICATION Extremely similar to Greater Sage Grouse and undoubtedly best identified by range, which lies to the south of Greater. It is the only sage grouse in SW Colorado and SE Utah, where it is very localised. Compared to Greater Sage Grouse both sexes are c.30% smaller, but only lekking males exhibit significant differences. Most striking is the more clearly and evenly barred tail of Gunnison: relatively broad, neat whitish cross-bars on a grey-brown background make it appear paler than rest of upperparts; most apparent when fanned in display. Greater has much more irregular and finer broken buffy barring on a darker background. Female tail similarly differs, but seldom visible under normal field conditions. In display, male has elongated black filoplumes, erected above white ruff: these are few and inconspicuous in Greater, but form a thick black tuft (like a pony-tail) in Gunnison. There are also significant differences in male display (see Voice & Habits).

DESCRIPTION Much as Greater Sage Grouse except smaller size and differences mentioned above. Bill also appreciably smaller than in Greater.

GEOGRAPHICAL VARIATION Monotypic.

MEASUREMENTS Length: male 55–64 cm, female 45–50 cm. Males: tail 347 (mean), weight 1727–2435. Females: weight 1622–2176. Other data unavailable.

HABITAT Sagebrush *Artemisia* spp. (especially *A. tridenta*) plains below 3000 m. In winter in shrubby sagebrush areas with mix of oaks, junipers and pines; sometimes in cultivation in more disturbed areas, i.e. alfalfa and bean fields.

VOICE & HABITS Basically much as larger species, but not known to wander far from natal areas, being largely sedentary throughout year. Certain elements of male display differ from Greater Sage Grouse: though call sequences similar in length, Gunnison possesses nine quicker low-pitched popping sounds (two in Greater) and three weak wing-swishes (two stronger swishes in Greater); Gunnison also freely raises and shakes pony-tail of filoplumes forward over head, and sometimes terminates display by shaking tail, neither behaviour is shown by Greater.

BREEDING Considered much as larger species; interestingly, despite smaller size of Gunnison female, the eggs of both sage grouse appear similar in size.

DISTRIBUTION W USA: known only from isolated populations in SW Colorado and SE Utah.

STATUS Endangered. Currently known in 6–7 counties in SW Colorado and one county in adjacent SE Utah, with total range <500 km². Entire breeding population estimated at fewer than 5000 birds, with most (c.2500–3000) in Gunnison Basin of Gunnison and Saguache counties in Colorado. Elsewhere populations number fewer than 300, with fewer than 150 in Utah (severely compromising genetic diversity); it has disappeared from several pockets since 1980, with overall decline of over 60% in males attending leks since 1953 in Gunnison Basin. Formerly, believed to have been considerably more widespread across S USA with sage grouse populations that once inhabited New Mexico, NE Arizona, SW Kansas and Oklahoma all possibly belonging to this form. Loss and fragmentation of pristine areas of sagebrush habitat through overgrazing by both stock and deer, and land development are main reasons for decline. Hunting now curtailed and a conservation plan developed to manage Gunnison Basin will hopefully improve habitat and reverse decline of this fascinating grouse.

REFERENCE Young *et al.* (2000).

Genus *TYMPANUCHUS*: prairie-chickens

Small to medium-sized grouse of open grasslands or brush in North America; all are overall mottled and barred brown and whitish, lacking bold plumage features. Males sport colourful neck sacs and feather tufts, which are inflated and erected during lekking displays.

186 SHARP-TAILED GROUSE
Tympanuchus phasianellus (Linnaeus, 1758)   Plate 52

Sometimes considered to form a monotypic genus *Pedioecetes*, this distinctive grouse has adapted well to forest clearance over the north of its range but has disappeared from much of the southern portion through agricultural intensification.

IDENTIFICATION Occurs in wooded, bushy grasslands in N and C USA and Canada. A small, mottled brownish and whitish, rather featureless grouse with little sexual dimorphism. Easily identified in flight by pointed whitish tail formed by elongated brown-barred central feathers and shorter, but often striking, buffy-and-white tail-sides and ventral region. Superficially similar prairie-chickens have short, rounded dark tails. On ground exhibits almost unmarked or, at most, mottled and spotted rather than barred appearance, especially to underparts. In display, male dances while inflating purplish neck sacs and cocking long tail to expose white undertail-coverts and tail base. Confusion momentarily possible with female Common Pheasant in flight, but latter much more uniform in colour and lacks whitish in tail or on rear underparts. Compare also Ruffed Grouse. Hybridises with Greater Prairie-chicken surprisingly frequently.

DESCRIPTION *T. p. phasianellus*. Small with graduated tail, the central pair of feathers elongated but blunt tipped. Tail-coverts conceal all but longest feathers when tail closed. Crown feathers slightly elongated giving ruffled appearance when erect. Male has pinkish-purple to violet patch of bare skin on upper neck-sides, concealed by slightly longer surrounding feathers when at rest, but visible as purplish sac when inflated in display. Tarsi feathered to base of toes. Comb inconspicuous (even in male), orange-yellow. Bill weak horn-brown. Irides dark brown. Feet pale brown (tarsi feathered grey-brown). Sexes differ but plumage patterns similar. **Adult male:** Forehead and crown darkish brown, mottled buff, with buffy-white loral stripe and supercilium, the latter interrupted by yellow comb. Lower loral stripe dull dark brown merging with ear-coverts as band through eye. Chin and throat almost unmarked buffy-white; lower throat and breast buffy-white, marked with increasingly heavy dark chevrons at breast-sides. Rest of underparts whitish, washed very slightly buff; flanks, belly and lateral undertail-coverts marked by dark chevrons and streaks; vent particularly whitish. Upperparts, including wing-coverts, closely marked whitish, buff, brown and black; wing-coverts have particularly large whitish spots forming rows on spread wing. Primary-coverts and primaries plain brown, with whitish spots on outer webs. Uppertail-coverts almost uniform very pale grey-brown, with faintly darker markings. Central tail feathers brown with tawny, black and buff markings and very pale tips; the rest almost unmarked whitish. **Adult female:** Like male, but smaller, with less contrasting facial and throat patterns but difficult to reliably sex. Female has more even barring on central tail feathers, whereas male has broader areas of tawny-brown and more blotched black markings. Crown of male very dark with only very narrow pale feather edges, while female has crown evenly barred brown and buff. **Juvenile:** Resembles small version of female but central tail hardly elongated and outer tail feathers barred and mottled brown, not whitish as adult.

GEOGRAPHICAL VARIATION Varies in basic ground colour, depending to some extent on coloration of soils and amount of rainfall. Northern and western populations darkest, possessing very heavy blackish spotting and chevrons below, and bold whitish spotting on dark brown ground colour to back and wings; in contrast those from semi-arid plains and prairies of interior are paler brown, with less strongly contrasting markings.

    T. p. caurus (Friedmann, 1943) occurs in Alaska east to S Yukon, N British Columbia and N Alberta; darker than nominate.

    T. p. kennicotti (Suckley, 1861) occurs in Mackenzie (Yukon, Canada).

    T. p. phasianellus (Linnaeus, 1758) occurs from N Manitoba east to WC Quebec; a paler brown form.

    T. p. campestris (Ridgway, 1884) occurs in C Canada (S Manitoba and S Ontario) south to NC USA (Minnesota, Wisconsin and Michigan); a distinctly pale and buffy form.

    T. p. jamesi (Lincoln, 1917) occurs in N Alberta and C Saskatchewan south to Wyoming and Nebraska; a pale brown form.

    T. p. columbianus (Ord, 1815) occurs in NC British Columbia, south to Utah and Colorado; overall rather cold greyish-brown.

MEASUREMENTS Length 38-48 cm, female slightly smaller. *T. p. phasianellus*. Males: wing 194–223, tail 110–135, weight c.950. Females: wing 186–221, tail 92–126, weight c.815.

HABITAT Variety of open habitats, including steppe, shrub-steppe, savanna, shrubland, aspen parkland and early successional forest. In summer, occurs in open prairie and in winter in more closed habitats, though amount of vegetation cover varies and ranges from semi-desert (*columbianus*) to up to 50% woody cover (some populations of *campestris*).

VOICE Male produces variety of calls at lek. When females present, a sound similar to a cork popping is uttered to attract females. Neighbouring males may give sharp 'bark' *chilk*, and jump several feet into air. These carry great distances, as does short 'cooing' call and 'gobbling' *lock-a-lock*, which has 3–5 notes. Latter two often associated with aggressive situations. Female vocalisations not well known, though they may 'gobble' and give brood calls. Both sexes cackle, the female when approaching the lek, and also give a three-note call when taking flight, *whucker-whucker-whucker*.

HABITS Largely sedentary, though snow may enforce local movements from open to more closed habitats in winter. Males establish leks in September–October and then may move according to snowfall. Return to territories in April–May and display mainly on fairly open, elevated land. In display, male performs complex series of postures and manoeuvres, involving cocking and spreading tail, exposing white under- and pale uppertail-coverts; spreading wings forward, indulging in head-down 'clockwork' runs synchronised with tail-rattling, in addition to remarkable vocalisations (see Johnsgard (1983) for fuller summary and especially Hjorth (1970) for details). Males emerge onto lek c.35–40 minutes before sunrise, remain for 2–4 hours and then forage until mid-afternoon. Feeds principally on buds and catkins of birches, willows and poplars in winter, clambering on branches with remarkable agility; but in spring and summer is basically terrestrial, taking greater variety of plant material, with high percentage of dandelions and buttercups, and some insects (especially grasshoppers). In late afternoon, either forage or attend lek. In winter, may remain in snow burrows for prolonged periods during bad weather. Often remarkably indifferent to humans, and adapted well to cleared areas as settlers penetrated North America. Even now, birds may even enter farmsteads and towns in search of grain if hard-pressed. Usually more wary, flushing suddenly from almost underfoot with roar of wings and flying away at high speed.

BREEDING Promiscuous, with males forming leks. Female mostly nests on ground under cover of, for example, shrub or small tree. Nest a slight scrape, often lined with moss, grass, other plant material and feathers. Lays in April–June. Clutch 5–17, usually 10–13. Eggs oval and fawn with ruddy-rufous to chocolate-brown wash; sometimes finely speckled. Incubation 21–24 days by female alone.

DISTRIBUTION North America, from C Alaska and Yukon east to W Quebec, and south to Great Plains of interior USA, avoiding lusher Pacific Northwest and E USA. Isolated populations at northern and southern limits, those in north being more poorly known.

STATUS Has disappeared from large tracts of original range, mainly in southwest, due to agricultural intensification. Extinct in eight states of USA and occupies less than half of original range in another nine. In north (Canada) it is fairly common. Numbers appear to have increased in Idaho and Utah since 1980s and USA populations of *campestris* and *jamesi* have increased through direct conservation action. Pressures on habitat persist, mainly as result of overgrazing, alteration of fire-management regimes and changes in plant communities as invasive weeds become established, all of which produce decline in habitat quality. Small population sizes have inbuilt negative effects, and use of chemicals to control plants on rangeland habitats is suggested to have both direct and indirect effects.

REFERENCES Connelly *et al.* (1998), Hjorth (1970), Johnsgard (1983), de Juana (1994), Storch (2000).

187 GREATER PRAIRIE-CHICKEN
Tympanuchus cupido (Linnaeus, 1758)   Plate 52

Alternative names: Pinnated Grouse, Prairie Grouse, Attwater's Prairie-chicken (*attwateri*), Heath Hen (nominate).

The two prairie-chickens are very similar and some authorities have questioned the validity of their being considered separate species. Their ranges no longer overlap.

IDENTIFICATION Now very localised in prairie grasslands of C USA with an isolated remnant in coastal Texas. A brown and narrowly whitish-barred grouse, basically similar in all plumages and recalling Sharp-tailed Grouse, but latter appears spotted above and below and has prominent whitish rear with brown central projection. Prairie-chickens have very short tails (dark in male, barred in female, but mostly concealed by barred uppertail-coverts). Elongated feathers form 'shawl' of black and pale buff on neck-sides in both sexes; these most developed in male and erect into 'rabbit ears' during display. Most easily found in early spring when males gather for 'booming' lek and inflate yellow-orange neck sacs. See very similar Lesser Prairie-chicken.

DESCRIPTION *T. c. pinnatus.* Small grouse with short rounded tail, the latter almost concealed by long tail-coverts, the central undertail-coverts virtually reaching tail tip. Crown feathers slightly elongated giving ragged appearance when erect. Male has yellow-orange bare skin on neck-sides, considerably inflated into air-sacs in display, but concealed by shawl of elongated and broadened pinnae, the latter erected into 'rabbit ears' during display. Tarsi feathered to base of toes. Comb (conspicuous only in male) orange-yellow. Bill weak horn-brown. Irides dark brown. Feet yellow-brown (tarsi feathered grey-brown). Sexes differ but plumage patterns similar. **Adult male:** Forehead and crown darkish brown, mottled buff, with buffy-white loral stripe and supercilium, the latter mostly obscured by yellow-orange comb. Lower loral stripe dull dark brown merging into ear-

coverts as band through eye. Chin and throat almost unmarked buffy-white except dusky malar patch. Neck, breast and entire underparts cleanly and almost evenly barred grey-brown and off-white; undertail-coverts enlarged and blunt tipped, pure white but blackish band at base of feather breaks pattern when tail erect. Upperparts, including wing-coverts and uppertail-coverts closely barred whitish, buff, brown and black; wing-coverts have whitish spots forming rows on spread wing. Primary-coverts and primaries uniform brown with whitish spots on outer webs. Tail dark brown, with weak marbling at base of feathers, concealed by tail-coverts. **Adult female:** Like male, but smaller, with shorter pinnae, indistinct comb and less contrasting facial and throat patterns, but difficult to reliably sex. Female has barred tail, which appears all dark in male in field (though concealed bases have some barring). Crown of male very dark with only very narrow pale feather edges, while female has crown evenly barred brown and buff. **Juvenile:** Resembles small version of female but upperparts have whitish shaft streaks.

GEOGRAPHICAL VARIATION Three subspecies recognised, with the two coastal populations darker than those of the interior, however, one of these (Heath Hen) is extinct, and the other is almost so.
  T. c. attwateri Bendire, 1893 (Attwater's Prairie-chicken) occurs in coastal Texas; smaller and darker brown than *pinnatus*, with relatively shorter pinnae.
  T. c. pinnatus (Brewster, 1885) occurs in NC USA from North Dakota south to Kansas and Missouri; described above.
  T. c. cupido (Linnaeus, 1758) (Heath Hen) is now extinct, but formerly occurred on bushy coastal plains of E USA, from Boston south to Washington DC (extirpated on mainland by c.1835, but survived on Martha's Vineyard until last report in 1932); more boldly barred rustier brown and pinnae narrower than in *pinnatus*.

MEASUREMENTS Length 41–47 cm; female smaller. *T. c. pinnatus.* Males: wing 217–241, weight c.990. Females: wing 208–220, weight c.770.

HABITAT Now restricted to a patchwork of prairie and cropland, as native woodland prairie mosaic has largely been converted to agriculture. Native vegetation required for roosting.

VOICE Male produces trisyllabic 'boom' *whhooo-doodoooohh* at end of 'booming' display. In open areas audible over several kilometres. Other calls given in breeding season include 'whoops' *pwoik* when female near and cackles during other displays. Female recorded to give three calls: a *kuk* at display or nest site, *brirrrb* to bring chicks together and *kwerr* as warning to young concerning predators.

HABITS Usually in groups, males at leks during breeding season, to which females visit in groups. Leks usually sited in native vegetation and males tend to utter 'booming' display on elevated ground with short vegetation. In display male performs complex series of postures and manoeuvres: 'booms' with head down, air-sacs inflated, pinnae erect and forward, with tail cocked to expose white undertail-coverts as it footstamps and runs forward briefly, quickly fanning tail open several times at both beginning and end of each display sequence. Combatants frequently jump into air, perhaps more so in areas where at low density (see Johnsgard (1983) for fuller summary and especially Hjorth (1970) for details). In autumn, some move considerable distances, though most largely sedentary. Form mixed flocks at this season that gather as larger packs in winter; numbers largest on cold mornings. Feed terrestrially, usually in early morning and afternoon, but fly between feeding areas, roosts etc. In winter, roosts by tunnelling in snow.

BREEDING Promiscuous, with leks having mean of 8–9 males and up to 70 recorded. Female mostly nests on ground in dense grassland. Nest a shallow depression, lined with feathers, plant material and twigs. Eggs laid late March–early April (*attwateri*) and mid-April–early June (*pinnatus*). Clutch usually 8–13, though up to 17 recorded. Eggs oval and smooth, usually tawny-olive to horn, with umber speckles. Incubation 23–25 days, by female alone.

DISTRIBUTION C North America in remnant prairies of Michigan, Wisconsin and Illinois, and from E North Dakota and NW Minnesota south to W Missouri and Oklahoma and parts of Texas coast. Extinct in Canada where formerly occurred from Alberta to SE Ontario.

STATUS Subspecies *cupido* extinct by 1932 following sustained sharp decline. Subspecies *attwateri* declined from 8700 individuals in 1937 to 1070 in 1967; by 1998 only 56 remained in three isolated populations, which were largely maintained by released captive-reared birds; it is severely threatened. Nominate *pinnatus* has declined in many states, but current populations overall appear reasonably stable. Threatened largely by loss and degradation of habitat in which native vegetation is replaced by cropland on large scale or overgrazing, changes in fire management or invasion by weeds. Overall population of *pinnatus* estimated at c.500,000 individuals in autumn in late 1970s, with at least 60,000 killed annually by hunters at that time. Due to its small isolated populations, this species is perhaps at greater risk from effects of small population size than most other grouse.

REFERENCES de Juana (1994), Schroeder & Robb (1993), Storch (2000).

---

188 LESSER PRAIRIE-CHICKEN
Tympanuchus pallidicinctus (Ridgway, 1873)   Plate 52

The prairie-chicken of dry short-grass prairie in the Texas panhandle and parts of adjacent states, largely southwest of the range of Greater, with no overlap.

IDENTIFICATION Dry shrubby grasslands of N Texas and nearby areas of adjacent states. Very similar to Greater Prairie-chicken, which it replaces in semi-arid, short-grass prairie and sagebrush southwest of the lusher long-grass prairie and oak woodland favoured by Greater. Though the two come very close in C Kansas and C Oklahoma, they are ecologically separated and do not overlap. Slightly smaller than *pinnatus* Greater (but larger than many *attwateri*), with distinctly paler, sandier brown, close barring, and narrower black barring on upperparts (merely black edging to brown bars). Barring becomes paler and more diffuse on central belly, making 'hidden' portion of belly paler. Greater has bold barring over entire belly. Differences difficult to appreciate in field, but lekking male has redder, sometimes almost reddish-violet, neck-sacs, contrasting with relatively larger yellow-orange comb; Greater has both comb and neck sacs

yellow-orange. There are subtle vocal differences and slight differences in display movements, which add to impression that the two are separate species.

DESCRIPTION Largely as Greater Prairie-chicken, with exceptions detailed above.

GEOGRAPHICAL VARIATION Monotypic. Formerly treated as conspecific with *T. cupido.*

MEASUREMENTS Length 38–41 cm, male rather larger. Males: wing 207–220, weight c.790. Females: wing 195–201, weight c.700.

HABITAT Originally found throughout dry grasslands intermixed with shinnery oak *Quercus havardii* or sand sagebrush *Artemisia filifolia.* Now most common in sandy, dwarf shrub–mixed grass vegetation, sometimes interspersed with short-grass habitats. Some occur in patches of farmland and, in winter, small fields are used.

VOICE Similar to Greater Prairie-chicken, though vocalisations appear generally higher pitched and shorter than latter. Boom has been described as a bubbling hoot, which is in contrast to the low droning notes of Greater.

HABITS Mainly sedentary, with few movements beyond 10 km and most less than 6–7 km. Movements greater in winter. Territories established in autumn, with older males showing high degree of site fidelity. Male 'booms' on territory. Display postures much the same in both prairie-chickens, with subtle differences. Though postures similar, Lesser has quicker, shorter displays including only briefly fanning tail at start of each display sequence (Greater spreads tail at both start and end of each sequence). during booming (Sharpe 1968). Often feeds on crops (such as grain) in winter when there is heavy snow for several days. Shinnery oak is most important food source (catkins) and cover year-round. During heavy snow, roosts in burrows in snow.

BREEDING Promiscuous, with males forming leks of usually 10–15, but occasionally more than 40. Nest a shallow depression in grass, usually bluestem *Andropogon hallii*. Clutch typically 12–14 very pale buff eggs, though later clutches (probably re-nests) contain 7–10 eggs. Lays April–May. Incubation lasts c.24 days.

DISTRIBUTION Historically, throughout southwest Great Plains, in SE Colorado, SW Kansas, W Oklahoma, N Texas and E New Mexico. Now, however, restricted to less than 10% of this distribution and occurs only in small, scattered populations

STATUS Vulnerable. Overall has declined substantially since European settlement of Great Plains. Its range initially increased as agriculture was introduced, but decline thought to be over 90% since 19th century and nearly 80% since early 1960s; in 1980 occupied 27,300 km² (only 8% of original). Spread of intensive agriculture into shinnery oak and sand sagebrush rangeland is overriding reason for decline, while overgrazing resulting in reduction of habitat quality and herbicide use, which reduce acorn production, are major problems. Overall population estimated at 42,500–55,500 individuals in autumn 1979, with 5700 killed annually by hunters at that time, but only 10,000–25,000 in 1999 (by which time most were in Texas and Kansas), when hunting restrictions had reduced annual 'bag' to 1000 birds. As most populations comprise fewer than 1000, small population size is likely to be a long-term problem.

REFERENCES Giesen (1998), Johnsgard (1983), de Juana (1994), Storch (2000).

FAMILY ODONTOPHORIDAE
New World Quails

American quails were formerly included in the Phasianidae. However, recent DNA-DNA hybridisation studies demonstrate, as some authorities had anticipated, that they are only quite distantly related to the Old World galliformes. Most species sport some form of crest, be it a ruffled lump on the rear crown (as in wood-quails), or an elaborate set of head-plumes (like California Quail). Certain features set them apart from Old World species, notably their very stout bills, which have slightly serrated cutting edges, their relatively long, slender toes and short tarsus (the latter never developing spurs).

Genus *DENDRORTYX*: tree-quails

Three montane forest, medium-sized largely allopatric species of Mexico, with one extending into C America south to Costa Rica. Long tails of 12 rectrices, in some as long as the rounded wings, which have the fifth and sixth primaries the longest. Sexes are similar among adults. All are declining through deforestation and other pressures on their montane habitats, with one classified as globally threatened.

189 BEARDED TREE-QUAIL
Dendrortyx barbatus Gould, 1846

Plate 56

Alternative name: Bearded Wood-partridge.

Endemic to EC Mexico, where now very rare. Its recent discovery at new localities in Querétaro and Oaxaca gives some hope that it may be more widespread than previously supposed.

IDENTIFICATION Distinctive reddish-brown tree-quail, with a predominantly blue-grey face and throat, which is now extremely rare in EC Mexico due to the loss of most of its cloud forest habitat. Has obviously shorter tail than congeners. Potentially overlaps with Long-tailed Tree-quail (which see) and certainly Singing Quail, which is smaller, with a different head

pattern, shorter tail and rarely flushes.

DESCRIPTION Short crest. Rounded wing and shorter tail than congeners of 12 rectrices. Irides yellowish or greyish-olive, with orange-red orbital skin slightly elongated, especially at rear. Relatively stout red bill. Legs and feet dull orange-red to bright red. Sexes similar, though female smaller with shorter tail. **Adult (both sexes):** Crown and crest grey-brown, streaked rufous on hindneck; face, throat and foreneck blue-grey. Underparts cinnamon or reddish-brown, with breast-sides streaked rufous, grey-brown mottling on thighs and flanks and dark undertail-coverts tipped whitish. Mantle

385

streaked rufous and rest of upperparts cryptically patterned buff, grey-brown, blackish and pale grey, with rufous flight feathers and outer rectrices. **Juvenile:** Largely as adult, but has dark brown barring and spotting on flanks, duller breast, primaries frayed and pointed and buffy tips to greater primary-coverts.

GEOGRAPHICAL VARIATION Monotypic.

MEASUREMENTS Length 22–32 cm. Male larger. Males: wing 147–166, tail 117–121, weight 459. Females: wing 148–152, tail 110–119, weight 405.

HABITAT Humid montane forests with dense understorey in the subtropical and possibly lower temperate zones, principally in cloud forest, but also evergreen forest, pine–oak woodland and oak–sweetgum–tree-fern associations, at 1200–3100 m, but with reports to 900 m. Where potentially overlaps with Long-tailed Tree-quail, probably prefers lower elevation, more humid evergreen forest. May visit planted fields in forest gaps and apparently uses second growth, forest edge and narrow strips of suitable habitat along watercourses.

VOICE Gives loud whistles like congeners, repeated rapidly and often given in duet: male a lower pitched *ko-orrr-EE-EE* or *ko-orrr-EE*, to which female responds with quieter, but progressively louder *ko-or-ee-ee-ee-eee*, usually preceded by a number of softer notes only audible when close to. Considered difficult to distinguish on voice from Long-tailed Tree-quail. Particularly vocal, at least in captivity at dawn and dusk when choruses may last 15–20 minutes, but in wild may call for up to first four hours of daylight.

HABITS Behaviour almost unknown. Sedentary. Usually singly or in pairs in breeding season, but also forms small groups of 3–5 birds. Flushes on whirring wings. Takes seeds and small fruits and perhaps ripe black bean seeds. In captivity takes corn, black beans and soft fruits. Roosts in coveys or pairs in trees and tall shrubs.

BREEDING Poorly known. In captivity, constructs shallow scrape lined with palm leaves. No information on clutch size, but brood of 5 apparently taken in wild and eggs are dull white, incubated 28–30 days in captivity. No information on role of sexes or fledging period. Season perhaps April–June, with downy young recorded in latter month, but still very vocal in July in Querétaro.

DISTRIBUTION EC Mexico, SE San Luis Potosí and NC Hidalgo to Puebla, Veracruz; recently discovered in NE Querétaro and N Oaxaca.

STATUS Vulnerable; formerly classified as Endangered. Rapid deforestation, illegal hunting and even poisoning (as believed to feed on bean crops) have all contributed to significant decline, with comparatively few recent records from most parts of historical range. Prior to 1994–1998 surveys, situation appeared very dire and population suspected to number fewer than 1000 individuals, though considered very locally common, with no records in San Luis Potosí since 1951 and none in Veracruz, where historically most common, since 1968. Habitat loss in the latter state, through land conversion to monocultures, human settlement and livestock grazing has been unusually high. Recently (late 1990s) discovered at five localities in Querétaro, where the Sierra Gorda Biosphere Reserve may be of key importance for its survival, with a new record from San Luis Potosí, 11 localities being identified in Veracruz and the first record from Oaxaca (in the Sierra Mazateca). Records from Hidalgo in mid-1990s and Puebla 1977, but most cloud forest has been destroyed in the former. Despite the many important new findings and the consequent revision of its estimated population to 2500–10,000 individuals, the species remains at risk. In addition to the threats mentioned above, developments for tourists, road building and urbanisation all threaten the increasingly fragmented population.

REFERENCES BirdLife International (2000), Carroll (1994), Collar *et al.* (1992), Eitniear *et al.* (2000), Howell & Webb (1995), Johnsgard (1988), Rojas-Soto *et al.* (2001).

---

190 LONG-TAILED TREE-QUAIL
Dendrortyx macroura (Jardine & Selby, 1828)   Plate 56

Alternative name: Long-tailed (Tree-) Partridge.

Like other tree-quails, more often heard than seen; endemic to montane forests of WC Mexico, where it marginally overlaps with Bearded Tree-quail.

IDENTIFICATION Endemic to montane forests of WC Mexico. Peculiar greyish quail with long barred tail (held cocked when running) and black-and-white head pattern. Unmistakable if seen well, as black throat and very long tail unique within genus. Range marginally overlaps with Bearded Tree-quail (in C Veracruz and perhaps Puebla), but range of features, especially head pattern, easily distinguish it. In flight, concentrate on remiges and outer rectrices, which are grey-brown in this species, but rufous-brown in Bearded. Also overlaps with Singing Quail, but latter has much shorter tail, is overall smaller and lacks characteristic head pattern and crest of present species.

DESCRIPTION *D. m. macroura* Short crest. Rounded wing and long tail of 12 rectrices. Irides yellowish or greyish-olive, with orange-red orbital skin slightly elongated, especially at rear. Relatively stout red bill, with paler tip and cutting edges. Legs and feet dull orange-red to bright red. Sexes similar, though female smaller with shorter tail. **Adult (both sexes):** Forehead, head-sides, throat and foreneck deep black, with buff-streaked dark crown and two long white streaks above and below eye. Body overall chestnut and grey, with bluish-grey breast, spotted and streaked rufous on chest and flanks, grading much paler on rear flanks and belly, but has dusky-grey vent and undertail-coverts, tipped whitish. Mantle to upper back and wing-coverts chestnut with broad grey fringes to feathers, becoming dusky on rump and uppertail-coverts, and tail brownish with broad pale grey bars. Flight feathers brown with pale fringes. **Juvenile:** Largely as adult, but has dark brown spots on underparts, less chestnut on upperparts, primaries frayed and pointed and buffy tips to greater primary-coverts.

GEOGRAPHICAL VARIATION Six subspecies recognised, which vary in extent of rufous streaking on underparts and clarity of head pattern.

D. m. diversus Friedmann, 1943 occurs in NW Jalisco (WC Mexico); poorly differentiated form.

D. m. griseipectus Nelson, 1897 occurs on the Pacific slope, in Distrito Federal, México and Morelos (C Mexico); has narrow rufous shaft-streaks to breast feathers almost entirely concealed by broad grey fringes, back, rump, wings and flanks darker and more olive than nominate and flanks have indistinct rufous shafts.

D. m. macroura (Jardine & Selby, 1828) occurs in the valley of México and Veracruz (EC Mexico); described above.

D. m. striatus Nelson, 1897 occurs in S Jalisco to Michoacán and Guerrero (WC Mexico); see *inesperatus*.

D. m. inesperatus Phillips, 1966 occurs in Chilbancingo, Guerrero and the Sierra de Miahuatlán of S Oaxaca (S Mexico); most like *striatus*, but differs in distinctly white supercilium and malar, grey breast-sides and upper back, stronger contrast to breast feathers, reduced brown centres to tertials and has sootier brown rump and uppertail-coverts.

D. m. oaxacae Nelson, 1897 occurs in W Oaxaca (S Mexico); smaller than most forms, with longer, slenderer bill, darker tail, very dark back to uppertail-coverts, lacking whitish mottling, and has white face stripes often very indistinct, duller and less contrasting crown coloration and broader based bill.

MEASUREMENTS Length 29–39 cm. Male larger. Males: wing 151–166, tail 138–169, weight (mean) 433. Females: wing 141–158, tail 119–151, weight 374–446.

HABITAT Dense montane forest at 1200–3700 m, in cloud forest, pine–oak woodland, evergreen forest and occasionally in drier areas at lower limit of pine–oak zone; prefers heavy undergrowth.

VOICE Song mostly given at dusk and dawn (frequently from roost) is a series of five grunting hoot-like calls, increasing in volume and followed by a loud, ringing *kor-eee-oh*, repeated several times and often given in duet; also a similar series of phrases, spaced at c.1-second intervals, often given in chorus. Alarm is a shrill or squeaky *quid-it*, often rapidly repeated.

HABITS Sedentary. Usually singly or in pairs in breeding season, but forms small groups at other times. Coveys largely disband at start of breeding season, but no information on group size. Runs into cover at least sign of danger, with tail cocked, and is generally furtive and very shy; moves swiftly through dense cover. Rarely flushes, but does so with whirring wings. Takes legume seeds, flower buds, flowers and small fruits from arboreal perches, but also scratches leaf-litter on forest floor. Roosts in coveys or pairs in trees and tall shrubs.

BREEDING Few data, with no information on role of sexes, incubation and fledging periods. Four nests discovered (dates mid-April and July): two associated with rocky outcrops, another at base of a shrub, with one being sheltered by leaves of twigs from a fallen tree. Four to 6 whitish eggs, lightly speckled brown (6-egg clutch has been speculated as being work of two females). Season unclear, perhaps February–July (based on calls being more frequent at this season), but also listed as April possibly to December. Fledged young observed by early May, but also as late as December.

DISTRIBUTION WC to S Mexico: on Pacific slope from Jalisco to Oaxaca, in central mountains from Colima to Veracruz and on Atlantic slope from C Veracruz to Oaxaca.

STATUS Population probably declining, but not properly assessed, though thought to total between 20,000 and 200,000 individuals. Deforestation presumably threatens it in some portions of range, and is trapped and hunted for food in some areas. Considered overall fairly common to common, but rare or uncommon on those parts of range where heavily hunted or understorey has been overgrazed.

REFERENCES Binford (1989), Carroll (1994), Howell & Webb (1995), Hunn *et al.* (2001), Johnsgard (1988).

---

191 BUFFY-CROWNED TREE-QUAIL
Dendrortyx leucophrys (Gould, 1844)

Plate 56

Alternative names: Buff-fronted/Buffy-crowned Wood-partridge, Guatemala Partridge, Highland Partridge.

Being the only tree-quail south of Mexico, this is a readily identified species across most of its comparatively wide range.

IDENTIFICATION The only tree-quail that occurs south of Chiapas (Mexico). Dull grey-brown, long-tailed quail with black bill (reddish in other tree-quails) and variable rufous streaking on greyish body. Easily separated from Long-tailed Tree-quail (no overlap) by reddish-brown (rather than grey) wings and tail, and whitish-buff throat, forehead and long super-

cilium. Singing Quail is smaller with a stubby tail and rarely flushes, while Spotted Wood-quail has a largely dark head and also lacks the long tail of this species.

DESCRIPTION *D. l. leucophrys* Short crest. Rounded wing and long tail of 12 rectrices. Irides yellowish or greyish-olive, with orange-red orbital skin slightly elongated, especially at rear. Relatively stout black bill, with orange lower mandible. Legs and feet orange-red. Sexes similar, though female smaller with shorter tail. **Adult (both sexes):** Forecrown, throat and narrow, slightly downcurved supercilium pale buff to whitish, with finely pale-streaked blackish ear-coverts and malar; rest of crown, hindneck and neck-sides chestnut, streaked and spotted white (except crown). Underparts largely bluish-grey, becoming brownish on flanks and lower throat, foreneck and breast striped chestnut or black; belly dull grey-brown, vent buffy-brown and undertail-coverts sooty. Mantle, scapulars and back bluish-grey with bold chestnut stripes, becoming dusky or olive-brown on rump, uppertail-coverts and tail, of which outer rectrices are often reddish and sometimes narrowly barred. Flight feathers largely reddish-brown with slightly paler fringes, and rest of wings brownish. **Juvenile:** Largely as adult, but throat streaked dusky, body browner flecked white, primaries frayed and pointed, buffy tips to greater primary-coverts and wing-coverts barred buffy.

GEOGRAPHICAL VARIATION Two reasonably well-marked subspecies recognised; much variation is clinal with populations becoming darker north to south, but also many intermediates between two extremes on Pacific slope of Guatemala south to Nicaragua.
D. l. leucophrys (Gould, 1844) (includes '*nicaraguae*') occurs in montane SE Chiapas (S Mexico) south to W Nicaragua; described above.
D. l. hypospodius Salvin, 1896 occurs in montane N Costa Rica; larger, darker and greyer, especially on underparts, than nominate, with stripes on foreneck and breast darker (often black) and much narrower and has essentially uniform breast-sides, flanks and vent (shaft streaks reduced and lacking tawny borders).

MEASUREMENTS Length 28.0–35.6 cm. Male larger. Both forms. Males: wing 138–160, tail 113–149, tarsus 49–55, weight 397. Females: wing 130–153, tail 108–157, tarsus 49.0–55.5, weight 340.

HABITAT Favours humid to semi-humid montane pine–oak forests, as well as evergreen and cloud forests, with brushy undergrowth, at 300–3000 m. Apparently adapts to second growth (even prefers partially logged forest in Costa Rica), narrow 'tongues' of forest alongside streams on otherwise denuded hillsides and occasionally occurs in coffee plantations.

VOICE Much as congeners. Most data from Stiles & Skutch (1989). Loud, far-carrying, often-repeated

gabbling chorus of whistles, *whew, Whit-cha, cha-wa-WHAT-cha* and a soft, descending gobble in alarm when in covey. Often calls throughout day, but most frequently at dusk and dawn from roosts.

HABITS Largely sedentary, being encountered in coveys of 4–6 birds (probably family groups) most of year, but up to 12 in non-breeding season. Coveys probably largely disband at start of breeding season. Slinks into cover at least sign of danger and is generally furtive and very shy. Takes seeds, flower buds, small fruits and invertebrates. Few other data on feeding, but scratches vigorously in oak leaf-litter on forest floor. Roosts in coveys in trees and tall shrubs.

BREEDING Very few data. Nest apparently undescribed, but reputedly (and probably) on ground. Possibly 4–5 reddish-buff eggs, with reddish-brown spots. Season apparently May in Guatemala, April–July in Honduras (well-grown young) and February–March in El Salvador (young seen April–July); half-grown chicks observed in Costa Rica in June–September, where nesting apparently tied to rains.

DISTRIBUTION C America, from SE Chiapas (Mexico) south through Guatemala, Honduras and E El Salvador to W Nicaragua and N Costa Rica (perhaps as far south as Térraba). Reports from N Chiapas require verification.

STATUS Population probably declining, but not assessed, though thought to total between 20,000 and 200,000 individuals. Deforestation presumably threatens species in some portions of its range, but its ability to adapt to secondary and apparently quite small areas of habitat may stand it in good stead. Trapped and hunted for food in some parts of range, e.g. Guatemala. Considered common in parts of Costa Rica, 'by no means uncommon' in early 20th century in Guatemala, the most common of the highland quail in Honduras, and fairly common to common in restricted Mexican range (though only population estimate suggests it occurs at low densities).

REFERENCES Blake (1977), Carroll (1994), Griscom (1932), Howell & Webb (1995), Johnsgard (1988), Monroe (1968), Stiles & Skutch (1989).

Genus *OREORTYX*: Mountain Quail

Medium-sized montane North American quail, which is perhaps most closely related to Scaled Quail. Given its more striking plumage similarities to some of the other *Callipepla* species, this may appear to be a surprising conclusion.

192 MOUNTAIN QUAIL
Oreortyx pictus (Douglas, 1829)
Plate 57

Alternative names: Mountain Partridge, Painted/ Plumed Quail.

Highly distinctive and attractive, but rather secretive quail of montane W North America.

IDENTIFICATION W North American quail, which overlaps with two species of *Callipepla* quail: Gambel's and California Quails. Given reasonable view, identification should be straightforward given that both of the latter species have black, not cinnamon, throats, shorter, forward-curving crests, and significantly different upperparts and flank patterns. Rather different juvenile may be separated from juveniles of Gambel's and California by virtue of greyer underparts and longer head plumes than either of these species at this age.

DESCRIPTION *O. p. pictus* Rounded tail of 12 rectrices, about 60% of wing length. Wings also rounded, with sixth and seventh primaries being the longest. Long, strikingly erect narrow crest plumes. Dark irides. Bill black, with brown to dusky-flesh legs and feet. Sexes similar, but female usually has shorter and more brownish plumes, and browner grey hindneck. **Adult (both sexes):** Head pattern dominated by long black crest formed by two plumes; dark blue-grey forehead to mantle, scapulars, upper back, neck-sides and breast, with white around bill base and as line from eye around throat, encircling rufous-cinnamon chin and throat. Belly and flanks bright chestnut, with striking black-bordered white flank bars, and blackish undertail-coverts. Lower back to tail olive-brown, concolorous with wing-coverts and flight feathers, which have striking white line on inner webs of tertials. **Juvenile:** Dull version of adult, lacking boldly patterned flanks, rich face and throat markings, and has grey-brown and buff upperparts, and buff-tipped greater primary-coverts, with two outermost primaries more pointed and frayed than rest.

GEOGRAPHICAL VARIATION Five subspecies listed here; they differ in general coloration, principally of the back and breast. The forms '*palmeri*' and *plumiferus* have both been submerged within the nominate.

    O. p. pictus (Douglas, 1829) (including '*palmeri*') occurs from SW Washington to the Sierra Nevada of C California (locally introduced to Vancouver I. British Columbia and W Washington state); described above.

    O. p. plumiferus (Gould, 1838) occurs from S Washington and extreme W Nevada south to NE and NC California.

    O. p. confinis Anthony, 1889 occurs in Baja California.

    O. p. eremophila van Rossem, 1937 occurs in S and WC California, and in extreme SW Nevada south to extreme N Baja California.

    O. p. russelli Miller, 1946 occurs in Riverside and San Bernadino counties (S California).

MEASUREMENTS Length 24–29 cm. Male slightly larger. Males: wing 125–140, tail 73–92, weight (mean) 235. Females: wing 126–138, tail 71–86, weight (mean) 230.

HABITAT Apparently prefers mixed evergreen forest in California, with a much lesser preference for chaparral, foothill or riparian woodlands or their ecotones. Compared to California Quail, prefers areas of steeper slopes, greater ground, shrub and canopy cover, more and larger trees, and fewer herbs, and generally shuns open country and grassland. Occurs at 500–3000 m.

VOICE Apparently incompletely known. Male advertising call is a loud clear and often-repeated whistle, *plu-ark*, which is also given in early autumn, as well as spring (commencing in February in California). Audible over 1 km. Most frequently heard is a rallying call, which is an extended series of *kow* or *cle* notes. Also a 'squealing twitter' when flushed.

HABITS Reasonably secretive, best seen in late summer when small family parties may occasionally venture onto roadsides. Forms small social units of 5–9 birds, with occasionally up to 20; family coveys usually consist of a pair and up to five young. Seeds, then bulbs and acorns form principal diet, with flowers, fruit, green herbage, animal material and fungi of much lesser importance. Six genera of plants (*Lithophragma*, *Quercus*, *Stellaria*, *Erodium*, *Trifolium* and *Rhus*) may form over 60% of diet in some areas, but fruits more important in Washington and Idaho. Arthropods form only tiny fraction of diet, even of young. Forages diurnally, principally early morning and late afternoon, digging for bulbs, plucking fruits and seeds, shelling acorns and also clambering up trees. Mobile, tends to escape uphill, by running or, to a lesser extent, flying (sometimes up to 500 m). Performs well-defined but short (up to 50 km) seasonal movements to lower altitudes in winter in some areas. Daily movements rarely exceed a few hundred metres, but typically visits water on daily basis, in late morning or late afternoon. Usually arrive at water source on foot and in single file, but in the most arid regions such areas may attract hundreds and perhaps even thousands of individuals.

BREEDING Coveys disband in February–March, with pairs assuming breeding territories of 2–20 ha and most nests being constructed in April. Nest usually well concealed in dense vegetation, typically within close proximity to water. Clutch probably usually 6–10 unmarked white to pale reddish-buff eggs. Incubation period 21–25 days, but no information on fledging rates. Male guards nest, defends brood and may, rather exceptionally, incubate eggs. May lay replacement clutches (up to two), if first attempt unsuccessful. Season generally March–July, earlier in south and later in north, with peak hatching in May–June.

DISTRIBUTION W USA from S Washington and SW Nevada south to Baja California (Mexico), with introduced populations in Idaho, W Washington and Vancouver I. British Columbia (Canada).

STATUS Overall population considered to number up to 1 million individuals and is an important gamebird in several areas. Overgrazing threatens its future in Mexico and other threats include agricultural conversion, dam construction, impoundments, which have led to significant decline in Idaho (only three small populations remain), and other extinctions and declines.

REFERENCES Carroll (1994), Howell & Webb (1995), Johnsgard (1988).

Genus *CALLIPEPLA*: crested quails

Group of four largely allopatric bulky short-tailed quails of the SW USA and Mexico, where they inhabit dry habitats. All are crested; one has extravagant sword-like vertical feathers and two others, forward-drooping crests, while the other has much less noticeable, slightly bushy crown feathers.

193 SCALED QUAIL
Callipepla squamata (Vigors, 1830)   Plate 57

Alternative name: Blue Quail, Chestnut-bellied Quail (*castanogastris*), Scaled Partridge.

Most closely related to allopatric Elegant Quail; the two have been considered conspecific, but the only known hybrids between the two have proved sterile.

IDENTIFICATION Plump, rather short-tailed quail of semi-arid country in S USA and N and C Mexico, which should be readily identifiable given reasonable view. Sandy bluish-grey in overall plumage with short prominent whitish crest and heavily scaled body, though appears rather plain looking at distance. Other allopatric or partially sympatric quails all have much more strikingly marked plumages, usually with diagnostically different head patterns and some with dramatic crests.

DESCRIPTION *C. s hargravi* Rounded wings and moderately long tail of 12–14 rectrices. Variably exposed crest, usually longer in male. Bill blackish and legs and feet grey. Sexes largely alike. **Adult (both sexes):** Head and upperparts grey-brown, with whitish-tipped crest and grey tail. Blue-grey neck and breast, boldly scaled black and whitish-streaked grey-brown flanks, grading to buff on belly and undertail-coverts, which are scaled black. Female may tend to have dusky shaft-streaks on throat, buffier crest, indistinct buff mottling on outer fringes of secondaries and black marginal line to white fringes on inner webs of secondaries. **Juvenile:** Much as adult, but lacks bold black scaling and has shorter crest (without white tip), indistinct brownish barring on underparts, white-streaked upperparts, wing-coverts and tertials vermiculated black, whitish-barred tail, and buff-tipped greater primary-coverts, with outermost primaries more pointed and frayed than rest.

GEOGRAPHICAL VARIATION Four subspecies recognised, based on upperparts coloration.

   C. s. hargravi Rea, 1973 occurs from SE Colorado and SW Kansas through N New Mexico to W Oklahoma and NW Texas (USA); described above.
   C. s. pallida Brewster, 1881 occurs from S Arizona, S New Mexico and W Texas (USA) south to N Chihuahua and N Sonora (NW Mexico); has upperparts palest of the four races.
   C. s. squamata (Vigors, 1830) occurs from N Sonora and N Tamaulipas south to the Mexico Valley (Mexico); most similar to *hargravi*.
   C. s. castanogastris Brewster, 1883 occurs from S Texas (USA) south to E Coahuila (NE Mexico); upperparts tone darkest of the four races and further distinguished by chestnut belly.

MEASUREMENTS Length 22–29 cm. Sexes apparently similar. Males: wing 109–121, tail 75–90, weight 151–202. Females: wing 109.5–120.0, tail 75–88, weight 130–274.

HABITAT Desert grasslands, arid brush and thorn scrub from sea level to 2450 m, and from 1000 to 2000 m in Mexico. Prefers areas dominated by shrubs 1–7 m tall and will use sites with man-made structures; often in reasonably close proximity to a water source.

VOICE Male advertising call a hoarse, wheezing repeated *rrehh*, sometimes alternated with dry nasal, rhythmic clucking *chow-chowk chow-chowk…* or *cow-cow-h cow-cow-h…* (probably only given by unmated birds); also gives a dry *chek-ah*, a sharp metallic *ching* in alarm and *pey-cos* as separation or rallying call between group or pair members.

HABITS Relatively sedentary, though movements of up to 100 km reported; coveys usually occupying winter territories of 9.6–33.6 ha (mean 20.8 ha in one study), with little interchange between members of different groups and only slight overlap in home ranges. Large winter coveys (10–40 birds, occasionally up to 200) disband at start of breeding season. Prefers to run rather than fly from perceived danger, but will flush if surprised (especially away from cover) and seeks shade during middle of day. Regularly dust-bathes in summer. Primarily takes wide range of weed and grass seeds (e.g. *Panicum, Croton* and *Bidens* in Mexico), principally herbaceous legumes, as well as tree seeds and fruits, e.g. of *Acacia, Celtis, Atriplex* and *Mahonia*, but these of much less importance in overall diet. Green herbage important in winter and autumn, but overall the species seems to be relatively catholic and opportunistic. Arthropods taken in small quantities, at least by adults.

BREEDING Nest usually within cover or shrubs, rather than open grassland. Lays mean 12–14 (range 9–16 in Mexico, 12.7–14.0 in USA) dull whitish eggs, usually speckled brown and incubated for a mean of 23 days. Young fledge rapidly, being adult-sized by 77–105 days. Role of sexes largely unknown, but in one instance male raised first brood, while female laid second clutch, and latter takes virtually sole responsibility for incubation duties. Mean brood size in USA 7.8–11.5. Season apparently late, June–September (October), and presumably timed to take advantage of summer and early autumn rainfall within its range, and perhaps to facilitate replacement clutches or even a second brood.

DISTRIBUTION From SE Arizona, N New Mexico, EC Colorado and SW Kansas south through W Oklahoma, WC and S Texas (USA) to N and C Mexico, from NE Sonora, Chihuahua and Coahuila east to Nuevo León and Tamaulipas, south through Durango and San Luis Potosí to NE Jalisco, Guanajuato, Querétaro and NW Hidalgo. Introduced with uncertain success to Hawaii, C Washington, E Nevada and Nebraska.

STATUS Few data, though total population estimated at over one million individuals. It is an important gamebird in the SW USA, where it has declined rather dramatically since 1960 due to degradation of arid grasslands and mesquite control. Considered common to fairly common in Mexican range, where has benefited, at least formerly, from forest clearance and overgrazing.

REFERENCES Carroll (1994), Howell & Webb (1995), Johnsgard (1988).

---

194 ELEGANT QUAIL
Callipepla douglasii (Vigors, 1829)   Plate 58

Alternative names: Douglas/Benson's Quail.

Endemic to NW Mexico, where it is usually reasonably common. See Scaled Quail (above) for comments relating to its possible relationship to that species.

IDENTIFICATION Plump greyish quail of arid and semi-humid habitats in NW Mexico, with bold white-spotted underparts, forward-pointing tawny (male) or dusky (female) crest. Male has chestnut on wings and flanks, and streaking on head and neck. Range does not overlap with smaller Banded Quail or California Quail, but does so with Gambel's Quail, from which it is easily distinguished by lack of striking black-and-white head pattern, overall coloration and underparts pattern.

DESCRIPTION *C. d. douglasii* Rounded wing and moderately long tail of 12–14 rectrices. Forward-pointing crest (tawny/orange-buff in male and dusky in female), usually longer in male. Bill dark grey, legs and feet grey. Sexes differ. **Adult male:** Face and throat whitish, streaked and spotted black, becoming blue-grey on hindneck, mottled chestnut. Underparts grey to blue-grey, with lower breast, belly and flanks boldly spotted white, and flanks and sometimes breast-sides mottled rufous. Upperparts grey to blue-grey, scapulars and tertials mottled chestnut and fringed whitish, and wing-coverts, flight feathers and tail greyish-brown. **Adult female:** Like adult male, but overall much browner, with head-sides and nape olive-brown, finer white spotting on chin and throat, mantle and rest of upperparts washed greyish and mottled whitish-buff, scapulars and tertials patterned blackish, buff and rufous-brown, wing-coverts fringed and vermiculated buff, outer secondaries deep blackish-brown, mottled rufous and fringed buff, tail vermiculated pale grey-brown, and underparts washed brown, with whitish spotting usually reaching upper breast. **Juvenile:** Much as adult female, but has unspotted whitish throat, back streaked whitish, underparts whitish with grey-brown mottling on breast and dark brown barring on flanks, buff-tipped greater primary-coverts, with outermost primaries more pointed and frayed than rest.

GEOGRAPHICAL VARIATION Five subspecies often recognised and listed here, separable according to coloration, especially of breast, and wing length, but validity of *languens* is perceived as questionable and status and relationships of nominate and *impedita* also demand further research.

C. d. bensoni Ridgway, 1887 occurs in Sonora (NW Mexico).

C. d. languens (Friedmann, 1943) occurs in W Chihuahua (NW Mexico); distinguished by indistinct pale spotting on breast, but see above.
C. d. douglasii (Vigors, 1829) occurs in S Sonora, Sinaloa, NW Durango and N Nayarit (W Mexico). Described above.
C. d. impedita (Friedmann, 1943) occurs in C and S Nayarit (W Mexico).
C. d. teres (Friedmann, 1943) occurs in NW Jalisco (WC Mexico).

MEASUREMENTS Length 22.0–25.5 cm. Sexes apparently similar in size. Males: wing 101–115, tail 66–94, weight (mean) 175. Females: wing 98–115, tail 65–87, weight (mean) 169, both sexes 160–196.

HABITAT Prefers arid to semi-humid brushy deciduous woodland, thorn forest, dense scrub in tropical forest and overgrown fields from sea level to 1000 m.

VOICE Male advertising call is a hollow, ringing and repeated *whoi* or *hoik* (very similar to that of Scaled Quail). Also gives a sharp, nasal clucking *keh teh-wek keh teh-wek…* or *whirr ki-dik…*, often uttered in series. When nervous, an emphatic *hui'ka hui'ka*, or a more excited *huit huit…* and a *ca-cow* uttered by separated members of pair or group in series of 2–5 notes (also like that given in similar circumstances by Scaled Quail).

HABITS Presumed sedentary. Coveys number 6–20 individuals, but disband in mid-April at start of breeding season. Habits considered to be much like Scaled Quail (which see). Takes wide range of herb seeds, fruits and insects, with legume seeds perhaps most favoured. Often forages alongside roads, scratching at ground, and will also visit cultivated areas to feed. Roosts above ground in thick bush or vine tangle.

BREEDING Few data. Nest reportedly on ground. Typically lays 8–12 white eggs, speckled pale brown, but sometimes as few as 4 and up to 20 found in single nest; latter presumably the result of two females laying in same scrape. In captivity lays one egg per day. Incubation period 22–23 days. Season commences in April–May.

DISTRIBUTION Mexico, from C and SE Sonora and SW Chihuahua south through Sinaloa, NW Durango and Nayarit to NW Jalisco.

STATUS Few data and status poorly known. Total population postulated as being 50,000–100,000 individuals and reportedly common in several areas, including some sites close to large towns and busy roads, with forest clearance and other human activities perhaps benefiting the species, at least locally. No evidence to suggest that it is threatened by over-hunting, but data are very sparse.

REFERENCES Brooks (2000), Carroll (1994), Howell & Webb (1995), Johnsgard (1988).

195 CALIFORNIA QUAIL
Callipepla californica (Shaw, 1798)   Plate 58

Alternative names: Valley Quail, San Lucas Quail (*achrustera*), Santa Catalina Quail (*catalinensis*), Warner Valley Quail (*orecta*).

Replaces Gambel's Quail in much of Baja California, California and the NW USA; occasional hybrids between the two from limited area of overlap in SE California may have chestnut throat patch, like Mountain Quail, but features otherwise much like one or other of parents (see Plate 58).

IDENTIFICATION Attractive stocky quail of arid country in W USA and Baja California, where it largely replaces closely related Gambel's Quail. Principal confusion risk is with latter in areas of overlap: both have striking black-and-white bridled head pattern and forward-pointing, drooping black crest. Both sexes of California have diagnostic pale or golden, scaled belly and central underparts (usually becoming chestnut at centre) and strongly speckled nape. Tawny-brown crown of male California differs slightly in coloration from that of Gambel's and other useful supporting features are the dense blackish scaling and fine white spotting on the hindneck and brown flanks. Hybrids occur where ranges meet. These show mixed features, such as a combination of black belly patch and scaled underparts. Sympatric Mountain Quail has very long, straight (not forward-drooping) crest, chestnut (not black) face, with white border, and chestnut flanks boldly barred white.

DESCRIPTION *C. g. californica* Rounded wings and moderately long tail of 12–14 rectrices. Forward-pointing, comma-shaped black crest (shorter and browner in female), usually more obvious in male. Bill blackish and legs grey. Sexes differ. **Adult male:** Pale forehead, black crest, tawny-brown crown with white border, and black face and throat also have white border. Hindneck, breast, flanks and upperparts grey-brown, with dense white spotting and black scales on hindneck, white streaks on flanks, and tail grey. Rest of underparts buff, grading to whitish on belly, which is heavily scaled black and has dark rufous centre, and coarsely streaked darker on undertail-coverts. Overall wings brown with whitish edges to inner webs of tertials forming contrasting stripes. **Adult female:** Much as adult male, but overall browner, and lacks dark central patch of belly and black-and-white head pattern (replaced by dirty white feathers with dark centres) and has brownish-grey neck, mantle and breast. **Juvenile:** Much as adult, but lacks boldly patterned flanks and has cryptically patterned upperparts, consisting of pale grey-brown, white and blackish, buff-tipped greater primary-coverts, and outermost primaries more pointed and frayed than rest.

GEOGRAPHICAL VARIATION Eight subspecies recognised and listed here. They differ to some extent

according to size, but principally in general coloration, especially in the tone of greyish or brownish on the mantle and back; such differences are most obvious in females.

C. c. californica (Shaw, 1798) occurs from N Oregon and W Nevada (NW USA) south to Baja California (NW Mexico), and probably introduced to SE British Columbia (SW Canada) southeast to Colorado (WC USA).

C. c. orecta (Oberholser, 1932) occurs in SE Oregon and extreme NW California (W USA).

C. c. brunnescens (Ridgway, 1884) occurs from coastal N California south to SC California (W USA) and probably introduced to Vancouver I. (Canada).

C. c. catalinensis (Grinnell, 1906) occurs on Santa Catalina I. (SW California) and nearby Santa Rosa and Santa Cruz islands, where probably introduced.

C. c. canfieldae (van Rossem, 1946) occurs in EC California (W USA).

C. c. plumbea (Grinnell, 1926) occurs from S California (W USA) to N Baja California (NW Mexico).

C. c. decoloratus (van Rossem, 1946) occurs in C and S Baja California (NW Mexico) between c.25°N and 30°N.

C. c. achrustera (Peters, 1923) occurs in extreme S Baja California (NW Mexico) and introduced to Chile, Argentina, New Zealand, Australia (King I.) and Hawaii.

MEASUREMENTS Length 23–27 cm. Male slightly larger. Males: wing 102–119, tail 77.0–95.5, weight (mean) 176. Females: wing 101–117, tail 78–92, weight (mean) 162.

HABITAT Uses variety of habitats, including arid to semi-arid scrub, grassland (perhaps most common in USA), agricultural land, understorey of open and mixed pine forest, riparian woodland and chaparral from sea level to 2800 m. Compared to Mountain Quail, with which it overlaps to great extent, uses less steep slopes, areas with less dense crown, shrub and ground cover and generally more open regions, edge and transitional habitats. Proximity of standing water is important.

VOICE Bears close similarity to Gambel's Quail: a loud crowing *ka-kwa* and *ka ka-kwah*, with accent on second part, also a single *k-yowh*, sharp clucking and spluttering calls.

HABITS Highly sedentary. Maximum recorded movement 27 km. Forms large, stable coveys of 25–40 individuals (but up to 1000 recorded) in non-breeding season (with little interchange between groups and with home territories of 6.8–18.0 ha), which disband from late February. Pairs, which may form in late winter within the covey, assume breeding territories of 4.8–10.0 ha that decrease to 1.2–4.0 ha with onset of nesting, but only unmated males appear to engage in strict territory defence. Takes forbs, legumes and seeds, with green herbage forming majority of diet in winter and spring. Legumes such as *Medicago*, *Trifolium*, *Lotus* and *Lupinus* are all of importance for their leaves and/or seeds. In California, *Erodium* spp. seeds are of some importance, while acorns may also be consumed in considerable quantities, as well as, locally, fruits. Scratches litter for seeds, takes barley and plucks leaves from live plants.

BREEDING Nests in sheltered location; a simple depression lined with grass among dry grass or at base of rock pile. Lays 6–17 (mean in various studies 10.9–14.2) creamy to pale buff eggs, spotted brown. Incubation in captivity 22–23 days (latter more common). Male assists with chick-rearing and may take sole responsibility for brood at two weeks if pair attempts a second clutch, but incubation is largely by female alone. Double-brooding perhaps not uncommon in favourable years/certain areas, but few verified instances and breeding success is reportedly often low. Chicks fledge at 14 days and have acquired full juvenile plumage at 70 days. Adult-like plumage is assumed at 21 weeks. Season from April (in south of range) or May–June (north) to July–August.

DISTRIBUTION SE British Columbia including Vancouver I. (where probably introduced), through Washington, Idaho, Oregon (some populations introduced), Nevada, Utah and California, including some offshore islands, to coastal Baja California south to Cape San Lucas. Introduced to Chile, from Atacama south to Concepción and spread to W Argentina, from San Juan south to Río Negro and much of Neuquén; King I. (Australia), New Zealand, Hawaii and, unsuccessfully, to Europe.

STATUS Few data, but considered to have undergone significant decline in USA since 1960, where it is an important gamebird with up to two million harvested annually. Overgrazing known to be detrimental in some areas, but equally undergrazed mesic habitats also may become unsuitable. Apparently still common in Baja California.

REFERENCES Carroll (1994), Howell & Webb (1995), Johnsgard (1988).

196 GAMBEL'S QUAIL
Callipepla gambelii (Gambel, 1843)

Plate 58

Alternative names: Desert/Arizona Quail, Fulvous-breasted Quail (*fulvipectus*), Tiburon Island Quail (*pembertoni*).

This species, which like California Quail has been placed in the genus *Lophortyx*, is restricted to SW USA and NW Mexico, where it is generally common in arid habitats.

IDENTIFICATION Arid-land crested quail of SW USA and NW Mexico, which is largely allopatric with similar California Quail, but is slightly larger and markedly greyer. Both sexes have plain yellowish-buff belly and central rear underparts, lacking scaly pattern of California. Male also has black (not pale) forehead, brighter chestnut crown and flanks, and distinctive blackish belly patch. Hybrids occur where ranges of California and Gambel's meet. These show mixed features, such as a combination of black belly patch and scaled underparts. Also overlaps with Mountain Quail, but latter has very long, straight crest, chestnut (not black) face, with white border, and chestnut flanks boldly barred white.

DESCRIPTION *C. g. gambelii* Rounded wings and moderately long tail of 12–14 rectrices. Forward-pointing, comma-shaped black crest, usually more obvious in male. Bill blackish, legs grey. Sexes differ. **Adult male:** Forehead and crest black, becoming rufous on crown with white border and striking black face and throat also have white border. Hindneck, breast and upperparts blue-grey, with slight black scales on hindneck. Rest of underparts buff, with blackish central belly, chestnut flanks boldly streaked white and coarsely dark-streaked undertail-coverts. Tail grey-brown. Overall wings brown with whitish edges to inner webs of tertials forming contrasting stripes. **Adult female:** Much as adult male, but overall browner, with plain greyish face and throat and lacks dark central patch of belly, which is finely streaked dark brown. **Juvenile:** Much as adult female, but lacks boldly patterned flanks and has cryptically patterned upperparts, consisting of pale grey-brown, white and blackish, buff-tipped greater primary-coverts, with outermost primaries more pointed and frayed than rest.

GEOGRAPHICAL VARIATION Seven subspecies recognised and listed here, which vary in grey tone to upperparts and that of buff to belly.
　　C. g. gambelii (Gambel, 1843) occurs from S Utah and Nevada (W USA) south to Baja California (NW Mexico), and also introduced to Idaho (NW USA). Described above.
　　C. g. sana (Mearns, 1914) occurs in W Colorado (WC USA).
　　C. g. ignoscens (Friedmann, 1943) occurs in S New Mexico and extreme W Texas (S USA).
　　C. g. pembertoni (van Rossem, 1932) occurs on Tiburón I. in Gulf of California (NW Mexico).
　　C. g. fulvipectus Nelson, 1899 occurs from NC to SW Sonora (NW Mexico) and possibly this race in SE Arizona and SW New Mexico (SW USA).
　　C. g. stephensi (Phillips, 1959) occurs in S Sonora (NW Mexico).
　　C. g. friedmanni (Moore, 1947) occurs in coastal and NW Sinaloa (NW Mexico).

MEASUREMENTS Length 23–27 cm. Male slightly larger. Males: wing 106–122, tail 81–107, weight (mean) 161. Females: wing 105–118, tail 83–102, weight (mean) 156, both sexes 160–176.

HABITAT Occurs in arid warm-desert scrub, typically in valleys with mesquite *Prosopsis* vegetation, uplands dominated by *Acacia*, *Yucca* and *Opuntia* (annual precipitation in such regions rarely exceeds 250 mm, but is usually above 125 mm per annum) or sagebrush *Artemisia* and other alkaline-adapted scrub (winter temperatures may be sub-freezing with prolonged periods of snow cover); also bushy riparian woodland and irrigated agricultural areas, from sea level to at least 1800 m. May require standing water if moist and succulent plants are unavailable.

VOICE Much like California Quail. Male gives a loud, crowing advertising call, *ka-kya*, *ka kah-ha*, with accent usually on second part; also a single *ka-owh* or *ka-aah*, a loud *chi-ca-go-go* uttered by separated members of covey or pair, sharp clucking and liquid chattering calls.

HABITS Sedentary, with maximum recorded movement of 16 km. Small winter coveys (mean 12.5 birds in one study, but up to 40 reported) constitute family groups, or multiples thereof, and home ranges (typically 7.6–38 ha, mean 14.3 ha) rarely overlap, though especially in late winter (as coveys begin to disband), there is considerable inter-group movement, especially among young males. Consumes wide variety of plants, flowers and leafy materials, especially legumes (in common with rest of genus), with seeds being the most important food item (particularly *Lotus*, *Erodium*, *Medicago* and *Acacia*). Probably reasonably catholic, permitting it to persist in agricultural as well as undeveloped desert areas, though, with exception of young, takes few insects.

BREEDING Monogamous, though high mortality rates presumably force many birds to select new partners each year. Nest a simple depression scratched under shelter of vegetation. Lays on near-daily basis, usually 4–6 eggs on each of three days, with a day between each. Clutch comprises 9–16 (occasionally up to 19) creamy to pale buff eggs, spotted brown/purplish-brown and incubated by female alone for 23 days. Male assumes guard duties or may take over first brood's care in order that female can attempt a second clutch. Season commences late April and continues until August.

DISTRIBUTION From EC California, S Nevada, S Utah and WC Colorado south to SE California, Arizona, New Mexico and extreme SW Texas (USA), thence south into Mexico, in NE Baja California, Sonora (including Tiburón I.), coastal Sinaloa and N Chihuahua. Introduced Hawaii, San Clemente I. off S California, and NC Idaho.

STATUS Few data, but total population estimated at over one million individuals and considered stable in USA since 1960s. Being an important gamebird in this country, populations and habitats are, to some extent, managed on behalf of the species. More tolerant than congenerics of conversion of natural habitats to cropland, though heavy grazing may have caused local declines.

REFERENCES Carroll (1994), Howell & Webb (1995), Johnsgard (1988).

Genus *PHILORTYX*: Banded Quail

The sole member of this genus is a drab, brownish quail with uniquely barred plumage, forward-pointing crest and moderately long tail. Latter features are indicative of *Callipepla* quails, but its uniqueness is confirmed by having skeletal features of closer affinity to the tree-quails *Dendrortyx*.

197 BANDED QUAIL
Philortyx fasciatus (Gould, 1844)

Plate 57

Alternative name: Barred Quail.

Peculiar small crested quail of arid country in S Mexico, where it is the ecological equivalent of the bobwhites.

IDENTIFICATION Small quail of dry scrubby habitats, endemic to Río Balsas drainage in WC Mexico where it replaces bobwhites; though both it and 'Black-headed' Northern Bobwhite of race *salvini* occur in vicinity of Acapulco. Its rather full tail and prominent upright blackish crest suggest a miniature Elegant Quail, but ranges do not overlap and Banded has boldly barred blackish and whitish underparts, whereas those of Elegant are spotted. Sexes remarkably similar, with whitish throats, but immature can be quite confusing, differing markedly in having blackish face and throat (perhaps suggesting *salvini* Northern Bobwhite). Fortunately habitat and limited distribution make it unlikely to be confused.

DESCRIPTION Small quail with straight, narrow crest. Tail moderately long, of 12 feathers. Bill blackish. Irides dark brown. Legs flesh-pink. Sexes similar. Juvenile and immature differ. **Adult:** Crest blackish. Rest of head, neck and upper breast cinnamon-brown, except whitish throat and weak whitish barring on breast. Rest of underparts whitish, boldly barred blackish. Upperparts, including wings, grey-brown, narrowly barred buff and more broadly barred black. Tail grey-brown with narrow buff bars. Sexes similar, though female has shorter crest. **Juvenile:** Initially has whitish shaft streaks and whitish throat, moulting into immature plumage at 8–12 weeks, which is closer to adult, but has blackish face and throat, finally becoming like adult at 16–20 weeks.

GEOGRAPHICAL VARIATION Monotypic.

MEASUREMENTS Length 19–21 cm. Sexes similar. Males: wing 95–102, weight (mean) 130. Females: wing 94–104, weight (mean) 126.

HABITAT Dry arid to semi-arid country, from weedy agricultural land with scattered bushes and trees to open thorn scrub, from sea level to 1600 m.

VOICE Advertising call a loud ringing *k-yah* or *keeah* often repeated. Another version is sharper and rapidly repeated. Latter might be same as low, repeated *ca-ut-la* reportedly given by scattered birds when flushed. Coveys 'explode' with loud squealing *wheer whee'ar* or *wheer-pee-pee-pee-peer*. Also a low growl in alarm.

HABITS Like bobwhites, generally shy and keeps well hidden in grassy cover. Largest coveys of up to 30 form in non-breeding season, but c.12 is usual. Coveys gather at roost sites towards dusk, usually roosting in trees. Keeps close to rank vegetation at field borders, from which coveys venture to forage in more open situations in early morning and evening, spending most of day in cover; runs across roads or tracks to nearby cover. Flushes suddenly, with birds scattering, generally over short distance

before returning to cover; sometimes flies to trees when flushed. Diet basically seeds of low-growing plants, augmented by insects in summer.

BREEDING Wild nest undocumented. Presumed monogamous. Nest a depression simply lined and lightly roofed with grasses. Clutch 3–7 white eggs, incubated by female alone for 21–23 days. Season chiefly July–September, which is rather later than Northern Bobwhite in the same area (around Acapulco).

DISTRIBUTION Endemic to Mexico, throughout drainage of Río Balsas, from S Jalisco and Colima to SW Pueblo and C Guerrero.

STATUS Locally common to frequent in restricted range, which suggests that population is stable. Little studied, but potential threats such as habitat degradation through overgrazing and agricultural intensification mean that this unique species could repay closer investigation.

REFERENCES Howell & Webb (1995), Johnsgard (1988).

Genus *COLINUS*: bobwhites

Plump, rather short-tailed New World quails of open, grassy country, and perhaps the most familiar and most geographically variable of American gamebirds. They are strongly sexually dimorphic. The c.45 taxa form a superspecies complex, which extends from the equator north to Maine; they have been grouped into four allopatric species, but a review is long overdue.

198 NORTHERN BOBWHITE
Colinus virginianus (Linnaeus, 1758)   Plate 59

Alternative name: Common Bobwhite (see also Geographical Variation).

This species exhibits the most remarkable range of geographical variation of all galliformes. Very well known in North America, it has been successfully introduced to various parts of the world.

IDENTIFICATION Bobwhites occur in open, grassy country and while far more often heard than seen, are perhaps the most familiar of North American gamebirds. Northern races present few problems, the white or buffish-white throat and supercilium, and mottled rufous-brown body prevents confusion with all other North American 'quails', most of which also have longer tails and crests. Southern races have rich rufous underparts with variable head and throat patterns, the most extreme having a solid blackish face and throat. Despite complexity of variation, identification presents little problem in field as range does not overlap with congeners. Introduced populations (e.g. France) also unlikely to be confused, being between partridges and Common Quail in size, but small juveniles with weakly-defined head pattern could be confused with Common Quail; latter has more pointed wings, if seen in flight, is smaller and has virtually tailless, pointed rear. Compare other bobwhites, especially Black-throated in Mexico.

DESCRIPTION *C. v. virginianus.* Crown feathers can form ruffled crest when erect. Irides dark brown. Bill

blackish. Legs flesh. Sexes differ. **Adult male:** Crown and nape chestnut, with blackish sides; supercilium long and broad from base of bill to nape, white. Chin and throat unmarked white; ear-coverts and lores blackish-chestnut, extending on neck-sides to form band across upper breast. Neck-sides and breast finely flecked white, breast and flanks rufous, with white scalloping on breast and black-and-white shaft streaks on flanks, and central underparts buffish-white, with fine blackish-grey scaling. Upperparts reddish-brown, vermiculated black and buff; tail, relatively short, greyish-brown. **Adult female:** Resembles male but overall duller, supercilium and throat unmarked warm buff, and crown and head-sides less blackish, darker reddish-brown. **Juvenile:** Like female in overall coloration, but all markings less distinct; has prominent buffish supercilium, but throat may be washed brownish.

GEOGRAPHICAL VARIATION Remarkably complex, differences striking in males, though all females similar, having buffish throats. In Mexico situation becomes extremely complex, with no fewer than 16 subspecies recognised. Some authorities have advocated treating southern and northern groups as separate species, and more radical opinions have proposed up to four species, despite interbreeding where forms meet.

Northern races: described above, basically five similar races extending over North America, south to N Mexico and including Cuba.

C. v. virginianus (Linnaeus, 1758) (includes *marilandicus*) occurs over most of E USA, south to N Florida; described above.
C. v. floridanus (Coues, 1872) occurs in peninsular Florida.
C. v. cubanensis (Gray, 1846) occurs in Cuba and the Isle of Pines.
C. v. taylori Lincoln, 1915 occurs in South Dakota, N Texas, NW Arkansas east to W Missouri.
C. v. texanus (Lawrence, 1853) occurs in SW Texas and extreme N Mexico.

Southern races: these inhabit most of Mexico and have almost unmarked rich rufous-chestnut underparts, but head and throat patterns vary geographically. For field purposes they can be subdivided into three groups.
C. v. ridgwayi Brewster, 1855 (Masked Bobwhite) occurs in C Sonora, where now very rare; has forehead, throat and face blackish, with diffuse supercilium behind eye.

The *pectoralis* group (Rufous-bellied Bobwhite) occurs over most of Mexican range, with exception of areas inhabited by Masked and Black-headed forms and extreme north, which is inhabited by *texanus* of Northern group; has white supercilium and throat, black facial mask and chest (black extending over entire breast in southernmost forms).
C. v. maculatus Nelson, 1899 occurs in C Tamaulipas, south to N Veracruz, west to SE San Luis Potosí.
C. v. aridus Aldrich, 1942 occurs in W and WC Tamaulipas south to SE San Luis Potosí.
C. v. graysoni (Lawrence, 1867) occurs in SE Nayarit and S Jalisco south to Morelos, S Hidalgo and SC San Luis Potosí.
C. v. nigripectus Nelson, 1897 occurs in Puebla, Morelos and México.
C. v. pectoralis (Gould, 1843) occurs in C Veracruz, on east slope of mountains.
C. v. godmani Nelson, 1897 occurs in lowlands of Veracruz.
C. v. minor Nelson, 1901 occurs in NE Chiapas and adjacent Tabasco.

The *atriceps* group (Black-headed Bobwhite) occurs in Oaxaca and S Chiapas, extending just into Guatemala; similar to Masked, but black more extensive on head and extending over breast.
C. v. atriceps (Ogilvie-Grant, 1893) occurs in interior W Oaxaca.
C. v. thayeri Bangs & Peters, 1928 occurs in NE Oaxaca.
C. v. harrisoni Orr & Webster, 1968 occurs in SW Oaxaca.
C. v. coyolcos (Müller, 1776) occurs on Pacific coast of Oaxaca and Chiapas.
C. v. salvini Nelson, 1897 occurs in coastal S Chiapas.
C. v. insignis Nelson, 1897 (includes *nelsoni*) occurs in S Chiapas and adjacent Río Chiapas valley in Guatemala.

MEASUREMENTS Length 24–28 cm. Sexes similar. Mexican races tend to be smaller than northern forms. USA wing 98–119, weight (mean) 171; Mexico wing 90–114, weight 129–159.

HABITAT Inhabits variety of semi-open to open country, from grassland with scattered bushes and trees to open woodland and forest clearings; also prairies, but avoids dense forest. Found both on plains and slopes of scrubby hillsides and canyons.

VOICE Advertising call a whistled *bob-WHITE* or *bob-bob-WHITE*, rising on the 'white'. Coveys reassemble once scattered by keeping in contact with repeated anxious, enquiring *a-loi-kee* or similar, which becomes increasingly loud as birds regroup. Variety of other calls, including raucous squealing in male territorial disputes.

HABITS Generally shy and keeps well hidden in grassy cover. Proclaims presence by voice, calling repeatedly in spring and summer from perch such as fence post or small tree. Largest coveys of up to 30 form in non-breeding season, but c.12 is usual. Coveys gather at roost sites towards dusk, roosting in tight circle on ground under thickets, facing outwards with tails up. Coveys disband at onset of breeding. Keeps close to rank vegetation at field borders, from which coveys forage in more open situations in early morning and evening, spending most of day under cover; runs across roads or tracks to adjacent cover. Flushes suddenly, with birds scattering, flying rapidly on downcurved whirring wings, generally keeping low. Diet varied over broad range, but typically seeds of low-growing plants, augmented by insects in summer.

BREEDING Monogamous. Nest a scrape, lined with grasses and with a grassy, arched roof, well concealed in grassy cover, often under fence post. Constructed by both sexes. Clutch 14–16 white eggs, incubated by female for 18–20 days. Rarely double-brooded, but often re-lays if first clutch predated. Season chiefly April–August, but varies somewhat over wide range (e.g. May–July in Cuba).

DISTRIBUTION North and C America. Native range extends from extreme SE Canada (S Ontario), south over E USA, west to South Dakota and SE Wyoming and into Mexico. Widespread over most of E, C and S Mexico, with isolated population in Sonora; range extends just into Guatemala (Chiapas Valley). In West Indies, occurs on Cuba and adjacent Isle of Pines. Widely introduced in various parts of world with varying success; currently established in parts of W North America (e.g. British Columbia and Oregon), several West Indian islands, France and New Zealand. Other introductions briefly flourished before dying out (e.g. British Isles).

STATUS Locally common, but northern and western populations particularly subject to fluctuations in abundance depending on severity of winters. Intensification of agriculture has produced dramatic declines over most of range, mirrored to largest degree in near extinction of race *ridgwayi* (Masked Bobwhite) of Sonora, which disappeared from adjacent Arizona by 1900. Remaining habitat in C Sonora now severely depleted through overgrazing by excessive cattle ranching to supply North American demand for beef. Remnants of wild population now restricted to few remaining ranches with extensive native grassland; attempts to reintroduce this form into Arizona have thus far failed as creation of extensive areas of native grassland appears to be only option to secure its ultimate survival.

REFERENCES Bent (1932), Johnsgard (1973), King (1979).

199 YUCATAN BOBWHITE
Colinus nigrogularis (Gould, 1843) Plate 59

Alternative name: Black-throated Bobwhite.

Closely related to both Northern and Spot-bellied Bobwhites, with series of isolated populations in Mexico to Nicaragua, none of which overlaps with congeners.

IDENTIFICATION Only bobwhite within restricted patchy range. Male has black throat and eye-band contrasting with bold white supercilium and head-sides; black and rufous underparts heavily spotted white. Adjacent races of Northern Bobwhite almost unmarked rufous below and have blackish heads. Females of the two very similar, sharing unmarked buff supercilium and throat, but in *nigrogularis* ground colour of underparts whiter, enhancing pattern. Lacks mottled throat of female Spot-bellied, but best distinguished by range and males. In Mexico, where Northern is widespread, Yucatan replaces it in Yucatán Peninsula. Elsewhere in C America, Yucatan occurs in dry savannas in two further areas north of central highlands, being replaced to south by Spot-bellied.

DESCRIPTION *C. n. caboti.* Crown feathers can form ruffled crest when erect. Bill blackish. Irides dark brown. Legs fleshy-grey. Sexes differ. **Adult male:** Crown and nape reddish-brown, supercilium white, forehead, band through eye, chin and throat black, and ear-coverts white. Breast and most of underparts white, each feather having prominent black terminal border forming heavy scaling; flanks rufous with white shaft streaks. Upperparts reddish-brown with grey-brown and fine black vermiculations, and weak buff fringing; tail greyish-brown. **Adult female:** Crown and nape brown, with black feather centres, chin, throat and supercilium buffish, unmarked; band through eye, extending on neck-sides and forming breast-band, brownish-buff closely marked with dark streaks. Rest of underparts buffish-white, with dark scalloping much less intense than male. Upperparts brown, vermiculated black and grey. **Juvenile:** Resembles female in overall coloration, but all markings less distinct; buff tips to primary-coverts.

GEOGRAPHICAL VARIATION Four subspecies recognised over fragmented range.

C. n. nigrogularis (Gould, 1843) occurs in Belize and adjacent Guatemala; similar to next but darker.
C. n. caboti Van Tyne & Trautman, 1941 occurs over most of Yucatán Peninsula of Mexico; described above.

C. n. persiccus Van Tyne & Trautman, 1941 occurs in Progresso area of Yucatán (Mexico); palest form, with sandy upperparts, and larger white markings and narrower black edging to underparts feathering giving delicately patterned appearance.
C. n. segoviensis Ridgway, 1888 occurs in NW Nicaragua and adjacent Honduras.

MEASUREMENTS Length 22–24 cm. Sexes similar. *C. n. caboti.* Both sexes: wing 95–103, weight 126–144 (male mean 137, female mean 139).

HABITAT Savanna grassland with bushes and trees, chiefly in form of weedy cultivation with scattered *Agave* clumps.

VOICE Advertising call a rising, whistled *bobWHITE* or *WHITE*, with rising inflection on the 'white'; though similar to Northern Bobwhite, is uttered more quickly and frequently lacks the 'bob'. All calls usually higher pitched than Northern and appears to lack caterwauling squealing call, which is replaced by a low *churr*, thus recalling Crested in this respect.

HABITS Generally shy and keeps well hidden. Proclaims presence by voice, calling repeatedly in spring and summer from perch such as fence post or small tree. Like Northern, coveys appear to average c.12. Little dependence on water, seemingly acquiring moisture from vegetation, but in dry season coveys are usually near water sources. General behaviour apparently much as Northern Bobwhite.

BREEDING Little studied in wild. Probably monogamous. Nest a depression lined with grasses, typically well concealed in cover beneath *Agave* clumps. Season appears prolonged, in Mexico at least April–August. Eggs white to pale buff, often with dark spotting, but poorly documented.

DISTRIBUTION C America. Three discrete populations: northernmost widespread over Yucatán and E Campeche (Mexico), with another pocket in Belize extending just into NE Guatemala, while the third inhabits extreme NW Nicaragua and adjacent NE Honduras.

STATUS Few data, but in Yucatán Peninsula appears locally frequent, with population density estimated at one bird per acre in prime areas.

REFERENCES Howell & Webb (1995), Johnsgard (1988).

Alternative names: see Geographical Variation.

Northern counterpart of Crested Bobwhite, with which it may be conspecific, but latter at northern limit of range is most different from Spot-bellied suggesting that their specific separation is valid. Following recent range expansion of Crested into Costa Rica, the two forms may overlap in the near future.

IDENTIFICATION Only bobwhite within restricted patchy range, which almost meets that of Crested in Costa Rica. Males have geographically variable head and breast patterns, from white throat, breast and central underparts to black throat, white malar stripe and spotted underparts; all have conspicuous white supercilium, spotted lower underparts and short crest. In Costa Rica the form *dickeyi* differs from Crested in having shorter crest, whitish (not rufous) supercilium and throat, and brown (not rufous) ground colour to underparts; additionally Spot-bellied is common in west and Central Valley, whereas Crested is known only from extreme east near Panama border, but appears to be spreading west. Females very similar, but supercilium and throat whiter in Spot-bellied.

DESCRIPTION *C. l. dickeyi*. Crown feathers form short, spiky crest when erect. Bill blackish. Irides dark brown. Legs grey. Sexes differ. Considerable geographical variation (see below). **Adult male:** Crown and nape brown, supercilium long and broad, white, and band through eye, extending over ear-coverts and on neck-sides, dark brown. Chin and throat whitish, mottled black and rufous; neck-sides black, with white mottling. Breast cinnamon-brown, finely mottled black, and rest of underparts brown, each feather with black-bordered white spot, largest and most obvious on flanks. Upperparts dull grey-brown, vermiculated grey, black and white. **Adult female:** Duller and less strongly marked than male, with greyer, but well-spotted underparts and buffier supercilium and throat, the latter mottled and streaked black. **Juvenile:** Like female in overall coloration, but underparts markings buffier and less distinct; buff tips to primary-coverts.

GEOGRAPHICAL VARIATION Six taxa usually considered valid, males differing in coloration and pattern of throat and breast, but female differences less striking. Extreme taxonomic opinions include lumping all forms with Crested Bobwhite of South America or treating them as two or four species. For field purposes they fall into four groups.

White-breasted Bobwhite (*hypoleucos* group): has throat, breast and central underparts white, flanks and body-sides brown with white spotting.
  C. l. incanus Friedmann, 1944 occurs in S Guatemala.

C. l. hypoleucos (Gould, 1860) occurs in W El Salvador.

White-faced Bobwhite: throat white, breast and underparts brown with white spotting.
  C. l. leucopogon (Lesson, 1842) occurs in E El Salvador.

Dickey's Bobwhite: throat white, mottled black and rufous, breast and underparts brown with white spotting.
  C. l. dickeyi Conover, 1932 occurs in Costa Rica; described above.

Sclater's Bobwhite (*sclateri* group): throat brownish-black, breast and underparts brown with white spotting.
  C. l. sclateri (Bonaparte, 1856) occurs in Nicaragua.
  C. l. leylandi Moore, 1849 occurs in Honduras.

MEASUREMENTS Length 22–24 cm. Sexes similar. Wing (both sexes) 95–107, weight (mean male) c.144, (mean female) c.115.

HABITAT Variety of open and semi-open country. Savanna grassland with bushes and trees, weedy cultivation and open woodland. From sea level to 1500 m.

VOICE Advertising call a throaty, scratchy *bobWHITE* or *bob-bobWHITE*; also a series of hoarse, throaty phrases: *pipi JEE pi JER* or *JER pi JEE*. Coveys maintain contact with clucking, cheeping and chattering notes. When alarmed, makes twittering sounds, which change to a *prrrt* as anxiety increases, and when flushed utter soft, repeated *chit* notes in flight.

HABITS Generally shy and keeps well hidden. Typically seen dashing across roads and tracks. Proclaims presence by voice, calling repeatedly before and during breeding season from perch such as fence post or small tree. Coveys forage in early morning and evening, retiring to dense cover for rest of day. Covey size 3–15. When alarmed, covey gathers before running, but flushes if hard-pressed, flying low with 'buzzy' flight for short distances.

BREEDING Little studied in wild. Probably monogamous. Nest a hollow of grass stems, hidden under a thick tussock. Clutch c.10 white eggs. Season May–September (slightly later in El Salvador).

DISTRIBUTION C America, from S Guatemala, through El Salvador and S and C Honduras to NW Nicaragua, with another population on Pacific slope of W Costa Rica extending into the highlands of Central Valley and even reaching upper limits of Caribbean slope.

STATUS Few recent data from most of range, but in Costa Rica quite common and widespread, and even described as an occasional pest of bean and rice crops.

REFERENCE Stiles & Skutch (1989).

Alternative names: see Geographical Variation.

The southernmost member of the genus, widespread over N South America, it exhibits considerable racial variation, southern forms in particular approaching certain races of Spot-bellied in plumage, but where ranges of two are closest their differences are most marked. Both voice and egg colour also appear to differ, reinforcing the impression that they constitute two species.

IDENTIFICATION Only bobwhite in South America (with seemingly isolated population in W Panama); range does not overlap with other bobwhites. Only problem area is Costa Rica, where Crested is a relatively recent colonist having spread from Panama; here Crested is only known from Pacific lowlands of Golfo Duce in extreme E Costa Rica, where Spot-bellied absent. Male of this population differs from Spot-bellied in much longer crest, rufous (not whitish) supercilium and throat, and darker upperparts and rufous, rather than dull brown ground colour to underparts. Elsewhere, crest and throat creamy or buff, with variable whitish or rufous patterning. Some have blackish bands from eye to (blackish white-spotted) collar; most have heavily spotted underparts, but some have breast or central underparts unspotted, with plain background colour. Female generally less variable than male, except in basic colour saturation; similar to Spot-bellied but has throat and supercilium usually more rufous, and a longer crest.

DESCRIPTION *C. c. sonnini.* Crown feathers form long, prominent often 'double-spiked' crest when erect. Bill blackish. Irides dark brown. Legs greyish-brown. Sexes differ. Males show considerable geographical variation, females less so. **Adult male:** Crest dirty whitish, becoming whiter on forehead and lores, and rufous-cinnamon near eye, extending as supercilium onto neck-sides and over most of throat, becoming whiter on chin and upper ear-coverts, and interrupted by black and white spotting bordering ear-coverts, merging with black-and-white spotted nape, and lower neck-sides and extending to narrowly border lower throat. Rest of underparts pinkish-chestnut, uniform and unmarked across breast, but heavily spotted with black-edged white markings on flanks and rest of underparts. Upperparts, including wings and tail, dull brown, vermiculated grey, black and white. **Adult female:** Duller and less strongly marked than male, with buffier, but quite strongly marked head and underparts; face and throat mottled and streaked black. Crest brownish and shorter but well developed. **Juvenile:** Resembles female in overall coloration, but underparts markings less distinct; buff tips to primary-coverts.

GEOGRAPHICAL VARIATION Considerable, chiefly in coloration of throat and breast, face pattern and length of crest. Given large number of described subspecies (c.14), it is perhaps surprising that differences are not more striking; indeed most differences are rather clinal and future work may unite some forms. Races in E Andes are darkest, e.g. *parvicristatus*, having the richest chestnut underparts, with *barnesi* even

having a dark brown crest. Other populations markedly paler, with *continentis* of NW Venezuela having buff underparts, with black scaling rather than bold spotting, while *sonnini* over most of eastern range has longest crest.

Central American races.
  C. c. mariae Wetmore, 1962 occurs in W Panama (Chiriquí).
  C. c. panamensis Dickey & van Rossem, 1930 occurs in western lowlands of Panama and adjacent Golfo Duce region of Costa Rica.

South American races.
  C. c. decoratus (Todd, 1917) occurs on Caribbean coast of Colombia.
  C. c. littoralis (Todd, 1917) occurs at north base of Santa Marta Mountains (Colombia).
  C. c. cristatus (Linnaeus, 1766) occurs at east base of Santa Marta Mountains and Guajira Peninsula (Colombia).
  C. c. badius Conover, 1938 occurs from Cauca Valley along Pacific slope of W Andes (Colombia).
  C. c. leucotis (Gould, 1844) occurs in Magdalena and Sinú valleys (Colombia).
  C. c. bogotensis Dugand, 1943 occurs in Boyacá and Cundinamarca (Colombia).
  C. c. parvicristatus (Gould, 1843) occurs on east slope of E Andes of Colombia and W Venezuela (N Amazonas, NW Bolívar and upper Apure Valley).
  C. c. horvathi Madaràsz, 1904 occurs in Mérida Andes of Venezuela.
  C. c. continentis Cory, 1913 occurs in coastal NW Venezuela, Aruba and Curaçao.
  C. c. barnesi Gilleard, 1940 occurs in NC Venezuela.
  C. c. mocquerysi (Hartert, 1894) occurs in NE Venezuela.
  C. c. sonnini (Temminck, 1815) occurs in coastal N Venezuela, east through Guianas to extreme N Brazil (upper Rio Branco); described above.

MEASUREMENTS Length 18–23 cm. Sexes similar, but male averages larger. *C. c. sonnini.* Males: wing 95–120, weight 132–153. Females: wing 92–119, weight 131–141.

HABITAT Variety of open and semi-open country, from semi-arid lowlands with weedy cultivation, through savanna grasslands with bushes and trees, to woodland fringes. From sea level to 1500 m, locally to 3200 m in Colombia.

VOICE Advertising call resembles Northern Bobwhite but voice less rich and mellow, and sequence faster. Compared to voice of Spot-bellied in Costa Rica described as clearer, less throaty and transcribed *pwit pwit PWEET*; also gives wheezy *WHEEcher* repeated up to six times, this more clipped than equivalent in Northern but very similar to Yucatan Bobwhite. Coveys maintain contact with chirping and cheeping notes.

HABITS Like congeners: generally shy and keeps well hidden, but where unmolested may become remarkably confiding, e.g. in N Brazil reported coming to houses for food. Proclaims presence by voice, but though said to be less vocal than Northern Bobwhite, calls throughout year. Usually in pairs or small coveys, generally of fewer than ten, i.e. smaller in number than Northern Bobwhite.

BREEDING Little studied in wild. Probably monogamous. Nest a hollow of grass stems, hidden under thick tussock. Clutches of 8–16 recorded; eggs creamy-buff, usually blotched dark brown. Incubation 22–23 days. Breeds chiefly in wet season, but recorded in most months in various parts of Colombia, i.e. February and April–September.

DISTRIBUTION N South America, with isolated population in W Panama and adjacent Costa Rica, but strangely absent from E Panama. Widespread over most of Colombia and Venezuela, through Surinam and Guyana and into adjacent N Brazil (N Rio Branco and Amapá). Introduced to several West Indian islands but perhaps only survives on Mustique (where current status unclear). Also recorded on Aruba and Curaçao where also possibly introduced.

STATUS Locally common in most of range. In Colombia reported to be locally common in valleys of interior, and spreading in lowlands through forest clearance; conversely habitat degradation has lead to some highland populations becoming rare and fragmented. Similar situation in Venezuela. From Panama, its spread into Costa Rica has been aided by forest clearance and agricultural conversion of lowlands.

REFERENCES Carroll (1994), Hilty & Brown (1986), Meyer de Schauensee & Phelps (1978), Stiles & Skutch (1989).

Genus *ODONTOPHORUS*: wood-quails

Medium-sized dark partridge-like birds of Neotropical rain- and cloud forests, with a distribution centred on humid forests of the N Andes of Colombia and cordilleras of C America. All are very dark, often blackish-brown or deep chestnut, with short tails, relatively stout bills and heavy, almost square-topped heads, the latter an effect of the elongated crown feathers that form a ruffled rear crown; in some species the crown feathers may be conspicuously crested when erected.

Sociable by nature, they are usually encountered in small coveys, which are basically family parties. They inhabit dense undergrowth of primary forest and are among the most difficult of all gamebirds to observe in the wild. Coveys maintain contact with bubbly calls, often uttered in noisy choruses as coveys define their feeding territories in early morning, or assemble to roost well concealed in low tree canopy at dusk. Often vocalisations are only clue to presence, but waiting quietly by forest trails toward dusk and dawn sometimes permits glimpses as they scratch noisily at edges of cover or cross open spaces in single file. Few species appear to occur in true sympatry, being either separated geographically or by altitude, but most are so poorly known that broader overlap possibly occurs. Knowledge of most is based on specimens, and field observations may greatly contribute to our understanding of their ecology and future conservation; several wood-quails are threatened by deforestation.

If seen well, unlikely to be confused with other Neotropical gamebirds, only much smaller Singing Quail in C America and more widespread Tawny-faced Quail share similar habitats. Latter is smaller, with orange head-sides and grey breast (male), or has prominently barred rear underparts (female). Smaller species of tinamou have different overall shape, with smaller head on thinner neck and more bulbous, tailless, body.

Wood-quails comprise 15 species as treated here but 9 form two superspecies complexes of allopatric forms (as indicated below).

Chestnut group
O. melanotis (Black-eared)
O. erythrops (Rufous-fronted)
O. hyperythrus (Chestnut)
O. melanonotus (Dark-backed)
O. speciosus (Rufous-breasted)

Dusky group
O. dialeucos (Tacarcuna)
O. strophium (Gorgeted)
O. columbianus (Venezuelan)
O. leucolaemus (Black-breasted)

202 MARBLED WOOD-QUAIL
Odontophorus gujanensis (Gmelin, 1789)   Plate 60

The best-studied and most widespread wood-quail, with a range extending from Costa Rica to C Brazil.

IDENTIFICATION Dull brownish plumage and reddish-orange facial skin unique within range, but acquiring adequate views of any wood-quail always problematic. Over most of range is only wood-quail, but confusion possible in C America and W South American range where it meets other species; its relatively dull coloration and lack of any white on head and throat separates it from most others, except Starred, which has white spotting on breast and upper flanks, unbarred underparts and relatively plain, pale grey head and throat, with rufous crown tuft.

DESCRIPTION *O. g. gujanensis*. Loose-crested appearance; though feathers relatively short they give ruffled appearance to crown. Bill stout, blackish (reddish in juvenile). Irides russet to dark brown. Bare skin around eye reddish or orange. Legs bluish-lead or grey. Sexes similar. **Adult:** Loose-crested crown feathers vermiculated dark brown. Upperparts dull brown, vermiculated blackish, and indistinct pale spotting on rump and uppertail-coverts, becoming greyish on mantle and nape. Underparts dull or buffish-brown with indistinct close dull buff and dark barring. Head-sides and forecrown almost unmarked dull rufous (duller in females) with pale buff mark behind eye. Sexes similar, but female slightly smaller and duller rufous on head-sides and throat. **Juvenile:** Similar, but bill reddish-orange (not blackish) and crown feathers warmer brown, lacking vermiculations of adult.

GEOGRAPHICAL VARIATION Quite marked in degree of colour saturation over wide range with eight races currently recognised. Nominate *gujanensis* and *medius* of eastern part of range dark and richly-coloured, with tawny underparts and darkish grey mantle. Western and northern races most uniform and less dark, with mantle indistinctly, or lighter, grey.

O. g. gujanensis (Gmelin, 1789) occurs in E Venezuela through Guianas, N and W Brazil to NE Paraguay; described above.

O. g. medius Chapman, 1929 occurs in Amazonas (S Venezuela) to NW Brazil; ochraceous-tawny below (like nominate), with head-sides and throat greyish (as in *buckleyi*), and underparts brighter than *marmoratus*, as well as lacking white spotting and barring on throat of latter.

O. g. marmoratus (Gould, 1844) occurs in E Panama, N Colombia and NW Venezuela; most like *castigatus*, but crown and crest duskier, often flecked cinnamon, neck and upper back black and grey, rear underparts more conspicuously barred, and chin and throat more extensively spotted and bared white/grey.

O. g. castigatus Bangs, 1901 occurs in SW Costa Rica and W Chiriquí (extreme W Panama); most like *marmoratus*, but crown and crest more uniform, often inclining to reddish-brown, neck and upper back brown or olivaceous, and chin and throat darker, with less grey or white spotting and barring.

O. g. buckleyi Chubb, 1919 occurs in E and S Colombia, E Ecuador to N Peru; head-sides and throat grey to greyish-buff, being overall similar to nominate, but duller, with heavier duskier markings.

O. g. pachyrhynchus Tschudi, 1844 occurs in EC Peru and probably this form discovered in W Bolivia; head-sides, chin and throat rufous (like nominate), but underparts darker and more obviously barred, and has deeper based bill.

O. g. rufogularis Blake, 1959 occurs in NE Peru; most like previous form or *buckleyi*, but head- and neck-sides and throat rufous-chestnut, and has greyer and duskier underparts, with little barring, darker olive rump and uppertail-coverts, and a heavier bill.

O. g. simonsi Chubb, 1919 occurs in E Bolivia; the palest form, being less reddish above than nominate, with duller, more greyish-brown crown, crest tipped black, head-sides and chin tawny (not rufous), throat and foreneck greyish, breast pale tawny, becoming buffy-grey on rest of underparts, and lacks dark markings on vent.

MEASUREMENTS Length 23–29 cm. Male averages larger. All races. Males: wing 130–155, tail 51.0–77.5, tarsus 39–48, weight 313–380. Females: wing 130–149, tail 51–75, tarsus 41–46, weight (n=1) 298.

HABITAT Rain- and cloud-forest undergrowth, preferring lowland hill forest, from sea level to 900 m (Ecuador), but to 1000 m (Panama), at least 1300 m (Colombia) and 1800 m (Venezuela). Locally in tall secondary forest, especially mature *terra firme* in Ecuador.

VOICE Advertising call far carrying; a fast, rhythmic, musical and resonant duet, rapidly repeated for prolonged periods and audible over up to 0.5 km. Likened to '*burst the BUBble, burst the BUBble*' or '*corocoroVADo, corocoroVADo*', the male uttering first part ('*burst the*') and female the latter ('*BUBble*'). Coveys maintain contact with low, soft notes while feeding. Other calls include a soft *witty witty witty* and a prolonged cackling *caaa caaa caaa*, as well as a confusingly hollow repeated *koo-kororo, koo-kororo, koo-kororo*, which is similar to rarer Starred Wood-quail. Its varied vocabulary also includes a rising and swelling *too-too-too-too-too-too-too*.

HABITS Generally shy, but locally confiding where not persecuted. Voice betrays presence, calling repeatedly towards dawn and dusk, sometimes in daytime and often on moonlit nights. Often in small parties of 5–8 on forest floor or slope, walking in single file, scratching in leaf-litter for invertebrates and fallen fruits. Occasionally visits riverside sand bank in early morning to drink. Keeps close to shade of dense ground vegetation or fallen trees. Normally crouches or walks quietly away when approached, but if suddenly surprised at close range covey may flush and scatter as far as 80 m before landing and running. Probably roosts in trees, well concealed in canopy.

BREEDING Probably monogamous. Nest a scrape with roof of dead leaves and sticks, at base of tree among tree roots. Clutch 4 pure white, glossy or unglossed oval eggs, often with some brown spotting, which is occasionally heavy. Season January–August at least in north and west of range.

DISTRIBUTION Widespread in humid forested areas of C America and N South America, from Pacific slope of Costa Rica, through Panama, north and east of Andes in Colombia, most of Venezuela (except central-north), the Guianas, E Ecuador, E and C Peru, N and E Bolivia and N Brazil (south to N and W Mato Grosso and NE Pará).

STATUS Locally quite common, but forest destruction and hunting responsible for dramatic decreases in some areas (e.g. Panama where now feared extinct). Indeed future of northernmost subspecies *castigatus* appears gloomy, as if lost from Panama is now confined to small isolated area of SW Costa Rica, where local decreases also reported (e.g. appears to have disappeared from Carara Biological Reserve at extreme northern limit of range). Overall, given its relatively extensive range, this is the least endangered of the wood-quails.

REFERENCES Blake (1977), Hilty & Brown (1986), Johnsgard (1988), Ridgely & Greenfield (2001), Stiles *et al.* (1999), Stiles & Skutch (1989), Wetmore (1965).

203 SPOT-WINGED WOOD-QUAIL
Odontophorus capueira (Spix, 1825)   Plate 60

The most southerly wood-quail; considering its relatively wide range, surprisingly little appears to be known concerning its habits or current status.

IDENTIFICATION Except tinamous, no other gamebirds occur within its range; the former have tiny heads on thin necks and more bulbous, tailless bodies and thus unlikely to be confused. Dark slate-grey wood-quail with bare red skin around eye and cinnamon supercilium, most similar to Marbled Wood-quail of N Brazil, but unmarked dark grey underparts and clear white spotting on upperparts provide easy distinctions if seen well, and ranges do not overlap.

DESCRIPTION *O. c. capueira*. Loose crest gives ruffled appearance to rear crown. Bill stout, blackish (reddish in juvenile). Irides dark brown. Bare skin around eye reddish. Legs dark grey. Sexes similar. **Adult:** Crown, including loose crest, ruddy-brown, spotted buff. Supercilium and frontal band cinnamon-rufous. Throat, head-sides and entire underparts slate-grey. Upperparts grey-brown, with blackish vermiculations and spotting, and white shaft streaks on nape, mantle, back and scapulars; rump and uppertail-coverts plainer, buffier and unstreaked, and wing-coverts spotted white. Female very similar, but slightly smaller. **Juvenile:** Similar, but has reddish bill, broader and more conspicuous pale shaft streaks on upperparts and grey underparts washed rufousbrown and freckled white.

GEOGRAPHICAL VARIATION Probably best regarded as monotypic, though an ill-defined subspecies has been described from NE Brazil.

O. c. capueira (Spix, 1825) occurs over most of range; described above.

O. c. plumbeicollis Cory, 1915 occurs in Ceará and Alagoas (NE Brazil;) paler, more buff-toned underparts than nominate, with less-defined whitish streaking above, throat and foreneck vermiculated blackish, and narrower supercilium and frontal band.

MEASUREMENTS Length 26.5–30.0 cm; males average larger. *O. c. capueira*. Males: wing 151–172, tail 75–82, weight c.457. Females: wing 144–153, tail 70–77, weight c.396.

HABITAT Lowland dry, dense tropical forest, including mature secondary growth, to 1600 m.

VOICE Poorly documented. Advertising call 3–4 flute-like, sometimes very slow sustained notes *uru...uru...uru...uru*, repeated and far carrying; given in duet (commenced by male with monosyllabic *kloh-kloh-kloh*) and most usually heard close to dawn and dusk, especially on moonlit nights, when coveys assemble to feed or roost. Given from roost in breeding season. Loud *wit, wit, wit* in alarm, and also gives weak tremulous *bew, bew, bew* at roost.

HABITS Largely unstudied in wild, but appear very similar to those of Marbled Wood-quail. Occurs in pairs or small coveys (principally family groups), usually of 6–8, but 10–15 also reported; these remain constant even when female nesting. Prefers to flee from danger, especially when with small young, and may sometimes hide by crouching on ground. Disturbed birds may return to food source. Takes nuts, especially *Araucaria*, berries, principally *Phytolacca decandra* and presumably insects. Roosts on narrow horizontal branches, at mid-height in trees.

BREEDING Monogamous. Few wild data. Nests on ground, sometimes in hole and always constructs shelter of dry leaves, with side entrance and secure roof. Eggs white, becoming yellowish or even reddish with dirt. More than one female may lay in same nest as clutches of up to 12 reported. Season August–November. Captive birds constructed a domed nest and laid 5 and 3 white eggs in a clutch, the smaller clutch being laid after the first had been removed. Incubation by female alone 18–19 days, and female also assumes responsibility for chick care.

DISTRIBUTION E Brazil, from Ceará and Alagoas in north, south to Rio Grande do Sul and west to SE Mato Grosso; extending into Paraguay in Campos Cerrados, Central Paraguay and Alto Paraná, and extreme NE Argentina in Misiones.

STATUS Few recent reports from Argentina or Paraguay and its rather specialised Atlantic lowland forest habitat is threatened in Brazil. Formerly hunted with snares. However, appears locally quite common in protected forests, though extreme northeastern population *plumbeicollis* is certainly at risk, given extensive deforestation within its range.

REFERENCES Belton (1984), Blake (1977), Carroll (1994), Hayes (1995), Hellmayr (1929), Johnsgard (1988), Sick (1993).

---

204 BLACK-EARED WOOD-QUAIL
Odontophorus melanotis Salvin, 1865   Plate 61

Closely related to Rufous-fronted Wood-quail with which it is usually considered conspecific, but their ranges possibly meet on the Panama/Colombia border, apparently without intergradation.

IDENTIFICATION Inhabits low to mid-altitude forests on Caribbean slope of C America. Appears all

dark in forest gloom, but closer views should reveal unspotted chestnut crown and underparts, and blackish throat and head-sides. Overlaps with Marbled Wood-quail, which has dull underparts, lacking blackish face and throat, and reddish (not bluish or dusky) orbital skin; and Spotted, which has brighter, more orange crest and white-spotted underparts. Suspected to meet Rufous-fronted in extreme NW Colombia, which differs in having bold white throat crescent and dusky crown, but lacks black throat. Ecuadorian race of Rufous-fronted very similar to Black-eared, differing chiefly in having rufous ear-coverts and blackish-brown crown.

DESCRIPTION *O. m. melanotis.* Loose crest gives ruffled appearance to rear crown. Bill stout, blackish (perhaps brownish-red in juveniles). Irides dark brown, varying from deep reddish-brown in male to coffee-brown in female. Bare skin around eye purplish (male) or bluish-black (female). Legs grey, with blue-black feet. Sexes basically similar. **Adult male:** Loose-crested chestnut crown feathers dark tipped and relatively short, but afford ruffled appearance to crown. Upperparts dull brown, with indistinct buffish and blackish vermiculations, and feather centres. Head-sides and throat dull black. Breast and most of underparts rich chestnut, becoming brownish, finely barred blackish on lower flanks and belly to undertail-coverts. **Adult female:** Slightly smaller and duller, with some mottling on underparts, less intense blackish face and throat (can entirely lack blackish) and blacker orbital skin. **Juvenile:** Duller, bill reddish-brown (specimens), upperparts have buffish shaft streaks, and underparts more extensive black barring and spotting.

GEOGRAPHICAL VARIATION Slight; two subspecies generally recognised.
 O. m. melanotis Salvin, 1865 (includes '*coloratus*') occurs from Honduras (separated from *verecundus* by the Aguán Valley) and Nicaragua to Panama; described above.
 O. m. verecundus Peters, 1929 occurs in Honduras; colder, greyer upperparts than nominate, with less conspicuous black scapular and wing-covert markings, and more obsolete dark tibial bars.

MEASUREMENTS Length 22–28 cm; male averages fractionally larger. *O. m. melanotis.* Males: wing 130–153, tail 42–60, tarsus 43–47, weight c.340. Females: wing 131–149, tail 50–53, tarsus 44–47, weight c.329.

HABITAT Tropical and subtropical forest of lowlands and foothills, reaching 1000 m in Costa Rica and 1600 m in Panama, but to just 500 m in Honduras. Locally in dense secondary growth.

VOICE Advertising call far carrying; a rhythmic, musical, ringing, cheery duet (two or more individuals simultaneously in gabbling chorus), rapidly repeated up to 12 or more times. Likened to *kooLAWlik kooLAWlik, kooKLAWK kooKLAWK* or *LAWcooKLAWcoo.* Coveys maintain contact with low, soft, cooing and peeping conversational notes. Other calls described include a liquid alarm rattle.

HABITS Generally shy and elusive, betraying presence by voice, calling repeatedly in early morning and towards dusk. Typically in coveys of up to 12 on forest floor, walking in single file when crossing open patches, or ascending slopes. Keeps close to shade of dense ground vegetation, scratching in leaf-litter for insects and fallen fruits. Normally 'freezes' or runs rapidly if approached, flushing with great reluctance; if flushed, covey tends to break up, flying away in twos and threes.

BREEDING Little known. Probably monogamous. A Costa Rican nest was a scrape lined with leaves and grasses at foot of large tree. Clutch 4 creamy-white eggs, at least sometimes spotted brown. In Panama breeding commences in late dry season.

DISTRIBUTION Caribbean slope of C America from NC Honduras, through N Nicaragua, Costa Rica and Panama; also on Pacific slope in E Panama. Range suspected to extend over border into extreme NW Colombia.

STATUS Formerly not uncommon, but forest destruction has produced marked decrease throughout its range. In Costa Rica and Panama now described as scarce and local. Shuns human habitation and rapidly disappears from settled areas. Long considered uncommon in Honduras.

REFERENCES Blake (1977), Carroll (1994), Monroe (1968), Stiles & Skutch (1989), Wetmore (1965).

205 RUFOUS-FRONTED WOOD-QUAIL
Odontophorus erythrops Gould, 1859   Plate 61

Rusty-rufous wood-quail of Pacific slope of Colombia and Ecuador.

IDENTIFICATION Low to mid-altitude forests of W Colombia and Ecuador. Most of head and underparts unspotted chestnut, with dull brown upperparts; bare orbital skin dark. Rich rufous head-sides and underparts and white throat bar distinguish it from Black-fronted. Nominate Ecuadorian race of Rufous-fronted may lack white throat bar of Colombian form and is very similar to Black-eared, differing chiefly in having rufous ear-coverts and blacker brown crown (ranges quite different). Virtually unknown Gorgeted is similar but has black-and-white head-sides, and white spots on breast; Chestnut lacks black and white on throat (as may female Rufous-fronted), and has

bare whitish skin around eye; neither known to occur within range of Rufous-fronted. Dark-backed of NW Ecuador and extreme SW Colombia occurs at higher altitudes, has rufous only on throat and breast, darker upperparts and lacks white throat bar. Ranges of other wood-quails do not meet Rufous-fronted.

DESCRIPTION *O. e. parambae.* Loose-crested crown feathers relatively short but give ruffled appearance to crown. Bill stout, blackish (perhaps reddish-brown in juvenile). Irides dark brown. Bare skin around eye purplish (male) or blackish (female). Legs grey. Sexes basically similar, though female duller. **Adult male:** Loose-crested chestnut crown feathers dark tipped and relatively short. Upperparts dull brown, with indistinct buffish and blackish vermiculations,

GEOGRAPHICAL VARIATION Monotypic.

MEASUREMENTS Length 22–25 cm; male averages fractionally larger. Males: wing 129–131, tail 50–54, tarsus 45–48, weight c.264. Females: wing 126–132, tail 46–50, tarsus 44.5–49.0, weight c.258.

HABITAT Humid subtropical forest, at 1050–1450 m.

VOICE Virtually undescribed. When flushed reported to utter low, rapid, alarm calls typical of genus.

HABITS Little known. Occurs in pairs or parties of up to eight within undergrowth on forest floor. Will flush if hard-pressed, one seen flying to perch in tree at height of c.5 m

BREEDING Undescribed. A juvenile was collected in early June.

DISTRIBUTION Confined to Darién Highlands of Panama–Colombia border; in E Panama known from Cerro Tacarcuna and Cerro Mali. In 1982 discovered on slopes of Cerro Tacarcuna on Colombian side of border.

STATUS Vulnerable. Population estimated at fewer than 10,000 individuals, but considered probably stable. Given incredibly restricted range, threatened by forest destruction for mining, agriculture, coca production (though perhaps not yet within species' altitudinal range) and potential completion of Pan-American Highway, but appears safe at present as its range is relatively inaccessible and uninhabited. Darién National Park nominally protects virtually entire Colombian range, but protected area's integrity is far from secure. In 1965 it was described as quite numerous on these two mountains, and there has probably been little change since.

REFERENCES BirdLife International (2000), Blake (1977), Ridgely (1976), Wege (1996), Wetmore (1965).

---

211 GORGETED WOOD-QUAIL
Odontophorus strophium (Gould, 1844)   Plate 63

A Colombian endemic recently rediscovered after having been 'lost' for nearly 60 years. Despite the renewed hope, it could still disappear unless restrictions on forest clearance within its limited range are enforced.

IDENTIFICATION C Colombia where not known to come into contact with other wood-quails, though approaches regions inhabited by both Rufous-fronted and Black-fronted. Gorgeted easily distinguished if seen well by black-and-white variegated head pattern and white chest-band; Rufous-fronted also has a white collar but occurs at lower elevations, has chestnut head-sides and lacks white breast spotting of Gorgeted. Closely related Tacarcuna occurs only near Panama border of Colombia.

DESCRIPTION Crown feathers short but probably impart somewhat ruffled appearance. Bill stout, blackish. Irides dark brown. Lacks obvious bare orbital skin. Legs dusky-grey. Sexes differ. **Adult male:** Crown feathers blackish-brown. Supercilium, head-sides and throat chiefly white, with blackish band running back from eye and mottled blackish throat centre, blackish extending below white ear-coverts; band of white forms collar on lower throat, bordered below by blackish. Rest of underparts rufous-chestnut, with bold white spotting on breast. Upperparts dark warm brown with buff shaft streaks and blackish spotting. **Adult female:** Head pattern similar to male, but more mottled, throat centre whiter, less solid blackish and underparts dark grey. **Juvenile:** Resembles female, but more brownish-grey below and has fewer and smaller, diamond-shaped pale spotting, buff with black border.

GEOGRAPHICAL VARIATION Monotypic.

MEASUREMENTS Length 25–28 cm; male averages fractionally larger. Males: wing 127–151, tail 56–58, weight c.302. Females: wing 135–146, tail (n=1) 59, weight c.302.

HABITAT Humid subtropical forest dominated by oak and laurels, at 1750–2050 m, through speculated to occupy range of 1500–2500 m, and is known to use degraded and secondary areas.

VOICE Typical loud rollicking song of genus, usually given in early morning, but no other details.

HABITS Largely undescribed, but presumably typical of genus. Forages for fruit, seeds and arthropods within dense undergrowth on forest floor.

BREEDING Probably March–May and again September–November, coinciding with peaks in rains; male with chicks observed in May.

DISTRIBUTION Known from only four sites on west slope of E Andes of C Colombia between Betulia (Santander) and Bogotá Subia (Cundinamarca).

STATUS Critical. Population recently estimated at possibly fewer than 1000 individuals. Prior to 1970 largely known only from specimens and considered possibly extinct as forest in areas where these taken by then severely depleted. Rediscovered in Cuchilla del Ramo (Santander) in May 1970, when male with young captured, and Guanentá–Alto Río Fonce Flora and Fauna Sanctuary, where a female was collected in November 1979, a young female in December 1979 and a male in March 1981. Though forest in Bogotá area has been mostly cleared and there have been no records in Cundinamarca since 1954, sufficient suitable forest remains in Santander to support it. Some of this is now protected; though hunting and selective logging affect lower parts of the 100 km² Guanentá–Alto Río Fonce Flora and Fauna Sanctuary, areas above 1900 m are largely intact.

REFERENCES Andrade & Repizzo (1994), BirdLife International (2000), Collar *et al.* (1992), Hilty & Brown (1986), Romero-Zambrano (1983).

212 VENEZUELAN WOOD-QUAIL
Odontophorus columbianus Gould, 1850
Plate 62

Closely related to Gorgeted and Tacarcuna, replacing them in cloud forests of N Venezuela.

IDENTIFICATION Dark reddish and brownish wood-quail with striking whitish throat and heavily spotted underparts; range does not overlap with two other Venezuelan wood-quails. Black-fronted, which is only known further north (in Zulia), has blackish face and throat, and Marbled, of lower altitudes, has unspotted underparts, lacks white throat and has reddish orbital skin.

DESCRIPTION Crown feathers ruffled especially at rear. Bill stout, blackish (reddish in juveniles). Irides dark brown. Lacks obvious bare orbital skin. Legs dusky-grey. Sexes differ. **Adult male:** Crown feathers dark brown, freckled black, short but impart somewhat ruffled appearance to crown. Chin and throat white, mottled blackish at sides, with blackish lower border. Indistinct mottled buff-and-black band behind eye, above dusky ear-coverts. Rest of underparts dark reddish-brown, clearly marked with black-bordered white arrowhead spots, except on rear underparts, which are buffish, freckled black. Upperparts grey-brown, with buff shaft streaks, edged black; nape chestnut and scapulars have heavier black spotting. **Adult female:** Like male but underparts plainer brown, with sparser, smaller spots. **Juvenile:** Similar to female, but buff shaft streaks on upperparts weak or absent, and smaller or no spots on underparts; bill reddish.

GEOGRAPHICAL VARIATION Monotypic.

MEASUREMENTS Length 25–30 cm; male averages fractionally larger. Males: wing 134–150, tail 45–62, weight c.343. Females: wing 132–150, tail 50–60, weight c.336.

HABITAT Highland subtropical cloud forest, at 800–2400 m.

VOICE Undescribed.

HABITS Little known. Found in parties of up to 12 within undergrowth on forest floor. Seen to go to roost in palm fronds.

BREEDING Few data. One nest was a chamber with 'roof' of vegetation, placed at foot of palm tree. Clutch 6 white eggs, incubated 30 days. Season stated to be May–late July.

DISTRIBUTION Endemic to Venezuela. Known from along the Río Chiquito in SW Táchira and through northern coastal cordillera, from Carabobo to W Miranda.

STATUS Near Threatened. Like all wood-quails, destruction of its forest habitats is greatest threat, especially in view of restricted range. While extensive habitat remains in some areas of the northern cordillera, habitat loss around Caracas and other human settlements has been severe, and deforestation in Táchira has also been heavy. Present in several protected areas, recently reported as apparently quite numerous in parts of Henri Pittier National Park.

REFERENCES BirdLife International (2000), Blake (1977), Carroll (1994), Johnsgard (1988), Meyer de Schauensee & Phelps (1978).

213 BLACK-BREASTED WOOD-QUAIL
Odontophorus leucolaemus Salvin, 1867
Plate 62

Alternative name: White-throated Wood-quail.

Despite tiny range (it is almost endemic to Costa Rica), this dark wood-quail is quite numerous in montane forests.

IDENTIFICATION Exceedingly dark plumage and restricted range make identification relatively straightforward. Entire plumage dusky-brown, inclining to blackish on head and underparts, usually with striking white throat, but latter often small, diffuse or even absent. Range does not meet similar Tacarcuna Wood-quail of E Panama, which has variegated black-and-white face and throat, and is overall less blackish. Inhabits forest zone between higher altitude Rufous-fronted and lowland Spotted, overlapping to certain extent with both, but most widely with Spotted.

DESCRIPTION Crown feathers short but give ruffled appearance. Bill stout, blackish. Irides dark brown. Lacks obvious bare orbital skin. Legs dusky-grey. Sexes similar. **Adult:** Crown, nape and entire upperparts almost uniform dark brown, vermiculated

black, rufous and buff; larger black spotting on scapulars. Face and most of underparts blackish, becoming dark brown on belly, rear flanks and vent; whitish feather fringes on lower breast and belly form indistinct whitish barring. Face often mottled white, chin and throat usually pure white, contrasting strongly with blackish head and underparts, but amount of white varies individually, some lack any. **Juvenile:** Similar, but breast dark chestnut-brown rather than blackish, white throat obscured by dusky mottling, upperparts closely barred rufous and bill tip cinnamon to buffy-brown.

GEOGRAPHICAL VARIATION Monotypic. Occurrence of very dark birds throughout range invalidates 'smithianus', the name given to the rather isolated population around Dota (Costa Rica).

MEASUREMENTS Length 22.0–25.5 cm; male averages fractionally larger. Males: wing 118–130, tail 44–59, tarsus 44.5–48.0, weight c.226. Females: wing 125–130, tail 46–50, tarsus 43.0–45.5, weight c.220.

HABITAT Cool, wet highland forest at 700–1850 m.

VOICE Advertising call a gabbled *kee-a WOWa kee-a WOWa* or *coweep-CHOweep*, which has been likened to 'where-ARE-you where-ARE-you', punctuated by low, hoarse, chucking or clicking notes. Coveys call in rushing, gabbled chorus. Conversational contact notes consist of soft, upslurred peeps and chirps. Metallic, rattling alarm trill and growling *CUH-k'rrr* in aggression also noted.

HABITS Shy and elusive, betraying presence by voice, calling repeatedly in early morning and at dusk. Typically in coveys of 10–15 within undergrowth on slopes of forest interior. Feed scattered over small area, maintaining contact with calls and early-morning choruses. At dusk assemble and fly to low branches to roost. If approached walks rapidly away within cover, flushing with great reluctance.

BREEDING Little known. Probably monogamous but parties of adults apparently guard nest. A Costa Rican nest was situated on sloping bank of small stream, a round hollow in leaf-litter with entrance pointing slightly down. Clutch 5 white (becoming stained brown) eggs. Incubation 16–17 days. Season June (though vocalisations reportedly most intense in March–April).

DISTRIBUTION Costa Rica and Panama, over central range of Costa Rica, from Cordillera de Guanacaste south, chiefly on Caribbean slope but in northern cordilleras occurs on both slopes, with isolated population in region of Dota. Extends into W Panama, where recorded chiefly from Caribbean slope east to Coclé province.

STATUS Locally quite common in parts of Costa Rica, but scarce and poorly known, probably extinct, in Panama where not reported since 1933.

REFERENCES Blake (1977), Stiles & Skutch (1989), Wetmore (1965).

---

214 STRIPE-FACED WOOD-QUAIL
Odontophorus balliviani Gould, 1846   Plate 63

Another virtually unknown wood-quail, isolated from all others on Andean slopes of the Amazon basin in extreme S Peru and adjacent Bolivia. It exhibits affinities closest to Starred, but clearly has evolved to become very distinct.

IDENTIFICATION Only wood-quail in restricted range. Relatively dark chestnut with prominently white-spotted underparts. Replaced by Starred much further north in Peru, which lacks extensive white spotting below and has much more conspicuous crest. Overlaps with Rufous-breasted Wood-quail, which has similar vocalisations, but latter appears to principally occur at lower altitudes, at least in Bolivia.

DESCRIPTION Somewhat elongated crown feathers probably form ruffled crest at rear. Bill stout, blackish. Irides dark brown. Bare orbital skin reddish-orange. Legs dusky-grey. Sexes basically similar. **Adult male:** Crown rufous-chestnut. Head-sides blackish. Supercilium and lower head-sides rufous-cinnamon. Rest of underparts dark chestnut becoming blackish on throat, each feather with diamond-shaped white subterminal spot and black tip. Upperparts reddish-brown, vermiculated black, with black spotting on mantle and scapulars. **Adult female:** Somewhat paler, more rufous below and paler brown above. **Juvenile:** Undescribed.

GEOGRAPHICAL VARIATION Monotypic.

MEASUREMENTS Length 26–28 cm; male averages fractionally smaller. Males: wing 141–152, tail 57–71, weight c.311. Females: wing 142–156, tail 59–75, weight c.324.

HABITAT Both humid and seasonally dry montane forests, with tree ferns, bamboos and epiphytes, at c.1000–3050 m. Appears to be able to tolerate young second growth.

VOICE Advertising call described as a rapidly repeated bubbling *whydlyi-i, whydlyi-i..*, considered similar to, but faster than Rufous-breasted Wood-quail.

HABITS Few data. Very difficult to observe, favouring dense undergrowth in steep gullies. Calls chiefly towards dawn and dusk. Occurs in small groups, which may flush upon close approach; runs across roads.

BREEDING Undescribed. Song regular in May, in Bolivia.

DISTRIBUTION SE Peru and W Bolivia. Known only from Cordillera Vilcabamba and E Andean slope of Cuzco and Puno region of Peru and in Yungas of Cochabamba in Bolivia.

STATUS Unknown. In great need of investigation.

REFERENCES Blake (1977), Fjeldså & Krabbe (1990), Johnsgard (1988).

215 STARRED WOOD-QUAIL
Odontophorus stellatus (Gould, 1843)   Plate 60

Widespread in forests of Amazon basin; it replaces Marbled to some extent, though the two do overlap in some regions.

IDENTIFICATION Rufous-and-grey wood-quail with prominent rufous crest and inconspicuously spotted breast. Only wood-quail over most of its range, marginally overlapping Marbled and Rufous-breasted in E Ecuador and probably in Peru. Marbled is overall dull brownish and has weaker crest and more extensive reddish orbital skin. Rufous-breasted occurs at higher elevations and is not proven to overlap; if seen well there should be no confusion as it is considerably darker, has blackish face and throat, and short crest.

DESCRIPTION Relatively long crown feathers form conspicuous crest at rear. Bill stout, blackish (reddish-yellow in juvenile). Irides dark brown. Bare skin around eye orange-yellow, but insignificant. Legs grey. Sexes basically similar. **Adult male:** Relatively long crown feathers form conspicuous rufous-chestnut crest at rear. Forecrown dark brown. Most of head, throat, neck and mantle grey. Rest of underparts rufous-chestnut, with blackish barring on vent and fine white spotting on breast-sides. Upperparts vermiculated olive-brown, paler and more uniform on rump; wings and scapulars darker brown with large black markings on scapulars and tertials, and fine buffish-white spotting on wing-coverts. **Adult female:** Resembles male but crown blackish-brown (not rufous-chestnut). **Juvenile:** Similar, but bill reddish-yellow, young male has rufous crest.

GEOGRAPHICAL VARIATION Monotypic; despite relatively extensive range no subspecies recognised.

MEASUREMENTS Length 24–28 cm; male averages larger. Males: wing 138–150, tail 56–72, tarsus 40, weight c.358. Females: wing 134–142, tail 57–65, weight c.315.

HABITAT Lowland humid forest, including *terra firme*, transitional and flood-plain forest below 1050 m, though usually lower (e.g. no records above 400 m from Ecuador).

VOICE Advertising call a low, bubbly, musical, somewhat resonant disyllabic *kor-korralo, kor-korralo, kor-korralo...*, with a tremor at end of second syllable, repeated for prolonged periods. Delivery slower than similar calls of Marbled Wood-quail.

HABITS Shy and elusive, betrays presence by voice, calling repeatedly near dusk. Small parties of 5–8 on forest floor, scratching in leaf-litter for insects and fallen fruits. Keeps close to shade of dense ground vegetation, crossing trails or open areas in single file. Usually scuttles into dense cover if alarmed.

BREEDING Apparently undescribed.

DISTRIBUTION Widespread in tropical lowland forest of W Amazonia, from SE Ecuador south through lowlands of E Peru and W Brazil, north to Amazon and east to Rio Madeira, and south into adjacent N Bolivia in Beni.

STATUS Locally quite common, but rare and little known in Ecuador, and forest destruction must have caused dramatic decreases in some areas.

REFERENCES Blake (1977), Johnsgard (1988), Ridgely & Greenfield (2001).

216 SPOTTED WOOD-QUAIL
Odontophorus guttatus (Gould, 1838)   Plate 60

Widespread in forests of C America, with range extending much further north than congeners. Unlike most other wood-quails, it exhibits no close affinities to group of species.

IDENTIFICATION Rufous-brown wood-quail with orange-rufous crest and heavily white-spotted underparts. Only C American wood-quail that is heavily spotted below, though spots perhaps difficult to discern in forest gloom. Altitudinally overlaps widely only with Rufous-fronted, which has solid blackish face and throat, and unspotted underparts, and marginally with darker Black-breasted, which usually has whiter throat; both have inconspicuous crests. Compare also Singing Quail.

DESCRIPTION Relatively long crown feathers form conspicuous crest at rear. Bill stout, blackish (reddish-yellow in juvenile). Irides dark brown. Bare skin around eye bluish-grey, but insignificant. Legs grey. Sexes rather similar. **Adult male:** Relatively long crown feathers form conspicuous rusty-orange crest at rear. Forecrown dark brown. Ear-coverts and upper head-sides chestnut. Throat and lower head-sides streaked black and white. Rest of underparts olive-brown (typical phase) or rufous (rufous phase), with bold white, black-edged spots on each feather, and vent finely barred blackish. Upperparts dull brown (typical phase) or reddish-brown (rufous phase), vermiculated darker, with bolder black spotting on scapulars and tertials, and fine whitish shaft streaks on mantle and back. **Adult female:** Like male but has dull blackish crown and crest, and duller grey-brown (or occasionally dull cinnamon) underparts. **Juvenile:** Reddish-yellow bill, rufous crest (like adult male), underparts spotting smaller and buffier, throat mottled whitish rather than streaked, and flanks and breast barred black.

GEOGRAPHICAL VARIATION Monotypic (includes '*matudae*'); despite relatively extensive range no subspecies now recognised.

411

Genus *CYRTONYX*: ocellated quails

Relatively stocky quails, with stout bills, short soft tails of 12 feathers and soft floppy crests on rear crown. Legs are short and stout for New World quails, but toes and claws are relatively long. Males have black-and-white facial patterns and boldly spotted underparts. The two species are allopatric and form a super-species—in view of the intermediate appearance of *sallei* they could be considered conspecific.

218 MONTEZUMA QUAIL
Cyrtonyx montezumae (Vigors, 1830)   Plate 64

Alternative names: Harlequin Quail (American), Salle's Quail (*sallei*), Mearns's Quail (*mearnsi*).

One of the New World's most attractive quails, the strikingly marked male plumage provides a surprisingly cryptic pattern in dappled light as they forage under shady shrubs.

IDENTIFICATION Plump quail of bushy semi-arid grasslands and open woodland in S USA and Mexico. Bushy ruffle on rear crown creates large-headed appearance, this and the stunning plumage pattern, particularly of male, renders it quite unmistakable in range. Male has stunning black-and-white head pattern ('clown-like') and blackish-and-chestnut underparts, profusely spotted white. Female duller, quite tawny below, marked with whitish streaks; differs from female bobwhites in head shape, including very stout bill, and by having 'ghost' of male head pattern. Southern race *sallei* (Salle's Quail) rather different, male bluish-grey below with rufous and buff spots, and suggests link with Ocellated Quail in underparts coloration (see latter for discussion). Flushes from almost underfoot, having strongly patterned wings in comparison to bobwhites, which have almost unmarked wings and longer tails.

DESCRIPTION *C. m. mearnsi*. Crown feathers elongated into soft bushy tuft at rear. Tail inconspicuous. Bill blackish, with steel-grey lower mandible and sides at base of upper mandible. Irides dark brown. Legs whitish-grey. Sexes differ. **Adult male:** Crown tawny-buff. Head and throat chalky-white, with striking black crescents and throat centre. Boldly patterned below throat, having chestnut central underparts, becoming blackish over vent, but whole dominated by blackish-grey breast-sides and flanks, marked with relatively large white spots, which may become buff on flanks. Upperparts tawny-brown, marked by dark-bordered buff shaft streaks and darker cross bars. Wings greyish-buff with paired black spots on each feather, being particularly large and noticeable on tertials. Primaries heavily spotted whitish-buff. Tail narrowly barred buff and dark grey-brown. **Adult female:** Lacks bold facial pattern and both upper- and underparts spotting of male. Crown centre streaked and spotted black. Area around eye and supercilium whitish, face and throat buffy-white, mottled black at sides and weakly bordered blackish. Underparts tawny-buff, streaked whitish, becoming paler on vent. Upperparts much more finely and weakly patterned than male, lacking bold spotting. **Juvenile:** Resembles female in overall coloration, but underparts duller and greyer, less

tawny, and more heavily spotted and barred blackish. Young male soon acquires adult male underparts and much as adult by first-winter, though head pattern remains obscured for several months.

GEOGRAPHICAL VARIATION Five quite well-differentiated forms, differing principally in male plumage pattern. Race *sallei* is somewhat intermediate between Montezuma and Ocellated Quails in appearance, lending weight to proposal that the two comprise one species. Conversely, others have suggested that *sallei* deserves species-level treatment. Two groups of races, with some intermediates where ranges meet.

Northern group (Mearns's Quail) Males have dark purplish or blackish-grey ground colour to underparts, heavily spotted white, or white and pale buff. Relatively larger than southern populations.
  C. m. mearnsi Nelson, 1900 occurs in S USA and N Mexico.
  C. m. montezumae (Vigors, 1830) occurs in Tamaulipas south to Oaxaca (Mexico).
  C. m. merriami Nelson, 1897 occurs on Mt Orizaba, Veracruz (Mexico).

Southern group (Salle's Quail) Males have blue-grey flanks, spotted whitish and buff, becoming heavily marked with rufous on rear flanks; upperparts have bright rufous streaking.
  C. m. sallei Verreaux, 1859 occurs in S Michoachán, Guerrero and W Oaxaca (Mexico).
  C. m. rowleyi Phillips, 1966 occurs in Sierra de Miahuatlán, Guerrero and Oaxaca (Mexico).

MEASUREMENTS Length 21–23 cm; male rather larger. *C. m. mearnsi*. Males: wing 113–131, mean weight 209. Females: wing 111–126, mean weight 193.

HABITAT Inhabits variety of semi-open, dry bushy grassland, chiefly on slopes, and open pine–oak woodland, with grassy understorey. Found chiefly at 1000–3000 m.

VOICE Advertising call an almost insect-like descending buzzing whistle. Coveys maintain contact with series of descending, quavering whinnies. Also a twitering *whi-whi, whi-hu* in alarm.

HABITS Generally shy and wary, remaining within bushy or grassy cover; usually encountered dust-bathing on dry dusty tracks and paths, when can be remarkably confiding in areas where not disturbed. Sits tight, flushing from almost underfoot, with wings making loud 'popping' sound. Roosts on ground under bushes, coveys facing outwards in a circle. Most coveys are generally of 7–8, rarely up to 25. Feeds on ground, raking with their long toes and claws for small bulbs, tubers, fruits and seeds of various low-growing plants (notably *Oxalis*); invertebrates readily taken in summer.

BREEDING Monogamous. Nest a scrape, lined with grasses with a grassy arched roof, well concealed under a grass clump or other dense herbage; side entrance has a grassy 'hinged' door, which totally conceals incubating bird. Male apparently assists with its construction. Clutch 6–28 (mean 11) whitish eggs, incubated for 25–26 days. Season chiefly June–September in USA, but begins late March in Mexico, where it may be double-brooded. Both sexes tend chicks.

DISTRIBUTION Mexico and extreme S USA, from extreme SW Texas, S New Mexico and SE Arizona, south through central hills and mountains of Mexico, from Sonora and Coahuila south to C Oaxaca to the Isthmus of Tehuantepec (east of which it is replaced by similar Ocellated Quail).

STATUS Uncommon and distinctly local in USA at northern limit of its range. Widespread but decreasing in Mexico, with chief concern being habitat degradation through overgrazing but also, to some extent, hunting. Salle's Quail (*sallei*), may warrant specific treatment, could be threatened.

REFERENCES Harrison (1978), Howell & Webb (1995), Johnsgard (1973).

219 OCELLATED QUAIL
Cyrtonyx ocellatus (Gould, 1837)   Plate 64

This close relative of Montezuma Quail is perhaps better treated as a well-marked form within the latter, as their ranges do not meet.

IDENTIFICATION Similar to Montezuma Quail, which it replaces from E Mexico to Nicaragua. Male readily distinguished from northern populations of Montezuma by extensive rufous-buff underparts, almost completely obscuring blackish or dark grey, which is reduced to indistinct barring on flanks. Chest much paler cinnamon, rather than chestnut of Montezuma. Note that form *sallei* of Montezuma approaches Ocellated in range and coloration, being paler, bluish-grey below with rufous spotting—in field appears less heavily spotted and more rufous than northern populations. It differs from Ocellated in having rufous spotting on blue-grey background, whereas latter appears basically rufous below, with merely a small area of pale spotting at breast-sides. Females of the two very similar, and female Ocellated is probably not safely separable from *sallei* Montezuma, but compared to northern forms, usually paler and more pinkish, less buffish below than Montezuma, with warmer buff shaft streaks on upperparts. Ranges separated by Isthmus of Tehuantepec, with *sallei* Montezuma south to C Oaxaca and Ocellated reaching its northern (and western) limit in extreme E Oaxaca. Possible vocal differences between the two require clarification.

DESCRIPTION Crown feathers elongated into soft bushy tuft at rear. Tail inconspicuous. Bill blackish, with steel-grey lower mandible and sides at base of upper mandible. Irides dark brown. Legs grey. Sexes differ. **Adult male:** Crown olive-brown. Head and throat chalky-white, with striking black and blackish-grey facial crescents and throat centre. Underparts below throat mostly rufous or rufous-buff, becoming warm buff on centre of breast and brighter rufous on belly and flanks. Breast-sides and fore flanks have blue-grey and pale buff spotting, but elsewhere blue-grey restricted to indistinct barring and tipping on flanks. Vent and lower belly blackish. Upperparts grey-brown, marked by dark-bordered chestnut shaft streaks and darker cross bars. Wings greyish-buff with paired grey-black spots on each feather, particularly large and noticeable on tertials. Primaries heavily spotted whitish. Tail narrowly barred buff and dark grey-brown. **Adult female:** Lacks bold facial pattern and upperparts spotting of male. Crown centre streaked and spotted black. Area around eye and supercilium whitish, face and throat warm buff, mottled black at sides and weakly bordered blackish. Underparts pinkish, mottled and streaked blackish. Upperparts much more finely and weakly patterned than male, lacking bold spotting. **Juvenile:** Probably not safely separable from that of Montezuma.

GEOGRAPHICAL VARIATION Monotypic. Honduran population has been named '*differens*' but not usually recognised.

MEASUREMENTS Length 19–23 cm; male rather larger. Males: wing 114–130, tail 48.0–57.5, tarsus 30–33, mean weight c.218. Females: wing 110.5–119.5, tail 45.0–55.5, tarsus 29–32, mean weight c.182.

HABITAT Very much as Montezuma Quail. Inhabits dry brushy fields and open pine–oak woodland at 750–3050 m.

VOICE Poorly documented. Reported to give a whistled *preeet*, perhaps equivalent of the buzzy advertising call of Montezuma Quail, but appears to lack descending whinny. A sweet whistled *pico-de-oro* or similar. Lack of vocal information is surprising given that it is (or was) a popular cage-bird in S Mexico, prized for its voice!

HABITS Much as Montezuma Quail.

BREEDING Virtually undocumented, believed to be much as Montezuma Quail. Season April–August in Guatemala.

DISTRIBUTION C America, from extreme E Oaxaca through C Chiapas (Mexico) and Guatemala, extreme N El Salvador, to C Honduras and formerly just entering adjacent N Nicaragua.

narrowly barred pale cinnamon, with fine pale buff streaks on forehead; pale buff central crown-stripe, head- and neck-sides pale buff, finely speckled dark grey-brown, and chin and throat off-white. Breast-sides cinnamon with pale buff spots and dull black streaks and bars, becoming even paler buff dorsally, each feather with large V- or heart-shaped black subterminal spot. Central breast cinnamon-orange, flanks warm yellow-buff, deepening to cinnamon on undertail-coverts, sometimes with black subterminal spots, and belly and vent cream-white. Hindneck and upper mantle pale cinnamon finely streaked pale buff and indistinctly barred darker; rest of upperparts, including tertials and tail closely barred black and cinnamon, with off-white fringes and grey tips, especially on mantle and scapulars; tertials blotched pale buff. Wing-coverts cinnamon dotted black and have broad pale buff or cream-white fringes, and some pale buff on feather centres and inner webs, especially on inner coverts. Flight feathers dark sepia with paler inner webs and faint and irregular cream-white, pale grey, pale cinnamon or buff fringes. Underwing-coverts and axillaries pale buff. When worn, cinnamon parts of plumage bleach to pale buff and off-white streaks and grey fringes on upperparts become less distinct, while generally paler in non-breeding plumage. **Adult female:** Darker and brighter than breeding male, being predominantly chestnut, rather than cinnamon and buff. Crown chestnut with narrow off-white fringes and black bases; spots on head-sides, neck and line above eye heavier and darker. Lower throat, breast-sides, flanks and undertail-coverts deep rusty-cinnamon, rather than pale cinnamon-orange; belly and vent pinkish-buff. Hindneck and upper mantle chestnut with more obvious pale buff streaks, and rest of upperparts, tail and tertials black, with broader and richer chestnut barring, pale streaks more distinct and no grey wash. Black subterminal spots on wing-coverts and breast-sides larger and rounder. In non-breeding plumage similar but upperparts paler chestnut with less coarse black vermiculations and narrower off-white streaks. **Juvenile:** More like adult male, but buff breast-patch less distinct and blackish spots or dark brown streaks on breast. Forehead to hindneck cinnamon, with slight dusky-brown tips and indistinct pale buff central crown-stripe. Line above eye, head- and neck-sides pale buff, finely marked cinnamon; chin and throat off-white. Breast-sides pale cinnamon, feathers black at tip with white spots, and rest of underparts cream-white, streaked black on central breast, except buff undertail-coverts. Mantle, scapulars, upperwing-coverts and tertials pale cinnamon, finely vermiculated black, each feather with white lateral spot, which form rows. Back, rump uppertail-coverts and tail black tipped and sometimes finely marked cinnamon. Flight feathers largely as adult.

GEOGRAPHICAL VARIATION Nine races generally recognised, principally based on overall body size (those in SE Asia are generally much smaller than elsewhere), upperparts coloration and that of breast-sides. Significant individual variation may exist as Iberian birds are considered to be noticeably darker than those that formerly occurred on Sicily and persist locally in NW Africa. The following forms have usually been regarded as synonyms: 'alleni' and 'arenaria' (with lepurana) and 'mikado' (with davidi), though several recent

authors, including Robson (2000), have followed Peters in recognising the latter form. Some taxonomic confusion persists (see above) and race celestinoi of SE Philippines sometimes included within Red-backed Buttonquail, where overlaps with form 'masaaki' on Mindanao. Latter race was formerly ascribed to Red-backed Buttonquail, but is now regarded as a synonym of celestinoi and both forms ascribed to T. sylvatica.

T. s. sylvatica (Desfontaines, 1787) occurs in S Spain and NW Africa; described above.

T. s. lepurana (A. Smith, 1836) occurs in sub-Saharan Africa; smaller than nominate, with more or less strongly marked upperparts, a paler cinnamon tone to breast-sides and smaller breast spots.

T. s. dussumieri (Temminck, 1828) occurs in India and Myanmar; overall smaller and less heavily marked than nominate, being streaked rather than barred, and generally paler above than preceding forms with more prominent rufous-chestnut and buff on hindneck/mantle.

T. s. davidi Delacour & Jabouille, 1930 occurs in Indochina, S China in Guangdong, Taiwan and Hainan; most closely resembles dussumieri, but is overall larger and more richly coloured.

T. s. whiteheadi Ogilvie-Grant, 1897 occurs on Luzon, Philippines; principally differs in upperparts coloration, being brown barred dull rufous, while female has collar mottled rufous and is darker chestnut on breast.

T. s. nigrorum duPont, 1976 occurs on Negros, Philippines; generally intermediate between 'masaaki' (=celestinoi) and whiteheadi and female differs from latter in having dark brown fringes to black crown feathers, darker chestnut collar, overall blacker mantle with darker brown barring, underparts spotting larger, rounder and less V shaped and wing-coverts spots less linear, while male also differs from whiteheadi in shape and pattern of underparts spotting.

T. s. celestinoi McGregor, 1907 occurs in Bohol and C Mindanao, Philippines; upperparts coloration distinctive being black barred dark chestnut, chin and throat feathers tipped buff and breast-sides broadly barred black.

T. s. suluensis Mearns, 1905 occurs on the Sulu Is, southwest of Mindanao; has spots on breast-sides dark chestnut, paler breast, more rufous wing-coverts and blacker lower back, uppertail-coverts and tail.

T. s. bartelsorum Neumann, 1929 occurs on Java and Bali; differs from dussumieri in being shorter winged and darker both above and below, with pale isabelline fringes to upperparts feathers (rather than ochre-yellowish in dussumieri). Female differs from male in being larger and has an obvious rusty-red nuchal collar, and forehead, central crown-stripe and area around eyes barred white and black; in male forehead and crown-stripe are unbarred pale yellowish and the head-sides yellowish with a few black spots.

MEASUREMENTS Length 13–16 cm. Female larger. T. s. sylvatica. Males: wing 83–92, tail 36–43, tarsus 22–25, mean weight c.60. Females: wing 91–101, tail 40–46, tarsus 22–26, mean weight c.70. Other races: male wing 62–80, tail 25–33, tarsus 17.0–20.5, weight

418

(*T. s. lepurana*) 32.2–43.5; female wing 68–92, tail 31–40, tarsus 19.0–23.0, weight (*T. s. lepurana*) 39–54. *T. s. dussumieri* weight (both sexes) 36–43.

HABITAT Inhabits dry grassland and scrub and grass bordering cultivation (to 1150 m in SE Asia and 2400 m in India), always on dry warm soils, avoiding wetlands and forests, and sparsely-vegetated desert. In W Palearctic, formerly occurred principally in dwarf palm or palmetto *Chamerops humilis* scrub, or among asphodel (Liliaceae) and other coastal scrub communities, stubble and sugar beet, but now restricted to a probably suboptimal Mediterranean scrub including *Halimium halimifolium*, *Pistacia lentiscus* and *Quercus suber* on coastal sands. In Asia, uses grass-and-scrub jungle bordering cultivation and grassland, and in E Africa frequents savanna bush with long grass and overgrown cultivation; also sandy grass-covered plains, plantations and rank, grassy areas near temporary pools and seasonal watercourses.

VOICE Advertising call, by female, is a loud, ventriloquial resonant one-second boom, likened to the distant lowing of cattle, repeated every 1–3 seconds for upwards of 30 seconds, and sometimes given all day, but principally in early morning and late evening. Also a double *oo-up* variant and rattling *terrrr* perhaps also to attract male, which responds with a *tuc-tuc-tuc* or a sustained *triii* and may be given in duet. Various rattling low-pitched calls are given by both sexes, as well as a low-pitched *cree-cree cree* when together in cover, but only male appears to utter soft chuckling in defence of young. Apparently little variation in female advertising song across range.

HABITS Terrestrial. Usually recorded singly or in pairs, occasionally small groups or scattered flocks in winter. Slow creeping walk while feeding. When not feeding, walk can be surprisingly upright and this is particularly noticeable when crossing bare/burnt ground. Prefers to run from perceived danger, only flushing a very short distance on whirring wings. Courtship is remarkable in that the female has been reported to occasionally mount the male during copulation. Populations differ in their movements, with those in Iberia and NW Africa being resident, but both sedentary and an intra-tropical migrant within rest of Africa. Local movements reported in many W and S African countries and is wet-season breeding visitor to drier areas in N Afrotropics and dry-season non-breeding visitor to parts of C and S Africa (where numbers increase significantly at this season), but probably does not perform longer, trans-equatorial movements and evidence from South African region suggests that it is more irruptive than seasonally dispersive. Formerly regarded as a summer migrant breeder in SW Arabia, but some more recent authors consider it to be probably sedentary there. Nomadic or semi-migratory throughout Asia, e.g. a wet-season breeding visitor to NW India. Migrates nocturnally. Takes seeds, especially grasses and invertebrates, including ants, scratched from ground. Latter often important (e.g. 50% in Spanish study), though sometimes takes equal quantities of seeds. Young are entirely insectivorous during first ten days. Mealworms, fruits and pigeon pellets taken in captivity. Most active

in early morning and late afternoon in Africa, but perhaps partially nocturnal in W Palearctic range. Captive birds roost in pairs, sometimes with other pairs.

BREEDING Shallow, well-concealed scrape, lined with grass, beneath a grass tussock or low vegetation, selected by female. Nests are usually separated by 1 ha or more from adjacent pair. Standing grass is often pulled over to form a loose canopy. Female usually polyandrous, mating sequentially with several males and, in captivity, capable of producing over 100 eggs in a seven-month period, but sustained monogamy has also been observed in captivity (few detailed observations in wild). Four eggs (range 2–5) normal in Palearctic, 3–4 (2–7) in Africa and 4 (4–5) in Asia, incubated for 12–15 days. Eggs cream to greyish-white, marked with chocolate-brown to black, or yellowish-brown (SE Asia). Laid at one-day intervals. One instance, from Tsavo National Park, Kenya, of an apparent Harlequin Quail egg within a nest of this species. Male alone usually takes responsibility for incubation and chick care, unless climatic or other conditions dictate need for female participation. Young are precocial and nidifugous, capable of self-feeding at 2–3 days (but, at least in captivity, often reliant on male for food until day 10), flight at 7–15 days and are independent at 18–20 days, before becoming fully grown (35 days), and capable of breeding at four months, though sexually mature at 37 days. Season is April–August in W Palearctic and all months in Africa and Asia, but locally only during rainy season especially in S Africa (e.g. January–July with February peak in Namibia).

DISTRIBUTION Africa and S Asia. Isolated population in S Iberia and NW Africa, from N Morocco east to N Tunisia and perhaps Libya. In sub-Saharan Africa, from S Mali and Senegambia east to S Sudan, Ethiopia, Eritrea and Somalia (and Yemen and SW Saudi in extreme SW Arabia), thence south locally in W and C Africa, in Gabon, Congo and N Cameroon to Angola, and more widespread in E and S Africa, from Rwanda, Burundi and Uganda to S Namibia and N South Africa. Also in lowlands to 2400 m, from E Pakistan, in Sind, and India, except extreme SE, north to Himalayas, east to SE China, Hainan I., Taiwan and south to S Myanmar, C Thailand and Indochina, as well as W Java, Bali and the Philippines (Luzon, Negros, Bohol, Mindanao and Jolo, with a recent record presumably of this species from Sanga-Sanga). Vagrant Iran, Oman and elsewhere.

STATUS Uncommon to common throughout Asian range, with local extinctions reported in, e.g. Bangladesh and very local in SW Arabia. Scarce to locally abundant in Africa, where widespread in W, E and S Africa, and common to abundant in Zambia, Zimbabwe and Malawi, but very rare in Lesotho where overgrazing appears responsible for decline. Nominate *sylvatica* is rare and declining, and persists only very locally in SW Spain (5–10 pairs in Doñana National Park) and coastal NW Africa (where perhaps extirpated in Tunisia and always rare and local in Libya), and extinct in Sicily since at least 1920 due to hunting and habitat destruction. No records since 1973 from Portugal where always rare in north of country and status now unclear, but possibly extinct. In the Philippines, the form *suluensis* is known from just the type-specimen, though its collector, Mearns, noted it to be 'truly abundant' in the dry uplands, but also recorded it in marshy areas, and both *celestinoi* and *whiteheadi* have been recorded at very few localities.

REFERENCES Brooks & Dutson (1997), Cramp & Simmons (1980), Debus (1996), duPont (1971), Flieg (1973), Grimmett *et al.* (1998), Hagemeijer & Blair (1997), Jennings (1995), Johnsgard (1991), Robson (2000), Urban *et al.* (1986).

222 RED-BACKED BUTTONQUAIL
Turnix maculosa (Temminck, 1815)   Plate 67

Alternative names: Black-backed/Black-spotted /Orange-breasted Buttonquail.

This species, which enjoys a moderately broad distribution in coastal N and E Australia, the New Guinea region and Wallacea, has been considered conspecific with Small Buttonquail, though it may be closer to Yellow-legged Buttonquail in its relationships, and exhibits complex geographical variation; subspecies limits are poorly known, in some cases complex and surely deserve reappraisal.

IDENTIFICATION A small buttonquail, which overlaps quite widely with Brown and King Quails and, in Australia, with Australian Little and Red-chested Buttonquails. Key features are the rufous-brown or chestnut hindneck and shoulders, and, in flight, the clearly defined and prominent buff panel on the inner wing-coverts, all of which are diagnostic. The fine yellow bill and boldly marked buff flanks, breast-sides and wing-coverts offer useful confirmatory field marks, if seen at rest. Female King and both sexes of Brown Quails, which share same habitats in Australia, New Guinea and S Indonesia, may be confused with this species, being generally dark above, but latter significantly larger, more uniform, with narrower and more pointed wings lacking characteristic coverts pattern, and also lacks rufous-brown hindneck/shoulder patch. Male King Quail is not confusable with Red-backed Buttonquail, but female is relatively similar; though size is closer to the buttonquail, the same features useful for distinguishing Brown Quail may be used to separate the two. Within Australia, the most serious confusion risk is perhaps Red-chested Buttonquail, but this species is slightly larger, with a much deeper based, darker bill, largely grey-brown above and orange-rufous below extending to undertail-coverts. Other Australian buttonquails should not pose significant identification problems if seen well and, in flight, lack the distinctive upperwing-coverts pattern of Red-backed. For identification from Sumba Buttonquail see that species.

DESCRIPTION *T. m. melanota.* Short tail, of 12 rectrices, and short, round-tipped wings. Irides cream (black-brown in juvenile); bill pale yellow with broad grey to dark grey culmen and tip (brighter and more extensively yellow in female; grey-black in young), and buffish-yellow tarsus and feet (dirty pink in juvenile). Sexes differ. **Adult male:** Forehead to nape blackish, scalloped grey and with narrow buff crown-stripe; head-sides, neck and throat brownish-buff and rufous-brown collar extends from hindneck and upper mantle to neck-sides. Chin and throat white, grading to buff on breast to undertail-coverts, with breast-sides and flanks boldly spotted and scalloped black, and belly more whitish.

Lower mantle to tail slate-grey, with variable, but usually narrow and dense, rufous-brown and black barring, forming blotches on back and some scapulars. Flight feathers similar. Inner wing-coverts buff with black central spot or bar to each feather. Underwing ash-grey, with pale greyish-brown lining. **Adult female:** Much as male, but differs in brighter, more uniform and broader rufous-brown hindneck collar, extending well onto breast-sides, brighter yellow bill, more restricted median crown-stripe, which may be entirely absent, and brighter buff, inclining to pale rufous-brown face, head-sides and sometimes throat. **Juvenile:** Differs from adult in being overall much darker: blackish mantle, back and scapulars, barred grey-brown to rufous-brown, with blackish inner wing-coverts coarsely spotted and barred white, black breast and flanks barred and irregularly spotted white, and generally dark greyish-brown above, without pale upperwing-coverts panel.

GEOGRAPHICAL VARIATION Represented by 14 disjunct races. The forms '*yorki*' (from NE Australia) and '*pseutes*' (NW Australia) are now considered synonyms of *melanota*, while *mayri* has sometimes been subsumed within the similar *horsbrughi*; form *celestinoi* of Small Buttonquail has been included within *T. maculosa* (see that species).

    T. m. beccarii Salvadori, 1875 occurs in Sulawesi and adjacent Muna and Tukangbesi islands; characterised by poorly developed neck collar and black back speckled and barred yellowish-rusty.

    T. m. kinneari Neumann, 1939 occurs on Peleng in the Banggai Is (Indonesia); a large form, with broad and dark rusty neck collar, black-and-grey back with dark rusty-brown spots and bars, and underparts dark ochraceous-rusty.

    T. m. obiensis Sutter, 1955 occurs on Obi and Kai (Moluccas) and Babar (Lesser Sundas); female characterised by poorly defined rusty collar, dark grey fringes to black back, with dark rust-coloured spots and broken barring, and largely pale underparts with rusty-ochre foreneck.

    T. m. sumbana Sutter, 1955 occurs on Sumba (Lesser Sundas); well differentiated among forms from this region as lacks rusty neck collar and has upperparts dark ashy and blackish olive-grey, with dark brownish-rusty spots and bars.

    T. m. floresiana Sutter, 1955 occurs on Sumbawa, Komodo, Padar, Flores and Alor (Lesser Sundas); very close to *savuensis*, but considered smaller and darker above than other Wallacean forms, with broad blackish olive-grey fringes to upperparts feathers and ochraceous-rust vent.

    T. m. maculosa (Temminck, 1815) occurs on Timor, Wetar, Kisar and Moa (Lesser Sundas);

characterised by broad rusty collar, coarse black and rusty pattern to back with pale grey/brownish-grey fringes, bright golden-rust fringes to wing-coverts and yellowish-rust underparts.

T. m. savuensis Sutter, 1955 occurs on Sawu (Lesser Sundas); slightly paler dorsally than preceding form with less pronounced collar.

T. m. saturata Forbes, 1882 occurs on New Britain and Duke of York Is; differs from the nominate in being generally darker above and slightly deeper rufous below (the latter coloration extending to the chin and throat), with a deeper rufous supercilium and more curved, deeper based, dirty yellow bill.

T. m. furva Parkes, 1949 occurs on the Huon Peninsula, in NE New Guinea; female has almost entire underparts rusty-chestnut, overall much darker upperparts, including scapulars and crown, more obvious contrast between central black spot and buff surround to greater coverts and more noticeable, but restricted, black scalloping to breast-sides and upper flanks.

T. m. giluwensis Sims, 1954 occurs in CE New Guinea; lacks chestnut collar of *horsbrughi* and is smaller than *furva*, being paler below than both these forms, but at least one apparent intermediate between *giluwensis* and *horsbrughi* has been collected within the supposed range of the former.

T. m. horsbrughi Ingram, 1909 occurs in S New Guinea; similar in some respects to *furva*, female has noticeable chestnut collar, reduced black scalloping on breast-sides and upper flanks, extensively rusty-chestnut underparts, but less boldly patterned wing-coverts and overall paler upperparts.

T. m. mayri Sutter, 1955 occurs on the Louisiade Is; female has noticeable chestnut collar, but is duller and less well defined than *horsbrughi*, even paler upperparts and underparts than latter form, whitish central belly-patch and virtually all-yellow bill.

T. m. salamonis Mayr, 1938 occurs on Guadalcanal in the Solomon Is; similar to *horsbrughi*, but larger (wing 85) and deeper rufous below, particularly on flanks and central belly, with well-developed collar, very broad grey fringes to crown feathers, back dark grey with rather large black spots and narrow vermiculations, outer edges of tertials and upperwing-coverts deep ochraceous; and differs from *saturata* in greyer, less blackish back and rufous collar.

T. m. melanota (Gould, 1837) occurs in N and E Australia; described above.

MEASUREMENTS Length 12–16 cm. Female larger. All races. Males: wing 65–82, tail 21–30, tarsus 16.9–21.5, weight 23–39. Females: wing 72–89, tail 26.0–33.5, tarsus 19–23, weight 32–51.

HABITAT Inhabits grassland, woodland and cropped areas in coastal and subcoastal regions generally to 1200 m (but form *giluwensis* inhabits interior mountains at 1600–2450 m). Often in areas with tussock grass in Australia and frequently in dense grass near water. Will apparently use recently burnt areas, at least occasionally. In Australia only occurs in regions with 400 mm or more summer rain and appears to be resident in those with at least 800 mm at this season.

VOICE Principally female during breeding season. Advertising call a frequent subdued *oom*, higher pitched and more cooing than similar vocalisation of Painted Buttonquail. Repeated at c.0.5 second intervals over long periods, each note being slightly upslurred at end. Given day and night in spring. No other information.

HABITS Wholly terrestrial. Recorded singly, in pairs and family groups of up to five. Prefers to hide and freeze, rather than flush, which it does reluctantly and usually only over short distances, though it is capable of longer flights. Reported as 'tame' in some areas. Resident, migratory and dispersive populations known, but very few specific data on temporal movements available: known to concentrate in coastal areas of Australian tropics in dry season, is reportedly more widespread in NW Australia during wet season, and only recorded in Kimberley Division, Western Australia, in June–March. Probably a nocturnal migrant. Takes grass seeds, e.g. *Vicia, Swainsona, Rumex* and *Polygonum avicularae*, green shoots and insects by gleaning and scratching in leaf-litter. Latter more important in diet than most *Turnix*. Grit, earth and sand are used to aid seed digestion. Principally nocturnal and crepuscular.

BREEDING Always close to wet areas and usually in tall grass formations. Shallow depression on ground under grass tussock, herb or shrub, and lined with grass, eucalypt leaves and cattle dung. Surrounding grass may be woven into a canopy or dome with a side entrance. Females are sequentially polyandrous in captivity, laying second clutch 14 days after first, but nests are solitary. Two to 4 oval eggs (mean 3.6), greyish-white to yellowish largely obscured by pale brown or grey speckles, and incubated for 14 days, commenced once last egg has been laid. Male alone assumes incubation and chick-care duties, though one captive male mated with two females and neglected incubation, forcing one female to brood eggs for a short period. Young are precocial and nidifugous. Able to feed themselves at 10 days, capable of flight at two weeks and fully feathered at six; they reach adult size at seven weeks and attain sexual maturity at four months. Lays October–June.

DISTRIBUTION Indonesia and Australasia. Lowlands to 2450 m in Sulawesi, including offshore Muna, Butung, Peleng and Tukangbesi islands; Mindanao in S Philippines; the Lesser Sundas from Sumbawa and Sumba east to Kisar, Moa and Babar, Obi I. in C Moluccas, Kai Is, C and SE New Guinea, Louisiade Archipelago, New Britain and Duke of York Is, Guadalcanal in Solomon Is, and N and E Australia, from NE Western Australia west to the Kimberleys and east to North Territory (in Arnhem Land), and from E Queensland north to Cape York, inland to Atherton Tableland and south to NE New South Wales, including islands in Torres Strait and Great Barrier Reef, Groote Eylandt and Fraser I.

STATUS Remains common and generally widespread in N Australia, and common in extant habitat in Solomon Is, but most of latter has now been destroyed and race *salamonis* may be threatened. In Northern Territory sometimes recorded at extraordinary densities in small areas of extant habitat following fires. Elsewhere, uncommon and infrequently recorded in E Australia and may have disappeared from southeast extremity of Australian range, but suggested decline perhaps exaggerated, and status in, e.g. SE Queensland and NE New South Wales considered subject to long-term variability.

REFERENCES Debus (1996), Diamond (1972), Johnsgard (1991), Marchant & Higgins (1993), White & Bruce (1986).

223 BLACK-RUMPED BUTTONQUAIL
Turnix hottentotta (Temminck, 1815)   Plate 65

Alternative name: Hottentot Buttonquail.

Endemic to sub-Saharan Africa where generally less common than frequently sympatric, though ecologically separated Small Buttonquail; two species may be involved given differences in plumage, eye colour and migratory habits between nominate *hottentotta* and more widespread *nana*.

IDENTIFICATION This comparatively widespread resident and intra-African migrant buttonquail overlaps extensively with the *lepurana* form of Small Buttonquail, as well as Small, Harlequin and Blue Quails. Separation from the former is usually reasonably straightforward given reasonable views (see that species) and Böhm's Flufftail *Sarothrura boehmi*, which may occasionally cause confusion, especially in flight, has slower wingbeats, a longer body and neck, red head (in male), overall white-streaked blackish plumage and long, trailing legs. Of the three *Coturnix* species, only female and immature Blue Quail may offer more significant identification problems, but all are readily distinguished by larger size, bulkier bodies, less noticeable neck and pale central crown-stripe; also tend to call when flushed (unlike *Turnix*) and fly further and higher, being more readily provoked into flight on a second occasion than any buttonquail (though some *hottentotta* appear to readily flush a second time). Immature and female Blue Quail, which may present the most serious challenge, clearly have unpatterned upperparts and are larger, with a distinctive *Coturnix* structure that should immediately eliminate confusion for the experienced observer.

DESCRIPTION *T. h. nana*. Short tail, of 12 rectrices, and short, round-tipped wings. Irides pale blue to silvery-white (pale brown in juvenile), and has dark brown bill with yellowish-grey cutting edges and lower mandible, and dark tip, and pale flesh to dusky-white tarsus and feet (dark flesh in juvenile). Sexes differ. **Adult male:** Forehead to crown blackish with white fringes and dull rufous-brown tips; lores and face orange-rufous with blackish feather tips, becoming intricately patterned on malar and neck-sides; nape dark sepia, spotted white or buff and barred rufous-brown and blackish; and chin and throat white to golden-buff. Breast golden-buff to orange-rufous, grading to white, tinged golden-buff/orange-rufous on lower breast to rear flanks and belly, with undertail-coverts as breast. Mantle and scapulars to rump and uppertail-coverts blackish, with grey-brown feather tips and irregular rufous-brown barring on mantle and back, broad white/golden-buff fringes to scapulars and more regular barring, and golden-buff tips to dorsal surfaces. Tail blackish with golden-buff fringes and stripes to each feather. Flight feathers dark (darkest on primaries) with variable white to buff spots, creamy-buff to orange-rufous fringes and tips and variably barred on tertials. Lesser and median coverts rufous with variable white tips and subterminal blackish-brown barring, and greater coverts dull brown, with broad rufous-buff fringes. Axillaries grey-brown, fringed golden-buff and underwing-coverts buff to grey, washed golden-buff, with dark silvery-grey underside to flight feathers. **Adult female:** Like male, but forehead, supercilium, face and breast orange-rufous, deepest on breast and palest on chin and throat; median and greater coverts also orange-rufous with golden-buff subterminal spotting and blackish bars; and breast barring confined to sides and also less extensive on flanks than in male. **Juvenile:** Also much as adult male, but less rufous and more heavily marked underparts; face and supercilium washed pale orange-rufous, spotted white, scapulars fringed white or buff, no golden-buff on rump-sides and upperwing-coverts have prominent white or buffish-white spotting. Male has chin to belly white, sometimes golden-buff on upper breast, and is heavily barred dark brown on breast and blackish and white on flanks. Female has breast washed orange-rufous and is less extensively barred.

GEOGRAPHICAL VARIATION Two reasonably well-marked races, which have recently been considered as separate species, but such treatment is still not without controversy and further studies certainly desirable. Urban *et al.* (1986) and others included '*luciana*' and '*insolata*' within *nana*; evidence that southern populations within the latter's range are paler is available, but regional subdivisions unclear and there is obviously extensive individual variation within *nana*.

T. h. nana (Sundevall, 1851) occurs from Nigeria to Uganda and Kenya and south to Angola and E South Africa as far south as East London; described above.

T. h. hottentotta (Temminck, 1815) occurs in S and SW Western Cape Province east to Port Elizabeth (S South Africa); compared to previous form has paler upperparts, especially the rump which is usually pale brown (and never appears noticeably dark in flight, unlike in *nana*, which does look dark/black, befitting the species' name), with conspicuous black breast, flanks and belly spots on a paler rufous background and yellow eye.

MEASUREMENTS Length 14–16 cm. Female larger. *T. h. nana*. Males: wing 71–77, tail 21–27, tarsus 19–21, weight (n=2) 40. Females: wing 77–86, tail 28–32, tarsus 19–21, weight (n=2) 57.5–62.5.

HABITAT The form *nana* uses open grassland and savanna on dark, clayey (occasionally sandy) soils and marshy areas (dambos) in woodland to 1800 m, but generally avoids standing water. Uses thicket edge, close to grassland and short-grazed areas with 25–50 cm-tall dense ground cover and occasionally fallow crop fields and sugar cane fields. In Zambia, *nana* almost always prefers open, typically wet grassland (though never more than a couple of millimetres of surface water), as well as dry sandy plains (in this region Small Buttonquail tends to avoid open plains and often occurs in grassland with some scrub). In contrast, *hottentotta* occurs in mountain fynbos, preferring low, relatively sparse restionaceous vegetation. There is some evidence to suggest that it may depart areas when vegetation reaches certain age and becomes too dense, and local movements may hence track fire cycles. In coastal strandveld, also prefers relatively open, sparse vegetation.

VOICE Advertising call, by female, is reportedly a low *hoom hoom hoom* uttered at a rate of 1.6 per second with very little pause between notes, or a flufftail *Sarothrura*-like *oooooop-oooooop*, perhaps shorter and delivered in faster series than Small Buttonquail. This call is considered indicative of breeding, but a low-pitched humming noise, which continues on same pitch for up to a minute or more has also been ascribed to *nana*. No other information.

HABITS Terrestrial. Recorded singly or in pairs, occasionally in loose groups. Gait similar to *sylvatica*, a slow creeping walk when feeding. Very difficult to flush, preferring to run from danger but if extremely hard-pressed will erupt from cover in fast, low whirring flight, before swiftly returning to cover and running on. An intra-African migrant, which only appears in many areas during wet season (to breed), though nominate race is a resident, with possibility of local movements, and elsewhere is sedentary in Kenya, Uganda and South Africa (being still regular around Morgan Bay at least). Data from other areas, e.g. Zambia, very complex: though essentially sedentary in latter country, local movements probably occur if suitable habitat is burnt or flooded and a dry-season influx from the Kalahari Basin may occur. Clearly tolerates dry areas in this part of its range, if other conditions are suitable. Nocturnal migrant. Few dietary data available, but apparently takes grass and weed seeds, as well as insects and their larvae.

BREEDING Shallow scrape or natural hollow lined with grass, under a tussock with stems bent to form loose canopy, or under fallen grass without dome. Race *nana* breeds in seasonally wet grasslands, while *hottentotta*

occurs in fynbos and strandveld. Typically 3 eggs (range 2–6), yellowish-grey marked with grey-brown (rather than dark brown as in Small Buttonquail in area of overlap) and incubated for 12–14 days by male alone. Captive-bred young fledge in 32–35 days, being capable of flight at 12 days. Female is possibly polyandrous, but nests solitary. Laying recorded in most months, but principally during or at end of rainy season (e.g. September–February and mainly December–January in Zimbabwe). Nominate *hottentotta* recorded nesting in October–December.

DISTRIBUTION W Africa from Sierra Leone east to SW Central African Republic, Gabon, Congo and Zaïre, and in E and SE Africa from Rwanda, Uganda and NW Kenya south through Angola, Zambia, Malawi and Mozambique to Zimbabwe and E South Africa.

STATUS Less numerous than partially sympatric *T. sylvatica*, and is uncommon to locally common, e.g. conservative estimate that suitable habitat in Liuwa Plain National Park, Zambia held c.1 bird/ha, or 40,000 individuals in the entire park. In South Africa, where range has contracted significantly, probably due to overgrazing, human settlement, trampling and excessive burning of habitat, it may no longer breed and is considered Endangered in this country. Few records in Kenya since 1950. Uncommon and local in W Africa (where perhaps only a vagrant in some areas), Mozambique and Zimbabwe; locally common in many parts of C and S Africa, but alleged occurrence in Botswana is unconfirmed. While overgrazing may be a problem in some areas, the species' association with dry heavily grazed grassland, and areas disturbed by cattle suggest that it is likely to be secure. Nominate *hottentotta* has very restricted range, is poorly known and was, until recently, even considered possibly extinct, with last breeding record in 1968, but significant numbers discovered recently, e.g. c.310 estimated in 25 km² of suitable montane fynbos habitat in Cape of Good Hope Nature Reserve and is also present in coastal strandveld vegetation. Given the latter, population estimates that only consider mountain fynbos distribution may be too conservative. While large areas of montane fynbos habitats are managed for conservation, the coastal fynbos and strandveld habitats are under immediate threat of transformation.

REFERENCES Aspinwall (1978), Beel (1996), Debus (1996), Demey (in press), Johnsgard (1991), Leonard (1999), Ryan & Hockey (1995), Spottiswoode & Cohen (in prep. and in litt. 2001), Tarboton (2001), Taylor (2000), Urban *et al.* (1986).

224 YELLOW-LEGGED BUTTONQUAIL
Turnix tanki Blyth, 1843   Plate 66

The most northerly breeding buttonquail, reaching NE China, Korea and extreme SE Russia in summer, though most of its range lies within the Oriental region, where it is generally not uncommon.

IDENTIFICATION Within widespread Indian and E Asian range, usually easily identified from congeners and small *Coturnix* quail (which have striking white dorsal shaft streaks) through use of a number of features. A small buttonquail with a comparatively large, deep-based yellow bill and strong yellow legs (both brighter in female), deep buff breast-band, rufous nuchal collar (in female alone), unbarred underparts and sandy-buff upperwing-coverts with large black spots. Latter feature is diagnostic among overlapping congeners, but other plumage marks assist identification. Generally darker and more greyish on dorsal surface than Small or Barred Buttonquails, while latter has black on breast (and throat of female) and former is generally more barred and streaked, rather than spotted. In flight, exhibits more considerable contrast between paler wing-coverts and darker flight feathers than all confusion species in range.

DESCRIPTION *T. t. blanfordii*. Short tail, of 12 rectrices, and short, round-tipped wings. Irides whitish (straw-yellow to creamy-white in female), and has pale horn-brown to yellow bill (with distal portion of upper mandible reddish-brown), brighter in female, and chrome-yellow tarsus and toes (former paler in male). Sexes differ. **Adult male:** Forehead, supercilium and head-sides buff, with black feather tips; crown black, fringed buff, sometimes with central buff stripe. Throat whitish-buff with throat-sides and breast rufous-buff, breast-sides having small round black spots, thereafter becoming paler on flanks and white on belly to undertail-coverts. Nape and scapulars to uppertail-coverts and tail greyish-brown with traces of rufous and irregular darker brown/black spotting and vermiculations. Flight feathers blackish-brown with narrow buff fringes to outer webs, and wing-coverts buff, marked with subterminal black spots, especially on lesser and median coverts. **Adult female:** Much as adult male but generally has brighter bare parts (see above) and well-defined rufous nuchal collar in breeding plumage, while black markings on upperparts may be less heavy and dense. Non-breeding plumage consists of buff crown-stripe, with rufous collar admixed grey and less well defined than in breeding plumage, greyish mantle and scapulars irregularly marked black, diffusely rufous and has some buff fringes. **Juvenile:** Most similar to male, with less distinct breast-patch, faint narrow greyish bars on lower throat and breast, less pronounced, but more numerous wing-covert spots and overall duller plumage.

GEOGRAPHICAL VARIATION Two subspecies recognised, though these are not particularly well marked and may plausibly intergrade in Myanmar and elsewhere. Closest relatives unclear.

T. t. tanki Blyth, 1843 occurs in the Indian subcontinent, the Andaman and Nicobar islands; smaller with less distinct dorsal markings.

T. t. blanfordii Blyth, 1863 occurs from Myanmar to Indochina and SW, S, C and E China north to Korea and extreme SE Russia in Amurland and Ussuriland; described above.

MEASUREMENTS Length 15–18 cm. Female larger. *T. t. tanki*. Males: wing 71–84, tail c.26, tarsus c.23. Females:

wing 79–93, tail 30–40, tarsus 25–28. Weight (both sexes) 36–43. Eastern *blanfordii*: male wing 85.5–91.0, tail 30–33, tarsus 23–25, weight 35–78; female wing 96–100, tail 33–34, tarsus 26–27, weight 93–113.

HABITAT Principally in grassy areas, scrub, slightly marshy grassland, cultivation, especially rice fields and second growth (particularly on migration); also to 2150 m in undergrowth of pine forest in Myanmar.

VOICE Advertising call, by female, is a low-pitched 10–15-second moaning hooting sometimes increasing in strength, when considered almost human-like; also a far-carrying *off-off-off*, which is more subdued. A *pook-pook* is perhaps only given by male.

HABITS Terrestrial. Generally solitary or in pairs. Flushes very reluctantly from almost underfoot, flying short distance on thrumming wings before returning to cover and running on. Resident in most areas but nomadic or migratory in dry parts of Indian subcontinent, where is a breeding visitor during the rainy season. Also known only as a summer migrant breeder in northeast of range, with these birds wintering in SE Asia. Migrates nocturnally. Omnivorous, taking grain seeds, green shoots and a variety of invertebrates, including ants, small beetles and grasshoppers, though seeds are principal constituent of species' diet. Young largely fed on small insects, but also some seeds.

BREEDING Shallow depression lined with grass, sometimes with surrounding stems bent to form rough dome with side entrance, probably selected by both sexes. Usually 4 pear-shaped eggs, greyish-white and variably marked with yellowish, pale mauve, brownish and black, and incubated for 12–16 days by male alone. Young, also tended solely by male, self-feed after 5–6 days, are capable of flight at 10 days and attain adult plumage at seven weeks. Female is sequentially polyandrous and nests solitary. Season March–November, occasionally other months and perhaps all year in SE Asia, but principally in June–October rainy season.

DISTRIBUTION S and E Asia, from India subcontinent east to SE China, SE Siberia and N Korea, south to Andaman and Nicobar Is, Myanmar (except SW, peninsula and NE), Thailand (except Peninsula) and Indochina. Principally occurs below 950 m, but locally to 2150 m in Himalayas and Myanmar.

STATUS Few data. Widespread and apparently common, e.g. in Thailand and Nepal, but uncommon in much of India, irregular in Pakistan, only one recent record in Bangladesh and considered rare in Russian portion of range. Apparently common in Malaysia, but no breeding records and only an uncommon migrant (no breeding records) in E Tonkin and N Annam. Prefers disturbed and cultivated areas, and species therefore apparently secure.

REFERENCES Debus (1996), Grimmett *et al.* (2000), Johnsgard (1991), Robson (2000).

Alternative name: Ocellated Buttonquail.

Distinctive buttonquail of the N Philippines where it is apparently reasonably common, though it is comparatively infrequently recorded by ornithologists.

IDENTIFICATION The largest buttonquail known from the Philippines, where it is restricted to Luzon and, perhaps doubtfully, Negros (some doubt exists concerning the collector of the single specimen reportedly taken on the latter). Fairly large brown buttonquail, with a strongly patterned head, unmarked rufous breast and boldly spotted wings; the female is typically even brighter, having even more boldly marked head and more prominent rufous nuchal collar. Smaller Worcester's Buttonquail, which overlaps on Luzon, is distinguished by virtue of its rufous flanks and undertail-coverts, but other *Turnix* species in range should be easily distinguished, especially given a good view.

DESCRIPTION *T. o. ocellata*. Short tail, of 12 rectrices, and short, round-tipped wings. Irides yellowish-white, and has horn or greenish-yellow bill (with pale yellow cutting edges and grey lower mandible base) and pale orange-yellow tarsus and toes (brighter in female). Sexes differ. **Adult male:** Crown to nape black, with brown fringes to feathers, white median crown-stripe and supercilium, and white face and throat-sides, all feathers tipped black. Throat whitish with indistinct dark bars or spots, breast dull rufous sometimes with subterminal black spots to some or all feathers, greyish-brown flanks, grading to dirty buff on belly and paler on undertail-coverts. Mantle, scapulars and back brown, feathers vermiculated and spotted black and fringed buff; rump, uppertail-coverts and tail brown finely barred black. Flight feathers dark to blackish-brown, with pale buff fringes especially on outer webs, tertials as scapulars and wing-coverts buffy boldly and heavily spotted black, with whitish-buff fringes. **Adult female:** Similar to male, but more boldly patterned. Crown to nape black with three distinctive white stripes and rufous-brown fringes, and entire face black prominently and irregularly spotted white; black throat. With age entire face apparently becomes more or less uniform black. Extensive rufous breast, extending around hindneck as well-developed broad collar and grading into greyish-buff belly and undertail-coverts. Wing-coverts have fewer and smaller black spots. **Juvenile:** Young male has throat largely spotted black and most breast feathers with subterminal black spots, while female has throat variably spotted white; both sexes may have darker irides than adults. With age both sexes acquire subterminal blotches of upper back and pale-buff fringed scapulars, chin and throat become largely white and upperparts markings more distinct.

GEOGRAPHICAL VARIATION Two races recognised, apparently principally varying in size, but some evidence of intergradation in NE Luzon, from where an intermediate-sized specimen originates. The only specimen (and record) from Negros has been assigned to the nominate, but doubt exists concerning the provenance of this individual (see above).

   T. o. benguetensis Parkes, 1968 occurs in montane N Luzon and lowland NE Luzon; has smaller wings and bill, but more extensive chestnut on lower breast and collar than nominate.

   T. o. ocellata (Scopoli, 1786) occurs in lowland S and C Luzon and perhaps Negros; described above.

MEASUREMENTS Length 17–18 cm. Female larger. Both races. Males: wing 88–102, tail 35–41, tarsus 27–28. Females: wing 97–111, tail 43–46, tarsus 28–30, weight (n=1) 110.

HABITAT Occurs in broad variety of areas, to 2200 m, in gardens and scrub to dry-forest ravines and edge, including bamboo.

VOICE No data.

HABITS Very few data. Terrestrial. Flushes reluctantly, usually at less than 1 m from perceived danger, flying a short distance and then either running or 'freezing'. May feed relatively unconcernedly a few metres from observers. Presumed resident, as no records outside limited range. Information on diet is wholly lacking, but recent field observations indicate a preference for foraging in grassy borders at forest edge, and on dirt trails and roads in forest.

BREEDING Very few data. Season May–August and February (chick), but no vocalisations heard in February–March. Nest is a depression lined with leaves on ground, concealed by sticks, or slightly elevated among root stems of shrub. Lays 2–4 greyish-white eggs, densely speckled grey to purple. Female polyandrous.

DISTRIBUTION Philippines. Endemic to N and C Luzon, and perhaps Negros.

STATUS Formerly considered Near Threatened and currently known from perhaps as few as 16 localities, but treated as common by Kennedy *et al.* (2000). Few data on status and comparatively rarely recorded by ornithologists, though it appears to be relatively frequent around Subic Bay, Luzon and appears tolerant of second growth. Subject to some human predation, but relatively frequent capture suggests that it is reasonably common. Recently (March 1990) discovered on Negros (see above) and in lowlands around Pasaleng, N Luzon, suggesting that the species may also await discovery in other poorly surveyed areas.

REFERENCES Debus (1996), duPont (1971), Johnsgard (1991), Kennedy *et al.* (2000).

226 BARRED BUTTONQUAIL
Turnix suscitator (Gmelin, 1789)   Plate 66

Alternative name: Dusky Buttonquail.

Medium-sized buttonquail, which is widespread in Asia from the Indian subcontinent east and south to the Philippines, Sulawesi and the Lesser Sundas, and is subject to extensive geographical variation.

IDENTIFICATION This, the most widespread buttonquail in SE Asia, is usually readily identified, if seen well, by virtue of a number of features unique within its range. Like other buttonquails, female is the more strikingly marked of the two sexes, in this species having black throat and centre of upper breast, heavy blackish bars on rest of breast and upper flanks, heavily barred coverts and deep rufous-buff vent and undertail-coverts; male lacks black on throat and breast and has slightly duller rear underparts. The heavy underparts and wing-covert barring, rear underparts coloration and, in female, black throat-patch immediately identify this species from all sympatric congeners. Even given a brief flight view, it should be identifiable from smaller Small Buttonquail and *Coturnix* quails by virtue of greater contrast between coverts and rest of wing and blunt tail, with Yellow-legged Buttonquail exhibiting greater contrast on this surface, while both species are easily separated by head and underparts patterns at rest. In Philippines, heavily barred breast and upper belly, and rufous undertail-coverts are diagnostic among overlapping congeners, namely Spotted, Worcester's and Small Buttonquail.

DESCRIPTION *T. s. taigoor.* Short tail, of 12 rectrices, and short, round-tipped wings. Irides pale yellow (paler in male), and has black bill with yellow base (yellow with greenish tip in female) and bluish-flesh to brownish-/greenish-yellow tarsus and toes (marginally darker in female). Sexes differ. **Adult male:** Forehead, lores, head-sides and entire throat and neck greyish-/buffish-white, with subterminal black spots and lores sometimes all black; crown to hindneck greyish-brown to rufous with white central crown-stripe. Foreneck and entire breast barred black and buff, grading to rusty-buff or pale buff across entire rest of underparts, paler on central belly and vent sometimes barred. Mantle and scapulars to uppertail-coverts and tail greyish-brown to rufous, barred and vermiculated black, with scapulars and some outer feathers dorsally having whitish-buff fringes. Flight feathers and primary-coverts blackish-brown, narrowly fringed buff or white on outer webs and wing-coverts rufous or brown, barred black and with buff outer webs. **Adult female:** Forehead, lores, head-sides, throat and neck white, with subterminal black spot on all feathers and lores occasionally all black; crown to hindneck greyish-brown to rufous with white central crown-stripe. Centre of throat and foreneck deep black, with neck- and breast-sides buff barred black, grading to rusty-buff or pale buff across entire rest of underparts and sometimes extending as rufous collar on hindneck, paler in central belly and vent sometimes barred. Mantle and scapulars to uppertail-coverts and tail greyish-brown to rufous, barred and vermiculated black, with scapulars and some outer feathers dorsally having

whitish-buff fringes. Flight feathers and primary-coverts blackish-brown, narrowly fringed buff or white on outer webs and wing-coverts rufous or brown, barred black and with buff outer webs. **Juvenile:** Most resembles male, but female gradually acquires black throat-patch and both sexes have V-shaped or rounded black spots on breast, not bars, more buff on wing-coverts and outer edges of flight feathers more broadly and irregularly fringed buff.

GEOGRAPHICAL VARIATION Eighteen races recognised, though some such as *interrumpens* and *baweanus* may be of doubtful validity, most differing in extent of black and rufous markings on upperparts, coloration of belly and flanks, presence or not of black throat in female, and females of two races have duller non-breeding plumages; overall size, especially of wing also varies. Those in N Sumatra have sometimes been referred to *atrogularis* and highly distinctive *powelli* may warrant specific status.

T. s. taigoor (Sykes, 1832) occurs in India; described above.

T. s. leggei Stuart Baker, 1920 occurs in Sri Lanka; yellow base to bill more extensive and noticeable than in many forms, with brighter, more rufous upperparts, especially scapulars, particularly bold white fringes to wing-coverts, and ground colour to breast and breast-sides perhaps whiter than in *taigoor.*

T. s. plumbipes (Hodgson, 1837) occurs from Nepal to Assam, Bangladesh and W Myanmar, also China in SW Yunnan and SE Xizang; a rather poorly-differentiated form.

T. s. bengalensis Blyth, 1852 occurs in lower W Bengal; has generally very uniform grey-brown upperparts, rufous-buff ground colour to most of underparts, deep-based bill, largely plain grey-white face with black feather tips and extensive black throat reaching neck-sides.

T. s. okinavensis Phillips, 1947 occurs from S Kyushu south to Ryukyu (Japan); resembles *blakistoni* but has a heavier bill (recalling *thai*) and is rather paler brown above than other races from E Asia.

T. s. rostrata Swinhoe, 1865 occurs on Taiwan; female has duller non-breeding plumage.

T. s. blakistoni (Swinhoe, 1871) occurs from Myanmar through N Vietnam to S China and Hainan, and winters south to NW Thailand and N Indochina; both sexes have buffier underparts than other forms in SE Asia and richer chestnut ground colour to upperparts, and female has duller non-breeding plumage.

T. s. pallescens Robinson & Stuart Baker, 1928 occurs in SC Myanmar; generally pale, with black-and-rufous upperparts markings highly indistinct, broad white bars (rather than streaks) on scapulars and inner wing-coverts and overall rather rufescent.

T. s. thai Deignan, 1946 occurs in C Thailand; differs from *blakistoni* and *atrogularis* in having upperparts brownish-grey (rather than rufous or greyish-brown), with a bill intermediate between the two latter forms.

T. s. interrumpens Robinson & Stuart Baker, 1928 occurs in peninsular Myanmar and Thailand; has very uniform upperparts, lacking both rich rufous markings of *blakistoni* and black bars of *suscitator* and *atrogularis*.

T. s. atrogularis (Eyton, 1839) occurs in S Thailand and the Malay Peninsula; has richer buff underparts than other forms in SE Asia and pale buff on wings is paler and more extensive than in *suscitator*.

T. s. suscitator (Gmelin, 1789) occurs in Sumatra and offshore islands, Java and Bali (includes '*kuiperi*' on Belitung off E Sumatra and '*machetes*' in much of Sumatra); male has white throat, white breast and belly, former scalloped dark brown/black, rufous lower flanks and undertail-coverts and predominantly brown upperparts, while female has rather dark crown, heavy deep-based bill, very extensive black chin and throat, otherwise similar underparts to male, but breast more heavily scalloped, and boldly marked buff, black and white on larger wing-coverts.

T. s. baweanus Hoogerwerf, 1962 occurs on Bawean I. (off Java); male has bill shorter than in other races and both sexes have the bill less deep based, female has black on throat and foreneck less extensive than in most forms, with underparts barring less coarse, rest of underparts duller and less extensively buff than in *suscitator* and upperparts markings overall fewer in number than latter, and male and young female differ in similar respects from similar plumages of neighbouring taxa.

T. s. fasciata Temminck, 1815 occurs in the N Philippines, from Luzon south to Masbate; male has greyish central crown-stripe, slight chestnut collar and pale chestnut undertail-coverts, while female has black throat and chestnut collar.

T. s. haynaldi Blasius, 1888 occurs on Palawan and the Calamian group (Philippines); overall rather small with a long bill and in plumage most similar to *rufilata*.

T. s. nigrescens Tweeddale, 1878 occurs in the CE Philippines from Panay south to Negros and Cebu; female has broader chestnut hind collar than *haynaldi* and generally darker upperparts than other races, with extensively dark head and throat.

T. s. rufilata Wallace, 1865 occurs on Sulawesi; sexes alike, with white throat, grey breast, and usually barred black and rufous-buff on flanks.

T. s. powelli Guillemard, 1885 occurs in the Lesser Sundas from Lombok east to Alor; overall much darker grey than forms in mainland SE Asia, with restricted, but very neat black-bordered white spots on larger wing-coverts, and differs from *rufilata* in its greyish flanks and black upper throat in female.

MEASUREMENTS Length 13.5–17.5 cm. Female larger. *T. s. taigoor.* Males: wing 72–85, tail 35–37, tarsus 22–23, weight (*T. s. leggei*) 35–52. Females: wing 77–90, tail 33–41, tarsus 22–25, weight (*T. s. leggei*)

47–68. Race *haynaldi* in Philippines smaller (both sexes): wing 73–81, tail 22–24, tarsus 21–24; while wing of *rufilata* on Sulawesi (both sexes) is 89–102.

HABITAT Inhabits dry grassy and cultivated areas including sugar cane and coffee and tea plantations, scrub and second growth, generally below 300 m, but occurs to 1650 m in SE Asia and 2500 m in Himalayas.

VOICE Female advertising call, often given at night, has been likened to a distant motorbike, a ventriloquial *drr-r-r-r-r-r*, prefaced by 3–4 long deep *groo* notes, given at half-second intervals and the whole lasting upwards of 15 seconds before ending abruptly; also a far-carrying *hoon-hoon-hoon-hoon* variation.

HABITS Terrestrial. Solitary or in pairs. Rarely flies from danger and drops back into cover within 10–20 m if flushed. Resident in most of range, but some continental populations may be locally migratory or dispersive, perhaps to avoid rains. Limited evidence of nocturnal activity from Malaysia. Takes grass and weed seeds, insects, snails and green shoots from among grass and leaf-litter, making circular scrapes in mud. It commutes to foraging sites along clearly marked and well-used trails and dirt roads.

BREEDING Pad of grass in shallow depression, often in grass tuft with stems bent to form thin dome and side entrance. Typically 4 eggs (range 2–6, usually 2–3 in Philippines), grey-olive densely marked with brown especially at broader end, and sometimes lavender and purplish-black, and incubated for 12–16 days by male alone, who also assumes chick-care responsibilities. Young reach adult size at 40–60 days. Female is sequentially polyandrous, but nests are solitary. Lays in all months (December–September in continental SE Asia and February–September in Philippines), with local peaks according to seasonal conditions, e.g. April–May in Japan, and may not breed at height of rains or in driest months.

DISTRIBUTION S Asia, Indonesia and the Philippines, from Indian subcontinent to SE China and Hainan I., Taiwan and Japan (C and S Ryukyu Is to S Kyushu); Philippines, on Luzon, Mindoro, Calamian Is, Palawan, Sibuyan, Masbate, Panay, Cebu and Negros; and Indonesia on Sulawesi, Sumatra (including Riau and Lingga Is), Java, Bali, Lombok, Sumbawa, Flores, Lomblen and Alor.

STATUS Apparently widespread and common in India, Sri Lanka and most of SE Asia, e.g. very common in Thailand. Relatively common within restricted Japanese range, and in Malaysia. Persists in areas around habitation and apparently benefits locally from cutting, grazing, cropping and even fires, though perhaps declining in cultivated areas in Malaysia, due to effects of herbicide usage.

REFERENCES Debus (1996), Grimmett *et al.* (2000), Johnsgard (1991), Kennedy *et al.* (2000), MacKinnon & Phillipps (2000), van Marle & Voous (1988), Robson (2000), White & Bruce (1986).

Other names: Madagascan/Black-necked Buttonquail.

The only buttonquail on Madagascar and related islands, and therefore unlikely to be confused by experienced observers.

IDENTIFICATION Only confusable with the two *Coturnix* species that occur in Madagascar, Common and Harlequin Quails, and readily distinguished from both given a reasonable view. Neither of the two confusion species are known from the other islands within Madagascar Buttonquail's range. Both sexes tiny and plump, principally grey-brown with darker, black barring on upperparts and white-spotted wing-coverts, while female has obvious white moustachial area and orange-rufous breast patch. Both *Coturnix* species are slightly larger than Madagascar Buttonquail, with more direct and powerful flight patterns; Common Quail is more richly patterned in both sexes, especially the head and lacks rufous breast of female Madagascar Buttonquail, while both sexes of Harlequin Quail have highly distinctive head patterns, including long white supercilia and extensive white throat patches, while male has strikingly patterned black-and-rufous breast. Given close ground views, Madagascar Buttonquail has a paler bill and whitish iris, which are not shared by either of the *Coturnix*.

DESCRIPTION Relatively short winged and short tailed. Irides creamy-/greyish-white, with bill dull bluish-grey and tarsus whitish-grey to grey-blue. Tarsus is unique among buttonquail, being longer than middle toe and claw. Sexes differ. **Adult male:** Forehead, crown and nape dark grey or black, with narrow central stripe and broadly edged buff, and heavily mottled, grey face with slight whitish-grey moustachial. Pale buff underparts with narrow black bars on throat broadening on breast, becoming even paler on belly and vent; breast-sides washed pale rufous. Black mantle and scapulars, barred rufous and feathers fringed whitish or buff, while back, rump and uppertail-coverts brownish-grey, admixed rufous with intricate black barring and black and white streaks. Tail and primary-coverts blackish-brown, with buff outer webs to tail feathers. Rufous-brown wing-coverts and tertials, with irregular white spots outlined black. Greyish-brown flight feathers. **Adult female:** Forehead and lores black, barred white, crown chestnut with black streaks. Nape dark grey. Face and upperparts largely as male, but feathers tipped black; overall brighter and more rufous, especially on wing-coverts, and with more obvious whitish moustachial stripe extending from base of lower mandible. Lower throat and upper breast black, with bright rufous breast-sides (much more extensive and richer than male) and upper flanks, rest of breast and flanks grey, belly white and undertail-coverts rufous. **Juvenile:** Differs from male in having outer webs of secondaries rufous, vermiculated black, with black-edged white spots on fringes.

GEOGRAPHICAL VARIATION Monotypic.

MEASUREMENTS Length 13–16 cm. Female larger. Males: wing 72–82, weight 60–72. Females: wing 81–88, weight 59–84. Tail (both sexes) 34–36, tarsus (both sexes) 20.

HABITAT Recorded in open grassland, savanna, heath and littoral and spiny forests fringing humid forest to 1900 m (to 1660 m on Réunion), and most common in grasses and second growth of closed-canopy gallery forest with a deep leaf-litter. Often sympatric with Madagascar Partridge in grassland and inhabits dry cultivated areas and disturbed woodland.

VOICE Relatively silent, though female gives deep, humming advertising call, lasting c.3 seconds before abruptly ending.

HABITS Terrestrial. If disturbed, runs or flies a short distance and runs on. Considered sedentary, but perhaps locally dispersive, it being unclear whether populations on islands other than Madagascar were self-introduced or the product of human intervention (or both). Usually in pairs or small groups. Diet includes seeds and insects, including a variety of beetles, flies and Lepidoptera larvae, taken while scratching and pivoting over well-defined circular or conical scrapes in leaf-litter. Diurnal, in contrast to several congeners.

BREEDING Shallow depression or scrape lined with grass, beneath tussock or within grass below small tree or bush, and often with canopy and side entrance, or even tunnel. Three to 5 eggs, buff marked with brown and black, and incubated for 13–16 days by male alone. Young can feed themselves at two weeks, are fully feathered and capable of flight at three weeks, and wholly independent one week later. Solitary breeder. Lays in late August–February, with downy young reported as late as early April in Madagascar. Reportedly breeds year-round on Réunion.

DISTRIBUTION Endemic to Madagascar. Introduced on Mauritius, Réunion (where an indigenous population may have already existed) and Glorieuses Is.

STATUS Common in N, W and SW Madagascar, but less frequent in east and on High Plateau. Reportedly common around Toliara, Zombitse and Ampijoroa. Possibly now extinct on Mauritius, but common on Réunion. Prefers a wide variety of disturbed, cultivated and secondary habitats, and species therefore probably secure. Threats include hunting, with both walk-in traps and slingshots reportedly used by local people to capture it.

REFERENCES Barré *et al.* (1996), Debus (1996), Goodman *et al.* (1997), Johnsgard (1991), Morris & Hawkins (1998).

Alternative name: Black-fronted Buttonquail.

This large, boldly patterned and relatively unmistakable buttonquail is now very rare and perhaps restricted to SE Queensland, where its preferred habitat of drier forest-types has been rather little incorporated within the protected areas network.

IDENTIFICATION This rare and highly range-restricted buttonquail should be very difficult to confuse with overlapping congeners, even similar-sized Painted Buttonquail, given black head, neck and breast of female, boldly barred and spotted white, and large size, pale eyes, ash-grey rest of underparts, generally dark upperparts and general lack of solid brighter rufous-brown markings. Rather 'open' whitish face, black-and-white barred breast and generally dark upperparts readily distinguish male from other buttonquail of similar size.

DESCRIPTION Short tail, of 12 rectrices, and short, round-tipped wings. Irides creamy-white (bluish-grey in juvenile), with mid-grey bill and darker culmen, and dull yellow legs and feet. Sexes differ. **Adult male:** Forehead, head-sides and neck white, finely speckled blackish, with darker ear-coverts patch; crown and nape brownish-grey, scalloped rufous-brown and has black lateral stripes and chin and throat white. Breast coarsely spotted and barred black and white, mottled rufous-brown on sides, becoming ash-grey, with fine dark barring across entire rest of underparts. Mantle and scapulars to uppertail-coverts and tail predominantly brownish-grey, barred rufous-brown and black with white streaks and narrow grey-brown fringes to upper half, becoming more uniform with finer barring and less-distinct streaks dorsally. Dark grey-brown flight feathers, with rufous-brown central wing-coverts, marked with white spots and fringes and black subterminal streaks. Underwing ash-grey. **Adult female:** Much as male, but entire head black, washed chestnut on rear crown and nape, with fine white spotting forming weak supercilium and moustachial stripe. Hindneck and neck-sides also black, boldly spotted white, continuing onto black breast as bars and becoming sparser. Underparts generally darker ash-grey than male. Upperparts identical to male, except white-spotted (rather than streaked) central inner wing-coverts. **Juvenile:** Similar to adult male, but inner wing-coverts duller brown with relatively broader white streaking and hook-shaped black subterminal markings to each feather, and duller brownish-grey upperparts characterised by heavier black blotching on outer back and scapulars and pale streaking much reduced.

GEOGRAPHICAL VARIATION Monotypic. Form '*goweri*' from Queensland merely representative of individual variation, which may be relatively marked given existence of several, relatively isolated populations.

MEASUREMENTS Length 17–19 cm. Female larger. Males: wing 104–117, tail 36–49, tarsus 22.7–25.5, weight 50–87. Females: wing 112–120, tail 43–50, tarsus 23.5–27.6, weight 80–119.

HABITAT Favours dry bottletree *Brachychiton rupestris* scrub intermixed with other low tree species, in rainforests and drier forests, e.g. semi-evergreen vine thickets, low microphyll vine forest and araucarian notophyll forest, with a closed canopy and sparse understorey. Also seeks refuge in *Lantana* thickets and very occasionally recorded in stubble some distance from forest. Principally restricted to areas receiving 770–1200 mm annual rainfall.

VOICE Advertising (booming) call of female is a low, tremulous drumming series of 5–7 rapid *oo-oom, oo-oom, oo-oom* notes, lasting 1.5–2.0 seconds and repeated 1–4, or more frequently 14–21 times. Inaudible at distances above 50 m and only given in response to 100 mm of rain over a few days in any month. Also a soft whistle to juveniles. Males utter a variety of high-pitched clucking and staccato notes, usually to defend or rally young, occasionally in female's presence, while young also possess a number of piping or chirping calls, used in response to danger or to stimulate feeding.

HABITS Terrestrial. Recorded singly, in pairs, family groups of up to seven and coveys of 4–5. Runs or freezes in response to danger, only occasionally flying a short distance. Locally irruptive but perhaps principally sedentary on basis of limited radio-tagging data, with no evidence for seasonal or long-distance movements. Principally takes invertebrates: beetles, including weevils, ants and spiders apparently most important items, but centipedes, millipedes and land snails also reported in diet. Also takes seeds, including grain. Feeds, diurnally and at night, by gleaning, scratching and pecking in litter and, like other species of buttonquail, digs characteristic saucer-shaped feeding scrapes by pivoting on one foot while raking ground with the other. Direction of scratching is occasionally reversed, and it may also shade ground with outstretched wings, perhaps to delay retreat of exposed prey. Depressions may be as close as 50 mm, or up to 30 cm apart, with clusters of such scrapes generally being 10 m distant. Between one and 100 scrapes within a feeding area may be used, with 10–40 being typical. Roosts at daytime feeding site or in nest.

BREEDING Scrape, lined with grass and leaves and placed under low bush or coarse grass tussock, often with substantial dome and side entrance, is constructed by both sexes within one day. Solitary breeder, but female is sequentially polyandrous. Typically 3–4 round or oval eggs, pale buffy-white marked with brown, purplish-grey and black blotching, laid at 1–2-day intervals and incubated for 15–16 days once clutch is complete. Groups of 4–7 feathered juveniles with one female are assumed to be amalgamated broods. Male assumes entire incubation and majority of chick-care responsibilities. Young precocial and nidifugous, capable of feeding themselves at 8–11 days but may be fed for two weeks, attain adult plumage at 8–12 weeks and can breed at 3–5 months. Lays August–February (or March) in wild, but if sufficiently warm will breed in all months, principally September–April in captivity.

DISTRIBUTION Endemic to coastal CE Australia in SE Queensland, north to Rockhampton district, and south to extreme NE New South Wales in Northern Rivers and Tableland; perhaps extinct in latter state.

STATUS Classified as Vulnerable, but not listed as endangered under Australian national or regional legislation. Population currently estimated at c.5000 within severely fragmented range of 750 km². Appears much reduced in N New South Wales, where possibly now extinct, and Dawson and Fitzroy River catchments. Records from Fraser I. National Park, where c.2000 individuals may survive, are perhaps indicative of recent range expansion, but its preferred habitat of drier forms of rainforest within large tracts of moist forest is rarely included in national parks or other conservation zones. Data on habitat requirements, breeding biology, territory size and post-breeding dispersal are urgently required. The species has presumably declined dramatically due to habitat clearance for agriculture and silviculture (bottletree scrub has diminished from several hundred thousand to just a few thousand ha, with 90% of its habitat having been cleared since European settlement), and while it may be adapting to plantations and *Lantana*, it is unclear whether these are suitable for breeding. Survival in fragmented landscapes, especially those with relatively small patches of forest may be dependent on availability of a well-developed shrub layer between patches of vine forest. Landscapes managed for timber production often possess a much higher connectivity between sites, apparently making these more suitable. Small populations are threatened by fire, and probably cat and fox predation. The species is also taken by several raptors and reptiles may predate nests. Disturbance, particularly during drought, by cattle, horses, feral pigs and wallabies, which has increased as a result of partial forest clearance, is probably also detrimental. Research on the impact of forestry and fire, and inventories and management of dry rainforest remnants are ongoing, as is research to determine whether the species is able to persist within introduced hoop pine *Araucaria cunninghamii* plantations.

REFERENCES BirdLife International (2000), Debus (1996), Johnsgard (1991), Marchant & Higgins (1993), Smyth & Pavey (2001).

229 CHESTNUT-BACKED BUTTONQUAIL
Turnix castanota (Gould, 1840)   Plate 67

Alternative name: Thick-billed Quail.

One of a number of Australian buttonquail considered to be globally threatened, this rather poorly known species is restricted to the north coast of the country.

IDENTIFICATION A relatively little-known, medium to large buttonquail of N Australia, which is intermediate in size between larger Brown Quail and Red-backed Buttonquail. Easily distinguished from former by virtue of being overall paler and brighter plumaged, with a heavier bill, more uniform underparts, paler irides and a preference for drier habitats; even given brief flight views it should be distinguishable by smaller size and more contrasting upperwing pattern. Range overlaps with several congeners, all of which lack solidly rich rufous back and wings, dark lateral crown-stripes and white-spotted grey underparts, and more closely recalls Little and, especially, Painted Buttonquails, but no known sympatry with either. Former is smaller, with more white streaking on upperparts and lacks dark leading edge to upperwing of Chestnut-backed, while Painted lacks dark lateral crown-stripes, has much more black in upperparts, especially on crown and nape, and is unlikely to come into contact with *castanota*.

DESCRIPTION Short tail, of 12 rectrices, and short, round-tipped wings. Irides bright yellow with broad greyish orbital ring, pale brownish-grey bill and yellow tarsus and feet. Sexes differ. **Adult male:** Forehead densely spotted black and white, grading to grey with dark lateral stripes on crown and nape, tinged pale rufous-brown; hindneck rufous-brown heavily spotted black and white, with white head- and neck-sides, spotted black. Throat off-white, with rufous-brown breast, spotted white, becoming olive-grey spotted creamy on lower breast and grading to buffy-white on belly to undertail-coverts, though more whitish in centre. Mantle and scapulars rufous-brown, streaked paler and blotched black, becoming rufous-brown washed grey dorsally to uppertail-coverts and tail. Dark blackish flight feathers, contrasting with rufous-brown wing-coverts, boldly spotted white and having narrow black subterminal markings. **Adult female:** Resembles male, but in breeding plumage has forehead and head-sides blackish, spotted and streaked white, and grey hindneck, spotted white, which reaches onto upper mantle and even back in some. Slightly darker grey-olive breast and flanks, with more sharply defined and elongated creamy-white markings, while upperparts are brighter rufous-brown with fewer black markings and smaller white spots on inner wing-coverts, forming a less marked pale central panel in flight. Acquires more black in upperparts in non-breeding season, with paler whitish head-sides and is thus more like male. **Juvenile:** Apparently undescribed but probably recalls male, if perhaps overall duller.

GEOGRAPHICAL VARIATION Monotypic: races '*magnifica*' (NW Australia), '*melvillensis*' (Melville I.) and '*alligator*' (N Australia) all now regarded as invalid, being merely representative of individual variation.

MEASUREMENTS Length 14–20 cm. Female larger. Males: wing 88–93, tail 33–37, tarsus 20–23, weight 68–70. Females: wing 95–103, tail 31–41, tarsus 22–25, weight 87–124.

HABITAT Recorded from subcoastal forested and wooded areas subject to a monsoon climate, mostly in areas with above 800 mm summer rainfall, though noted in some regions that receive as little as 200 mm at this season. Often favours dry elevated quartzite sand-stone ridges, escarpments and plateaux, usually with short open-grass cover; occasionally occupies *Eucalyptus* forests (e.g. lateritic country with *Eucalyptus miniata* dominant) and woodland adjacent to recently burnt areas, and attracted to vine thickets and small rainforest patches within all habitat types.

VOICE Exceptionally poorly known. No recordings available. A low moaning *oom* reported from a separated group. Only other data concerns timing, February.

HABITS Terrestrial. Behaviour little known. Recorded singly, in pairs and coveys of up to 20. If disturbed runs with head high or, if hard-pressed, flushes over short distance; coveys run or take flight in unison. Extraordinary rocking motion observed when moving through open or semi-open country: an individual will move its entire body, including head and neck, backwards and forwards 3–4 times before taking each step. Apparently sedentary, e.g. in Kakadu National Park, even following grass fires, and no specific evidence for seasonal fluctuations or dispersal is available. Nocturnal and crepuscular. Few dietary data are known, but takes grass seeds, *Triodia*, beetles, ants and their eggs by scratching and gleaning in leaf-litter. Often feeds in groups. Grit, pebbles and sand are swallowed to aid digestion.

BREEDING Few data and those given below have been questioned as to whether they certainly relate to this species. Solitary breeder. Depression in long grass at base of shrub or grass clump, and often near water. May be domed with a side entrance, and is lined with grass and leaves. Typically 4 round eggs, white to greenish-white, finely or heavily marked with brown to black blotching, and reportedly incubated for 14–15 days. Breeds in wet season (December–May), with eggs recorded in January.

DISTRIBUTION Endemic to coastal N Australia, in NE Western Australia in the Kimberleys and N Dampier Peninsula, and N North Territory east to Arnhem Land and Groote Eylandt.

STATUS Near Threatened. Population may number 100,000. Large-scale changes in habitat, e.g. grazing by introduced herbivores, or more regular fires and associated spread of annual *Sorghum* spp., may be having significant adverse effects on the species, and have perhaps caused its disappearance from extreme southeast of range, where it was common in early 20th century. Regarded as uncommon in North Territory. Density of 0.4 birds per 10 ha in Kakadu National Park. Research urgently required on distribution, status and threats.

REFERENCES BirdLife International (2000), Debus (1996), Johnsgard (1991), Marchant & Higgins (1993).

230 BUFF-BREASTED BUTTONQUAIL
Turnix olivei Robinson, 1900   Plate 67

Alternative names: Buff-backed/Olive's Buttonquail.

Formerly treated as a subspecies of Chestnut-backed Buttonquail, this globally threatened Australian endemic is restricted to a tiny area of N Queensland where its population is under pressure due to habitat changes and associated degradation.

IDENTIFICATION This highly range-restricted and globally threatened buttonquail is unlikely to be mistaken by any observer sufficiently fortunate to encounter one (the population is now considered to be tiny). No other species within its declining range on the Cape York Peninsula shares its combination of uniform olive-buff foreneck and breast and generally plain pale rufous upperparts. It overlaps marginally with Brown Quail and Painted Buttonquail, but prefers more stony habitats and woodland with a less dense understorey to the latter and is, in any case, otherwise easily separated by plumage. Painted has more variegated black, rufous-brown and grey upperparts, more distinct rufous-brown breast-sides, a grey foreneck and breast with elongated pale spotting, dark red eyes and a finer, shorter bill. Even in flight the generally much darker and less uniform upperparts, grey-tinged rump (pale rufous in Buff-breasted), largely grey breast (often visible on landing), more tapered tail and less striking pale central coverts panel should be relatively obvious. Larger than either Painted Buttonquail or Brown Quail, and has slightly longer legs than either. No known overlap with Chestnut-backed Buttonquail, which is usually smaller, with markedly shorter (but equally deep-based) bill, while

both sexes have a white-spotted forehead, larger white marks on the hindneck, mantle and back, overall darker rufous upperparts, with more dark streaking, and dull white-spotted/streaked breast; breeding-plumage female can be further distinguished by olive-grey breast marked with cream, drop-shaped spots.

DESCRIPTION Short tail, of 12 rectrices, and short, round-tipped wings. Irides yellow, with largely brown bill, except bluish-white cutting edges and lower mandible, and yellow tarsus and feet. Sexes differ. **Adult male:** Forehead to hindneck grey with prominent black lateral crown-stripes reaching nape; head- and neck-sides off-white, finely speckled black. Dull white throat and olive-grey breast, merging with rufous-brown on breast-sides, and grading to off-white on flanks and belly to undertail-coverts. Mantle to uppertail-coverts and tail rufous-brown, with short white streaks on mantle becoming longer on back and scapulars, which have broad pale grey fringes, and overall ground colour is paler dorsally. Greyish-black flight feathers and pale rufous-brown wing-coverts, marked with black subterminally and large, bold white spots near tips, forming pale central panel to wing, which is obvious in flight and offers contrast with dark flight feathers and leading edge. Underwing pale grey. **Adult female:** Much as male, but has forehead darker grey, mostly chestnut lateral crown-stripes, darker head- and neck-sides with less white speckling, comparatively less heavily marked and overall brighter rufous-brown upperparts, and fewer and smaller white

431

spots on wing-coverts, forming less marked pale panel in flight. **Juvenile:** Undescribed, but as in similar species is perhaps most likely to recall male.

GEOGRAPHICAL VARIATION Monotypic. Form '*coenensis*' from north of range merely reflects individual variation and is no longer considered valid.

MEASUREMENTS Length 18–22 cm. Female larger by c.10%. Male (n=1) wing 101, tail 41, tarsus 22.8. Females: wing 112–113, tail 43–48, tarsus 23.5–27.2. No weight data.

HABITAT Apparently favours lowland, subcoastal grassland and wooded areas to 400 m. Dependent on suitable grassy woodlands especially of *Melaleuca*, *Acacia*, *Alphitonia* or *Tristania* and rarely uses recently burnt areas; some occupied sites possess a ground cover of 1 m-high *Heteropogon*, but also found on wooded stony hillsides with much sparser ground cover and almost no leaf-litter.

VOICE No recordings or studies available, but reasonably well known. Advertising (booming) call by female is a *ooom-oom-oom*, repeated up to 20 times, the notes becoming gradually louder (indeed, the initial notes may be almost inaudible), higher pitched and shorter, and the whole lasting up to 30 seconds. Male responds with deep, rapid *chu-chu-chu* whistle. Also a deep humming *gug-gug-gug* variously attributed to both male and female, and a soft *chirp-chirp-chirp* and a longer louder *kwaare-kwaare* given by both sexes.

HABITS Terrestrial. Recorded singly, in pairs or coveys of 3–8 (exceptionally 20). Walks or runs from danger, and only performs short (50–80 m, rarely as short as 15 m), low flights if hard-pressed to within 2–5 m, though it is capable of longer flights. Level take-off is followed by an initial 'leap', a further climb and then levels-off at c.3 m. Apparently resident but may move

south from C Cape York Peninsula in wet summers and local movements perhaps in response to habitat changes. Data on food largely absent, but takes seeds and insects, and uses sand to aid digestion.

BREEDING Few data. Solitary breeder. Shallow depression with dome of grasses and side entrance, lined with grass and leaves, well hidden in grass, low shrubs or beneath tussock in open *Acacia*, *Alphitonia*, *Melaleuca* or *Tristania* woodland within rainforest. Lays 2–4 (usually 3) round eggs, whitish and speckled chestnut, bluish-grey or black, but incubation period unknown. Male suspected to assume all incubation and chick-care duties. Young precocial and nidifugous. Season January–March, though male with two chicks seen in late December.

DISTRIBUTION Endemic to extreme NE Australia, in N Queensland from near Coen to Mareeba west of Cairns.

STATUS Endangered. Population currently estimated at 500 individuals within historical range of 2070 km², but very few records, known only from eight localities and no measures of abundance available. Apparently extirpated from early collecting sites at Coen and near Cooktown, and less common within last decade at Mt Molloy stronghold. Perhaps threatened by overgrazing and some sites may have been rendered unsuitable by extensive fire regimes that promote occlusion of grasslands and grassy woodland by woody weeds. Like other threatened Australian buttonquails, rarely encountered by birdwatchers and biology is poorly known; survey and research work are urgently required.

REFERENCES BirdLife International (2000), Debus (1996), Johnsgard (1991), Marchant & Higgins (1993), Rogers (1995).

---

231 PAINTED BUTTONQUAIL
Turnix varia (Latham, 1801)

Plate 67

Alternative names: Scrub/Speckled/Varied Buttonquail.

This comparatively widespread and attractive Australian buttonquail is declining across much of its range, despite its protected status, and an outlying population in New Caledonia appears to be on the verge of extinction.

IDENTIFICATION Like other Australian buttonquails, this intricately patterned species is relatively distinctive given a reasonable view and with experience. It is a large buttonquail, though its bill is less deep based than similar-sized species of *Turnix*, which should be easily recognised given range and habitat by virtue of its dark eye, rufous-brown shoulder patches and pale-spotted forehead and breast. Its range does not overlap with most similar Chestnut-backed Buttonquail and only marginally with Buff-breasted Buttonquail (see those species for distinguishing features). Also overlaps with highly range-restricted

Black-breasted Buttonquail, but should be easily separated in all plumages (see above).

DESCRIPTION *T. v. varia*. Short tail, of 12 rectrices, and short, round-tipped wings. Irides red when breeding, becoming paler reddish-orange to deep pink at other seasons (blue-grey becoming creamy-orange with age in juvenile), with pale grey bill, grading to grey-black on culmen and deep/chrome-yellow tarsus and feet (duller in juvenile and dirty pink in some). Sexes differ. **Adult male:** Forehead to nape and hindneck brownish-grey, finely spotted white, increasing on hindneck, scalloped rufous-brown and has broad black lateral crown-stripes; neck-sides and head otherwise white finely speckled black. Throat white, with dull rufous-brown shoulder patches extending to breast-sides, sparingly spotted white, and rest of underparts grey, densely marked with black-bordered buff spots, becoming unmarked cream on belly and vent, and buff on undertail-coverts. Mantle and scapulars to uppertail-coverts and tail brownish-grey, heavily blotched black, barred rufous-brown and streaked white, but black and white markings becoming less prominent dorsally, and rump and tail appear largely grey in flight. Grey-black flight feathers and leading edge to wing contrast with chestnut wing-coverts on ground and in flight. Wing-coverts have black subterminal bar and broad white tips. Underwing dark grey. **Adult female:** Resembles adult male, but entire forehead black with bolder white spotting, which extends to grey crown, mostly chestnut lateral crown-stripes, brighter, more solid and more extensive rufous-brown upperparts, especially on mantle, which grades into breast-sides. **Juvenile:** Smaller than adult male and otherwise differs in heavy black scalloping on white foreneck, breast and flanks, less conspicuous cream upperparts streaking and colour of bare parts (see above).

GEOGRAPHICAL VARIATION Three races recognised here. The forms '*stirlingi*' (SW Australia) and '*subminuta*' (NE Australia) are now regarded as invalid, as representative of individual variation and not reflective of geographical differences.

T. v. varia (Latham, 1801) occurs throughout mainland Australia and Tasmania; described above.

T. v. scintillans (Gould, 1845) occurs on the Houtman Abrolhos Is, off Western Australia; considerably smaller than previous form with paler and less grey upperparts crossed by narrower black-brown barring, but overall pattern bolder due to more conspicuous white streaking on same surface.

T. v. novaecaledoniae Ogilvie-Grant, 1893 occurs in New Caledonia; apparently smaller than both preceding forms, with mainly black upperparts marked by whitish or buffish fringes to feathers.

MEASUREMENTS Length 17–23 cm. Female larger. *T. v. varia.* Males: wing 96–106, tail 40–47, tarsus 19.7–23.9, weight 53–94. Females: wing 106–116, tail 40–53, tarsus 21–25, weight 72–134. *T. v. scintillans* (based on three males and two females, all but one of latter being immature). Males: wing 90–92, tail 34–37, tarsus 18.8–20.3. Females: wing 97–98, tail 38–45, tarsus 21, weight (both sexes) 52–82. One *T. v. novaecaledoniae* had wing c.82.

HABITAT Occupies forest and woodland in subcoastal areas below 800 m, favouring dry open or more closed, mature *Banksia* or *Acacia* forests, usually with a sparse or not too dense understorey but deep plant litter, open and closed heath and shrublands (up to 2 m tall). In wetter forests appears to only use dry ridges and slopes; also occasionally in coastal-dune scrub, cropped areas and grassland. Uses clearings within forest and occasionally recorded in suburban gardens and other atypical habitats in autumn, when presumably on migration.

VOICE Advertising (booming) call by female is a loud, low-pitched *oom*, usually repeated up to 8 (exceptionally 27) times at 1.5-second intervals, to which male may respond with a faint *cluck*. Booming most frequent at dusk and night, in June–February (especially October–December), though also given during day. Volume and intensity of notes increases if male nearby, when accompanied by feet stamping. Female also gives rapid drumming during courtship

feeding, or in response to imitation of booming song, as well as various other soft clucking and chattering notes near nest or in display. Male also utters various harsh churring notes when defending chicks. A captive-bred female was capable of booming song at c.6 months. Flapping flight, unlike other buttonquail, is accompanied by a whistled or metallic *whirr* of wings.

HABITS Terrestrial. Recorded singly, in pairs and small coveys or family parties of up to six. Freezes or runs in response to danger, and is only occasionally flushed, when it usually flies swiftly low between trees, though it is capable of longer flights at up to 6 m off the ground. May create permanent roosting depression, sheltered by tussock or rushes. Largely resident, though numbers appear to fluctuate in many areas suggesting that true situation is more complex and may be linked to seasonal factors such as rainfall and food availability. In south of range, especially highland areas, is a summer breeding migrant. Conducts nocturnal movements, but evidence does not suggest that it is an altitudinal or long-distance north–south migrant. Principally active at night, but also crepuscular and less commonly diurnal. Forages on seeds of grasses, *Avena*, Fabaceae, *Trifolium*, *Erodium* and *Acacia*, fruits of *Solanum* and other wild berries, green shoots and insects, including fly pupae, grasshoppers, ants, beetles, weevils, bugs, moths, larvae and aquatic insects. Feeds, usually in pairs, by scratching and gleaning in litter and, like many congeners, forms characteristic circular scrapes by pivoting on one foot, occasionally reversing direction. Up to 15 such depressions may be created within 1.5 m². Grit and sand are ingested in order to assist food breakdown.

BREEDING Cup of grass and fine plant, leaf- and stick litter on ground, partially domed and walled, in a scrape at base of grass tussock, rock or small shrub. In captivity, female constructs nest and is sequentially polyandrous, mating with up to 3–4 males, though there is some evidence of long-term pair bonds (up to eight months) in wild. Three to 4 (rarely 5) oval eggs, faint buffy to greyish-white and variably speckled chestnut, dull violet, grey or black. Laid at 1–3-day intervals and incubated, on completion of clutch, for 13–14 days, usually by male alone. Young precocial and nidifugous. Typically fed and guarded by male alone, but are able to self-feed and fly at 7–10 days, are fully independent at 16 days and reach adult size at c.23 days, though adults have been observed feeding fledged young. Of 16 nests for which clutch size and outcome were known, a mean of 2.6 young was raised per clutch. Breeds throughout year in N Australia, if conditions suitable, but typically August–February in most areas.

DISTRIBUTION Coastal SW, E and SE Australia, in SW Western Australia north to Houtman Abrolhos Is and Shark Bay; and from E Queensland north to Cairns, south to Victoria and Tasmania and west to Eyre Peninsula in South Australia, also Kangaroo and King Is, and New Caledonia. Unsuccessfully introduced to Hawaii in 1922.

STATUS Uncommon to locally common, but probably declining in south of range, in Western Australia, New South Wales and SE South Australia, and especially in Tasmania, where now very rare. Tiny population on Abrolhos Is considered vulnerable to extinction, while *novaecaledoniae* on New Caledonia is rare or perhaps already extinct. Habitat clearance and degradation through agricultural intensification, urbanisation, grazing and fire are principal threats, though effects of hunting, introduced predators around human habitation and domestic grazing animals may also be significant. Obviously susceptible to disturbance; often departing such areas for up to two months. Usually reappears at burnt areas within three months to two years, but after particularly severe fires may go unrecorded for up to eight years. Formally protected in Australia.

REFERENCES Debus (1996), Hall (1974), Johnsgard (1991), Marchant & Higgins (1993).

232 WORCESTER'S BUTTONQUAIL
Turnix worcesteri McGregor, 1904

Plate 66

Alternative name: Luzon Buttonquail.

This taxon has enjoyed a confused history, being initially considered a form of Small Buttonquail and then conspecific with Sumba and Red-chested Buttonquails, but is now generally regarded as a separate species. Nonetheless it is still one of the most poorly known Oriental birds, with virtually all available information coming from trappers and all pre-1960s specimens having been destroyed.

IDENTIFICATION Virtually unknown in life, this small buttonquail endemic to the Philippine island of Luzon has a relatively short stout bill and comparatively poorly marked plumage. Male Spotted Buttonquail is larger, with rufous breast, but lacks rufous flanks and undertail-coverts, while female has largely black-and-white head and rufous collar. Both sexes of Barred Buttonquail are also larger and both have strongly barred underparts, and female a largely dark head.

DESCRIPTION Short tail, of 12 rectrices, and short, round-tipped wings. Irides pale yellow and has bluish bill and pinkish flesh-coloured legs. Sexes differ. **Adult male:** Forehead, crown and nape dark brown with paler feather fringes, and former spotted white, incomplete buff median crown-stripe and supercilium, lores and face black spotted pale buff, and neck-sides and moustachial black, former with subterminal white bar to each feather. Throat white, with sides streaked dark brown, rufous and buff breast, flanks and undertail-coverts rusty-buff, surrounding white belly and vent-sides partially barred blackish-brown. Virtually entire upperparts and wing-coverts dark brown, finely barred buff and feathers broadly fringed buff, forming streaks, and flight feathers pale grey-brown, narrowly fringed whitish, especially on outer webs; tail black with buff fringes, and scapulars and tertials fringed whitish-buff. **Adult female:** Very similar to male, but lores and face spotted white and throat pale rufous continuous with underparts, except white belly. **Juvenile:** Unknown.

GEOGRAPHICAL VARIATION Monotypic.

MEASUREMENTS Length 12–14 cm. Female larger. Males: wing 62–70, tail 20–25, tarsus 14–18. Females: wing 67–74, tail 19–35, tarsus 15–17. No weight data.

HABITAT Considered to be a grassland species and possibly restricted to highlands, where taken at 1100 m at Dalton Pass, but neither is confirmed and it is possible that it is a forest species, like some of the Australian buttonquails.

VOICE Unknown.

HABITS Terrestrial. Movements unknown, though a single record from a montane pass perhaps suggests local migration may occur. Diet and feeding behaviour presumably as congeners, but specific information relating to this species is almost entirely lacking. Data from one specimen suggests that insects are taken.

BREEDING No information available, but presumed to breed in north of island in April–July, dispersing south in July–March. One male, taken in March, had slightly enlarged sexual organs.

DISTRIBUTION Philippines. Endemic to N and C Luzon.

STATUS Classified as Data Deficient. Extremely little known and rarely recorded by birdwatchers. Records are available from just six localities, at which individuals have been found at only three in the last 20 years. Presumed to breed in N Luzon in April–June, with at least some apparently dispersing south in July–March, but perhaps confined to grasslands in highlands of Cordillera Central, though possibility that it frequents forested (non-grassland) habitats cannot be eliminated. Certainly subject to human predation, as most records are made by trappers (e.g. at the migratory funnel and notorious bird-catching area of Dalton Pass), but extent of this and other potential threats unclear. Populations perhaps await discovery on other islands and extensive research on all aspects of the species' behaviour and biology is urgently required.

REFERENCES BirdLife International (2000, 2001), Debus (1996), Johnsgard (1991), Kennedy *et al.* (2000).

Restricted to the island of the same name, Sumba Buttonquail is the least known of the three threatened species found only in the Sumba Endemic Bird Area.

IDENTIFICATION Endemic to Sumba, in the Lesser Sundas, where confusion is possible only with the ecologically sympatric *sumbana* race of Red-backed Buttonquail (which is the only other buttonquail to occur on the island), from which it is best distinguished in the field (given a good view) by virtue of its heavy blue-grey bill (slimmer and yellow in the latter), flesh-pink (not yellow) legs and rather plain, slightly scaled wing-coverts (boldly black spotted in *sumbana*). Sumba also has a somewhat diffuse dark eye-stripe and upper border to ear-coverts. Both species are dumpy button-quails with orange-red breasts, with *sumbana* lacking the chestnut nape collar of most forms of the Red-backed group and thus complicating its separation from *everetti*. Both Brown and Blue-breasted Quails also occupy the same habitats as Sumba Buttonquail, but both appear larger, even in flight, and usually call when flushed, unlike either species of *Turnix*.

DESCRIPTION Short tail, of 12 rectrices, and short, round-tipped wings. Irides bright yellow or whitish-yellow in female, and has dark to blue-grey bill and flesh-coloured tarsus and feet (with yellowish tinge in young male specimen). Sexes differ. **Adult male:** Description is based on young male. Crown black with broad reddish-brown fringes and obvious white central crown-stripe; lores and malar whitish flecked brown and supercilium and ear-coverts lightly marked cinnamon-brown, with small black band extending from ear-coverts onto neck-sides; and chin and throat whitish, marked blackish. Neck-sides and breast yellow-ochre barred black and white, becoming deeper coloured on latter and grading to white on belly and flanks, and reddish-yellow on undertail-coverts. Mantle black with broad whitish fringes and rest of upper-parts generally similar, though fringes become more cinnamon-brown dorsally. Pointed tail with whitish fringes. Flight feathers largely brownish-black with variable-width buff fringes, and scapulars and wing-coverts cinnamon-brown fringed white. **Adult female:** Description is based on young female. Crown black with broad reddish-brown fringes and obvious ochre central crown-stripe; lores and malar whitish flecked brown, and supercilium and ear-coverts lightly marked cinnamon-brown, with small black band extending from ear-coverts onto neck-sides; and chin and throat whitish. Neck-sides and breast yellow-ochre barred black and white, becoming deeper coloured on latter and grading to white on belly and flanks, and reddish-yellow on undertail-coverts. Mantle and scapulars, with broad cinnamon-brown fringes and rest of upperparts generally similar, though coloration of fringes varies somewhat dorsally. Flight feathers largely brownish-black with variable-width

buff fringes and wing-coverts cinnamon-brown fringed white with black tips and black-bordered cinnamon flecks. **Juvenile:** No specific information concerning differences from adults (but see above).

GEOGRAPHICAL VARIATION Monotypic. Formerly treated as conspecific with both Worcester's and Red-chested Buttonquails.

MEASUREMENTS Length c.14 cm. Female larger. One male wing 65, tarsus 15, weight 28. One female wing 76, tail 21, tarsus 17.5, weight 28.

HABITAT Recorded in scrubby grassland, usually with a sward height of 0.5–0.7 m, and fields to 220 m, and, at least occasionally, in fallow fields.

VOICE No data.

HABITS Very few data. Terrestrial. Appears to share habitat with Red-backed Buttonquail, Blue-breasted and Brown Quails. Presumably a strict resident. Information on food and feeding behaviour is extremely sparse, with no data on dietary constituents other than it takes seeds and that its relatively heavy bill may permit it to take larger items than ecologically sympatric Red-backed Buttonquail and Blue-breasted Quail. Known to forage in pairs. May occasionally seek bushy cover upon being flushed.

BREEDING No information available, other than that villagers have reported nests with 2–3 eggs in the dry season (July–October) and two juveniles taken in 1949 had hatched in late June or July.

DISTRIBUTION Indonesia. Endemic to Sumba I. in the Lesser Sundas.

STATUS Vulnerable. Known from three specimens, taken in 1896 and 1949, and several sight records since 1989, all from four localities, while unidentified buttonquails, quite possibly this species, were recorded at five other sites during fieldwork in 1992, suggesting it is widespread and locally common on the island. Identical habitat to that known to be used by the species has been identified in other areas of Sumba. Occurs in some man-modified grasslands and may reach densities of at least 2/ha in suitable habitat, e.g. around Yumbu and Waingapu in northeast of the island. Limited shifting cultivation may have increased available habitat, as may repeated burns to create grazing land. However, intensive grazing and fires during breeding season are probably deleterious. Some human predation probably occurs. Resource portioning and effects of potential competition with Red-backed Buttonquail unknown. It has been suggested that populations may await discovery on other islands and further research is therefore required.

REFERENCES BirdLife International (2000, 2001), Debus (1996), Johnsgard (1991), Marsden & Peters (1992), White & Bruce (1986).

Alternative names: Chestnut-breasted/Red-breasted Buttonquail.

Formerly considered conspecific with Sumba and Worcester's Buttonquails, but such treatment appears unwarranted under any species concept and does little to highlight the perilous conservation status of the other two taxa.

IDENTIFICATION A small, relatively wide-ranging buttonquail with a stout bill and obvious white irides, which is very slightly larger than partially sympatric Red-backed and Little Buttonquails. Largely grey-brown above and rufous-brown below; in flight from behind it is easily distinguished from the other two small species of buttonquail by its uniform grey-brown upperparts, orange-rufous visible underparts and only slightly paler central upperwing-coverts panel. At rest, additional features become useful, in particular the heavy grey bill and black-and-white breast scalloping are diagnostic among similar-sized species of *Turnix*. Most frequently confused with Little Buttonquail, which has similar upperwing pattern, but paler central coverts are more prominent and this species lacks orange-rufous on dorsal underparts. Red-backed Buttonquail has a finer, yellow bill, a rufous-brown collar, slate-grey upperparts (appearing darker in flight), bolder back barring on underparts extending to flanks, and much more sharply defined and more prominent central upperwing-coverts; it also generally occupies wetter habitats and denser vegetation.

DESCRIPTION Short tail, of 12 rectrices, and short, round-tipped wings. Irides white to cream or pale lemon-yellow (darker blue in juvenile) and has blue-grey bill with dusky culmen and paler lower mandible, and pale pink or creamy-buff tarsus and feet (brownish tinged in juvenile). Sexes differ. **Adult male:** Forehead to nape grey-brown, blotched black with narrow buff median crown-stripe reaching bill base, becoming more uniform, streaked white, on hindneck; supercilium, lores and ear-coverts rufous-buff, with white neck-sides and moustachial stripe, finely scalloped black and clean white chin and throat. Breast to undertail-coverts orange-rufous with white belly and black-and-white scalloping on flanks and upper breast-sides. Mantle and scapulars grey-brown, grading to black on rump, upper-tail-coverts and tail, with conspicuous off-white to buff streaking and black blotches on upper body and fine rufous-brown barring throughout; creamy-white streaks much fainter dorsally. Dark ashy-grey flight feathers contrasting with pale rufous-brown central wing-coverts, which have black subterminal bars and broad off-white fringes that form indistinct central wing panel most obvious in flight. Underwing largely ash-grey. **Adult female:** More brightly coloured than male: forehead and forecrown finely spotted black and white and rest of crown and nape more uniform grey-brown, with narrower pale median crown-stripe and less black mottling; head- and neck-sides white, finely scalloped black. Generally more extensive and brighter orange-rufous upperparts and upper breast area, with narrower and

closer black-and-white barring on flanks and breast-sides, rarely extending onto breast as scalloping. **Juvenile:** Upperparts darker than adult, being generally white-streaked chestnut, with hindneck and crown mottled black and chestnut and bold white median crown-stripe reaching base of nape; rufous-brown streaks on white head- and neck-sides and finely black-speckled face. Black barring on white-streaked chestnut upperparts most obvious on back to uppertail-coverts and scapulars; white spots on some wing-coverts bolder than adult male. White underparts with rufous-brown gorget, mottled darker, with dark brown chevrons on upper breast. Bare-parts coloration also differs.

GEOGRAPHICAL VARIATION Monotypic. Forms '*berneyi*' (NW Australia) and '*intermedia*' (Queensland) have been proposed, but reflect individual, not geographical, variation.

MEASUREMENTS Length 12–16 cm. Female larger. Males: wing 74–82, tail 27–36, tarsus 17–21, weight 27–46. Females: wing 64–89, tail 27–38, tarsus 17–21, weight 31–83.

HABITAT Known from subcoastal and semi-arid grassland and open *Acacia*, *Eucalyptus* and *Melaleuca* woodland with up to 1 m-tall understorey, to 900 m. Prefers dense and sometimes damp native grasslands, at edge of flood plains and swamps, with little or no tree cover, especially for breeding, but also frequently uses tussock grassland, mallee scrub, irrigated pastures, crops, stubble and lucerne.

VOICE Very little known and no recordings available. Advertising call, reportedly given by female, is a rapidly repeated booming *oom*, which increases in pitch and intensity. A sharp chatter is uttered by flushed birds, and a variety of soft whistles and chirrups, of unknown significance, have also been described. Young give a feeble, chicken-like note when handled.

HABITS Terrestrial. Recorded singly, in pairs or small coveys of up to five. Frequently sits motionless in response to perceived danger, but if hard-pressed flushes fast and low over a variable distance. Populations are resident, erratic or nomadic, occurring only in spring and summer in southern areas, and as an austral winter migrant in tropical north. Nocturnal migrant, which is chiefly active at night, dawn and dusk, and only occasionally diurnally. Takes seeds of grasses, *Triticum*, *Panicum* and Malvaceae, and insects, including cockroaches, ants, flies and their larvae. Forages by scratching and gleaning in litter. Like congeners makes circular feeding scrapes by pivoting on one foot while raking the ground with the other. Pairs may roost together, occupying a small circular scrape.

BREEDING Few data. Solitary breeder though female is sequentially polyandrous. Depression lined with grass, domed and sheltered by tussock, usually constructed by female in sedge-grass, 'Spinifex' or *Melaleuca* woodland, or standing crops. Four oval eggs usual but 2–5 recorded; white with chestnut-brown markings, laid at one- or two-day intervals in captivity, and incubated for 13–18 days when clutch complete, most often by male alone, who usually assumes sole responsibility for chick care. Young are precocial and nidifugous; they reach adult size by 6–8 weeks and attain adult plumage at 2–3 months. Seasonality poorly known, with eggs recorded in February–July and September in north of range, and September–February further south.

DISTRIBUTION Largely endemic to N and E Australia, from Kimberley Division, Western Australia, N North Territory west to Arnhem Land, and NW and C Queensland south through New South Wales to W Victoria and SE South Australia east of Adelaide. Ranges south to SE Victoria.

STATUS Generally uncommon, occasionally locally common during irruptions. Perhaps declining in south of range due to conversion of native grassland to agriculture, where very uncommon in South Australia and infrequent in coastal New South Wales, but evidence for fluctuations in range and abundance has been disputed. Few records in Victoria, where considered threatened and 95% of native grassland has disappeared or is degraded. More frequent and widespread in north, though considered sparse in much of Queensland, especially coastal areas. Formerly hunted for food and sport, and is occasionally killed by cats. Nests in crops may be destroyed during harvesting. Densities of 0.2 to 5.0 individuals per ha reported.

REFERENCES Debus (1996), Hall (1974), Johnsgard (1991), Marchant & Higgins (1993).

235 LITTLE BUTTONQUAIL
Turnix velox (Gould, 1841)   Plate 68

Alternative names: Australian Little/Butterfly/Swift-flying/White-bellied Quail.

The most extensively distributed of the Australian endemic buttonquail, but its broad range belies local declines, general rarity in eastern coastal areas, and little-known nomadic and irruptive behaviour in many regions.

IDENTIFICATION Usually the most frequent buttonquail over much of its pan-Australian range. A small buttonquail with a relatively stout blue-grey bill, pale eyes and strongly white-streaked pale rufous upperparts. Most closely resembles partially overlapping other small buttonquails, Red-backed and Red-chested Buttonquails (which see). Even in flight, and with experience, readily distinguished from these species and smaller *Coturnix* by diagnostic combination of uniform pale rufous-brown upperparts, white rear flanks, vent and undertail-coverts and strongly contrasting upperwing pattern (with much paler coverts). Stubble Quail is much larger, with longer and less rounded wings, more conspicuous white upperparts streaking and much less contrasting upperwing pattern. Red-backed Buttonquail is much darker above, with paler and more sharply defined pale central upperwing-coverts panel with rich buff rear underparts, and also prefers wetter habitats, while Red-chested Buttonquail is more grey-brown above, with duller and less prominent central upperwing-coverts panel (distinction is relatively subtle) and striking rufous-orange rear flanks, vent and undertail-coverts.

DESCRIPTION Short tail, of 12 rectrices, and short, round-tipped wings. Irides cream or yellow (grey-blue in juvenile), and has pale grey or brown bill with paler cutting edges and dusky culmen and tip, and pale pink or brownish tarsus and feet. Sexes differ, with some seasonal variation in female plumage. **Adult male:** Forehead to nape rufous-brown, with white median crown-stripe and black blotching and white streaking; indistinct dusky eye-stripe and buff head-sides, white chin and throat. Upper breast to upper flanks buff, faintly scalloped rufous-brown, with bolder black-and-cream scalloping on breast-sides and rest of underparts to undertail-coverts white. Entire upperparts from mantle to tail rufous-brown, with fine black barring and bold white streaking, and buff mottling restricted to longest scapulars and lower back. Dark-grey flight feathers and primary-coverts contrast strongly with unbarred pale rufous-brown wing-coverts, which are paler centrally, forming diffuse paler panel in flight. Underwing pale grey. **Adult female:** Has distinct non-breeding plumage, though both this and breeding attire are similar to adult male. More brightly coloured when breeding: entire head and neck more uniform rufous-brown with no median crown-stripe or supercilium and little black mottling on these surfaces; upperparts have heavier black barring largely restricted to scapulars and breast is more pale rufous-brown, grading to buff in centre and usually less or entirely devoid of black barring, especially on central breast. Non-breeders more closely resemble adult male, but have less blackish mottling on breast-sides, less contrasting median crown-stripe, fewer blackish speckles on throat, and more subtly and still less extensively barred breast and foreneck. **Juvenile:** Rather similar to corresponding adult plumages and differ in same respects, but ground colour of breast pale rufous-brown with white tip and blackish subterminal band to each feather, giving much darker overall appearance to breast, which contrasts more strongly with rest of underparts.

GEOGRAPHICAL VARIATION Monotypic. Forms '*picturata*' and '*vinotincta*' (both from NW Australia), and '*leucogaster*' (C Australia) have been proposed, but reflect individual, not geographical, variation.

MEASUREMENTS Length 12–16 cm. Female larger. Males: wing 72–83, tail 27–34, tarsus 15.6–20.6, weight 28–44. Females: wing 78–90, tail 28–39, tarsus 16.9–19.9, weight 39–64.

HABITAT Occurs patchily in arid and semi-arid grassland and woodland, exceptionally to 800 m. Prefers native grasslands for breeding, especially tussocks of *Danthonia* and *Stipa*, and may be attracted to recently burnt areas. Also uses *Acacia* and *Eucalyptus* woodlands at this season, as well as ripe crops and stubble (especially in wet years when these provide dense cover, but swiftly abandon such areas following harvesting), mallee scrub, coastal shrublands and even urban parks. Utilises similar habitats in non-breeding season, but probably more dependent upon tussock and 'Spinifex' grasslands and *Acacia* woodland.

VOICE Poorly studied and sexual differences unknown. Advertising call is a loud, low-pitched booming, *oo-ah* or *coo-oo* given continuously for several minutes. A squeaking *chip chip chip* is given when flushed and by juveniles. Female rises on sharply whirring wings.

HABITS Terrestrial. Recorded singly, in pairs or coveys of up to 10, but groups of 30–50 also noted and exceptionally hundreds or thousands may occur during large irruptions, when sometimes directly associates with Stubble Quail and Red-chested Buttonquail. Flushes reluctantly (for up to 200 m) and very rarely more than once, preferring to run close to the ground or squat within cover on approach of danger. Movements appear complex, with sedentary, migratory and dispersive populations known, and appears erratic or irruptive in some areas, depending on local rains and associated plant growth. Moves south and toward coast in spring and summer, i.e. those regions with winter rainfall, and inland and north in winter to areas experiencing 100–400 mm of summer rainfall. Migrates nocturnally on broad front, and principally active at night, but also diurnal and crepuscular. Largely dependent on grass seeds, including grain (*Triticum, Triodia, Danthonia, Chloris, Eragrostis, Panicum, Stipa, Sida, Rumex, Portulaca* and Juncaceae all recorded), green shoots of *Citrullus* and *Cucumis* seedlings, and insects, including crickets, grasshoppers, bugs, beetles, ants and moth larvae. Gleans and scratches in leaf-litter, and uses grit and sand to aid digestion.

BREEDING Not well known. Solitary breeder though female is sequentially polyandrous. Scrape, created by female, is sometimes lined and domed with grass and fine sticks, or consists of a domed structure with side runway entrance, placed beneath grass tussock, small shrub or fallen branch, or within dense grass or crops. Three or 4 oval eggs, white to buff or greyish marked with chestnut and violet-grey blotches, laid at two-day intervals in captivity, and incubated for 15 days once clutch complete. Incubation and chick-care responsibilities assumed entirely by male. Chicks precocial and nidifugous, attempt to self-feed at three days and sexually mature at three months. Breeding activity recorded in most months, but probably seasonal in S and E Australia, and usually August–December (March–November in wet years) in Western Australia and January–May in Northern Territory.

DISTRIBUTION Endemic to Australia, but absent from NE Western Australia in the Kimberleys, N Northern Territory in Arnhem Land and N Queensland on Cape York Peninsula, and generally rare on E coast.

STATUS Uncommon to common and even locally abundant during irruptions. Declines evident in areas under intensive cultivation in south of range, e.g. inland Western Australia and E Australia, but range has expanded in others, due to forest and scrub clearance. May be attracted to recently burnt areas, though fires are known to destroy many nests. Heavy mortality due to farm machinery during harvesting, with birds crushed or caught on barbed wire when trying to escape; and also subject to predation by cats. Recorded densities vary from 0.01 to 0.41 birds per ha.

REFERENCES Debus (1996), Hall (1974), Johnsgard (1991), Marchant & Higgins (1993).

Genus *ORTYXELOS*: Quail-plover

This monotypic genus has longer and broader wings than *Turnix*, which are distinctively and boldly patterned with black and white and has pale brownish and rufous plumage above. The tail is longer than in *Turnix*, with stiff pale rufous rectrices, the two outermost having a buffy fringe and the others tipped buff and having buff-and-black markings. It is a solitary nester, with no evidence of polyandry (unlike in many *Turnix*), though the male takes responsibility for incubation. Sibley (1996) suggests that it may not be a turnicid.

236 QUAIL-PLOVER
Ortyxelos meiffrenii (Vieillot, 1819)   Plate 65

Alternative names: Lark-like Quail, Lark Buttonquail.

Given this species' striking pattern in flight, the relative paucity of records from its principally Sahelian range suggest that it is genuinely scarce and local, rather than subject to severe under-recording.

IDENTIFICATION Quail-plover is a very small, short-tailed grassland species that superficially recalls a miniature courser when seen running on ground.

Both sexes are principally sandy-rufous above and whitish/golden-buff below, but the distinctive wing pattern of white greater coverts, contrasting with blackish, white-tipped remiges that form a conspicuous diagonal band on upperwing, and the jerky, fluttering flight, reminiscent of a bush-lark *Mirafra* or butterfly, provide easy identification aids. Readily distinguished from all *Turnix* buttonquails by combination of striking wing pattern, slightly smaller size and radically different flight pattern, being much less direct and more erratic than buttonquails.

DESCRIPTION Relatively long, white-tipped tail and striking wing pattern. Irides pale to deep brown, with yellowish-horn to pale green bill and whitish-flesh to creamy-yellow tarsus and toes. Sexes differ. **Adult male:** Forehead to nape and hindneck rufous-brown, with cream feather fringes, lores, face and supercilium cream, tinged golden-buff, rufous-brown streak from eye to neck-sides and pale rufous-brown ear-coverts. Throat white with pale golden-buff feather tips, becoming golden-buff on breast and more rufous-brown with black-bordered cream spots on breast-sides, grading to cream on belly, and white on flanks and undertail-coverts. Mantle, scapulars and back feathers rufous-brown, broadly fringed black, bordered cream and sometimes with spots or bars, grading to pale rufous-brown with narrow buff tips on rump and uppertail-coverts, and tail also pale rufous-brown, with creamy tips and subterminal bars, and two outermost feathers having buff or white fringes and outermost a dusky-brown subterminal area. Flight feathers largely blackish, with whitish fringes and tips (some buff on primaries) and tertials rufous-brown with cream tips and bars and black borders. Lesser and median wing-coverts cream and greater coverts white. Underwing-coverts cream with white axillaries. **Adult female:** Differs little from male, but possesses deeper rufous-brown breast, and outer three tail feathers narrow towards tips and have dusky-brown subterminal marks and broad white fringes. **Juvenile:** Much as adult, but more spotted (rather than streaked) above, with considerably paler, more sandy and less rufous upperparts, each feather more vermiculated and broadly fringed white; paler rufous on breast-sides and wing markings less even.

GEOGRAPHICAL VARIATION Monotypic.

MEASUREMENTS Length 10–13 cm. Female larger. Males: wing 72–76, tail 29–32, tarsus 17–19, weight 15.7–19.5. Females: wing 76–80, tail 33–36, tarsus 18–20, no weight data.

HABITAT Savanna, particularly of *Acacia* and *Chrysopogon* and grassland habitats, where grass cover exceeds 25%, in semi-arid and arid regions to 2000 m, but usually below 1200 m in E Africa. In some areas of W Africa favours sandy localities with *Cenchrus* and *Aristida* spp., often without surface water, but also extends into wetter coastal grasslands, bushier, thorn scrub areas and sometimes sites with a few scattered trees.

VOICE Very few data. A soft, low whistle, which lacks the booming quality of most buttonquail and has been likened to wind blowing through a pipe. Apparently silent when flushed but perhaps particularly vocal on moonlit nights (see below).

HABITS Terrestrial. Recorded singly or in pairs in non-breeding season. Stands erect and runs rapidly though a slow, rocking motion is used on bare ground or in sparse cover. If disturbed, crouches in frozen posture but if hard-pressed flushes silently in slightly undulating, high, erratic escape flight before dropping into cover. Movements little understood. Although resident in some areas of E and, less usually, W Africa, it is an intra-African migrant in others, being variously present in either the dry (e.g. coastal Ghana, N Nigeria) or wet season in many regions. At least partially nocturnal, especially on moonlit nights. Data on food and feeding behaviour is almost non-existent, though it is known to take grass seeds and insects, including termites, and appears to derive sufficient moisture from these to live far from water.

BREEDING Few data. Solitary, probably monogamous, breeder, though male incubation may suggest a polyandrous system. Scrape on bare ground or firm sand, lined with leaves and stalks, and placed near base of plant within lightly vegetated areas. Nest sometimes rimmed by small stones. Two oval eggs, cream with black, brown and grey blotching, incubated by male alone. Downy young otherwise undescribed. Generally lays in September–March during cool dry season at inland and coastal locations.

DISTRIBUTION Africa in the Sahel zone, from Senegambia and S Mali east to N Cameroon, S Chad and S Sudan, and discontinuously through SW Ethiopia, Uganda, N and SE Kenya and NE Tanzania. A vagrant to coastal Côte d'Ivoire, Gambia and Togo.

STATUS Uncommon or occasionally locally common and is expanding range in some areas, possibly due to desertification and woodland clearance, e.g. in Mali, Chad and Sudan, and locally spreading south in Kenya, where considered local and uncommon, though perhaps reasonably common in Tsavo East National Park in the 1970s. Uncommon and local in much of W African range and may have become less common in Sénégal since the 1930s. No threats currently known.

REFERENCES Borrow & Demey (in press), Debus (1996), Johnsgard (1991), Urban *et al.* (1986).

FAMILY PEDIONOMIDAE
Plains-wanderer

A monotypic family that was long considered to be most closely associated with the buttonquails (Turnicidae), with which it shares many plumage and behavioural similarities, but its morphological characters, the pattern of its downy young and DNA analysis demonstrate that it is most closely related to the seedsnipe (Thinocoridae) and thus belongs among the Charadriiformes. Plumage is cryptic pattern of black, buff and rufous, with spots and bars. Female is larger and more colourful, with a white-spotted black collar and rufous breast.

237 PLAINS-WANDERER
Pedionomus torquatus Gould, 1840   Plate 68

Alternative names: Collared Plains-wanderer, Turkey Quail.

A remarkably buttonquail-like bird endemic to SE Australia, where its numbers are in decline; its enigmatic and apparently nocturnal lifestyle, coupled with its attractive plumage and classification within a monotypic family, make it a key attraction among visiting birders.

IDENTIFICATION Highly distinctive and threatened Australian endemic, which is unmistakable if seen well. Like buttonquails, reversed sex roles mean female is larger and brighter, with chestnut breast, black-and-white neck collar, rather 'open' facial expression (emphasised by pale eye), predominantly brown upperparts and lower underparts marked by brown crescents. Male duller, being principally buff and white and having only a very inconspicuous collar. Its general shape and plumage resembles buttonquails, but it is much more inclined to stand boldly upright, with neck upstretched, and has a markedly finer bill and much longer legs (with hindtoe) than either true quails or buttonquail. Slightly larger than Little *Turnix velox* or Red-chested *T. pyrrhothorax* Buttonquails, being about the same size as Stubble Quail *Coturnix pectoralis*; all share the same habitats as Plains-wanderer. Female distinctive, due to breast patch and bold pied collar, and unlikely to be confused when seen on ground, and even duller male, if seen well, is sufficiently different, due to bill structure and coloration, long legs, rather plain upperparts and less boldly marked underparts (white streaks do not align to form 'tramlines' as in quail and buttonquail), to cause few identification problems. Even in flight both sexes are readily distinguished from confusion species by distinctive upperwing pattern, especially white primary patch and broad pale trailing edge, and more laboured progress with feet projecting beyond tail, before fluttering descent (unlike whirring flight and direct landing of quail).

DESCRIPTION Wings short and rounded; the 2–3 outer secondaries shorter and weaker than proximal secondaries. Also has 10 primaries and 12 short rectrices. Irides cream (yellower in female), with narrow and cream-coloured orbital ring (brighter in female). Bill medium length, slender and cream to pale yellow with dark brown culmen (brighter in female with dark brown confined to basal half of culmen), and cream to

pale yellow tarsus (yellow-orange in female in breeding season) and feet (four toes, including hindtoe), with grey-brown claws. Bare-parts coloration intensifies in breeding season. Juvenile has bare parts much as adult male. Sexes differ. **Adult male:** Forehead to nape and hindneck pale brown, scalloped blackish and streaked white, becoming more boldly marked rearwards; head-sides whitish to buff, with heavy black-brown streaking on cheeks and ear-coverts, and white chin and throat, becoming buff or buff-white, finely spotted black-brown on foreneck and neck-sides. Breast, flanks and undertail-coverts buff to orange-buff, with black-brown crescents and each feather having central black-brown spot or streak, grading to unmarked white on belly. Upperparts and lesser coverts pale brown vermiculated black-brown and streaked white, becoming creamy-buff on larger coverts, with diagonal band extending inwards from carpal. Dark flight feathers, with pale patch at base of primaries visible in flight, as is broad creamy-buff trailing edge to secondaries and inner primaries. Underwing mostly pale grey, with greyish-white band across centre of wing and darker buffy leading edge to inner wing. **Adult female:** Most of plumage like male, but much more brightly coloured. Has diagnostic broad black collar, heavily streaked and spotted white and broad rufous upper breast patch. Head-sides brighter and buffier, with upper edge of collar richer rufous-brown and similarly coloured stripe extending from nape to eye along upper edge of ear-coverts. **Juvenile:** Much as adult male, but principal differences as follows: white scalloping on crown less distinct, black streaking on ear-coverts and supercilium finer and less conspicuous, more finely and widely spaced vermiculations on yellower rest of upperparts, whiter underparts grading to warm buff on upper breast and to cream on undertail-coverts, with heavier dark brown chevrons throughout, and has broader grey-white fringes and yellower and broader tips to remiges.

GEOGRAPHICAL VARIATION Monotypic.

MEASUREMENTS Length 15–19 cm. Female larger (male usually 15–17 cm). Males: wing 79–104, tail 28–33, tarsus 22.5–28.4, weight 40–80. Females: wing 95–109, tail 26–35, tarsus 23–31, weight 55–95.

HABITAT Almost exclusively prefers open native grasslands, with ephemeral and perennial grasses and herbs, especially *Stipa, Danthonia, Helipterum, Helichrysum*,

Chrysocephalum and *Calocephalus*, but structure is of paramount importance. Favours short-grass sward, where c.94% of vegetation is <5–8 cm tall, usually but not essentially with larger (10–40 cm-high) plants 10–20 cm apart, c.50% bare soil between plants and 10% litter, on red-brown earths (primarily brown, red and grey clays), which are found mainly on elevated plains, or along levees and associated swamps. Suitable habitat tends to be small (50–300 ha) patches that do not support dense pasture growth under any seasonal conditions. Improved or denser grasslands are rarely, if ever utilised, but cereal crops and lightly grazed agricultural areas may be used.

VOICE Not well known and apparently few recordings. Most obvious call is a repeated, low-pitched resonant *oo* (slightly dove-like and also reported to resemble tapping on a cask), given day and night in spring, possibly only by female. A similar call reported when about to lay. Also a soft *chuck* when perceives danger to chicks, a quiet *irr-irr* in response to chick distress calls and a drawn-out piping used to summon young.

HABITS Seldom seen by day, and considered principally crepuscular and nocturnal, but rather active in day when in captivity. Usually solitary, but pairs sometimes together in breeding season and family parties occasional post-breeding. Crouches motionless in alarm, or adopts head down and forward posture and runs quickly away, sometimes with wings spread and fluffed-out body feathers. Flight more ponderous than quail and rarely flushes, unless particularly hard-pressed. Flies on bowed wings, with slow sideways twisting of body. Occasionally lands on low fence post or another vantage point. Rarely flies during day and when does so, flight more dipping and uneven than at night, presumably as a defence against raptors such as Black *Falco subniger* and Brown Falcons *F. berigora* and Spotted Harrier *Circus assimilis*, all of which may take the species. When walking, frequently pauses with head upright and on tiptoe to survey surroundings. Can be captured at night by hand or in a butterfly net if blinded by light. Takes wide range of seeds (both fallen and ripe), leaves, insects and spiders, taking moisture from leaves. Takes arthropods and seeds year-round, but proportions vary seasonally: grass seeds predominate in summer, saltbush seeds in winter and arthropods in spring. Grit, gravel and broken pebbles used to aid digestion. Principally sedentary. Claims of local seasonal movements, nomadism and migration unsupported, though will vacate habitat subject to overgrazing, fires, cultivation or drought. Radio-tracking and ringing studies demonstrate very strong site fidelity under normal circumstances. In wild may spend day in flattened scrape on ground or in dense grass, but in captivity roosts by night in sparse grass.

BREEDING Female appears, at least occasionally, to be serially polyandrous, but may form strong pair-bonds in captivity. Selects site in ephemeral and perennial herbs and grasses, sometimes denser vegetation; also barley stubble, and crops of wheat and oats. Nests in hollow constructed by female, lined with straw and fine grass (once horse manure), and sometimes with grass pulled over top to form canopy. Twice, during wet conditions, recorded on raised grass nests c.30 mm above ground.

Lays 2–5 (usually 4) greenish-white eggs, spotted and blotched brown and grey. In captivity may lay replacement clutch. Male undertakes incubation duties (with some help from female in captivity) and also appears to take virtually sole responsibility for chick-care and guarding duties. Young independent by two months, when primaries fully grown. Season: apparently all months, but no records in March–April; eggs late August–November (sometimes second brood in January–February) in New South Wales, mid-August and early January in South Australia, early October in Victoria and autumn–early winter in Queensland. In New South Wales, studies by Phil Maher have revealed the following: in years of average rainfall, pair formation occurs in July, with eggs in August and young by September. If conditions wet in August–September, more likely to breed in October–November, and continues to breed throughout summer in years with good rains. Breeding may also occur in autumn, particularly if success has been poor in spring and summer. Most successful in years of average rainfall, rather than excessively wet or dry years. In S Riverina area of New South Wales, appears not to have bred in spring and summer of drought years (1982–1983 and 1994), and with little success in wet years (1990–1992). Young breed in first year.

DISTRIBUTION Endemic to E and S Australia, mainly from SW and C Queensland, W and C Victoria and SE New South Wales, with few recent records from South Australia and unconfirmed recent records from Northern Territory and Western Australia.

STATUS Endangered. Population assessed at c.11,000 individuals in late 1980s, but now considered to number approximately 8000 and is confined to a 33,000 km² range (though only c.1000 km² of this may be actually occupied). The population may decline to 2500 following years with lower than average rainfall. High densities persist only in Riverina region of New South Wales, where between 1000 and 5500 birds occur (numbers appear to vary dramatically between 'good' and 'bad' years, determined by rainfall). Fewer than 500 are estimated to remain in N Victoria and only low densities are known from SW and C Queensland. Considered effectively extinct by late 1990s in SE South Australia, SW Victoria, E New South Wales and SE Queensland. Fragmentation and destruction of native grasslands due to increased cultivation is principal reason for decline; even when subsequently left to recover, such grasslands may take decades to become suitable again. High-level grazing may increase the species' vulnerability to predators and certainly leads to it abandoning such areas, while foxes may be significant predators in cropped areas and pesticides, used in locust control, may directly or indirectly kill birds. Extensive research into the species' habitat requirements and populations is underway in several parts of its range, but a key short-term priority must be the purchase and management of substantial areas of its native short-sward grasslands in the Riverina region.

REFERENCES Baker-Gabb (1998), BirdLife International (2000), Garnett & Crowley (2000), P. Maher website (http://www.philipmaher.com), Marchant & Higgins (1993), Sibley & Ahlquist (1990).

Best known among European ornithologists for its formerly periodic irruptions, which brought the species, sometimes in large numbers and even to breed, far to the west of its usual range.

IDENTIFICATION Large, bulky sandgrouse with feathered toes, of C and E Asia, which is easily identified given a good view. Male has pastel-grey crown, nape and breast, with deep orange face, narrow dark pectoral-band, black ventral patch, largely sandy-pink wings and closely marked upperparts. Female is better camouflaged, having bolder upperparts and wing markings, a largely orange-yellow head, dull pinkish breast, white belly and black vent. Both sexes have pin-like central tail feathers, longest in male. Only Tibetan Sandgrouse shares feathered toes and lack of hind toe, but the two are readily separated (see above) and those species of sandgrouse occurring sympatrically in C Asia all possess quite different plumage and do not offer a confusion risk, except given extremely poor views.

DESCRIPTION Structure differs from *Pterocles* sandgrouse: has rather smaller head and long tail, making wings appear set further forward in flight. Quite large and relatively attenuated, with diagnostic combination of entirely pale underwing and underbody, except bold black patch on rear belly. Remarkable, acute elongated outer primaries. Sixteen to 18 rectrices with central tail feathers elongated. Bill greyish-blue. Irides brown with dark bluish-grey eye-ring. Tarsus and toes feathered white; lacks hind toe. Sexes differ. **Adult male:** Head orange-ochre, with grey rear crown, from eye to neck, and on breast; lower breast delimited by transverse small black bars. Rear underparts buff-white with bold, broad black band on belly and long white ventral patch. Back, entire wing-coverts, secondaries, rump and tail sandy-buff, with bold black chevrons on back and scapulars, and black or black-brown spots or lines on inner median and greater wing-coverts, inner secondaries, primary-coverts and inner primaries. Primaries pale dove-grey. In flight, upperwing has chestnut bar across inner wing and dark trailing edge to secondaries and inner primaries. Underwing also virtually unpatterned, with black-spotted, pale sand-buff axillaries and wing-coverts contrasting little with pale ash-grey flight feathers and entire wing only narrowly bordered dusky. Shorter tail feathers have pale outer margins. **Adult female:** Like male but duller, with speckles and spots on crown, rear ear-coverts, hindneck and all wing-coverts. Belly patch purple-brown and has short black bar bordering buff throat, but lacks deep grey chest. **Juvenile:** Much as adult female but with blackish-brown neck and breast markings, a less distinct head pattern, less regular barring and spotting on the scapulars and wing-coverts, indistinct fringes and centres to the inner remiges and primary-coverts, and browner primaries with buffy tips and darker freckling.

GEOGRAPHICAL VARIATION Monotypic.

MEASUREMENTS Length 30–41 cm. Male wing 243–259, tail 165–228, tarsus 20–23, weight 250–300; female wing 214–235, tail 131–160, tarsus 19–23, weight 200–270.

HABITAT Arid open country, including steppes, semi-desert and also cultivated areas. Avoids extensive areas of waterless desert, preferring flat or hilly grassy shrub semi-deserts with either wormwood *Artemisia absinthium* or the xerophytic chenopod *Agriophyllum gobicum*. Within its native range, principally occurs at 1300–3250 m in summer, lower in winter and only to 2400 m in NW Mongolia. Reports of its occurrence to 5500 m appear false.

VOICE Vocalisations include a trisyllabic, rapidly repeated low-pitched *cu-ruu cu-ruu cu-ou-ruu*, as well as variety of mono- and disyllabic notes, likened to those of a flock of shorebirds. The wings produce a distinctive whistling sound in flight, which is presumably created by the specialised outermost primaries.

HABITS Gregarious, being recorded in flocks of up to several hundred throughout non-breeding season, while non-breeders may form summer flocks. Not wary. Partial migrant, which is also subject to occasional irruptive behaviour. Northernmost breeding areas vacated in winter (during September/October to March/April), but extent of movements depends on amount of snowfall. Irregular irruptions have reached as far as W Europe, most notably in 1863, 1888–89 (following which it bred in several countries) and 1908, N China (1860), Manchuria (1912–13 and 1922–23) and Japan. The cause of such long-distance movements is unknown, but is presumably related to food supply, connected to snow cover, prolonged drought, or failing seed crops. Feeds on seeds and green shoots of many plant species, including Leguminosae, Polygonaceae, Chenopodiaceae, Cruciferae and Gramineae, as well as, in some areas, cultivated grain crops such as *Triticum* and *Panicum*. Insect pupae appear to be taken only incidentally, although captive-bred chicks take mealworms with relish. Will dig for food, like a domestic chicken. Occasionally comes to drink in evening, and regularly in morning, usually between 06:00 and 10:00 hrs (peaking 09:00–10:00 hrs and always terminated by noon).

BREEDING Unlined ground nest, sometimes in shelter of bush or grasses, in rubble-covered substrate. Generally breeds in small, loose colonies, where nests may be just 4–6 m apart. Two to 3 elliptical eggs, pale buff or yellowish-ochre with brown markings, laid over a 4–5-day period and incubated for 22–28 days once clutch is initiated, probably by female alone, although males with brood patches have been reported. Male probably responsible for watering chicks, like other sandgrouse species. Young capable of flight at 25 days and attain immature plumage at three months. Breeds in first summer. Lays late March to July, with downy young observed as late as early August. Unclear whether later dates reflect second or even third broods, replacement clutches or simply late laying.

DISTRIBUTION C and E Asia, from NE shore of Caspian Sea at 38–50°N east to Aral Sea, Turkestan and Kazakhstan, thence to SW Siberia, S and W Mongolia and N China, south to NE Tibet. Some evidence to indicate that part of the population moves slightly further south in winter. Highly irruptive and has bred irregularly west to British Is, Faeroes and W Europe.

STATUS Few data. Sporadic occurrence within C Asian and Siberian range although breeding territories may be densely occupied. Widely considered to have declined in western part of range during latter part of 20th century but few, if any, quantitative data to support such suggestions, although incursions into Europe have been rarer and markedly smaller since early 20th century. Irregular throughout vast Chinese range but is common in some years. Increasing overgrazing of marginal lands in China and, probably, Russia may affect this species. Overall, extensive range and remote, sparsely populated habitat probably make it relatively safe.

REFERENCES Cramp (1985), Johnsgard (1991), de Juana (1997).

Genus *PTEROCLES*: African and south Asian sandgrouse

Males of this genus of primarily African and Middle Eastern sandgrouse have well-marked and bold plumage patterns, tails of 14–16 feathers and most differ markedly from the usually more cryptically patterned females; some males have bold breast or head patterns and several species possess elongated central tail filaments, like *Syrrhaptes*. At least two subgenera have been recognised, based on close basic plumage patterns evident in some species, but at least two species appear to have no obviously close relatives within the genus, and one of these, Burchell's Sandgrouse, has occasionally been placed within the monotypic genus, *Calopterocles*. Though close to *Syrrhaptes* they differ in having 'normal' toes, though the hind toe is comparatively small and slightly raised, and their tarsi are only feathered at the front. Most other physical characteristics are shared by the two genera.

240 PIN-TAILED SANDGROUSE
Pterocles alchata (Linnaeus, 1766)   Plate 69

Alternative name: Large Pin-tailed Sandgrouse.

One of only two species of sandgrouse to breed in Europe, this beautifully marked bird is arguably the most attractive, and certainly the longest tailed of the pin-tailed group. Males are unique among sandgrouse in possessing a distinct non-breeding plumage.

IDENTIFICATION Supremely attractive sandgrouse of the southern W Palearctic and Middle Asia, which is usually readily identified due to its long central tail feathers and richly patterned plumage. The gleaming white underwings and belly of both sexes serve as a useful identification mark in flight. On the ground, both sexes possess a broad chestnut breast-band, bordered above and below by black lines. Males have a well-marked head pattern, although the black throat is lost in winter (when the black eye-stripe is reduced or absent and yellow back and wing spots are also lost), and uniquely largely green wings and upperparts. Females are overall duller, with an additional band on the underparts, at lower throat level, and heavily barred and patterned upperparts and wings, which lack the predominantly green coloration of males. Most frequently occurs in close sympatry with Black-bellied Sandgrouse, with which it often shares the same water sources and winter-feeding grounds, but the two could only be confused with great difficulty.

DESCRIPTION *P. a. alchata.* Rather large sandgrouse, with strikingly white underbody and underwing-coverts and most intricately patterned and colourful fore- and upperparts in genus. Sixteen rectrices with central tail feathers elongated. Bill dull brown or slate and irides brown, with blue-grey eye-ring. White tarsus. Sexes differ. **Adult male:** In breeding plumage, crown, most of neck, back and fore- and innerwing-coverts bright oily-green, with obvious yellow spots on scapulars and central back, with black fringes to wing-coverts. Face chestnut-yellow, with black line through eye and black central throat. In winter, when moult from breeding plumage complete, upperparts (including crown and upper face) patterned as rump and tail but become buff, and chin white or partially so. Rest of plumage not subject to seasonal change. Broad chestnut-buff breast-band outlined black. Outerwing-coverts vinous-chestnut, outlined white and black. Primaries grey-black, with pale cast and edges so obvious that in flight upperwing has black trailing edge to inner primaries and secondaries. Unlike other sandgrouse, pure white underbody and mainly white underwing combine to form marked contrast with black outer primaries and dusky trailing and leading edges of wing. Rump and tail boldly barred yellow and black, except dusky tail-streamers. **Adult female:** In breeding plumage has chin white, with golden-buff face, neck and breast, black line through eye, broad black bar on lower throat and narrow black line across neck (forming double neck-ring), and broad black bar below breast. Entire upperparts barred and spotted black and pearl-grey on buff and yellow background, reaching wing-coverts as bars that broaden dorsally, from lesser to greater coverts, ending in sharply etched black-and-white outer feathers at lower edge of folded wing. Rest of plumage as breeding male, except rump and tail less distinctly barred and central tail-feathers shorter. In non-breeding plumage loses pearl-grey bars on upperparts and throat becomes spotted. **Juvenile:** Paler and more uniform than adult; brown breast lacks black upper border and lower border very weak. Male has shorter central tail feathers than adult and black throat patch with some white feathers; crown, scapular and back feathers are barred black rather than grey (also evident in scapulars of young female). Sexes distinguishable, like adults, by their greater wing-coverts patterns: male has deep brown to chestnut outer webs with a yellow line at their margin, while female has golden to brown outer webs, fringed black. Both sexes retain juvenile primaries until their second-calendar year.

GEOGRAPHICAL VARIATION Two weakly differentiated subspecies recognised. Appears to form a group with Chestnut-bellied, Spotted and Namaqua Sandgrouse, all of which possess long central rectrices, though Urban *et al.* (1986) considered it to be of independent origin.

P. a. alchata (Linnaeus, 1766) occurs in Iberia and S France; described above.

P. a. caudacutus (S. G. Gmelin, 1774) occurs in NW Africa and SE Turkey through Iraq and Iran to Uzbekistan and S Kazakhstan; the male generally has duller face and underparts patterns than nominate, with more obvious white fringes to the lesser and median coverts and yellower centres to the greater coverts, while the female has the median coverts and secondaries white, rather than yellow as in nominate; both sexes have longer wings.

MEASUREMENTS Length 31–39 cm. *P. a. alchata*. Males: wing 205–214, tail 147–173, tarsus 27–30, weight (*P. a. caudacutus*) 250–408. Females: wing 201–211, tail 129–146, tarsus 25–27, weight (*P. a. caudacutus*) 207–274.

HABITAT Uses stony plateaux and treeless plains, dryland cultivation, stony areas on the edges of deserts, arid flats and even dried mudflats around marshes, with a winter and spring rainfall regime of c.20 cm per annum. Much overlap with Black-bellied Sandgrouse but prefers sandier soils and is much less reliant on areas with vegetational cover. Occasionally uses fallow areas and ploughed land, especially in winter. Shuns hilly areas and higher altitudes above 1000 m.

VOICE Flight calls described as a loud *catar-catar*, a nasal *ga-ga-ga* and guttural *gang gang*, lower pitched than other sandgrouse. Also a *twoi-twoi-twoi* reported in alarm. Usually silent on ground.

HABITS Gregarious, especially at waterholes when flocks of many thousands recorded, but group size on migration is much smaller, usually a few dozens up to 150. While sedentary or nomadic in Europe, N Africa and the Middle East, it is principally a migrant in Turkestan and other northernmost parts breeding areas, where it is only present between March/April and October/November. Predominantly a seed-eater, but also takes green shoots and leaves. Strong preference for Leguminosae, as well as *Polygonum, Fagopyrum, Salicornia, Artemisia, Alhagi, Helianthemum* and *Asphodelus*, but in cultivated areas also takes cereal grain and agricultural legumes. Insects and other invertebrate products, principally beetles, appear to be taken only incidentally. Grit is commonly ingested and forms up to 30% by weight of stomach contents of some individuals. Principally drinks in morning, in Spain usually c.2.75 hours after dawn and, during particularly hot weather, some also 1.3 hours prior to dusk.

BREEDING Occasionally loosely colonial. Shallow, usually unlined, scrape or natural depression, such as hoof-print. Stones, feathers and droppings are rarely used as lining. Three (occasionally two) elliptical eggs, usually creamy-buff spotted brown and pale grey, laid at one- or two-day intervals and incubated, upon clutch completion, for 19–25 days (21–23 days in captivity). Incubation is shared, with male sitting from c.50 minutes before sunset to 3.5–4 hours after sunrise. Both sexes care for chicks, but only male provides water. Young self-feed at less than a week, can fly at c.25 days, but are dependent on parents for at least two months and do not acquire adult plumage until four months. Single-brooded except, perhaps, occasionally in N Africa and up to two replacement clutches may be attempted in captivity. Season varies slightly geographically: mid-April–early August across entire range, but season usually commences in late April and is more constricted in former USSR and N Africa, and may start during May in some parts of Middle East.

DISTRIBUTION SW Europe, N Africa and SW Asia. Disjunct populations occur locally in E Portugal, Spain (except NW), SE coastal France (Camargue), and NW Africa from C Morocco east to S Tunisia and NW Libya; also in SW Asia, from SE Turkey and Levant east to S Transcaucasus, Transcaspia, Aral Sea, Turkestan, SW Iran and Iraq. Some winter south to C Arabia, Pakistan (tiny numbers may breed) and W India, and also appears more numerous in Jordan during winter suggesting immigration. Several recent records in United Arab Emirates, and a vagrant to Lebanon and Oman.

STATUS European population endangered and widespread decline, with local extinctions noted throughout most of W Palearctic due to changes in farming practices, but remains common in parts of Spain (Ebro Valley and Southern Meseta, and overall population estimated at 10,000–15,000 birds), and, at least formerly, numerous in Morocco (c.200,000 birds on Haut Plateau in 1964, although it appears to have become exceptionally scarce in the west of the country during the last decade), Algeria, Iraq, Iran and Turkestan, where concentrations of tens of thousands occasionally reported. Range perhaps expanding in SE Turkey, in response to habitat changes within core range. Has declined sharply in France, where 165–175 pairs persist at La Crau, the only known site for the species. Now fewer than 100 pairs in Portugal, where restricted to two diminishing areas of suitable habitat. Evidence for a decline in S Israel in recent years. Scarce and declining resident in Tunisia, Libya and Arabia (though locally common in Northern Desert during winter), and a scarce and local winter visitor to Pakistan and only straggles to India. Hunting and habitat degradation, as well as deliberate pesticide poisoning have been reported as threats in Golestan province, Iran, where a significant percentage of the possibly declining C Asian population winters.

REFERENCES Cramp (1985), Hagemeijer & Blair (1997), Johnsgard (1991), de Juana (1997), Urban *et al.* (1986).

446

241 NAMAQUA SANDGROUSE
Pterocles namaqua (J. F. Gmelin, 1789)   **Plate 70**

One of three sandgrouse restricted to southern Africa, this species is considerably darker than Burchell's Sandgrouse and the sharp pin-like tail of the male points to its closer relationship with several more northerly forms.

IDENTIFICATION Given good views this rather small, dark sandgrouse of SW Africa is easily distinguished from the only sympatric species, Double-banded and Burchell's Sandgrouse. Male has narrow white and chestnut pectoral-bands, a brown belly, weakly patterned head and heavily spotted scapulars, wing-coverts and tertials. Female is cryptically marked, being heavily mottled above, with closely barred underparts and richly white, buff and black spangled wings. Both sexes are readily distinguished from Double-banded and Burchell's Sandgrouse, by virtue of their projecting central tail feathers. In addition, the former has a white and black barred forehead, broader pectoral bands, a black and white barred belly and more uniformly patterned wings, with white-tipped coverts. Burchell's is even more easily separated, given its white- and grey-spotted overall reddish plumage and the grey face and yellow orbital ring of the male.

DESCRIPTION Sixteen rectrices with central tail feathers elongated. Irides dark brown, with yellow eye-ring and pale greyish-horn bill. Pale buff tarsus. Sexes differ. **Adult male:** Crown to nape and neck-sides buffy-olive to olive-yellow, with pale buffy-brown face and chin and throat rusty-yellow. Breast pale ochre-yellow, becoming increasingly greyish dorsally, bordered below by an upper band of white and lower band of deep red-brown, with belly greyish becoming chestnut to blackish dorsally and pale buff undertail-coverts. Mantle, back, scapulars, tertials, rump and uppertail-coverts pale brownish-olive, darker on tertials and scapulars and these feathers spotted bluish-silver with brownish surround, while rump and uppertail-coverts have paler feather centres. Tail olive-brown broadly tipped white and mottled pale buff on outer webs, except 2–3 central pairs, which are pale brownish-olive with pinky-buff base and elongated black filaments. Primaries and primary-coverts dark brown, former paler on inner webs and innermost with white tip; secondaries dark brown tipped white and wing-coverts brownish-olive with pale buff/cream terminal spot on each feather, edged chestnut and some lesser and median coverts with metallic silver spots. Underwing pale buffy-brown. **Adult female:** Mottled above with yellow-buff face and throat finely speckled black, olive-yellow crown and nape streaked black and pinkish-buff breast streaked dark brown; belly dull whitish barred dark brown, washed sepia in centre, and undertail-coverts pale buff. Mantle, scapulars, back, rump and uppertail-coverts olive-yellow barred blackish-brown; scapulars with cream subterminal spot and chestnut tips. Tail heavily barred and tertials and wing-coverts barred olive-yellow and greyish-black, the latter tipped cream. **Juvenile:** Similar to adult female, but even more cryptically coloured. Male has a barred head and back, with the head and underparts patterns more akin to adult male (but throat paler, breast more rufous and

brown belly vermiculated sepia); also buff-tipped primaries and shorter central rectrices. Female is very similar to respective adult, but with a paler tail, initially lacking elongated central feathers, and wing-coverts broadly fringed and tipped buffy-white.

GEOGRAPHICAL VARIATION Monotypic. Those from north of range formerly separated as '*ngami*' and populations in south and southeast as '*furvus*', but neither currently regarded as valid. Considered to form a species-group with Crowned, Chestnut-bellied and Spotted Sandgrouse, and may form a subgenus (*Namapterocles*) with the second named.

MEASUREMENTS Length c.28 cm. Males: wing 167–179, tail 89–124, tarsus 21–24, weight 166–191. Females: wing 163–173, tail 88–106, tarsus 20–23, weight 143–192.

HABITAT Principally occurs in areas with an annual precipitation of less than 30 cm, in open steppe and similar landscapes with sandy soils, often stony areas with low, sparse grasses and thin, well-spaced xeromorphic scrub, but occasionally in areas with denser ground vegetation.

VOICE Five adult calls: a series of sharp *quip* notes on take-off, a trisyllabic *kwelkiewyn* in flight, a *ki-kiii* in alarm, a high-pitched call used in the nest distraction display by both sexes and a softly repeated *quip* used to summon chicks.

HABITS Gregarious, particularly in non-breeding season when flocks of up to 30 and occasionally hundreds recorded at waterholes, which appear to act as 'information centres', given that significant percentages of some flocks visiting these areas do not appear to drink. Sedentary and locally nomadic, while southern populations are migratory, moving north from the Karoo to N Cape Province, Botswana and Namibia. Feeds on small, dry seeds, with a strong preference for 1–2 mm-diameter *Tephrosia dregana* and *Cleome diandra* and *C. luederitziana* (in Namibia and South Africa) and *Lophio carpus burchelli* in Kalahari. Insects, fruits and mollusc parts probably ingested by chance or as grit to aid digestion. Drinks at good-quality water sites in morning, between 08:00 and 10:00 hrs, with some also visiting waterholes in late afternoon, but is apparently able to survive without water for long periods of up to one month (regularly 3–5 days). Roosts in closely spaced groups, arriving over an hour before sunset at such sites; much of the rest of the day is spent at favoured feeding areas, but activity patterns in this respect vary between breeding and non-breeding seasons. Flocks act in highly synchronised manner during latter.

BREEDING Shallow, usually unlined scrape on bare soil or sand, or among stones, grass tufts or scrub. Small, loose colonies, with nests occasionally as close as 22 m apart, but more usually solitary. Two or 3 (mean 2.9) eggs, greyish-green or pinkish-grey marked with brown or grey, laid at one- or two-day intervals and incubated, perhaps upon initiation but at least in some only when complete, for 21–23 days by both sexes, with male

Clearly one of the pin-tailed species-group, nevertheless the closest affinities of this species, which is widespread from NW Africa to the NW Indian subcontinent, are like many of its congenerics subject to speculation.

IDENTIFICATION This species, while common in many areas, is rarely the most abundant within most of its range, but is like most of the genus easily separated from potentially confusing congeners given reasonable views. The combination of pin-like tail, largely fawn-coloured underparts and pale ochre underwings and black belly, which is only ever conspicuous in flight when the dark trailing edge to the wing is also noticeable, should readily distinguish it. Male has unique pastel-grey and yellow head and upper breast pattern and extensively sandy-yellow fringed grey scapulars, wing-coverts and tertials. Female is an understated version of the male, the grey areas of the plumage being replaced by darker spotted, brown feathering, though this is difficult to appreciate at long range. Readily separated from most congeners by upperwing pattern (largely pale with dark trailing edge) and by underparts pattern from Chestnut-bellied and Black-bellied Sandgrouse, neither of which are likely to pose real identification problems. Crowned Sandgrouse may offer the most significant challenge, but even this species is not really confusable, given its black frontal band, much warmer orange face and quite different underparts and wing patterns in male, and much less boldly spotted upperparts and breast in female, and different upperwing pattern and lack of pin-like tail in both sexes.

DESCRIPTION Fairly large sandgrouse, with both sexes having long black division to plain, pale lower belly. Slightly longer bodied, but much bulkier, than Crowned Sandgrouse and shorter tailed than Pin-tailed Sandgrouse. Sixteen rectrices with central tail feathers elongated. Irides brown, with yellow eye-ring, and bluish-white to bluish-grey bill. White tarsus. Sexes differ. **Adult male:** Head yellow-ochre, with broad pale grey supercilium and pink-brown crown visible only at close range. Body and tail mainly sandy-isabelline, with grey marbling on scapulars, grey upper breast and neck and brown bases to median and greater wing-coverts, which along with scapulars have yellow-buff tips, creating obvious pale spots at distance and give overall olive cast to back. Pale buff edges to grey-brown primaries afford little contrast with rest of folded wing. Central belly black, contrasting with isabelline flanks, but obvious only in flight and at close range. Underwing pattern lacks clear white centre, being pale buff with greyer flight feathers. **Adult female:** Differs from male in that only lower face is yellowish-white to ochre, ground colour of plumage is paler on underparts and pinker above than male, with obvious dark streaks on crown and hindneck, dull and intense black spots scattered over entire breast, mantle, back, rump, tail and wing-coverts, being boldest on breast-sides, scapulars, and median and greater wing-coverts. **Juvenile:** Similar to adult female but lacks elongated central tail feathers and has white throat, barred and dark-streaked upperparts, U-shaped marks on breast and pale buff

outer webs to the primaries, which are also mottled brown or buff at their tips. With age assumes respective adult plumage, but duller and paler.

GEOGRAPHICAL VARIATION Monotypic. Those in India formerly separated as '*remotus*', based on their slightly paler and more greyish plumage, but this form no longer considered valid. Adult plumage characters suggest that it is most closely related to Chestnut-bellied Sandgrouse and usually considered to form a species-group with this species, Crowned and Namaqua Sandgrouse, though tentatively placed close to Pin-tailed Sandgrouse by Johnsgard (1991).

MEASUREMENTS Length 29–36 cm. Males: wing 203–212, tail 120–167, tarsus 21–24. Females: wing 189–203, tail 99–120, tarsus 21–22. Weight (both sexes) 250–340.

HABITAT Inhabits deserts, including those with only rare and erratic rainfall, semi-deserts, low foothills and stony plains. Does not appear to use adjacent arable lands, unlike often sympatric Pin-tailed and Black-bellied Sandgrouse, and also avoids very hilly or mountainous areas.

VOICE Slower and louder calls than many sympatric sandgrouse species. A liquid double note, *cuddle-cuddle* or *waku-waku*. Flocks in flight give an extended series of staccato notes, likened to a small dog yapping.

HABITS Gregarious and usually recorded in flocks of more than 100 in non-breeding season in Indian subcontinent; exceptionally up to 5000 in Oman. Mostly sedentary and/or nomadic, especially during dry season (see Distribution). Primarily feeds on small, hard seeds, with a distinct preference for those of *Euphorbia guyoniana* and *Asphodelus tenuifolius* in Morocco and barley grain in Iraq, with two principal species in one crop from United Arab Emirates being *Emex spinosus* and *Tephrosia purpurea*. Insects also recorded in India. Grit or small stones are also ingested. Usually feeds early morning and late afternoon, and drinks in morning during 06:30 to 10:30 hrs and again in evening in hot weather. Drinking is usually completed in 15 seconds. Some authors have noted males and females arriving in separate flocks at watering sites. Foraging birds may roost in groups of up to 50.

BREEDING Scrape or natural depression on the ground, sometimes in a hoof-mark or near a stone, often near a waterhole in barren stony desert. Nesting pair densities of 12 per 1.5 km^2 have been reported, but very patchy in other areas. Typically 3 elliptical eggs, more occasionally 2 pale creamy-buff sparsely marked with pale/reddish-brown and purplish-grey, laid at 24–28-hour intervals and incubated for 27–31 days, with male assuming nocturnal duties (19:00–c.10:00 hrs). Incubation probably commences as soon as clutch is initiated. Male alone provides water, but both sexes brood the young, which are self-feeding within a few hours of hatching. Fledging period unknown but probably c.1 month. Rarely more than 2 young reared, but probably double-brooded in years with favourable rainfall. Lays in March–July, although season may extend to early August in some areas.

DISTRIBUTION S and C Morocco and S Algeria to Egypt, including Sinai, south to Mauritania and N Mali east to Eritrea, Djibouti and N Somalia; also in SW Asia from Arabia, Levant, S Iraq and S Iran to SW Afghanistan, W Pakistan and NW India. Principally resident, but some winter southeast to Pakistan and NW India (Thar), and, in Africa, in certain areas of Morocco and Algeria from which the species is absent in summer. It has wandered north to Italy and Turkey and south to Burkina Faso.

STATUS Widespread and common throughout most of range, e.g. in Israel (2000–3000 pairs in mid-1980s, though some evidence for a decline in the south of country since then) and Egypt (1000–10,000 pairs), but patchily distributed in Morocco and Algeria, scarce in Tunisia, where apparently hunted in summer at waterholes, and uncommon in Arabia. Perhaps decreasing in Syria and rather local in Iraq. Fairly common in C and S Oman, but only a vagrant in the north of that country. Apparently increasing in N Somalia. Common but erratic winter visitor and passage migrant in NW Indian subcontinent, and now known to be resident in Desert National Park, Rajasthan.

REFERENCES Cramp (1985), Johnsgard (1991), de Juana (1997), Prendergast (1993), Roberts (1991), Urban *et al.* (1986).

244 YELLOW-THROATED SANDGROUSE
Pterocles gutturalis A. Smith, 1836   Plate 71

Bulky sandgrouse of uncertain relationships, which occurs in a narrow and intermittent band from NE to southern Africa, and is generally uncommon throughout much of its sizeable range.

IDENTIFICATION Distinctive E and southern African sandgrouse, which is easily recognised among several overlapping conspecifics. Short, wedge-shaped tail in both sexes. Male is more diagnostically marked of the two, having an extensive buffish-yellow throat and face, bordered below by a broad black half collar, dark grey-and-chestnut underparts and wings and black underwings. Female more featureless with dull yellowish throat, barred underparts and richly but cryptically patterned upperparts. Unlikely to be confused given a good view: Chestnut-bellied Sandgrouse has an otherwise unmarked yellow face, pin-like tail and pale and dark pectoral-bands; other species without pin tails in range are less bulky and have bold breast patterns in both sexes, with black-and-white forehead-bands in males, while Black-faced Sandgrouse has a distinctive black frontal face-band and all have yellow (not grey) orbital rings; and potentially similar female Namaqua Sandgrouse has brighter yellow throat and pin tail.

DESCRIPTION *P. g. gutturalis.* Wedge-shaped tail. Irides dark brown with grey eye-ring and pale bluish-grey bill. Tarsus rufous-buff. Sexes differ. **Adult male:** Crown and nape greyish-yellow becoming dark olive-buff on neck-sides and hindneck; lores black; chin, throat, face and supercilium creamy-buff, latter narrowly edged black above and throat bordered below by obvious black band that reaches to neck-sides. Breast dull grey with olive-buff fringes to feathers and rest of underparts chestnut-brown, vermiculated black on flanks and undertail-coverts fringed rust. Mantle, scapulars and tertials dull greyish washed yellowish, back, rump and uppertail-coverts greyish-olive and tail black broadly tipped and barred buffy-white. Primaries brownish-black fringed and tipped whitish, secondaries blackish-brown and wing-coverts pale grey, broadly tipped clay and washed yellowish on greater coverts. Underwing brownish-black. **Adult female:** Crown and nape blackish-brown, becoming darker on hindneck, with face, chin, throat and supercilium creamy-buff and lores black. Upper breast pale ochre barred dark brown, becoming chestnut heavily barred black on rest of underparts to undertail-coverts, which are greenish-brown, with black fringes. Mantle, back, rump and uppertail-coverts mottled and barred blackish-brown and olive-buff. Tail black broadly tipped and barred buffy-white. Flight feathers and wing-coverts brownish-black, with off-white fringes to primaries and greater coverts greyer. **Juvenile:** Much as adult female, but upperparts spotting and barring is smaller and narrower, and primaries are broadly tipped and fringed, on outer web, with olive-buff.

GEOGRAPHICAL VARIATION Two comparatively weakly differentiated forms recognised, with a third, '*tanganjicae*' from east of Lake Tanganyika no longer recognised. Often considered to possess no particularly close relatives and to represent a monospecific phyletic lineage, though it has been placed in a separate subgenus with Black-bellied Sandgrouse.

    P. g. saturatior Hartert, 1900 occurs from Ethiopia south to extreme NE Zambia; has brighter, more cinnamon fringes to wing-coverts than nominate.
    P. g. gutturalis A. Smith, 1836 occurs from SE Angola, S Zambia and W Zimbabwe south to N Cape Province (South Africa); described above.

MEASUREMENTS Length 30 cm. *P. g. gutturalis.* Males: wing 208–228, tail 83.5–94.0, tarsus 28–32, weight 340–345. Females: wing 205–220, tail 75–88, tarsus 28–31, weight 285–400.

HABITAT Comparatively unusual among sandgrouse as it selects short-grass plains and black cotton soils, which are dark and contain high clay content, near rivers and swamps in flood plains. Also uses ploughed and (one-year) fallow fields (exclusively dependent upon such habitats within one area in South Africa), and recently-burnt areas to 2000 m.

VOICE Principal call is a far-carrying *ipi, aw-aw*, on a slightly descending scale, of which only the last two notes are uttered at waterholes. A growling sound has been reported for agitated individuals.

HABITS E African populations are principally sedentary, but those in S Africa are partial migrants, breeding in S Zambia (present April–December, with peak numbers in May–October) and N Botswana, where more sedentary, and principally wintering in Zimbabwe, SE Botswana, Transvaal and N Cape Province (though recently established as a resident in one area within latter). Takes cultivated grains and grasses, particularly early successional species and most importantly, Leguminosae, Gramineae, *Achyramthes*, *Amaranthus*, *Crotalaria* and *Bidens* seeds. Drinks in morning, arriving in groups of 10–50 between 07:00 and 10:00 hrs, and again in mid- to late afternoon when it may share waterholes with Chestnut-bellied and Burchell's Sandgrouse.

BREEDING Solitary nester, in flat treeless areas, with many weedy plants, though adjacent pairs may occasionally be within 40 m of one another. Shallow circular scrape or natural hollow in ground, occasionally in hoof-print and frequently partially concealed by grass or stubble. Typically 3 eggs, sometimes just 2, laid at two-day intervals and incubated, upon initiation of clutch, by both sexes (male at night, with changeovers in morning and evening) for 25–27 days. Male solely responsible for watering chicks. Young capable of flight at c.4 weeks, when approximately half adult size. Principally nests in dry season, April–October (peaks June–July), but timing varies through extensive range, with peak generally becoming later with latitude.

Predation and ploughing accounted for most nest losses in one area in South Africa.

DISTRIBUTION Local in E and S Africa, from W and C Ethiopia south through Kenya, Tanzania, Zambia, extreme SE Angola, N Namibia, SW Zimbabwe and Botswana to N South Africa, in Northern Cape and North West Provinces.

STATUS Local and generally uncommon throughout most of range (e.g. entirely absent from C Zambia), usually recorded in small parties, although occasionally forms larger flocks, principally on migration, e.g. 1000 moving south over Kafue Flats, Zambia. Has reportedly declined in Transvaal, where perhaps no longer annual in occurrence, now absent from N Cape Province and possibly declining on Kafue Flats, where altered flood regime (due to the construction of two large hydroelectric dams) may have affected foodplant cycles. Listed as Indeterminate in South African Red Data book. In parts of South Africa, significant numbers of nests may be destroyed during ploughing (8 of 13 in one study), but also considered relatively common in parts of North Cape Province, where the population may number tens of thousands of individuals and may even have the potential to be sustainably hunted.

REFERENCES Johnsgard (1991), de Juana (1997), Tarboton (2001), Tarboton *et al.* (1999), Urban *et al.* (1986).

---

245 BLACK-BELLIED SANDGROUSE
Pterocles orientalis (Linnaeus, 1758)

Plate 72

Alternative name: Imperial Sandgrouse.

One of the two European-breeding sandgrouse and the largest of the *Pterocles*, this distinctive and boldly patterned species is frequently one of the most common of sandgrouse, perhaps in part due to its ability to tolerate some low-level cultivation and modification of its dry-land habitats.

IDENTIFICATION This bulky and widely, but disjunctly distributed sandgrouse is easily identified from congeners due to the combination of its wedge-shaped tail and black belly and flanks. Among mixed groups of flying sandgrouse its large size is frequently noticable, as are the white underwing-coverts that contrast markedly with the black flight feathers and rear underparts. Plumage most strongly patterned of Western Palearctic sandgrouse. Male has sandy-buff breast and grey head and neck, distinct black pectoral-band, deep orange-yellow throat and well-marked gold and grey upperparts and wings. Female much duller, with heavily spotted brown upperparts, intricately marked, brown, gold and black wings and plain face. Chestnut-bellied and Spotted Sandgrouse are both smaller and slimmer with pin-like tails, and different underwing patterns. Given at-rest views, both sexes of the superficially similar Spotted Sandgrouse can also be seen to have different face and wing patterns, and also lack the narrow black pectoral-band of both sexes of Black-bellied. In areas where the species overlaps only with Pin-tailed Sandgrouse, more experienced observers

will be able to identify either species on call alone, but there is also a host of plumage features that separate the two.

DESCRIPTION *P. o. orientalis.* A large heavy-bodied sandgrouse with rather broad wings. Combination of large black belly patch and white underwing-coverts diagnostic within family. Sixteen rectrices form relatively short, wedge-shaped tail. Irides brown with lemon-yellow lids, and pale to dark lead bill. White tarsus. Sexes differ. **Adult male:** Head, neck and foreparts grey, paler on lower chest and has chestnut and black half-collar on lower throat and distinct black border to lower breast, sharply contrasting with wholly black belly and vent. Hindneck to rump, as well as tertials and wing-coverts, basically yellow-ochre, but olive-black centres obvious on all larger feathers except greater coverts. In flight, grey-black primaries and dusky primary-coverts contrast with grey-spotted yellow innerwing (on which yellowest greater coverts may appear as pale central panel). On underwing, black flight feathers contrast sharply with white coverts. Pointed but short tail barred yellow and black. **Adult female:** Pattern as male, but lacks chestnut half-collar and grey foreparts. Head and breast pale buff, streaked and spotted dark black-brown, with breast-marks contained by black line positioned as male, and entire upperparts yellow-ochre, closely barred and marbled dark brown or black. **Juvenile:** Overall paler. Male initially resembles adult female, and subsequently both sexes differ from respective adults by virtue of their buff-fringed primaries and primary-coverts, which are vermiculated black.

GEOGRAPHICAL VARIATION Weakly represented by two races and has been considered to be probably monotypic; all other previously described forms '*aragonica*', '*enigmaticus*', '*koslovae*' and '*bangsi*' are now subsumed within the nominate. Relationships to other sandgrouse unclear; sometimes placed in subgenus *Eremialector* with Yellow-throated Sandgrouse, but also considered sufficiently unique to occupy its own group or is placed within the pin-tailed group with which it shares features such as having 16 rectrices.

P. o. orientalis (Linnaeus, 1758) occurs in Iberia, the Canaries, NW Africa, Cyprus, Turkey, Armenia and Israel; described above.

P. o. arenarius (Pallas, 1775) occurs from NW Kazakhstan east to NW China and south to Pakistan; average paler and heavier, with males having back, rump and uppertail-coverts and fringes of upperwing-coverts and scapulars yellower, and breast greyer than nominate, while females are more whitish below the pectoral-band, but many are apparently indistinguishable.

MEASUREMENTS Length 33–39 cm. Both races. Males: wing 227–244, tail 88–101, tarsus 26–34, weight 400–550. Females: wing 221–242, tail 84–101, tarsus 26–35, weight 300–465.

HABITAT Uses plains, low hilly areas, saltflats, rough pastures, grassy steppes and semi-desert areas to 1300 m with an annual precipitation of 20–50 cm, avoiding areas devoid of vegetation and those with extensive trees or shrubs. Appears tolerant of limited agricultural development of such areas, but avoids montane habitats. In those parts of its range where it is a migrant, uses semi-desert plains with scattered large, spiny scrub in winter.

VOICE A soft gurgling *tchowrrr rerr-rerr* recorded on the ground, at water and in flight.

HABITS Gregarious, but flocks of fewer than ten are usual in April–October. Rarely very approachable, usually flushing at c.100 m distance from observer. Winter concentrations at waterholes are highly variable, but up to 8000 have been reported in India. Populations differ in degree of sedentariness, with those in Iberia and N Africa being strictly resident, those in the Middle East nomadic or partially migratory, and is principally a summer resident in C Asia and other northernmost breeding areas. Winters throughout Middle East, south to Sinai and Kuwait, and Pakistan and NW India, between September/October and February/March. Prefers small, hard seeds, typically of a variety of Leguminosae, as well as *Heliotropium, Polygonum, Sisymbrium, Salicornia, Ammodendron* and others. Like other species of sandgrouse, takes cereal grains and cultivated legumes in agricultural areas, as well as berries, termites, beetles and their larvae. Grit is ingested but insects unrecorded in diet. Drinks in morning (usually c.3 hours after dawn)

and, in hot weather, c.1 hour before dusk, flying up to 60 km to reach favoured waterholes.

BREEDING Scrape or natural depression, usually left unlined or has a circle of small stones, but frequently situated in shade of bush. Typically 3 elliptical eggs (mean 2.5 in Spain, 2.6 in N Africa and 3.0 in Turkey), greyish-green or cream-buff marked with brown and grey, and incubated for 21–24 days (23–28 in captivity), with male sitting from c.1 hour before sunset to c.4 hours after dawn. Incubation commences with first egg. Both parents tend chicks but, like other sandgrouse, only male supplies water. Young are capable of flight at c.1 month, when three-quarters of adult size and are fully grown at two months. Sexually mature at 12 months. Apparently single-brooded but replacement clutches not uncommon and genuine second broods claimed in several countries. Spanish study revealed that of 12 clutches and 19 broods, 86% of eggs hatched and 42% fledged young, while each pair produced a mean of 1.05 fledged young. Season, March–August, but apparently varies with latitude: mostly April in Canary Is, May in Pakistan, June in Spain and Russia, and with replacement clutches being initiated until September.

DISTRIBUTION SW Europe, NW Africa and W Asia, from Iberia (except W, N and NE coastal areas), E Canary Is and N Africa, from C Morocco east to S Tunisia and NW Libya; also from Israel and C Turkey and Cyprus east through C Asia, Iran and Afghanistan to NW China and W and S Pakistan. Northeast population winters southeast to Pakistan and west to NW India. Vagrant to S Europe, Lebanon and perhaps United Arab Emirates (escape likelihood unclear).

STATUS Frequently uncommon and usually occurs only in pairs or very small flocks, except in certain wintering areas. W Palearctic range and population undergoing decrease due to agricultural intensification and spread of irrigation, forestation practices and consequent habitat loss. Ultimately, some of these factors may also locally threaten its survival elsewhere. Considered threatened in Spain (10,000–20,000 pairs), where virtually extinct in Catalonia and population considered to have halved within last 30 years, and probably fewer than 1000 in E Portugal, where also decreasing and now restricted to three areas. In N Africa, uncommon or frequent in Algeria, uncommon in Tunisia, where hunted in summer at waterholes, frequent, at least formerly, in N Libya, and occasionally reaches Egypt in winter. Widely distributed and occasionally common in Russia and Turkey (perhaps as many as 50,000 pairs), and relatively common in deserts of Israel (1000–1500 pairs in mid-1980s). Decreases noted in Canaries (where now extirpated from Gran Canaria) and Cypriot populations, with very few recent records in latter. Rare in Xinjiang, W China, but still common to abundant at wintering locations in Punjab of Pakistan and NW India.

REFERENCES Hagemeijer & Blair (1997), Johnsgard (1991), de Juana (1997), Urban *et al.* (1986).

246 CROWNED SANDGROUSE
Pterocles coronatus Lichtenstein, 1823   **Plate 70**

Alternative name: Coroneted Sandgrouse.

Within its moderately extensive range from NW Africa east through Arabia to Pakistan, this attractive species is often one of the least common sandgrouse, being often local and sparsely distributed.

IDENTIFICATION A comparatively small, plump sandgrouse with a wedge-shaped tail that overlaps with a number of congeners within its Saharo-Sindian range. Male is wholly distinctive if seen well, due to black frontal-band, which is unique among sympatric sandgrouse. Also has rufous crown and face, long grey supercilium and otherwise sandy-grey plumage with boldly white-spotted wing-coverts and scapulars. Female lacks black mask, but has face and throat yellow with densely barred breast and upperparts, and largely unmarked belly and vent. Both sexes similar in overall colour to Spotted Sandgrouse but lack pin-like tail and black on belly, in addition to different head and breast patterns, while female is very like female Lichtenstein's, but is overall paler with more strongly patterned wings and an unmarked yellow throat patch.

DESCRIPTION *P. c. coronatus.* Slightly larger than Lichtenstein's Sandgrouse, but among those species recorded in Western Palearctic it is the second smallest. Sixteen rectrices in rounded tail. Irides dark brownish, with pale bluish-grey eye-ring and bill. Whitish-buff tarsus. Sexes differ. **Adult male:** Intricately patterned head, with pale red-brown crown encircled by pale blue diadem formed by broad supercilium, originating behind eye, meeting on nape; pale buff around eye and on forehead, black frontal-band from forehead to chin; and golden-yellow lower face and lower throat, extending as band below blue nape. Body and wing-coverts pink-isabelline, with fine brown marbling and off-white streaks and spots, indistinct on back, but obvious on scapulars and wing-coverts. Dark brown flight feathers and beautifully patterned head contrast markedly at close range. Tail brown-isabelline with white tips to outermost feathers. In flight, underwing pattern plainest of all male sandgrouse, with pale buff rear body and underwing-coverts, and dark brown undersurface to flight feathers. **Adult female:** Ground colour paler, especially of underparts, than male, with most of plumage flecked and close-barred black or dark brown. Face and throat yellow-ochre and faintly streaked. Barring more open and broader above and more obsolete on underparts. **Juvenile:** Much like adult female, but overall more rufous-buff and throat whitish, with coarser barring and little or none on belly, and male has buff secondary-coverts and tail feathers vermiculated black.

GEOGRAPHICAL VARIATION Varies within, as well as between races and apparently closely linked to soil colour, being more rufous in hot deserts and greyer in colder deserts. Five taxa recognised based on overall ground colour and amount of dark grey or black markings. The species' relationships appear somewhat confused given its various systematic treatments, it being sometimes placed in a species-group along with Spotted, Chestnut-bellied and Namaqua Sandgrouse, or within a black-faced group consisting of it, Black-faced and Madagascar Sandgrouse, and also at one time in the genus *Eremialector.*

P. c. coronatus Lichtenstein, 1823 occurs across the Sahara from S Morocco to N Sudan and the Red Sea; described above.

P. c. vastitas R. Meinertzhagen, 1928 occurs in Sinai and neighbouring Israel and Jordan; male has slightly browner and less rufous upperparts and is more heavily spotted dark grey, while female is more densely and darkly barred.

P. c. saturatus Kinnear, 1927 occurs in interior Oman; described as being even darker than *atratus,* the male being apparently very dark blackish and the female having more densely and darkly barred underparts.

P. c. atratus Hartert, 1902 occurs in S Arabia and Iran to Afghanistan; darker than nominate and *vastitas,* and has more richly patterned wings with white spots duller and bordered by grey and rufous, the male is more blackish-brown above and the female more densely and darkly barred above.

P. c. ladas Koelz, 1954 occurs in Pakistan; both sexes paler than *atratus,* with male less rufous and overall greyer and less strongly marked black, while female is less strongly barred, but paler and overall less rufous than *vastitas.*

MEASUREMENTS Length 25–30 cm. *P. c. coronatus.* Males: wing 193–205, tail 79–86, tarsus 22–24, weight (n=1) 300. Females: wing 183–195, tail 75–83, tarsus 23–24, no weight data.

HABITAT Adapted to highly arid areas, including some of the driest areas of the interior Sahara, but in Africa prefers stony deserts, rather than sand deserts, which it uses in the Asian portion of its range. Occupies slightly grassed areas in hilly and montane areas, as well as stony areas and ravines among lava fields.

VOICE Principal vocalisation is a far-carrying staccato series of *kla-kla-kla* notes. Also a descending *wheek* and various loud barking notes, all principally given in flight.

HABITS Gregarious, like other sandgrouse, being recorded in small flocks of up to 50, infrequently up to 175 and exceptionally 2000. Sedentary and nomadic like many other sandgrouse species. Occurs in NE Morocco only in October–March, most frequent in parts of Libya in June–September and moves north in Chad in April–June, while numbers in Pakistan increase in winter. Takes shoots, perhaps insects and, principally, small, hard seeds, favouring *Tephrosia apollinea* in Sudan and *Asphodelus tenuifolis* in S Morocco. Occasionally drinks in evening, and regularly in morning between 09:00 and 10:00 hrs (winter) and 07:00 and 09:00 hrs (summer), travelling up to 80 km to reach waterholes. Where two species co-exist, often shares such resources with Spotted Sandgrouse and arrives synchronously.

BREEDING Scrape among pebbles or a sandy depression, sometimes surrounded by a ring of small stones, and fully exposed. Three elliptical eggs typical, although clutches of 2 recorded; cream marked with pale brown and purplish-grey. Incubation period unknown but sexes share duties, with male sitting at night, taking over c.1 hour prior to sunset. Nidifugous young can self-feed upon hatching. Few other data although male (and perhaps female) provides chicks with water. Season is April–June, but breeding may occur opportunistically after significant rainfall.

DISTRIBUTION N Africa in the Sahara, from S Morocco east to N Egypt including Sinai, south to Mauritania, Niger and N Chad; also in S Asia, in Israel and S Arabia east through E Iran and Afghanistan to W Pakistan. Vagrant to Mali.

STATUS Usually widespread and relatively common, except in northern parts of W Africa, where generally uncommon. In Algeria, common to abundant in most areas of the country in 1930s–1950s, and also common in Egypt and Sudan. Common in Israeli deserts, though some evidence for a decline in recent years, and apparently very local in Jordan, status in S Iraq confused and rare in Saudi Arabia. Elsewhere in the peninsula, common in C Oman (endemic race *saturatus*) and Omani Dhofar, but few records from Gulf States. Locally common in Pakistan, but no records in India since 19th century.

REFERENCES Cramp (1985), Johnsgard (1991), de Juana (1997), Urban *et al.* (1986).

---

247 MADAGASCAR SANDGROUSE
Pterocles personatus Gould, 1843   **Plate 71**

Alternative names: Masked/Madagascan Sandgrouse.

This comparatively sedentary species is endemic to Madagascar where only common in the west and south of the island, and entirely absent from the east. It appears to be most closely related to Black-faced Sandgrouse.

IDENTIFICATION Restricted to Madagascar, where it is the only sandgrouse and thus unmistakable due to its waddling walk and generally plump appearance. Rather stocky. Male has striking black frontal-band and extremely bold yellow orbital ring, dark-brown upperparts, largely unmarked wing-coverts, pale rufous breast and narrow blackish belly barring. Female differs in lack of facial mask and orbital ring, and is more cryptically patterned with closely barred upperparts.

DESCRIPTION Rounded tail consisting of 14–16 rectrices. Irides brown, with striking yellow orbital ring and blue bill (bluish-black in female). Tarsus buff. Sexes differ. **Adult male:** Broad black frontal-band on face; crown to upper back dark isabelline, becoming yellowish on nape; throat buffish-white, becoming vinaceous-buff on breast, white breast-sides and rest of underparts rufous-buff closely barred black, with undertail-coverts buff. Scapulars vinaceous-brown and lower back to uppertail-coverts blackish-grey, densely spotted whitish-buff; tail similar with irregular bars and broadly tipped white. Flight feathers black and wing-coverts yellowish-buff, some median coverts with brown terminal band. Underwing dark brown with black axillaries. **Adult female:** Has top of head spotted blackish-brown, throat and face-sides buffy-white, breast vinous and flanks and belly barred black and white, becoming rufous and black on vent and undertail-coverts. Nape, upper back and lesser and median wing-coverts regularly and evenly barred blackish-brown, scapulars irregularly barred buff, greater coverts buff, irregularly barred black. Tail blackish-brown barred and tipped yellowish-white. **Juvenile:** Most similar to adult female but overall duller, with very pale buff wings barred black.

GEOGRAPHICAL VARIATION Monotypic. Appears closely related to Black-faced Sandgrouse, with which it shares a black forehead in males and an absence of

elongated central rectrices, and perhaps Crowned Sandgrouse. The three have been considered to form a species-group.

MEASUREMENTS Length 35 cm. Males: wing 216–248, tail 94–127, tarsus (both sexes) 25. Females: wing 203–216, tail 86–108. No weight data.

HABITAT Prefers slightly degraded or open spiny forest, or savanna areas of *Xerophyta* and introduced grasses around rocky ground. Also sparsely vegetated lake and river shores from sea level to 1200 m. Avoids more heavily wooded areas.

VOICE Flight call is a rapid, guttural *catch-catcha-catcha*; also given from the ground.

HABITS Group size is generally 2–6 to 20–40 individuals. Perhaps sedentary, no information on potential movements available. Seeds probably the most important food resource but very few precise data are known, and insects have also been reported. Principally arrives at waterholes in early morning (exceptionally observed at drinking sites throughout the day), particularly during the dry season, sometimes as many as 300–400 gathering at a favoured site.

BREEDING Scrape on ground often sparsely lined with grass, usually in flat terrain with sparse vegetation, even on lakeshores and within tide wrack on a sea beach. Three smooth, glossy vinaceous-buff eggs, with small blotches, spots and specks of brown and grey. Both sexes incubate, but no information on incubation or fledging periods. Nests found in June, August and October, and two juveniles noted in late May and late October, and probably nests throughout dry season.

DISTRIBUTION Endemic to lowlands, from sea level, of S and W Madagascar, east to Mahamavo and Tanambao-Ankatsaky.

STATUS Patchily distributed in north of island, but regarded as common and widespread in S and W Madagascar. Most regularly recorded around Toliara, south of Antsalova (where common), Berenty, Ampijoroa and Lake Amboromalandy. The species' local name, 'Katakatra' is onomatopoeic and flight calls

455

are easily impersonated, the birds responding to human versions of their calls; such generally confiding behaviour may make it vulnerable to subsistence and 'sport' hunting.

REFERENCES Goodman *et al.* (1997), Johnsgard (1991), de Juana (1997), Morris & Hawkins (1998), Rand (1936).

---

248 BLACK-FACED SANDGROUSE
Pterocles decoratus Cabanis, 1868

Plate 71

Alternative names: Bridled/Masked Sandgrouse.

Closely related to Crowned and Madagascar Sandgrouse, with which it shares a distinctive black frontal-band. This species, which is generally not uncommon within its E African range, also shares a number of plumage characters with the group of banded sandgrouse.

IDENTIFICATION Slightly less intricately patterned than many sympatric sandgrouse, this comparatively small-ranged E African species possesses a diagnostic black frontal-band in the male and distinctive gleaming white breast in both sexes. In addition, male has white supercilium, dark belly and less closely marked mantle and wings, while female lacks facial mask and has much more cryptically patterned plumage. Shares black mask with both Crowned and Madagascar Sandgrouse, but no overlap with either. Shares range with Chestnut-bellied and Yellow-throated Sandgrouse, but easily separated from both on a range of characters. Two other short-tailed species that overlap with it, Lichtenstein's and Four-banded Sandgrouse, are both much more closely barred, have wholly different breast patterns in both sexes and males have black-and-white forehead bands. Male Lichtenstein's also lacks white supercilium.

DESCRIPTION *P. d. decoratus.* Fourteen rectrices in rounded tail. Irides brown, with dull yellow eye-ring and deep yellow bill. Whitish-buff tarsus. Sexes differ. **Adult male:** Forehead barred black and white, with small buff patch above nostrils, white supercilium bordered below by black eye-stripe, black-streaked khaki crown to hindneck, centre of throat black and remaining face buff to yellowish-buff. Upper breast khaki bordered below by black band and broad gleaming white lower breast; belly dark brown with whitish feather tips and undertail-coverts khaki-buff with broad blackish-brown chevrons. Mantle, back, scapulars, rump, uppertail-coverts and tail khaki, largely barred brown and blackish, with buff tips to tail and broad blackish subterminal band. Flight feathers largely dark brown/khaki, primaries with whitish tips and wing-coverts similar with coarse blackish barring. Underwing whitish, washed brown with darker brown axillaries. **Adult female:** Largely similar to male, but more closely barred dorsally and has upper breast barred; lacks black frontal-band, supercilium and breast-band; while chin is yellowish and face and neck-sides are finely spotted blackish. **Juvenile:** Very similar to adult female but has darker, narrower and rustier barring on scapulars, inner secondaries and secondary-coverts; primaries have rusty tips, fringed whitish and tail is more irregularly barred. Following first moult, male

and female more like respective adults, but most feathers fringed whitish and male lacks white lower breast.

GEOGRAPHICAL VARIATION Three weakly differentiated taxa recognised, principally on the basis of overall plumage colorations; another subspecies '*katharinae*', from N Tanzania, is no longer recognised. Its intrageneric relationships are not wholly clear: variously treated as a member of a black-faced group, with Madagascar and Crowned Sandgrouse (also at one time placed in the genus *Eremialector* with the latter), or a banded group, containing Painted, Lichtenstein's and Double-banded Sandgrouse.

> *P. d. ellenbecki* Erlanger, 1905 occurs from NE Uganda and N Kenya to Ethiopia and Somalia; less heavily barred below, and overall paler, less brown and yellower than nominate.
> *P. d. decoratus* Cabanis, 1868 occurs in SE Kenya and E Tanzania; described above.
> *P. d. loveridgei* (Friedmann, 1928) occurs in W Kenya and W Tanzania; also paler than nominate, but is more greyish-sandy and less rusty than *ellenbecki*.

MEASUREMENTS Length 28 cm. All races. Both sexes: wing 154–175, tail 60–75, tarsus 25. Weight male 160–216, female 149–210.

HABITAT Inhabits dry savanna, thornbush, semi-deserts and coastal dunes, including bare areas within heavier vegetation, including *Commiphora* woodland and thickets. In areas where overlaps with Lichtenstein's and Four-banded Sandgrouse, prefers thicker bush and more wooded savannas, and also uses saline, poorly drained soils with scattered grasses and trees, and mean annual rainfall of 24–36 cm, most of it seasonal and causing abundant and rapid vegetational growth. Principally occurs below 1800 m.

VOICE A series of three *chukar* notes given in flight.

HABITS Relatively gregarious, but most groups are of fewer than 10, although up to 20 are occasionally recorded. Probably largely resident but few data on degree of sedentariness. Food also poorly known. Data from Tanzania indicate a preference for seeds, principally Leguminosae, mainly *Heliotropium undulatifolium*, *Indigofera* and *Trianthema*, and Boraginaceae. Drinks during first half of morning, e.g. from 07:00 hrs: onwards, usually arriving at waterholes in small parties of up to 12, or pairs, but much larger aggregations of up to 1000 individuals have been noted in Tsavo East, Kenya, during dry season.

BREEDING Unlined scrape on sandy or stony ground. Two or, more usually, 3 oval eggs; buff with reddish-brown blotches. Incubation and fledging

456

periods unknown, but evidence for suggested phenomena of juvenile breeding and double broods are scant. Nesting activity apparently peaks in dry season, e.g. June–August in Tanzania, where known to breed virtually year-round, between January and November, and July–August and December in Somalia.

DISTRIBUTION E Africa, from S Ethiopia and S Somalia south to NE Uganda, Kenya and SC Tanzania.

STATUS Few data. Most frequently recorded in pairs and small parties, and considered common to very common in Ethiopia and S Somalia, and locally so in Kenya, e.g. in Tsavo East, but absent from much of the west of the country. Most records in Tanzania are from the north and centre.

REFERENCES Johnsgard (1991), de Juana (1997), Urban *et al.* (1986).

249 DOUBLE-BANDED SANDGROUSE
Pterocles bicinctus Temminck, 1815   **Plate 72**

One of the banded group of sandgrouse and the only one to occur in southern Africa, this species appears to be most closely related to Painted Sandgrouse of the Indian subcontinent.

IDENTIFICATION This species' attractive plumage pattern places it firmly within the banded group of sandgrouse, but is unique within southern Africa, making it readily identifiable from its two overlapping congeners. Plumage closely recalls Painted Sandgrouse (no overlap): male has black-and-white forehead pattern, one black-and-white pectoral-band, broad white tips to dorsal feathering and sandy-buff breast and wing-coverts, while female is very cryptically patterned with crescent-shaped markings, and a paler belly. Only sympatric sandgrouse are Burchell's, which is overall reddish-brown, with a striking grey face and yellow orbital ring in the male and yellow face and throat in female and Namaqua Sandgrouse, which has a pin-like tail in both sexes and males lack the forehead banding, while females have striped, not barred, throat and neck and lack narrow yellow orbital ring of female Double-banded. There is also slight overlap with quite different Yellow-throated Sandgrouse.

DESCRIPTION *P. b. bicinctus.* Rounded tail of 14 (perhaps 16) rectrices. Irides brown with yellow eye-ring and yellowish or reddish bill with darker tip. Tarsus buffy-white. Sexes differ. **Adult male:** Forehead white with transverse black band; crown and nape deep rufous-buff streaked black, becoming olive-buff on hindneck; lores black and rest of face, chin and throat creamy-buff, becoming rufous-buff on lower throat. Upper breast pinkish-buff, bordered below by single bands of black and white, with belly whitish and blackish-brown and deep buff undertail-coverts barred dark brown. Mantle, scapulars and tertials blackish-brown, barred pale rufous and tipped white, being barred greyish-brown and rufous on back and rump, and uppertail-coverts and tail deep buff barred greyish-brown/blackish-brown, with buff tips to all but central rectrices. Flight feathers blackish-brown, with whitish tips to primaries and wing-coverts rufous-buff fringed olive-buff. Underwing greyish-brown with paler feather tips and grey axillaries. **Adult female:** Crown and nape pale rufous-buff, becoming pale buff on sides of neck and hindneck, and all tracts streaked black; face, chin and throat creamy-buff, becoming pinkish-buff on lower throat and extending to upper breast, where barred brownish-black. Rest of underparts off-white finely barred black, becoming deep buff, barred blackish-

brown, on undertail-coverts. Mantle, back, scapulars, rump, uppertail-coverts and tertials pale rufous-buff barred blackish-brown and tipped whitish; tail barred buff and black, tipped pale buff and has wavy black subterminal bar. Flight feathers brownish-black and wing-coverts pale pinkish-buff, barred dark brown and spotted white. **Juvenile:** Most similar to adult female, but overall less densely barred with most feathers edged buff; chin to breast pale pinkish-buff, rest of underparts off-white finely barred black, and primaries and primary-coverts blackish-brown, the former tipped buff.

GEOGRAPHICAL VARIATION Three subspecies recognised, with variation being most clearly expressed in overall size and plumage coloration. The forms '*chobiensis*' (from N Namibia and N Botswana), '*usheri*' (N Zimbabwe and Mozambique) and '*elizabethae*' (W Namibia) are now usually considered synonyms. Perhaps derived from ancient *lichtensteinii* stock but appears to possess strongest links with Painted Sandgrouse; both sexes share very similar plumage. Considered to form a species-group with other banded species, perhaps including Black-faced Sandgrouse.

P. b. ansorgei Benson, 1947 occurs in W Angola; smaller and paler than nominate.

P. b. bicinctus Temminck, 1815 occurs from SW Angola south to NW Cape Province (South Africa) and east to Botswana; described above.

P. b. multicolor Hartert, 1908 occurs from Zambia south to Transvaal; varies in size across range, becoming smaller further east, and has richer and more rufous plumage than nominate.

MEASUREMENTS Length 25 cm. *P. b. bicinctus.* Males: wing 172–187, tail 73.5–86.5, tarsus 22.0–26.5, weight 215–250. Females wing 171–185, tail 76.0–82.5, tarsus 22–26, weight 210–280.

HABITAT Prefers lightly-wooded savannas, mopane woodland (dominated by *Colophospermum mopane*), thornbush and similar areas with a ready water supply, rocky rather than sandy substrate and a moderately moist to quite arid climate; also less frequently found in desert-edge environments and in *Brachystegia* woodland, where apparently only a vagrant.

VOICE A series of harsh chuck-chuck notes in flight and, at drinking site, a complex phrase rendered as *Oh NO, he's gone and done it AGAIN* or *Don't weep so Charlie.*

HABITS Resident, being rarely recorded more than 100 km away from its core range, though may undertake some movements in search of water during dry season. Takes seeds of various grasses, herbs and weeds, including introduced *Bidens bidentata*, usually feeding within a limited area in early morning and late afternoon, and principally inactive during rest of day, often huddling in a loose group in shade. Their crepuscular activity pattern appears to be a development against diurnal predators, such as raptors, and perhaps to save energy and reduce evaporative water loss. Small groups probably visit waterholes daily, flying at low altitude, arriving after sunset and remaining until after dark. Studies in Namibia reveal a highly synchronised drinking pattern, with birds staying at water for a mean 28 minutes, mostly immediately after sunset and, to a lesser extent, at night and shortly before sunrise. Numbers at artificial waterholes decrease following rainfall. Nocturnal roosts consist of tightly packed groups.

BREEDING Scrape on ground in flat or hilly country, among sparse grasses or under shrub or tree, and sometimes scantly lined. Pairs nest solitarily. Two to 4 eggs (usually 3, mean 2.6 in Namibia), pinkish-buff marked with purplish-slate or reddish-brown, and incubated 23–24 days, though a captive female incubated infertile eggs for 33 days. Incubation shared, male at night and early morning, female late morning and afternoon. Commences when clutch is complete. Young provisioned by both sexes, but only male brings water. Fledge at c.4 weeks, but capable of flight well before they reach

adult size. In captivity, females incubated at night and fledging period was 33 days. Nests in winter dry season, in April–October, principally July–October in Angola, April–August in Zambia, May and October in Namibia, May–August in Botswana, and April–October in Transvaal and Zimbabwe (where peaks in August).

DISTRIBUTION S Africa, from W and S Angola, W Zambia (and the Luangwa Valley), S Malawi and W and S Mozambique (where the only sandgrouse) south through Namibia, Botswana (principally in north and east) and Zimbabwe to N South Africa in Northern Cape, North West Province, Gauteng, Northern Province and Mpumalanga.

STATUS Generally relatively common and widespread (e.g. in Namibia where only scarce in the south, Mozambique, Transvaal and Zimbabwe), occurring in scattered pairs in breeding season and in flocks of up to 50 at other times. Now only a rare vagrant in C Transvaal, where formerly quite common, but overall may have benefited from the construction of artificial watering holes in recent years. Evidence of overhunting within some parts of S African range has led South Africa, Botswana and Namibia to sign an international agreement to ensure that the species receives adequate protection and is hunted sustainably.

REFERENCES Dean (2000), Johnsgard (1991), de Juana (1997), Maclean & Herremans (1997), Tarboton (2001), Urban *et al.* (1986).

250 FOUR-BANDED SANDGROUSE
Pterocles quadricinctus Temminck, 1815   Plate 72

This species, another member of the banded group, which are distinguished by a series of black-and-white forehead-bands, forms a superspecies with Painted Sandgrouse, for which it is a clear geographic replacement in Sahelian Africa.

IDENTIFICATION Small, short-tailed sandgrouse, which recalls and partially overlaps with one other member of the banded group, Lichtenstein's Sandgrouse, but is more widespread in Africa immediately south of the Sahara. Male has black-and-white banded forehead and complex of breast bars. Female closely barred, but otherwise more like male than other banded sandgrouse, sharing similar dorsal plumage, being a very bold, open pattern. Like the previous species closely recalls Painted Sandgrouse (but no overlap). Only serious confusion risks are Black-faced and Lichtenstein's Sandgrouse, but male lacks barred throat and breast pattern of latter and female is easily distinguished by having unique combination of plain buff breast and barred belly. Black-faced male has different facial pattern, with black extending to the throat as a frontal-band, and both sexes have a much broader white breast-band and lack black wing-tips.

DESCRIPTION Rounded tail of 14 (perhaps 16) rectrices. Irides dark brown with yellow eye-ring and dull yellow bill (yellowish with darker tip or mostly brown/black in female). Whitish tarsus and yellow feet. Sexes differ. **Adult male:** Forehead white with broad transverse black

bar; crown rufous-buff heavily streaked black, becoming sandy-buff on nape, neck-sides and hindneck; and buff chin and throat, deepening in colour on lower throat. Breast khaki-buff, bordered below by single bands of chestnut, white and black, with belly finely barred black and white and ochre-yellow and black on undertail-coverts. Mantle, back and scapulars yellowish-buff, heavily barred black and rufous, becoming ochre-yellow and black on uppertail-coverts and tail. Flight feathers dark brown, with pale fringes to secondaries and plain ochre-yellow wing-coverts. Underwing-coverts and axillaries grey. **Adult female:** Generally similar to male, but lacks forehead pattern and breast-bands. Crown rufous-buff streaked black, becoming spotted on nape and barred on hindneck; face buff becoming whitish on chin and throat. Breast unbarred khaki-buff; rest of underparts as male. Upperparts paler and more closely barred than male, but wing-coverts deep buff barred black and underwing brown and white, grading to brownish-grey on coverts. **Juvenile:** Closely recalls adult female, but distinctly more rufous with finer black barring, mantle, back and scapulars tinged buff and primaries have broad rufous or whitish-buff tips.

GEOGRAPHICAL VARIATION Monotypic. Those east of Lake Chad were described as '*lowei*', but this taxon is no longer regarded as valid. May form a superspecies with Painted Sandgrouse, to which appears extremely closely related. Along with the previous species, may be derived from ancient *lichtensteinii* stock.

MEASUREMENTS Length 25–28 cm. Males: wing 175–182, tail 75–80, tarsus 25–26. Females: wing 176–184, tail 72–78, tarsus 23–25. No weight data.

HABITAT Avoids sandy substrates, instead occupying open or lightly-wooded savannas, bushy grasslands, coastal dune scrub and occasionally partially cultivated areas to 2000 m. Prefers more wooded habitats to partially sympatric Lichtenstein's Sandgrouse.

VOICE Loud twittering calls at water and a soft, shrill whistled *wur-wulli* or *pirrou-ee* in flight.

HABITS Largely resident, but moves north in much of W Africa during wet season (June–October in Chad) and has been recorded as vagrant in Sierra Leone suggesting at least localised nomadism. Flushes reluctantly and over short distance in zigzagging flight. Probably takes small dry seeds, in common with other sandgrouse, but no data available. A nocturnal feeder and largely active at night: it drinks in the evening, 20–50 minutes after dusk, and perhaps again before dawn. Relatively large numbers (up to 200) may congregate at favoured waterholes.

BREEDING Few data. Scrape on ground. In Sudan, often among dry pinkish leaves of *Bauhinia* trees, or in bare stony soil, among scrub or bushes. Two nests in E Africa had 3 oval eggs and another 2. Eggs salmon-buff spotted with orange-brown. Breeds in dry season, November–June, principally March in Senegambia, and February–March in Somalia and Ethiopia (perhaps also July–August and December in latter).

DISTRIBUTION Principally in W Africa, from S Mauritania and S Mali east to NE Cameroon, Central African Republic and Lake Chad, and from C and S Sudan, Ethiopia and Eritrea south to NE Uganda and NW Kenya.

STATUS Frequent throughout most of range, being recorded in pairs or small flocks. The commonest sandgrouse in W Africa, being regarded as common in Senegambia, Mali, N Côte d'Ivoire (dry season only), Nigeria, Chad (south of 16°N), Sudan, but apparently uncommon in Kenya, where few records. Perhaps at risk from increased bush fires, at least in W African portion of its range.

REFERENCES Johnsgard (1991), de Juana (1997), Urban *et al.* (1986).

251 PAINTED SANDGROUSE
Pterocles indicus (J. F. Gmelin 1789) — Plate 72

Alternative name: Indian Sandgrouse.

A member of the banded group of sandgrouse, Painted Sandgrouse is the only member of the family to be confined to the Indian subcontinent, where it is not uncommon and generally widespread.

IDENTIFICATION Both sexes of this boldly marked sandgrouse are easily distinguished within the species' Indian subcontinent range, where it overlaps extensively with only one congener, Chestnut-bellied Sandgrouse. Male Painted Sandgrouse has a white forehead with a black band, strongly banded breast and closely barred upperparts; the female is heavily barred throughout, and lacks the bold breast and forehead patterns of male. The only other banded sandgrouse to occur in the Indian subcontinent is Lichtenstein's, but the two do not appear to overlap (see Lichtenstein's Sandgrouse) and are further distinguished by a number of plumage features (see that species). Easily separated from widely sympatric Chestnut-bellied Sandgrouse, especially the duller females, by breast and forehead markings in male, lack of pin-like tail and grey, not dark underwing in both sexes. The latter feature also assists its recognition from Crowned Sandgrouse, though the two do not overlap and are separated by a number of other field marks.

DESCRIPTION Rounded or wedge-shaped tail of 16 rectrices. Irides brown with yellow to yellowish-green eye-ring and orange to orange-brown bill. Whitish-buff tarsus. Sexes differ. **Adult male:** Forehead white with broad black transverse band and lores and supercilium also white; crown buff with blackish shaft streaks; and throat and face yellowish-buff, merging into similarly

coloured breast. Lower breast bordered below by moderately broad chestnut pectoral-band, with broader bands of yellowish-buff and black, and belly to under-tail-coverts narrowly barred black and white. Mantle and upper back yellowish-buff, becoming black on rump to uppertail-coverts, entirely barred white to yellowish-white. Scapulars and tail black, barred rufous-buff and latter broadly tipped yellowish-buff. Flight feathers brownish-black narrowly fringed off-whitish. Some median and all lesser wing-coverts yellowish-buff; and rest of wing-coverts broadly barred white and dark grey with broad yellowish-buff tips. Underwing-coverts and axillaries medium grey, with slightly darker undersides to flight feathers. **Adult female:** Differs from male in lacking black-and-white forehead and pectoral-band, has neck-sides and throat spotted black, breast and upperparts rufous-buff closely barred black, scapulars and wing-coverts largely yellowish-buff and outermost primary bright buff. **Juvenile:** Most similar to adult female, but overall even more densely streaked and barred. In male, bars mostly appear as vermiculations, breast only has trace of pectoral-band and primaries are vermiculated black and buff. Female shares latter feature, but otherwise closely resembles respective adult.

GEOGRAPHICAL VARIATION Monotypic. Subspecies *arabicus* of Lichtenstein's Sandgrouse was formerly included within this species by some authors. Painted and Four-banded Sandgrouse appear to act as geographical replacements and have been considered to form a superspecies and a larger species-group with Lichtenstein's and Double-banded Sandgrouse, which has been variously treated at generic or subgeneric levels as *Nyctiperdix*.

459

MEASUREMENTS Length 28 cm. Both sexes: wing 158–184, tail 80–101, tarsus 23–25; weight male 166–208, female 166–176.

HABITAT Prefers bare, stony substrates rather than sandy soils and apparently avoids coastal locales, occupying dry country, rocky ravines and stony hillsides with sparse woodland, especially *Acacia* and *Ziziphus*, and scrub. Avoids mountainous areas.

VOICE Flight call is distinctive, a *chirik-chirik*, rising and falling at end; also a croaking, low-pitched *yek-yek-yek* when flushed.

HABITS Less gregarious than most sandgrouse species, being recorded in pairs and small groups of up to ten. Permits close approach and rarely flushes more than 200–300 m. Possibly nomadic, with concentrations reported from certain areas at end of the rainy season, but little specific evidence available for movements. Takes hard seeds of various weeds and grasses, shoots, some berries and insects, including termites in season. Drinks after sunset and around dawn, flying considerable distances, at low altitude, to water.

BREEDING Scrape among stones or earth, with scant or no lining (once a neat pad of grass), and commonly shaded by tree, bush or boulder. Two, more usually 3 eggs, pale cream to salmon-buff marked with purple-red and reddish-brown, and incubated by both sexes (male at night) for c.21–23 days. Young are nidifugous and can self-feed upon hatching. Scattered records in all months, except July and September, with peak perhaps in March–June.

DISTRIBUTION E Pakistan and W and C India, from W Gujurat to S Punjab east to E Orissa and throughout most of peninsula south to N Tamil Nadu; considered as a rare straggler to Persian Baluchistan by Zarudny (1911), but no confirmation of this.

STATUS Most frequently occurs in pairs and small groups, and regarded as moderately common in parts of India, where absent from the extreme south, but only locally so in Pakistan, where typically rare and largely confined to the north.

REFERENCES Grimmett *et al.* (1998), Johnsgard (1991), de Juana (1997), Roberts (1991).

252 LICHTENSTEIN'S SANDGROUSE
Pterocles lichtensteinii Temminck, 1825

Plate 72

Alternative name: Close-barred Sandgrouse.

Lichtenstein's is a member of the banded species-group and may form its ancestral type. Over large parts of its discontinuous N and E African and Middle Asian range it is one of the hardest sandgrouse to observe due to its semi-nocturnal lifestyle. Unlike many other sandgrouse it very rarely appears to form large groups, though it is frequently not uncommon.

IDENTIFICATION Another sandgrouse that is closely tied to the Saharo-Sindian zone, this species is finely barred above and below in both sexes. Lacks pin-like tail and has uniform grey underwings. Male almost entirely barred black with two black bands on white forehead, golden-buff wing-bars and yellowish-buff and black breast-bands. Female lacks breast and forehead patterns and is even more heavily barred black. The black-and-white forehead pattern of male is similar to Black-faced and Painted Sandgrouse, but lacks white supercilium and black throat of former and both have strikingly white, not buff breast-bands; further distinguished from latter by overall basal colours to plumage and lack of sympatry (only doubtfully overlaps with Painted Sandgrouse in North West Frontier Province). Female differs from Black-faced in lack of white breast-band and from female Painted in bill colour and overall greyish plumage coloration. In some parts of range, female may also require separation from female Crowned Sandgrouse, but lacks plain yellow face of latter and has much more finely barred plumage and less boldly marked wing spots.

DESCRIPTION *P. l. targius.* Head and body similar in size to small dove, with rather short graduated tail, of 14–16 rectrices, and is the smallest and shortest-tailed W Palearctic sandgrouse. Irides brown with noticeable

yellow eye-ring (paler or even greyish in female) and brownish-red bill. Tarsus pale buff to white. Sexes differ, but much less distinctly than most congenerics. **Adult male:** Off-white head, neck, and most of underparts, overall densely barred black, except on spotted and streaked crown, cheeks and lower throat. White supercilium and black-and-white bands on forehead are most obvious features on head. Yellow-buff back, rump and wing-coverts, also densely barred black (thus at some angles may appear dark-backed), with pale gold-buff bars on folded wing and similar patches or spots on scapulars, tertials and longest uppertail-coverts. Broad yellow-buff breast-band, with narrow black line across centre and at lower edge. In flight, wing has noticeably dark outer half, except pale bases to primaries and pale buff-grey underwing-coverts. **Adult female:** General plumage pattern and colours only slightly duller than male, but forehead and face yellow-buff, crown and neck more strongly spotted and chest-band absent or reduced to narrow yellow-buff line. **Juvenile:** Largely female-like, but more densely barred both above and below and has grey flight feathers. By first-winter both sexes are much like respective adults, but male may lack black-and-white forehead-bands and breast-bands usually more poorly defined.

GEOGRAPHICAL VARIATION Five taxa recognised, differing in overall coloration and strength and width of the underparts barring. Clearly closely related to Double-banded and Painted Sandgrouse, with which it was formerly regarded as conspecific by some authors and subspecies *arabicus* has been included within latter species. Four-banded and Black-faced are also close relatives and sometimes placed within the same species-group.

P. l. targius Geyr von Schweppenburg, 1916 occurs in the Sahara and Sahel from S Morocco to Chad; described above.
P. l. lichtensteinii Temminck, 1825 occurs patchily from S Israel to N Ethiopia and N Somalia, and Socotra I.; less rufous and has more yellowish-buff upperparts than nominate.
P. l. sukensis Neumann, 1909 occurs in SE Sudan and S Ethiopia and SW Somalia to C Kenya; the darkest race, with heavier black barring than the previous form, particularly on wings and underparts.
P. l. ingramsi Bates & Kinnear, 1937 occurs in E Yemen; the overall palest race, with upperparts and belly barring the least dense of the five forms, more brown and buff coloration on the wing-coverts, more extensive yellowish-buff breast and perhaps broader forehead bars.
P. l. arabicus Neumann, 1909 occurs in S Arabia east through Iran to Pakistan; overall darker and more closely barred than *ingramsi*, but distinctly paler than previous three forms.

MEASUREMENTS Length 22–26 cm. All races. Males: wing 187–195, tail 70–81, tarsus 26–28, weight (*P. l. sukensis*) 175–250. Females: wing 176–187, tail 66–72, tarsus 25, weight (*P. l. sukensis*) 190–230.

HABITAT Highly adapted to extreme desert environments, though it avoids open deserts lacking in vegetation and cultivated areas. Uses partially stony or sandy sites with some thorn scrub vegetation, as well as bushy wadis, bush-covered stony hillsides and clearings. To 1800 m in E Africa.

VOICE Calls include a repeated liquid *wheet-wheet-wheet* or *quitoo* in flight, more grating and lower pitched than other sandgrouse, and similar musical chattering notes when visiting water; also a guttural *krerwerwerwer* if flushed and a dry croaking *krre-krre-krre-krre* in alarm. Rarely vocalises during day.

HABITS Gregarious, but rarely recorded in large groups, though parties of up to 300 exceptionally reported in Oman. Chiefly sedentary, although there is limited evidence of nomadic movements from some parts of range. Typically, among sandgrouse, it is largely a seed-eater, principally favouring *Acacia sayal* and, when these are unavailable, those of *Asphodelus tenuifolis*, *Prosopia*, *Plantago*, *Reseda*, *Cassia* and *Salsola*, as well as flowers and leaves of *Mesembryanthemum*, insects, including beetles, ants, ant-lions, and their larvae. It is principally nocturnal, drinking at or just after dusk and again before dawn, typically performing considerable distance, low-altitude flights to such sources. Several arrived to drink at regular waterhole in Kenya in day

during a total solar eclipse, with smaller numbers than usual consequently visiting the same source that evening. Numbers visiting favoured water sources in Israel in October–February are lower than during the rest of the year, presumably due to reduced requirements. Remains within shade during much of day, though feeding parties are occasionally encountered.

BREEDING Poorly known. Scrape on ground, often among scattered trees or rocks, in open or under low shrub. Appears to prefer hillsides over level ground, sometimes in very close proximity to habitation, and may also occasionally nest in association with other pairs. Unlike other sandgrouse, tends to fly from the nest, rather than run, if approached too closely. Two or, more usually, three elliptical eggs, pinkish to buff marked with reddish-brown or purplish-grey, and incubated by both sexes (male at night). Male is probably also responsible for watering young and chick-care. Young are precocial and nidifugous, like other species of sandgrouse, but incubation and fledging periods unknown. Lays February–September, peaking May–July (and possibly also September in Kenya). In Kenya, at least, nest predation may be heavy.

DISTRIBUTION Local in NC Africa, mostly along south edge of Sahara, from S Morocco and W Mauritania east through Mali to C and NE Sudan, and SE Egypt to Somalia and Socotra I., thence south through SE Sudan to Uganda and C Kenya. Also in SW Asia, east from Sinai and S Israel to S Arabia, S Iran, S Afghanistan and W Pakistan; occurrence in North West Frontier province of India unconfirmed. Vagrant to N Sénégal.

STATUS Sparsely distributed, although often frequent or locally common (uncommon and patchily distributed in W Africa), and usually in pairs or small parties. Extremely localised in S Morocco, where may not breed in all years, apparently limited to Hoggar and Tassili in Algeria, uncommon and local in Sudan, patchily distributed and usually uncommon in Kenya, and scarce in E Sinai. Around Eilat, S Israel, where 50–100 pairs were estimated in the 1980s, the population appears to be increasing and perhaps spreading north due to the development of kibbutzim and the larger number of waterholes currently available. Occurrence in Jordan is probable. Elsewhere, reportedly abundant in N Chad, common in Adrar des Ifoghas, Mali, locally common in SE Egypt (100–1000 pairs reported in whole country), occasionally frequent in Ethiopia, relatively common in Somalia, Oman and United Arab Emirates, and locally frequent in Pakistan.

REFERENCES Johnsgard (1991), de Juana (1997), Shirihai *et al.* (1999), Urban *et al.* (1986).

253 BURCHELL'S SANDGROUSE
Pterocles burchelli W. L. Sclater, 1922   Plate 71

Alternative name: Spotted Sandgrouse.

One of three species of sandgrouse confined to southern Africa, Burchell's Sandgrouse is arguably the most attractive, least common and most poorly known of

these. It was also the last sandgrouse to be described, over 50 years after Black-faced.

IDENTIFICATION The sexes are relatively alike in this highly distinctive and rarely confusable southern

African species, which is comparatively long legged and short tailed among sandgrouse. Male striking, being overall reddish-brown with white spots, especially on wing-coverts, grey face and supercilium, and yellow orbital ring. Female largely similar but white spotting is more extensive and less bold, grey areas of face are yellowish-buff and belly overall paler. Overall salmon-red plumage readily distinguishes both sexes from only sympatric congeners, Double-banded and Namaqua Sandgrouse, of which latter also has elongated central tail feathers. Further distinguished from that species, by preference for less desertic habitats with red Kalahari soil, which provides good camouflage for Burchell's Sandgrouse.

DESCRIPTION Rounded tail of 14 rectrices. Irides brown with broad yellow eye-ring (reduced in female) and blackish bill. Buff-coloured tarsus. Sexes differ. **Adult male:** Crown and nape dark olive-brown with slight streaking; lores, face, chin, throat and supercilium pale blue-grey, and ear-coverts and neck-sides buffy-ochre streaked darker. Breast bright cinnamon, with faint grey banding and bold white subterminal spotting, appearing as even broader feather centres on lower breast, becoming greyish-rust with broad whitish centres on belly and buff on undertail-coverts. Mantle to uppertail-coverts and tertials olive-brown, with orange-yellow and white spotting on some feathers of mantle and back, and spots becoming principally white dorsally. Tail dark grey, barred pinkish-buff with dark subterminal band and broad whitish tips, except central feathers, which are tipped ochre. Rest of flight feathers blackish-brown, primaries with white tips and wing-coverts pale greyish olive-brown, with bold white spotting and broad orange-yellow to rufous tips. Underwing deep rufous becoming greyish at base of primaries. **Adult female:** Upperparts very similar to male, with deep yellow-buff face, supercilium, chin and throat, latter with some rusty spots; breast pinkish-cinnamon washed ochre and feathers with subterminal white spotting, becoming barred on lower breast; belly buffy-white narrowly barred pale brown and undertail-coverts deep buff. Wing-covert tips less rufous and has buffier tips to tail feathers, with underwing buffy-brown. **Juvenile:** Closely recall adults, the male having the throat and supercilium area tinged buff, duller and more diffuse wing spotting, and overall paler tipped feathering, especially noticeable on primaries.

GEOGRAPHICAL VARIATION Monotypic. Those from N Namibia and N Botswana are paler and were formerly separated as '*makarikari*', but this taxon is no longer usually regarded as valid, though a gap between the two forms, in N Cape Province through C and NE Botswana, apparently exists. No apparent close relatives within the genus, which has lead to its placement within the monotypic genus *Calopterocles*, but has also been included within formerly recognised genus *Eremialector*. It is retained within *Pterocles* here.

MEASUREMENTS Length 25 cm. Males: wing 163–175, tail 66–75, tarsus 23–29, weight 180–200. Females: wing 163–173, tail 63–72, tarsus 25–29, weight 160–185.

HABITAT Avoids true deserts, being most abundant in open, rolling grassy plains and Kalahari vegetation types, especially with 30–50 cm-high *Aristida, Stigagrostis* and *Asthenatherum*. Also uses lightly-wooded savannas in semi-deserts, sometimes far from water.

VOICE Calls include a mellow *kowk-wok* or *chok-lit*, the second syllable being higher pitched, in flight, a sharp repeated *quip* on take-off, and various cheeping notes on the ground. In comparison with other sandgrouse, it calls very infrequently in flight and may occasionally visit waterholes without vocalising.

HABITS Resident and nomadic (particularly in drier areas); only recorded in Zambia in dry season (though little relevant observer activity during this period). Takes dry seeds of grasses and shrubs but few specific data, although *Lophiocarpus burchelli* is known to be most important species in Kalahari. Hottest period of day is usually spent roosting. Drinks only in morning, 2–4 hours after dawn, sometimes flying 70–80 km at c.300 m above ground level, to visit waterholes; mostly in flocks of up to 50 and often sharing such sites with Namaqua and, to a lesser extent, Yellow-throated Sandgrouse. Usually arrives an hour later than former. Drinking visits are often extremely short and may be further curtailed in winter and during cloudy conditions.

BREEDING Few data. Favours grass-covered sandy soils, among trees and shrubs. Perhaps nests in loose assemblages, but solitary nesting also reported. Shallow ground scrape, excavated by female; often in short grass or stunted scrub, and very well concealed. Three, rarely 2, eggs; creamy-white or olive marked with greyish-mauve. Incubation and fledging periods unknown, but both sexes brood the eggs and chicks, while the male assumes responsibility for watering. Young capable of flight when half of adult size. Single-brooded. Lays after rains, mostly April–October (peak May–June), in winter dry season.

DISTRIBUTION S Africa, in extreme SE Angola, extreme S Zambia, N and E Namibia, Botswana, extreme NW Zimbabwe and CN South Africa, in Northern Cape, North West Province and Northern Province.

STATUS Large numbers are occasionally recorded at drinking sites, but usually recorded in pairs or small parties. Considered widespread and common in Botswana (but with evidence of locally massive declines due to hunting in north), relatively common at several localities in NW Transvaal (though not known to breed), common in E Namibia and abundant in Gemsbok National Park, but uncommon in Angola and may not breed in Zimbabwe. Known from only two localities in Zambia: the Cuando-Mashi flood plain, near Imusho, and Zambezi flood plain, near Simungoma, and quite common at the latter. Has probably benefited from provision of artificial watering sites. Evidence of overhunting (see above) within some parts of S African range has led South Africa, Botswana and Namibia to sign an international agreement to ensure that the species receives adequate protection and is hunted sustainably.

REFERENCES Johnsgard (1991), de Juana (1997), Maclean & Little (1997), Tarboton (2001), Urban *et al.* (1986).

BIBLIOGRAPHY

Abdusalyamov, I. A. (1971) [*Fauna of Tajik SSR*, Vol. 19 (1)]. Dushanbe, Donish [In Russian].

Aguilar-Rodríguez, S. H. (2000) Registro de la perdiz veracruzana o Chivizcoyo (*Dendrortyx barbatus* Gould) en la sierra norte de Oaxaca, México. *Huitzil* 1: 9–11.

Alaoui, M. Y. (1992) Ecologie de la ponte chez la perdix gambra (*Alectoris barbara*) au Maroc. Pp. 405–415 in Birkan, M., Potts, G. R., Aebischer, N. & Dowell, S. D. (eds.) *First International Symposium on Partridges, Quails and Francolins. Gibier Faune Sauvage* 9.

Alderton, D. (1992) *The Atlas of Quails*. T. F. H. Publications, Neptune City.

Aldrich, J. W. (1965) The Turkey. In Severy, M. (ed.) *Water, Prey and Gamebirds of North America*. National Geographic Society, Washington DC.

Ali, S. (1949) *Indian Hill Birds*. Oxford University Press, Bombay.

Ali, S. (1962) *Birds of Sikkim*. Oxford University Press, Bombay.

Ali, S. & Ripley, S. D. (1969) *Handbook of the Birds of India and Pakistan*, Vol. 2. Oxford University Press, Bombay.

Allan, D. G. & Colahan, B. D. (1997) Blackrumped Buttonquail. In Harrison, J. A., Allan, D. G., Underhill, L. G., Herremans, M., Tree, A. J., Parker, V. & Brown, C. J. (eds.) *The Atlas of Southern African Birds including Botswana, Lesotho, Namibia, South Africa, Swaziland and Zimbabwe*. BirdLife South Africa, Johannesburg.

Andrade, G. I. & Repizzo, A. (1994) Guanentá-Alto Río Fonce Fauna and Flora Sanctuary: a new protected area in the Colombian East Andes. *Cotinga* 2: 42–43.

Andreev, A. V. (1979) Reproductive behaviour in black-billed capercaillie compared to capercaillie. Pp. 135–139 in Lovel, T. W. I. (ed.) *Proc. First International Symposium on Grouse*. World Pheasant Association, Lamarsh.

Andreev, A. V. (1990) Beobachtungen zur Winterbiologie des asiatischen Sichelhuhns (*Falcipennis falcipennis*) im Primorje-Gebiet. *Zool. Zurn.* 69: 69–80.

Andreev, A. V. & Hafner, F. (1998) Zur Biologie des Sichelhuhns *Falcipennis falcipennis*. *Limicola* 12: 105–135.

Arshad, M. I. & Zakaria, M. (1998) Breeding ecology of Red Junglefowl. In *The International Symposium on Galliformes 1997*. Department of Wildlife and National Parks Peninsular Malaysia, Kuala Lumpur.

Ash, J. S. (1978) The undescribed female of Harwood's Francolin (*Francolinus harwoodi*) and other observations on the species. *Bull. Brit. Orn. Club* 98: 50–55.

Ash, J. S. (1992) The Galliform species of the Horn of Africa (Ethiopia, Somalia, Djibouti). Pp. 539–550 in Birkan, M., Potts, G. R., Aebischer, N. & Dowell, S. D. (eds.) *First International Symposium on Partridges, Quails and Francolins. Gibier Faune Sauvage* 9.

Ash, J. S. & Miskell, J. E. (1998) *Birds of Somalia*. Pica Press, Robertsbridge.

Aspinall, S. (1996) *Status and Conservation of the Breeding Birds of the United Arab Emirates*. Hobby Publications, Dubai & Warrington.

Aspinwall, D. R. (1978) Striped Crakes and some other dambo birds near Lusaka. *Bull. Zambian Orn. Soc.* 10: 52–56.

Aspinwall, D. R. (1979) MAC comments on Kurrichane Buttonquail. *Newsletter Zambian Orn. Soc.* 9: 126–127.

Ayeni, J. S. O. (1981) The biology of Helmeted Guineafowl (*Numida meleagris galeata* Pallas) in Nigeria. *J. World Pheasant Assoc.* 6: 31–39.

Ayeni, J. S. O. (1983) Home range size, breeding behaviour, and activities of Helmeted Guineafowl *Numida meleagris* in Nigeria. *Malimbus* 5: 37–43.

Baker, E. C. S. (1928) *The Fauna of British India, including Ceylon and Burma*, Vol. 5. Taylor & Francis, London.

Baker, E. C. S. (1930) *Game Birds of India, Burma and Ceylon*, Vol. 3. John Bale & Son, London.

Baker-Gabb, D. J. (1998) Native grasslands and the Plains-wanderer. Birds Australia Conservation Statement No. 1. *Wingspan* 8 (1): 1–8.

van Balen, B. (1992) Distribution, status and conservation of the forest partridges in the Greater Sundas (Indonesia) with special reference to the Chestnut-bellied Partridge (*Arborophila javanica*). Pp. 561–569 in Birkan, M., Potts, G. R., Aebischer, N. & Dowell, S. D. (eds.) *First International Symposium on Partridges, Quails and Francolins. Gibier Faune Sauvage* 9.

van Balen, B. (S) (1997) Status and conservation of the Green Peafowl *Pavo muticus* on Java. *Tragopan* 7: 18–20.

Balmer, D. & Betton, K. (compilers) (2001) Around the region. *Sandgrouse* 23: 157–160.

Bannerman, D. A. (1930) *The Birds of Tropical West Africa*, Vol. 1. Crown Agents, London.

Bannerman, D. A. (1953) *The Birds of West and Equatorial Africa*. 2 vols. Oliver & Boyd, Edinburgh & London.

Bannerman, D. A. (1963) *The Birds of the British Isles*, Vol. 12. Oliver & Boyd, Edinburgh & London.

Baral, H. S. (1998) Status, distribution and habitat preferences of Swamp Francolins *Francolinus gularis* in Nepal. *Ibisbill* 1: 35–70.

Barlow, C., Wacher, T. & Disley, T. (1997) *A Field Guide to the Birds of the Gambia and Senegal*. Pica Press, Robertsbridge.

Barré, N., Barau, A. & Jouanin, C. (1996) *Oiseaux de la Réunion*. Les Éditions du Pacifique, Paris.

Barua, M. & Sharma, P. (1999) Birds of Kaziranga National Park, India. *Forktail* 15: 47–60.

Bates, R. S. P. & Lowther, E. H. N. (1952) *Breeding Birds of Kashmir*. Oxford University Press, Bombay.

Baziev, D. K. (1978) [*The Snowcocks of the Caucasus: Ecology, Morphology, Evolution*]. Nauka, Leningrad [In Russian].

Davison, G. W. H. (1979) Studies of the Crested Argus III: Gunong Rabon 1977. *J. World Pheasant Assoc.* 4: 76–80.
Davison, G. W. H. (1979) The behaviour of the Barredback Pheasant *Syrmaticus humiae* Hume. *J. Bombay Nat. Hist. Soc.* 76: 439–446.
Davison, G. W. H. (1981) Diet and dispersion of the Great Argus *Argusianus argus. Ibis* 123: 485–494.
Davison, G. W. H. (1981) Sexual selection and the mating system of *Argusianus argus.* (Aves: Phasianidae). *Biol. J. Linn. Soc.* 15: 91–104.
Davison, G. W. H. (1982) Systematics within the genus *Arborophila* Hodgson. *Fed. Mus. J. (Malaya)* 27: 125–134.
Davison, G. W. H. (1983) Notes on the extinct *Argusianus bipunctatus* (Wood). *Bull. Brit. Orn. Club* 103: 86–88.
Davison, G. W. H. (1983) Behaviour of Malay Peacock Pheasant *Polyplectron malacense* (Aves: Phasianidae). *J. Zool., London* 201: 57–66.
Davison, G. W. H. (1986) Breeding behaviour of Crested Wood-partridges in captivity. *Avicult. Mag.* 92: 18–22.
Davison, G. W. H. (1987) Ecology and behaviour of Great Argus in sub-optimal habitats. Pp. 127–132 in Savage, C. D. W. & Ridley, M. W. (eds.) *Proc. Second International Symposium on Pheasants in Asia.* World Pheasant Association, Reading.
Davison, G. W. H. (1996) Why are *Lophura* pheasants so variable? *Tragopan* 5: 8–9.
Dean, W. R. J. (2000) *The Birds of Angola.* Checklist No. 18. British Ornithologists' Union, Tring.
Debus, S. J. S. (1996) Turnicidae (Buttonquails). Pp. 44–59 in del Hoyo, J., Elliott, A. & Sargatal, J. (eds.) *Handbook of the Birds of the World,* Vol. 3. Lynx Edicions, Barcelona.
Dee, T. J. (1986) *The Endemic Birds of Madagascar.* International Council for Bird Preservation, Cambridge.
Delacour, J. (1945) Notes on the eared-pheasants (*Crossoptilon*) with the description of a new subspecies. *Zoologica* 80: 30–45.
Delacour, J. (1949) The genus *Lophura. Ibis* 91: 188–200.
Delacour, J. (1977) *The Pheasants of the World* (2nd edn.). Spur Publications, Hindhead.
Delacour, J. & Jabouille, P. (1931) *Les Oiseaux de l'Indochina Française.* 4 vols. Exposition Coloniale Internationale, Paris.
Dement'ev, G. P. & Gladkov, N. A. (eds.) (1967) *Birds of the Soviet Union,* Vol. 4. Israel Program for Scientific Translation, Jerusalem.
Diamond, J. M. (1972) *Avifauna of the Eastern Highlands of New Guinea.* Nuttall Ornithological Club, Cambridge, Massachusetts.
Dinesen, L., Lehmberg, T., Svendsen, J. O., Hansen, L. A. & Fjeldså, J. (1994) A new genus and species of perdicine bird (Phasianidae, Perdicini) from Tanzania; a relict form with Indo-Malayan affinities. *Ibis* 136: 3–11.
Ding Chang-qing (1995) The mating system and breeding ecology of Cabot's Tragopan *Tragopan caboti. Tragopan* 2: 11–12.
Ding Chang-qing, Liang Wei, Zhao Lei-gang & Gong Hui-sheng (1998) The ecology of the Golden Pheasant in the 1996 breeding season. In *The International Symposium on Galliformes 1997.* Department of Wildlife and National Parks Peninsular Malaysia, Kuala Lumpur.
Ding Ping & Zhu ge Yang (1990) The ecology of Elliot's Pheasant in the wild. Pp. 65–68 in Hill, D. A., Garson, P. J. & Jenkins, D. (eds.) *Pheasants in Asia 1989.* World Pheasant Association, Reading.
Dolgushin, I. A., Gavrin, V. F., Korelov, M. N. & Kuz'mina, M. A. (1962) [*Birds of Kazakhstan*], Vol. 2. Alma Ata [In Russian].
Donegan, T. M. & Dávalos, L. M. (1999) Ornithological observations from Reserva Natural Tambito, Cauca, south-west Colombia. *Cotinga* 12: 48–55.
Dowell, S. D. (1998) The Sichuan Hill-partridge forest conservation project. *World Pheasant Assoc. News* 54: 14–16.
Dranzoa, C., Nkwasire, J. & Sande, E. (1999) Additional surveys of Nahan's Francolin *Francolinus nahani* in the tropical rainforests of Uganda. *Bull. Afr. Bird Club* 6: 52–55.
Dranzoa, C., Sande, E., Owiunji, I. & Plumptre, A. (1997) A survey of Nahan's Francolin *Francolinus nahani* in two tropical rainforests of Uganda. *Bull. Afr. Bird Club* 4: 90–92.
Duckworth, J. W., Tizard, R. J., Timmins, R. J., Thewlis, R. M., Robichaud, W. B. & Evans, T. D. (1998) Bird records from Laos, October 1994–August 1995. *Forktail* 13: 33–68.
DuPont, J. E. (1971) *Philippine Birds.* Delaware Museum of Natural History, Greenville.
Eames, J. (1996) Conservation management options for Edwards's Pheasant. *Tragopan* 4: 8.
Eames, J. (1997) Pheasant news: rediscovery of Edwards's Pheasant. *Tragopan* 7: 3.
Eitniear, J. C., Tapia, A. A., González, V., Pedraza, R. & Baccus, J. T. (2000) New galliformes for the Mexican state of Querétaro. *Cotinga* 13: 10–13.
Eriksen, J. & Sargeant, D. E. (2000) *Oman Bird List* (5th edn.). Oman Bird Records Committee, Muscat.
Evans, T. D. & Timmins, R. J. (1996) The status of the Green Peafowl *Pavo muticus* in Laos. *Forktail* 11: 11–32.
Evans, T. D. & Timmins, R. J. (1998) Bird records from Laos during January–July 1994. *Forktail* 13: 69–96.
Eynon, A. E. (1968) The antagonistic and sexual behaviour of captive Japanese Quail (*Coturnix coturnix japonica*). PhD dissertation, University of Wisconsin, Madison.
Fjeldså, J. & Krabbe, N. (1990) *The Birds of the High Andes.* Zoological Museum, University of Copenhagen, Copenhagen & Apollo Books, Svendborg.
Fjeldså, J. & Mayer, S. (1996) *Recent Ornithological Surveys in the Valles Region, Southern Bolivia.* Centre for Research on the Cultural and Biological Diversity of Andean Rainforests, Rønde.
Fleming Sr, R. L., Fleming Jr, R. L. & Bangdel, L. S. (1976) *The Birds of Nepal.* Fleming, Kathmandu.

Flieg, G. M. (1970) Observations on the first North American breeding of the Spot-winged Wood Quail (*Odontophorus capueira*). *Avicult. Mag.* 76: 1–4.

Flieg, G. M. (1973) Breeding biology and behaviour of the South African hemipode in captivity. *Avicult. Mag.* 79: 55–59.

Flint, P. R. & Stewart, P. F. (1992) *The Birds of Cyprus.* Check-list No. 6 (2nd edn.). British Ornithologists' Union, Tring.

Flint, V. E. (1995) Numbers of grouse and their conservation in Russia. Pp. 173 in Jenkins, D. (ed.) *Proc. International Symposium on Grouse 6.* World Pheasant Association, Reading.

Francis, I. S., Penford, N., Gartshore, M. E. & Jaramillo, A. (1992) The White-breasted Guineafowl *Agelastes meleagrides* in Taï National Park, Côte d'Ivoire. *Bird Conserv. Intern.* 2: 25–60.

Frith, H. J., Brown, B. K. & Morris, A. K. (1977) Food habits of the stubble quail *Coturnix pectoralis*, in south-eastern Australia. *CSIRO, Div. Wildl. Res., Tech. Pap.* 32.

Frith, H. J. & Carpenter, S. M. (1980) Breeding of the stubble quail *Coturnix pectoralis*, in south-eastern Australia. *Australian Wildl. Res.* 7: 117–137.

Fujimaki, Y. (1995) Status of the hazel grouse in Hokkaido, Japan in 1923–93. Pp. 168–169 in Jenkins, D. (ed.) *Proc. International Symposium on Grouse 6.* World Pheasant Association, Reading.

Gallagher, M. & Woodcock, M. W. (1980) *The Birds of Oman.* Quartet, London.

Gao Yu-ren (1998) Conservation status of endemic Galliformes on Hainan Island, China. *Bird Conserv. Intern.* 8: 411–416.

García del Rey, E. (2001) *Check-list of the Birds of the Canary Islands.* Turquesa, Santa Cruz de Tenerife.

Garnett, S. T. & Crowley, G. M. (2000) *The Action Plan for Australian Birds 2000.* Canberra, Environment Australia.

Garson, P. J. (1983) The Cheer Pheasant *Catreus wallichii* in Himachal Pradesh: an update. *J. World Pheasant Assoc.* 8: 29–39.

Garson, P. J. (2001) Pheasant taxonomy: a cunning way to remove species from the Red List. *Bull. Oriental Bird Club* 33: 52.

Gaston, A. J., Islam, K. & Crawford, J. A. (1983) The current status of the Western Tragopan *Tragopan melanocephalus. J. World Pheasant Assoc.* 8: 440–449.

Gatter, W. (1998) *Birds of Liberia.* Pica Press, Robertsbridge.

Gavrilov, E. I., Ivanchev, V. P. & Kotov, A. A. (1993) [*The Birds of Russia and contiguous regions: Pterocliformes, Columbiformes, Cuculiformes, Strigiformes*]. Nauka, Moscow [In Russian].

Ghaemi, R. (1999) The status of Pin-tailed Sandgrouse *Pterocles alchata* in Golestan Province, Iran. *Sandgrouse* 21: 180–181.

Giesen, K. M. (1998) Lesser Prairie-chicken. In Poole, A. F. & Gill, F. (eds.) *The Birds of North America,* No. 364. Academy of Natural Sciences, Philadelphia & American Ornithologists' Union, Washington DC.

Glenister, A. G. (1951) *The Birds of the Malay Peninsula, Singapore and Penang.* Oxford University Press, London.

Gonzalez, M. J., Quigley, H. B. & Taylor, C. I. (1998) Habitat use and reproductive ecology of the Ocellated Turkey in Tikal National Park, Guatemala. *Wilson Bull.* 110: 505–510.

Goodman, S. M., Pidgeon, M., Hawkins, A. F. A. & Schulenberg, T. S. (1997) The birds of southeastern Madagascar. *Fieldiana Zool.* New Ser. 87: 1–132.

Goodwin, D. (1953) Observations on voice and behaviour of the Red-legged Partridge *Alectoris rufa. Ibis* 95: 581–614.

Goodwin, D. (1954) Notes on captive Red-legged Partridges. *Avicult. Mag.* 60: 49–61.

Goodwin, D. (1958) Further notes on pairing and submissive behaviour of the Red-legged Partridge *Alectoris rufa. Ibis* 100: 59–66.

Gossow, H., Hafner, F., Pseiner-Petrjanos, S., Vonkilch, G. & Watzinger, G. (1992) The status of Grey Partridge (*Perdix perdix*) and Rock Partridge (*Alectoris graeca*) populations in relation to human land use in Austria: a review. Pp. 515–521 in Birkan, M., Potts, G. R., Aebischer, N. & Dowell, S. D. (eds.) *First International Symposium on Partridges, Quails and Francolins. Gibier Faune Sauvage* 9.

Grahame, I. (1969) Breeding of the Vulturine Guineafowl (*Acryllium vulturinum*) *Avicult. Mag.* 75: 24–26.

Grahame, I. (1971) *Blood Pheasant. A Himalayan Adventure.* Mitre Press, London.

Grahame, I. (1976) The Himalayan Blood Pheasant—some further observations. *J. World Pheasant Assoc.* 1: 15–22.

Green, I. (1993) Caucasian Black Grouse and Caspian Snowcocks in north-east Turkey. *Orn. Soc. Middle East Bull.* 31: 14–18.

Grimmett, R., Inskipp, C. & Inskipp, T. (1998) *The Birds of the Indian Subcontinent.* Christopher Helm, London.

Griscom, L. (1932) The distribution of bird-life in Guatemala. *Bull. Amer. Mus. Nat. Hist.* 64.

Hagemeijer, W. J. M. & Blair, M. J. (1997) *The EBCC Atlas of European Breeding Birds.* Poyser, London.

Hall, B. P. (1963) The francolins, a study in speciation. *Bull. Brit. Mus. Nat. Hist. (Zool.)* 10: 105–204.

Hall, B. P. (ed.) (1974) *Birds of the Harold Hall Australian Expeditions 1962–70.* British Museum (Natural History), London.

Han Lianxin, Yang Lan & Zheng Baolai (1988) [The sound spectrographic analyses on the calls of Lady Amherst's Pheasant *Chrysolophus amherstiae*]. *Zool. Res.* 9: 127–132 [In Chinese].

Hannon, S. J. & Eason, P. K. (1994) Willow Ptarmigan. In Poole, A. F. & Gill, F. (eds.) *The Birds of North America,* No. 369. Academy of Natural Sciences, Philadelphia & American Ornithologists' Union, Washington DC.

Harper, C. A. & Exum, J. H. (1999) Wild Turkeys (*Meleagris gallopavo*) renest after successful hatch. *Wilson Bull.* 111: 426–427.

Harrison, C. (1978) *A Field Guide to the Nests, Eggs and Nestlings of North American Birds.* Collins, London.

Hart, J. A. & Upoki, A. (1997) Distribution and conservation status of Congo Peafowl *Afropavo congensis* in eastern Zaïre. *Bird Conserv. Intern.* 7: 295–316.

Hayes, F. E. (1995) *Status, Distribution and Biogeography of the Birds of Paraguay.* Monogr. Field Orn. 1. American Birding Association, Colorado Springs.

Hazevoet, C. J. (1995) *The Birds of the Cape Verde Islands.* Check-list No. 13. British Ornithologists' Union, Tring.

He Fen-qi (1992) Conservation of the Sichuan Hill Partridge in China. *PQF News* 2: 7.

Hellmayr, C. E. (1929) A contribution to the ornithology of northeastern Brazil. *Field Mus. Nat. Hist. Zool. Ser. Publ.* 255, 12: 235–501.

Hennache, A., Randi, E. & Lucchini, V. (1998) Genetic diversity, conservation and phylogenetic relationships of Edwards's Pheasant. In *The International Symposium on Galliformes 1997.* Department of Wildlife and National Parks Peninsular Malaysia, Kuala Lumpur.

Henry, G. M. (1971) *A Guide to the Birds of Ceylon* (2nd edn.). Oxford University Press, London.

Herzog, S. K., Fjeldså, J., Kessler, M. & Balderrama, J. A. (1999) Ornithological surveys in the Cordillera Cocapata, depto. Cochabamba, Bolivia, a transition zone between humid and dry intermontane Andean habitats. *Bull. Brit. Orn. Club* 119: 162–177.

Hewitt, O. H. (ed.) (1967) *The Wild Turkey and its Management.* Wildlife Society, Washington DC.

Hill, D. A. & Robertson, P. A. (1988) *The Pheasant. Ecology, Management and Conservation.* Blackwell Scientific Publications, Oxford.

Hilty, S. L. & Brown, W. L. (1986) *A Guide to the Birds of Colombia.* Princeton University Press, Princeton.

Hinsley, S. & Ferns, P. (2000) Juvenile plumage of European sandgrouse. *Brit. Birds* 93: 91–93.

Hjorth, I. (1970) Reproductive behaviour in Tetraonidae, with special reference to males. *Viltrevy* 7: 183–596.

Holder, K. & Montgomerie, R. (1993) Rock Ptarmigan. In Poole, A. F. & Gill, F. (eds.) *The Birds of North America,* No. 51. Academy of Natural Sciences, Philadelphia & American Ornithologists' Union, Washington DC.

Hollom, P. A. D., Porter, R. F., Christensen, S. & Willis, I. (1988) *Birds of the Middle East and North Africa.* Poyser, Carlton.

Howell, S. N. G. & Webb, S. (1995) *The Birds of Mexico and northern Central America.* Oxford University Press, Oxford.

Huang Renxin, Shao Hongguang & Mi Erman (1991) [Preliminary observations of the ecology of the Altai Snowcock]. *Sichuan J. Zool.* 10: 36 [In Chinese].

Hume, A. O. & Marshall, C. H. T. (1879–81) *The Game Birds of India, Burma and Ceylon.* 3 vols. Acton, Calcutta.

Hunn, E. S., Vásquez, D. A. & Escalante, P. (2001) Birds of San Juan Mixtepec, district of Miahuatlán, Oaxaca, Mexico. *Cotinga* 16: 14–26.

Inskipp, C. & Inskipp, T. P. (1995) Birds recorded during a visit to Bhutan in spring 1993. *Forktail* 9: 121–142.

Inskipp, T., Lindsey, N. & Duckworth, W. (1996) *An Annotated Check-list of the Birds of the Oriental Region.* Oriental Bird Club, Sandy.

Iqubal, P., McGowan, P. & Rahmani, A. (1998) Nesting success of the Swamp Francolin *Francolinus gularis* in northern India. In *The International Symposium on Galliformes 1997.* Department of Wildlife and National Parks Peninsular Malaysia, Kuala Lumpur.

Iredale, T. (1956) *The Birds of New Guinea,* Vol. 1. Georgian House, Melbourne.

Irwin, M. P. S. (1981) *The Birds of Zimbabwe.* Quest Publishing, Harare.

Jansen, R., Little, R. M. & Crowe, T. M. (2001) Breeding biology of the Redwing Francolin in the highland grasslands of Mpumalanga Province, South Africa. *Ostrich* 72: 20–23.

Javed, S. (1998) Conservation status and distribution of Swamp Francolin in India. *J. Bombay Nat. Hist. Soc.* 96: 16–23.

Javed, S. (2001) Status and distribution of the Swamp Francolin in the north Indian terai [report to the Conservation Fund]. *Oriental Bird Club Bull.* 33: 16.

Javed, S., Kaul, R. & Khan, J. A. (1998) Ecology and conservation of Western Tragopan, *Tragopan melanocephalus,* in the western Himalaya, India. In *The International Symposium on Galliformes 1997.* Department of Wildlife and National Parks Peninsular Malaysia, Kuala Lumpur.

Javed, S. & Rahmani, A. (1991) Swamp Francolin in the north Indian terai. *World Pheasant Assoc. News* 34: 15–18.

Javed, S. & Rahmani, A. R. (1998) Conservation of the avifauna of Dudwa National Park, India. *Forktail* 14: 55–64.

Javed, S. & Rahmani, A. R. (1998) Flocking and habitat use patterns of Red Junglefowl. *Gallus gallus* in Dudwa National Park, India. In *The International Symposium on Galliformes 1997.* Department of Wildlife and National Parks Peninsular Malaysia, Kuala Lumpur.

Jeggo, D. (1975) Breeding the Palawan Peacock Pheasant at the Jersey Zoological Park. *Avicult. Mag.* 81: 8–12.

Jennings, M. C. (1995) *An Interim Atlas of the Breeding Birds of Arabia.* National Commission for Wildlife Conservation and Development, Riyadh.

Jia Chen-xi, Zheng Guang-mei, Zhou Xiao-ping & Zhang He-min (1998) Home range and habitat selection of Blood Pheasant. In *The International Symposium on Galliformes 1997.* Department of Wildlife and National Parks Peninsular Malaysia, Kuala Lumpur.

Johnsgard, P. A. (1983) *The Grouse of the World.* Croom Helm, London.

Johnsgard, P. A. (1986) *The Pheasants of the World.* Oxford University Press, Oxford.

Johnsgard, P. A. (1988) *The Quails, Partridges and Francolins of the World.* Oxford University Press, Oxford.

Johnsgard, P. A. (1991) *Bustards, Hemipodes and Sandgrouse. Birds of Dry Places.* Oxford University Press, Oxford.

de Juana, E. (1994) Tetraonidae (Grouse). Pp. 376–410 in del Hoyo, J., Elliott, A. & Sargatal, J. (eds.) *Handbook of the Birds of the World*, Vol. 2. Lynx Edicions, Barcelona.

de Juana, E. (1997) Pteroclidae (Grouse). Pp. 30–57 in del Hoyo, J., Elliott, A. & Sargatal, J. (eds.) *Handbook of the Birds of the World*, Vol. 4. Lynx Edicions, Barcelona.

Kalsi, R. & Kaul, R. (1998) Density index and habitat associations of the Cheer Pheasant *Catreus wallichii* in Himachal Pradesh, India. In *The International Symposium on Galliformes 1997*. Department of Wildlife and National Parks Peninsular Malaysia, Kuala Lumpur.

Kang, K. (1969) A note on Rickett's Hill Partridge, *Arborophila gingica* (Gmelin) in Taiwan. *Quart. J. Taiwan Mus.* 22: 121–123.

Kaul, R. (1992) Indian Mountain Quail: can we learn from Cheer Pheasant studies? *World Pheasant Assoc. News* 38: 18–19.

Kaul, R. & Howman, S. (1992) Distribution and habitat requirements of the Northern Painted Francolin *(Francolinus pictus pallidus)* in Jamnagar, India. Pp. 483–492 in Birkan, M., Potts, G. R., Aebischer, N. & Dowell, S. D. (eds.) *First International Symposium on Partridges, Quails and Francolins. Gibier Faune Sauvage* 9.

Kaul, R. & Shakya, S. (2001) Spring call counts of some galliformes in the Pipar Reserve, Nepal. *Forktail* 17: 75–80.

Kaul, R., Thanga, L. & Ahmed, A. (1998) Conservation initiatives to save Blyth's Tragopan in Mizoram, N. E. India. In *The International Symposium on Galliformes 1997*. Department of Wildlife and National Parks Peninsular Malaysia, Kuala Lumpur.

Kennedy, R. S., Gonzales, P. C., Dickinson, E. C., Miranda, H. C. & Fisher, T. H. (2000) *A Guide to the Birds of the Philippines*. Oxford University Press, Oxford.

Khaling, S., Kaul, R. & Saha, G. K. (1998) Spring call counts of Satyr Tragopan in the Singhalila National Park, India. In *The International Symposium on Galliformes 1997*. Department of Wildlife and National Parks Peninsular Malaysia, Kuala Lumpur.

King, B., Buck, H., Ferguson, R., Fisher, T., Goblet, C., Nickel, H. & Suter, W. (2001) Birds recorded during two expeditions to north Myanmar (Burma). *Forktail* 17: 29–40.

King, B., Dickinson, E. C. & Woodcock, M. (1975) *A Field Guide to the Birds of South-East Asia*. Collins, London.

King, W. B. (1979) *Endangered Birds of the World: the ICBP Bird Red Data Book*, Vol. 2. The World Conservation Union, Morges.

Kirwan, G. M. (compiler) (1999) Around the region. *Sandgrouse* 21: 108–112.

Kirwan, G. M. (2000) Spotted Sandgrouse at Birecik, Turkey, in June 1999. *Dutch Birding* 22: 17–18.

Kirwan, G. M., Martins, R. P., Eken, G. & Davidson, P. (1999) Check-list of the birds of Turkey. *Sandgrouse Suppl.* 1: 1–32.

Klaus, S., Scherzinger, W. & Sun Yue-Hua (1997) Ecology and behaviour of the Chinese Grouse. *Grouse News* 13: 20–21.

Klaus, S., Scherzinger, W. & Sun Yue-Hua (1998) Territorial und Werbeverhalten des Chinahaselhuhns (*Bonasa sewerzowi*). *J. Orn.* 139: 185–186.

Komen, J. & Meyer, E. (1984) Hartlaub's Francolin, a formal introduction to one of Namibia's 'specials'. *1984 SWA Annual*: 39–43.

Kopij, G., Nuttall, R. J. & de Swardt, D. H. (1999) Diet of the Namaqua Sandgrouse *Pterocles namaqua* and the Laughing Dove *Streptopelia senegalensis* in South Africa. *Mirafra* 16: 36–38.

Kren, J. (2000) *Birds of the Czech Republic*. Christopher Helm, London.

Kumar, R. S. & Singh, P. (1999) Discovery of a new monal from Arunachal Pradesh. *Oriental Bird Club Bull.* 30: 35–38.

Kumar, R. S. & Singh, P. (2000) More news on the new monal discovered from Arunachal Pradesh. *Oriental Bird Club Bull.* 32: 63–65.

Kuroda, N. (1981) The Japanese green pheasant *Phasianus (colchicus) versicolor* in Japan. *J World Pheasant Assoc.* 6: 60–72.

Kylänpää, J. (2000) Birds of Dera Ismail Khan district of North West Frontier province in Pakistan. *Forktail* 16: 15–28.

Lack, P. C. (1985) The ecology of the land-birds of Tsavo East National Park, Kenya. *Scopus* 9: 2–23.

Lambert, F. R. & Howes, J. R. (1989) A recent sighting of Salvadori's Pheasant. *Kukila* 4: 56–58.

Lambert, F. R., Eames, J. C. & Nguyen Cu (1994) *Surveys for Endemic Pheasants in the Annamese Lowlands of Vietnam, June–July, 1994*. The World Conservation Union, Gland & Cambridge.

Langrand, O. (1990) *Guide to the Birds of Madagascar*. Yale University Press, New Haven & London.

La Touche, J. D. D. (1931–1934) *A Handbook of the Birds of Eastern China*, Vol. 2. Taylor & Francis, London.

Laurent, A. (1990) *Catalogue Commenté des Oiseaux de Djibouti*. Office National du Tourisme et de l'Artisanat, République de Djibouti.

Lehmberg, T. & Dinesen, L. (1994) The bright sides of stumbling over a new bird species. *Bull. Afr. Bird Club* 1: 24–25.

Lekagul, B. & Round, P. D. (1991) *A Guide to the Birds of Thailand*. Saha Barn Bhaet, Bangkok.

Lelliott, A. D. (1981) Cheer Pheasants in west-central India. *J. World Pheasant Assoc.* 6: 89–95.

Leonard, P. M. (1999) Afrotropical bird movements in Zambia—part 1: grebes to nightjars. *Zambia Bird Report* 1998: 15–73.

Le Trong Trai (1997) Green Peafowl *Pavo muticus* in Vietnam. *Tragopan* 7: 16–18.

Lewis, A. & Pomeroy, D. (1989) *A Bird Atlas of Kenya*. Balkema, Rotterdam.

Lewis, J. C. (1973) *The World of the Wild Turkey*. Lippincott, Philadelphia.

Li Xiangtao & Lu Xiaoyi (1992) Status and ecology of the Snow Partridge (*Lerwa lerwa callipygia*) in southwestern China. Pp. 617–624 in Birkan, M., Potts, G. R., Aebischer, N. & Dowell, S. D. (eds.) *First International Symposium on Partridges, Quails and Francolins. Gibier Faune Sauvage* 9.

Li Xiao-Hui & Liang Qihua (1985) Ornithological survey of the southern part of Jiangxi. *Chinese J. Zool.* 20: 37–41.

Li Xiao-Hui, Tan Hong-Zhi, Chen Cai-An & Zhang Ai-Li (1990) Ecological studies on the White-browed Hill-partridge. *Chinese J. Zool.* 25: 22–26.

Li Xiao-Hui, Tan Hong-Zhi, Chen Cai-An & Zhang Ai-Li (1992) Domestication and breeding of the White-browed Hill Partridge (*Arborophila gingica*) in China. Pp. 765–771 in Birkan, M., Potts, G. R., Aebischer, N. & Dowell, S. D. (eds.) *First International Symposium on Partridges, Quails and Francolins. Gibier Faune Sauvage* 9.

Lippens, L. & Wille, H. (1976) *Les Oiseaux du Zaïre*. Lannoo, Tielt.

Little, R. M. (1997) Namaqua Sandgrouse. In Harrison, J. A., Allan, D. G., Underhill, L. G., Herremans, M., Tree, A. J., Parker, V. & Brown, C. J. (eds.) *The Atlas of Southern African Birds including Botswana, Lesotho, Namibia, South Africa, Swaziland and Zimbabwe*. BirdLife South Africa, Johannesburg.

Little, R. M. & Crowe, T. M. (1997) Habitat fragmentation limits the distribution of Cape Francolin *Francolinus capensis* on deciduous fruit farms in South Africa. *S. Afr. J. Zool.* 32: 82–991.

Liu Naifa (1984) On the taxonomic status of the Przewalski's Rock Partridge *Alectoris magna*. *Acta Zootaxonomica Sinica* 9: 212–218.

Liu Naifa (1992) Ecology of Przewalski's Rock Partridge (*Alectoris magna*). Pp. 605–615 in Birkan, M., Potts, G. R., Aebischer, N. & Dowell, S. D. (eds.) *First International Symposium on Partridges, Quails and Francolins. Gibier Faune Sauvage* 9.

Liu Naifa & Yang You-tao (1982) Ecological studies of *Alectoris graeca magna*. *Zool. Res.* 3: 69–76.

Liu Shaochu & Ciren (1993) Monal-partridge in Tibet. *Chinese Wildl.* 2.

Lloyd, P., Little, R. M. & Crowe, T. M. (2000) Daily activity pattern of a Namaqua Sandgrouse, *Pterocles namaqua*, population. *Ostrich* 71: 427–429.

Lovel, T. W. I. (1976) The present status of the Congo Peacock. *J. World Pheasant Assoc.* 1: 48–57.

Lu Xin (1997) Study of habitat selection and behaviour of Tibetan Eared-pheasant. *Tragopan* 7: 5–6.

Lu Xin & Zheng Guang-Mei (2000) Why do eared-pheasants of the eastern Qinghai-Tibet plateau show so much morphological variation? *Bird Conserv. Intern.* 10: 305–309.

Ludlow, F. & Kinnear, N. B. (1944) The birds of south-eastern Tibet. *Ibis* 86: 348–389.

Lukianov, Y. (1992) Ecology of the Altai Snowcock (*Tetraogallus altaicus*) in the Altai Mountains. Pp. 633–640 in Birkan, M., Potts, G. R., Aebischer, N. & Dowell, S. D. (eds.) *First International Symposium on Partridges, Quails and Francolins. Gibier Faune Sauvage* 9.

Lups, P. (1981) Is the Rock Partridge disappearing from the Alps? *Naturforschende Gesellschaft und Rheinaubund, Schaffhausen, Flugblatt* (Ser. II) 16: 1–22.

Lytoon, V. Y. & Flint, V. E. (1993) *Bearded Partridge*. Nauka, Moscow [In Russian].

Ma Li (1992) The breeding ecology of the Himalayan Snowcock (*Tetraogallus himalayensis*) in the Tian Shan Mountains (China). Pp. 625–632 in Birkan, M., Potts, G. R., Aebischer, N. & Dowell, S. D. (eds.) *First International Symposium on Partridges, Quails and Francolins. Gibier Faune Sauvage* 9.

Ma Ming (1998) Captive breeding of snowcocks in Xinjiang, China. In *The International Symposium on Galliformes 1997*. Department of Wildlife and National Parks Peninsular Malaysia, Kuala Lumpur.

MacKinnon, J. & Phillipps, K. (1993) *A Field Guide to the Birds of Borneo, Sumatra, Java and Bali*. Oxford University Press, Oxford.

MacKinnon, J. & Phillipps, K. (2000) *A Field Guide to the Birds of China*. Oxford University Press, Oxford.

Mackworth-Praed, C. W. & Grant, C. H. B. (1957) *African Handbook of Birds. Series One. Birds of Eastern and North Eastern Africa*, Vol. 1. Longman, London & New York.

Mackworth-Praed, C. W. & Grant, C. H. B. (1970) *African Handbook of Birds. Series Three. Birds of West Central and Western Africa*, Vol. 1. Longman, London & New York.

Maclean, G. L. (1967) Die systematische Stellung der Flughühner (Pteroclididae). *J. Orn.* 108: 203–217.

Maclean, G. L. (1985) *Roberts' Birds of Southern Africa*. John Voelcker Bird Book Fund, Cape Town.

Maclean, G. L. & Herremans, M. (1997) Doublebanded Sandgrouse. In Harrison, J. A., Allan, D. G., Underhill, L. G., Herremans, M., Tree, A. J., Parker, V. & Brown, C. J. (eds.) *The Atlas of Southern African Birds including Botswana, Lesotho, Namibia, South Africa, Swaziland and Zimbabwe*. BirdLife South Africa, Johannesburg.

Maclean, G. L. & Little, R. M. (1997) Burchell's Sandgrouse. In Harrison, J. A., Allan, D. G., Underhill, L. G., Herremans, M., Tree, A. J., Parker, V. & Brown, C. J. (eds.) *The Atlas of Southern African Birds including Botswana, Lesotho, Namibia, South Africa, Swaziland and Zimbabwe*. BirdLife South Africa, Johannesburg.

Maleshin, N. A. & Stakheev, V. A. (1981) [Altai Snowcock. Peculiarities of nesting and propagation]. In [*Rare, Disappearing and Poorly Studied Birds in the USSR*]. Nauka, Moscow [In Russian].

Mamat, I. H. J. & Yasak, M. N. (1998) The status and current distribution of Crested Argus *Rheinardia ocellata nigrescens* in Peninsular Malaysia. *Bird Conserv. Intern.* 8: 325–330.

Marchant, S. & Higgins, P. J. (eds.) (1993) *Handbook of Australian, New Zealand and Antarctic Birds*, Vol. 2. Oxford University Press, Melbourne.

van Marle, J. G. & Voous, K. H. (1988) *The Birds of Sumatra*. Check-list No. 10. British Ornithologists' Union, Tring.

Marsden, S. & Peters, S. (1992) Little-known bird: Sumba Buttonquail. *Bull. Oriental Bird Club* 15: 24–26.

Martínez, I. (1994) Numididae (Guineafowl). Pp. 554–567 in del Hoyo, J., Elliott, A. & Sargatal, J. (eds.) *Handbook of the Birds of the World*, Vol. 2. Lynx Edicions, Barcelona.

Martins, R. & Kirwan, G. M. (1996) Photospot: Philby's and Arabian Partridges. *Sandgrouse* 18: 18–21.

Mazar Barnett, J. & Kirwan, G. M. (compilers) (1999) Neotropical Notebook. *Cotinga* 11: 96–105.

McGowan, P. J. K. (1992) Status and micro-habitat use of the Crested Wood Partridge (*Rollulus rouloul*). Pp. 571–582 in Birkan, M., Potts, G. R., Aebischer, N. & Dowell, S. D. (eds.) *First International Symposium on Partridges, Quails and Francolins. Gibier Faune Sauvage* 9.

McGowan, P. J. K. (1994) Phasianidae (Pheasants and partridges). Pp. 434–552 in del Hoyo, J., Elliott, A. & Sargatal, J. (eds.) *Handbook of the Birds of the World*, Vol. 2. Lynx Edicions, Barcelona.

McGowan, P. J. K. (1998) Weights of some birds from the Malaysian forest floor. *Forktail* 14: 78.

McGowan, P. J. K., Dowell, S. D., Carroll, J. P. & Aebischer, N. J. (1995) *Partridges, Quails, Francolins, Snowcocks and Guineafowl: Status Survey and Conservation Action Plan 1995–1999*. The World Conservation Union, Gland & World Pheasant Association, Reading.

McGowan, P., Duckworth, W., Wen Xianji, van Balen, B., Yang Xiaojun, Mohd. Khan Momin Khan, Siti Hawa Yatim, Thanga, L., Setiawan, I. & Kaul, R. (1998) A review of the status of the Green Peafowl *Pavo muticus* and recommendations for future action. *Bird Conserv. Intern.* 8: 331–348.

McGowan, P. J. K. & Garson, P. J. (1995) *Pheasants: Status Survey and Conservation Action Plan 1995–1999*. The World Conservation Union, Gland & Cambridge.

McGowan, P. J. K., Hartley, I. R. & Girdler, R. P. (1989) Palawan Peacock Pheasant: habitat and pressures. *J. World Pheasant Assoc.* 14: 80–99.

McGowan, P. J. K. & Panchen, A. L. (1994) Plumage variation and geographical distribution in the Kalij and Silver Pheasants. *Bull. Brit. Orn. Club* 114: 113–123.

Medway, M. A. & Wells, D. R. (1976) *The Birds of the Malay Peninsula*, Vol. 5. Witherby, London.

Meinertzhagen, R. (1954) *The Birds of Arabia*. Oliver & Boyd, Edinburgh & London.

Mentis, M. T. & Bigalke, R. S. (1980) Breeding, social behaviour and management of greywing and redwing francolins. *S. Afr. J. Wildl. Res.* 10: 133–139.

Mentis, M. T. & Bigalke, R. S. (1981) Ecological isolation in greywing and redwing francolins. *Ostrich* 52: 84–97.

Menzdorf, A. (1982) Social behaviour of Rock Partridges (*Alectoris graeca*). *J. World Pheasant Assoc.* 7: 70–89.

Meyer, H. F. (1971) Notes on Coqui Francolin. *Honeyguide* 65: 29–30.

Meyer, H. F. (1971) Shelley's Francolin. *Honeyguide* 66: 27–28.

Meyer de Schauensee, R. & Phelps, W. L. (1978) *A Guide to the Birds of Venezuela*. Princeton University Press, Princeton.

Mirza, Z. B., Aleem, A. & Asghar, M. (1978) Pheasant surveys in Pakistan. *J. Bombay Nat. Hist. Soc.* 74: 292–296.

Mocci Demartis, A. (1992) Barbary Partridge *Alectoris barbara* (Bonnaterre 1790). In Brichetti, P., de Francesci, P. & Baccetti, N. (eds.) *Fauna d'Italia, Aves*, Vol. 1. Calderini, Bologna.

Monroe, B. L. (1968) *A Distributional Survey of the Birds of Honduras*. Orn. Monogr. 7. American Ornithologists' Union, Washington DC.

Moreau, R. E. & Wayre, P. (1968) On the Palearctic quails. *Ardea* 56: 209–227.

Morejohn, G. V. (1968) Study of the plumage of the four species of the genus *Gallus*. *Condor* 70: 56–65.

Morioka, H. (1957) The Hainan Tree-partridge *Arborophila ardens*. *Ibis* 99: 334–336.

Morris, P. & Hawkins, F. (1998) *Birds of Madagascar: a Photographic Guide*. Pica Press, Robertsbridge.

Morris, R. P. & Oatham, M. P. (1992) Chestnut-bellied Sandgrouse on Ghanadah island UAE. *Phoenix* 9: 9–10.

Munechika, I. (1998) Relationships of *Syrmaticus* and *Phasianus* by cyt-*b* gene array comparison. *Japanese J. Orn.* 47: 133–138.

Nechaev, V. A. (1991) [*Birds of Sakhalin Island*]. USSR Academy of Sciences, Vladivostok [In Russian].

van Niekerk, J. H. (1979) Social and breeding behaviour of Crowned Guineafowl in the Krugersdorp Game Reserve. *Ostrich* 50: 180–189.

Nijman, V. & Sözer, R. (1997) New information on the distribution of Chestnut-bellied Partridge *Arborophila javanica* in the central parts of Java. *Bird Conserv. Intern.* 7: 27–33.

Nuytemans, H. (1998) Notes on Philippine birds: interesting records from northern Luzon and Batan Island. *Forktail* 14: 37–40.

O'Brien, T. G., Winarni, N. L., Saanin, F. M., Kinnaird, M. F. & Jepson, P. (1998) Distribution and conservation status of Bornean Peacock-pheasant *Polyplectron schleiermacheri* in central Kalimantan, Indonesia. *Bird Conserv. Intern.* 8: 373–385.

Ogilvie, L. S. (1949) Nesting habits and early life of the Crested Green Wood Quail. *Malay. Nat. J.* 4: 80–84.

Ogilvie-Grant, W. R. (1896–1897) *A Handbook to the Game-birds*. 2 vols. Edward Lloyd, London.

Oman Bird Records Committee (1998) *Breeding Bird Atlas of Oman*. Oman Bird Records Committee, Muscat.

Palmer, S. C. F. & Bacon, P. J. (2001) The utilization of heather moorland by territorial Red Grouse *Lagopus lagopus scoticus*. *Ibis* 143: 222–232.

Paludan, K. (1959) On the birds of Afghanistan. *Vdensk Medd. Dansk Naturh. Foren.* 122: 1–332.

Parker, T. A., Stotz, D. F. & Fitzpatrick, J. W. (1996) Ecological and distributional databases for Neotropical birds. Pp. 132–407 in Stotz, D. F., Fitzpatrick, J. W., Parker, T. A. & Moskovits, D. K. (1996) *Neotropical Birds: Ecology and Conservation*. University of Chicago Press, Chicago.

Parkes, K. C. (1962) The Red Junglefowl of the Philippines—native or introduced? *Auk* 79: 479–481.

Patterson, R. L. (1952) *The Sage Grouse in Wyoming.* Sage Books, Denver.

de la Perche, N. (1992) Moroccan Double-spurred Francolin. *Dutch Birding* 14: 10–12.

Peters, J. L. (1934) *Check-list of Birds of the World,* Vol. 2. Museum of Comparative Zoology, Harvard University Press, Cambridge, Massachusetts.

Pfister, O. (2001) Birds recorded during visits to Ladakh, India, from 1994 to 1997. *Forktail* 17: 81–90.

Pinto, A. A. da R. (1983) *Ornitologia de Angola,* Vol. 1. Instituto de Investigação Científica Tropical, Lisbon.

Pizzey, G. & Knight, F. (1997) *The Field Guide to the Birds of Australia.* Angus & Robertson, Sydney.

Plumptre, A. J. (1996) Two nests of Nahan's Francolin in the Budonga Forest Reserve, Uganda. *Bull. Afr. Bird Club* 3: 37–38.

Poltack, D. (1972) In search of the Mikado Pheasant. *1972 Ann. Rep. Pheasant Trust & Norfolk Wildlife Park.*

Poole, C. M. (1999) Little-known Oriental bird: Chestnut-headed Partridge *Arborophila cambodiana. Oriental Bird Club Bull.* 30: 46–50.

Porter, R. F., Christensen, S. & Schiermacker-Hansen, P. (1996) *Field Guide to the Birds of the Middle East.* Poyser, London.

Porter, R. F., Martins, R. P., Shaw, K. D. & Sørensen, U. G. (1996) Status of non-passerines in southern Yemen. *Sandgrouse* 17: 22–53.

Porter, W. F. (1994) Meleagrididae (Turkeys). Pp. 364–375 in del Hoyo, J., Elliott, A. & Sargatal, J. (eds.) *Handbook of the Birds of the World,* Vol. 2. Lynx Edicions, Barcelona.

Potapov, R. L. (1985). [*Fauna of the USSR. Birds,* Vol. 3]. Leningrad. [In Russian].

Potapov, R. (1992) Adaptation to mountain conditions and evolution in snowcocks (*Tetraogallus* sp.) Pp. 647–660 in Birkan, M., Potts, G. R., Aebischer, N. & Dowell, S. D. (eds.) *First International Symposium on Partridges, Quails and Francolins. Gibier Faune Sauvage* 9.

Potapov, R. L. (2000) New information on the Snow Partridge *Lerwa lerwa* (Hodgson 1833) and its systematic position. *Bull. Brit. Orn. Club* 120: 112–120.

Potapov, R. L. & Flint, V. E. (1989) *Handbuch der Vögel der Sowjetunion.* Bd. 4. Ziemsen Verlag Wittenberg Lutherstadt.

Potts, G. R. (1986) *The Partridge.* Collins, London.

Potts, G. R. (1988) The impact of releasing hybrid partridges on wild Red-legged populations. *Game Conserv. Rev.* 20: 81–85.

Poulsen, J. G. (1998) Status, distribution and ecology of the Manipur Bush Quail (*Perdicula manipurensis*) in north-eastern India. In *The International Symposium on Galliformes 1997.* Department of Wildlife and National Parks Peninsular Malaysia, Kuala Lumpur.

Pratt, H. D., Bruner, P. L. & Berrett, D. G. (1987) *The Birds of Hawaii and the Tropical Pacific.* Princeton University Press, Princeton.

Prendergast, H. D. V. (1993) Crop contents of a Spotted Sandgrouse. *Orn. Soc. Middle East Bull.* 31: 29–31.

Raffaele, H., Wiley, J., Garrido, O., Keith, A. & Raffaele, J. (1998) *Birds of the West Indies.* Christopher Helm, London.

Raja, N. A., Davidson, P., Bean, N., Drijvers, R., Showler, D. A. & Barker, C. (1999) The birds of Palas, North-West Frontier Province, Pakistan. *Forktail* 15: 77–85.

Ramadan-Jaradi, G. & Ramadan-Jaradi, M. (1999) An updated check-list of the birds of Lebanon. *Sandgrouse* 21: 132–170.

Rand, A. L. (1936) The distribution and habits of Madagascar birds; summary of field notes on the Mission Zoologique Franco-Anglo-Americaine a Madagascar. *Bull. Amer. Mus. Nat. Hist.* 72: 143–499.

Rand, A. L. & Gilleard, E. T. (1967) *Handbook of New Guinea Birds.* Weidenfeld & Nicolson, London.

Rands, M. R. W. (1987) Philby's Rock Partridge in North Yemen. *Sandgrouse* 9: 67–68.

Rands, M. R. W. & Rands, G. F. (1987) The Arabian Red-legged Partridge in North Yemen. *Sandgrouse* 9: 69–73.

Rank, M. (1997) New information on Chestnut-throated Partridge in Tibet. *Oriental Bird Club Bull.* 25: 14.

Rasmussen, P. (1998) Is the Imperial Pheasant *Lophura imperialis* a hybrid? *Tragopan* 9: 8–10.

Ratcliffe, C. S. & Crowe, T. M. (2001) Habitat utilisation and home range size of helmeted guineafowl (*Numida meleagris*) in the Midlands of Kwa-Zulu-Natal province, South Africa. *Biol. Conserv.* 98: 333–345.

Ridgely, R. S. & Gwynne, J. A. (1981) *A Guide to the Birds of Panama.* Princeton University Press, Princeton.

Ridgely, R. S. & Greenfield, P. J. (2001) *The Birds of Ecuador.* 2 vols. Christopher Helm, London.

Ridgway, R. & Friedmann, H. (1946) *The birds of North and Middle America.* Part 10. US Natl. Mus. Bull. 50, Smithsonian Institution.

Rieger, I. & Walzthöny, D. (1992) The distribution of the Mountain Quail (*Ophrysia superciliosa*) in the last century. Pp. 585–590 in Birkan, M., Potts, G. R., Aebischer, N. & Dowell, S. D. (eds.) *First International Symposium on Partridges, Quails and Francolins. Gibier Faune Sauvage* 9.

Riley, J. H. (1930) Descriptions of three new birds from Siam. *Proc. Biol. Soc. Wash.* 43: 189–192.

Rimlinger, D. S., Landel, H., Cheng Cai Yun & Gou Geng (1998) Natural history of a marked population of Chinese Monal pheasant in Sichuan province, P. R. China. In *The International Symposium on Galliformes 1997.* Department of Wildlife and National Parks Peninsular Malaysia, Kuala Lumpur.

Robbins, G. E. S. (1998) *Partridges and Francolins: their Conservation, Breeding and Management.* World Pheasant Association, Reading.

Roberts, T. J. (1991) *The Birds of Pakistan,* Vol. 1. Oxford University Press, Karachi.

Robertson, I. (1989) The occurrence of Rain Quail, *Coturnix coromandelica,* in north-east Thailand. *Nat. Hist. Bull. Siam Soc.* 37: 257–258.

Robertson, P. A. & Carroll, P. (1989) Observations on the autumn densities of Chinese Ring-necked Pheasants in Shanxi Province. *J. World Pheasant Assoc.* 14: 101–106.

Robertson, P. A., Dellelegn, Y., Dejene, S., Shimelis, A., Mariam, T. & Alemayehu, M. (1997) Harwood's Francolin *Francolinus harwoodi*: recent observations on its status, distribution, habitat requirements, behaviour and threats. *Bird Conserv. Intern.* 7: 275–282.

Robinson, H. C. & Chasen, F. N. (1936) *The Birds of the Malay Peninsula*, Vol. 3. Witherby, London.

Robinson, H. C. & Kloss, C. B. (1924) On a large collection of birds chiefly from West Sumatra made by Mr E. Jacobson. *J. Fed. Malay States Mus.* 11: 89–349.

Robson, C. (compiler) (1997) From the field. *Oriental Bird Club Bull.* 26: 60–66.

Robson, C. (2000) *A Field Guide to the Birds of South-East Asia.* New Holland, London.

Robson, C. (compiler) (2001) From the field. *Oriental Bird Club Bull.* 33: 68–78.

Robson, C. R., Eames, J. C., Nguyen Cu & Truong Van La (1993) Further records of birds from Viet Nam. *Forktail* 8: 25–52.

Robson, C. R., Eames, J. C., Wolstencroft, J. A., Nguyen Cu & Truong Van La (1989) Recent records of birds from Viet Nam. *Forktail* 5: 71–98.

Rogers, D. (1995) A mystery with history: the Buff-breasted Buttonquail. *Wingspan* 14 (3): 26–31.

Rojas-Soto, O. R., Sahagún-Sánchez, F. J. & Navarro, S. A. G. (2001) Additional information on the avifauna of Querétaro, Mexico. *Cotinga* 15: 48–52.

Romero-Zambrano, H. (1983) Revisión del status zoogeográfico y redescripción de *Odontophorus strophium* (Gould) (Aves: Phasianidae). *Caldasia* 13: 777–786.

Rozendaal, F., Nguyen Cu, Truong Van La & Vo Quy (1991) Notes on Vietnamese pheasants, with description of female plumage of *Lophura hatinhensis*. *Dutch Birding* 13: 12–15.

Rusch, D., DeStefano, S. & Lauten, D. (1999) Ruffed Grouse. In Poole, A. F. & Gill, F. (eds.) *The Birds of North America*, No. 515. Academy of Natural Sciences, Philadelphia & American Ornithologists' Union, Washington DC.

Ryan, P. G. & Hockey, P. (1995) Is the Hottentot Buttonquail really endangered? *Ostrich* 66: 92–93.

Salaman, P. G. W., Donegan, T. M. & Cuervo, A. M. (1999) Ornithological surveys in Serrania de los Churumbelos, southern Colombia. *Cotinga* 12: 29–39.

Sankaran, R. (1990) Mountain Quail—a preliminary survey. Pp. 135–137 in *Status and Ecology of the Lesser and Bengal Floricans with Reports on Jerdon's Courser and Mountain Quail.* Bombay Natural History Society, Bombay.

Sara, M. (1988) Notes on the distribution of *Alectoris graeca whitakeri* in western Sicily. Pp. 207–216 in Spagnesi, M. & Tosa, S. (eds.) *Atti I Conv. Naz. Biol. Selvaggina (Suppl. Ric. Biol. Selvaggina, XIV).* Instituto Nazionale di Biologia, Bologna.

Schäfer, E. (1934) Zur Lebenweise der Fasanen des chinesisch-tibetischen Grenzlandes. *J. Orn.* 82: 487–509.

Schifferli, A., Geroudet, P. & Ninkler, R. (1980) *The Atlas of Breeding Birds in Switzerland.* Station Ornithologique Suisse de Sempach, Sempach.

Schodde, R., van Tets, G. F., Champion, C. R. & Hope, G. S. (1975) Observations on birds at glacial altitudes on the Carstenz Massif, western New Guinea. *Emu* 75: 65–72.

Schorger, A. W. (1966) *The Wild Turkey: its History and Domestication.* University of Oklahoma Press, Norman.

Schroeder, M. A. & Robb, L. A. (1993) Greater Prairie-chicken. In Poole, A. F. & Gill, F. (eds.) *The Birds of North America*, No. 36. Academy of Natural Sciences, Philadelphia & American Ornithologists' Union, Washington DC.

Seavy, N. E., Apodaca, C. K. & Balcomb, S. R. (2001) Associations of Crested Guineafowl *Guttera pucherani* and monkeys in Kibale National Park, Uganda. *Ibis* 143: 310–312.

Serez, M. (1992) Status, distribution and conservation of Phasianid species in Turkey. Pp. 523–526 in Birkan, M., Potts, G. R., Aebischer, N. & Dowell, S. D. (eds.) *First International Symposium on Partridges, Quails and Francolins. Gibier Faune Sauvage* 9.

Severinghaus, L. L. (1996) Swinhoe's Pheasant in Yushan National Park. *Tragopan* 5: 5–7.

Severinghaus, S. R. (1977) *A Study of the Swinhoe's and Mikado Pheasant in Taiwan with Recommendations for their Conservation.* PhD thesis. Cornell University, Ithaca.

Severinghaus, S. R. (1978) Recommendations for the conservation of the Swinhoe's and Mikado Pheasants in Taiwan. *J. World Pheasant Assoc.* 3: 79–89.

Severinghaus, S. R. (1980) Swinhoe's Pheasant in Taiwan. *Living Bird* 18: 189–209.

Sharpe, R. S. (1968) *The Evolutionary Relationships and Comparative Behavior of Prairie Chickens.* PhD thesis. University of Nebraska, Lincoln.

Shirihai, H. (1996) *The Birds of Israel.* Academic Press, London.

Shirihai, H., Yosef, R., Doherty, P. & Alon, D. (1999) Photospot: Lichtenstein's Sandgrouse. *Sandgrouse* 21: 5–8.

Short, L. L. (1967) A review of the genera of grouse (Aves: Tetraoninae). *Amer. Mus. Novit.* 2289: 1–39.

Short, L. L., Horne, J. F. M. & Muringo-Gichuki, C. (1990) Annotated check-list of the birds of East Africa. *West. Found. Vert. Zool.* 4.

Shrestha, T. K. (1992) Conservation status of the Swamp Partridge (*Francolinus gularis*) in Nepal. Pp. 553–539 in Birkan, M., Potts, G. R., Aebischer, N. & Dowell, S. D. (eds.) *First International Symposium on Partridges, Quails and Francolins. Gibier Faune Sauvage* 9.

Sibley, C. G. (1996) *Birds of the World.* 2.0. Thayer Birding Software, Cincinnati.

Sibley, C. G. & Ahlquist, J. (1990) *Phylogeny and Classification of Birds: a Study in Molecular Evolution*. Yale University Press, New Haven & London.

Sibley, C. G. & Monroe, B. L. (1990) *Distribution and Taxonomy of the Birds of the World*. Yale University Press, New Haven & London.

Sick, H. (1993) *Birds in Brazil*. Princeton University Press, Princeton.

Siegfried, W. R. (1966) Growth, plumage development and moult in the Crowned Guineafowl *Numida meleagris coronata* Gurney. *Dept. Nature Conserv. Investigation Rep.* 8: 1–52.

Siegfried, W. R. (1971) Chukar Partridge on Robben Island. *Ostrich* 42: 158.

da Silva, M. B., Dissanayake, S. R. B. & Santiapillai, C. (1993) The status of the Ceylon Junglefowl in Ruhuna National Park, Sri Lanka. *J. World Pheasant Assoc.* 17/18: 62–66.

Singh, P. (1994) Recent bird records from Arunachal Pradesh, India. *Forktail* 10: 65–104.

Skead, C. J. (1962) A study of the Crowned Guineafowl *Numida meleagris coronata* Gurney. *Ostrich* 33: 51–65.

Smyth, A. K. & Pavey, C. R. (2001) Foraging by the endangered black-breasted button-quail (*Turnix melanogaster*) within fragmented rainforest of an agricultural landscape. *Biol. Conserv.* 98: 149–157.

Smythies, B. E. (1953) *The Birds of Burma* (2nd edn.). Oliver & Boyd, Edinburgh & London.

Smythies, B. E. (1981) *The Birds of Borneo* (3rd edn.). The Sabah Society, Sabah & The Malayan Nature Society, Kuala Lumpur.

Smythies, B. E. (1986) *The Birds of Burma* (3rd edn.). Nimrod Press, Liss.

Snethlage, E. (1914) Catalogo das aves Amazonicas. *Bol. Museu Goeldi* 8.

Snow, D. W. (1978) *An Atlas of Speciation of African Non-Passerine Birds*. British Museum (Natural History), London.

Stepanyan, L. S. (1990) [*Conspectus of the Ornithological Fauna of the USSR*]. Nauka, Moscow [In Russian].

Stattersfield, A. J., Crosby, M. J., Long, A. J. & Wege, D. C. (1998) *Endemic Bird Areas of the World: Priorities for Biodiversity Conservation*. BirdLife International, Cambridge.

Stiles, F. G., Rosselli, L. & Bohórquez, C. I. (1999) New and noteworthy records of birds from the middle Magdalena valley of Colombia. *Bull. Brit. Orn. Club* 119: 113–129.

Stiles, F. G. & Skutch, A. F. (1989) *A Guide to the Birds of Costa Rica*. Christopher Helm, London.

Stokes, A. W. (1961) Voice and social behaviour of the Chukar Partridge. *Condor* 63: 111–127.

Storch, I. (2000) *Grouse: Status Survey and Conservation Action Plan*. The World Conservation Union, Gland & Cambridge.

Sun Yue-Hua & Fang Yun (1998) The ecology and behaviour of the Blood Pheasant at Lianhuashan. In *The International Symposium on Galliformes 1997*. Department of Wildlife and National Parks Peninsular Malaysia, Kuala Lumpur.

Sun Yue-Hua & Fang Yun (1998) A preliminary study on the Verreaux's Monal-partridge at Lianhuashan by radio-tracking. In *The International Symposium on Galliformes 1997*. Department of Wildlife and National Parks Peninsular Malaysia, Kuala Lumpur.

Taka-Tsukasa, N. (1967) *The Birds of Nippon*. Maruzen, Tokyo.

Tarboton, W. (2001) *A Guide to the Nests and Eggs of Southern African Birds*. Struik, Cape Town.

Tarboton, W. R., Blane, S. & Lloyd, P. (1999) The biology of the Yellow-throated Sandgrouse *Pterocles gutturalis* in a South African agricultural landscape. *Ostrich* 70: 214–219.

Taylor, B. (2000) Blackrumped Buttonquail. In Barnes, K. (ed.) *The Eskom Red Data Book of South Africa, Lesotho and Swaziland*. Johannesburg: BirdLife South Africa.

Temple Lang, J. & Cocker, M. (1992) A nest of the Caucasian Blackcock (*Tetrao mlokosiewiczi*) in Turkey. *Sandgrouse* 13: 102–103.

Thewlis, R. M., Duckworth, J. W., Anderson, G. Q. A., Dvorak, M., Evans, T. D., Nemeth, E., Timmins, R. J. & Wilkinson, R. J. (1996) Ornithological records from Laos 1992–1993. *Forktail* 11: 47–100.

Thewlis, R. M., Timmins, R. J., Evans, T. D. & Duckworth, J. W. (1998) The conservation status of birds in Laos: a review of key species. *Bird Conserv. Intern. Suppl.* 8: 1–159.

Thornhill, J. W. (1981) Captive breeding of Jungle Bush-quail *Perdicula asiatica*. *J. World Pheasant Assoc.* 6: 53–59.

Tobias, J. & Seddon, N. (in press) Reading the sand: identifying bird tracks in Madagascar's spiny forest. *Bull. Afr. Bird Club* 9.

Todd, W. E. C. & Carriker, M. A. (1922) The birds of the Santa Marta region of Colombia: a study in altitudinal distribution. *Ann. Carnegie Mus.* 14.

Trollope, J. (1966) Some observations on the Harlequin Quail (*Coturnix delegorguei*). *Avicult. Mag.* 72: 5–6.

Tucker, G. M. & Heath, M. F. (1994) *Birds in Europe: their Conservation Status*. BirdLife International, Cambridge.

Tymstra, R. B., Connop, S. & Tsering, C. (1997) Some bird observations from central Bhutan, May 1994. *Forktail* 12: 49–60.

Urban, E. K., Fry, C. H. & Keith, S. (eds.) (1986) *The Birds of Africa*, Vol. 2. Academic Press, London.

Vaurie, C. (1961) Systematic notes on Palearctic birds. No. 50: the Pteroclidae. *Amer. Mus. Novitates* 2071: 1–13.

Vaurie, C. (1964) A survey of the birds of Mongolia. *Bull. Amer. Mus. Nat. Hist.* 127: 103–144.

Vaurie, C. (1965) *The Birds of the Palearctic Fauna: Non Passeriformes*. Witherby, London.

Vaurie, C. (1972) *Tibet and its Birds*. Witherby, London.

Vuilleumier, F., LeCroy, M. & Mayr, E. (1992) New species of birds described from 1981 to 1990. *Bull. Brit. Orn. Club* 112A (Centenary Suppl.): 267–309.

Warner, D. W. & Harrell, B. E. (1957) The systematics and biology of the Singing Quail *Dactylortyx thoracicus*. *Wilson Bull.* 69: 123–148.

Watson, A. (1972) The behaviour of the Ptarmigan. *Brit. Birds* 65: 6–26, 93–117.

Watson, A. & Miller, G. R. (1976) *Grouse Management.* The Game Conservancy, Fordingbridge.

Watson, G. E. (1962a) Sympatry in Palearctic *Alectoris* partridges. *Evol.* 16: 11–19.

Watson, G. E. (1962b) Three sibling species of *Alectoris* partridges. *Ibis* 104: 353–367.

Wege, D. C. (1996) Threatened birds of the Darién Highlands, Panama: a reassessment. *Bird Conserv. Intern.* 6: 175–179.

Welch, G. & Welch, H. (1984) Birds seen on an expedition to Djibouti. *Sandgrouse* 6: 1–23.

Welch, G. & Welch, H. (1985) Observations on the endemic Djibouti Francolin *Francolinus ochropectus* with emphasis on potential threats to the population. *J. World Pheasant Assoc.* 10: 65–71.

Welch, G., Welch, H., Denton, M. & Cogilan, S. (1986) Djibouti II preliminary report. *World Pheasant Assoc. News* 12: 24–27.

Wells, D. R. (1999) *The Birds of the Thai-Malay Peninsula*, Vol. 1. Academic Press, London.

Wen Xian-ji, Yang Xiao-jun & Yang Lun (1998) The status and conservation of Green Peafowl in China. In *The International Symposium on Galliformes 1997*. Department of Wildlife and National Parks Peninsular Malaysia, Kuala Lumpur.

Wennrich, G. (1983) Hattung und Zucht der Frankolinwachtel (*Perdicula asiatica*). *Gefiederte Welt* 106: 321–324.

Wetmore, A. (1965) *The Birds of the Republic of Panama*, Vol. 1. Smithsonian Misc. Coll. 150.

Whale, R. (1997) Western Tragopan winter survey, Palas Valley. *Tragopan* 7: 11–13.

White, C. M. N. & Bruce, M. D. (1986) *The Birds of Wallacea*. Check-list No. 7. British Ornithologists' Union, London.

Wildash, P. (1968) *Birds of South Vietnam.* Tuttle & Co., Rutland & Tokyo, Japan.

Wilson, K. J. (1965) A note on the crop contents of two Crested Guineafowl *Guttera edouardi* (Hartlaub). *Ostrich* 36: 103–106.

Witherby, H. F., Jourdain, F. C. R., Ticehurst, N. F. & Tucker, B. W. (1941) *The Handbook of British Birds*, Vol. 5. Witherby, London.

Xu Wei-shu, Wu Zhi-kang & Li Zhu-mei (1990) Current status of the Reeves' or White-crowned Long-tailed Pheasant in China. Pp. 31–32 in Hill, D. A., Garson, P. J. & Jenkins, D. (eds.) *Pheasants in Asia 1989.* World Pheasant Association, Reading.

Yakovlev, E. P. (1976) [Rare, endangered and little-studied birds of the USSR]. [*Proc. Oka State Nature Reserve*] 13: 188–189. [In Russian].

Yamashina, Y. (1976) Notes on the Japanese Copper Pheasant. *J. World Pheasant Assoc.* 1: 23–42.

Yin Binggao & Liu Wulin (1993) *Wildlife Protection in Tibet.* China Forestry Publishing House, Beijing [In Chinese].

Young, J. R., Braun, C. E. & Schroeder, M. A. (1998) Sage Grouse. In Poole, A. F. & Gill, F. (eds.) *The Birds of North America*, No. 425. Academy of Natural Sciences, Philadelphia & American Ornithologists' Union, Washington DC.

Young, J. R., Braun, C. E., Oyler-McCance, S. J., Hupp, J. W. & Quinn, T. W. (2000) A new species of sage-grouse (Phasianidae: *Centrocercus*) from south-western Colorado. *Wilson Bull.* 112: 445–453.

Zacharias, V. J. (1997) Status of Grey Junglefowl *Gallus sonneratii* in Periyar Tiger Reserve, Kerala, S. India. *Tragopan* 7: 13–15.

Zacharias, V. J. & Gaston, A. J. (1999) The recent distribution of endemic, disjunct and globally uncommon birds in the forests of Kerala State, south-west India. *Bird Conserv. Intern.* 9: 191–225.

Zarudny, N. (1911) Verzeichnis der Vögel Persiens. *J. Orn.* 59: 185–241.

Zhang Zheng-wang & Wu Yie-ching (1992) The Daurian Partridge (*Perdix dauuricae* [sic]) in north-central China. Pp. 591–595 in Birkan, M., Potts, G. R., Aebischer, N. & Dowell, S. D. (eds.) *First International Symposium on Partridges, Quails and Francolins. Gibier Faune Sauvage* 9.

Zhang Zheng-wang, Zheng Guang-Mei, Yang Xiang-ming & Wu Jian-yong (1998) Clutch size and nesting survival of Brown Eared-pheasant. In *The International Symposium on Galliformes 1997*. Department of Wildlife and National Parks Peninsular Malaysia, Kuala Lumpur.

Zhao Zheng-Jie (1995) *A Handbook of the Birds of China.* Jilin Science & Technology Publishing House, Changchun [In Chinese].

Zhao Zheng-Jie, Wu Jingcai & Zhang Shuhua (1992) A traditional method for hunting the Daurian Partridge (*Perdix dauuricae* [sic] *suschkini*) in China. Pp. 831–835 in Birkan, M., Potts, G. R., Aebischer, N. & Dowell, S. D. (eds.) *First International Symposium on Partridges, Quails and Francolins. Gibier Faune Sauvage* 9.

Zhao Zheng-Jie, Zhang Shuhua & Feng Feng Kai (1992) The biology of the Daurian Partridge (*Perdix dauuricae* [sic] *suschkini*) in northeastern China. Pp. 597–604 in Birkan, M., Potts, G. R., Aebischer, N. & Dowell, S. D. (eds.) *First International Symposium on Partridges, Quails and Francolins. Gibier Faune Sauvage* 9.

Zimmerman, D. A., Turner, D. A. & Pearson, D. J. (1996) *Birds of Kenya and Northern Tanzania.* Christopher Helm, London.

Zwickel, F. C. (1992) Blue Grouse. In Poole, A. F., Setetteneheim, P. & Gill, F. (eds.) *The Birds of North America*, No. 15. Academy of Natural Sciences, Philadelphia & American Ornithologists' Union, Washington DC

INDEX